W9-CFU-499

Organizational
behaviour

An existential-systems approach

Organizational behaviour

An existential-systems approach

JOE KELLY

Professor of Management
Sir George Williams University

Revised Edition • 1974

RICHARD D. IRWIN, INC.   Homewood, Illinois   60430
Irwin-Dorsey International   Arundel, Sussex   BN18 9AB
Irwin-Dorsey Limited   Georgetown, Ontario   L7G 4B3

© RICHARD D. IRWIN, INC., 1969 and 1974

Revised Edition

First Printing, May 1974
Second Printing, March 1975
Third Printing, July 1975
Fourth Printing, September 1975
Fifth Printing, February 1976
Sixth Printing, August 1977

ISBN 0-256-01434-5
Library of Congress Catalog Card No. 73–89112
Printed in the United States of America

Preface

An editor persuades an author to write a revision and immediately demands, "Give this book a better, firmer structure." How do you build a better, firmer structure for a fledgling, schizophrenic, fragmented subject like organizational behaviour? You reach for a model, a yet-to-be-established suggestive framework, which encompasses everything you know and which, if it is intelligible, will pilot the reader through the morasses and mysteries of the marshy field of organizational behaviour.

The model which is developed in this book has three critical dimensions: structure, process, and values. These can be applied to four different levels of behavioural systems: the individual, the group, the organization, and society, and the end products of these systems can be cast into two categories—task and human.

The format for this Revised Edition has been changed by splitting chapters into topics, or minichapters, to allow the reader some choice in skipping and in sequence. Each chapter begins with an integrating theme which is meant to give some thread, thrust, and direction to the story line of organizational behaviour as the author sees it. All chapters include questions and exercises for research and review, as well as a glossary to help summarize the main concepts of each chapter.

The boxes have been updated and those of less relevance removed. The selected readings set off in boxes are meant to do a variety of things. Drawing on classical articles in the literature, most supply additional information on specific theoretical concepts; others give fuller accounts of particular research exercises which may be of interest to some readers if not all; a few contain illustrative material as a sort of digression from the narrower aspects of our subject, to remind us that there are other views of the world; a small number earn their place by being useful for either case discussion or problem-solving sessions.

Perhaps a word is in order in regard to a shift in the perspective and posture of the author. This revision reflects a movement away from the academic-purist position, where the sole concern is with theoretically significant empirical research, to a position which recognizes that organizational behaviour is a crossroads subject where traffic mainly from behavioural science and technology, operations research, computer technology, and economics occasionally coalesces with the ideas streaming out of organizational practice. The curious thing is that executives, without using the same esoteric concepts or semantics, frequently arrive at the same perspective and posture as the academic.

Aimed at the business student, both undergraduate and M.B.A., the book assumes little prior knowledge of behavioural science or of organizations. But, with this particular audience in mind, the book is addressed to the future role of these students as executives and seeks to deal with some of the executive's problems, including recruitment, selection, socialization, development, education and training, conflicts, and capacity for stress.

Every author owes a great deal to others in an intellectual sense and I am no exception. First, I would like to acknowledge the editorial guidance of Larry Cummings who drew my attention to a wide variety of theoretical concepts and research findings whose inclusion greatly strengthened the text. Professor Cummings also made many useful suggestions which, I hope, have added to the structure of the book. I would also like to recognize the assistance of graduate students of business at Sir George Williams University who have worked with me in developing and testing the ideas for this book. I would like to mention particularly Joe Ong and Joe Jany, especially the latter, who helped with the research and preparation of material. Bernard Queenan, my good friend, also helped with the research and proofreading. I would also like to recognize the administrative and intellectual support of Professors G. Brink and A. Berczi who, as deans at Sir George, helped to make this book an actuality. Finally, my wife Maureen kept my domestic life intact and I would again like to acknowledge her help in making this book become a reality.

April 1974   Joe Kelly

Contents

1

Organizational behaviour

The most important thing to know about organizations is that they do not exist—except in peoples' minds. For example, how does a group of workers become "organized labour"? The whole exercise is concerned with the establishment of their union's existence. Presumably, a small number get together to fight for better conditions. Guided by the slogan "united we stand, divided we fall," they decide to form a union. Their first problem is to find a name; secondly, they must make up their minds what they stand for—they must, as a movement, have an ideology. They set out to recruit members, who are given membership cards, and dues are levied; a rule book is made up and distributed to members; branches are formed, with chairmen, secretaries, regular meetings (where people address each other as comrade or brother), and minutes ("the meeting commenced . . . and brother Jones intimated to the meeting . . ."); national office holders are elected; the annual general meeting is arranged. We now have a fully blown union on our hands. But supposing management refuses to recognize its existence. The union decides to strike. A particular ceremonial ritual is acted out which involves the workers' marching through the plant, the election of strike leaders, the appointment of committees, the posting of pickets, and the general atmosphere of a Mardi Gras. Management executes its rituals, and the macabre dance is acted out in all its boring but necessary detail. Management decides to recognize the union. Organized labour has emerged. What has happened is that a group of people have gotten together to achieve a particular purpose; evolved an ideology; developed a structure of offices, authorities, and roles; worked out a process in terms of norms, procedures, and rules for doing things; and fleshed out the structures and process with a value system. An organization has been created which established its credibility by achieving some of its goals, thus demonstrating its power. Power essentially consists of the ability to restructure the perceptions of others to the effect that, irrespective of what they do, you are going to do what you say you are going to do. Now some odd things are going to happen to our union as it develops, but let's postpone this for the moment. What is important for the moment is the light which "winning recognition" throws on the definition of organizational behaviour.

It seems reasonable at this point to define organizational behaviour as the effect of the organization on the perceptions, emotions, and behaviour of its members and clients and how their actions and attitudes affect the achievement of the organization's goals.

But suppose that our union a few years later has a head office instead of a forwarding address, salaried officials, a constitution, and a social benefits plan, including sickness and pension arrangements. At the annual general meetings, some dissidents (who receive considerable applause from the back of the hall) claim that the head office is out of touch with the rank and file, that red tape is strangling the life blood of the union, and that the union has lost sight of its original mandate. Important salary increases are voted for the national officers. What has happened to transform a movement into an organization, which in turn has become a bureaucracy? A bureaucracy with a corporate oligarchy, leaders who insist on people going through channels, who are concerned about their superannuation, pension rights, job tenure, and gas allowances for their union cars? Why does the union now look very much like the bureaucracy which it was set up to fight? A possible explanation is that all organizations, irrespective of their democratic or autocratic origins, behave in the same way; which suggests a different definition of organizational behaviour.

Organizational behaviour can be understood through the study of how organizations begin, grow, and develop, and of how a structure, process, and value system emerge which enable them to learn and to adapt themselves to the environment. This view treats the organization as a living system, like a giant amoeba, which has a life of its own. The focus in this definition is on the behaviour of the organization; the focus in our first definition was on the behaviour of the member and how his behaviour affected the organization. As organizational behaviour develops as a subject, evolving more sophisticated theories, research methods, and data, it is increasingly the behaviour of the organization that will be the subject of the study.

Thus organizational behaviour may be defined as *the systematic study of the nature of organizations: how they begin, grow, and develop, and their effect on individual members, constituent groups, other organizations, and larger institutions.*

This definition contains within its confines the elements of the earlier academic efforts to understand the interactions and relations between "the organization" and individual "behaviour." It indicates that our subject takes in and goes beyond psychology, group dynamics, organizational psychology, and industrial sociology, as illustrated in Figure 1–1.

To understand how organizational behaviour has developed, it is necessary to review the short history of organization theory. In discussing organization theories, three points must always be kept in mind. For starters, organization theories are culturally bound, that is, they are products of the social and economic forces of their times. Just as bureaucracy can be understood better if it is seen as an administrative device which the Prussians borrowed from the French (shades of the Napoleonic Code) to unify and make Germany the central power of Europe in the 19th century, so adhocracy can be better understood as a purely American inven-

FIGURE 1–1
ORGANIZATIONAL BEHAVIOUR

Focus	Subject	Typical problem
Individual	Industrial psychology	The relation between individual productivity and illumination.
Group	Group dynamics	How the primary working group restricts production and develops a value-norm-reinforcement-sanction system.
Organization	Organizational psychology	How an organization structures perceptions of different work groups.
Society	Industrial sociology	Conflict between organizations such as unions versus businesses.

tion of the 20th century—an instant-build, immediate-destruct, turnkey system to get to the moon and back.

Secondly, "you get the organization you deserve." The needs of a particular age determine the kinds of organizations that emerge. For example, the concept of mass production—developed in the automobile assembly line with ideas Henry Ford borrowed from the Chicago meat processing factories, where the slaughtered animals were moved from one work station to another by overhead hook—is a peculiarly American triumph, summed up in the industry's tough motto "move the iron." But it was an American dream of production in mass, low prices, and first class wages which enabled a man to buy what he built. The whole idea made good sense in the 1920s and even in the early 1960s, but is now increasingly out of kilter with the expectations of the existential, hip young men on the line.

Thirdly, organization theory is derivative; it derives its concepts, language, and ideas from other disciplines. To grasp what organization theory is about requires at least a Cook's tour of behavioural science, econometrics, computer science, and operations research. For example, systems theory—which utilizes the computer analogy that requires a grasp of such terms as feedback, heuristic, and algorithim—presupposes some insight into such biological terms as adaptation, operations research concepts like the law of requisite variety ("it takes complexity to beat complexity"), and an understanding of such physics concepts as entropy.

THE ORGANIZATION THEORISTS: WEBER, TAYLOR, MAYO, AND SIMON

Conceivably, by a dramatic and drastic flourish of Ockham's famous razor (the principle of logical parsimony, where the theory with the least assumptions which can explain something wins) one could reduce the organization theory jungle to no more than four pivotal figures, legendary

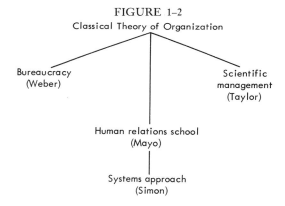

FIGURE 1–2
Classical Theory of Organization

theorists who were kings of the management theory jungle in their day and who left monuments dominating, overshadowing, and sometimes absorbing the contributions of lesser figures. Four men of such stature are Max Weber, Frederick Winslow Taylor, Elton Mayo, and H. A. Simon. As indicated in Figure 1–2, the first two orginated the art in the form of the classical theory, with its two great strands of bureaucracy and scientific management. Weber asserted that the ideal organization is a hierarchy of specialists run according to the book by a dedicated meritocracy with tenure, who act rationally but impersonally; in other words that bureaucracy is the ideal organization. Taylor's treatise on scientific management made work measurable by bringing the stop watch into the factory; in other words, time and motion study is the ideal way to get production out of the gate on time. Elton Mayo brought people back in, via the discovery that when human relations are driven out by treating people like machines in the beehive of bureaucracy, they reappear like Banquo's ghost in the guise of the informal organization. The fourth theorist, H. A. Simon, initiated the present revolution by treating organizations as information-processing systems which—by having hierarchical coalitions made up of cliques and cabals of technocrats managing different kinds of information, acting rationally most of the time by employing rather simple rule-of-thumb decision rules—achieve a variety of inconsistent goals by maximizing this and satisficing that as they respond to the imperatives of the environment.

THE GRAND DESIGN: THE PARADIGM OF MARRYING PARADOXES

Now, having had a sneak preview of what organization theory is all about, the reader may be somewhat puzzled as to how to proceed to acquire the necessary Bulgarian footdrill, as Voltaire's Candide might have put it. Fortunately Robert Dubin in his *Theory Building* offers two paradoxes between which a marriage can perhaps be effected which will offer a modus operandi for making organization theory operational. Dubin identifies two paradoxes: the first is the precision paradox, the fact that we can frequently "achieve precision in prediction without understanding how the predicted outcome was produced"; the second is the power paradox, the fact that it is frequently possible to achieve understanding of organizational behaviour "without being able to predict its character in specific circumstances."

To realize the prediction paradox, organizational theorists make the problem simpler by inventing models (which usually are made up of black boxes in dark regions), collecting data about specific variables which have been condensed into equations which function like the system, and then pumping this data through a computer; outputs emerge which describe the system state at some future time. That both executives and operations research specialists can carry through this process with some accuracy without necessarily knowing or even desiring to understand the system is the dramatic change in management in the last 20 years. Thus the student of organization has a deep and pervasive interest in the formulation of scenarios, models, and metaphors which work like organizations.

But measurement and precision, while necessary, are not sufficient. It is also necessary to enhance our power of understanding, and thus it is necessary to turn to behavioural science as a means of finding out "why." Why are particular variables interlocked? For example, why are "flat" structures effective in one business but not in another? To get "why" answers, the student of organization is compelled to look in some odd corners as he takes a guided tour of the mental hospital led by Erving Goffman, follows R. D. Laing through the mysteries of the "double bind" as an explanation of schizophrenia, and follows Mario Puzo through the mystique of the Mafia to learn that that organization is a sort of trade union whose members operate like any other organization men in a systematic, low-profile, careful way which is legitimate to them. What is being argued is that organizations work equally well for legal or illegal ends and moral or immoral purposes, but their activities must be legitimate to (fit the belief system of) their members. Hence the fact that executives of cigarette manufacturing companies and B-52 pilots can go on living and carrying out their duties; they are seen as legitimate. Hence the deep feelings of futility associated with war crime trials. So much for the power paradox of understanding.

But what organizational behaviour is attempting to do is to evolve a paradigm which will bring these two paradoxes together; the aim is a fruitful marriage of operations research in the form of systems and behavioural science in the form of existentialism. It is difficult to see how this mixed marriage is to be arranged, for neither discipline has reached maturity; the parties have still to be introduced; they speak different languages and read different journals; they belong to different "scientific" religions, within which the same word has different meanings. Such a marriage would have to be a bilingual and bicultural match.

Organizational Behaviour is offered as a preparation for both parties, and the subtitle "an existential systems approach" is intended to high-light the fact that the subject deals with two kinds of behaviour: the behaviour of organizations, which is what systems are all about, and the behaviour of man, choosing and being chosen, which is what existentialism is all about. As the Soviets would say, "all power to the matchmakers."

STRUCTURE OF CHAPTER I

Four topics are considered in this chapter. The first deals with the history of organization theory, and the object of the exercise is to put each of three theories into historical perspective.

Our second topic deals with the different levels of analysis pursued in organizational behaviour and describes the escalation of the focus of research from the individual to the group to the organization. To illustrate the interdisciplinary nature of our field, two different types of organization are examined in some detail: the mental hospital and the Mafia.

In Topic 3, a model for the study of organizational behaviour is evolved. The aim of this chapter is to explain the meaning of this model. Topic 4 brings the chapter to a close by setting out a new perspective and posture regarding organizational behaviour.

TOPIC 1
Theories of organization

It is not sufficient to record the behaviour of executives, no matter how accurate and detailed these records may be, or even to supplement these records with clinical interviews of the executives themselves or to reinforce one's data by carrying out surveys of their beliefs by scientifically constructed attitude scales. This by itself does not constitute science; organizational science demands the development of a coherent edifice of concepts and hypotheses about the managerial process. Too few managers as yet seem to realize that nothing is more efficient than a valid theory. This inadequate appreciation of the virtues of theory springs from the failure to appreciate the supreme importance that theory plays in the development of a science.

Organization theory—a sine qua non of corporate man. An organization theory is not a theory in the narrow physical science sense (for example, Dalton's atomic theory, which argues that matter is indestructible and cannot be created) but rather represents theory on the grand scale, which suggests a perspective for looking at organizations. Organization theory is painted in with a broad brush on a large canvas, with the "details" of personality theory, group dynamics, econometrics, and sociology fitted together like a set of Picasso eyes, squinting and looking askance at one another. But in spite of this imperfect congruence of its plural parts, organization theory is an excellent focus for cerebration.

For a start, jumping ahead of our tale, organizations have an autonomy of their own and live like giant amoebas, consuming part of their environment in terms of men, machines, money, and information, not to mention other smaller amoebas. Within the sovereignty of the organization, structures, processes, and value systems are developed which are peculiar to organizations and which can only be half understood by studying organizations. For the sociologist, organization theory is one of the missing links as he moves up the intellectual escalator from personality, the group, and the organization to the study of society.

For the executive, whether he be a general, archbishop, Don, chief psychiatrist, or just plain old-fashioned company president, a knowledge of organization theory—even if it only supplies him with the terminology, to say nothing of the ritual, rubrics, and routines—is vital if he is to assume the charismatic mantle of certainty and success which his underlings, followers, and lieutenants so earnestly crave. For the executive, the design of the optimal organization—which is constantly undergoing change, not to adapt to reality but to get a shade ahead of reality—is a compulsive preoccupation which leaves scant time for the pleasures of the bed, the table, or the golf course. The study of organization theory is a must, and the few crumbs and occasional crusts that have fallen from the tables of Robert (*Up the Organization*) Townsend, C. Northcote Parkinson, and Lawrence Peter have whetted his appetite for the meaty dishes of game theory, behavioural science, decision theory, and futurology that should be coming out of the highly capitalized, overresourced university business schools for which he has already paid so much. Suppose there is something in organization theory which he doesn't know and his competitor does. Or suppose there is nothing in it, but his competitors believe there is. All roads point to the need for a critical, if not dispassionate, review of organization theory.

Why not dispassionate? The answer is simply that the grand theories of organization do not lend themselves to unbiased analysis, for such theories are derivative, culturally bound, and influenced by the needs of organization members.

THREE THEORIES OF ORGANIZATION

Speaking in broad terms, three different theories have been identified in the brief history of management studies. Figure 1–3 illustrates these

FIGURE 1–3
THE RELATIONSHIP BETWEEN MANAGEMENT THEORY, SOURCE DISCIPLINE, AND
MANAGEMENT TECHNIQUES

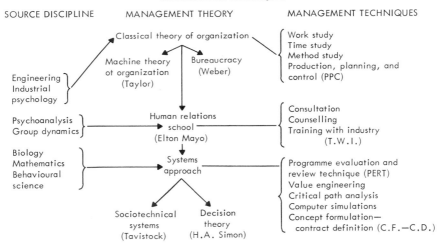

theories, the sources from which they drew, and the techniques they have produced. The first, the classical theory of organization (one strand of which is known as the machine theory of organization and is sometimes called Taylorism), treats work primarily as an economic activity and is obsessed with the scientific measurement of productivity to the neglect of the human aspect of work (see Box 1.1). The human relations school evolved essentially as a reaction to the excesses of Taylorism and argues that an industrial organization should be viewed as a social system with twin objectives: one, producing the product, and the other, generating and distributing satisfaction among employees, that is, achieving both economic effectiveness and job satisfaction.

The human relations school, believing that economic and technological aspects of business were adequately developed, concerned itself with

Box 1.1: Three theories of organization

March and Simon in *Organizations* have argued that propositions about organizational behavior can be grouped in three broad classes, on the basis of their assumptions:

1. Propositions assuming that organization members, and particularly employees, are primarily passive instruments, capable of performing work and accepting directions but not initiating action or exerting influence in any significant way.
2. Propositions assuming that members bring to their organization attitudes, values and goals; that they have to be motivated or induced to participate in the system of organization behavior; that there is incomplete parallelism between their personal goals and organization goals; and that actual or potential goal conflicts make power phenomena, attitudes, and morale centrally important in the explanation of organizational behavior.
3. Propositions assuming that organization members are decision makers and problem solvers, and that perception and thought processes are central to the explanation of behavior in organizations.

J. G. March and H. A. Simon, *Organizations* (New York: John Wiley & Sons, Inc. 1958).

developing better human relations within the firm. The human relations school has in turn given way to the systems approach, which, as Wilfred Brown has pointed out, is concerned with the development of optimal organizations within which "the work to be done and the resources available, both technical and human, determine the methods of work to be employed." In this context the effective executive is psychologically distant, reserved, task-oriented in his approach to his subordinates, and in a phrase would be described as a task specialist.

It is possible to see these theories as a reflection of the political, social, and cultural forces operative at the time. For example, Taylorism—with its implicit assumption that all other men are essentially lazy, passive, and unambitious and thus require tight supervision and policing of their behaviour before they will give of their best—is to be ranged alongside the Marxist comments on the conditions of the working classes and the implied class war, with the factory floor as the chosen arena for battle. To make use of a rather crude metaphor, it can be argued that the principal consequence of Taylorism was to exacerbate and extend the trench war between management and labour which many trade unionists regarded as a war of attrition to be won only by a victory on the political front.

The human relations school focused attention on the mechanisms which shop floor operatives developed to maintain the restriction of production, covert reactions that inevitably flowed from the worst excesses of Taylorism. Faced with a social blockage of this type, it was impossible for management to improve productivity by increasing direct supervision. What was required was a tangential approach, namely, an appeal for less direct supervision and a corresponding increase in human relations. In any case, with piece work, the job itself is the principal supervising mechanism of both output and behaviour, in the sense that it controls in an easily predictable manner the behaviour of the operative. The efficient supervisor apparently intuitively recognizes that organizational logic must take cognizance of technological realities (e.g., the supremacy of the factor of the speed of the assembly track in structuring behaviour) and operates on a flow-line concept of management, where the emphasis is on ensuring both an adequate flow of work into his section and an acceptable movement of output through the checkpoint of inspection into the next section. Within his section, he behaves like a sociotechnical realist.

It is quite possible that the human relations school would have held sway for a far longer period but for the traumatic threats which the West, particularly America, has experienced since the Korean War, especially from the success of the sputniks. These external threats not only have drawn attention to the inherent weakness of the "democratic" approach to leadership where the subordinates' personal needs are regarded as paramount, but have as well challenged the hitherto assumed technological supremacy of the West. This essentially Orwellian situation appears to be fading in 1973 compared with 1957, but nevertheless it has had a significant effect on managerial thinking.

CLASSICAL THEORY

Bureaucracy

Bureaucracy, essentially a 19th-century invention (although a product in the first instance of the revolution in France, spawned by the thought that science and rationality could also be applied to society and facilitated by the printing press, because things could be done "by the book"), represented an obvious antidote to the caprice and arbitrary fiat which characterized the divine right of kings. Bureaucracy promised rationality, order, system, and the reasonableness of merit applied to the business of government, the military, the law, and eventually education. Industrial organizations on a large scale, except in arsenals and naval dockyards, did not yet exist; but the state industries that were to emerge would be organized as bureaucracies which would become the prototypes for the Duponts, the I. G. Farbens, the Mitsubishis, the Krupps, and the General Motors Corporations of a hundred years later, who in turn would become the organizational blueprints for most other medium-sized and large businesses.

But the defeated learn most, and it was the Prussians who took the idea of the bureaucracy out of its prototypical state and fashioned a nation where births and deaths were registered and where conscription and mobilization could be achieved by throwing the right switches. Administrative machinery was invented, applied, and perfected with the German military machine, backed by the bureaucracy of Krupps, ready to astound the world in 1870, 1914, and again in 1940.

Therefore it can evoke no surprise to know that the academic par excellence of bureaucracy was Max Weber, a distinguished German sociologist who wrote the manual on bureaucracy. He spelled out the need for specialization, hierarchy, and rules ("the files"), all to be exercised in an impersonal atmosphere by men who had a career for life, where promotion was supposed to be by merit but more usually involved occupying dead men's shoes. The model for thinking about organizations was the railroad, which was the invention and hallmark of modernity in the late 19th century. Both Britain and the United States publicly regarded bureaucracy with a distaste bordering on horror, as an infringement of personal freedom and dignity. But the first World War, logistically a test of railroad systems, proved you can only beat bureaucracy with bigger and better bureaucracies. Out of the war came the giant chemical, engineering, and ship-building industries organized as bureaucracies in the United States, Britain, and Japan.

Scientific management

While Max Weber was writing his ponderous treatises on bureaucracy, Frederick Winslow Taylor, from a good middle-class family in Philadelphia, was working his way through an engineering shop first as clerk, then as operator, setter, and eventually foreman. To a genius like Taylor, the hit-or-miss methods of working, and above all the lack of shop management in terms of planning and controlling, were wholly unacceptable, but something that could be set right by the application of science to management. Taylor started at the other end of the scale from Weber and propounded the principles of scientific management which are still valid today. These principles include:

1. Select the right man for the job.
2. Emphasize that there is one right way of doing the job.
3. Appoint foremen who will specialize in planning methods and time study, getting the tools ready, installing incentive schemes, and so on.

Taylor discovered such elementary principles as the fact that you need one shovel for shovelling ashes and another for iron ore and, most important of all, that such matters can be settled scientifically (see Box 1.2). Machine speeds and cuts on lathes, for example, can be determined scientifically. Taylor was joined by Frank Gilbreth, who "invented" time study, and Henry Gantt, who "discovered" production planning and control.

Industrialists in the United States and elsewhere took up Taylorism with a vengeance, and Taylor made a personal fortune as a consultant, though he was reviled by the workers (whom he saw as continuously "soldiering," for "he never saw a smiling face among them"). Taylorism worked, but at a price, as the workers banded together in shop floor

Box 1.2: The case of the "pigs"

When Frederick Winslow Taylor started to introduce the principles of scientific management at the Bethlehem Steel Company, he was assigned the task of moving 80,000 tons of pig iron from an open field into the works. Taylor found that the gang on the average was loading about 12½ long tons per man-day, for which the wages were $1.15 a day. After studying the matter Taylor concluded that a first-class pig iron handler ought to be able to handle between 47 and 48 long tons per day, for which he proposed to pay him $1.85 a day. The method which Taylor used for selecting his first convert to this system is rather interesting.

. . . Finally we selected one from among the four as the most likely man to start with. He was a little Pennsylvania Dutchman who had been observed to trot back home for a mile or so after his work in the evening, about as fresh as he was when he came trotting down to work in the morning. We found that upon wages of $1.15 a day he had succeeded in buying a small plot of ground, and that he was engaged in putting up the walls of a house for himself in the morning before starting work and at night after leaving. He also had the reputation of being exceedingly "close," that is, of placing a very high value on the dollar. As one man whom we talked to about him said, " A penny looks about the size of a cartwheel to him." This man we will call Schmidt.

The task before us, then, narrowed itself down to getting Schmidt to handle 47 tons of pig iron per day and making him glad to do it. This was done as follows. Schmidt was called out from among the gang of pig iron handlers and talked to somewhat in this way:

"Schmidt, are you a high-priced man?"

"Vell, I don't know vat you mean."

"Oh yes you do. What I want to know is whether you are a high-priced man or not."

"Vell, I don't know what you mean."

"Oh, come now, you answer my questions. What I want to find out is whether you are a high-priced man or one of these cheap fellows here. What I want to find out is whether you want to earn $1.85 a day or whether you are satisfied with $1.15 just the same as all those cheap fellows are getting."

"Did I vant $1.85 a day? Vas dot a high-priced man? Vell, yes, I vas a high-priced man."

"Oh, you're aggravating me. Of course you want $1.85 a day—everyone wants it! You know perfectly well that has very little to do with your being a high-priced man. For goodness sake answer my questions, and don't waste any more of my time. Now come over here. You see that pile of pig iron?"

"Yes."

F. W. Taylor, *Scientific Management* (New York: Harper & Bros., 1947).

schemes to restrict production, showing an ingenuity that made management wonder what could they do if they used this ingenuity productively.

HUMAN RELATIONS

In both Europe and North America, executives, government administrators, and military technocrats in growing numbers turned hopefully to social scientists to explain and in some cases to solve their problems. The nature of the problem has varied from time to time. In Britain during

"You see that car?"

"Yes."

"Well if you are a high-priced man, you will load that pig iron on that car tomorrow for $1.85. Now do wake up and answer my question. Tell me whether you are a high-priced man or not."

"Vell—did I got $1.85 for loading dot pig iron on dot car tomorrow?"

"Yes, of course you do, and you get $1.85 for loading a pile like that every day right through the year. That is what a high-priced man does and you know it as well as I do."

"Vell, dot's all right. I could load dot pig iron on the car tomorrow for $1.85, and I get it every day don't I?"

"Certainly you do—certainly you do."

"Vell, den, I vas a high-priced man."

"Now, hold on, hold on. You know just as well as I do that a high-priced man has to do exactly as he's told from morning till night. You have seen this man here before, haven't you?"

"No, I never saw him."

"Well, if you are a high-priced man, you will do exactly as this man tells you tomorrow, from morning till night. When he tells you to pick up a pig and walk you pick it up and walk, and when he tells you to sit down and rest, you sit down and rest. You do that right straight through the day. And what's more no back talk. Now a high-priced man does just what he's told to do, and no back talk. Do you understand that? When this man tells you to walk, you walk; when he tells you to sit down you sit down, and you don't talk back to him. Now you come on to work here tomorrow morning and I'll know before night whether you are really a high-priced man or not."

This case illustrates Taylor's misconception in trying to obtain maximum productivity even at the expense of imposing on the worker a burden that would be exhausting to the average man. Several times in Taylor's writing it may be observed that there is some confusion between the normal goal to be reached and the "maximum amount of work which a first-rate man of [each workman's] class can do and thrive." When he turns to the problem of those workers who cannot reach such a standard, Taylor recommends that they be declared redundant, unless they can be found work in another part of the plant. While it is true that Taylorism did bring substantial financial rewards to those workers who eventually were selected, his fundamental mistake was to imagine that these methods could be generally applied. On this point, Taylor was bitterly opposed not only by the trade unions but by independent research workers.

World War I, the problem was to reduce fatigue and the incidence of accidents while increasing personal productivity—all through the adjustment of environmental variables such as temperature, humidity, and illumination. In the U.S. Army in 1917, American psychologists made a significant contribution to the Allied war effort and eventually to management practice by the use of psychological tests for selection purposes. In the interwar period these new techniques were applied in industry, but only to a limited extent, in Europe.

During World War II, the new psychological selection techniques were applied on a vast scale in both Britain and the United States. For example, a significant factor in waging the war was the selection and training of pilots, which involved the development of complex selection procedures. Similar procedures, using techniques from group dynamics, were developed for the selection of officers and specialists such as paratroopers and saboteurs.

In the United States another interesting development in supervisory training was taking place. To understand this development, it is necessary to go back to the mid-1920s and the Hawthorne Works of the Western Electric Corporation, where Elton Mayo's experiments on the relationship between productivity and illumination had produced the interesting finding that if you isolate two groups (experimental and control) in a large factory, you create two élites. The conclusion of this experiment was that the existence of an élite is a more potent factor affecting productivity than illumination, or any other physical factor for that matter. Thus the importance of human relations as a subject of inquiry was "discovered," and at an appropriate moment; for the isolation of the worker *as a thing* which the pundits of scientific management required for the study of the personal environmental factors affecting productivity had created a situation which forced the worker into a defensive posture of surreptitiously restricting production. A wasteful war of attrition was being waged between management and labour: management pushing for production through incentives, and the workers—terrified by the dangers of ratebusting—pressing for "a fair wage for a fair day's work" (on their scale).

In this stalemate, human relations provided the necessary outflanking strategy. It was soon realized that the effective supervisor did not talk about work with his subordinates but exploited a person-centered approach. With all the benefits of hindsight, it is possible to grasp that many supervisors unconsciously recognized the reality of the situation, particularly the futility of pressing for increasing production in a social environment designed to restrict production. In such circumstances, it is possible to guess that the best line when dealing with shop floor operatives was to exploit ambiguous phrases such as "How's it going?" in the hope that, after some human relations, there was an increased probability they might give you the production information you needed to be effective. The codifying and development of ideas such as the skills required of the employee-centered, democratic supervisor provided the basis of training within industry (T.W.I.). In the United States during World War II, T.W.I. was used to train a very large number of foremen. From training foremen, it was an easy step to the training of management.

The human relations movement was in full spate after World War II. The permissive society had arrived, in education, in industry, in the military, and in personal relations. Somehow or other the various institutions of society manage to keep in step. The "new look" in learning produced an educational system appropriate to age, aptitude, and ability as the three R's receded. In the army, table lamps were rustled up for recruits and man-management became the approved way. In industry, joint consultation, good communications, the fostering of good relations, and the other trappings of human relations can be easily understood in a society of overfull employment.

But human relations could not last. The Orwellian situation in which the world found itself in the cold war, with the East threatening the West and the West threatening the East, guaranteed this. The Korean War provides a convenient watershed; the human relations movement was confronted by scientific management (the Marxist state section) and the result was agonizing reappraisal. The climate had been set for the philosophy of task management. Fundamental shifts in the social sciences are rarely the results of single causes. The shift from human relations to systems management is no exception to this rule.

If industrial psychology was concerned with the individual and human relations with the group, then why should the process stop here? The focus of the industrial psychologist in the 1960s became man-in-organization-in-a-social-environment. Organizational psychology was making its debut.

Human relations: Right for its time

It is easy to take a somewhat superior (if not jaundiced) view of human relations as a management philosophy, but this is to pluck it out of its historical context. In its time, it was quite apposite. It might be appropriate to regard human relations as the infra-structure change in the primary group to correspond with Franklin Roosevelt's *cri de coeur* that "we have nothing to fear, but fear itself" which helped to get American economy of the 1930s going again under the New Deal. The philosophy of human relations helped to ease Western society into a post-capitalist and post-Marxian era in which the robber barons and the sweat-shop capitalists have all but disappeared.

But the old concepts of human relations do not fit the facts any longer. They no longer describe the managerial thinking of those men who run enterprises which are a mixture of public and private investment and who have learned that while they must strive for private profit, they must defer to public welfare. These epoch-making organizational changes have come so quickly and pervasively that the managers who have managed through the actual phases of the change are somewhat bewildered·by it all.

Transition to the systems approach

Management was pushed into accepting its present ideology, systems management, by the realization that the subject of management was shaking free of its status as an art and beginning to show the embryonic signs of an emerging science. New concepts were developed, such as the belief that the organization could be viewed as a sociotechnical system which required the conscious planning of a formal organization within which social and technical factors could interact to produce both high productivity and human satisfaction.

This new approach to management was greatly assisted by the development of more sophisticated operational techniques which I call the calculus of production. These included operations research, including linear programming, PERT systems, functional costing, and cost-effective studies. In this managerial world, the crucial question is, "Who is the person most capable of managing—the manager or the worker?" Many companies have still to regain the managerial initiative—to recognize that the shop floor worker is unlikely to have the necessary expertise and sophistication to be both the effective manager and the effective worker that the piece-work situation requires. In this phase of management ideology, the role of the personnel manager requires that he be steeped in the behavioural sciences—yet not too deep, in case he has lost sight of the logics of cost and technology. As organizational analyst he must discard the notion that he is the conscience of the firm stranded between management and labour; rather, he must think of himself as a staff officer whose responsibility to management can be summed up in the phrase "the organization's social scientist."

SYSTEMS THEORY

Systems theory is essentially concerned with the notion that an organization consists of a set of interrelated parts and functions like a living creature, in the sense that it is goal seeking and that it trades with its environment—importing materials, energy, and information, transforming them through a mysterious set of processes, and exporting them into the environment with value added, all for a profit.

Systems theory has a peculiar history, as befits such a complicated theory and one which reflects both developments in weapon systems and theorizing in metabiology. A brief glance at the military evolution of systems is in order. In talking about systems, the task is always the primary consideration which decides everything. The German military in 1940 were the first to recognize that combat formations should be designed, trained, applied to a particular task, and then disbanded. Their success in building task forces of combat engineers, armoured infantry, paratroopers, and dive bombers brought the static fortresses of France and Belgium to a state of ruin. Britain and the United States took up the idea with enthusiasm, and soon task forces—which cut across conventional military structures, processes, and values—were everywhere. With this concept of the task force, project management was just around the corner.

A more direct development was the creation of air defence systems which interlocked radar (sensor subsystem), the plotting room (data processing subsystem), the control centre (decision-making subsystem), the fighter squadrons (process subsystem), the strategic command (control subsystem), and the daily score of aircraft destroyed (memory subsystem). Figure 1–4 illustrates these subsystems, applicable to all systems.

The systems approach was beginning to arrive and soon organization analysts were no longer looking at organization charts (which are all about structure, and tell you who can speak to whom, who can initiate contacts, who can authorize expenditures, and so on) but were instead plotting and charting information flows (which tell you more about what was said and done, by whom, when, where, and why).

In the systems approach information (and access to it) became king, and conventional authority relations went by the board. In the new technostructure, a new logic emerged. The emphasis was on project management, and a new style of leader emerged who was a facilitator or consultant to a team of resource people of diverse skills who were working on a batch of assignments at any one time.

FIGURE 1–4
A SYSTEM AND ITS SUBSYSTEMS

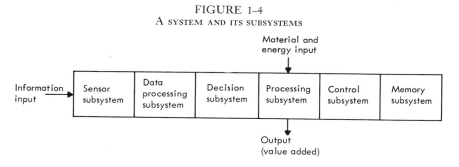

The aerospace industry, with its problems of rapid obsolescence, was the first to adapt the systems approach. In this adjustment it was greatly facilitated by the U.S. Air Force, which was locked into the systems approach by developments in weapon systems which had to have target identification, locking-on capacity, and fail-safe capability, all produced by zero defect programmes. The U.S. Air Force developed a programme of equipment acquisition which set the style for the aerospace firms.

Further, unlike the U.S. Navy, the Air Force did not have a bureau of planes, and thus the aerospace firms were faced with the problem of high innovativeness, which required self-targeting—lock-on systems that could invent, prototype build, and manufacture within tight cost and time schedules.

The RAND Corporation, a think tank, was set up partly by Air Force funding to provide guidance and counsel in the formulation of future policies. A new spirit of independence was emerging, where rationality and imagination were the aces. If organizational problems could be thrown into systems form, dramatic new exciting solutions apparently suggested themselves—which left more conventional analysts dazzled and overawed.

Robert McNamara typified the new breed of system theorists. He earned his spurs in the military during World War II, working with a team of operations research (O.R.) specialists who gave early signs of their collective genius by deciding to leave the military as an on-going team. They offered their services to the highest bidder in terms of challenge, prestige, and reward. They went to the Ford Motor Company and with Henry Ford II staged the great postwar come-back for Ford. McNamara became president of Ford, only to be called to Washington to serve as Secretary of Defense, which ensured a rapid assimilation of systems theory by government departments and their clients in private industry.

The most dramatic application of the systems approach was the Apollo Project to put a man on the moon. Project management was defined simply as "doing what we say we are going to do." The conventional loyalties of the NASA programme people on the one hand and the technical types from the aerospace manufacturing firms on the other broke down as the task became the focal point of their collective lives.

The systems approach has been spreading fairly quickly to other industries, facilitated by the widespread use of computers, which makes information a key raw material; encouraged by the success of PERT and other O.R. techniques; and dominated by the new organizational development (O.D.) man, committed to teaching change, aided and abetted by university business schools.

For the scholar, system theory was an attractive proposition, for it was both complex and complicated. It had its intellectual roots in biology through the use of such terms as adaptation and growth, and could borrow and use the concept of entropy from the field of thermodynamics. Systems theory demanded an interdisciplinary approach—which at times was somewhat confusing, for one could never be sure whether the expert was talking about the hydrogen molecule, DNA, the protein molecule, the virus, the amoeba, the paramecium, the automatic washing machine, James Watt's governor, the thermostat, the human personality, the group, the organization, or even society. And that's the beauty of general systems theory. If you discover a principle which is valid for one particular system, it may be possible to generalize it for all systems.

Systems theory and cybernetics

System theorists have been greatly influenced by the subject of cybernetics, which was defined by the late Norbert Wiener as "the science of control and communication in animals and machines."

It is generally accepted that the extreme complexity of the business organization, which requires for its efficient functioning that all the constituent parts should be related, can be treated as a cybernetic system. In this cybernetic approach, it is assumed that the system to some extent must be self-regulating, which would presume a feedback of information.

But these systems have become so complex that it is improbable that all the facts and relations will ever be known. To meet this particular difficulty, operations researchers have introduced the idea of the "black box." This somewhat unscientific term refers to the model of a system whose mechanisms are unknown but which can be thought of as a way of relating input variables to output variables, so that when the O.R. specialist manipulates the input data, he can first record and then predict output data without really knowing what is going on within (the black box).

In an essay entitled "The Cybernetic Approach in Business," Sir Rowland Whitehead from SIGMA (Science in General Management) Ltd., has concluded:

> From a management point of view, the cybernetics approach can help as follows:
> 1. Teach management to treat company as a complex inter-reacting whole—not a collection of unrelated units.
> 2. Show that aspects of this inter-acting whole will never be clearly understood. An approach of manipulation rather than dissection will be more successful.
> 3. Variety in the controlling system is the only way to kill the variety existing in the system itself.
> 4. Control, at any level must be implicit not explicit.
> 5. Feed-back of information is vital to the control of the system.

Sociotechnical systems treat the organization as an organism interacting with its environment

A most useful idea on which many behavioural scientists are working today is the notion that a business can be likened to an organism. The presumption in this analogy is that the organization as an organism ingests raw materials, does some complex operations on them, and produces more complex products which in turn become the raw material for other organizations.

To distinguish such organizations from mechanistic organizations which have more rigid structures and control systems, Professor Tom Burns, a sociologist from Edinburgh University, has suggested the title organic organizations for those businesses where the structure of roles has been left "unfrozen," and where people interact and evolve a structure which has survival value for the business in a changing technological environment.

In the organization-as-organism approach, it is vital to think of an enterprise as being influenced by its environment, its political climate, its markets, and government policy. In this approach, management (as the brain of the organism) must make decisions which will help the organism to solve the problems of a changing environment; this presumes that a business organization should be treated as an open system.

The Tavistock Institute of Human Relations (but more particularly

F. E. Emery and E. L. Trist) has demonstrated the value of studying enterprises as sociotechnical systems; in "Socio-Technical Systems" they reject the idea of a business as a "closed system" and argue that:

> The alternative conception of "open systems" carries the logical implications that such systems may spontaneously re-organize toward states of greater heterogeneity and complexity and that they achieve a "steady state" at a level where they can still do work. Enterprises appear to possess at least these characteristics of "open systems." They grow by processes of internal elaboration and manage to achieve a steady state while doing work, i.e., achieve a quasi-stationary equilibrium in which the enterprise as a whole remains constant, with a continuous "throughput," despite a considerable range of external changes.

In the open system business, management is responsible both for managing the internal system and organizing the external environment. This requires that the strategic decision must be made at the "boundary" of the system. Emery and Trist have further argued that:

> The strategic objective should be to place the enterprise in a position in its environment where it has some assured conditions for growth—unlike war the best position is not necessarily that of unchallenged monopoly. Achieving this position would be the *primary task* or overriding mission of the enterprise.

The organization as an organic open system

Treating an organization as an open system provides an excellent conceptual scheme (see Figure 1–5). It compels the executive to:

1. View an organization as a complex interacting whole, where parts are considered as subsystems which interact among themselves within the total system. The acheivement of synergy (the "$2 + 2 = 5$" principle) becomes a major focus of mental activity.
2. Think of an organization as an information-processing system where omniscience is not possible because the cost of capturing a total infor-

FIGURE 1–5
ORGANIZATION AS AN ORGANIC OPEN SYSTEM

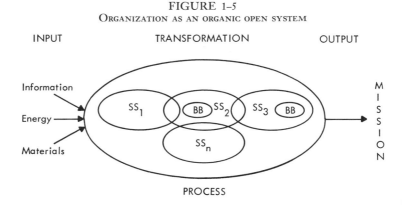

PROCESS

mation picture would be prohibitive. In fact an organization is only partially knowable, with many "dark regions"; to cope with this uncertainty, many parts must be treated as black boxes. Not all of the many variables can be quantified and many can be described only in qualitative terms.

3. Search for feedback loops which define how a subsystem influences other subsystems.

4. Try to define the boundaries of the system and the various transactions between the system and its environment.

5. Come to terms with the proposition that conflict and co-operation are inevitable both within and without the system. Since the subsystems are not completely knowable, the greatest measure of autonomy possible must be granted to each subsystem. The concepts of role, authority, and power must be defined in information terms. For example, authority can be defined as a mode in the information system where the role holder searches for, receives, analyses, and transmits particular signals. He represents a particular constituency, such as his subordinates, the customers, the government, or the whole system. His status is defined in terms of information privileges. His power is seen as his ability to deal with contigencies which may arise in the future.

6. Invent scenarios, construct models, find data for them, play with the models and come up with relevant game plans which he can then implement. His prime interest is in manipulation and control; he is interested in understanding only as it facilitates control. Identification of critical decision variables becomes a vital activity.

7. Accept that since the organization is not completely knowable, maximum autonomy is encouraged. The glue which holds the organization together must have the right level of consistency, should not be too sticky, and should be applied to cleanly defined surfaces. This social glue consists of values. Making sure that the organization has a value system which is appropriate to the social and technological mandates of the situation inevitably involves discussions of dilemmas such as long-term versus short-term, task versus human effectiveness, and integration versus differentiation.

8. Search for, identify, and evaluate the structure and processes of the system. Structure—how the system is shaped, who can speak to whom, who can initiate contacts, who pays, and so on—is usually well known. Traditionally books on management have dealt extensively with structural questions such as hierarchy, span of control, and so on. "Process" is a different kettle of fish; it describes the sequence of events from the moment a person, piece of information, or unit of energy or material enters the gate until it leaves. The process question is, What happened next?

But how can the executive as organizational analyst improve his effectiveness? An increasing number of executives have turned to the study of organizational behaviour for answers. Figure 1–6 illustrates the frame of reference for this study.

Models of man and organization theories

All organization theories seem to imply some sort of model of man. Both organization theorists and managers who subscribe to these theories carry around in their heads, albeit in some cases intuitively, a model of man which stuctures in their minds how man energizes, sustains, and directs his behaviour. Thus the classical theorists, at least disciples of Taylor, see man in the same terms as psychologist B. F. Skinner, as a set of S-R's

FIGURE 1–6
FRAME OF REFERENCE FOR ANALYSIS OF THE SUBJECT "ORGANIZATIONAL BEHAVIOUR"

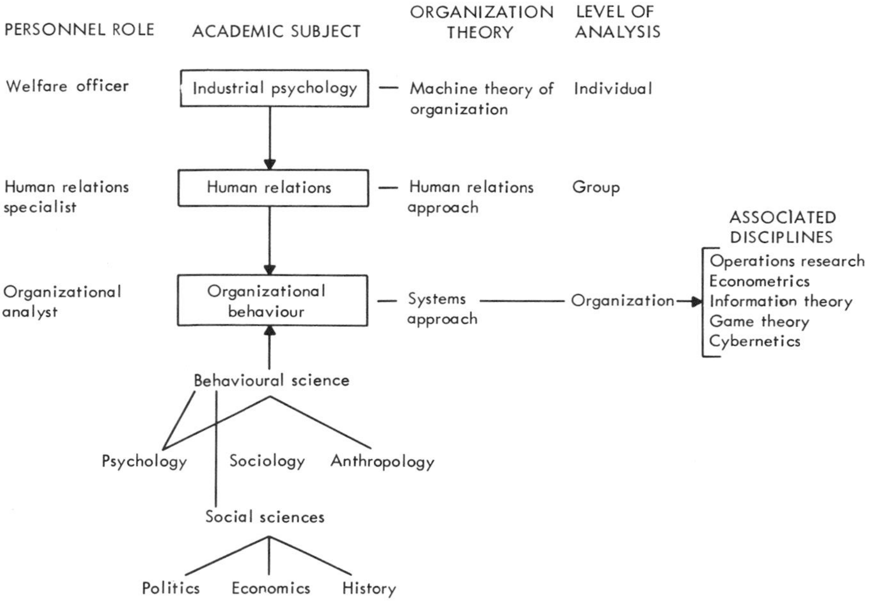

(stimulus-response), as a kind of vending machine. You put your money (reward or reinforcement) in one slot, the machine is triggered to recognize the relation between the stimulus and the response, and out pops the coffee. In Taylor's machine theory, men behave like vending machines or S-R systems; and all will go well if the right machine has been selected, properly programmed (the right S's connected to the desirable R's), and fed with just the right money. Occasionally, of course, the machine will get somewhat intransigent and have to be treated to a good kick. Thus a judicious mixture of rewards and kicks, or carrots and sticks, will keep S-R man going quite nicely.

Quite a different model of man is used by the human relations theorist, who sees man in S-O-R terms. The O stands for the organism, which is presumed to be full of values, attitudes, needs, and expectations. The presumption is that, since these motivational elements are welded into a psychic web which is difficult to disentangle because man places such a high value on integrity and "being together," the best method is to work through the group process. Participation allows the crises of negotiations associated with shifts in values and attitudes to appear to be self-inflicted wounds, while other group members help to reconcile the changee to the changes.

The system or task approach uses the P-G (path-goal) model of man. The path-goal approach represents a cognitive theory of motivation which makes a great deal more sense than a noncognitive S-R formulation. The presumption is that man can identify goals, set paths to these goals, and make choices in terms of paths and goals that reflect his interests. In other words, people have a good idea which tasks they enjoy doing, how they feel about specific task accomplishment, what rewards are valuable, and what will happen if they make a more significant effort. The critical problems for the behavioural scientist studying P-G man are to figure out in quantitative terms (1) how much enjoyment a man gets out of doing a task and attaining a goal, (2) what he expects in terms of external outcomes or rewards (say, for the moment, money), and (3) the trade-offs between pleasure and pay.

TOPIC 2
The manager, the psychiatrist, and the Godfather: They all manage organizations

What do students of organizational behaviour study? To answer this question it is necessary to say something about the level of analysis. As has already been indicated, organizational behaviour is a multilevel subject which employs an interdisciplinary approach. Basically, four levels of analysis are pursued in the field: the individual, the group, the organization, and society. Each of these different levels of analysis draws on a variety of academic disciplines, as shown in Figure 1–7. The history of organizational behaviour is essentially concerned with recording the shift in conceptual focus from the individual to the societal level.

THE INDIVIDUAL

Historically there is a close link between the classical theory of organization, particularly Taylor's scientific management, and industrial psychology. Industrial psychologists were the first to apply the principles of

FIGURE 1–7

Level	Academic discipline	Examples of related disciplines
The individual	Personality and motivation	Psychology
The group	Group dynamics	T groups, group psycho-therapy, encounter groups
The organization	Organization theory	Econometrics, decision theory, operations research
Society	Sociology	Industrial relations, social anthropology, social psychiatry

psychology to the study of work. They began their research on work by trying to measure the characteristics of the physical environment and relate them to such matters as productivity, job satisfaction, accident levels, scrap produced, and the experience of fatigue. Their intention was to measure several dimensions of the physical environment, including temperature, humidity, and level of illumination, and relate these to output factors in terms of changes in the worker's behaviour or attitudes. The basic paradigm (see Figure 1–8) was a very simple one—in fact, deceptively simple—but it led to a great deal of useful work which helped to define optimal working temperatures, humidity levels, and illumination and noise levels, as well as producing guidelines for rest periods.

The line of logic employed in this paradigm is of considerable interest. The presumption was that by manipulating the physical stimulus (the independent variable), the worker's behaviour and attitudes (the output or dependent variable) could be modified. But not all early industrial psychologists pursued this particular logic. A different approach is suggested when it is realized that people are different, that abilities, aptitudes, and attitudes are widely distributed within a given population. Thus the problem for the industrial psychologist becomes the identification of the best man for the job. The value of this approach was demonstrated in 1917 when the U.S. Army made extensive use of psychological tests to allocate recruits to different types of military roles.

These two approaches—the personnel psychologist on the one hand, who is trying "to find the right man for the job"; and the engineering psychologist on the other hand, who is trying "to make the job fit the man (any man)"—are still with us, even though in many ways they are diametrically opposed. The role of the personnel psychologist and the part he plays in the executive selection process, we will return to in considerable detail in Chapter 9. Engineering psychology (or ergonomics, as it is called in Europe), which begins from the proposition that the human being is not a perfectly adaptable organism, received a tremendous impetus during World War II, when it was discovered that radar operators were falling asleep at their sets, that pilots were landing their aircraft with the

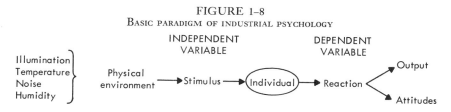

FIGURE 1–8

BASIC PARADIGM OF INDUSTRIAL PSYCHOLOGY

undercarriage still in the retracted position, and, more generally, that the man-machine system was not behaving itself properly. And today, engineering psychologists, when they are not designing weapons systems, are playing a part in designing such mundane things as baths, chairs, automobile interiors, and airline seats. They study the pilot in his pressure suit, the hospital patient in his iron lung, the student in his teaching machine, and the driver getting in and out of his truck. They have come up with a whole new vocabulary, including "display mode," "control mode," "control configuration," and "aided tracking time constant." Many of the problems (as their language reveals) are concerned with getting information into man and out of him. Unfortunately, the approach adopted has rested too strongly on the measurement of machine variables, which can be easily quantified, and neglected human variables (such as personality and motivation), which are not so easily quantified. It is necessary to look at what's happening inside the individual, and this is precisely what personality and motivation studies do.

PERSONALITY THEORY AND THE EXECUTIVE

At the individual level, executives were quick to realize the convenience of the extravert-introvert dichotomy. The only reservation worth making on this score is that many managers seem to have made a fetish of extraversion, presenting it as the only possible adjustment for the up and coming executive. This gross oversimplification ignores, for example, the use of the moderately adjusted introvert as an "ideas man" in the advertising agency. In any case, many senior managers are perfectly capable not only of recognizing and exploiting this distinction but of recognizing the hysterical and the obsessional as neurotic extensions of extraversion and introversion, respectively.

The obsessional is readily recognized, either in the dining room (polishing his knife or sawing his food into an infinity of minute morsels, each of which receives 32 chews) or in the office (scrupulously straightening his desk, counting paper clips, and so on). While the modern executive might be reluctant to accept the Freudian explanation for such behaviour —i.e., that it is anal-erotic, a consequence of excessive toilet training, possibly caused by an upper working-class mother in search of respectability—he has not been slow to recognize that such personality types can be employed very usefully as adjutants or as office and methods specialists, where their compulsive interest in detail will have its greatest payoff.

Again, the explanation of the etymology of hysteria—from the Greek *hystera* meaning womb—is not only greeted with gales of laughter by executives but also with nods of the head in recognition of the supposed sexual nature of hysteria. The modern graduate executive is not unaware of his own hysterical symptoms, such as imagined cardiac conditions conjured up by his misgiving about his possible obesity.

Much the same discussion can be repeated regarding the ego defence mechanisms, such as rationalization and projection. Motivation research findings are usually treated with very good humour but also with recognition that a good starting point for selling has been found. For example, the ideas that prunes should be sold as fertility symbols (in contradistinction to their appearance) and that spaghetti "won't sell" because it reminds housewives of human excreta are readily acknowledged as "good starters" for sales conferences.

Experience proves that not only can most executives who are sent to business schools for management education recognize the relevance and utility of findings from personality theory and research, but they are also willing to look at group dynamics as yet another source of intellectual hardware. Here the process has not been quite so successful.

Group psychotherapy, which is the seminal intellectual source of such diverse institutions as sensitivity training (discovering "who you are") and Alcoholics Anonymous groups ("talking about alcohol is almost as good as drinking the stuff"), requires a more complex theoretical analysis. Role theory, theories of cognitive dissonance, work and nonwork, sociograms, and graph theory sometimes prove too much not only for the line executive but also for his personnel colleagues.

THE GROUP

Our next level of analysis is the group. Why groups? One answer is that groups are nearly universal in organizations and that their power in influencing, shaping, and changing behaviour and attitude is well known. Another answer is that in theoretical terms the group is an intermediate mechanism between the individual and the organization and thus conceptually provides both a very useful unit of analysis and a meeting place for the organization and the individual. Not all theories of organization have recognized the role of the group as a natural stepping stone, both in theory and practice. Indeed a major criticism of the rational-economic approach of classical theory was its failure to consider the existence of groups.

Yet the curious thing is that the scientific study of groups began because of a typical industrial psychology experiment, measuring the relationship between illumination and productivity. This experiment called for setting up two groups of workers, an experimental group (where illumination would be varied) and a control group (illumination constant). The unexpected result was that the process created two élite groups who both worked extraordinarily well, not because of any change in illumination but because they believed they were members of élite experimental groups. The idea that groups are nothing more than the sum of the behaviours and attitudes of individual members was exploded. A new type of calculus was needed which could provide rules for assessing the additions and subtractions of effort and attitude which arise in the group.

Group dynamics, which was invented precisely for this new calculus, drew its inspiration from the Gestalt psychologists, who had been previously preoccupied with such matters as why one sees movement in the movies (a good name) when presented with a sequence of consecutive still pictures. The answer is that the process of perception adds something—"motion"—that wasn't there before. Likewise, in the group, something new emerges. Group dynamics is all about this something new, and

FIGURE 1–9
MODEL RELATING INPUT FACTORS TO OUTPUT FACTORS FOR A GROUP

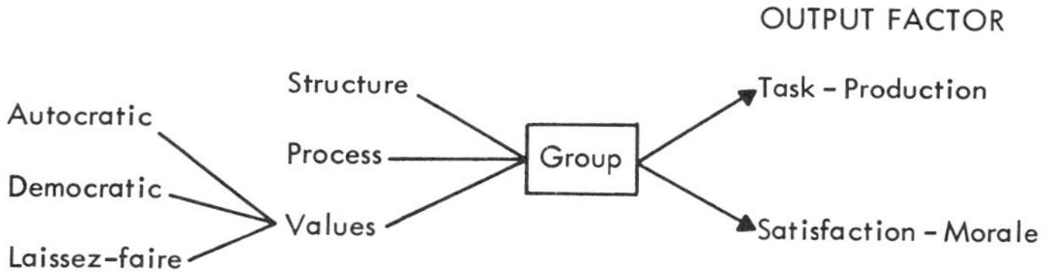

the whole objective of this rapidly growing field is to discover the properties of the primary group (e.g., one's work group) and the reference group (e.g., one's graduate class or any group used for comparison purposes).

The properties to be studied could include such structural factors as size, autonomy, homogeneity, intimacy, stability, stratification, and accessibility; such process considerations as how the group allows members to contribute in terms of effort; and such value considerations as whether the group is operating in an autocratic, democratic, or laissez-faire culture. Such properties could be organized into a model, such as Figure 1–9, which might suggest possible empirical investigations. And this was exactly what K. Lewin, R. Lippitt, and R. K. White, did in the 1930s, manipulating groups by changing their "political" climates (autocratic, democratic, and laissez-faire) and observing what happened. While this experiment did set those researchers and executives who did not study it too closely on the wrong track (they believed that it had been scientifically proved that democracy is more effective than autocracy in all circumstances), the vital point to emerge was that groups were "in" as far as research and theorizing were concerned. Soon the whole field of group dynamics was bursting with activity. During World War II, there was a sustained drive to apply this new discipline to such exciting problems as the selection of officers and saboteurs via leaderless groups, the treatment of combat neurosis by the technique of group psychotherapy, and the rehabilitation of P.O.W.'s by processing them through deconditioning groups.

After the war, group dynamics became a major growth industry for the employment of behavioural scientists. In the late 1940s the whole T group (T stands for training, not therapy—though there is a lot of therapy in the training) movement suddenly emerged and transformed the training situation for industry.

In the early 1950s R.F. Bales of Harvard published the seminal work in the whole field of group dynamics, setting out the structure, process, and value systems for small discussion groups. Data was collected by observation through a one-way screen, using categories which allowed other research workers to replicate his findings. And so it went, through the 1950s and 1960s, with one experiment following another as social psychologists figured out what factors favoured interpersonal attraction, how groups grow and develop, how size affects a group, how the task affects the group, how group pressures distort judgements, and how groups affect individual decision making.

But the essence of the whole approach described so far is the interaction between the group and the individual. What happens when a group interacts with another group? Another escalation in conceptual focus; and soon social psychologists were creating and breaking intergroup co-operation so that they could study what conditions favoured the reduction or increase of intergroup conflict. But to get into such matters as intergroup conflict, social psychologists had to extend their conceptual weapon systems. Fortunately, subjects like game theory and information theory were also rapidly developing, and many of the concepts that behavioural scientists employed were drawn from such cognate fields.

But, in spite of the brilliant work of people like George Homans, D. Cartwright and A. Zander, Rensis Likert, R.F. Bales, and Kurt Lewin in the United States and Elliott Jaques in Britain, group dynamics as a conceptual form is limited in its ability to explain organizational behaviour. In an organization we are dealing with a group of groups; and just as a group is more than the sum of its individuals, so an organization adds up to something more than a group of groups.

THE ORGANIZATION AND SOCIETY

An organization can be defined as a social system of two or more groups which has been deliberately constructed and reconstructed to achieve specific goals. To facilitate analysis, it is useful to see how effectively the discussion of structure, process, and values can be applied to the concept of organization.

STRUCTURE

Every organization has some kind of structure which sets out the nature and limitations of the authority and communication networks. This kind of structural information is usually presented in the form of an organization chart which spells out the various departments, divisions, or subunits and how they are connected. The nature of an organization's structure is related to its goal structures. If an organization has production, maintenance, marketing, research and development goals, the way in which such goals interlock in a particular structure will be reflected in a specific arrangement of authority. If structure and goals are compatible, the organization can achieve its purposes.

When there is a significant degree of incompatibility, more scope is created for the emergence of the informal organization, the system of groups which have purposes different from the formal goals and achieve their aims through a structure of cliques and cabals. This kind of informal organization exists in every institution, but is most formidable in situations where there is a sharp discordance between goals and structure. For example, in the New York City Police Department a significant and major effort is currently being made to achieve a higher degree of congruence between the factors of structure and goals. Where previously a charge of corruption would be investigated by the headquarters unit, now the division chief of the policemen being charged is required to conduct the investigation. With the autonomy of the division enhanced, the possibility of the supervising officers and policemen combining together in an informal group to fight the headquarters unit is diminished.

The advantage of the organization as a conceptual unit of analysis now becomes clear. A major limitation of the group approach is that group theorists have so little to say about power relations, which in fact are of critical importance for the understanding of corporate *real-politik*. As a result of Cartwright and others voicing this criticism that social psychologists were being "soft on power," a dramatic shift of gears took place in organizational studies, with power becoming a major variable. Thus the modern approach views organizations as having both an authority system and an identifiable power system, with both systems overlapping but not coinciding.

The structure, of course, is not immune to pressures which may arise internally from changes in the power distribution or externally from changes in environment.

PROCESS

The goals of an organization determine the processes—the actual sequences of events that describe the means used to reach the goals. March and Simon in *Organizations* (see Box 1.1) have described organizations as groups of coalitions which are bound together by the self-interest of pursuing a particular task and which with limited rationality satisficed this then that, all by rather relatively crude rules of thumb. What is important to note for the moment is that coalition members achieve their particular goals by processing information. So information becomes the key raw material of the organizational process. What March and Simon are arguing is that the material which flows along the structure is information and (contrary to what happens in society at large, where the information is subject to considerable diffusion) in an organization it flows along particular channels which reflect the distribution of power. D. Katz and R. L. Kahn ("The Social Psychology of Organizations") have further elaborated the idea of an organization as a social system consisting of the patterned activities of a number of groups.

VALUES

Values are articulated in statements about the aims of individuals or groups which assist members in thinking about what they ought to do. Values are of necessity vague, inchoate, and ambiguous, for otherwise man would be condemned to the fate of a computer program. This indefinite nature allows man both freedom and flexibility.

Exactly the same point is valid for the organization; value statements give its members a measure of discretion which enables the organization to enjoy the freeedom which is essential for coping with the uncertainties of the contemporary turbulent environment. The values which individuals derive from organizational membership are usually described as "climate," and include perception of autonomy, structure, reward orientation, and support.

INTERACTION WITH SOCIETY

The organizational theorist sees the whole society both as a context of the organization and as a source of raw material. Organizational psychologists presume an interdisciplinary approach and argue that no academic discipline should be left unturned.

For the executive, at first sight, the anthropologist in Samoa or New Guinea must seem irrelevant. But Sune Carlson, who carried out the first study of executive behaviour by observation, begins his account of the study of the behaviour of his group of Swedish managing directors by comparing them with the Arapesh people studied by Margaret Mead, the famous American cultural anthropologist. When we learn from her study of the Arapesh that they were extremely friendly, that aggression was virtually unknown, and that the Arapesh, when they wanted someone to act as leader for some festive occasion (fiestas are nearly as important as food), experienced considerable difficulty in persuading someone to fill this role, then the excursion into anthropology can be understood.

Again, the now-classic relation between psychological distance and executive effectiveness was suggested by an investigation which had as its objective an assessment of the effectiveness of different psychotherapists. It was found that the ineffective therapist was the one who said something like this "Let's face it, there is something wrong with you. You're different from me—from other people." The effective therapist, on the other hand, might say, "Well, that's not too bad—we are more or less in the same boat." In the therapeutic context, the psychologically closer therapist is more effective. But what happens in business? In an organizational setting, this suggested that the psychologically distant executive (the task specialist) might be more efficient. The researcher went on to measure psychological distance and then to study basketball teams (losing teams have human relations specialists as leaders, i.e., the psychologically closer type), then tank crews and bomber crews, then the managers of co-operatives.

Organization theorists study all kinds of organizations

Organization theorists do not confine their interest only to the industrial organization, but believe that much can be learned from the study of different types of organization. For example in studying socialization (or how members assimilate values, norms, and attitudes), the student of organizational behaviour would inevitably want to look at how patients become institutionalized in a mental hospital, how priests are prepared for ordination, how officers are produced at cadet schools, and how budding *Mafiosi* "make their bones," as well as worrying about how the IBM man gets the IBM look. The same subjects would be a fruitful field for anthropologists (studying initiation rites in primitive tribes), social psychiatrists (researching "anti-hospitals" to find out how doctors learn their new role as patient), and social psychologists (studying how new group members negotiate access to groups).

To show how widely researchers in this field have cast their nets, two quite different organizations have been selected as illustrations—the mental hospital and the Mafia.

MENTAL HOSPITALS AS ORGANIZATIONS

What do the running of a hospital and the management of a business have in common? A good example of the virtue of such a comparison has been provided by a study of the value of insulin therapy for patients in mental hospitals.

The background for this type of therapy lay in the fact that it was discovered that a low dosage of insulin had a good effect on the patient by restoring or improving his appetite, which (when gratified) made the patient feel better; so this therapy was sometimes used while the psychiatrist was deciding on an appropriate treatment. Psychiatrists, like social scientists and managers, are forced to try a wide range of methods in a spirit of trial and error. Insulin in larger doses was tried as a cure for carefully selected schizophrenics and found to be successful in a proportion of cases (however, the treatment induced a state of coma and as many as 60 treatments might be required; and some patients died on account of the severity of the treatment).

In these first experiments, only the insulin dosage was considered as the therapeutic agent. But further experimentation using a control group who were treated with tranquilizers suggested that insulin might not be the therapeutic agent. In *Administrative Therapy* (with the intriguing subtitle "The Role of the Doctor in the Therapeutic Community") David H. Clark suggested another explanation which a business executive would readily understand. He reviewed the history of insulin shock therapy and came up with a very interesting conclusion as to the true therapeutic agent. It was found that the people making up the "insulin unit" were a warm, closely knit group within the hospital. In effect, what was happening was that a life or death crisis was being induced and a group composed of the patient and a dedicated band of doctors and nurses joined forces to try to save the patient's life—a good example of group dynamics, with values, norms, and roles inevitably emerging. This intense situation was group dynamics with a difference, compared with the normal laboratory situation where groups of students cut up pieces of cardboard and rewards were pitched at the level of $1 an hour. Only members of a group who have lived through a crisis of this type can appreciate the significance of the bonds that the task generates.

Total institutions

What actually happens in a mental hospital? A social anthropologist, Caudill, entered a small neurosis unit as a "patient," as a "participative observer," and reported what happened to him. His account of his experiences has a distinct Hawthorne ring about it and is reminiscent of accounts of other social scientists' experience in the workshop as operators. Caudill tells how the other patients taught him what his role was to be, what "cover stories" he was to feed the staff, and in general codified the mores, values, norms, and sanctions of the inmates.

A brilliant sociologist, Erving Goffman, has compared mental hospitals with other "total institutions" such as prisons, boarding schools, and officer cadet schools. Clark in *Administrative Therapy* observes that:

> Goffman points out that all these total institutions develop certain social patterns—a psychological isolation from the outside world; a denial of previous social or educational differences; a "stripping process" in which the entrant loses all those things that gave him his previous identity (clothes, money, personal belongings, hair) and is dressed in uniform garb,

a private jargon; a unique and peculiar system of rewards and punishments for actions not regarded as exceptional in the outside world; a system of special roles such as "court jester"; and special Saturnalia-like festivals.

The question that must spring to the minds of many managers is, "To what extent are our large companies total institutions?"

The schizophrenic—The elected psychotic of the family

The subject of schizophrenia, at first sight, might seem an improbable and unprofitable focus for the behavioural scientist looking at organizations. But the *avant-garde* among psychiatrists now see schizophrenia as having one of its causes in the development of a particular role in the family group; its cure is closely interlocked with organizational matters.

Instead of the traditional view of schizophrenia as a pathological organic state whose nature is as yet unknown but which is largely determined by genetic and constitutional factors, this disease was seen as partly a product of the family situation where the patient's sentiments and evaluations were not given approval, but on the contrary were confused by the very penetrating and inescapable ambiguities of the "double-bind" situation: the "do me a favour—drop dead" type of instruction. The conclusion was that schizophrenia was not a disease of one person but rather a group phenomenon where a whole family behaved in a crazy way. David Cooper in "The Anti-Hospital: An Experiment in Psychiatry" has presented his argument:

> For the emerging view is that acute schizophrenia is not a disease process with as yet undetermined somatic or psychological causes, but rather that it is a *Microsocial crisis situation* in which one member of a group, usually a family group, is elected by a process which is often violent and arbitrary to become the patient.

To unravel this complication of personal relations underlying schizophrenia he set up an anti-hospital "where traditional notions of authority have been upended, with 'results' that seem to be favourable." In the anti-hospital,

> there was a progressive blurring of role between nurses, doctor, occupational therapist, and patients which brought into focus a number of disturbing and apparently paradoxical questions: for example, can patients "treat" other patients and can they even treat staff? Can staff realise quite frankly and acknowledge in the community their own areas of incapacity and "illness" and their need for "treatment"? If they did what would happen next and who would control it?

It does not follow from this brief account of Cooper's ideas that environmental factors such as the double-bind situation are widely accepted as the only cause of schizophrenia; undoubtedly constitutional and genetic factors are of paramount importance in the complex causation of schizophrenia. The value of Cooper's ideas lies in his identification of organizational factors in the onset and treatment of schizophrenia.

In general terms, what is being argued is that mental hospitals are organizations with hierarchies, roles, and values; in fact, with all the conceptual paraphernalia found in organizations everywhere. Therefore their problems and solutions which have organizational implications are of great interest to both behavioural scientists and executives, who have a profound interest in becoming aware of such experiments. This exchange of concepts is a two-way affair. Psychiatrists and hospital administrators have a considerable interest in organization theory, for hospitals and businesses have much in common.

A variety of management systems are employed in mental hospitals, reflecting different organization theories. The more advanced are using the concept of the therapeutic community; less sophisticated hospitals are at the human relations stage; and many are still at the custodial phase. It is within this common frame of reference that Cooper's work must be judged.

For Cooper the significant problem of the psychiatric hospital is the need to distinguish between authentic and inauthentic authority.

> The "official" practice of psychiatry in this country, whatever progressive mantle it may don, aims only too often at enforcing conformism to the rigid, stereotyped dictates and needs of authority persons who refract on to the patient massified and alienated social expectations and hidden injunctions as to who and what he may be. The authority of the authority person is granted him by arbitrary social definition rather than on the basis of any real expertise he may possess. If staff have the courage to shift themselves from this false position they may discover real sources of authority in themselves. They may also discover such sources of authority in "the others" who are defined as their patients.

The most important mark of authentic leadership is the denial of the impulse to dominate others. The lesson for management does not have to be underlined.

Many of our senior managers, especially those who are products of such "total institutions" as the Ivy League university and business schools, have been brought up in an environment where every gesture, both conscious and unconscious, has the effect of structuring roles so that a steep authority gradient is created. This may be no bad thing in a static business situation which is predictable and capable of high definition, where coordination is prime and innovation of minimal importance.

In the contemporary dynamic business, authority is where you find it. This is especially true in the science-based industries, where by design the authority structure is frequently left unfrozen so that the innovating point of success can be reinforced. The management of innovation assumes that authentic authority cannot be equated with structural authority but must be thought of as having an affinity with sapiential authority.

THE MAFIA AS AN ORGANIZATION

Mario Puzo in *The Godfather* has given us a study of a powerful organization. Our discussion is based purely on this fictional work, but there is reason to believe the fiction is solidly grounded in real life and that we can learn from it. (It should also be noted that our use of the term Mafia is simply shorthand for organized crime in America; while the name applies to the Sicilian original, it is disputed as a correct term for American activities.)

As an organization, the Mafia must be comparable to others; and we can use the criteria of structure, process, and values as the means of comparison.

The structure is basically the unit called a Family, headed, as shown in Figure 1–10, by a Don. Puzo's book centres around Don Corleone, leader

FIGURE 1–10
STRUCTURE OF THE MAFIA FAMILY

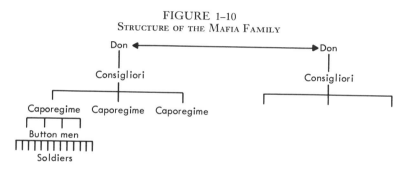

of one of five Families in New York City. The Don's authority is much like that of a feudal lord—more than a company president but somewhat less than a monarch. A role peculiar to this structure is that of the *Consigliori* (counsellor). He is, like many other aides, a trusted, reliable, capable second to his chief; but because of the nature of the activities, he is also vital as an insulation from betrayal. As the sole channel of communication from the Don to the rest of the organization, he ensures that orders to perform illegal acts can be traced only so far—and Puzo avers that no *Consigliori* has ever been known to betray his Don. The next rank is that of *caporegime (capo)*, a position much like that of vice president. Each *capo* heads a *regime* of "soldiers" (the rank-and-file worker), and each has particularly reliable lieutenants or assistants called "button men." Don Corleone is described as having three *capos*, each of whom can, when necessary, muster about 500 men.

At the upper levels, the Family portrayed in *The Godfather* is closely knit and often related by blood and marriage. Being of Sicilian origin is considered very important, although there are notable exceptions—Don Corleone's *Consigliori*, for example. One of his *capos* is the Don's oldest son; nepotism operates as in many other organizations—it is a factor, but ability and inclination may supersede it. The Don may also, like other fathers, be torn betweeen wanting his sons in the family business and wanting for them "better things" (only sons are of interest; in this complete patriarchy, female chattels stay on domestic pedestals and keep up a sort of grim pretence that they're not sure what the menfolk do for a living). Moving down in the ranks, it becomes less important whether the soldier identifies so completely with the Family, has the right ethnic background, or even is a full-time employee—but at every level, loyalty is considered the paramount value.

FIGURE 1–11
ORGANIZATION PROCESSES

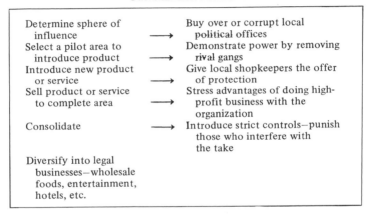

Determine sphere of influence	Buy over or corrupt local political offices
Select a pilot area to introduce product	Demonstrate power by removing rival gangs
Introduce new product or service	Give local shopkeepers the offer of protection
Sell product or service to complete area	Stress advantages of doing high-profit business with the organization
Consolidate	Introduce strict controls—punish those who interfere with the take
Diversify into legal businesses—wholesale foods, entertainment, hotels, etc.	

The relationships between Families are ambiguous. Rivalry within a city may lead to full-scale war; truces are uneasy at best. On a national scale, the book portrays one meeting designed to form a trade alliance between cities, but it seems only a weak confederation making some general agreements and allocations of territory (Miami and Las Vegas are designated "open cities").

The processes of the organization may be roughly described as in Figure 1–11. There are many points of comparison to other businesses if one can put aside the knowledge that the products and services are such items as drugs, prostitution, gambling, and juice loans and that salesmanship is carried out through extortion, concrete life-jackets, and the like. Each Family controls particular areas or particular activities in its city (an allocation achieved by force exerted against other Families; one process is thus the coming-of-age or initiation rite in which a member "makes his bones" by killing a member of an enemy Family).

It is the value system of organized crime which most sets it apart in a behavioural sense. Whatever outsiders may think, the Mafia member lives by a code which is valid to him, and Puzo makes us understand many aspects of it. Poor inhabitants of our city slums have looked to the Mafia in much the same way others looked to trade unions and other legitimate avenues to a livelihood and to "success." It cannot be denied that the U.S. experiment in enforcing "morality" in the guise of Prohibition was the greatest impetus to the founding (and condoning) of large, well-organized underworld groups. Those unable to "make it" in other ways could often turn to these groups for jobs, many forms of assistance, and even a chance at becoming powerful and respected in that milieu.

The value system incorporates many qualities society in general regards as virtues—as mentioned, loyalty above all, friendship, family love, honouring one's word, chastity in young daughters, and so on (all, as with humanity in general, routinely violated although revered). To be a "man of respect" is the great ideal; Don Corleone is such, and is pictured as courteous and courtly in personal relationships (hence the affectionate name "Godfather").

The organization and society

Perhaps most interesting of all is the attitude of outsiders towards this portrayal of organized crime. *The Godfather* as a book was a best-seller and as a movie one of the greatest box-office attractions of all time. Why? Social critics see in it parallels to legitimate activities, and it is recommended as a study in organizational behaviour; but those can scarcely be the reasons it attracted droves of paying customers. It is true that it has generous lacings of sex and violence, always popular ingredients. But it is not unreasonable to suspect something more: that the straight citizen is not as sure of his own value system as he might be. Not only the poor immigrant may be looking at the rich, powerful hoodlum in his expensive clothes, car, and home and feeling something at least akin to envy. Money and its concomitants are so common to value systems that we may almost forget to list them as such, and to acknowledge that in truth far too many of us worship at the bank of our choice and have ambivalent attitudes when being law-abiding faces direct competition from "grab what you can."

Some such attitudes must account for the observable tolerance for illegal activities and the political and social corruption necessary for their existence. The Mafia man might well echo the slogan that he "gives the public what it wants," for he could not stay in business without the patronage of "honest" citizens. It is not fiction but fact that the Don Corleones of America live in our best suburbs, hobnob with celebrities in legitimate circles, and have less to fear from the law than the small-time burglars and streetwalkers at the bottom of their structural heap. Here, then, is a good example of how studying an organization can escalate our focus to a consideration of the structure, process, and value system of society itself.

THE DOUBLE BIND:
THE ORGANIZATIONAL VERSUS THE EXISTENTIAL SIGNAL

What does this brief trip around the mental hospital and the Mafia tell us about organizational life? The first point to note (which is more obvious in the case of the Mafia but is valid for all organizations, including mental hospitals) is that all organizations have a structure, process, and value system. Structure can be thought of as the anatomy of the system and process as its physiology; the value system defines goals, norms, and appropriate reinforcements and sanctions.

To catch a snapshot of how organizations operate we have briefly reviewed two cases of total institutions which have highly unusual processes and value systems. To grasp what is happening in these apparently bizarre processes necessitates some knowledge of what psychiatrists, psychoanalysts, and social anthropologists have discovered from their research.

For example, an experienced executive has little difficulty in understanding the relevance of R.D. Laing's double bind, for that is how organizations frequently operate—sending signals to members which send them scuttling back into their roles while their innermost beings are sending a different kind of signal which in effect is saying, "Are you a man or a mouse? Stand up and be counted." The complexities, ambiguities, and anxieties of the double bind are best reviewed in the process of socialization—how people get into their roles and the inevitable human reactions as they struggle to avoid existential hell, to maintain their centres, to stay aware and authentic, to be what destiny meant them to be, to be in good faith and good standing with their fellows.

The double bind—two contradictory signals, one systemic and the other existential—represents the crucial problem of organizations. As our examples show, peeople identify with an organization not because it is "normal" or "legal" but because it has a structure, process, and value system which works for them and fits with the history of their socialization.

TOPIC 3
A contingency model for the study of organizational behaviour

Organizational behaviour is a very complicated subject, with all sorts of convoluted theories, ranging from the naive and simplistic to the complex. The theories have varying empirical bases (some have none), with the data collected in a wide variety of ways, stretching all the way from casual observation to careful interviewing to computer analysis of documents. To add further complication, studies in different environmental milieux are integrated without adequate qualification. The basic difficulty is that few theorists in this field have faced up to the problem of developing an adequate taxonomy of framework to organize the intelligence available.

A comprehensive model of organizational behaviour would have many advantages. It would suggest to the researcher and practitioner what to look for, what has been left out, what research strategies to use, and how to experiment with and then integrate different findings. In developing such a model, the theorist must consider certain questions, including:

1. What is the conceptual level of the system? Is the individual, the group, or the organization the subject of the model?
2. What are the critical dimensions of the model? For example, in physics, once it had beeen recognized that the critical dimensions were force, mass, space, and time, the subject made dramatic progress. In organizational behaviour, the problem is more complex because the question is about the critical dimensions of a living system.
3. Is productivity, human satisfaction, or some combination of task and human satisfaction the end product which is measured? The answer to this question will prove useful and relevant in determining the critical dimensions.
4. How did you find out what you found out? What kind of research method was used—case study, field study, laboratory experiment? How were the data collected—by observation, interview, examination of documents?
5. What was the environmental milieu of the subject (individual, group, or organization)?

How each of these questions is answered determines the kind of model that will emerge.

SYSTEM LEVEL

As we have already noted, there has been a steady escalation of conceptual focus from the individual to the group to the organization. Figure 1–12 again diagrams this shift in focus and its results. In this section, we have omitted society as a level because its consideration is less structured, often impinging at other levels or simply serving as what we here call environment.

CRITICAL DIMENSIONS

The three most powerful, pervasive, and fundamental dimensions of organizational behaviour are structure, process, and values. We have already described these factors as they pertain to organizations; now we look at them again as dimensions of a system, within a wider frame of reference. What is important to note in this frame of reference is the use of

FIGURE 1–12
SYSTEM LEVEL OF THE MODEL

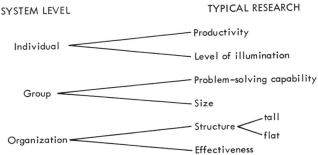

the term *behaviour systems*. Behaviour systems include the three system levels, as shown in Figure 1–13.

To fit each dimension into this systems frame, we must be aware that structure is essentially theological in character and usually tells us what *ought* to happen, whereas process is essentially what *is* happening. In the technical language of the behavioural scientist, structure is normative and contains "ought" propositions; process is positive and contains "is" propositions.

We identify structure and process as corresponding to the statics and dynamics of the physicist, the form and content of the logician, or, if you like, the anatomy and physiology of the medical student. Why bring in values? The need for values as an explanatory dimension becomes obvious when it is recognized that behaviour systems are teleological in nature: purpose is built into the interaction between structure and process. The structure and process and their interactions have built into them a programmed purpose which makes the system goal-seeking.

STRUCTURE

Structure describes the shape, the anatomy, the framework which holds the system together. Structure is essentially static in nature and refers to

FIGURE 1–13
CRITICAL DIMENSIONS OF A BEHAVIOUR SYSTEM

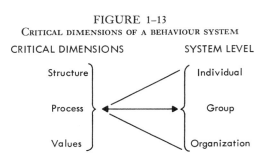

the network of relations. Structure is like the apparatus which you might use to carry out an experiment in chemistry. It describes the round-bottomed flask, connecting glass tubes, filters, gas jars, and so on. But nothing happens until you pour in the chemicals. Then the process begins; the action starts and things begin to happen—some of them unexpected, if you don't get the proportions right.

Much the same happens in behaviour systems. The process, the sequence of activities, frequently bubbles over the structure. The process is the physiology of behaviour and is much less predictable than the structure.

PROCESS

Thinking about organizations in meaningful terms is greatly facilitated by treating organizations as information-processing systems. We have noted that the raw material of organizations is information. The organization is essentially a network of roles which is structured in a particular way so that information flows through it according to definite paths, depending on which activity or function is being evoked.

Essentially, as Figure 1–14 shows, structure is the network of information flows; process defines what is done to the information at each stage.

For example, Figure 1–15 illustrates how the doctor-patient relationship can be studied structurally (the middle column) in terms of the rules, roles, and relationships. The right-hand column indicates how it can also be studied in terms of the processing of information.

In more general terms, all organizational processes can be described in systems terms. Using a model such as Figure 1–16, it is possible to record the actual sequence and phasing of events and critically examine the effectiveness of the process.

VALUES

The third critical dimension of organizational analysis is values. Values are involved in the selection of aims, and the existence of a value system helps an organizational member to choose between conflicting activities or

FIGURE 1–14

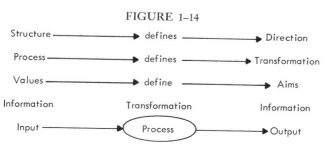

FIGURE 1–15
DOCTOR-PATIENT PROCESS

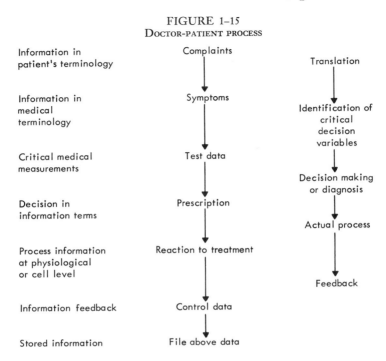

Information in patient's terminology	Complaints	Translation
Information in medical terminology	Symptoms	Identification of critical decision variables
Critical medical measurements	Test data	Decision making or diagnosis
Decision in information terms	Prescription	Actual process
Process information at physiological or cell level	Reaction to treatment	Feedback
Information feedback	Control data	
Stored information	File above data	

purposes. Values of necessity must always be vague, indefinite, ambiguous statements phrased in the form of moral injunctions or imperatives, because it is impossible to state in clear, unambiguous terms what the purposes of an organization, group, or individual are. If life were otherwise, it would be possible to spell out in mechanical or computer terms what actually is happening and what will happen next. Behavioural science can produce such descriptions and predictions only in probability terms for a limited number of variables (usually two) in very restricted circumstances (usually in the laboratory with captive students).

FIGURE 1–16
SYSTEMS WITH SUBSYSTEMS

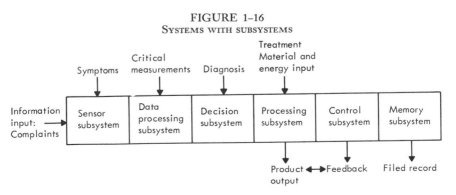

If it is accepted for the moment that values are vague descriptions or imperatives, what form do they actually take? They usually emerge in the form of slogans:

STEAM TOWARDS THE SOUND OF GUNFIRE
OFFENCE IS THE BEST FORM OF DEFENCE
WHEN IN DOUBT, ATTACK
ANY GOOD SCIENTIFIC PROJECT WILL GET SUPPORT
THE CUSTOMER IS ALWAYS RIGHT
WHAT'S GOOD FOR GENERAL MOTORS IS GOOD FOR THE COUNTRY
PUBLISH OR PERISH
PUBLISH AND BE DAMNED
THINK
WE'RE NUMBER TWO—WE TRY HARDER

An example: Structure, process, and values of a problem-solving group

Turning to the group to illustrate the dimensions of structure, process, and values, R.F. Bales of Harvard has provided an excellent analysis of what happens when a group is given the task of solving a problem. In terms of structure, as shown in Figure 1–17, a task specialist (*TS*)

FIGURE 1–17
ROLES IN A PROBLEM-SOLVING GROUP

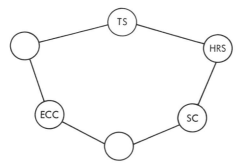

emerges who spends his time "zeroing in on the problem," "getting the show on the road," and generally "tying up loose ends." Meanwhile the human relations specialist (*HRS*) is rushing up with plasma to treat the wounded whom the task specialist has hit on his way to solving the problem. The eccentric (*ECC*) is being funny by introducing bizarre but potentially useful ideas. The scapegoat (*SC*) is picking up the spare hostility floating around the group. The various roles are welded into a particular structure which allows the group to work on its two problems of work (task) and nonwork (human relations).

But as the structure evolves, the group is also working through the process, which in this case consists of:

1. Clarification—What is the problem?
2. Evaluation—How do we feeel about it?
3. Decision—What are we going to do about it?

At the same time, a value system is evolving. A useful paradigm for looking at values, norms, reinforcements, and sanctions is shown in Figure 1–18. Here the overriding value is democracy in the group.

The group as a behaviour system can be described in greater detail, but our point here is only to show that these dimensions of structure, process, and values can be applied to a group. The same kind of analysis can be applied to a football team, an infantry platoon, an assembly line work group, a cell in the Communist Party, or a Family in the Mafia.

FIGURE 1–18
VALUE SYSTEM IN THE GROUP

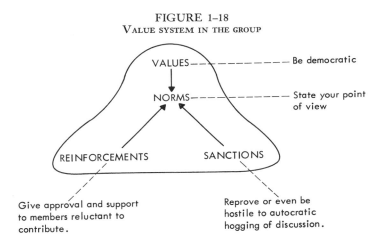

END PRODUCTS: TASK AND HUMAN

All living systems are goal-oriented. The system achieves (or at least attempts to achieve) its goals by working on a task or set of tasks. In the process of working on the task, the organism experiences a degree of satisfaction or dissatisfaction. In the behavioural sciences, a major effort is made to measure task achievement and human satisfaction and also to ascertain the relations between them.

Tasks can be categorized in a wide variety of ways (see Figure 1–19). A major factor is task structure, and tasks can be plotted on a continuum from highly structured (such as the assembly of a bicycle pump) to the relatively unstructured (such as designing a new type of bicycle pump with no mechanical moving parts). Another major factor is complexity. There are obviously different levels of complexity; for example, compare the complexity of starting up a stalled car with that of starting up a stalled heavy water plant. Tasks can also be defined in terms of clarity, feedback (the extent to which achievement can be measured), number of goal

FIGURE 1–19
EXAMPLES OF TASKS

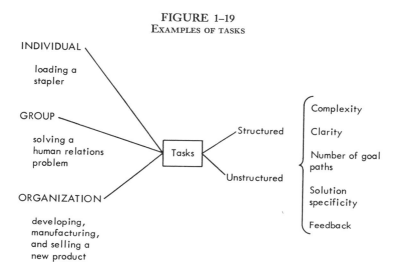

paths (means available for achievement), and solution specificity (number of correct solutions).

As shown in Figure 1–20, the task end products are productivity and profitability. The human end product of systems activity is measured in terms of job satisfaction at the individual level, group satisfaction at the group level, and morale at the organizational level. These end products are indicated by such measures as absenteeism, labour turnover, and number of grievances. A major issue in organizational behaviour is the relationship between productivity and job satisfaction, which will be considered at a later stage.

FIGURE 1–20
MEASURES OF END PRODUCTS

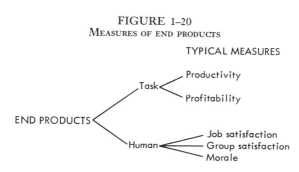

RESEARCH METHOD

The type of research method employed will to some extent determine the research findings and therefore the concepts generated. Figure 1–21 illustrates three principal methods used at any of the conceptual levels.

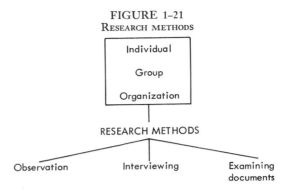

FIGURE 1–21
RESEARCH METHODS

While the whole subject of research methods will be gone into in considerable detail early in the text, perhaps it is sufficient to illustrate this vital consideration by pointing out that two entirely different pictures of the effective executive emerge depending on whether the data are collected by asking his subordinates for a description or by observing him in action.

ENVIRONMENT

The kind of setting in which the data are collected will have a significant effect on the relations being studied. While it is obvious that there are important differences in environments between a study conducted in the 1920s in Chicago (to measure the relation between productivity and group norms) and a similar study conducted in Japan in the 1970s, some theorists are inclined to gloss over such differences. Environment is often the societal conceptual level—the relationships between all of the other factors and the society as a whole.

THE CONTINGENCY MODEL FOR THIS TEXT

It is now possible to fit all these different factors together and come up with a model for this text. Figure 1–22 is our contingency model of an organizational behaviour system. The items in parentheses indicate features (not yet discussed) which will sometimes be added—the model is intended to be flexible and adaptable to systems which will not always fit this "skeleton" in exact details.

The model has been described as a contingency model because it is tied to the view that it is no longer possible to accept the simplistic view that X causes Y under all conditions; the conditions $(C_1, C_2, \ldots C_n)$ under which the relation holds have to be specified. The model employed in the text is meant to direct the reader's attention to the fact for example that structure is a function of technology and that structure in turn signifi-

FIGURE 1–22
MODEL FOR THE STUDY OF ORGANIZATIONAL BEHAVIOUR

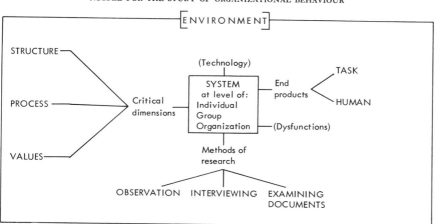

cantly affects process (how people communicate) which in turn affects organizational values. Structure, process and values collectively and individually affect end products (much depends on how you measure them). But all this depends on how you found out (the research method employed). The "It-all-depends" type proposition is what the contingency approach is all about. Hopefully the contingency approach will be clearer when the reader has reviewed; the relation between the structure of the firm and technology in Chapter 2; the connection between the norm of restricting production and the social class of the workers in the primary working group in Chapter 3; the conditions which favour one leadership style in Chapter 9; and so on. The important point now is not only to get the reader worrying about relation of the form:

$$X \longrightarrow Y \text{ under conditions } C_1, C_2, \ldots, C_n$$

but also to suggest which other variables constitute the conditions. Our contingency model spells out the set of variables to be considered for organizational relations.

The purpose of introducing the model early in the text is to provide the reader with a frame of reference which will help him to organize the diverse material in our field of inquiry. Each chapter uses the model as a means of integrating and putting together concepts and research findings developed in that chapter. The whole object of the model is to stimulate the reader to conceptualize in structure, process, and value terms when he looks at the behaviour of individuals, groups, and organizations; and to try to link these factors to the end products, task and human. The model also highlights the importance of both the environment and the way the system was studied, i.e., the methods of research. In many cases it will include the effect of technology on the system or show the dysfunctions of a particular system. Having set out our model, we now turn to the specification of the perspective and posture with which we will approach organizational behaviour.

TOPIC 4
A new perspective and posture toward organizational behaviour

Conventional wisdom as revealed in standard texts on management theory and practice appears largely irrelevant for dealing with organizational realities. An entirely different perspective and posture are required if we are to escape from the current mechanical, wooden explanations of events and get into the real craziness of organizational realities, the true world beyond the looking-glass. The traditional analysis of organizations has been carried through by hard-headed, logical people who have typically approached the problem looking for linear trains of causal events and have adopted an essentially imperialist view of organizations. Their world is made up of line and staff, spans of control, one man–one boss, defined delegation, and authority commensurate with responsibility. It is a world of double-entry bookkeeping and engineering blueprints applied to the human organization.

Meanwhile, back at the firm, organizations were doing all sorts of crazy things they shouldn't do—Ford producing the Edsel, the English and the French producing the Concorde, U.S. combat units in Vietnam putting peace signs on their tanks, transport systems not transporting, police distributing drugs, university students chasing presidents out of their offices, jumbo jets swamping airport facilities, prisons becoming officer cadet schools for criminals, mental hospitals making inmates mentally ill, high schools providing a marketplace for drugs and sex and a theatre for students to thumb their noses at authority, and the Mafia diversifying into straight legal businesses. By beginning with the psychopathology of organizations, the intention is to develop a more relevant way of looking at organizations.

A NEW PERSPECTIVE

The study of organizational behaviour takes place on two levels, macro and micro. The most striking change in this study in the last five years has been the growing recognition that our field of enquiry at the macro level deals primarily with the behaviour of the organization itself, as if it had a separate life of its own, its own personality—with all that that implies in terms of structure, process, and values, to say nothing of more esoteric matters such as climate and culture. With the emergence of systems theory, students of organizational affairs have been given a dramatic new metaphor to get at this kind of macro behaviour. While we are getting to know more about macro behaviour—as theoreticians and researchers speculate about, observe, manipulate, and play with organizations, real and simulated—in fact, organizational behaviour at the micro level is still largely concerned with the behaviour of people in organizations, about which we know a great deal. A curious thing about our subject is that frequently the conditions that favour effective macro behaviour are those that inhibit healthy micro behaviour.

From the new optic, the traditional behaviouristic approach of North American psychologists (as proposed in Skinner's S-R paradigm) is seen as a form of *reductio ad trivia* which has scant relevance for the student of organizational actualities. The new outlook on organizational behaviour is making a vigorous effort to get to the realities of organizational life; and no focuses, no avenues of approach, no maps, no methods are being rejected a priori, because variables are hard to identify and, even worse, when identified difficult to measure. In fact, our field of study is going through a period of convulsive therapy where all kinds of different organizational milieux are being examined by a plethora of techniques—a few rigorously scientific, many somewhat less scientific but occasionally treating subjects of great interest, and a substantial minority whose sole claim to scientific merit lies in the employment of pseudoscientific jargon to disguise the delusory recollections of the executive or academic. Thus a student in this area faces a rather large literature which must be sampled with some discretion if he is going to be encouraged to develop a gourmet taste for good theories and interesting but relevant findings. Presumably the good student is both fastidious about his preparation in terms of methodology and keen to sample the really succulent dishes hidden in the journals from which the material must be extracted.

THE SCOPE OF ORGANIZATIONAL THEORY

The first thing that strikes a student of organizational behaviour as soon as he is a little way into the subject is the breathtaking vastness of its scope. It takes in behavioural sciences (which includes the whole of social psychology), large chunks of sociology, and a dash of social psychiatry. It uses maps drawn from computer science and tries to speak in divers tongues by using the argot of information theory. In its finest presentations, it cuts back and forth effortlessly from Taylor's pig-iron movers at the Bethlehem Steel Works at the turn of the century, being time-studied into productiviy; to Mayo's soldermen and wiremen at Hawthorne in the 1920s, stubbornly resisting dehumanization; to the project managers at NASA in the 1970s, putting together their ad hoc "fly me to the moon." It is easily, equally at home in the Lubianka prison with Solzhenitsyn, evading undesirable encounters with the guards; in the corporate dining room, planning the next merger; and in the mental hospital, figuring out why that psychiatrist is mentally ill. The ultimate aim of organizational behaviour is to illuminate and—on good days—to explain what is happening in all these happenings. To achieve this purpose, it interweaves behavioural science with econometrics and operations research, usually in complex and sophisticated ways.

The idea that binds all these different events together is the notion of organizational theory: the belief that at different stages of our history following the industrial revolution, men have evolved particular perceptual frames of reference for viewing organizational life. Our new perspective does not discard all of this history and "old" theory and groundwork; it rather aims to assimilate and use them in new ways, toward new ends.

A NEW POSTURE

Taking a new posture, a new approach, towards the study of organizational behaviour primarily means understanding the orientations and stances discussed in the following sections.

THE CONTINGENCY APPROACH

Modern organizational behaviour employs a contingency approach. The presumption is that it is not sufficient to know the relationship between X and Y but it is also necessary to state the conditions under which this relation holds. For example, contrary to common prejudice, two way communication is not always superior to one way; "it all depends"; it depends (is contingent) upon certain factors such as the kind of problem being tackled, the people involved, time available, method of measuring performance, and so on. The important point to note is that relations in organizational behaviour are of the form:

$$X \xrightarrow{\text{causes}} Y \text{ under conditions } \begin{matrix} C_1 \\ C_2 \\ C_3 \end{matrix}$$

The contingency approach has transformed organizational behaviour into a much more precise discipline which has led researchers to specify in a much more definitive way not only "what causes what" but also under which conditions. Therefore the received wisdom in our field tells us which group of employees prefer to restrict production; which levels prefer human relations; when democratic leadership is most effective; which spatial layouts facilitate interaction; which technology of production has the highest hierarchy and the broadest broadarchy (span of control); which personality type gets a coronary; and which change strategy is most relevant. The contingency approach can handle more complexity in organizational behaviour and handle it with a measure of subtlety missing in earlier theoretical efforts. To get the contingency approach into action in this text, we have developed the model shown in Figure 1–22, which will be used to pull together the findings and concepts of each chapter.

INFORMATION IS SYSTEM-ORIENTED

The currency of organizational behaviour is information. And information is infinite in quantity; expensive to collect; must be treated selectively; can only be picked up with a taxonomy (classification) based on yesterday's experience (and thus is to some extent irrelevant); causes surprise (which is how we measure it); and fraught with uncertainty. The best way to deal with information is to use the systems approach shown in Figure 1–23. The uncertainty cannot be removed, but it can be reduced.

FIGURE 1–23
THE INFORMATION-PROCESSING SYSTEM

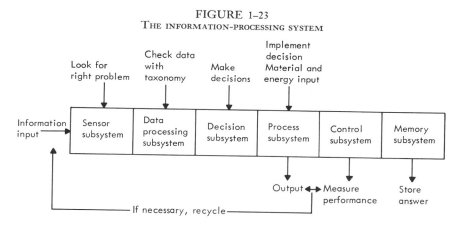

Using the systems approach, the new-style organizational analyst keeps his cool and allows the problem to run over him, hoping that he will pick up the right problem and so on. His dilemmas include:

1. The right problem may be hard to even visualize, while the wrong problem is easily capable of analysis and solution.
2. The taxonomy may be known, but some of the facts won't fit it.
3. Perhaps a decision should be made now; perhaps it should be postponed.
4. Tight control is desirable, but it may stifle innovation.
5. The memory subsystem may be storing aging information, when what is needed is an entirely new framework.
6. The system may be recycling the old problem when it should instead be used to try a new problem.

It was with the appearance of H. A. Simon's seminal papers and books on organizations that the true dimensions of organizational behaviour, the scope of its concern, the multiplicity of its source disciplines, and its potential payoff became apparent. Reading Simon after reading the human relations literature of the 1940s and the industrial psychology papers of the 1920s was like acquiring stereoscopic vision and the ability to see a full range of colours after staring for decades at a blurred black-and-white image. The world had suddenly become larger, as our subject slipped its moorings to the group and sailed into the sea of organizations in societies. Its final port of call may never be reached, but it traverses an infinitely more interesting world where all sorts of people come together to study organizations.

ORGANIZATIONS ARE CHANGE-ORIENTED

The new approach presumes that the chance of gaining a full understanding of how organizations work is slim. They are too complex and complicated to be completely knowable; they are suffused with black regions and black boxes. For organizations "You play it as it lays." Or, more technically, a symbiotic interaction takes place between the executive or researcher and the organization. Like head-over-heels passion, nothing is understood at the time, but what has happened can be explained in tranquillity later. So you shoot for manipulation rather than understanding, hoping that the understanding will come retrospectively.

ORGANIZATIONS ARE DILEMMA-ORIENTED

The organizational analyst and the executive both live in a world suffused with ambiguity and conflict, which are both absolutely essential to the process of organizing. Opposing tendencies are built into organizations, and without them organizations cannot survive, grow, or prosper. Some of the dilemmas are:

1. Integration versus differentiation.
2. Productivity versus quality.
3. Long-term versus short-term.
4. Participation versus timely decision.
6. Control versus innovation.

The contemporary organizational analyst recognizes that both elements in the dilemma have survival relevance and both must be retained. To operate effectively, alternate expressions of these opposed elements are required, rather than a compromise solution.

GOALS ARE REACTIVE

The new approach focuses on the process rather then the typical traditional, theological approach to management which begins with a statement of the objective and then the invention of the means. The new view presumes that statements of objectives are derived reactively from what has happened and describe outputs that have already emerged. Purposes, for the student of organizational behaviour, are largely accounts of fictions which have been pulled together reactively.

BEHAVIOUR IS EXISTENTIAL

The new posture towards organizational behaviour requires an existential approach, with the emphasis on decision (refusal to choose to act unfree), authenticity (real, not phoney, relations must structure the solution), and good faith (maximum information made available to all parties involved). People are accepted as they are and are not prejudged using stereotypes.

Answers (of the type to be found at the back of the book) are not as important as the process used to reach for them. Problems are not regarded as incapable of solution, but a dialectical approach is invoked with the presumption that evolving solutions will generate new problems, and so on. The whole process must be approached in good faith. As Eldridge Cleaver put it, "If you are part of the problem, you have to decide if you want to be part of the solution."

OVERVIEW

Organizational behaviour as a field of enquiry and operation is only just beginning. All sorts of interesting problems in such diverse fields as the military, the women's movement, public administration, education, the commune, the church, and the kibbutz await exploration, creation, and simulation. A whole new field is mushrooming in a wild way which is going to have traumatic effects—both for the traditional academic psychologist puttering in his lab with rats and mazes, and for the staid executive who has lived with relative certainty in worlds of low technological complexity, with complaisant consumers and no Young Turks bent on playing the new systems game at his throat. The game is up. A dramatic intellectual escalation has emerged. Be there.

REVIEW AND RESEARCH

1. Explain the sequence: industrial psychology, human relations, organizational behaviour.
2. Draw up a continuum of organizations ranging from small groups (e.g., a football team) to large and complex organizations (e.g., universities, large corporations). Make a comparison table based on the headings specialization and co-ordination.
3. Organizational behaviour research and theorizing has developed very rapidly in North America. What conditions in North America have favoured this rapid growth?

4. Develop a model for the interview showing the different choice points and feedback loops. Develop a strategy for job hunting from this model.
5. Compare and contrast the structure, process, and values of any two of the following: the Catholic Church, an infantry division, the Mafia, a mental hospital.
6. Review the last four issues of the following periodicals: *The Administrative Science Quarterly*, *The Journal of Management*, and *Management International*. List the various articles that relate to organization theory.
7. What are the characteristics of the systems approach? Develop a systems description of the interaction between a methadone treatment centre and the pusher's network on the street. Specify structure, process, and values for each subsystem and show how they interact.
8. Describe the experience of being institutionalized in one of the following organizations: the military, the church, a school of business, the Scouts, or a large corporation such as IBM.
9. Review the last 12 issues of the *Harvard Business Review* and *Fortune*. Compare and contrast these two journals under the following headings: editorial point of view, readability, focus of interest, depth of analysis, relevance, and omissions. Cite examples to support your judgements.
10. Develop definitions of alienation, anomie, and apathy. To what extent do they apply to your own experience? If they do not, why?
11. What is existentialism? What does it have for you?
    a. What gives your life meaning?
    b. Try to state what your three most fundamental values are.
    c. What are the choices which you face today?
    d. What holds you back from making these choices?
    e. Write down the names of two people you understand and two people you do not understand. Try to list their respective values, attitudes, needs, and expectations.

GLOSSARY OF TERMS

Black box. A term used by systems analysts to denote that part of a particular system whose internal mechanism is unknown to him. The analyst knows the input-output relationship pertaining to the black box but he does not know how the input is transformed into the output.

Contingency approach. In organizational behaviour this is the presumption that a relationship can only be valid under certain conditions or contingencies. More specifically;

$$X \xrightarrow{\text{causes}} Y \text{ under conditions } C_1, C_2, \ldots, C_h$$

For example, one way communication is more effective than two way when the task is simple, the group is structured, the status gradient is clear, and communication is restricted (e.g. by radio).

Cybernetics. This term, coined by Norbert Wiener and derived from a Greek word meaning steersman, refers to the science of feedback mechanisms. It may also be viewed as the study that attempts to explain how systems achieve a balance while pursuing a mission.

Ergonomics. This new science, sometimes known as human factor engineering, is concerned with designing the job to suit the man.

Existentialism. A new approach in the area of psychology-philosophy-ethics where the emphasis is on a holistic view of man ("man supersedes the sum of his parts") in an interpersonal setting. The purpose of existentialism is to make man more aware of the choices open to him, to stop him from choosing to act unfree, and to make life more meaningful by the perceptive acceptance of reality as something which is seen through value-loaded senses.

Game. An organized activity in which the players or decision makers act within a simulated environment which may or may not be programmed. The nature of a game is usually competitive.

Group therapy. The treatment of neuroses by means of group interaction.

Management theories. 1. The *classical theory of organization* has two major variants. (a) The *machine theory of organization* is sometimes known as the physiological organization theory because it is concerned with a narrow range of relatively simple physiological tasks and emphasizes a limited number of variables. In this approach man is thought of as a machine motivated exclusively by economic considerations. (*b*) The *administrative management theory*, developed by Urwick, is based on the theory of departmentalization which assumes that an organization, given an overall mission, will be able to identify the required tasks, allocate and co-ordinate these tasks by giving jobs to sections, place the sections within units, unite the units within departments, and co-ordinate departments under a board, all in the most economic manner.

2. The *human relations school* argues that an organization should be considered as a social system which has both economic and human dimensions. Effectiveness is achieved by arranging matters so that people feel that they count, that they belong, and that work can be made meaningful.

3. The *systems approach* treats an organization as a sociotechnical system and is concerned with the development of optimal organizations within which the objective and the available resources, both human and technical, determine the activities to be performed and the methods of work to be employed. Three propositions illustrative of the terse economic excellence in the systems approach are: (*a*) technology is a major determinant of industrial behavior, (*b*) optimal organization is not a function of personality, and (*e*) generally, any attempt to optimize an end-product variable will cause other end-product variables to become increasingly suboptimal. Production blitzes are frequently achieved at the expense of product mix, maintenance, or morale. In this context the major management problem is the definition of acceptable margins of suboptimality in the significant variables.

Organization. A social system of two or more groups constructed for the purpose of achieving goals.

Organizational behaviour. The systematic study of the nature of organizations: how they begin, grow, and develop, and their effect on individual members, constituent groups, other organizations, and larger institutions.

Power paradox. The fact that it is frequently possible to achieve understanding of organizational behaviour without being able to predict its character in specific circumstances.

Precision paradox. The fact that we can frequently achieve precision in prediction without understanding how the predicted outcome was produced.

Process. This term refers to the physiology of a system, how the states of a system are changed. Specifically, process describes the technological and organizational activities for transforming inputs into outputs. Men, material, money and information constitute the raw material of the process.

Structure. The shape, anatomy, or framework of a system.

System. Any part of the universe on which the investigator may choose to focus his attention. A *social system* is defined with respect to a decision maker who pursues a goal. A *closed system* is one that has no interaction with its environment. An *open system* is one that interacts with its environment.

Steady state. A system is said to be in a steady state if the internal structure or parameters of the system remain constant over time despite a considerable range of external changes.

Values. An important class of beliefs held by members of an organization or society concerning what is desirable or "good." Values result from choices between competing human interests in pursuit of goals. A traditional value system may emphasize integrity, independence, and hard work; another may underscore authenticity, awareness, and interdependence; and so on.

part one

Theories, methods, and technologies

THEORIES

In Chapters 2, 3, and 4, which are devoted to the classical theory, human relations approach, and systems theory, respectively, we quickly set out the issues, processes, and consequences of each theory.

		Topics
Chapter 2 The Classical Theory	1.	Scientific management and administrative management theory
	2.	Bureaucracy
	3.	Technology and organization structure
	4.	Evaluation of classical theory
Chapter 3 Human Relations	1.	The Hawthorne experiment
	2.	Theory X and Theory Y
	3.	Alienation
	4.	Evaluation of human relations thory
Chapter 4 Systems Theory	1.	The new perspective of open systems
	2.	The organization as an information-processing system
	3.	Evaluation of all three theories

METHODS

In Chapter 5 we define the scope, methods, and limitations of the behavioural sciences and discuss the three basic methods of research. We review the theme of action research in organizations through a detailed look at the Harwood and Glacier studies.

	Topics
Chapter 5	1. The behavioural sciences
Behavioural Science	2. Action research in organizations
	3. The integration of behavioural science and technology

TECHNOLOGIES

Chapter 6 reviews the change strategies behavioural scientists have devised to control, monitor, and manipulate behaviour, beginning with an overview of how the various models of man link to the three theoretical schools.

	Topics
Chapter 6	1. S-R technology: Skinnerism
Behavioural Technology	2. S-O-R technology: The VANE model
	3. P-G man: The path-goal model
	4. Learning and the new training technique
	5. A critical review of behavioural technology

2

The classical
theory

A surprising characteristic of organization theory is that, in spite of the contemporary sustained discussions of adhocracy, matrix management, and project management, so many businesses and all kinds of other institutions are still structured according to the classical theory. What apparently happens in practice is that managers, when they become aware of new developments either in human relations or systems theory, try to assimilate them into the classical structure. Thus it seems reasonable to begin by asking why the classical form has survived so well.

It has been argued that the classical theory persists essentially because it provides a pro-management ethos which gives the manager the initiative in decision making and only requires consultation with subordinates as an optional extra. Further, the classical approach—with its division of personnel into such categories as officers and men, salaried and hourly paid, and line and staff—gives a nice cosy feeling to the officers.

The classical theory as we know it to-day had its origins in the political changes introduced in France after the Revolution of 1789, which were seized upon by the Prussians as a means of unifying their nation into an efficient instrument of military and industrial power. Max Weber (1864–1920), a German sociologist who is best known for his treatise *The Protestant Ethic and the Spirit of Capitalism*, made the most significant contribution to the development of classical theory by setting out his ideas on the "ideal organization," which he called bureaucracy. But developments in management thought were not an exclusively German activity. Henry Fayol (1841–1925), a leading French industrialist, published in

1916 at the age of 75 his most famous treatise, *Administration Industrielle et Générale,* in which he proposed a general theory of administration which, while it did not have a wide dissemination in the United States until 1949, had a profound effect on management thought. Fayol's unique contribution was his analysis of administrative activities into five primary elements: planning, organizing, command, co-ordination, and control. While Fayol did not present his ideas as a systematic management theory, he did emphasize that the principles underlying the management process could be applied in any organizational setting.

Following the pattern set by Fayol, Luther Gulick and Lyndall Urwick co-operated in 1937 in editing *Papers on the Science of Administration,"* which helped to get the idea abroad that bureaucratic principles of administrative management theory could be applied to all types of organizations.

STRUCTURE OF CHAPTER 2

Three interlocked topics and a critical review of them are discussed in this chapter. The first topic is scientific management and administrative management theory. It sets forth the contributions made by Frederick Taylor, Lyndall Urwick, and others to the classical principles of management theory.

Topic 2 maps out how bureaucracy emerged both as a historical actuality in 19th-century Germany and as a theoretical concept of the ideal organization in the 20th century.

In our third topic, the impact of technology on organizational structure is reviewed, with particular attention being paid to the work of the British school and to the measurement of end products and the dysfunctions of control systems.

Topic 4 closes the chapter with an evaluation of the classical theory.

TOPIC 1
Scientific management and administrative management theory

SCIENTIFIC MANAGEMENT

Many of the techniques used today by managers, including production planning and control, work study (time and method study), incentive plans, and quality control, have their origins in the scientific management movement that created enormous enthusiasm among managers and considerable despondency among trade unionists in the first two decades of this century. Frederick W. Taylor, who has been called the father of modern management and who was the first management consultant, created and developed a new field of industrial engineering which he called scientific management. Taylor's concept of the working man was strongly influenced by the so-called Protestant ethic, which emphasizes the values of achievement, deferment of consumption, economic rationality, and individualism. Taylor basically assumed that the working man would work flat out to maximize his economic interest and thus would welcome any process that facilitated this achievement.

Based on his actual work experiences at the Midvale Steel Company, Bethlehem Steel Company, and as a consultant to many firms, Taylor formulated specific solutions to the problems of management, including:

1. Selecting the right man for the job.
2. Deciding by method study on the one best way to do the job.
3. Developing differential piece-work plans that reward effort.
4. Careful planning of the actual work process.
5. Developing line and functional specialization.

Applying these principles, Taylor was able to achieve dramatic increases in productivity.

Taylor's ideas had a significant and sustained impact on management when he promulgated them, and to-day his principles are still built into most organizations. Helping him to spread the gospel of scientific management were his associates, Henry Gantt, Frank and Lillian Gilbreth, and Harrington Emerson. Their combined efforts in their several fields produced developments in management techniques. (A good example of this teamwork was the marriage of Frank and Lillian Gilbreth, the engineer and the psychologist, who—to the subsequent delight of many readers—practised such techniques on their *Cheaper by the Dozen* family.)

While Taylor was not an organization theorist, he did provide a number of explicit concepts concerning management which were absorbed into the development of classical theory. For example, in 1895 Taylor wrote a paper for the American Society of Mechanical Engineers about the importance of separating planning from operating from which can be derived the modern concept of line and staff work.

Coincidentally with the work of the fathers of scientific management, industrial psychologists were investigating hours of work and fatigue, devising selection tests, and generally trying to apply psychological principles to the problems of the industrial engineer.

ADMINISTRATIVE MANAGEMENT

While scientific management was essentially concerned with optimizing effort at the shop floor level, administrative management theory was focused on the development of broad administrative principles applicable at higher management levels. Administrative management theory was developed by Lyndall F. Urwick (born in 1891), who had extensive experience as an executive both in industry and in the military. He was greatly influenced by Taylor, whom he first read during World War I while in France and who was to have a tremendous effect on his whole career. The first World War was a test of management theories at the macro level—a test of the ability of one bureaucracy to destroy another by attrition. At the micro level, desperate efforts in the field of industrial psychology were made (at least in England and the United States) to find the principles and procedures which would facilitate maximum effort from shop floor workers and improve the selection process. Urwick, who immediately recognized the relevance of Taylor's ideas to what he was doing, became director (after the war) of the International Management Institute in Geneva and subsequently took up an appointment as the head of a well-known firm of management consultants.

Urwick's views on management principles and practices became better known in North America when he published, with Gulick, in 1937, a collection of papers on the science of administration. As well as drawing on Taylor, Urwick was influenced by Fayol and by J. D. Mooney and A. C. Reiley, whose book *Onward Industry* had been published in 1931.

Urwick's position in the management literature is not primarily due to his ability to develop new ideas; his place is assured because of a masterful ability to categorize and synthesize the fragmented work of other thinkers and from this material develop a coherent edifice of propositions about management structure and process. Through his writings he popularized such principles as fitting people to the organization structure; the need for unity of command, the use of special and general staffs; departmentalization by purpose, process, persons, and place; the principles of delegation; the balancing of authority and responsibility; and the definition of the span of control.

Integral to Urwick's approach is the paradigm of rationality—the idea that logical analysis rather than personalities should determine how organizations should be structured. For example, the theory of departmentalization assumes that an organization planner, given a purpose, will be able to identify the required tasks and thus the jobs, to organize the jobs in sections, to place the sections within units, to unite the units within departments, and to co-ordinate departments under a board—all in the most economic manner.

Efficiency is to be achieved by task specialization, and three kinds of formal relations—line, functional, and staff—are recognized. Line management is responsible for production and includes the general manager, department manager, foremen, and shop floor workers. Functional management includes managers who deal, not with a product, but with a function such as planning or programming. Staff managers have neither direct line nor functional responsibilities, but derive their purpose from a senior manager for whom they think (by preparing plans) and, on specific occasions, act. In developing such concepts Urwick was greatly influenced by his experience of the army, which is largely organized in this way, even to-day. For such matters as routine administration and separation of line and staff, and above all for a definition of what constitutes completed staff work, the military is not to be surpassed; most textbooks on the management process, even in the 1970s, reflect this source of concept, experience, and practice. The concepts of line, functional, and staff management are almost universally accepted today; and in the past they provided a useful semantic device for conducting discussions to clarify rules, roles, and relations in industrial organizations. But that day has now passed and a different perspective is emerging, where information and process are aces.

What is important to understand about Urwick's work is that he provided managers with a vocabulary which could describe relations in terms of line, function, and staff; he set out the concepts of span of control and unity of command; and he gave management formal guidance on how delegation and co-ordination should be achieved. Figure 2–1 is an example of how an organization chart might show levels of management, functions, and even a break-down of operations.

Two important consequences flowed from Urwick's work, one practical, the other theoretical. The practical consequences can be found in various treatises on management and organization which have appeared on both sides of the Atlantic. For example, E. F. L. Brech's *Organization— The Framework of Management* is to be found on the shelves of the offices of many senior managers both in Britain and the United States. In this compendium Brech, who takes up and updates most of Urwick's views, has produced a systematic and consistent statement of management roles and functions. What is of particular value in Brech's work is the extremely comprehensive set of role descriptions which spell out duties, decisions, responsibilities, and relations with other positions. In fact, a great deal of management activity in the 1940s and 1950s was concerned with the preparation of role descriptions which were hardly ever less than 4 or 5 pages in length and could run to 20 or 30—which had the effect of wonderfully concentrating the manager's mind on both his own job and the organization of his subordinates' jobs. This role description writing, coupled with the drawing up of organization charts spelling out authority in line, functional, and staff terms, greatly cleared the manager's mind to consider such matters as the optimal number of levels in the organization, the best span of control, the definition of what was to be delegated, and the methods of measuring accountability.

Not only did Urwick's work have practical relevance, it also had considerable theoretical impact; it suggested useful concepts such as the span of control, which could be measured empirically. If the measurement could be tied to effectiveness, perhaps the optimal span could be defined.

In the United States the significant inputs to the body of administration management theory came from two General Motors executives, James D. Mooney and Allan C. Reiley, who by their writings had a very considerable effect not only on management practice in the United States

FIGURE 2–1
EXAMPLE OF AN ORGANIZATION CHART

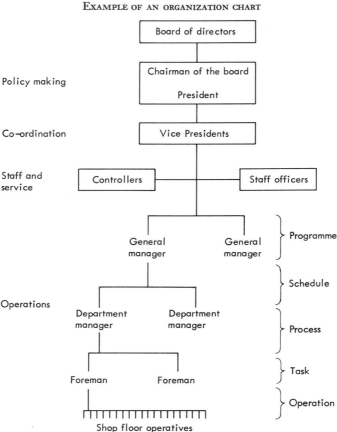

but also in Europe, for they argued that they were drawing up a set of principles which were valid for all organizations. A good illustration of their acumen is revealed in their treatment of co-ordination, which was defined as "the orderly arrangement of group effort, to provide unity of purpose in the pursuit of a common purpose." For Mooney, the very essence of organization is co-ordinated effort, which cannot be achieved unless employees have the high *esprit de corps* which can only be achieved if the organization's members are imbued with its purposes and values.

Contemporary management practice still makes considerable use of the principles of administrative management theory. Presidents still draw up organization charts and talk in terms of line, functional, and staff authority, but less than before. Careful attention is still paid to the writing of role descriptions; though the terminology now being used reflects a different concept of work, requiring the use of such terms as kinds of decisions to be made, time span of discretion, and review mechanism. Both academics and executives still speculate about and occasionally explore the relationship between "tall" and "broad" structures and effectiveness. A great deal of work has gone into such matters as the specification of product organization (where management activities are grouped according to products manufactured or services sold) and process operations (where management activities are arranged on the basis of operational sequence). More recent developments in management practice, such as task groups, project management, and even Alvin Toffler's (*Future Shock*) adhocracy, can be connected to administrative management theories.

While the basic assumptions of administrative management theory, both about man and about the similarities of organizations, are going to be challenged in a moment, consideration of this particular point of view provides an excellent point of departure for study of the evolution of organization theory. Not only for study, but also for practice—for almost all organizations have attempted to assimilate new ideas on human relations and systems theory into the old framework of administrative management theory.

To bring this discussion to a close, it is necessary to draw the reader's attention to an odd characteristic that marks the relationship between management theorizing and practice. In some curious way, which is not understood at all, the two entities seem to proceed on parallel tracks but with only tenuous connections between them. For example, Weber's theory of bureaucracy, which was published posthumously in 1921 in German, appears to owe little or nothing to classical theory, with which in fact it has much in common. As George B. Strother points out in *Social Science Approaches to Business Behavior*, classical theory had lost its élan by 1930, if not before. Yet the world of the organization theorist was held back in its development until the 1940s when R. K. Merton, a sociologist, demonstrated to the rest of the academic and corporate world what a powerful conceptual tool Max Weber had invented in his concept of bureaucracy. But, in fact, executives and government officials had already created bureaucracies which were exhibiting almost all of the characteristics that Weber had inferred from his ideal type. The concept of bureaucracy is a revealing example of the twin-track, parallel but somewhat separate, developments of theory and practice. The same phenomenon can be observed to-day in business, with many executives having already swung over to a style of management based on the concept of an organization as an information-processing system without being aware of a parallel development in organization theory.

But this is to jump ahead of our story. What is important at this juncture is to assess the relevance of Weber's concept of bureaucracy as a construct for developing the classical theory. Also significant is the need to be aware of the social, economic, and political backgrounds which generate management theories and practices. Thus we begin our next topic, bureaucracy, by trying to present it in its proper historical and political context.

TOPIC 2
Bureaucracy

It is almost impossible to carry on a rational discussion of organizational concepts because so many of the required terms, such as bureaucracy and democracy, have emotive connotations in everday parlance. For starters, as every student knows, we hate bureaucracy and love democracy. And yet, as every neophyte organizational analyst also knows, it is impossible to pursue any thorough analysis of organizational forms without using the term bureaucracy. American businessmen hate it; it is a term of derision in the British House of Commons; students feel victimized by it in the universities; in the Soviet Union, bureaucrats are the hated class. But bureaucracy is not simply an emotional catchword, but a technical term which has a respected position in the development of administrative theory.

Bureaucracies appear to have been with us for a very long time. We know from history that from 165 B.C. Chinese officials were chosen by examination; and even in those days matters of seniority, merit ratings, and the establishment of written reports and files were not unknown. In modern times, as early as 1764 the French philosopher Baron de Grimm was complaining about the red tape of his day and was already wondering "who existed for whom" when he noted of the 18th-century French: "here the offices, clerks, secretaries, inspectors and intendants are not appointed to benefit the public interest, indeed the public interest appears to have been established so that offices might exist."

In the language of the 18th century, bureau—as well as meaning a desk—also meant a place where officials worked. And naturally, with words like democracy and aristocracy in common use, the word bureaucracy soon emerged—for the French *bureaucratie,* for the Germans *Bureaukratie* (later *Burokratie*), and for the Italians *burocrazia.* But it was Prussia in the early 19th century which adopted bureaucracy with a vengeance.

In England in the 19th century, Walter Bagehot warned against undue admiration of the bureaucracy of the Prussian state. But in spite of the "essentially un-English nature of bureaucracy," bureaucratic forms of organization were emerging on a large scale in England in the early 20th century, just as Max Weber was writing his classic doctrine on the subject.

To understand Max Weber's ideas on bureaucracy it is necessary to keep in mind that radical and dramatic changes in the theory and practice of administration followed the defeat of Prussia by Napoleon in 1806, and as a consequence Prussia embraced bureaucracy as a means of public administration. As Germany got more experience of large-scale organization, the undoubted advantage of bureaucracy in terms of efficiency became clear. But as Robert Michels, a friend and contemporary of Max Weber, pointed out in his famous aphorism: "Who says organization, says oligarchy."

BUREAUCRACY: THE ADMINISTRATIVE MACHINE

Traditional classical theory (especially as developed by Taylor), which was essentially seen as a development of industrial engineering, had by 1930 lost most of its élan, largely because it lacked any significant theoretical base. Max Weber had developed a sociological theory of organizations which could have provided just such a theoretical base if academics and executives writing in this field had known of his work; but his seminal theorizing did not have much effect in English-speaking countries until the 1940s. There were several reasons for this delay. One reason was that Weber wrote in a ponderous, legalistic, convoluted style, which made it difficult to unscramble and tease out the relevant concepts for organization theory. The other reason was that Weber treated bureaucracy as an ideal type. We shall return to this idea in a moment.

First a word about his background. Max Weber, who qualified in law and was on the staff of the University of Berlin, was the son of a lawyer who was a member of the Prussian Diet and National Liberal member of the Reichstag. His mother was from a Westphalian family of scholars. Perhaps his home background partly explains both his scientific interest in religious phenomena and his passionate interest in the fate of modern nations. In any case, in his parents' home in his youth, he met men eminent in political and academic life who apparently spent a good part of their time debating what directions the new industrial states of their day should take. In all these discussions, there was one academic above all who was taken seriously and that was Karl Marx, whose radical views German scholars took seriously long before they attracted serious attention in either England or America. Though Weber was not a socialist, he was strongly influenced by Marx's analysis of modern society. As Albert Salomon put it, "Max Weber became a sociologist in a long and intense dialogue with the ghost of Karl Marx" (quoted in G. Duncan Mitchell, *A Hundred Years of Sociology*).

To begin his sociological studies and to avoid vagueness, Weber introduced the concept of the ideal type of bureaucracy which, after it had been rigorously defined, would facilitate the comparison of existing cases to the type. It was just this notion of bureaucracy as an ideal type which turned off so many scholars and postponed serious consideration of Weber's ideas. Yet these ideas, as events showed, were to be of tremendous value in integrating organizational thinking and in suggesting useful theoretical frames for important empirical work.

Weber's interest in bureaucracy at first was peripheral, for his first concern was the distinctive features of modern Western capitalism—which, from his historical studies, he realized was only one form of capitalism. In his famous book *Wirtschaft und Gesellschaft* (*Economy and Society*), Weber developed six types of capitalist activities. He argued that the changes in values resulting from the Reformation provided an ethical, and hence an economic, climate which was facilitative of the development of modern capitalism. Weber put forward the view that the Protestant environment in England, and later in New England was the significant reason why these areas developed so rapidly industrially. For Weber, Protestantism—with its emphasis on the virtues of hard work, sobriety, and accumulation of material goods, all as signs of God's grace—gave a society the edge in mobilizing human energies to produce goods, not for personal consumption but as a means of getting to heaven.

But modern Western capitalism achieves its excellence by the employment of rationally constructed organizations which are strikingly different in character from earlier types of organizations, for example, those used in feudal England. To get into this problem, Weber's methodological preference for comparative analysis suggested to him a study of types of law and administration in different historical societies.

The key question behind Weber's analysis of organization is, Why do people obey authority? Fundamentally, he argued, there is always a conception of authority, but the basis of that authority is different in different kinds of institutions. In any institution, one person or a small number of individuals give orders and others obey, and what is vital to understand in this context is that the person giving the orders expects to be obeyed. Why? The reason is that both the official and the subordinate share certain beliefs about the rightness of the process; in short, the authority is seen to be legitimate.

BUREAUCRATIC ORGANIZATIONS

Bureaucracy is the term often used in textbooks of sociology to refer to organizations possessing some sort of administrative machinery and specialized secretariat to keep the organization working. To get a proper understanding of Weber's work it is necessary to distinguish between power and authority. In this context, power refers to the probability that one actor within a social relationship will be in a position to carry out his own will despite resistance from the other party. Weber uses this concept in a rather general way. Authority, on the other hand assumes both voluntary compliance with legitimate demands and suspension of judgment.

Weber recognizes three sources of authority, traditional, charismatic, and legal.

Traditional

In the traditional analysis of authority the social system is viewed as sacred, eternal, and not to be broken. The subject is bound to the ruler by personal loyalty (e.g. divine right of kings), and is usually required to pay homage periodically. It goes without saying that this experience of expressing deference is one which few executives can avoid.

Charismatic

A person acting on the basis of charismatic authority is a missionary inspired by supernatural powers. The leader is usually a visionary with a number of disciples (e.g., Hitler). This authority normally operates as a revolutionary force, rejecting traditional values. Such movements tend to be anarchistic, although as time goes on there is the "routinization of the charisma," which requires setting up institutions to sustain organizational fictions.

Legal

Belief in supremacy of the law. Obedience is not owed to a person but to a set of legal principles. In this system of authority, government is by law, not by men.

Loren Baritz, writing in *The Servants of Power, A History of the Use of Social Science in American Industry*, describes how Alfred Krupp saw in the idea of bureaucracy his chance:

> As the industrial organization was wedged into a carefully designed plan, as managers began to think about lines of authority and communication as well as the problems of meeting a payroll and cutting costs, the bureaucratic pattern emerged. Levels of authority were carefully defined; job roles and positions were analyzed and assigned their predetermined places in the pyramid; relations among and between managers and workers were institutionalized as far as the nature of many would allow. Individualism obviously could not be planned or predicted or controlled and was, for the bureaucratic mentality, outlawed. Alfred Krupp, the German steel manufacturer, early gave this position its classic formulation: "What I shall attempt to bring about (in the Krupp Works) is, that nothing be dependent on the life or existence of any particular person; that nothing of importance shall happen or be caused to happen without the foreknowledge and approval of the management; that the past and the determinable future of the establishment can be learned in the files of the management without asking a question of any mortal." The goal

was to create an organization so perfect that, in the language of classic liberalism, it would be run by law, not by men.

Weber's theory of bureaucracy has five characteristics or marks:

a. Tasks are distributed among various members of the group as official duties, usually accompanied with division of labour and specialization of function. As Weber observes (the following quotations are from H. H. Gerth and C. Wright Mills's *From Max Weber*):

> Modern officialdom functions in the following specific manner:
> There is the principle of fixed and official jurisdictional areas, which are generally ordered by rules, that is, by laws or administrative regulations.
> 1. The regular activities required for the purposes of the bureaucratically governed structure are distributed in a fixed way as official duties.
> 2. The authority to give the commands required for the discharge of these duties is distributed in a stable way and is strictly delimited by rules concerning the coercive means, physical, sacerdotal, or otherwise, which may be placed at the disposal of officials.
> 3. Methodical provision is made for the regular and continuous fulfilment of these duties and for the execution of the corresponding rights; only persons who have the generally regulated qualifications to serve are employed.

b. Offices or roles are organized into hierarchical structures where the scope of authority of superordinates over subordinates is clearly defined. Weber argues that:

> The principles of office hierarchy and of levels of graded authority mean a firmly ordered system of super- and subordination in which there is a supervision of the lower offices by the higher ones. Such a system offers the governed the possibility of appealing the decision of a lower office to its higher authority, in a definitely regulated manner. With the full development of the bureaucratic type, the office hierarchy is monocratically organized. The principle of hierarchial office authority is found in all bureaucratic structures: in state and ecclesiastical structures as well as in large party organizations and private enterprises. It does not matter for the character of bureaucracy whether its authority is called "private" or "public."

c. A formal set of rules governing behaviour is specified which ensures uniformity of organization.

> The management of the modern office is based upon written documents ("the files"), which are preserved in their original or draft form. There is, therefore, a staff of subaltern officials and scribes of all sorts. The body of officials actively engaged in a "public" office, along with the respective apparatus of material implements and the files, make up a "bureau." In private enterprise, "the bureau" is often called "the office."

d. Officials are required to assume an impersonal attitude in contacts with both other officials and clients, which inevitably produces a considerable measure of psychological distance between superiors and subordinates.

e. Employment in a bureaucracy is usually assumed to be a career for life and promotion is by merit.

THE BUREAUCRAT

The bureaucrats or officials who run the bureaucracies are personally free but they must act impersonally, according to the rule which defines their specific areas of competence. They are selected according to merit, receive special training for their posts, and enjoy corporate tenure. They are not elected to their posts but are appointed according to their qualifications, usually measured by examination. They are paid a salary, with increases according to age and experience, and receive a pension when they retire.

What happens to the personalities of the officials who work in bureaucracies? In a classic article entitled "Bureaucratic Structure and Personality," Robert K. Merton, an American sociologist, spelled out the dysfunctions of bureaucracy in terms of "trained incapacity," "occupational psychosis," and "professional deformation." Such terms are used to describe the socializing effect of clinging to corporate problem-solving styles which, while they may have been appropriate in the past, are no longer relevant in the immediate context. Bureaucrats locked in a web of red tape of their own making are unable to cope with the exigencies of a changed situation. The issue, as they used to put it in the British Army, is not the question "Are you fit?" but the response "Fit for what?"

What happens in a bureaucracy is that the mind of the official develops a particular perceptual frame of reference within which going by the book becomes *de rigueur* (see Box 2.1). This condition induces a kind of astigmatism which makes him see the real world in such a way that both his self-interest (in terms of seniority, tenure, and salary) and his administrative convenience (in terms of finding blanket generalized solutions to problems that facilitate record keeping) become paramount.

The problem of the bureaucrat is essentially theoretical in origin and can be seen as flowing from Weber's structural preoccupation with the goals of precision, reliability, and efficiency. Weber made these goals primary without realizing that the process of achieving them is subject to human needs for security (avoiding risk) and administrative convenience (standardizing and simplifying procedures).

As Merton points out, the bureaucratic structure exerts pressure upon the personality of the official to be "methodical, prudent, disciplined." But so much pressure is put on him to conform to patterned obligations (the rules) that his attention and interest slip decisively from the ends

Box 2.1: Parkinson's law—The rising pyramid

Work expands so as to fill the time available for its completion. "It is the busiest man who has time to spare." Thus, an elderly lady of leisure can spend the entire day in writing and dispatching a post card to her niece at Bognor Regis. An hour will be spent in finding the post card, another in hunting for spectacles, half an hour in a search for the address and so on. The total effort that would occupy a busy man for three minutes all told may in this fashion leave another person prostrate after a day of doubt, anxiety, and toil.

Granted that work (and especially paper work) is thus elastic in its demands on time, it is manifest that there need be little or no relationship between the work to be done and the size of the staff to which it may be assigned. A lack of real activity does not, of necessity, result in leisure. A lack of occupation is not necessarily revealed by a manifest idleness. The thing to be done swells in importance and complexity in a direct ratio with the time to be spent. Politicians and taxpayers have assumed that a rising total in the number of civil servants must reflect a growing volume of work to be done. Cynics, in questioning this belief, have imagined that multiplication of officials must have left some of them idle or all of them able to work for shorter hours. The fact is that the number of officials and the quantity of the work are not related to each other at all. The rise in the total of those employed is governed by Parkinson's Law and would be much the same whether the volume of the work were to increase, diminish, or even disappear. The importance of Parkinson's Law lies in the fact that it is a law of growth based upon an analysis of the factor by which that growth is controlled.

Omitting technicalities, we may distinguish at the outset two motive forces. They can be represented for the present purpose by two almost axiomatic statements, thus (1) "An official wants to multiply subordinates, not rivals" and (2) Officials make work for each other.

To comprehend Factor (1) we must picture a civil servant, called A, who finds himself overworked. For this real or imagined overwork there are three possible remedies. He may resign, he may ask to halve the work with a colleague called B; he may demand the assistance of two subordinates to be called C and D. By resignation he would lose his pension rights. By having B appointed, he would merely bring in a rival for promotion

C. Northcote Parkinson, *Parkinson's Law* (Boston: Houghton Mifflin Co., 1957).

(the goals) to the means. As Merton points out in "Bureaucratic Structure and Personality":

> Adherence to the rules, originally conceived as a means, becomes transformed into an end in itself; there occurs the familiar process of *displacement of goals* whereby "an instrumental value becomes a terminal value." Discipline, readily interpreted as conformance with regulations, whatever the situation, is seen not as a measure designed for specific purposes but as an immediate value in the life-organization of the bureaucrat. This emphasis, resulting from the displacement of the original goals, develops into rigidities and an inability to adjust readily. Formalism, even ritualism, ensues with an unchallenged insistence upon punctilious adherence to formalized procedures. This may be exaggerated to the point that primary concern with conformity to the rules interferes with the achievement of the purposes of the organization, in which case we have the familiar phenomenon of the technicism or red tape of the

to W's vacancy when W retires. So A would rather have C and D, junior men below him. It is essential to realize at this point that C and D are inseparable. To appoint C alone would have been impossible. Why? Because C, if by himself, would divide the work with A and so assume almost the equal status that has been refused in the first instance to B. Subordinates must thus number two or more, each being thus kept in order by fear of the other's promotion. Where C complains in turn of being overworked, A will, with the concurrence of C, advise the appointment of two assistants to help C. But he can then avert internal friction only by advising the appointment of two more assistants to help D; with the recruitment of E, F, G, and H the promotion of A is now practically certain.

Seven officials are now doing what one did before. This is where Factor 2 comes into operation. For these seven make so much work for each other that all are fully occupied and A is actually working harder than ever. An incoming document may well come before each of them in turn. Official E decides that it falls within the province of F, who places a draft reply before C, who amends it drastically before consulting D and so on, before it finally reaches A.

What does A do? He would have every excuse for signing the thing unread, for he has many other matters on his mind. Knowing now that he is to succeed W next year, he has to decide whether C or D should succeed to his own office. He has looked pale recently—partly because of his domestic trouble. Then there is the business of F's special increment of salary for the period of the conference and E's application for transfer to the Ministry of Pensions. A has heard that D is in love with a married typist and that G and F are no longer on speaking terms. So A might be tempted to sign C's draft and have done with it. But he is a conscientious man. He reads through the draft with care and deletes the fussy paragraphs added by C and H. He corrects the English and finally produces the same reply he would have written if officials C to H had never been born. Far more people have taken far longer to produce the same result. No one has been idle. All have done their best.

The last of the office lights are being turned off in the gathering dusk that marks the end of another day's administrative toil. Among the last to leave, A reflects that late hours, like gray hairs, are among the penalties of success.

official. An extreme product of this process of displacement of goals in the bureaucratic virtuoso, who never forgets a single rule binding his action and hence is unable to assist many of his clients.

A further curious feature of the bureaucracy is that the informal organization has as its main goal the protection of the entrenched interest of officials in their own states and administrative convenience rather than the needs of their clients or the aspirations of higher officials. One of the most devastating contemporary examples of this phenomenon was a secret informal organization of the lower ranks of the New York City police which made it virtually impossible for proper investigations to be made of charges of corruption, because the parties who might be able to testify had taken an oath of silence where the interests of their colleagues were involved. The solution to this kind of problem probably is to be found not in the abolition of bureaucracy but in rearranging it. As described in Chapter 1, the solution being tried in New York is to give divisional chiefs more autonomy in the form of responsibility for investigating such charges themselves instead of bringing in the headquarters unit. Bringing in perceived "outsiders" only causes the "insiders" to close ranks and go through the motions of reporting "seeing and hearing no evil."

The police in every society illustrate another criticism of bureaucracy, namely, that the bureaucrat (in spite of signing his letters to clients "I remain your faithful servant") belongs to an informal organization which has a particular *esprit de corps* which presumes that when a bureaucrat acts, irrespective of his rank, he is acting for the whole structure. This *esprit de corps* puts the client at a considerable disadvantage and leaves him with little room for manœuvre, for he will gain little support or sustenance by turning to other officials or agencies.

Merton's stricture on this point (of bureaucrats banding together to protect their status and administrative convenience) was illustrated with examples taken from the Greenwich Employment Exchange where, as in offices of this type all over the world, the clerks give the unemployed a hard time. In British Labour Exchanges in the 1930s (Merton published his article in 1940), the walls were decorated with large signs saying "Don't spit—it spreads consumption" and "If you have not worked since your last visit, don't wait to be asked, say NO WORK"—which had the effect of getting the clients ready for what they were about to receive.

The way in which officials, policemen, doctors, executives, and civil servants handle their clients is also a function of the power the client can bring to bear on the official. There are many examples of this consideration everywhere—the police proceeding carefully with middle-class clients, military officers watching out in case recruits get their fathers to write to their M.P.'s or congressmen. In Britain, for example, the National Health Service, which provides "free medical attention for all," is more effectively exploited by the executives and professionals of the middle class, who are more expert at using the system; they can, for example, get their pregnant wives into hospitals more easily to have their babies, indirectly compelling more working-class mothers to have their babies at home (though the latter may well be running bigger risks and have fewer resources to cope with them). The same kinds of things happen with regard to bureaucracy in the Soviet Union; the social class of the client is a major determinant of how the bureaucrat is likely to respond. In the 1970s bureaucracies, both industrial and governmental, have made significant and sustained efforts in management training and policy formation to meet Merton's criticism; how successful such efforts have been is a matter of speculation. But what is not a matter of speculation is the effect that technology has had on bureaucratic organization.

TOPIC 3
Technology and organization structure

The rapid rate of technological change has left most people in the new industrial state more than a little breathless. For most people, technology has become a threat rather than a challenge. At an individual level the problem is acute, and at the organizational level a serious and continuing problem. Just as many people have stereotypes about foreigners, in thinking about organizations most managers and many organization theorists talk about structure as if all organizations were arranged the same way. It would not be too great an exaggeration to say that for many the model they carry around in their heads is a composite made up partly of the organization of an infantry division and partly of what General Motors looked like in the 1930s.

In fact, as modern organizational science has shown, technology and structure are very closely interlocked. In spite of this scientific fact—which research centres like the Tavistock Institute of Human Relations, on the basis of observational study of work, have been propounding for at least 20 years—many (if not most) managers seem to have in mind as a model an ideal organization with rigid hierarchies, one man–one boss, and line and staff clearly defined; their model has all the hallmarks of a thoroughgoing bureaucracy. What has to be understood is that the lines on organization charts are not drawn on stone; they are not prescriptions for all time, but must be thought of as "rules of the game" which can and must be changed as the game changes and new players and new technologies appear on the scene.

How can technology be defined? Joan Woodward in "Industrial Behaviour—Is There a Science?" has argued:

> One variable which it is possible to isolate, and which may prove to be the most important single determinant of industrial behaviour, is technology. Technology has been defined by some American sociologists, in particular Dubin, by dividing it into two major phases—firstly, the tools, instruments, machines, plant or technical formula basic to the performance of the work, and secondly, the body of ideas which express the goals of the work, its functional importance and the rationale of the methods employed.

To allow this discussion to proceed it is necessary to classify organizations in terms of technology. It is difficult to come up with a classification system which covers the complexity of the real situation, especially when nonindustrial organizations such as hospitals and schools are taken into consideration. James D. Thompson in *Organizations in Action* has produced a useful classification system which is applicable to a wide variety of organizations:

Long-linked technology. This type of technology involves serial inter-dependence between the various production units and is typified by the mass production assembly line. The fully automated production line would be the final stage in the development of longlinked technology.

Mediating technology. This technology involves the joining of clients, customers, or others who are otherwise independents. For example, the bank provides an interchange between depositors and borrowers. The telephone company and post office also provide a mediating or inter-change function between various members of the society.

Intensive technology. A variety of techniques is drawn upon in order to achieve a change in some object or to deal with a specific problem; it is a custom technology. This is the type utilized by the general hospital or the research and development laboratory.

In spite of the complexity of technologies, management theorists have ignored the technological factors in thinking about structure. For many, Weber's idea of a bureaucracy was considered to provide a universal plan for all organizations irrespective of the specific technology. The human relations school considered both the technological and economic factors to be so well developed that they could be ignored. In fact, as anyone who has ever used a copying machine knows, technology has had a tremendous effect on behavioural systems, including the way people think.

Marshall McLuhan (*The Gutenberg Galaxy—The Making of Typo-graphic Man*) has written eloquently about the impact of technology on cognitive processes. McLuhan has argued that:

> Any technology tends to create a new human environment. Script and papyrus created the social environment we think of in connection with the empires of the ancient world. The stirrup and the wheel created unique environments of enormous scope. Technological environments are not merely passive containers of people but are active processes that reshape people and other technologies alike.

TECHNOLOGY AT INDIVIDUAL, GROUP, AND ORGANIZATION LEVELS

A useful way of thinking about the impact of technology on behaviour is to view this relation at three levels: the individual, the group, and the organization.

THE INDIVIDUAL: MAN-MACHINE INTERFACE

At the individual level, in terms of what is now called the man-machine interface, the interlocking can be so complete that the operator becomes part of the machine. For one of the best illustrations of this integration of the individual into the machine, consider the fast-acting type of tool, such as the use of a bottle labeler in the pharmaceutical industry with which the operator feeds and picks off bottles at the rate of 40 or 50 a minute. This symbiotic activity between the person and the machine may fill the more sensitive university student making a factory visit with horror; but to those operators who can do it, it is frequently accepted both as a status achievement and an activity which is really slick and effective. At a more sophisticated level, J. C. R. Licklider has come up with the man-computer symbiotic concept, which has a neat division of labour. The more mechanical aspects of human thinking and problem solving (e.g., searching, calculating, transforming, and plotting, which are largely clerical in nature) are performed by the hard-working, thorough, keen computer, while the lazy, relaxed, open-minded man sets goals, formulates hypotheses, asks questions, builds models, defines criteria, correlates performance, and in general handles low-probability events. Ideally, in such symbiotic relationships it is necessary for the man and the machine to be able to talk to each other. To achieve this man-computer love affair, Licklider believes that man and his machine ought to be able to write notes and equations to each other on a common display surface. Or the computer might have an automatic speech recognition system.

Put in the most general terms, man is capable of acting like a machine. Contrary to the thinking of a good number of sensitive souls who themselves enjoy driving thousands of miles each year as part of the automobile traffic system in a highly programmed way, machine operators frequently enjoy the responsibility of a fixed routine. Not only do many people enjoy working like machines, but they like to think that they think like machines. In fact the prestige of technology is so pervasive that "you think like a computer" is often regarded as a compliment. It's said that people grow to resemble those they live with; so if you live in a world where your best relations are machines—well, after a while a man may begin to look like his computer.

THE GROUP: TECHNOLOGY BOSSES THE GROUP

If technology fits man to the machine at the individual level, then at the group level it fits individuals into their roles, gives commands, sets production levels, and punishes those who disregard the fiats of the technological fiefdom. Any production manager who has ever had his finger on the rheostat controlling the speed of a conveyor system and has let it slip progressively to see just how far human beings can be absorbed into the system knows the validity of the technological mandate on group behaviour. C. R. Walker and R. H. Guest have shown in their study of a motor car assembly line plant how dominant technology is in determining behaviour and social relations, including such critical matters as size, function, and interactions of work groups. Who talks to whom, where and when; and who gets what, in terms not only of breaks but also of wages, is largely a question of task, technology, and territory. The most striking factor in the whole car mass production scene is that technology becomes the boss and calls the shots, with the foreman playing a fairly limited role, largely concerned either with the logistics of getting material onto the line or clearing stoppages on the line.

In automobile assembly line production, alienation and dissatisfaction can rise to such levels that active sabotage born of frustration is not unknown; a worker may even seal a milk bottle into the gas tank. That technology can generate alienation from work was shown by the studies of the British Tavistock Institute of Human Relations, which pioneered the concept of the sociotechnical system to describe the intimate relationship between technology and the social system in the work place.

In an early Tavistock study, E. L. Trist and K. W. Bamworth studied the introduction of the long-wall method of coal mining in Britain's nationalized mines. The new method required a dramatic change from the traditional method of working. Previously, small independent teams of miners who strongly identified with one another had worked together with relatively primitive equipment to win the coal from the face. The work was hard and dangerous; productivity was low, but group morale was high. The development of new technology which required larger teams using coal cutting machines produced dramatic dysfunctional changes in relations. Groups numbering 40 to 50 miners now worked at a task requiring more specialization; and, being spread over a wider area, the work groups not unnaturally began to exhibit signs of wear and tear. Close interpersonal relationships and group identification were difficult to develop in such a work context. Productivity suffered and morale fell. To meet these difficulties the composite long-wall method of production, which restored many of the old relations displaced by technology, was introduced. The miners, who now shared a common pay, were able to switch job and shifts with their mates according to their own rules. With this newly won autonomy, the miners' morale and productivity went up and absenteeism and accidents went down.

As Trist and Bamworth point out, careful analysis of technology is a necessary prerequisite when planning how work groups should be structured. Merely maximizing group autonomy or generating "good human relations" may only lead to further problems. The critical consideration is achieving the task and designing structures and roles which facilitate getting the job done, bearing in mind that the stress generated has to be dealt with by some supportive element in the structure. Put another way: people don't like playing soldiers or miners in systems which are designed by others supposedly to make them feel good.

THE ORGANIZATION: MECHANISTIC AND ORGANIC

At the organizational level, the impact of technology is more obvious. Contrary to the views of early theorists, it is not possible to establish universal structures and laws which are valid irrespective of matters of technology. The classicists, such as Fayol, Gulick, Urwick, and Mooney—drawing heavily on their experience of early 20th-century technology and organization and taking intellectual sustenance from Taylor's notions of scientific management—recommended that work be divided according to function (for example, sales, production, maintenance, personnel). For them the central issues were the span of control, unity of command, and the need for a sharp division between line and staff.

In modern terms such organizations would be described as mechanistic, following the well-known classification system developed by T. Burns and G. M. Stalker in *The Management of Innovation*. They identify two systems of management operation: the mechanistic, which is appropriate to relatively stable conditions and has all the characteristics of the classical pattern; and the organic, which is more appropriate to an environment of dynamic change and innovation such as is found in science-based industries (electronics, aerospace):

> In mechanistic systems the problems and tasks facing the concern as a whole are broken down into specialisms. Each individual pursues his task as something distinct from the real tasks of the concern as a whole, as if it were the subject of a sub-contract. "Somebody at the top" is responsible for seeing to its relevance. The technical methods, duties, and powers attached to each functional role are precisely defined. Interaction within management tends to be vertical, i.e., between superior and subordinate. Operations and working behaviour are governed by instructions and decisions issued by superiors. This command hierarchy is maintained by the implicit assumption that all knowledge about the situation of the firm and its tasks is, or should be, available only to the head of the firm. Management, often visualized as the complex hierarchy familiar in organization charts, operates a simple control system, with information flowing up through a succession of amplifiers.
>
> Organic systems are adapted to unstable conditions, when problems and requirements for action arise which cannot be broken down and distributed among specialists roles within a clearly defined hierarchy. Individuals have to perform their special tasks in the light of their knowledge of the tasks of the firm as a whole. Jobs lose much of their formal definition in terms of methods, duties, and powers, which have to be redefined continually by interaction with others participating in a task. Interaction runs laterally as much as vertically. Communication between people of different ranks tends to resemble lateral consultation rather than vertical command. Omniscience can no longer be imputed to the head of the concern.

In a careful study of Scottish firms which were interested in entering the electronics field, Burns and Stalker were able to illuminate the problems of switching from a mechanistic to an organic system of management. The unstructured and highly dynamic environment of the organic system often created widespread anxiety and insecurity among the "rear mirror driving" old-style managers, whose whole political and status system was threatened. In just such circumstances, the high ground for power is the control of some scarce resource, which in this case turned out to be technical information. And thus organizational fire fights broke out between laboratory groups (research-development-design) and production and sales groups.

The organic system, which is much more market-oriented, recruits development engineers for sales liaison, avoids jurisdictional disputes (both by not having rigid product divisions and by appointing liaison managers who can bridge departmental boundaries), and above all regards the market as a source of design idea.

But such organizational changes are achieved at a price for the individual, as Burns and Stalker point out:

> Developing a system of organized industrial activity capable of surviving under the competitive pressures of technical progress, therefore, is paid for by the increased constraint on the individual's existence. In Freudian terms, men's conduct becomes increasingly "alienated"; "they work for a system they do not control, which operates as an independent power to which individuals must submit." Such submission is all the more absolute when it is made voluntarily, even enthusiastically.

TECHNOLOGY AND STRUCTURE—THE WOODWARD STUDIES

A central problem in the development of a comprehensive organization theory is to determine in what ways particular types of technology constrain organizational structures. As a first step in this direction it is necessary to produce a classification of technology. Professor Joan Woodward, of the Imperial College of Science and Technology in London, tackled this problem in an extensive study of 100 industrial firms in the south of England. She divided the firms surveyed into three categories according to their technology. The three main groups were (1) firms that produced units or small batches, generally to the customers' individual orders; (2) large batch and mass production firms; and (3) firms producing on a continuous process basis. Using the data collected in this brilliant research, Joan Woodward and her research associates were able to demonstrate a clear relation between level of technology and a number of organization factors, as described in "Industrial Behaviour—Is There a Science?":

> Among the organizational characteristics showing a direct relationship with technical advance were: the length of the line of command; the span of control of the chief executive; the percentage of total turnover allocated to the payment of wages and salaries, and the ratios of managers to total personnel, of clerical and administrative staff to manual workers, of direct to indirect labour, and of graduate to non-graduate supervision in production departments. . . .

My own work in south Essex demonstrated the closeness of the link between technology and industrial behaviour at both management and operator levels. It showed, too, that the most intractable problems of organization and industrial relations seemed to occur in two types of production—batch production and line production based on the assembly of components. It also suggested that organizational and behavioural patterns are much more consistent at what might be called the extremes of the technical scale, in unit production and process industry, than they are in these middle ranges. Variations in behaviour observed in the batch production area appeared to be related to the procedures used to rationalize production and to predict results.

For example, the number of levels of management in direct production departments increased with technical advance, process plants having the longest lines. Woodward's empirical analysis of the actual number of hierarchical levels in an industrial organization makes the claim of management theorists that there are n levels (usually 5) and only n levels in the ideal organization look naive.

The span of control concept did not stand up any better to rigorous investigation. Technical factors also seemed to explain the wide variations in the span of control of chief executives, the people responsible to the policy-forming body for the conduct of their firm's business. In unit production firms the number of people directly responsible to the chief executive ranged from 2 to 9, the median being 4; in large batch and mass production firms the range was from 4 to 13, the median being 7; and in process production firms the range was from 5 to 19, the median being 10.

MEASUREMENT OF END PRODUCTS

The greatest single problem facing organizational planners is measurement of effectiveness. In any assessment of organizational effectiveness the main difficulty relates to the problem of definition and evaluation of criteria. Organizations may be thought of as social devices for achieving definite ends. We are concerned not only as to how organizational effectiveness can be defined and measured, but also the dysfunctional consequences of overdefinition of effectiveness.

In organization theory, in econometrics, and in operations research a major and sustained effort is being made to quantify as many as possible of the variables with which management must deal. Inherent in this approach is the belief that progress in increasing productivity will be seriously hampered unless effectiveness can be defined and measured.

As has already been stated, it is possible to think of end products as being of two types, task and human. Task end products in turn can be divided into two basic categories. The first category of task end product is usually measured in terms of productivity, cost, quality, scrap, etc.; the other major task variable is the capacity of the organization to innovate. Human end products may be thought of in terms of job satisfaction and morale, and may be measured only crudely by such indices as labour turnover, rates of absenteeism, and incidences of sickness, accidents, and neurosis.

We might summarize these by saying that organizational effectiveness may be measured against the following broad criteria:

a. Organizational productivity.
b. The ability of the organization to innovate.
c. The control of both inter- and intraorganizational stress.

Many managers rather naively imagine that it is possible to define in rather a precise way what is meant by productivity. The usual presumption of such managers is that productivity may be measured in terms of output per man-hour. To the economist specializing in productivity measurement, this type of definition represents one extreme of ultrasimplified inadequacy. A more sophisticated measure is based on the concept of value added in production. Many large companies have come to the conclusion that it is an extremely difficult exercise to produce a reliable and useful measure of productivity, which is ultimately based on the ratio of output to input.

In general terms, considerable effort has been expended on the development of composite criteria of effectiveness. Composite criteria become necessary when it is realized that effectiveness in one dimension is usually achieved at the cost of ineffectiveness (or more technically, suboptimal performance) in some other dimension. For example, in manufacturing organizations productivity is very often achieved at the expense of maintenance. When senior officials become aware of this dysfunction, it is not uncommon for some control to be applied to maintenance. Many modern organization research studies suggest that if this control in regard to maintenance is properly applied, relations within the manufacturing plant will be significantly changed. As the organization grows more sophisticated further attempts will be made to monitor and control other variables such as scrap, quality, and overhead costs. When all these various factors are brought under some measure of control, the degree of discretion available to subordinate managers is considerably circumscribed and personal relations begin to change in a dramatic way. The result may well be less effective overall performance. A major area of development in organizational behaviour is the study of dysfunctions produced by complex control systems (see Box 2.2).

V. F. Ridgway in "Dysfunctional Consequences of Performance Measurements," has made this important observation in regard to the measurement of performance:

> The mounting interest in and application of tools such as operations research, linear programming, and statistical decision making, all of which

2.2: The price of copylation

Rolf Meyersohn provides a modern illustration of the dysfunctional consequences of trying to introduce an apparently efficient technique by consideration of the use made of xeroxing by clerical staff and secretaries. The process of photocopying represents a brilliant technological break-through which enables organizations to reproduce at relatively small cost not only simple letters, receipts, and invoices, but also complex legal documents such as wills and patent applications.

So far so good. Where are the dysfunctional consequences? The "bad" implications become immediately obvious when it is realized that secretaries frequently photocopy blank pages instead of going to the stationery store. Yet another more significant consequence is that they may well, and frequently do, prepare additional unsolicited copies. What are the reasons for overproduction? Is overproduction a form of play, where the secretary can set her own rules for the game of submission to orders, of outwitting her boss by anticipating his needs (will he request an additional two copies just when the secretary has returned from her walking trip to the machine)? Is she motivated by an urge to be infractionary, committing petty white-collar crime? Is it sagacity, use of a kind of mother-wit, this anticipation of her employer's requests? Or is it merely careless-ness, an indifference bordering on hostility, malingering at the controls of the machine whose dial can as easily be set at 10 copies as at 2)? Some of these copies are pre-sented gratuitously to management; others are filed away, presumably as insurance against the possibility of an unpredicted demand arising.

All this could raise the cost of xeroxing considerably. In general terms, management finds it extremely difficult to police this kind of activity. Yet another unanticipated con-sequence of photocopying flows from the fact that workers apparently regard photo-copying as a means of alleviating the boredom of office routine, and journeys to the photocopying machine are frequently made via the restaurant or some more interesting part of the office.

This problem of proliferation of documents may also produce difficulties in regard to secrecy, security, and professional confidence. The general conclusion arising from consideration of the photocopying process reveals that not only may there be significant dysfunctional consequences in terms of increased and unnecessary cost in regard to material, of valuable personnel time consumed, and of storage space taken up; it may also have unpredicted human consequences in the sense that the act of photocopying may assume the significance of a diversionary and recreational activity. Management response in such circumstances is not only to police the activity more carefully by asking designers to build meters and control devices into the machine but also to explain to the secretaries and clerks what the real situation is in regard to the use of such machines.

Rolf Meyersohn, "The Price of Copylation," *New Society*, Vol. 4 (January, 1968).

require quantifiable variables, foster the idea that if progress toward goals can be measured, efforts and resources can be more rationally man-aged. This has led to the development of quantitative performance measurements for all levels within organizations, up to and including measurements of the performance of a division manager with profit responsibility in a decentralized company. Measurements at lower levels in the organization may be in terms of amount of work, quality of work, time required, and so on.

Quantitative measures of performance are tools, and are undoubtedly useful. But research indicates that indiscriminate use and undue confidence and reliance in them result from insufficient knowledge of the full effects and consequences. Judicious use of a tool requires awareness of possible side effects and reactions. Otherwise, indiscriminate use may result in side effects and reactions outweighing the benefits, as was the case when penicillin was first hailed as a wonder drug. The cure is sometimes worse than the disease.

In general terms, it is possible to argue that some dysfunctions of technological devices are required to allow bureaucracies to function efficiently or at least to allow some human satisfaction. In fact, in most organizations a good deal of sport is achieved discussing the abuse of organization resources; e.g., the exploitation of company telephones or cars, claims for expense allowances, the use of engineering machines for "homers," and the use and abuse of company planes. Executives similarly revel in discussion of Parkinson's law and the adventitious growth of staff and empire building it examines. It is precisely the existence of organizational slack (of resources which have not been allocated to legitimate organizational ends) that allows organizations to accept a "10 per cent cut across the board."

The problem becomes a good deal more complex when questions of innovation are introduced. There seems to be some evidence that innovation is impeded by tight control. It is possible to summarize the situation by thinking of the organization in terms of the two main end products, task and human. A very high task effectiveness is apparently achieved at the cost of some human dysfunctions. Within the task itself, high productivity is very often achieved at the expense of maintenance (high scrap costs and heavy overheads). The problem of task effectiveness is further complicated by the need of organizations to innovate. The attempt to put all this measurement of end-product effectiveness on a quantitative basis may in itself produce dysfunctional consequences. This problem of measurement of effectiveness is complex and complicated and remains open for further development; this is the area of organizational research most likely to attract the greatest resources.

TOPIC 4
Evaluation of classical theory

In the classical approach, Taylor, Gulick, and Weber set out to study organizations with scientific precepts. Figure 2-2 illustrates how we can evaluate this approach using the elements contained in the systems model developed in Chapter 1.

In terms of structure, to the classical theorist the key to precision and effectiveness lay in defining a centralized pyramidal authority structure, with the number of hierarchical levels, spans of control, and line-staff relations carefully defined. Thus the first thing a classical theorist did

FIGURE 2–2
CLASSICAL APPROACH

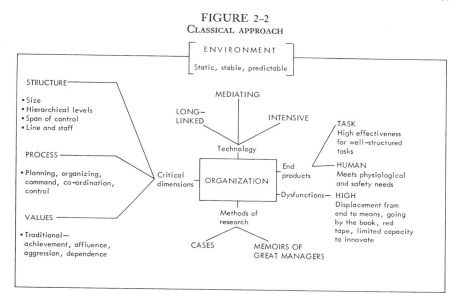

when setting up an organization was to draw up an organization chart with line (vertical) and staff (lateral) relations clearly laid out and write up long, elaborate job specifications setting out the incumbent's authority, responsibilities, functions, rank, and duties. This was it. This was the organization, the formal organization. With theological certainty, the organization had been defined in scientific terms. Gulick and Urwick spelled out the structural relationships among the factors of production, personnel, and logistics and introduced the ideas of departmentalization, specialization, and control. Weber codified the whole classical system in terms of staffing and structure: efficiency is achieved by arranging offices according to hierarchy and jurisdiction; experts are appointed to these offices who, guided by the book (precedent), deal with clients (the customer); and the bureaucrat comes into the organization by examination, moves through it by merit, and retires from it (he cannot be fired) with a pension.

So much for structure. What about the process? The total task of management can be broken into four elements, to use the up-to-date classical analysis: planning, organizing, leading (command and co-ordination) and control. Planning is a key activity which classifies objectives and sets goals for each subdivision. Through the plan, the policies, procedures, programmes, strategies, and schedules are established. Planning, when it was developed by Taylor, took the form of production planning and control and represented a significant move forward for management. In its modern form it can be better understood in terms of how an organization makes a strategic decision: diagnosing the problem, finding alternatives, projecting the results of each, and selecting a specific alternative. Organizing is the design of the organization chart and the writing of role specifications. Leading refers to the actual process of commanding and co-ordinating, and in the classical approach is essentially a matter of delegation, good staff work, and careful decision making. All this leading has to be backed up with nerves of steel, a cool analytical brain, a charismatic aloofness, and an infinite capacity for hard work, rounded out with a concern for man management. With this formidable personal equipment and the certainties of the classical structure, success ultimately depends upon efficient control to measure progress towards the objectives. If operations are not so progressing, one goes back to the plan to take the necessary, if need be painful, corrective action to get back on course. This last step, the corrective phase, is the essence of control.

In this essentially bureaucratic approach, the value system presumes that classical man will always act in the best interests of the firm and behave rationally. With the Calvinist work ethic built into him and guided by monetary inducements, the presumption was that the classical manager would get his work done by providing his subordinates (who were presumed to be lazy and unambitious) with work programmes which had been scientifically designed by methods engineers. The value system was based on four elements; achievement, self-control, independence, and endurance of pain and distress. It would be wrong to presume that the work ethic is dead in America. For example, a recent Daniel Yankelovitch survey found that 79 per cent of U.S. college students feel a meaningful career is an important element in a person's life.

In the term of end products, the presumption is that increasing productivity or profitability will bring satisfaction in its wake; following the Calvinist work ethic, "work is joy." But when productivity falls, management puts on the pressure by tightening up controls. Increasing controls, especially through the use of general and impersonal rules, can generate dysfunctional consequences—including, as F. J. Jasinski pointed out, wasted time, higher maintenance costs, figure fudging, poor morale, impaired personnel recruitment, higher unit costs, and lowered product quality. The dysfunctional consequences of control have a spiraling effect: management, as it becomes aware of further falls in productivity (the shop floor workers do the bare minimum that will avoid punishment) increases the pressure, which in turn increases the visibility of power relations. And this show of force makes the workers more determined than ever "to do the least for the most."

It would be wrong to imagine that the classical theory deals with ancient history. In fact, most businesses and public organizations are still organized along classical lines. As the Department of Health, Education, and Welfare's task force on employment points out, monotonous tasks and bleak regimentation are common to both the shop floor and office, to workers and managers, to men and women, and to black and white. The cost of this excessive routinization of work is immense. Their report, "Work in America" points out:

> Characterologically, the hierarchical organization requires workers to follow orders, which calls for submissive traits, while the selection of managers calls for authoritarian and controlling traits. . . .
>
> The more democratic and self-affirmative an individual is, the less he will stand for boring, dehumanized and authoritarian work. Under such conditions, the workers either protest or give in, at some cost to their psychological well-being. Anger that does not erupt may be frozen into schizoid, depressed characters who escape into general alienation, drugs and fantasies.

Thus, not unexpectedly, management and workers have turned to human relations for a way out.

REVIEW AND RESEARCH

1. Why did the theory of bureaucracy develop at the turn of the century in Germany?
2. Can Consciousness III people work in bureaucracies without undermining them? Discuss.
3. Select any large-scale organization in business, government, or the military, and assess the degree to which it conforms to bureaucratic principles.
4. Draw up a taxonomy of technologies, starting with the least complex and going to the most complex.
5. Why is it frequently better for a company to be "second in technology and first in management"?
6. Discuss the relationship between technology and structure. What are the basic structural differences between the firm with established routine technology and fixed markets and the firm with dynamic innovative technological needs in an uncertain environment?
7. Compare and contrast organic and mechanistic organization systems. Explain why Burns coined the term "organic" while studying electronics firms.
8. In problem solving, which functions should be given to the computer and which to man?
9. How will the computer affect management organization?
10. Why was project management invented? What "projects" are suitable for project management? List the pros and cons of project management.
11. What is matrix management? What organizational problems are best tackled by matrix management?
12. What is an adhocracy (a coined term which should be decipherable)? Which industries are most suitable to be treated as adhocracies? Why?
13. Describe the personality of the adhocracy man. How does it compare with the organization man of the 1950s?

14. Describe and explain the human reaction to working in the automobile industry.
15. How do conglomerates like I.T.T. manage such diversified interests?

GLOSSARY OF TERMS

Administrative management. A management system which includes such principles as fitting people to the organization structure; need for unity of command; use of special and general staffs; departmentalization by purpose, process, persons, and places; delegation; balancing of authority and responsibility; definition of the span of control.

Bureaucracy. Organization structure possessing some sort of administrative machinery and specialized secretariat to keep the organization working. Weber's theory of bureaucracy has five characteristics or marks:
a. Tasks are distributed among various members of the group as official duties, usually accompanied with division of labour and specialization of function.
b. Offices or roles are organized into a hierarchical structure where the scope of authority of superordinates over subordinates is clearly defined.
c. A formal set of rules governing behaviour is specified which ensures uniformity of organization.
d. Officials are required to assume an impersonal attitude in contacts with both other officials and clients.
e. Employment in a bureaucracy is usually assumed to be a career for life and promotion is by merit.

Dysfunctions. These are unanticipated end results which are not congruent with the original intention of the organizational goal. For example, increased quality control on car manufacture can lead to the dysfunctions of slower production and the concealing of defects.

Effectiveness. This refers to the optimal mix of productivity, innovation and control of inter- and intraorganizational stress.

Formal organization. A hierarchical differentiated system of interrelated groups and roles which has been designed by the chief executive as an efficient system for accomplishing the mission of the organization. The two principal determinants of the behaviour of members are the structure and values of organization. Structure specifies communication routes, defines authority, and sets methods of redress of grievance. The network of social relations is defined between individuals and groups. The value system helps to define the goals for which organizational members strive and specifies their ideals.

Informal organization. Informal organization is the inevitable antibody of formal organization and represents the backlash of the organized against the organizers. Patterns of interpersonal and intergroup relations always develop within and parallel to the formal organization. The informal organization inevitably will not have the same aims as the formal organization, and usually includes cliques and cabals. An informal organization is likely to develop when the formal organization proves to be inefficient or when it fails to meet important human needs of its members.

Mechanistic organization. A management system in stable conditions where the emphasis is on (1) co-ordination of different functions by hierarchical control; (2) vertical communications through a well-structured authority system with responsibilities clearly defined; and (3) insistence on loyalty to the organization.

Organic organization. A management system appropriate to a rapidly changing technological and social environment where (1) the emphasis is on expertise as opposed to structural authority; (2) roles are loosely defined and successful innovation becomes the focus for a temporary structure with which to carry out the project; (3) organizational omniscience is rejected; (4) horizontal communications are the order of the day and take the form of information and advice rather than instructions; and (5) loyalty is to the ethos of technological excellence rather than the organization.

Scientific management. A management system which includes such principles as selecting the right man for the job, deciding by method study on the one best way to do the job, developing differential piece-work processes, careful planning of the actual work process, and developing line and functional specialization.

Social organization. A loosely organized set of interrelated groups which has emerged to achieve a particular purpose (e.g., a political party).

Technology, which is a crucial variable in organizational behaviour, can be defined in two ways—firstly as tools, instruments, machines, plants or technical know-how and secondly as a corpus of knowledge derived from applied science (social and physical) for transforming particular problems in aerospace, the military, and so on. J. D. Thompson has identified three types: long-linked technology (car assembly automated track), mediating technology (telephone exchange system), and intensive technology (research laboratory).

Types of organization. P. Blau and W. R. Scott in *Formal Organizations* have developed a clasification system based on the principle of the "prime beneficiary":

a. Mutual benefit associations (prime beneficiary is member).

b. Business concerns (prime beneficiary is owner).

c. Service organizations (prime beneficiary is client).

d. Commonweal organizations (prime beneficiary is public at large).

Amitai Etzioni has classified organizations according to whether their predominant pattern of *compliance* is coercive, utilitarian, or normative.

3

Human relations

It was not as a pious hope that managers turned to human relations, but in the hope both of bringing about a better understanding between management and labour and of reducing frustration and conflict. The purpose of this chapter is to present an outline of the principles of human relations and the evidence on which this philosophy is based so that the reader may make an objective critique of their validity, relevance, and utility.

On the debit side, human relations has come under fire from two different points of reference. One group of critics takes the view that human relations represents a form of organizational paternalism which leaves managers behaving as "Dutch uncles" and treats subordinates as "immature adolescents" by virtue of its refusal to recognize that conflict is an inevitable consequence of the natural diversity of talents and a necessary prerequisite of innovation. The absence of conflict leaves the organization like "a slab of colloidal jelly," uniform and incapable of withstanding much pressure. The other great group of critics takes the view that human relations is a new form of manipulation, which draws its strength from "group think," pseudoparticipation, and phony democracy. But the major and significant criticism of human relations is neither that it is a new form of organizational paternalism ("the soft option" as it is sometimes termed) nor that it represents a form of manipulation, but rather that it does not go far enough to explain organizational actualities.

Nevertheless, it is more realistic and sensible to start from the proposition that it is an essential phase of managerial evolution and that most organizations and individuals, if they are to achieve maturity, must pass through this stage. It is perhaps a curiosity, but apparently managers and institutions seem to recapitulate the history of managerial philosophy. If the validity of this proposition is granted, for the moment at least (in suspense of prejudice), it is right and proper to begin by stating the case for human relations.

THE STRUCTURE OF THIS CHAPTER

Our review of human relations begins by presenting as Topic 1 the famous experiment carried out at the Hawthorne works of the Western Electric Company near Chicago in the 1920s and 1930s, which has been described as the largest, most expensive, most painstaking experiment in the history of the social sciences. The Hawthorne studies, while they have been heavily criticized, provide the experimental data and findings on which the whole human relations approach is founded. The discussion reviews the critical studies of H. A. Landsberger and Alex Carey.

With the experimental base identified, Topic 2 turns to one particular view of human relations, Douglas McGregor's concepts of Theory X (structured bureaucratic approach appropriate to passive, indolent workers) and Theory Y (complex adaptable approach appropriate to workers with a need for autonomy, growth, achievement, and self-actualization). McGregor's theories are related to A. H. Maslow's hierarchical theory of motivation, which presumes that all men are basically motivated by the same hierarchy of needs—physiological and safety needs, social needs, ego needs, and above all the need for self-actualization. How are these needs to be mobilized? According to this approach, by extending the autonomy of jobs through job enlargement or job enrichment and by increasing participation via management-by-objectives programmes.

But the basic supposition of this approach is that all employees share the same basic needs. And the exactly opposite point of view is what the study of our third topic, alienation, suggests. Some employees (but not all) are alienated from their work. The basic idea of alienation takes us back to the ideas of Karl Marx and Max Weber, who were both preoccupied with this issue. Alienation, which has the dimensions of powerlessness, meaninglessness, normlessness, isolation, and self-estrangement, is shown to be a function not only of the work itself but of the values and attitudes which employees bring to work. If the proposition that alienated workers from an urban working-class environment prefer low-skill, nonchallenging, but well-paid work with little involvement is true, a different approach must be taken both to the idea of a basic common theory of motivation and to the generally received theory of human relations. It is also argued that the kinds of relations preferred at work are a function of organizational level.

Topic 4 ends the chapter with an evaluation of human relations theory, using the systems model developed in Chapter 1.

TOPIC 1
The Hawthorne studies

The theoretical basis of the human relations school was established through the Hawthorne experiment, which is considered a classic by virtue of its scope, significance, and design. The actual experiments were carried out at the Western Electric Company's Hawthorne Works near Chicago and are usually closely linked with the name of Elton Mayo, who, as professor of industrial research at the Harvard School of Business Administration, was the person most responsible for developing these experiments and publicizing their significance.

The Hawthorne Studies can be considered under four headings. These are (1) the experiments on illumination, (2) the relay assembly test room, (3) the interviewing programme, and (4) the bank wiring observation room.

THE EXPERIMENTS ON ILLUMINATION

The experiments on illumination provide a classical illustration of the consequence of applying scientific method, as used in the physical sciences, to a social problem. The object of the experiment at the outset was to ascertain the relationship between productivity and illumination. To this end, productivity was measured at various levels of illumination. Contrary to expectation, the results showed that the output rose and fell without direct relation to the intensity of illumination. The experimenters showed true scientific caution and concluded there must be additional factors which were affecting productivity and which would have to be eliminated or suppressed before the experiment could be considered scientific. Following the traditions of good experimental psychologists, to overcome these difficulties two groups were set up—a test group and a control group. The test group worked under varying illumination and the control group under constant illumination. It is interesting to note that the groups were located in different buildings to eliminate any spirit of competition. But analysis of the results of this test showed very appreciable increases in productivity in both groups. In fact, the difference in efficiency between the two groups was not statistically significant.

Something odd was happening which puzzled the researchers. What was it? The standard psychological technique of experimentation had been used; it stood to reason illumination must affect productivity. The researchers decided to look at their problem again.

Several other fascinating experiments were conducted; for example, in one experiment two women worked in a locker room under reduced illumination—in fact, the amount of light was approximately equal to that of ordinary moonlight—and yet the women were still able to maintain production and reported no eyestrain or fatigue. In yet another intriguing experiment, an electrician changed the light bulbs in one particular department, but in fact replaced them with bulbs of the same wattage. Here again the women's response was favourable. The net result of these early experiments was the conclusion that illumination was only a minor factor affecting productivity. But more important and significant was the fact that the experiments focused attention on the need to gain more knowledge concerning the human factors that affect production.

THE RELAY ASSEMBLY TEST ROOM

In this part of the experiment it was decided to isolate a small group of women in a separate room away from the regular working force, where their behaviour could be more scientifically investigated. The task chosen was the assembly of small telephone relays. The rate of output was then 5 relays in six minutes (approximately 500 a day), so that even small changes in productivity would be immediately obvious.

The way the team was selected is important. Two operators who were friendly with each other chose three other assemblers and a layout operator. The only other person in the room was a research assistant who kept records of production, rejects, weather, temperature, and a log of hour-by-hour happenings. The chairs, fixtures, and work layout were similar to those in a normal department.

What in fact happened in this experiment was that the investigators, in setting up a scientific experiment, had of necessity to isolate a small group of operators, who began to think of themselves as an élite in the midst of a sea of mass production. In other words, scientific structuring of a social situation turned out not to be as "clinical" as most psychologists had thought. In fact, one might go further and say that the rationale of social psychology is to be found in the proposition that all group situations are loaded.

Stuart Chase in *Men at Work* has captured the atmosphere of the relay assembly test room when he writes:

> It was decided to use a group of girls assembling telephone relays. A telephone relay is a small gadget, looking something like a pocket whistle, made up of thirty-five separate parts. The task of the girls was to take these parts out of trays and put them together. It was a typical machine-age repetitive job.
>
> Two girls were selected who were skilled at assembling relays, and they picked four companions. Five of the group were about twenty years old, three of Polish families, one of Italian, one of Czech. The sixth had been born in Norway, and was about thirty years old. They were all moved into a special room separated by a thin partition from the big relay department where 100 employees worked.
>
> Here the six girls sit, at one long bench, trays of tiny metal parts in

front of them. Their nimble fingers fly. Every minute or so a relay is finished, dropped into a chute, and carried out into a box on the floor, where it is collected. On each girl's chute is placed a little machine operating a kind of ticker tape which counts every relay coming through. For five years these tickers will click—from 1927 to 1932—giving an accurate record of hourly, daily, weekly output.

Five of the girls were assemblers, while the sixth was the "layout operator," who prepared the trays of parts so the girls could assemble them more easily. A seventh person was also in the room—the observer. He represented the research staff. His job was to record everything of significance that happened. He was to be the counselor and friend of the girls, telling them about the experiment, talking over proposed changes, inviting their comments, listening to their complaints.

The relay assembly study started with six questions:

1. Do employees actually get tired out?
2. Are rest pauses desirable?
3. Is a shorter working day desirable?
4. What is the attitude of the employees towards their work and towards the company?
5. What is the effect of changing the type of work equipment?
6. Why does production fall off in the afternoon?

To answer these questions 23 test periods were introduced:

Period 1: A record kept of production of each woman without her knowledge for two weeks before going into test-room. This showed productive ability under usual conditions.

Period 2: After the workers entered the test-room, no change in working conditions for five weeks. This was meant to show changes as a result of transfer.

Period 3: A change in method of payment, relating pay more closely to individual effort; this lasted eight weeks.

Period 4: Two rest pauses of five minutes, one mid-morning, other early afternoon.

Period 5: Rest pauses lengthened to 10 minutes each.

Period 6: Six five-minute rests.

Period 7: Light lunches provided mid-morning and mid-afternoon.

Period 8: Work stopped half-hour earlier—at 4:30 P.M.

Period 9: Stopped at 4 P.M.

Period 10: Conditions returned to period 7.

Period 11: Five-day work week established.

Period 12: Conditions returned to period 3.

Periods 4–12 all lasted several weeks.

Period 13: November, 1928 to June, 1929. Return to conditions of period 7.

Periods 14–23: June, 1929 to July, 1932, continuation of period 13.

RESULTS AND CONCLUSIONS

The most significant result to emerge from this part of the research was that throughout the study the average hourly output of the employees continued to rise. No matter what change was introduced, the output continued to rise until it stabilized at a high level. A number of explanations have been offered to explain these somewhat unexpected effects.

1. Perhaps not too surprisingly, the women liked to work in the test-room; they thought "it was fun." Though each knew that she was producing more than in her regular department, each said it was not due to any conscious effort.

2. A new supervisory relationship had developed which apparently enabled the women to work freely without anxiety. Although they were really far more thoroughly supervised than before, to their mind the character and purpose of supervision were different. They regarded the test-room observer as a friendly representative of management and not as a supervisor who "bawls you out."

3. To their delight, the operators felt that they were a kind of élite and further that they were taking an important part in an interesting experiment which "proved" that management was interested in them. They were consulted on all the different changes, their opinions were sought, and they were even allowed to vote on changes. Therefore, in this respect, by the standards of the time, a different relationship had been created between the workers and management.

4. Over the experimental period there was a strengthening of the group bonds that held the women together; e.g., four of them started going out together both in the evenings and at weekends, and they all helped each other at work.

5. It can come as no surprise to learn that the group developed leadership and a common purpose (increase in output rate).

A devastating criticism of the Hawthorne Studies has been made by Alex Carey of the University of New South Wales, who has made a detailed comparison between Hawthorne conclusions and Hawthorne evidence (see Box 3.1). What Carey challenges is:

> . . . that social satisfactions arising out of human association in work were more important determinants of work behaviour in general and output in particular than were any of the physical and economic aspects of the work situation to which their attention had originally been limited. This conclusion came as "the great *éclaircissement* . . . an illumination quite different from what they had expected from the illumination studies." It is the central and distinctive finding from which the fame and influence of the Hawthorne studies derive.

Carey came up with this startling conclusion:

> A detailed comparison between the Hawthorne conclusions and the Hawthorne evidence shows these conclusions to be almost wholly

Box 3.1: A closer look at friendly supervision in action

Alex Carey's Hawthorne critique points out that the whole of the Hawthorne claim, that friendly supervision and resulting work-group social relations and satisfactions are over-whelmingly important for work behaviour, rests on whatever evidence can be extracted from the relay assembly test room (RATR) study, since that is the only study in the series which exhibits even a surface association between the introduction of such factors and increased output. The RATR study began with five women specially selected for being both "thoroughly experienced" and "willing and cooperative," so there was no reason to expect this group to be more than ordinarily co-operative and competent. Yet from very early in the study "the amount of talking indulged in by all the operators" had constituted a "problem," because it "involved a lack of attention to work and a preference for conversing together for considerable periods of time."

From now on the operators, especially 1A and 2A, were threatened with disciplinary action and subjected to continual reprimands. "Almost daily," 2A was "reproved" for her "low output and behaviour." The investigators decided 1A and 2A did not have the "right" mental attitude. 1A and 2A were replaced by two workers chosen by the foreman "who were experienced relay assemblers and desirous of participating in the test." These two women (designated Operators 1 and 2) were transferred to the test room on January 25th, 1928. They both immediately produced an output much greater (in total and in rate per hour) than that achieved by any of the original five operators and much above the performance at any time of the two women they replaced.

Operators 1 and 2 had been friends in the main shop. Operator 2 was the only Italian in the group; she was young (21) and her mother died shortly after she joined the test

Alex Carey, "The Hawthorne Studies: A Radical Criticism," *American Sociological Review*, Vol. pp. 403–16.

unsupported. The evidence reported by the Hawthorne investigators is found to be consistent with the view that material, and especially financial, reward is the principal influence on work morale and behavior. Questions are raised about how it was possible for studies so nearly devoid of scientific merit, and conclusions so little supported by evidence, to gain so influential and respected a place within scientific disciplines and to hold this place for so long.

THE INTERVIEWING PROGRAMME

While much concerning the Hawthorne studies has been criticized, the interviewing programme has come through this criticism very well. The critical point demonstrated by the interviewing programme, which is central to the whole human relations movement, is that if you let people talk about things which are important to them, they frequently come up with issues that surprise you because they are at first sight unconnected with their work. These issues relate to such matters as how their kids are doing at school, how the family is going to manage with all the medical bills, what their friends think of their jobs, and so on. Talking about such matters to a sympathetic listener, who does not interpret, is therapeutic. And this is precisely what happened at Hawthorne, where a nondirective

room; after this "Operator 2 earned the larger part of the family income." "From now on the history of the test room revolves around the personality of Operator 2." Operator 2 rapidly (i.e., without any delay during which she might have been affected by the new supervision) adopted and maintained a strong and effective disciplinary role with respect to the rest of the group, and led the way in increased output in every period from her arrival till the end of the study. In this she was closely followed by the other new worker, Operator 1.

CONCLUSION

(1) The dismissed workers were replaced by two women of a special motivation and character who immediately led the rest in a sustained acceleration of output. One, who had a special need for extra money, rapidly adopted and maintained a strong disciplinary role with respect to the rest of the group. The two new operators led the way in increased output from their arrival till the end of the study.

(2) Total output per week showed a significant and sustained increase only after the two operators who had the lowest output were dismissed and replaced by selected output leaders who account for the major part of the group's increase, both in output rate and in total output, over the next 17 months of the study.

(3) After the arrival of the new workers and the associated increase in output, official supervision became friendly and relaxed once more. The investigators, however, provide no evidence that output increased because supervision became more friendly rather than vice versa. In any case, friendly supervision took a very tangible turn by paying the operators for time not worked; the piece-rate was in effect increased.

interviewing strategy was adopted. So successful was this strategy that more than 20,000 employees were interviewed.

Above all the interviewing programme showed that the attitudes which people bring to their work are as important as those they pick up at work. Nevertheless a major criticism of the Hawthorne researchers was that they did not pay sufficient heed to what was going on in Cicero (a suburb bordering Chicago) at the time of their study. For Chicago was right in the middle of Prohibition and the bootlegging, gangsterism, organized crime, and political corruption which characterized the roaring twenties. It is hard to believe that researchers like Elton Mayo were not aware of this wider social context, which certainly affected workers' attitudes. Not only was it staring the man in the street in the face, but sociologists from such top schools as the University of Chicago were addressing themselves to the study of such matters as "social disorganization."

Whatever criticism can be levelled against the researchers for not looking outside the workplace, they did come up with a wealth of data about what was going on inside the plant. Having failed to find the Mafia outside, they did find mafia-like structures inside, in the primary working groups. These informed groups were organized like gangs, with bosses and side-kicks who had built an elaborate social apparatus to ensure that just the right amount was produced. If somebody stepped out of line, he was given "the message" and then "the hammer." This discovery of the

informal organization—the elaborate apparatus to control production, with
its own convoluted rules, its own particular hierarchy of *capos* and button
men—was the critical discovery of the studies. It was to find out more
about how the informal organization operated that the bank wiring room
experiment was set up.

THE BANK WIRING OBSERVATION ROOM

The interviewing programme had focused attention on the importance
of informal groupings, and in order to obtain more exact and detailed
information about the nature and function of such groups, the bank wiring
observation room was set up. The research procedure in this part of the
experiment was rather similar to the relay assembly test room method
except that it was male operators who were being studied in this case. The
workers in this group consisted of nine wiremen, three soldermen, and
two inspectors, who were engaged in the assembly of terminal banks for
use in telephone exchanges.

The workers were invited to co-operate in this experiment and at first
the men worked or appeared to be working all the time. But they adopted
a very cautious attitude towards the observer. Not surprisingly, three
weeks elapsed before the men started to relax and behave as they did in
their normal department.

As far as production was concerned, the management had introduced a
complicated wage incentive plan that assumed that the workers would
seek their own economic interests by maximizing productivity. But in
fact, the employees had their own idea of what was a proper day's work.
They defined a day's work as the wiring of two units and as soon as they
thought they could manage this they slacked off. This was more marked
among the faster than the slower workmen. As it turned out, no relationship was found between productivity and intelligence, finger dexterity,
or other skills. The graph of output tended to be a straight line. The men
reported more or less than what they had produced. They also claimed
excessive day work allowances for stoppages beyond their control.

Why was the wage incentive scheme not working? The men believed
that if they turned out an excessive amount of work, management would
lower the piece-work rate so that the men would be doing more for
approximately the same pay.

The method which the men had devised for controlling production is
rather interesting. Two techniques were used, one semantic, the other
physical; nicknames were given to workers who produced too much or
minor physical punishments were awarded. An example of the latter was
the technique of "binging." A bing is a very hard blow applied to the
muscles of the upper arm. The person "binged" has the right to bing back
if he wishes.

If we consider the mores or value system of the work group, the central

ox 3.2: The shop floor mafia

They (the employees) went on at great length explaining that adjustments were almost impossible in many cases because of variations in the quality and quantity of piece parts available, until I wondered how they were able to accomplish anything. I also noticed a general dissatisfaction or unrest. In some, this was expressed by demands for advancement or transfers; in others, by a complaint about their lot in being kept on the job.

These serious continuous defects, about which they talked a great deal, were not reflected by variations in their output curves. In other words, it looked as if they were limiting their output to a figure just below the bogey; and evidently this output could be accomplished even though machines were running poorly.

I then noticed that two of the workers in particular held rather privileged positions in the group and were looked up to by the rest of the members. On these two the group seemed to place considerable responsibility. Of A they said: "He can handle the engineers, inspectors, and the supervisors. They have to come to him if they want to know anything." In speaking of B they expressed admiration for his work habits and capacities. The common remarks about him were: "He taught me my job"; "When he adjusts a machine, he never raises his eyes until it works"; "So-and-so talked too much a while ago, and B shut him up." Quite frequently B shows them an easy way to make an adjustment that is difficult because of a variation in the piece parts. All expressed appreciation of his willingness to help them.

A, in his interviews, told of fights with supervisors and arguments with engineers and inspectors which usually resulted in their making the changes he recommended. In referring to one case he said, "I made several machines work after an expert from the East said an adjustment was impossible." B told of helping other adjusters. He said that he threatened to punch one operator in the nose because he had let the supervisor know that he had finished early.

From observations and from conversations with the supervisors I observed that the group chief consults with either A or B when a change is contemplated. The group chief defends the group in general whenever the foreman expresses dissatisfaction with their work, and he never bawls them out. On one occasion the foreman asked him why he didn't bawl them out when the quality chart showed an increase in defects. The group chief answered that he passed the quality record around the group so that they all could see it: "They know when they are slipping without my telling them." The bulk of the group chief's time is occupied in obtaining an even flow of work so that all are kept busy. The section chief and the assistant foreman have adopted a "hands off" policy. They say that the group has a "union" and that it could turn out much more than it does, but they don't know what to do about it, so they leave the men alone. (Interviewer's report at Hawthorne.)

F. J. Roethlisberger, and W. J. Dickson, *Management and the Worker* (Cambridge, Mass.: Harvard versity Press, 1939).

part played by the need to restrict production immediately becomes obvious (see Box 3.2). These mores or beliefs can be listed under four headings:

1. Don't be a rate-buster (you should not turn out too much work).
2. Don't be a chiseller (you should not turn out too little work).
3. Don't be a squealer (you should not tell your superiors anything that would harm an associate).
4. Don't act officiously (you must conform to the mandates of the informal group).

These four simple categorical imperatives served as the defence mechanism of the informal social organization, a mechanism the group developed to protect themselves both from within and without.

THE DEVELOPMENT OF CLIQUES

An interesting and intriguing manifestation of informal organization is the development of cliques. For example, two cliques were noted in the bank wiring room (Figure 3–1). The first consisted of four wiremen, one solderman, and an inspector; this group usually gambled. The second consisted of one solderman and three to five wiremen; this group preferred "binging." Job trading was only allowed within cliques. For those interested in snobbery, it may be of some interest to know that the first

FIGURE 3–1
INFORMAL ORGANIZATION WITHIN THE GROUP

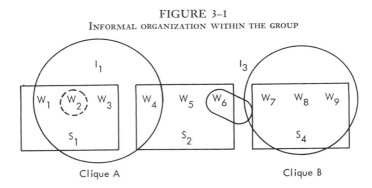

group considered themselves superior to the second; they thought their conversation was on a higher plane. Apparently the second group spent a lot of time not only binging but quarrelling over the opening and shutting of windows. To many who would "never waste their time in such a futile way," this appears to be a stupid and infantile method of dissipating energy. But it may also be viewed as telling evidence of the reaction to the repressions and frustrations that appear to be an inevitable part of modern industrial life.

A REVIEW OF HAWTHORNE

Professor H. A. Landsberger in *Hawthorne Revisited* has presented a brilliant review and assessment of the Hawthorne experiment. Landsberger sets out to make a genuine evaluation—neither an outright attack nor a defence of the work of Elton Mayo. On the debit side, Landsberger argues that while the Hawthorne study proved to be a seminal piece of research which triggered off a number of investigations, it has also been heavily criticized for providing the empirical and ideological basis of the human relations school. According to Landsberger:

> The most far-reaching charge against the Mayo group in particular and against the human relations group in general is that of inadequate conceptualization of the major problems in industrial relations. This is due to a logically prior inadequate view of the development of anomie in modern society. . . . Specifically, the critics point out, the group has failed to recognize the problem of conflict and conflicting interests of the parties in industrial relations and has therefore failed to look for the causes as well as the implications of this conflict. As a consequence the energy, attention and enthusiasm of the group have been directed toward concepts and phenomena which are, by comparison, superficial and even trivial: status strivings of employees, relationships in informal groups in the factory, the need for catharsis through a counselor and improving "communications. . . ."

In brief, the human relations school fails ultimately because it does not have a proper frame of reference; it fails to acknowledge the importance of sociological forces; it fails because it does not recognize the importance of conflict as a creative force in society. In particular the idea that conflict is always bad warrants closer examination. Perfect organizational health is not freedom from conflict. Conflict, if properly handled, can lead to more effective and appropriate adjustments.

At the sociological level, the Hawthorne researchers gave inadequate attention to the attitudes that people bring to work. The "us versus them" feeling, the sense of class consciousness that unites shop floor workers receives scant attention. This failure on the part of Elton Mayo to analyse the causes of social unrest—coupled with his idea that society is in a state of anomie (i.e., composed of morally confused, isolated people in a society disorganized and full of confusion) where "conflict is a social disease" and co-operation is social health—represents the main criticism levelled against Mayo.

Secondly, the Hawthorne experiment has been criticized for presuming that an ideal arrangement would be shop floor acceptance of management's goals and management treating the worker as somebody who can be manipulated. The worker is seen as a means to an end, not an end in himself. To the critics of Hawthorne, this reduces the social science of industry to a sort of "cow sociology."

Landsberger refers to Elton Mayo's lack of reference both to collective bargaining and to the role of the unions when he observes that:

> Some critics have voiced the suspicion that statements of Mayo and his colleagues suggest an actively antiunion attitude. But the general charge—and it is levelled by several critics, only some of whom seem to be ardent union partisans—is that the Mayo group, in both its theorizing and its research, has made the serious mistake of ignoring unions. Thus, a lead-

ing character is missing from their drama of industrial relations, and a major force in the life of the worker is left out.

Landsberger further points out that:

> Mayo's work in particular has about it an air of omniscience and finality which, rightly or wrongly, has rubbed many a reader the wrong way. Definitiveness is bound to be felt as inappropriate when dealing with problems as manifestly complicated as industrial unrest. The very titles of Mayo's works suggest that a complete diagnosis of the ills of our society is now available for, after all, not much (except the economic!) remains after writing about the human, social, and political problems of our industrial civilization.

According to Landsberger, the data presented by Roethlisberger and Dickson in *Management and the Worker*

> are such as to leave the reader with the impression that Western Electric was a thoroughly unpleasant place at which to work during those years and that the authors knew it. . . . Many of those who worked at Hawthorne thought of it as a semi-sweated beehive, with individuals at all levels—including lower and middle supervision—transferred arbitrarily from job to job and department to department. Favoritism was not infrequent and serious personal tragedies were often callously ignored.

Landsberger also criticizes the human relations schoolmen for emphasizing shop floor strivings for status and prestige at the expense of their desire for power, control, and economic advantage.

In passing, Landsberger takes a gentle sideswipe at the Hawthorne researchers for giving advice to managers on how to manipulate subordinates. This how-to-do-it aspect of *Management and the Worker* is regarded as a very dangerous practice. Landsberger's criticisms can be summarized under four headings:

1. The Hawthorne frame of reference is inadequate because it is pitched at the level of the individual-in-the-group and gives inadequate recognition to sociological forces, especially extra-plant forces such as class consciousness, collective bargaining, and the role of the unions.
2. The Hawthorne plant was a thoroughly unpleasant place in which to work, and thus not necessarily typical.
3. The human relations school placed too much emphasis on prestige and status and undervalued both power and economic advantage as motives.
4. Human relations as a practice smacks of manipulation.

CONCLUSION

The scientific status of the Hawthorne studies has been widely challenged and with good reason. Laboratory psychologists challenge both the experimental design employed and the validity of the findings. The studies can be defended on this count by arguing, as Alan Cubbon does, that the researchers were "contextualists"; i.e., they were mapping out the social forces of the primary working group in a particular setting or context rather than carrying out an exact scientific experiment. But this defence leaves them open to the attack of the sociologists who charge the researchers with failure to place the Hawthorne studies in a wider social context.

To the social scientist, the most perplexing and worrying aspect of the subject is why studies which exercised so much influence on the thinking of social scientists, executives and social reformers were not subjected to the most searching and sceptical scrutiny. Why did most authors of textbooks and most teachers of courses on organization theory fail to recognize the discrepancy between Hawthorne evidence and Hawthorne conclusions? Only a partial answer is provided by arguing that what the industrial world wanted at the time was human relations. The odd thing is that there are still academics alive who could help to unravel this mystery. Perhaps the answer is to persuade these academics to write their autobiographies and tell all.

At any rate, it is important to set out what the Hawthorne researchers did conclude, for their conclusions set the tone of the social science of organizations for a generation.

TOPIC 2
Theory X and Theory Y

Douglas McGregor in *The Human Side of Enterprise* has presented an interesting and insightful picture of how human endeavour can be mobilized more fruitfully to produce more effective management. His theories have been very well received in both North America and Europe. In his approach to human relations, McGregor takes as his point of departure the traditional management view which, in the interests of objectivity and to avoid a pejorative title, he labels "Theory X." He then explores the weaknesses of this traditional approach. To pursue his analysis, McGregor makes use of Maslow's hierarchical theory of motivation which, for his purposes, breaks motivation into four basic categories: physiological and safety needs, social needs, ego needs, and self-actualizing needs. Theory X only satisfies the employees' physiological and safety needs and to a lesser extent his social needs. He argues that a more comprehensive theory of human behaviour, which he labels "Theory Y," is required if we are in fact to mobilize fully the resources which the individual brings to work. McGregor's concept of human relations warrants closer examination, if only because his ideas have gained such wide currency in managerial ranks.

THEORY X

McGregor introduces Theory X by listing three fundamental propositions held by conventional management:

1. Management is held responsible for organizing the elements of production—money, material, men, and machines—all in the interest of maximizing economic returns. This is usually described as the organization of the four M's for economic reasons.
2. This process requires the directing of employees' efforts—motivating them and controlling and modifying their behaviour to suit the requirements of the organization. The implication is quite clear: "people can and must be manipulated."
3. Inherent in Theory X is the proposition that people are passive and even resistant to the needs of the firm unless they are persuaded, punished, or controlled. This conventional conception of management's role can be summed up by saying that management consists of "getting things done through other people."

Underlying this conventional theory are certain implicit assumptions regarding human nature, some of which most sensitive managers are usually prepared to acknowledge they have believed at some stage in their personal development.

a. The average employee is by nature indolent and lazy—he prefers to get by, doing as little as possible. The average worker is an "8 to 5" man who never "takes off his jacket" unless he has to.
b. He is seen as having scant ambition, little need for responsibility, and much need to be led. He works only to get three square meals a day, a roof over his head, and his "fags and beer." To make this policy effective, he plays the average, keeps his nose clean, and minds his own business.
c. He is presumed to be innately self-centred, and somewhat unconcerned about the needs of the organization. "Each man is an island" and "I'm all right, Jack" are his slogans. Other common expressions indicating this attitude are "I just couldn't care less," "I'm fireproof," and "I am maximizing ME."
d. He is fundamentally resistant to change. The presumption is that change is anathema to him: "I'm in a rut and I'm going to stay there."
e. He is assumed to be gullible and easily led by the demagogue; hence the success of the communists. Implicit in this approach is a sharp division between leaders and followers.

According to McGregor, management employing the conventional approach has two alternatives: it can take either a hard or a soft line.

Managers can be the hawks or the doves of organizational life. The hard approach, which requires devising tight controls, has one unfortunate disadvantage in that it breeds counterforce, restrictive practices, and antagonism. The soft approach is also unsatisfactory in the sense that we are all aware of organizations where relationships are excellent, morale high, and tensions low, yet nothing much in a productive way seems to be happening. In one such firm, which had an excellent and justified reputation for first-class consultation procedures, it was not uncommon for the men when asked, "What does the company produce?" to reply, "Consultation."

McGregor challenges this conventional view of management wisdom by arguing that it is advanced on a mistaken notion as to what is cause and what is effect. His considered view is that the assumptions on which Theory X is predicated may be accurate descriptions of employee behaviour and attitudes at the moment, but they are not innate; they represent the responses of the individual to organizational forces—behavioural effects of particular managerial attitudes.

McGregor, following Maslow, assumes that all motivation can be broken into four basic categories: (1) physiological and safety needs, (2) social needs, (3) ego needs, and (4) self-fulfilment needs.

PHYSIOLOGICAL AND SAFETY NEEDS

Physiological needs are man's needs for food, drink, warmth, shelter, sex, and so on. It is assumed that once these needs have been met, then the safety needs will require to be satisfied. Implicit in this approach is the idea that a satisfied need is not a motivator of behaviour. Maslow argues that when the physiological needs have been satisfied, needs at the next higher level begin to monitor man's behaviour.

The safety needs include protection against danger, threat, or deprivation. McGregor argues that when these needs are met the individual is more willing to take risks; it is only when a person feels threatened that his greatest need is for guarantees.

SOCIAL NEEDS

When man's physiological and safety needs have been met, his social needs become more important. Most executives are already aware of the existence of social needs, but it usually takes something going wrong in the organization before they will give full recognition to their importance. Evidence of these social needs is provided by the existence of informal organizations within the formal organization. These social needs include the need to belong, to associate with other people, to win approval, and so on. McGregor argues with some force that when man's social needs are thwarted, he responds in such a way that he blocks the organization from achieving its objectives. But the important point to bear in mind is that such behaviour is a consequence, not a cause.

Ego needs

Above the social needs in his model of motivation McGregor has listed the ego needs, which are of two basic kinds. The first is the need for self-esteem, that is, for self-confidence, independence, and achievement. The second relates to one's reputation—the need for approval, prestige, and recognition of one's work. It is obvious that as far as the rank-and-file members are concerned, the typical business organization offers scant opportunity for the satisfaction of ego needs. Indeed, the conventional way of organizing work militates against meeting ego needs except in a very limited way and for a fairly select group of senior managers.

Self-fulfilment needs

At the top of the hierarchy are to be found the self-fulfilment needs, which have a co-ordinating role. These are the needs for realizing the full extent of one's potentialities, including the need for self-development and the need to be creative. "What I can be, I must be," represents the essence of this need.

Central to this approach is a belief that while conventional management usually meets physiological and safety needs, and to a very limited extent social needs, it frequently fails to organize affairs so that people can work to satisfy some of these higher level needs. Inevitably in such circumstances frustration and conflict are generated, and as a consequence the organization is unable to function effectively. This particular preoccupation with physiological and safety needs can be identified with carrot-and-stick motivation. By focusing on this narrow aspect of motivation, management unfortunately has denied to itself the possibility of exploiting the full range of motives and talents that people bring to work.

The carrot-and-stick concept of control warrants a moment's consideration. Most managers who have some sense of self-awareness are, in my opinion, prepared to admit at least privately that they have used this strategy. But what is implied by this approach? Just that man is like a donkey; "give him the stick; if that doesn't work give him some carrots; if that doesn't work, give him both; if that doesn't work, get a bigger stick," and so on. The philosophy of conventional management is inadequate to fully motivate employees because human needs are much more complex than the implicit assumptions of Theory X would lead one to expect.

THEORY Y

The assumptions of Theory Y include:

1. Management is responsible for organizing production, that is, for the integration of money, materials, men, and machines in the interests of economic objectives.
2. People are not naturally passive or resistant to organizational needs. If they are, it is because of their experience in organizations.
3. Management has the onus or responsibility to exploit the complexity of human motivation, including the need that people have for autonomy—the need to direct their own behaviour and to assume some responsibility for their own destinies.
4. The principal responsibility of management is to organize matters so that people can meet and achieve their own goals by directing their own efforts towards organizational objectives.

McGregor was not unaware of the difficulties involved in making Theory Y a living and dynamic actuality in contemporary industry, and he recognized that it would take some time and would require extensive modification of the attitudes of both management and labour before such revolutionary ideas would become acceptable as a basis for organizational policy.

Nevertheless, he was essentially optimistic and in *The Human Side of Enterprise* drew our attention to some innovative ideas which he regarded as consistent with Theory Y, including:

1. Decentralization and delegation.
2. Job enlargement.
3. Performance appraisal.

Theory Y can be illustrated by its approach to the problem of performance appraisal. The individual is held responsible not only for setting targets or objectives for himself but also for playing a significant part in the evaluation of his performance. McGregor was quick to point out that this still leaves his superior an important role in the process of assessment. He rightly argued that by this method of "self-targeting," where a subordinate is held responsible for setting his own standards, the employee is encouraged to take a larger responsibility for defining and planning his own contribution to business, and in this way the company is able to exploit his egotistic and self-fulfilment needs.

Fundamental to McGregor's approach is the idea that management ought not only to think again about the assumptions of current managerial philosophies but should also depart from the carrot-and-stick theory of motivation and move over to a more sophisticated picture of the employee's motivation. McGregor's message is clear, "Management must assume the onus of developing conditions of employment for their people so that they feel free to exploit their self-fulfilment needs. This is an ambitious and optimistic hope." If such conditions are not developed, many employees, at all levels, may well experience the modern disease of alienation.

TOPIC 3
Alienation

The concept of alienation is extremely important for the student of organizational behaviour. The curious thing about researchers who get interested in alienation is that they are all drawn like moths to the candle flame of Karl Marx's idea of alienation. According to Marx, the market economy has a tendency to transform everything into commodities. Marx called this tendency the "fetishism of commodities." According to Marx, man becomes a cog in the industrial or bureaucratic machine; and with this loss of freedom, he is alienated from his human nature and becomes a thing. Marx describes alienation in the following manner:

> In what does this alienation of labour consist? First that the work is external to the worker, that it is not a part of his nature, that consequently he does not fulfil himself in his work but denies himself, has a feeling of misery, not of well being, does not develop freely a physical and mental energy, but is physically exhausted and mentally debased. The worker therefore feels himself at home only during his leisure, whereas at work he feels homeless. (T. B. Bottomore and M. Rubel, *Karl Marx: Selected Writings*.)

For Marx, man is alienated from his human nature by the economic process. In the process of alienation, man begins to act like a machine—perhaps, in our contemporary context, like a computer. When the process goes on long enough, man develops a "false consciousness." Marx uses the concept of false consciousness in a very complex and subtle way, but the term can be crudely interpreted as a view of the world which is at variance with reality.

Max Weber, like Karl Marx, was obsessed with the idea of alienation. As T. Burns and G. M. Stalker note in *The Management of Innovation*:

> Bureaucracy is often said to have played the part in Weber's sociology that social class did in Marx's. But both men were preoccupied, beyond these notions, with the idea of "alienation"—the moral, intellectual and social constraints exercised over men's natural instinctual inclinations by the immense apparatus of the social order.

Max Weber in developing his idea of formal rationality, which is the basic ingredient of his idea of bureaucracy, argues for a "value-free" approach and introduces the term the "demystification of social life." Weber invented the administrative machine par excellence, within which human needs would be subordinated to the system.

Alienation has also been defined in psychological terms. Erich Fromm has argued that rapid technological and economic changes have estranged man from his real nature. In *The Sane Society*, Fromm points out that:

> By alienation is meant a mode of experience in which the person experiences himself as alien. He has become, one might say, estranged from himself, he does not experience himself as the creator of his world, as the creator of his own acts—but his acts and their consequences have become his masters, whom he obeys, or whom he may even worship. The alienated person is out of touch with himself as he is out of touch with any other person. He, like the others, is experienced as things are experienced; with the senses and with common senses, but at the same time without being related to oneself and the world outside productively.

THE DIMENSIONS OF ALIENATION

M. Seeman has advanced the view that alienation is not a uniform experience but that it is a concept which can be better understood in terms of experiencing five dimensions: powerlessness, meaninglessness, normlessness, isolation, and self-estrangement.

POWERLESSNESS

Powerlessness refers to the essentially Marxist view of the worker's condition in a capitalist society, where the individual feels that he has no say or control over outcomes significant to his life; e.g., the powerlessness of the assembly line worker in an automobile plant.

MEANINGLESSNESS

Meaninglessness arises when the individual is unable to devise cognitive maps or models which facilitate predictions of his own acts. Repetitive work, maximal task break-downs, and limited responsibility create this loss of insight or understanding.

NORMLESSNESS

Normlessness, for example, arises in a society where there are strong and pervasive pressures to move upwards socially but inadequate means are available to do the actual climbing. In such circumstances, an individual may be virtually forced into using illegal or nonlegitimate means. The breach of legitimacy facilitates normlessness.

ɩ\

ISOLATION

Isolation develops when the individual not only rejects the legitimate means but also the goals of the organization or society. For example, in a bureaucratic organization an official may cling slavishly to the rules even though in doing so he is impeding the organization from achieving its goals.

SELF-ESTRANGEMENT

With self-estrangement, a person is alienated from some conception of himself and he is no longer interested in work or involved in it. Self-estrangement is closely linked to meaninglessness and powerlessness.

Using these five dimensions, R. Blauner has collected data on alienation among American industrial workers. Like most sociologists, Blauner believes that while the working class in the United States is not a potentially revolutionary force, nevertheless Marx's idea of alienation in the work process is valid. In *Alienation and Freedom*, Blauner argues that, "Today, most social scientists would say that alienation is not a consequence of capitalism per se but of employment in the large-scale organizations and impersonal bureaucracies that pervade all industrial societies." Having established that alienation does not necessarily follow from the capitalist mode of production, Blauner goes on to argue that it is wrong to assume that the worker must be alienated or nonalienated. The important point is to state the conditions under which alienation will arise. Since there are structural differences within modern industry, it can be assumed that certain conditions are more alienating than others.

In his researches, Blauner compared four industries using different forms of technology: a printing firm with a great variety of products, which meant that the work process had not been standardized; a textile plant with spinning and weaving as its chief processes; a company in the automobile industry; and an oil refinery where the main task of the process personnel was the supervision and monitoring of the control panels. Blauner categorizes these enterprises according to level of technology, division of labour, degree of bureaucratization, and economic standing (factors of market competition, concentration within industry, profit margin, and rate of growth).

Using data collected for another purpose which were published in *Fortune* magazine in 1947, Blauner found what he set out to find: that the degree of dissatisfaction and the lack of morale varies from industry to industry. For example the printers, partly because of the strength of their trade unions, had the most secure position. Because of their level of technology, which allowed them to exercise some freedom and control over work processes, they did not complain much about work pressures. Thus the experience of meaninglessness was reduced for them. Predictably, in the car industry Blauner found a higher level of alienation and indeed, for him, the automobile worker is the prototype of the alienated worker (see Box 3.3). The most satisfied group of workers were the process workers in the oil refinery, who, being highly trained and not engaged in hard physical work, had considerable freedom and discretion in spite of the fact that the production processes were automated. As Blauner points out, while alienation remains a widespread characteristic of factory life, "for most factory workers the picture is probably less black and white than for workers in the automobile and textile industries, where they tend to be highly alienated, and the printing and chemical industries, where freedom and integration are so striking."

ALIENATION AND THE ENVIRONMENT

The environment from which organizational members come has a significant say in how the workers are likely to respond in the work situation. Individuals from a particular environment or community bring a particu-

FIGURE 3–2
ALIENATION

lar set of values and attitudes to their work, which in turn significantly affect their behaviour in regard to such matters as whether they will observe or reject the production norms of a group or how they will respond to a job enrichment programme. As Figure 3–2 diagrams, alienation is a function of both the task and the environment.

The culture a person brings to work is partly responsible for the values and attitudes he displays there. But what is culture? In the language of the sociologist, it is usually thought of as some kind of vague, complex, inchoate cognitive map which people of a particular community carry around in their heads, albeit unconsciously, that gives a particular style to everything they do, feel, or think. Culture is synonymous with the learned and shared ways of believing and behaving which are part of the community's life style and give social meaning to the lives of its members.

The particular community from which a person comes may well affect his level of alienation. For example, it has been established that job satisfaction is higher in communities with substantial slum areas, since presumably when such a worker compares the alternative positions available to him, his present job is seen as relatively more attractive.

Box 3.3: The Lordstown syndrome: Blue collar blues on the auto assembly line

Since Henry Ford put the first car assembly line into action in 1914, social scientists, laymen, and car workers themselves have been struck with horror at what mechanization can do to people. Wage rates were and still are high, but not high enough to stop absenteeism, which is now running at 5 to 6 percent compared with 2 to 3 percent in 1965. On Fridays and Mondays, in many plants up to 15 percent do not report for work.

The most dramatic illustration of the monotony of car assembly work has been provided by the General Motors Corporation plant at Lordstown, Ohio, where resistance to the discipline of a highly automated line by young workers has led to sabotage and a 22-day strike. The dispute arose because the men accused management of eliminating jobs and redistributing the work among the remaining men. Agis Salpukas, who has made a special study of automobile assembly line problems for the *New York Times,* reports:

> Management has also accused workers of sabotage, such as breaking windshields, breaking off rear-view mirrors, slashing upholstery, bending signal levers, putting washers in carburetors and breaking off ignition keys,
>
> In the last four weeks a lot that holds about 2,000 cars has often been filled with Vegas that had to be taken back into the plant for repair work before they could be shipped to dealers. Sales of Vegas in the last two weeks have been cut about in half.
>
> The union, which concedes that there may have been some sabotage by a few angry workers, maintains that the bulk of the problems with the cars were a result of cutbacks in numbers of workers in a drive by management to increase efficiency and cut costs.
>
> According to the union, the remaining workers have had to absorb the extra work and cannot keep up with the the assembly line. The result, the union men say, is improperly assembled cars.

The basic underlying cause of this problem in the car industry is that contemporary North American man can no longer accept the boredom and inhumanity of the work. Salpukas illustrates this problem with two human cases from the Ford plant at Wixom:

> Mike Kingsley goes to the assembly plant about an hour before his shift every day and takes out his worn little Bible to read and meditate before he faces his job.

Agis Salpukas, *New York Times,* January 23, June 19, 1972.

CLASS IDENTIFICATION

A good illustration of how social class, as well as community, affects job behaviour is revealed by considering two shop floor types, restrictors and rate-busters. W. F. Whyte has pointed out that the social and family backgrounds of the restrictors were urban and working-class, whereas rate-busters were from farms or lower middle-class families. M. Dalton has also argued that while overproducers are likely to hold middle-class aspirations, underproducers do not.

Thus it seems reasonable to argue that a worker's class identification may affect his behaviour and attitudes at work. To test this proposition, Milton R. Blood and Charles L. Hulin, in "Alienation, Environmental Characteristics and Worker Responses," developed a construct which can be viewed on a continuum running from "integration with middle-class

"You've got to prepare yourself mentally," he said as he paused by the Ford assembly plant at Wixom. After three and a half years in the plant assembling dashboards, he feels he has reached a dead end.

"I'm going back to school at the end of the summer," he said. "There's only three ways out of here. You either conform and become deader each day, or you rebel, or you quit."

Willy Raines and two of his friends sat in an Oldsmobile on a parking lot outside the Wixom plant sipping Teachers Scotch from paper cups. It was 11 a.m. and this is the way they usually spend their half-hour lunch break.

Mr. Raines, on the assembly line for 17 years, had spent the morning glancing at a computer sheet that told him what kind of tires were needed for the Lincolns moving down the line.

His job is to take tires off a rack and hang them on hooks that move by at waist level. "I don't know what it is they can do, but they got to change these jobs," he said. "If you don't get a break off that line, you can go crazy."

Like many older workers who have built up seniority and benefits and have limited education he sees no choice but to keep his job. His hope is to put in his 30 years and retire at $500 a month in benefits at the age of 58.

IS JOB ENRICHMENT THE ANSWER?

One proposal put forward by the unions—that a team of workers should assemble a complete car or a large unit of the car—has been met by management's response that this would raise the price of the average car to $10,000 and foreign competition would put the U.S. car industry out of business. But Chrysler Corporation has been experimenting with the idea of giving auto workers a voice in assembly line management by allowing workers to supervise their own assembly lines, letting them control the flow of materials on the line. Salpukas describes other experiments in worker self-targeting:

At the Hamtramck plant, for example, some workers are no longer punished for taking an unexcused day off.

Instead, large calendars have been put up in one part of the plant and workers are asked to mark the day in advance when they want to take off.

Management can then juggle its schedules by knowing when a man will be

norms" to "alienation from middle-class norms." At the integrated end of the construct are to be found those workers who are involved and upwardly mobile; at the alienated end are those workers who view their jobs instrumentally, as a means to an end, who want good money for their work but in return for minimal involvement.

Blood and Hulin found that workers living in communities fostering alienation from middle-class norms (i.e., communities with more slum conditions, higher urbanization, greater urban growth) predictably organize their lives differently from workers from communities fostering integration. Thus the alienated workers have norms, but they are not the middle-class norms which are presumed to prevail at most places of work. Support for this thesis is provided by A. N. Turner and P. R. Lawrence, who, while studying job satisfaction, were puzzled to find "high job satisfaction with complex work in Town settings and high job satisfaction with

absent, instead of having to scramble around at the last minute to fill in for absent workers.

For two months absenteeism dropped, but then it crept up again to near its old rate. One advantage has remained. Half of the men now notify the company ahead when they take a day off.

One foreman objected so vociferously to the program that he resigned. Older workers, who often have more skilled jobs and do them with ease, have objected to proposals such as letting men rotate in different jobs. And some supervisors fear that their jobs will be eliminated through the program.

At the Detroit Gear and Axle plant, workers are being allowed to control the flow of assembly lines. William White, a 44-year-old worker, sat on a stool in front of a line where gear assemblies moved past him. There was a pedal he could hit with his foot to stop the line if he wanted to get a drink of water or take a break.

He is still expected to turn out 1,000 units a day, but now has a choice of working ahead and then shutting off the line for a while. "It's better," he said. "You've got more control now."

REVIEW

Results are difficult to assess in operational changes such as those introduced b Chrysler in their car plants, because in fact no major changes have been made in th way the workers work. The management does not expect a dramatic increase in pro ductivity. But there are definite advantages:

1. Workers feel more involved if they are consulted.
2. Workers like to use their skills, be creative, and learn new things.
3. Scheduling can be improved if workers advise management in advance about thei days off.
4. Giving workers some control of assembly line speeds allows them to work at differen rates across the day.
5. "A worker likes to work with his head and heart as well as his hands and feet."

The critical issue is whether such job enrichment programmes can be devised witl sufficient imagination to get the production needed to stave off foreign competition. I other countries car workers are still in highly traditional structures and quite happy t work at paces which North Americans can no longer manage. Nobody knows th answer yet.

---

simple work in City settings." In *Industrial Jobs and the Worker*, Turner and Lawrence point out:

> The positive relationship for Town workers between task attribute scores and Job Satisfaction indicates that what they wanted out of their job experience was a relatively large amount of variety, autonomy, inter-action, skill, and responsibility. Put in other terms, they were seeking a work environment in which they were expected or permitted a rela-tively rich and varied behavioral pattern in terms of activities, interac-tions, and mental states. Apparently they were predisposed to respond favorably to a relatively "challenging" or "involving" work environment, in which more of their potential ways of behaving could be constructively engaged with the task.
>
> We have repeatedly been forced to the conclusion that in a somewhat crude way the Town-City dichotomy we discovered in the course of analyzing our data points to some important and relatively deep-seated

differences in the perceived salience of task attributes. It seems as if these differences can best be explained by supposing that our City subcultures produce and reinforce an attitude of relative noninvolvement with the job, in which work is not perceived as a relevant means for attaining goals that are central to the individual's way of thinking about himself.

CONCLUSION

HUMAN RELATIONS AND SOCIAL CLASS

The inescapable conclusion of the research work on alienation is that both academics and executives have been naive in their view of what "the workers" expect from their work. Basically, what it amounts to is that

FIGURE 3–3
MODEL OF THE RELATIONS AMONG ALIENATION, MCI (MIDDLE-CLASS IDENTIFICATION), JOB SATISFACTION, AND NATURE OF THE TASK

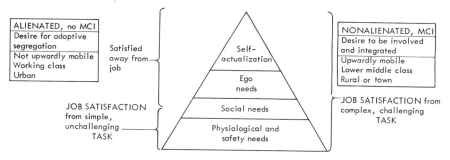

they have seen the workers as enjoying the same middle-class values as they hold themselves. Thus the solution to most problems at work is to be found in improving human relations—for example by pursuing the Theory Y rather than the Theory X approach, which will have the effect of mobilizing the workers' supposed need for self-actualization. And presumably all this can be achieved through increased participation.

But research data do not support such a simple, naive view. A more complex model, on the order of Figure 3–3, is needed, which basically recognizes that the workers are not all alike. They have different class identifications and different expectations from work. For example, alienated workers prefer simple, nonchallenging, but well-paid work which does not demand too much in terms of involvement (they may prefer adaptive segregation). Presumably they get their satisfaction in nonwork situations, for example working about the house or on their cars, or watching sports on TV while drinking beer. The nub of the matter is that it may be wrong to talk about basic human needs as Maslow does, as if all workers share the same needs for self-actualization and autonomy, and for work which is both challenging and complex.

The theory of human relations needs to be modified to take into consideration the values and attitudes which people bring to work. Further, it would be wrong to presume that this environmental constraint applies only to the shop floor workers. There is considerable evidence to support the view that organizational level structures the attitude which employees take to human relations.

HUMAN RELATIONS AND ORGANIZATIONAL LEVEL

An important point on human relations as a personal style should be mentioned: this kind of personal adjustment finds less favour as one ascends the hierarchy of an organization. In its simplest form, this means that shop floor workers, foremen, and some junior managers prefer human relations; more senior management men prefer good human resources planning. In other words, the typical senior manager prefers to operate in a situation which makes the best use of his resources, stretches him to the limit, but ensures that he is properly rewarded for his efforts *even though*, in the short run, conflict may be produced and considerable anxiety generated. Research findings suggest, on the other hand, that if junior managers are invited to describe the "manager they liked working for best," they describe a personnel-oriented executive who is supportive in personal relations and behaves in a generally considerate way which usually involves a fair amount of consultation and participation. For top managers, Wilfred Brown's idea of optimal organization represents a step beyond good human resources planning. For Brown, optimal organization is a function of the task and the resources available to achieve the task (technical, human and economic), not a function of personality:

$$\text{Optimal organization} = f(T, R)$$

In summary, it is possible to argue that human relations is best suited for some shop floor workers, good human resource planning for senior management, and optimal organization for top management.

As yet the experimental evidence is slim for this proposition (that as you ascend the hierarchy of a business organization, the need for human relations diminishes). Nevertheless, behavioural scientists cannot fail to be impressed by the fact that top management seems more capable of describing business behavior in objective terms; appears to be less involved in emotional terms; and seems to be capable of more dispassionate analysis of organizational problems, spanning a longer period of time.

TOPIC 4
Evaluation of human relations theory

What is this thing called human relations? Some saw it as a new reformation which would dramatically transform all social relations if only man's nature were properly recognized. The new reformation was to be built on man's intractability—and potentiality. Studying his intractability revealed the existence of informal shop floor organizations with their own sets of rules, roles, and relations. Behavioural scientists soon realized that these were not exclusively a blue-collar phenomenon; soon sightings of cliques and coalitions among archbishops, executives, and commissars were being reported in the literature. Thus, the dichotomy of formal and informal organization emerged, compelling the executives of the 1940s and 1950s to live in a split-level universe conceived by the humanistic behavioural scientist (who was also a rationalist).

Executives were taught that the bureaucracy, the well-ordered, structured world of classical organization, was ready for the organ transplant of human relations. The operation was a limited success except for a few dramatic cases—for example, the Glacier studies in England and the Harwood action research in the United States (both discussed in Chapter 5). In most cases the host organization was a tradition-loving culture which gave preeminence to a well-ordered hierarchy of specialists who had been selected on merit, promoted on performance, had corporate tenure, "did it their way"—and rejected the transplanted tissue of human relations.

Occasionally human relations did survive in pockets of devotees here and there. These devotees were regarded by their more hard-headed colleagues as odd fellows who were not to be trusted with the realities of life, such as getting the work out the gate on schedule, meeting the payroll week in and week out, and generating increasing dividends for 25 quarters in a row (as Harold Geneen did at I.T.T.).

A whole new science of organizational immunology emerged which was concerned with changing the corporate climate to facilitate the assimilation of human relations. Frederick Herzberg invented motivation-hygiene theory; R. R. Blake and J. S. Mouton evolved the managerial grid; the British tried work councils at the Glacier company; the Americans made participation a way of life at the Harwood company; and Rensis Likert came up with his "System 4," which presumed trust, participation, linking of groups, and supportiveness as prerequisites of effectiveness, not only for complex technologies manned by the new technocrats with their existential life styles, but also for the traditional organizations manned by the Archie Bunkers.

But human relations in the 1960s and 1970s has been looked at with an increasingly jaundiced eye by both sophisticated academics and informed executives, who have concluded that the basic model is too simple and its empirical base too weak. Our systems model set out in Figure 3–4 helps to illustrate the criticisms. Technology does matter. The structure of an oil refinery is one thing; that of a car assembly plant is another. (An oil refinery is largely automated and employs a minute number of process workers who, dressed in spotless white coveralls, spend their days gazing at dials; hence labour costs are a very small proportion of overall produc-

FIGURE 3-4
HUMAN RELATIONS AS A SYSTEM

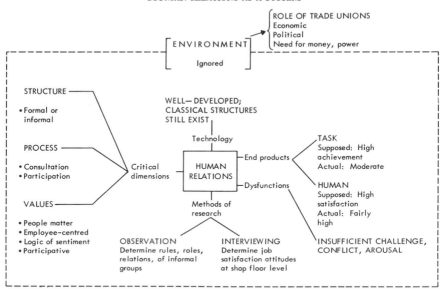

tion costs.) In the structures with high labour costs, the environment, particularly the role of trade unions, cannot be ignored. The General Motors plant at Lordstown, Ohio, shows that the irate long-hairs on the auto assembly line are importing a new, "hippie" life style into the plant, and it generated 5,000 grievances in a six-month period in 1973. The Lordstown plant was producing 103 cars an hour when the shop floor workers suddenly decided (after "everything behavioural" had been settled scientifically) to work half-time by a process called "doubling up" and still maintain quality (a baffling—and impossible—notion). A new blue-collar life style is slipping into the plant from the environment.

Another central belief of the human relations school is the proposition that if a worker is experiencing satisfaction at his work, he will be more productive—that morale and productivity are related. But A. H. Brayfield and W. H. Crockett carried out an extensive and systematic review of the literature and concluded than there is little evidence to support the view that employee attitudes, as measured in morale surveys, bear any appreciable relation to job performance.

The critical dimensions and other properties of the organization do "seep into" members' attitudes and behaviour, but the relationships are multidirectional and interacting, as our systems models indicate. The human relations school assumed simplistic, unidirectional causal flows, such as the assumption that the effects (improved job satisfaction, causing enhanced task effectiveness) flowed almost entirely from changes in the organization's process. Contemporary research supports the view that the relationships are interdependent. Underlying this one-sided aspect of human relations was the acceptance of a global personality theory, which gave the whole approach a closed system aspect. Not unexpectedly, in a closed system, theorists end up proposing "the one best solution" for all organizational problems.

Two other criticisms of the human relations school relate to the unit of analysis, the group, and the principal research method, typically the collection of data by interviewing shop floor workers. Focusing on the group inevitably seemed to mean focusing on the informal organization; since the informal group's purpose was reaction against the formal organization, any serious attempt at integration was blocked. Indeed this bias in human relations against Taylorism and administrative management theory has had the bad effect of impeding the assimilation of principles derived from information theory.

DEMISE AND RESURRECTION

Academics, both large and small, have been writing the obituary of human relations since its birth as a management philosophy in the 1930s. Ridiculed by unions as a form of "cow sociology" which turned factories into unthinking places of comfort; scorned by hard-headed managers who saw human relations as the soft option which destroyed the challenge of creative conflict (which, to their way of thinking, got things done even if a little angst was generated on the way); hammered into the ground by tough-minded behavioural scientists who defined the effective executive as a psychologically distant task specialist who rejected subordinates for poor performance—the demise of human relations always seemed to be just around the corner.

Yet in some curious, little-understood way, it has managed to survive. Rejected as a science, it has reemerged as a religion in the form of the human potential movement. The human potential movement is a newly emerging, quasi-scientific religion which is attracting growing support among the middle classes of North America in the 1970s. It is a burgeoning movement which is largely leaderless, inchoate, and ill-defined, but which includes sensitivity training, T groups, and encounter groups. Some of the more sensational terms used to describe this movement include "therapy for normals" and "the acidless trip." According to its high priests, it represents a reaction to the alienation of affluence, to the mobile, ambitious ethos that was presumed to be a prerequisite of the new industrial society. One of the consequences of a highly mobile society dedicated to high achievement and affluence has been a break-down of the intimacy between people, facilitated by the contraction of the extended family into the nuclear family.

Faced with a life that is largely barren in an intimate emotional sense, people were at one time likely to form their emotional values from the mass media, particularly TV and the movies. Now, in increasing numbers, many have responded to this emotional sterility with a desire to move in the direction of increased awakening of the senses, fuller appreciation of life's experiences, and keener insight into the human psyche. They have turned to the encounter group to experience what they are currently missing in their lives, hoping to achieve a new level of personal effectiveness and a higher degree of health and well-being. To many, the realization of such desiderata has been made possible through the emergence of the human potential movement, which explores man's unawakened resources. The movement focuses on the behaviour, feelings, and interactions of individuals in a group milieu. Devotees of this new cult achieve a higher level of emotional intensity and they come away, in some cases at least, with the feeling of having been "turned on."

As recent experiments in the laboratories of experimental psychologists have shown, man has a fundamental need for a minimal level of stimulus, arousal, or novelty. According to some psychologists, man, if placed in an environment of sensory deprivation for more than a few hours, lapses into a form of temporary madness and is unable to think clearly and make rational choices. Apparently this demand for stimulation represents a basic need—which has the interesting peculiarity that the more you get, the more you need. This has led to the curious situation of the mobile American who travels from sensitivity group to sensitivity group to maintain this "high."

And, perhaps not surprisingly, this movement for arousal and self-actualization has grown into a fantastically profitable business with some six million customers; it is regarded as a growth industry of the 1970s. Aided by the tremendous publicity generated by movies such as "Bob & Carol & Ted & Alice," this pay-as-you-go intimacy is spreading explosively. For example, "growth centres" like Esalen in San Francisco and Big Sur, south of Carmel in California, attract some 25,000 pilgrims a year. Centres have sprung up in most large cities in the United States, including New York, Chicago, Houston, and Austin. For those unwilling or unable to travel, do-it-yourself kits have been provided by books with titles such as *Conduct Your Own Awareness Sessions*, which include such fundamental awareness games as "Full-Length Mirror," "Body Magic," and "I Touch You and You Touch Me." Unfortunately and unhappily, people in our North American society have literally gotten out of touch with one another and become more distant. This physical untouchability has been accompanied by emotional remoteness.

It is not that good human relations are not sorely needed. This organizational approach, which could have helped to restore man's dignity, failed because the economic mandates of the organization preclude executives from supporting good human relations in times of trial, when the chips are down.

Summing up, human relations was right for its time and represented a necessary correction to the excesses of classical theory. By treating organizations as human systems, it argued for participation, creativity, and commitment, which was all to the good. The basic criticism of human relations is that the model of the organization employed left out important variables and made assumptions about causality that have turned out to be simplistic. Human relations failed because it was insufficient and provided too narrow a perspective; but it was a necessary step in the evolution of organization theory, for it paved the way for the systems approach.

REVIEW AND RESEARCH

1. Describe the strategy of a person who has very effective human relations skills.

2. Why do managers prefer human resources planning to human relations?

3. Describe a situation where you have deliberately restricted production. Why did you do so? List your answers under the headings: the primary working group's (*a*) values, (*b*) norms, (*c*) reinforcements, (*d*) sanctions.

4. Why was human relations right for its time?

5. Why did human relations as a management philosophy fail?

6. Compare and contrast the value systems inside the Hawthorne plant with the value systems outside, in the immediate environs of the plant. In your opinion, why did the Hawthorne researchers choose to ignore the attitudes people brought to their work?

7. Why do most North Americans still prefer human relations as a statement of their personal style in spite of its clash with the realities of the world?

8. Compare and contrast human relations as a personal style, as a management philosophy, and as a religion.

9. Describe "management by objectives." How should such a programme be introduced to a company? What role should a consultant play in such a programme? What are its advantages and disadvantages?

GLOSSARY OF TERMS

Alienation. Estrangement felt by a person—from his real nature, from others, from his work, or from groups or society. The dimensions of alienation are powerlessness, meaninglessness, normlessness, isolation, and self-estrangement.

Human potential movement. A quasi-scientific, quasi-religious movement focusing on the behaviour, feelings, and interactions of persons in a group setting, with the intent of increasing sensitivity, awareness, insight, etc.

Human resource planning. This is a more sophisticated view of "human relations." It is widely held by middle and senior management where the emphasis is on effective use of talent to achieve the organizational mission through the exploitation of human resources in a way which facilitates personal development, even if considerable conflict is developed in the process.

Informal group. A group formed within an organization but unrelated to its formal structure; typically, in business organizations, an interaction of lower level workers to promote their common interests. The informal group represents the reaction of the organized against the organizers.

Meaningful work. That type of work which enables an individual to identify himself with his work and to derive a feeling of worth from his work role.

Needs. Theory X and Theory Y presuppose four basic categories of needs (developed from Maslow's motivation theory): (1) physiological and safety needs, (2) social needs, (3) ego needs, and (4) self-actualizing needs.

Task specialist. One who adopts a structuring role which concentrates on task accomplishment above all other work considerations.

Theory X. One of two theories presented by Douglas McGregor in *The Human Side of Enterprise,* Theory X embodies classic, traditional views, approaches, and behaviour. It may be summarized as task-oriented and quite rigid.

Theory Y. McGregor's second theory embodies his concepts of better management approaches, including not only the organization of production but attempts to meet human needs such as autonomy and self-fulfilment. Theory Y may be summarized as more human relations–oriented and flexible.

4

Systems
theory

Increasing disenchantment with both the classical theory and the human relations approach led theorists in the late 1950s to search for a different optic, a new perspective, a dramatic new approach which would enable organization theory to move forward and escape from the sharply defined claustrophobia of the classical theory without falling into the marshmallow of human relations. Open systems theory, which required treating the organization as an organism which trades with its environment—importing inputs, transforming them, and exporting a product (person, thing, idea, or energy) to the environment—was the approach to which behavioural scientists turned in the hope of making a fresh beginning in organization theory. As Daniel Katz and R. L. Kahn point out in *The Social Psychology of Organizations*:

> In some respects open-system theory is not a theory at all; it does not pretend to the specific sequences of cause and effect, the specific hypotheses and tests of hypotheses which are the basic elements of theory. Open-system theory is rather a framework, a meta-theory, a model in the broadest sense of that overused term. Open-system theory is an approach and a conceptual language for understanding and describing many kinds and levels of phenomena. It is used to describe and explain the behavior of living organisms and combinations of organisms, but it is applicable to any dynamic, recurring process, any patterned sequence of events.

There are two basic arguments for adopting a systems approach. As F. E. Emery has argued in *Systems Thinking*, organization theorists adopted the systems approach because

123

. . . such an approach will reveal the "Gestalten" properties that characterize the higher levels of organization which we call "living systems."
. . . Second has been the argument that many of these Gestalten properties are common to the different levels of organization of living matter (from bacteria to human societies) and hence provide a valid and powerful form of generalization.)

Open systems theory draws its inspiration from the biological sciences, which have replaced the physical sciences as a main source of metaphor for the social sciences. We can look at the organization-as-organism metaphor from three aspects. The first aspect focuses attention on the interaction between the organization and its environment and sees the essential task of management as the managing of the boundary conditions, that is, the interchange between the external realities and the internal processes. This first aspect focuses on the concept of openness. The second aspect turns on the word "system" and argues the idea of interrelatedness—that everything that does or can occur is dependent on everything else that does or can occur. All organizational events are interlocked. The third aspect follows from the second and is essentially negative. It represents a rejection of linear causal trains as a means of explaining organizational phenomena; the concept of simple cause and effect is discarded.

ONE DEFINITION OF SYSTEM

First of all: What is a system? A hard question for the layman and a very hard question for the systems theorist. Everyone can point to examples of systems. A beautiful example of a system is the hydrogen atom, with its microscopic positive proton at the centre and the negatively charged electron flying round in a circle in perfect balance, its centripetal force perfectly balanced by electrostatic force. Going up the evolutionary scale of the physical sciences, a molecule represents yet another system, with all sorts of subsystems.

Taking a quantum leap, deoxyribonucleic acid (DNA) is a more complex system which by virtue of its complexity has the ability to reproduce itself. The DNA molecular system exists in the form of a double helix of matching parts (each basically a negative of the other); and the molecule has the capacity as it unwinds to allow each half of the helix to serve as a template which a new matching half can latch onto. DNA is, in turn, part of a larger system; it serves as a template for ribonucleic acid (RNA), which guides metabolism in the cell. Taking further quantum leaps, unicellular organisms like amoebas are systems, and examples of behavioural systems include human beings, groups, and organizations.

We still have not defined systems. In the 1956 edition of "General Systems, the Yearbook of the Society for General Systems Research," A. D. Hall and R. E. Fagen define a system as a set of objects together with relationships between the objects and between their attributes. This definition, though it emphasizes relationships and implies the holistic (hanging together) aspects of systems, is too terse for our purpose.

Thus if we define a system as any entity which consists of interdependent parts, we must add several qualifications. There are two basic types of systems, closed and open. Living systems are open systems, i.e., open to matter-energy-information exchanges with an environment. Human organizations are living systems and can be analysed accordingly. As Katz and Kahn put it, "Our theoretical model for the understanding of organizations is that of an energic input–output system in which the energic return from the output reactivates the system. Social organizations are flagrantly open systems in that the input of energies and the conversion of output into further energic input consist of transactions between the organization and its environment." (*The Social Psychology of Organizations.*)

HANDLING COMPLEXITY

As organizational analysts we are interested in complex open systems which exchange materials, energies, and information with their environments. Such systems are made up of a large number of parts that interact in a nonsimple way, and this complexity usually emerges in some form of hierarchy. The question then arises as to how we can handle this kind of complexity. Ludwig von Bertalanffy, the "inventor" and chief architect of general systems theory, proposed in 1947 a particularly abstract and daring idea—what some might call a *coup de théâtre* in scientific strategy or cynics might call just the old wine in new, bigger, and better bottles; at any rate, to many scientists a heady mixture which, when the hangover was over, was still a breath of new life. Von Bertalanffy's brilliant insight was that if we could discover the laws, concepts, and theories valid for systems in general, then we could make predictions with reasonable accuracy about how a particular biological or behavioural system (or any other similar system, for that matter) might work. Von Bertalanffy drew his inspiration from the biological sciences and tried to push beyond the limitations in man's thinking imposed by the use of a "billiard ball" physical science model of the world. The "world as billiard balls" is typically concerned with linear causal trains (the first cause-uncaused argument for the existence of God) or two-variable problems (Boyle's law that the volume of a gas is inversely proportional to its pressure at a constant temperature).

Goodbye physics . . .

The physics model of the world was incredibly successful in many applications; but unfortunately it is not applicable to the social sciences, and perhaps not to many areas of the biological sciences either. Instead of pursuing the traditional physical science method of breaking wholes into parts—which may turn out to destroy the essence of the problem we are studying—a more useful line of attack with biological and social systems is to try to develop a framework called "general systems" which includes all sciences. This general systems approach has turned out to be useful and productive in the social sciences, where the researcher must deal with the wholeness of the unit to be studied, and in general an extremely useful frame of reference in many fields. It is of particular interest to the student of organizations.

... Hallo biology

By and large, biology has now taken over from physics the central place which physics occupied in the 1920s and 1930s. This is largely a consequence of the Darwinian revolution, perhaps deferred to some extent by the gigantic achievements of atomic physics in the 1940s. This switch from a physics to a biological model has had a tremendous impact on organizational science. The shift has been made from the Newtonian certainties of the classical theories to the biological metaphors of Von Bertalanffy, where controlling uncertainties, transmitting information, and meeting complexity with complexity has become the order of the day.

Organizational scientists—impressed by the recent spectacular achievements of molecular biology, genetics, and neurochemistry—have been devising new metaphors and scenarios to help them to understand organizations better. For example, biologists now have a growing understanding of how the cybernetic network operates in human beings, i.e., how the genetic information and the constraints on which organic life depends are coded, transmitted, and selected in the evolutionary process. In more general terms, living systems are different from all nonliving structures in the universe. The unique difference is that they are endowed with purpose, which is built into their structures.

Exactly the same argument applies in a properly functioning, healthy organization. Somehow or other the structures (the roles and communication system), values, and processes seem to take up and incorporate into their very nature the purpose of the enterprise. Just as to-day the biologist can give us new information about the purpose of life more effectively than theologians, so can the behavioural scientist, by proper study and understanding of the structure and processes of groups, throw significant light on organizational purposes.

So the biological model is an extremely attractive one for the behavioural scientist studying organizations. It draws his attention to the actual processes, and from them he may be able to infer purposes. What the biologists have done in unravelling the molecular structure of DNA and RNA, behavioural scientists must do in the study of roles, role set, information flow, and control.

In organizational science a start—not a real beginning—has been made. The present plateau in organizational behaviour stems directly from this lack of beginning, this fatal gap between what science can tell us and what we imagine is actuality in our daily lives. What we need is an "ethic of knowledge" which builds on competence—competence in terms of understanding the organizational process. A genuine beginning will take place when we escape from the theological sterility of classical organization theory and write out a theory of organizations based on the information sciences. This is precisely the option offered to us by general systems theory.

STRUCTURE OF CHAPTER 4

Three topics are considered in this chapter. Topic 1 sets out the new perspective of open systems theory and argues the advantages of treating the organization as an organism. After differentiating among systems according to the level of abstraction involved, the characteristics of open systems are listed. These characteristics are: interrelation among component objects, attributes, and events; holism; goal seeking; input, transformation, and output; negative entropy; information processing; regulation; differentiation; and equifinality.

The second topic is the organization as an information-processing system. Beginning from the computer metaphor (that the organization is the computer writ large), it is argued that an organization has six subsystems: a sensor subsystem, a data processing subsystem, a decision subsystem, a processing subsystem, a control subsystem, and a memory subsystem. The critical role played by information as the life-blood of organizations is gone into in considerable detail, and man's role as a processor of information is discussed as a necessary preliminary for consideration of management information systems. What is being argued in this topic is that the critical shortage in our contemporary society is not capital, but information and its management.

Topic 3 concludes the three chapters which have dealt with classical theory, human relations, and systems theory with a comparative review and an evaluation of the three theories of organization.

TOPIC 1
The new perspective of open systems theory

There are two decisive consequences of adopting open systems theory. The first relates to the idea of openness. A major misconception flowing from the view that organizations can be treated as closed systems is that the linking of the structure, process, and values of organizations to goal achievement can be explained without reference to environmental influences. In the closed system approach, there has been serious neglect of the relationship between environmental variables and internal organizational variables. Thus the first principle of open systems theory is the principle of openness, which directs the attention of the researcher to the transactions with the environment. Walter Buckley, in *Sociology and Modern Systems Theory*, sets out the meaning of system openness:

> That a system is *open* means, not simply that it engages in interchanges with the environment, but that this interchange is *an essential factor* underlying the system's viability, its reproductive ability or continuity, and its ability to change.

Thus the systems approach requires that an organization be viewed as a subsystem of a larger system. Katz and Kahn (*The Social Psychology of Oraginzations*) have set out the virtues of this strategy:

> The first step should always be to go to the next higher level of system organization, to study the dependence of the system in question upon the supersystem of which it is a part, for the supersystem sets the limits of variance of behavior of the dependent system.

The other major consequence of adopting the open systems approach is the acceptance of the proposition that everything that happens or changes affects everything else; that is, that all events are correlated. Essentially

FIGURE 4–1
HUMAN RELATIONS CAUSAL TRAIN

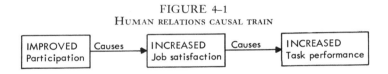

what the open systems optic requires is the rejection of analysis based on one-way causal trains. For example, the human relations paradigm shown in Figure 4–1 would be rejected by a student following the systems approach. A systems student would develop a different kind of model, such as that in Figure 4–2, which shows (*a*) some of the linkages between variables and (*b*) other variables being ignored (question marks).

In essence, the notion of interrelatedness argues that all elements in the system change when one element is changed. As T. M. Newcomb has pointed out in "Individual Systems of Orientation":

> I have chosen to emphasize "system properties" rather than single variables which contribute to them, and consequently none of the variables has an enduring status either as independent or as dependent . . . a change in one system variable is likely (under certain conditions) to be followed by a specified change in another system variable, but according to others a change in the second is a precondition for a change in the first.

THE ORGANIZATION AS AN ORGANISM

The idea of an organization as an organism derives considerable force and thrust from the fact that even the smallest part of any living system,

FIGURE 4-2
SYSTEMS MODEL OF FIGURE 4-1

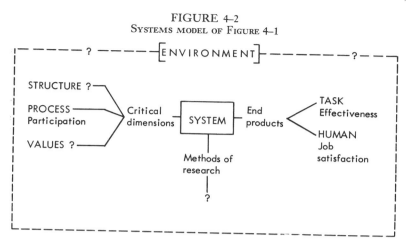

the individual cell, seems to have built into it the whole programme for building the complete organism. That each cell contains a library of information telling it what to do is validated by the recent work of biologists who have coaxed individual brain cells of mice apart, using enzymes, and then put the separated cells into a growth-sustaining solution. Carefully incubated, curious things happen; the cells begin to join and organize themselves into a pattern similiar to the original tissue. The reconstructed tissue forms synapses (chemical communication bonds that transmit messages) and myelin insulation to stop "noise" from other cells filtering in. Consider further that the human brain, which far surpasses in complexity the most intricate computer ever built, contains single cells which may be "wired up" to as many as 60,000 other cells. Which travel agent do such cells turn to? Apparently they programme their own travels.

The capacity built into individual cells to programme and position themselves inevitably has a fascination for organizational analysts, because this interlocking self-programming principle is precisely what organizational elements need to function in a purposeful way. This is what organizational behaviour is all about: to get each element (human being, group, or suborganization) to self-target by assimilating the correct programme (instructions) and posture (direction) and to lock into the other correct elements so the whole thing works. The emotional-logical enzyme that facilitates this process is called culture, and its constituents are values.

Experienced managers know all this biological–organizational analogy stuff intuitively; they know, for example, that people seek out and attach meaning to their every twitch, the smallest movement of lips or eyelids. Thus it is not for nothing that the Communist party and resistance groups are organized as cells; that politicians talk about the party apparatus; that soldiers in training run around all day shouting "kill the enemy" to condition their reflexes.

A large, well-structured, carefully designed and trained organization (like the Wehrmacht at the end of World War II) will hang on to the bitter end and have to be beaten by attrition. Against such well-structured, value-infused organizations there are no quick victories. Experienced generals believe that "things cannot be as good or as bad as they look at first sight" because they know that organizations have a resilience and survival capacity which rarely evaporates in the early moments of a struggle.

This resilience and survival capability, reinforced by some kind of organizational inertia, exists in nonmilitary organizations; no easy victories are won in the interorganizational struggles of giants such as General Motors versus the United Automobile Workers, Douglas versus Boeing, or IBM versus the Department of Justice (plus "competitive" gnats).

TYPES OF SYSTEM

It is possible to differentiate among systems according to the level of abstraction involved. Following Kenneth Boulding's thesis in his "General Systems Theory—The Skeleton of Science," systems can be classified in the following manner.

At the most elementary level we can identify structures or frameworks which help to identify parts and relationships in a static fashion—for example, charts showing the anatomy of the body; genus-species classification systems for rocks, plants, and animals; and in our field, organization charts and role descriptions. This level is essentially static.

The next level is that of the simple dynamic system, where the parts move and do something in a fixed and predetermined way. This might be called the level of clockworks.

The next stage is typified by the control mechanism which is essentially a cybernetic system, which Boulding refers to as the level of the thermostat. It is here we study mechanisms, dynamics, and servomechanisms. We can apply our findings to devise, for example, a system for controlling the booking of airline seats. The system is self-regulating in maintaining equilibrium.

The fourth level is that of the open system, where we are concerned not only with the intended purpose but also whether it is actually being achieved. This is the level at which life begins to differentiate from nonlife. Quickly other levels need to be added to include plants and animals. The animal system is characterized by increased mobility, teleological behaviour, and self-awareness. At the next level, the human level, the individual human being may be considered as a system with self-awareness, a sophisticated language, and the ability to use symbols in complex ways.

As we move to more complex systems, it is necessary to look at the social system. This involves consideration of how meaning is transmitted, how value systems evolve, how tradition is established, and how art forms emerge.

CHARACTERISTICS OF OPEN SYSTEMS

INTERRELATION AMONG COMPONENT OBJECTS, ATTRIBUTES, AND EVENTS

Essentially, what is asserted is that the system hangs together. If one element in the system changes, the system will be disturbed and other elements will have to adjust. For example, if you speed up productivity in the paint shop of a car plant by introducing an incentive bonus, it may well have repercussions in other parts of the plant. Increasing through-put will create a demand for bodies to paint, or the next assembly station will be overloaded, or shop floor operatives will have the opportunity of making an issue of pay differentials (see Box 4.1).

HOLISM

For the modern-minded executive, holism is usually put forward as synergism—that the whole, usually the executive team, produces more than the arithmetical sum of the individual executives' efforts. Taking an example from chemistry, H_2O is composed of two atoms of hydrogen and one of oxygen, but it has vastly different qualities from what you would expect if you had never seen the liquid (water) before and were only familiar with the gases (hydrogen and oxygen).

Turning to the behavioural sciences, personality may be thought of as the dynamic organization of behavioural elements such as behaviour, attitudes, feelings, and perceptions. The capacity for integration may become not only a need in itself, but an escalating process which continually requires exercise, compelling changes in behaviour, emotions, and perceptions.

GOAL SEEKING

In the old days (a few years ago), it appeared that large, complex systems such as business organizations had considerable stability. The example often cited was of corporations which repeatedly paid quarterly dividends to their stockholders for periods as long as 30 or 40 years. That was before the Penn Central collapse, the Rolls-Royce bankruptcy, and the Lockheed cost bind.

In any case, complex systems have multiple goals, not all of which can be satisfied to the same extent simultaneously. This principle of suboptimality in regard to the several dimensions for measuring performance usually involves trade-offs, and business systems may lose control and founder because their current cash flow failures weaken the will of bankers, investors, customers, and governments to bail them out. Organizations, like organisms, die. Though the mortality rate is rising for large,

Box 4.1: Too much production can be a problem

Problems of organizational behaviour, until very recently, have been viewed from one perspective or another rather than from an integrated organizational or systems point of view. Alex Bavelas, a distinguished social psychologist, tells of one of his experiences as consultant to a toy firm. His case is an excellent example of how professional bias can influence the mode of resolution of a production problem, which in turn can lead to dysfunctions within both the subsystem and the total system.

The case presented by Bavelas and Strauss centered around the reengineering of painting operations. The painting was only an intermittent operation, but constituted an integral part of the total manufacturing process. The new painting operation, as designed by engineers, was as follows:

. . . the eight girls who did the painting sat in a line by an endless chain of hooks. These hooks were in continuous motion, past the line of girls and into a long horizontal oven. Each girl sat at her own painting booth so designed as to carry away fumes and to backstop excess paint. The girl would take a toy from the tray beside her, position it in a jig inside the painting cubicle, spray on the color according to a pattern, then release the toy and hang it on the hook passing by. The rate at which the hooks moved had been calculated by the engineers so that each girl, when fully trained, would be able to hang a painted toy on each hook before it passed beyond her reach.

The engineer's design failed to take into account the interaction of the painting department with adjoining departments. It also emphasized the technical aspects of the operation but ignored critical human variables relevant to the designing of any new man-machine system.

The introduction of change is usually accompanied by transitional economical or psychological effects. Management did recognize that the women would inevitably go through a learning phase but assumed that the "learning bonus" would maximize motivation. They introduced the following transitional bonus scheme:

The girls working in the paint room were on a group-bonus plan. Since the operation was new to them, they were receiving a learning bonus which decreased by regular amounts each month. The learning bonus was scheduled to vanish in six months, by which time it was expected that they would be . . . able to meet the standard and to earn a group bonus when they exceeded it.

Alex Bavelas and George Strauss, "Group Dynamics and Intergroup Relations," in W. F. Why et al., *Money and Motivation* (New York: Harper & Row, 1955), pp. 90, 91.

complex systems, organization analysts cannot fill out the death certificates yet because our knowledge of systems pathology and senescence is minuscule.

INPUT, TRANSFORMATION, AND OUTPUT

Open systems, like biological organisms, must import some form of energy from the external environment. Just as the body requires oxygen to survive, so the human personality is dependent on an optimal level of stimulation to prosper. Once having secured the input, open systems then transform it by a through-put process; the through-put of an organization

But shortly after the new plan was put into operation, the painting department was plagued by absenteeism, considerable labour turnover, low morale, and unanticipated poor production. A consultant, a human relations specialist, was called in to resolve this problem—to increase both production and employee morale in the painting department. The consultant arranged discussion meetings with the women and their foreman. One significant factor emerged from these discussions: the women wanted to have some control over the speed of the belt on which they had to hang the toys. This shop floor right to control belt speed was introduced and led to considerable employee satisfaction, and to an average belt speed and production output above the standards set by the engineers. Where's the rub?

The consultant managed to solve the problems of the painting department, but at the same time to create considerable unrest in the rest of the organization. The new bonus scheme, coupled with the increased output, enabled the workers in the painting department to earn considerably more than their fellows in other departments, which triggered off considerable disturbance elsewhere on the shop floor. Furthermore, the increased output in the painting department disrupted the smooth flow of items from one department to the next by making excessive demands on the preceding operation and causing stockpiles in the next department.

These dysfunctions were caused by a very basic wrong assumption made by the consultant: that the painting department was an independent unit divorced from the rest of the manufacturing process and from general company policies. This led him to sub-optimize the painting process with respect to output, when in fact output was a constraint for the painting department.

The whole situation became intolerable to management. They threw out the consultant's recommendations and reverted to the original engineering design. This led to several shop floor resignations and the resignation of the foreman.

This case illustrates the fact that neither the engineer, the organizational behaviourist, nor management had any real understanding of the implications of change. The engineer's design analysed the painting operation only from a steady-state point of view emphasizing technological and economic considerations; the organizational behaviourist assumed that the painting department could be treated as a separate entity; and management reacted to both these developments in a stopgap fashion rather than in a coordinated way.

may be the production of a new person, place, thing, or service. Following the transformation, the open system exports some output into the environment. The simplest input-transformation-output model is presented in Figure 4–3.

When this simple model is applied to an economic organization, as in Figure 4–4, the inputs are energy, material, information, and people; the transformation process describes the various activities called work; and this process changes the inputs into output. The output is worth more than the input—in economic terms, value has been added.

The question then arises as to whether the actual output was up to the expected output. If a significant difference exists between actual and expected, management deals with the difference by installing a control element with feedback built in (see Figure 4–5).

FIGURE 4–3
SIMPLE INPUT-OUTPUT MODEL

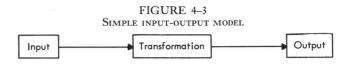

NEGATIVE ENTROPY

Open systems are characterized by patterns of activities that are cyclic in nature. The product sold in the market allows the purchase of new inputs, and so the cycle continues. As Katz and Kahn point out in *The Social Psychology of Organizations*, this recycling gives structure a dynamic quality:

> It is events rather than things which are structured, so that social structure is a dynamic rather than a static concept. Activities are structured so that they comprise a unity in their completion or closure. A simple linear stimulus-response exchange between two people would not constitute social structure. To create structure, the responses of A would have to elicit B's reactions in such a manner that the responses of the latter would stimulate A to further responses.

But to survive, an open system must be able to elude the forces of entropy. In thermodynamics, entropy is a curious factor which shows up when a system (strictly speaking, a closed system) is losing energy. The presence of entropy means that some of the system's energy is no longer available; hence entropy is a conceptual synonym for the "running down" or disorganization of a system. The open system can import more energy from the environment than it expends, store the energy, and thus escape entropy. Thus when Katz and Kahn speak of "negative entropy," the concept is one of increasing order or organization—a growth or betterment of the system.

INFORMATION PROCESSING

Systems not only input energy but also establish information and coding processes to translate the incoming information into forms useful and relevant to the system. To operate, effective systems utilize negative feedback loops which allow the system to correct its deviations from

FIGURE 4–4
ORGANIZATIONAL INPUT-OUTPUT MODEL

FIGURE 4–5
INPUT-OUTPUT SYSTEM WITH CONTROL ELEMENT

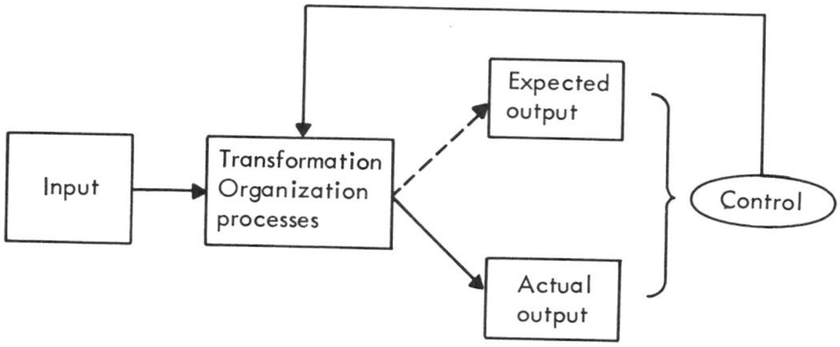

course. Figure 4–6 shows both input and process feedback loops. When an organism's feedback stops, its equilibrium is upset and the organism eventually dies.

REGULATION

Systems are capable of self-regulation through adjustment, control, and learning. The open system is characterized by a steady state and dynamic homeostasis—not motionlessness or static equilibrium, but rather a balance between external pressures and internal elaboration. This ratio of "the energy exchange" to "the relations between the parts," as Katz and Kahn put it, remains the same. The steady state is most clearly demonstrated in the homeostatic process for the regulation of body temperature. Organic homeostasis, according to W. B. Cannon, is the set of regulations which act to maintain the organism's steady state and frequently appear to act against the laws of physics and chemistry. For example, when the body temperature drops below 37° centigrade, the chemical reactions in the body (contrary to what one might expect from physical chemistry) begin to speed up. As Katz and Kahn point out in *The Social Psychology of Organizations:*

> Though the tendency toward a steady state in its simplest form is homeostatic, as in the preservation of a constant body temperature, the basic principle is *the preservation of the character of the system.* The

FIGURE 4–6
INPUT-OUTPUT MODEL WITH FEEDBACK

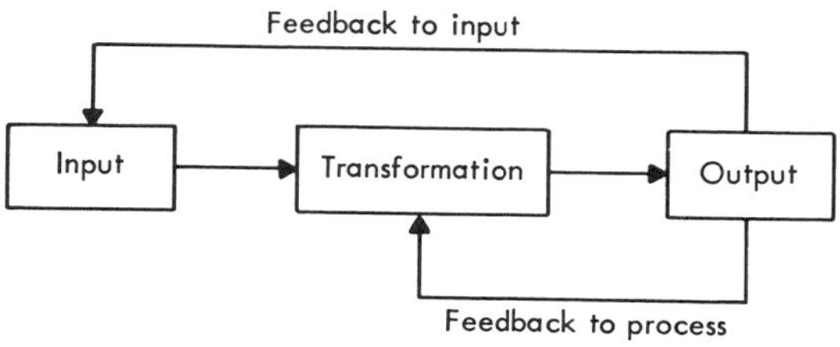

equilibrium which complex systems approach is often that of a quasi-stationary equilibrium, to use Lewin's concept. . . . An adjustment in one direction is countered by a movement in the opposite direction and both movements are approximate rather than precise in their compensatory nature. Thus a temporal chart of activity will show a series of ups and downs rather than a smooth curve.

In preserving the character of the system, moreover, the structure will tend to import more energy than is required for its output, as we have already noted in discussing negative entropy. To insure survival, systems will operate to acquire some margin of safety beyond the immediate level of existence. The body will store fat, the social organization will build up reserves, the society will increase its technological and cultural base. Miller . . . has formulated the proposition that the rate of growth of a system—within certain ranges—is exponential if it exists in a medium which makes available unrestricted amounts of energy for input.

DIFFERENTIATION

To cope with the problems of adaptation, systems become more differentiated. Just as the human body develops complexity through specialization of function, so the human personality evolves elaborate structures and processes such as the defence mechanisms which allow it some measure of privacy and autonomy. Groups (varying all the way from dyadic lovers to orgies, to take sexual groups for an example) reveal a significant capacity for differentiation. A modern university reveals the extent of differentiation needed to cope with the knowledge explosion.

EQUIFINALITY

Finally, open systems are characterized by the principle of "equi-finality," which was postulated by Von Bertalanffy in 1940 and which states that a system can achieve the same final state from a variety of different first states. In a closed system, if the initial state can be specified, the final state can be unequivocally specified. Not so in an open system. An initial state can have several end states, and a particular end state may be achieved from several points of departure. There is more than one way of skinning a cat.

TOPIC 2
The organization as an information-processing system

THE COMPUTER ANALOGY

The computer celebrated its silver anniversary in 1973; just 25 years since the late J. von Neumann designed the first fully modern electronic computer. The computer—which promised or threatened, depending on your point of view, to transform our world more than any other techno-logical advance—has in fact reached into nearly every realm of human development and in the process has transformed not only the shape of society but also the way man thinks. A new state of mind has emerged: an outlook which takes the view that man and the computer are two species of a more abstract genus called the information-processing system. Now this brilliant insight put forward by George A. Miller, professor of psy-chology at Rockefeller University, can be extended to cover not only men, groups, and organizations, but all sorts of other systems, even tissues, cells, and viruses.

Biologists have established that a living organism begins with a set of instructions. With this programme, written in the genetic code, a series of chemical computations are gone through which produce not another chemical but a living creature.

Perhaps the study of very simple living systems can provide better clues for understanding how other behavioural systems operate. Since World War II, there have been two main, well-concentrated, often highly mathematical theoretical pursuits of universals that are applicable to both living systems and machines. The two principal developments are cyber-netics and bionics. Cybernetics represents an attempt to understand living systems by making analogies to machines; bionics attempts to understand and build machines through the biological analogy.

SIX SUBSYSTEMS

The information-processing aspect of the computer has a general analogy in the biological field. As noted in Chapter 1, every organism has the following subsystems.

1. A *sensor* subsystem which is concerned with the reception and recog-nition of information.
2. A *data processing* subsystem which is concerned with breaking down this information into terms and categories which are meaningful and relevant to the organism.
3. A *decision* subsystem where decisions are made which may involve:
   a. Self-regulatory or homeostatic processes.
   b. Adaptive or learning processes.
   c. Integrative processes.
4. A *processing* subsystem which integrates information, energy, men, and materials to implement the decisions, accomplish tasks, and produce output.
5. A *control* subsystem which ties the whole system together by a set of feedback loops. These loops incorporate the equations of the critical decision variables which, if not respected, lead to lack of growth and the eventual demise of the organism.

6. A *memory* subsystem which is concerned with the storage and re-
trieval of information.

The subsystems in a living system are paralleled in the computer, as
shown in Figure 4–7. But because the computer can only deal with input
information that has been encoded in mathematical terms in rigorously
defined ways, the computer forces its users to review carefully the quality
of the information they work with. This informational discipline has a
salutory effect on behavioural theorists, who are compelled to examine
their terminology afresh to ensure that their logic is relevant.

FIGURE 4–7
BASIC COMPUTER PROCESS MODULES

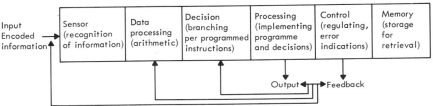

A new generation of researchers and executives are coming forward
who in some respects are more familiar with FORTRAN, a computer
language, than with English. Their cognitive processes seem to slip in
heuristics (rule-of-thumb guide-lines for human problem solving) somewhat more easily than the generation before them, who were brought up
on slide-rules.

The great difference between the computer system and the organic
system which must be noted has to do with the purely mechanical operation of the former. All of the critical variables—the decisions to be made,
the regulatory standards, what is to be done in processing the information
—must be fed into the machine by its human programmers. Thus the
mechanized slave seems alternately brilliant (incredibly swift mathematical computation) and stupid (incapacity to make even the simplest independent judgement or adaptation) to its human creators and manipula-
tors. Better programmes and mechanical self-regulations are, of course,
being built almost daily—through human ingenuity.

INFORMATION: THE CRITICAL INPUT

An organization may be defined as a hierarchically structured group of
people who have been brought together to achieve a particular purpose.
For our present purposes, the critical word in this definition is "structured." Indeed the whole notion of structure is integral to gaining an
understanding of what is meant by organization. We have already de-

scribed structure in various analogies to anatomy or framework; in our present context it is useful to think of it as the lattice of the interrelationships that exist between roles in an organization and to ask, "What is transmitted between these roles?" The answer is, "Information."

The modern view is one which stresses the organization as a system of information flows. The exchange of information, the transmission of meaning, and the orientation of decision-making processes to changing environments represent the very essence of organizational life. What this means essentially is that every organization is a communications system, and thus every organization is in the communications business. It is obvious that universities, publishing houses, television companies, and newspaper businesses are in the communication business, i.e., they acquire information, process it, and transmit it. What is not so obvious is that it is possible to think of any organization as being in the communication business.

For example, it is possible to think of an engineering company manufacturing plain bearings which are used in the assembly of the internal combustion engine as an information system. The significant difference in this case is that the information (which the company has acquired either through research or by purchase) is not transmitted in the form of paper or celluloid or magnetic tape, but is contained in the product, the bearing itself. The contents of the information relate to such matters as the material and the thickness of the surface of the bearing, the location and dimensions of the oil groove, and the inclusion and definition of the locating nick. The information is contained in the properties of the bearing and these properties have the effect of influencing in a significant way how the engine operates. Speaking generally, a product has information locked up in it and that is what the customer pays for when he buys a product. Alternatively, it is possible to think that the productivity which is added to a product in its transmission through an organization can be thought of as added value, and added value can be measured in information terms.

Put another way, the product can be thought of as carrying meaning in so far as it is able to meet the needs and wants of the consumer. Pursuing further the idea of the organization as an information system, it is useful to take the view that information results when uncertainty is removed. But any item of information is capable of a number of interpretations. If any action is to be taken, the degree of uncertainty must be reduced: Organizing is concerned with removing uncertainty from information and structuring relations so that this removal can be achieved.

INFORMATION—AN ECONOMIC FACTOR

In classical economics the three great factors of production were land, labour, and capital. At different times each of these has been the key factor. The successful entrepreneur of any given time has had to acquire and exploit the key input.

Until the middle of the 18th century the key inputs were labour and land. With the coming of the industrial revolution, the key input became capital. All the great entrepreneurs of the railroad-steamship age, such as Hudson, Carnegie, and Rockefeller, were great capitalists. Capital was the critical input well into the first half of the 20th century; but as skilled workers became scarce and new methods in metallurgy and electronics required less capital, knowledge replaced capital as the critical factor.

It is useful to think of information as an economic commodity to be bought and sold, stored, exchanged, and consumed. Like currency, it must be managed. Some social scientists have argued that money will go out of fashion and only information will change hands. Of course, this is already a tradition of the very rich, who rarely carry money.

As knowledge, or information, became the critical input, the emergence of the digital computer in 1954 changed the complete frame of reference. The new view of the firm was of an information-processing system. In this new context, various occupational figures attempted to dominate the organizational scene.

Managers, of course, work towards maximizing not only their salaries and status but also their information privileges. The notion of job enlargement can be readily understood in information terms. The effect of enlarging or enriching a job is to expand the information sources and to increase the information transfer functions and the responsibility for the management of information. For example, clerks in an airline ticket office selling tickets have a highly routinized type of operation. But if the ticket salesman is given the responsibility of preparing new office layouts that will maximize the effectiveness of the office—taking into consideration that there is a variation of traffic between international and domestic routes across the year—his job has been enriched. The informational opportunities presented to the salesman can be readily recognized; his prestige is increased by working with larger generalizations that encompass more subclasses.

In organizations, hierarchies of information access exist, and an executive's prestige is increased by working with larger generalizations. Many forms of information privilege can be shared by an executive group. And though computerized information dissemination tends to be pretty wide, the structuring and timing of the distribution is still a critical management operation. For example, it is not unknown for a sales manager to contact a particular salesman in the field on a Friday afternoon when the previous month's sales figures by territory have been printed out but not yet mailed to the salesman. A critical intervention like this, where one side has all the information and the other party has only inspired guesses, gives a good illustration of how the availability of information is related to the amount of power that an executive holds.

Some information is not or cannot be shared; and it is safe to say that the less widely shared information is, the greater its value.

THE YEAR OF THE INFORMATION REVOLUTION

The year 1948 can be identified as the date of birth of modern scientifically established information theory, for it was in that year that C. E. Shannon published his two-part paper "A Mathematical Theory of Communication." And it was also in that year that Norbert Wiener published his *Cybernetics*. In the following year Warren Weaver drew attention to these developments and helped to get the idea abroad that information and uncertainty could be measured accurately. In the 1950s and 1960s a spate of papers and conferences dealt with the use of information theory in psychology. It is now recognized that information theory developed out of nearly simultaneous work in control engineering, statistical theory, and communications engineering. But it was communications engineering that provided the greatest impact on its growth.

Weaver uses "communications" in a "broad sense to include all of the procedures by which one mind may affect another." For Weaver there are three distinct levels of communication: (1) the technical level—how accurately the symbols of communication can be transmitted; (2) the semantic level—how precisely the transmitted symbols convey the desired meaning; and (3) the effectiveness level—how effectively the received meaning affects conduct in a desired way. When information is received effectively, uncertainty is reduced. Whenever information is aimed and uncertainty reduced, communication has taken place. Management, of course, has a tremendous interest in controlling uncertainty levels.

One way of measuring the amount of information a message contains is to ascertain the degree of surprise it elicits in the receiver. The degree of surprise induced depends on what the receiver already knows. People tend to operate best in an environment where there is an optimal level of surprise or novelty, and not too well in an environment which is too flat. However, management does not want to be too surprised.

If management receives essentially the same information day in and day out, increasingly small amounts of information utility are added. In such conditions of minimal information, growth can be compared to a ticking clock—the message becomes background noise and it is only when the clock stops that new information is generated.

DEFINING "TO INFORM"

What does the word "information" mean? It is a rather vague, diffuse, portmanteau word which is difficult to define in clear, unambiguous terms. Information is a kind of metaconcept, like "space" and "time" in physics. It is useful to define what it is not. Information is not matter; it is not energy. A good starting point is to think of information as knowledge in a person's head. Writing, holes in punched cards, readings on meters, and pictures are all sources of information. But, like Bishop Berkeley's tree in the quad, they do not exist as information until someone begins to react to them. Information is in the brain behind the eye of the beholder.

COMMUNICATION

Imagine for a moment that you live in a world where you can only communicate in a language made up of two messages, yes and no. How would you communicate with another person in this binary world? If you were clever enough, you might work up something like the Morse code, where two signals put an alphabet, and thus a complex language, at your disposal.

FIGURE 4–8
A COMMUNICATION PROCESS

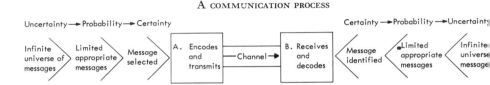

Or suppose you are subject to a cost constraint and can only send the other person a five-letter word. You decide to send the word HALLO (or HELLO). But the other person, because of noise on the line, receives only H-L-O. There is still a good probability he will be able to guess what your message is. The probability that one letter follows another can be computed statistically, and people who speak a language are aware of its word structures—diphthongs, doubled letters, common letters and words, and so on.

Essentially this is how communication takes place. As shown in Figure 4–8, out of an infinite universe of choices, made finite by their particular point in time and space, A selects a particular message which is encoded and transmitted as a signal over a channel to B, who decodes the message (with certainty, with probability limiting to a narrow range, or with uncertainty—the message was lost).

The purpose of communication is to introduce some order and direction into the world—to beat the entropy in the system. Systems tend to regress to the state of equilibrium which is least complex. For example, think of a pack of cards being shuffled; each shuffling makes it less likely that any two cards will appear in sequence. When you pick up your hand in a card game and sort the cards out by the different classification systems, you have reversed entropy and are then in a position to send a message.

Let us consider the concept of "noise" and its effect on information gain or uncertainty reduction. Noise is entropy raising its ugly head and trying to garble the message (static in the radio, snow on the TV screen, and so on). Suppose, going back to our model, that A selects message *K* from his portfolio of *n* possible messages for transmission over a noisy channel. When B gets the signal, because of the noise he cannot be certain just exactly what the message is. Let's say it could be *J*, *K*, or *L*. In brief, some communication has taken place and uncertainty has been reduced in this case; B's uncertainty has been reduced from a width of *n* messages to a set of three equally likely messages.

The more complex the message (the sequence of yes-no choices), the lower the probability that it will occur. The lower the probability, the more chances the message has of getting through. If you send "Please help me," the chances are that it may get garbled en route. But if you send a complex message such as "England expects every man will do his duty," there is a good chance that enough clues to the message will get through that it can be figured out. A significant reason why the English language has survived so long and pervaded so many cultures is that it is 50 per cent redundant—even if half the message is lost, the message can probably be figured out if it is long enough.

To prove this point in the technical language of information theory, the amount of information in a sequence of *n* symbols, according to the Wiener-Shannon formula, would be:

$$H_n = - \Sigma \, p_1 \log p_1$$

when p_1 is the probability of each symbol in a set of symbols. The message contained in this formula is that the least probable, least expected message contains the most information to the recipient. Thus, information may be measured by the degree of surprise which it induces.

Nature has designed man so that when he is functioning properly he gets an optimal amount of surprise. This is achieved by designing into man a limited span of attention (or, as it was called in the 19th century, span of apprehension). This constraint on perception makes man a serial processor of information. He is always in an environment where he has more information than he can respond to.

MAN AS A PROCESSOR OF INFORMATION

If a man is over- or understimulated in terms of sensory data, there is an increase of the distortion with which he perceives reality. Man requires a ceaseless flow of sensory data about his environment, both external and internal, to function properly. When he is subject to an information overload, he behaves in odd ways rather similar to the behaviour of schizophrenics. It is a well-known fact that in some forms of schizophrenia

—which is generally characterized by withdrawal symptoms, i.e., cutting off large sources of sensory data—the patient prefers to operate in a relatively sensory-deprived environment. For example, some schizophrenics are quite happy to watch TV with the sound switched off. Basically, the normal environment presents the schizophrenic with an information overload.

The question then suggests itself: Is it possible that normal subjects working under forced-pace, high-information inputs would exhibit the same pattern of errors that characterizes schizophrenics? There is, in fact, experimental evidence to support this conclusion. James G. Millar, director of the Mental Health Research Institute of the University of Michigan, has concluded that hitting a person with more information than he can handle may be related to various forms of mental disease. Millar has speculated that schizophrenics may have some metabolic fault which increases the amount of neural noise in their systems.

Therefore the first and most important point to note about man as an information processor is that he selectively organizes his perceptions and thus the information on which he works. This organization of perception is based on his values, attitudes, needs, and expectations. Since his expectations are formed to a large extent by other people's expectations, he may lose sight of his own wants; this is precisely what sensitivity training tries to help him to rediscover, by putting him in touch with himself.

In order to function effectively, both man and the organizations he forms must set up critical decision rules to help him decide what he should pay attention to. In an organizational context, this is what a management information system sets out to do. Thus information is the raw material of the processes of planning, organizing, and controlling.

THE INFORMATION PROCESS

Organizations function by collecting information, processing it, storing some of it, and taking action and formulating plans based on it so that they can start the cycle again. Looking at organizations in this model selectively organizes one's perceptions in a particular way. A beautiful illustration of the virtues of this line of approach is provided by the analysis of how a short-order restaurant might deal with an information overload. [See Box 4.2.]

The management information system

What the parable of the spindle illustrates is that the texture of managerial life is information. Management is preoccupied with the problems of bringing its environment, which essentially consists of a flow of information, under some measure of control. Fortunately, this kind of intelligence exercise, under the code name computerized management information system (MIS), is attracting some of the best brains in both business and academia. Yet, in fact, few computerized MIS's have been put into operation; and of those that have been, few have lived up to expectations.

Five common and erroneous assumptions built into the design of most MIS's have been identified by Russell L. Ackoff in a brilliant short article entitled "Management Misinformation Systems." It should be compulsory reading for top management considering or reviewing installation of an MIS. Ackoff, who is in the corner of the hard-pressed user-manager, begins his attack on the theme that most managers suffer from an over-abundance of irrelevant information. He illustrates from his own experience, pointing out that in an average week he receives 43 hours' worth of unsolicited reading material and about half as much solicited material. Many managers are inundated with status reports of inventories, budgets, and production performance in the form of computer print-outs. Condensation and filtration of this data should be a first concern of any effective MIS. Ackoff gives a penetrating example of how this overload of irrelevant information can be controlled (see Box 4.3).

From both Ackoff's observations and our own, it is clear that a basic need is for the MIS designer and the manager who will use it to co-operate and pool their talents in the interest of producing the best possible system. Unfortunately, too often the actuality has been more like Figure 4–9, with designer and user squaring off in exploitative and defensive roles. Ackoff's article details some ideas on co-ordination:

> For example, market researchers in a major oil company once asked their marketing managers what variables they thought were relevant in estimating the sales volume of future service stations. Almost seventy variables were identified. The market researchers then added about half again this many variables and performed a large multiple linear regression analysis of sales of existing stations against these variables and found about thirty-five to be statistically significant. A forecasting equation was based on this analysis. An OR [operations research] team subse-

FIGURE 4–9
How to produce "management misinformation systems"

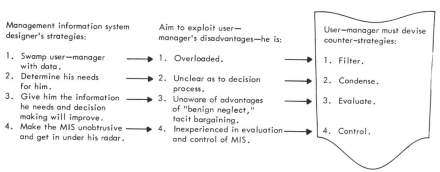

Management information system designer's strategies:	Aim to exploit user—manager's disadvantages—he is:	User—manager must devise counter-strategies:
1. Swamp user—manager with data.	1. Overloaded.	1. Filter.
2. Determine his needs for him.	2. Unclear as to decision process.	2. Condense.
3. Give him the information he needs and decision making will improve.	3. Unaware of advantages of "benign neglect," tacit bargaining.	3. Evaluate.
4. Make the MIS unobtrusive and get in under his radar.	4. Inexperienced in evaluation and control of MIS.	4. Control.

Box 4.2: The parable of the spindle

More and more we hear the word systems used in discussions of business problems. Just what is a system in the business sense? Elias Porter has provided a parable from the restaurant industry, and the implications of the parable will be discussed to answer the question.

Once upon a time the president of a large chain of short-order restaurants invited a team of consultants, namely a sociologist, a psychologist, and an anthropologist to contribute to the solution of the human relations problems in his restaurants.

The first to report was the sociologist. In his report he said:

It is during the rush hours that your human relations problems arise. We can see one thing which, sociologically speaking, doesn't seem right. The manager has the highest status in the restaurant. The cook has the next highest status. The waitresses . . . have the lowest status and yet they give orders to the cook.

It doesn't seem right for a lower status person to give orders to a higher status person. We've got to find a way to break up the face-to-face relationship between the waitresses and the cook. Now my idea is to put a spindle on the order counter. The wheel on the spindle has clips on it so the girls can simply put their orders on the wheel rather than calling out orders to the cook.

The psychologist was next to return and in his report he said:

It is during the rush hours that your human relations problems arise.

Psychologically speaking, we can see that the manager is the father figure, the cook is the son, and the waitress is the daughter. Now we know that in our culture you can't have daughters giving orders to the sons. It louses up their ego structure.

The psychologist then offered the same solution of the spindle wheel.

In the anthropologist's diagnosis of the situation he reported that:

It is during the rush hours that your human relations problems arise.

Man behaves according to his value system. Now, the manager holds as a central value the continued growth and development of the restaurant organization. The cooks tend to share this central value system, for as the organization prospers, so do they. But the waitresses, they couldn't care less whether the organization thrives or not as long as it's a decent place to work. Now, you can't have a non-central value system giving orders to a central value system.

The anthropologist then offered the same spindle wheel solution as the other two scientists.

Let us now observe the functions which the spindle fulfills.

First of all, the spindle acts as a memory device as well as a buffering device for

Elias H. Porter, "The Parable of the Spindle," *Harvard Business Review*, Vol. 40 (1962), pp. 58–

quently constructed a model based on only one of these variables, traffic flow, which predicted sales better than the thirty-five variable regression equation. The team went on to *explain* sales at service stations in terms of the customers' perception of the amount of time lost by stopping for service. The relevance of all but a few of the variables used by the market researchers could be explained by their effect on such perception.

The moral is simple: one cannot specify what information is required for decision making until an explanatory model of the decision process and the system involved has been constructed and tested. Information

the cook. Secondly it acts as a queuing device, as it provides proper waiting time and does all the standing in line for the waitresses. Thirdly, the spindle permits a visual display of all the orders waiting to be filled. By reason of having random access to all orders, the cook is able to organize his work around several orders simultaneously. The last function of the spindle is to provide feedback to both waitresses and cook regarding errors. The spindle markedly alters the emotional relationship and redirects the learning process.

It is significant that in our parable the three scientists each discovered that human relations problems arose mostly during the rush hours, in the period of "information overload." How a system responds to conditions of overload depends on how the system is designed.

One of the most common adjustments that a system makes to an excess input load is to increase the number of channels for handling the information. Restaurants put more waitresses and cooks on the job to handle rush-hour loads. But there comes a time when just increasing the number of channels is not enough. Then we see another common adjustment process, that of queuing or forming a waiting line. We have already seen that the spindle makes it unnecessary for the waitresses to queue to give orders.

The hostess can make another adjustment by keeping a list of waiting customers; by jotting down the size of the group, she can selectively pull groups out of the queue according to the size of the table last vacated.

A system can be so designed as to permit omissions, a simple rejection or non-acceptance of an input. In restaurants, when waiting lines get too long, customers will turn away. Also when people are in the queue, they are not spending money. One solution is to install a bar. This permits the customers to spend while waiting.

Another big time-saver in the restaurant system is the use of the "chunking" adjustment process. Big chunks of information can be predetermined by special arrangements. You may find a menu so printed that it asks you to order by number.

A rather unusual adjustment process that a system can adopt to cope with overload is to accept an increase in the number of errors made. It's better to make mistakes then not to deal with the input.

This article looks at organizations as systems which (1) process information—transform the information from one form into another, and (2) are or are not designed to cope with the conditions of overload that may be imposed on them. This new frame of reference is expressed as an interest in how the structure or design of an organization dynamically influences the operating characteristics and the capacities of the system to handle various conditions of information overload.

systems are subsystems of control systems. They cannot be designed adequately without taking control in account. Furthermore, whatever else regression analyses can yield, they cannot yield understanding and explanation of phenomena. They describe and, at best, predict.

In sum, Ackoff is arguing for a better understanding of how the system, particularly the decision-making subsystem, operates. This can only be achieved with a proper model of the organization as an information-processing system, spelling out the critical dimensions and their interaction with the end products of the system.

Box 4.3: A case of misinformation

A Chairman of a Board of a medium-size company asked for help on the following problem. One of his larger (decentralized) divisions had installed a computerized production-inventory control and manufacturing-manager information system about a year earlier. It had acquired about $2,000,000 worth of equipment to do so. The Board Chairman had just received a request from the Division for permission to replace the original equipment with newly announced equipment which would cost several times the original amount. An extensive "justification" for so doing was provided with the request. The Chairman wanted to know whether the request was really justified. He admitted to complete incompetence in this connection.

A meeting was arranged at the Division at which I was subjected to an extended and detailed briefing. The system was large but relatively simple. At the heart of it was a reorder point for each item and a maximum allowable stock level. Reorder quantities took lead-time as well as the allowable maximum into account. The computer kept track of stock, ordered items when required, and generated numerous reports on both the state of the system it controlled and its own "actions."

When the briefing was over I was asked if I had any questions. I did. First I asked if when the system had been installed, there had been many parts whose stock level exceeded the maximum amount possible under the new system. I was told there were many. I asked for a list of about thirty and for some graph paper. Both were provided. With the help of the system designer and volumes of old daily reports I began to plot the stock level of the first listed item over time. When this item reached the maximum "allowable" stock level it had been reordered. The system designer was surprised and said that by sheer "luck" I had found one of the few errors made by the system. Continued plotting showed that because of repeated premature reordering the item had never gone much below the maximum stock level. Clearly the program was confusing the maximum allowable stock level and the reorder point. This turned out to be the case in more than half of the items on the list.

Before the day was out it was possible to show by some quick and dirty calculations that the new computerized system was costing the company almost $150,000 per month more than the hand system which it had replaced, most of this in excess inventories.

The recommendation was that the system be redesigned as quickly as possible and that the new equipment not be authorized for the time being.

The questions asked of the system had been obvious and simple ones. Managers should have been able to ask them but—and this is the point—they felt themselves incompetent to do so. They would not have allowed a handoperated system to get so far out of their control.

No MIS should ever be installed unless the managers for whom it is intended are trained to evaluate and hence control it rather than be controlled by it.

The erroneous assumptions I have tried to reveal in the preceding discussion can, I believe, be avoided by an appropriate design procedure.

Russell Ackoff, "Management Misinformation Systems," *Management Science,* Vol. 14 (December 1967).

Conclusion

What has this brief review of information theory to tell us that is relevant to the study of organizational behaviour? First, that information, which is becoming the critical input in industry and pushing capital into second place as a factor of production, is something which can be mea-

FIGURE 4–10
SYSTEMS APPROACH TO INFORMATION

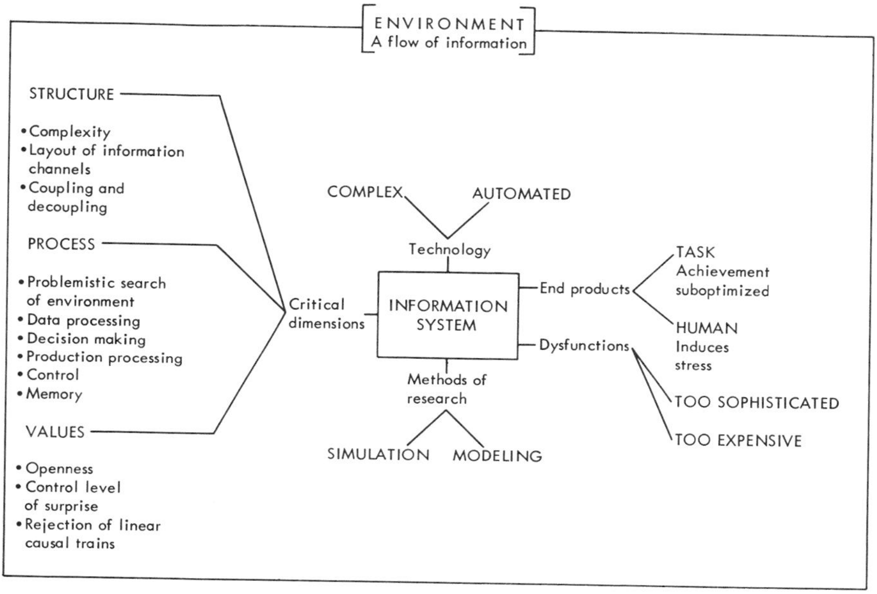

sured. And information is measured by the amount of surprise that it elicits. When information is received, uncertainty is reduced.

Management, because it has a critical interest in controlling its level of uncertainty, has a sustained and growing interest in managing information systems. This is precisely what the computer analogy is all about: living systems can also be thought of as information-processing systems. If you understand how any information-processing system operates and works, it will provide a good guide for the study of the individual, the group, and the organization as information processors. In this study, it will be useful to chart an information system according to the systems model developed in Chapter 1, as we have done in Figure 4–10.

TOPIC 3
Evaluation of all three theories

THE CLASSICAL THEORY

A useful tactic for reviewing organization theories is to compare how the different theories handle the basic issues of differentiation (how jobs are broken down) and integration (how jobs are held together or co-ordinated). The classical theory, the earliest and the longest lasting approach to the study of formal organizations, gives central importance to the paradigm of rationality in an attempt to find principles which contribute to the effectiveness and efficiency of organizations. Bureaucracy, the macro version of classical theory, represents the first systematic attempt to determine the structure of the ideal organization by discussing such matters as the ideal "height" of the hierarchy, the "width" of the span of control, and the need for unity of command. The machine theory, which is ultimately based on accounting and industrial engineering model, reinforces the idea of maximum task analysis. There are, of course, tremendous advantages in the machine approach. For a start, it focuses attention on the scientific measurement of productivity, which in turn suggests such techniques as production planning and control, work study (including method study and time study), quality control, rate fixing, and piece work.

Given these pillars of organization theory, how does the chief architect resolve the dilemma of integration versus differentiation? The answer in classical theory is to input more mechanisms of control via more detailed role specifications, more complicated organization charts, and more manuals to define such matters as delegation, the relation between line and staff, and how accountability should be measured.

Taylor, the principal proponent of the machine theory, introduced the principle of functional management. In general, it represents an attempt to break the total job down in a rational manner and introduces a balanced system of authority and responsibility. Mason Haire comments in "The Concept of Power and the Concept of Man":

> In principle, a certain amount of authority is pumped into each one of the boxes [in the organization chart] and along with this goes a responsibility to beam out a certain amount of productivity. This kind of double-entry system of input and output seems to be one of the first essentials.

EVALUATION

The main criticism of the classical theory is that it overcentralizes authority, maximizes neatness and control, and assumes men to be relatively homogeneous and relatively unmodifiable.

"Boxitis" is the term used to describe the system of management that assumes that when an organization chart has been constructed, a simple picture of authority and responsibility has been created. In other words, the system fails to recognize the problems that arise at the boundary between one command area and another, the consequences of the development of the informal organization. Basically, this first theory underestimates the difficulties of balancing authority and responsibility.

The division between line and function management can become too rigid. There is a tendency to think that line has the exclusive responsibility for producing the product and that staff is there to advise and provide expert assistance to line. Therefore the staff has no authority except within the staff group. It would seem if we accept the argument that authority and responsibility are balanced then the staff, because they are lacking in authority, have no responsibility. This picture is obviously unrealistic.

This early approach, which puts special emphasis on the avoidance of error rather than on the necessary acceptance of calculated risks, encourages a negative attitude and does not necessarily maximize efficiency. In general this organization theory is based on the belief that there are people (but not oneself) who are unfortunately lazy, and consequently will not do anything unless they are forced to do so.

Some unsolved problems of the classical theory revolve around the following questions. How much specialization should be developed? How can you achieve unity of command when a subordinate receives two orders from different superiors which are at variance with one another? How do you determine the optimum span of control?

In spite of these criticisms, many organizations are still based on these principles, and most organizations still try to assimilate the "new principles of management" within a classical frame.

HUMAN RELATIONS

The human relations school brought to the study of organizations a quite different orientation which presumed that economic incentives were relatively unimportant and that while the employee wants a minimum to provide a basic security for himself and his family, his central needs are for group membership, participation, and self-actualization. The human relations approach rejects the organization model built on the accounting and the industrial engineering analogy and gives central place to the individual and the primary working group.

Its advantages include the fact that this approach emphasizes initiative and innovation. Particular emphasis is placed on the need to facilitate self-actualization. Definitions of rules, roles, and relations of the informal group are held to be vital in management research. It seeks to maximize individual participation by encouraging consultation.

In order not to stifle initiative, it assumes that individuals will make mistakes but does not assume that this will necessarily maximize error. Inherent in the human relations approach is the proposition that man is modifiable, and the theory seeks to provide a climate within which the worker may meet his social needs—particularly the need to belong, to win approval, and to feel secure. The ideal type of organization is decentralized.

EVALUATION

The arguments against human relations as a management philosophy include: because it lays such great emphasis on getting the worker involved, it may lead to pseudoparticipation; i.e., participation which looks like, but is not, real participation. True participation means in fact that subordinates can observe the rules and yet feel free to make appropriate contributions.

Many human relations–oriented managers fail to realize that shop floor workers may prefer "adaptive segregation" to overinvolvement in organizational matters. Perhaps more important is the objection that this philosophy can encourage the wrong type of executive, one who thinks his responsibility is to keep everybody happy instead of getting his work done. And it may well breed patronizing attitudes towards subordinates because of a faulty understanding of what kind of relationships people expect. It tends to be unrealistic assuming that organizations can prosper without proper role definitions; for without these accurate and comprehensive job descriptions, it is impossible to anticipate and minimize the conflicts that arise at the boundary between the functions of one role and another.

The human relations school has also been criticized for contributing to the manipulation of employees through the use of Dale Carnegie techniques in personal relations, "music while you work" programmes to speed up productivity, and myths such as "we are just one big happy family here."

It must be stressed that although human relations has been discredited by many academics as an organization philosophy, people still need to be treated as human beings. Presumably this is the explanation for the human potential movement and many similar activities. If people can't have human relations at work, they are going to have them after work in the form of religion, recreation, cults, or whatever "latest thing" is presented. In fact, they should have them at work too, within an appropriate framework.

THE SYSTEMS APPROACH

The systems approach, which could not have emerged as an acceptable theory of organization without the two previous systems having run their historical course, represents a fusion of the best features of both its predecessors.

The systems theorists felt that both earlier approaches were incomplete and that a more fruitful point of departure was the idea that an organization could be treated as an open system which traded with its environment: importing inputs in the form of energy, material, information, and people; transforming them; and exporting to the environment a product with value added. Information and its detection, selection, structuring, processing, and transmission become the critical factors. Organizations are viewed as systems of black boxes in dark regions which are not completely knowable, but which work according to a particular logic that has more to do with biology than physics.

SOME CHARACTERISTICS OF THE SYSTEMS APPROACH

The title "task approach" gained currency in World War II, where special formations which cut across traditional organizational lines were called task forces; they were designed to achieve a particular task or mission. The advantages of the task, or systems, approach can be summarized under the following headings.

Optimum organization. The systems approach focuses attention on developing an optimum organization by considering both the task to be done and the resources available. The resources available can be divided into three categories: personnel, technical, and economic. Great care and effort are expended to ensure that specialists are properly used. The basic misuse of functional specialists that arises in the classical theory is avoided. The traditional division of line and staff is treated as irrelevant. Systems theory formalizes consultative procedures at every level through staff consultation and (where appropriate) work councils. This theory minimizes the importance of personality and assumes that roles can be objectified; thus efficiency is maximized and conflict minimized.

Sociotechnical systems. The systems approach assimilates the advantages of both the classical approach and the human relations school. Human relations is reserved for shop floor operatives; good human resources planning for middle management; and optimal organization for top management. The concept of sociotechnical systems, borrowed from Tavistock, is used to describe and predict organizational behaviour. Organizations are seen as giant molecules with roles for atoms.

Effectiveness and efficiency. Effectiveness and efficiency are seen as measures of the choice of goals and the ability to exploit the means to achieve these goals, respectively. The relation between effectiveness and efficiency is seen as both complex and complicated. Extensive use is made of models which simulate the business environment, quantify the factors structuring outcomes, frequently involve the use of computers, and enable executives to operate in a meaningful way on their environment. Technology is seen as a major determinant of organizational behaviour.

C.F.–C.D.: Concept formulation–contract definition. A fruitful marriage appears to have taken place in the United States between the sociotechnical system concept and the total marketing concept. A new approach to management has been developed by U.S. aerospace companies, who have to decide which business they are in and think the problem through. This has led to the development of C.F.–C.D., concept formulation–contract definition. This very successful frame of analysis has led to the development of the gourmet organization, which specializes in finding "interesting problems" and then solving them.

The objective: A set of inconsistent goals. In the task-oriented organization, there are the presumptions (1) of bounded rationality, (2) that information is expensive, and (3) that organizations work by programmed decisions. The technostructure is in command and the objective—to satisfy a number of variables rather than maximize profit—is achieved by the formation of coalitions which, overlapping one another, achieve a number of inconsistent goals.

An organic model. These new organizations will approximate the organic model of Burns and Stalker in *The Management of Innovation,* where the emphasis will be on:

> (*i*) A lateral rather than a vertical direction of communication through the organization; also, communication between people of different rank, resembling consultation rather than command; (*ii*) a content of communication which consists of information and advice rather than instructions and decisions; (*iii*) a commitment to the concern's tasks and to the "technological ethos" of material progress and expansion, which is more highly valued than loyalty and obedience; and (*iv*) an importance and a prestige which attach to affiliations, and an expertise valid in the industrial, technical, and commercial milieux external to the firm.

Research and development. In the task-oriented organization, R. & D. can be exactly defined and therefore managed; objectives are specified; programmes produced and policed. Research standards are of necessity less detailed, but both modern organizational investigation and experience confirm that scientists and technologists are able and willing to work within such a discipline. Integral to this approach are the notions that research can be evaluated on a cost-benefit-analysis basis and that technological pioneering does not create automatic commercial supremacy. Efficient production techniques coupled with aggressive marketing may make being second in the field a distinct advantage. In the systems approach, scientists are taken out of back rooms and ivory towers and treated, not as prima donnas (good old paternalistic days) but as technocrats who manage innovative information used to achieve the organization's objectives.

EVALUATION

Systems theory, then, has many advantages. In addition to those listed here, we can recall from Chapter 1 the wide-ranging interest the systems man takes in any academic disciplines which offer clues to organizational behaviour—anthropology, psychology, and so on. He is interested in the topic of socialization—the actual process of getting people into organizations, into roles, into the web of expectations that constitutes the actual nature of institutionalization. All of these, and the systems model we have been working with, tell us that this approach looks at organizations in a complex and many-faceted way that comes much closer than the older theories to the reality of diverse, interrelated, interacting factors.

A disadvantage of the systems approach is that the system may become too efficient in the short run by being too tough. It will encourage resistance among both workers and managers, and at the individual and the group level, if this is so. If the task is too great for the human resources available, it may foster the development of informal organizations which are directed against the best interests of the firm. At the individual level, tasks pitched too high may result in increased labour turnover or psychosomatic disorders.

But there is a further disadvantage of systems theory; and since it applies to all theories (and elements of all theories are present in most organizations), we need to take it up as a final evaluation of organization theory in general. It is, indeed, the conflict between theories about organizations on the one hand and existential man on the other.

ORGANIZATIONS AND EXISTENTIAL MAN

Organizations are, to a large extent, the environment of man, and certainly almost the exclusive environment of working man. The organization, with its giant radars of behavioural science, its computers to monitor performance and progress, and its corporate oligarchs to pick up what the machines miss, has locked on man as its target. This "locked-onto target" feeling is the prevailing experience of working in and for organizations.

Systems theory in fact represents an advance over older theories; but it too presents man with deep conflicts. It seeks to treat the largest autonomous unit it can cope with. It works best with larger and larger Gestalts, not all elements of which are knowable (nor need to be known). The system moves, prodded by a turbulent environment; man, caught up in its processes, asks, What is it doing? Can it be controlled?

But one element of the organizational Gestalt is existential man—man asserting his basic inalienable rights, fighting to be free, striving to give meaning to his life in the face of the absurdities of competitive power relations, trying to become whatever destiny has in mind for him. Like the man condemned to the gallows who studies his predecessors, hoping to beat "the big drop," existential man studies the history which has brought him to the actuality of future shock. Technology has served up his conflicts and his locked-onto feelings; can it also offer him new organizational behaviour structures and processes that will free up his values? That will let him control, rather than be controlled?

If we are to build on the basis of systems theory (keeping within it the best elements of the older theories), it must be in the direction of dealing with the questions of existential man and his value systems—taking them into account in the way organizations are structured, and hoping for the widest possible overlap between the value systems of organizations and the people who make them and work within them.

REVIEW AND RESEARCH

1. Describe the main subsystems of any system. Consider the organization of a hospital or a police force and identify the organizational elements that correspond to each of these subsystems. How is performance monitored?
2. Define a system. Compare and contrast open and closed systems. Give examples of systems that fit each level of Boulding's hierarchy of systems.
3. What is the computer analogy? Compare and contrast the organization, the group, and the individual as information-processing systems.
4. Using the systems model, describe the structure, process, and values of any organization that you are familiar with. How are end products measured? What dysfunctions are generated?
5. How are the traditional concepts of management related to the systems concept?
6. The Planning, Programming, Budgeting Systems (PPBS) has been widely used in government. Does PPBS have equal applicability in business? If not, why not?
7. How would you use the systems approach to describe these types of organizations? Use a process flow chart to identify the critical choices and decision variables.
   a. An air defence system (subsystems include: radar, data-plotting room, command group of officers, fighter aircraft and missiles, ground control of aircraft, statistical evaluations group).
   b. A manufacturing company (subsystems include: market research, R.&D., production planning and control, management decision groups, production shops, quality control and inspection, and accounting).
8. The problem is to relate planning to systems analysis. Select an organization with which you are familiar. List the different kinds of plans that are developed according to level (company, plant, department, section, squad, individual) and function (production, technical, and personnel). Use the systems approach to draw a diagram to integrate the plans. Can they be integrated? How much integration is needed? How should it be achieved?
9. What is the purpose of a management information system? Why is such a system so important? How would you design a MIS? Why did accountants *not* invent the idea of the MIS?
10. Compare the three theories of organization under the following headings: structure, process, values, level of analysis, measurement of end products, impact of the environment, and dysfunctions.

GLOSSARY OF TERMS

Communication. In a broad sense, all of the procedures by which one mind may affect another. The three levels of communication are the technical, the semantic, and the effectiveness levels. All organizations are communication systems.

Computer analogy. The concept that man and the computer are two species of a more abstract genus called the information-processing system.

Control. The methods used by an organization to police performance and monitor the behaviours and attitudes of its members; the feedback subsystem.

Information process. The process by which a system collects information, processes it, stores it, and takes action and formulates plans based on it. All systems may be thought of as information processors; for all, information is the key input and its management a critical process.

Open system. A system which trades with its environment and has the following main characteristics: (1) interrelation among component objects, attributes, and events; (2) holism; (3) goal seeking; (4) input, transformation, and output; (5) negative entropy; (6) information processing; (7) regulation; (8) differentiation; and (9) equifinality.

Organizational effectiveness. The achievement of goals, measured against the following criteria: (1) organizational productivity, (2) the ability of the organization to innovate, and (3) the control of inter- and intraorganizational stress.

Organizational objectives. The multiple set of hierarchical goals or ends which the organization tries to achieve, recognizing that the ascription of a single simple objective to an enterprise is no longer appropriate.

System. Any entity which consists of interdependent parts, qualified as to whether it is an open or closed system and is organic, mechanistic, human, etc.

System subsystems. Systems have the following subsystems: (1) sensor, (2) data processing, (3) decision, (4) processing, (5) control, and (6) memory.

5

Behavioural
science

The supreme beauty of behavioural science is that it focuses primarily on behaviour and only secondarily, if at all, on what is going on inside a person's head. Thus at one stroke it concerns itself with what can be observed (rather than inferred) and what is (rather than what ought to be). The presumption is that behaviour is caused, motivated, and goal-directed and is thus subject to rules which can be determined by observation followed by cogitation.

But why use the term behavioural science? Isn't behavioural science the same as psychology? The answer is that behavioural science incorporates those parts of psychology that deal with human behaviour—such as the study of personality and groups (but excluding, for example, physiological psychology)—as well as relevant elements of anthropology and sociology. But behavioural science is not primarily concerned with academic pedigree, and it borrows concepts and research findings from all sorts of sources, including social psychiatry and computer technology. Behavioural science is a walking demarcation dispute which adopts an interdisciplinary approach to the study, resolution, and implementation of problem-solving processes about human behaviour.

So behavioural science is the study of actual human behaviour, by observation, using an interdisciplinary approach where the focus—behaviour—is the key variable, not the academic specialty of the investigator. But it is research for a purpose, to solve some problem. Since behavioural science is problem-oriented, practical, and pragmatic, it has had the most rapid growth in the new business schools, which are now making significant contributions to the literature of a wide variety of academic disciplines.

Since behavioural science has an applied side concerned with problem solving, it may come as no surprise to learn that many of the most significant contributions in this field have come from nonacademic people as well as academics in diverse fields. This is true of many disciplines; the list of medical advances made by persons outside (and often scorned by) the medical profession is startling. But especially in fields relating to behaviour, people who have neither time nor a taste for erudite, "ivory tower" research will turn eagerly to writers with a gift for popularizing (witness an earlier generation's interest in Dale Carnegie's *How to Win Friends and Influence People*) or the ability to express, say, a psychoanalytic theory in clear and interesting ways (witness Eric Berne's *Games People Play* and Thomas Harris's *I'm OK—you're OK* in recent years). The serious student and the layman will often be found side by side in the paperback bookstore picking up R. D. Laing for an explanation of the double bind, Carl Rogers on handling human encounters, Alex Comfort for sexual guidance, or any number of "how-to" books (ranging from the excellent to the trivial).

The essence of the matter is that people tend to be interested in the technology, rather than the science, of behaviour. The technology of behaviour is preeminently concerned with control and prediction and only secondarily with understanding. Engineering consent and making things happen your way is more immediately relevant to individual needs than complex, pseudomathematical psychological theories which have been "proved" with rats.

Both behavioural science and technology, under the alias of action research in organizations, have been ploughing ahead since the 1940s. Action research (a paradoxical term) began during World War II as a field of enquiry and change concerned with developing new selection and training strategies for officers and saboteurs, monitoring and changing attitudes (propaganda), psychological warfare, and myriad other military matters. After the war came T groups, group dynamics, organizational development, confrontation and intervention techniques, and process consultancy. But there can be no technology (or applied science) without a science, and thus there is a complex set of connective and supportive relationship between behavioural technology and science, as shown in Figure 5–1. In this chapter, we focus on the "research" (science); in Chapter 6 we will focus on the "action" (technology).

STRUCTURE OF CHAPTER 5

Topic I deals with the behavioural sciences, setting out their scope, direction, thrust, and methods. Particular attention is paid to three basic methods of research: observation, interviewing, and examination of docu-

FIGURE 5–1

	Behavioural science	Behavioural technology
OBJECTIVES:	Understanding Explanation Prediction	Controlling Monitoring Manipulation
FOCUS:	Theories, concepts— consider small problem in depth	Problem solving— consider large problems·shallowly
PRACTITIONER:	Researcher	Consultant
APPROACH:	Analysis	Synthesis
EXAMPLES:	Psychology Psychotherapy Research	Transactional analysis T groups Synectics

ments. This brief review of behavioural methods is intended to help the student to recognize the restrictions that data collecting procedures impose on the findings that emerge from research studies.

Our second topic deals with action research in organizations, with particular emphasis on two major organizational studies, the Glacier and Harwood studies. The role of the client as philosopher-king is explored with a view to clarifying the complex, convoluted, and difficult relation that exists between consultant and client. This discussion concludes by exploring the puzzle of participative management, which apparently works in a nonsimple way whose nature is still a subject of guess-work rather than scientific fact.

Topic 3 closes the chapter by returning to the integration of behavioural science and technology (see Figure 5–1 and the discussion above). Behavioural science is modeled as a system, as a review of Chapter 5 and preparation for Chapter 6.

TOPIC 1
The behavioural sciences

Before discussing what the behavioural scientists have to say about behaviour perhaps it would be as well to say a word about the field itself— its scope, history, and present state. As the term is used here, behavioural sciences should not be equated with social sciences. The social sciences include the disciplines of anthropology, economics, history, political science, psychology, and sociology; the behavioural sciences are mainly concerned with the disciplines of anthropology, psychology, and sociology. In short, our subject is concerned with scientific research that deals directly with human behaviour, but in a dispassionate, systematic, and painstaking way.

Behavioural science is a booming subject which is becoming increasingly empirical and increasingly relevant for students of organizational life. In Europe, it is being taught in the new business schools to a new generation of executives who, it is hoped, will do for the European economy what their Harvard counterparts have done for the American.

What methods of inquiry do behavioural scientists use? Some readers may wonder why is it necessary to ask this question. Some cynics, critical of the behavioural sciences, complain that no other science has so many methods and so few hard findings. But it is just as well to remember that only by asking questions relating to methodology is it possible to maintain a proper balance between empiricism and theoretical development. In this context, certain questions automatically suggest themselves. For example, is it possible to make observations about behaviour without changing the very actions which the observations are supposed to define? Is man capable of being objective about his own behaviour? For that matter, is a science of human behaviour possible at all?

Why do methodological questions loom so large in behavioural science? There are two reasons. The first is that the methods which the behavioural scientist uses help to define the nature of the field itself. The second is that an intelligent and critical evaluation of research findings requires some knowledge of the assumptions and evidence on which they are based. If behavioural science is to establish itself as a source of hard knowledge about human behaviour, it must (as far as possible) satisfy the criteria that other sciences are required to meet. First, the procedures must be available for publication; not only the results but the methods must be both communicable and communicated. Behavioural science reports must contain a full and detailed description of just what was done and how. To achieve this first objective, a uniform and definitive language is required which is both terse and unambiguous. Further, the research methods must be objective and reliable, i.e., they must be checked for internal consistency.

Where possible, it is most beneficial if research findings of fact are capable of replication by other behavioural scientists. But science is not merely the collecting and enumeration of facts, no matter how accurate this process may be; theory is also needed and there must be a proper balance between theoretical development and empirical observation. It must be recognized that the mere collection of empirical data is not necessarily the most efficient way to proceed. There is the necessity to create a theoretical structure which employs central concepts and produces an organized system of verified and coherent propositions. A good theory, to have any relevance and utility, must have some power of prediction.

Even a casual review of the literature of behavioural science cannot but impress the reader with the great ingenuity that has been employed in designing research methods. The phenomena of organizational life have been subject to study by means of many different techniques, and each new publication brings reports of some new method. Three basic designs have been extensively used—the experiment, the sample survey, and the case study. The experiment has a central place in the history of science. Of particular interest to the behavioural scientist are experiments carried out with artificial groups in the laboratory. This type of research method enables the behavioural scientist to isolate variables and manipulate them under controlled conditions.

Yet, as we will see, the laboratory study and other "scientific" methods contain insidious traps for any researcher who gets so carried away with empiricism and objectivity that he forgets the nature of his raw material. Human beings are neither rats nor molecules. "The proper study of mankind" presents riddles, upsets, and unanswerable conundrums at every turn. If this is frustrating, it also has the virtue of seldom being dull.

METHODS OF RESEARCH

Perhaps it is just as well to remember that behavioural science is only now progressing beyond the stage of armchair theorizing and casual empiricism. Since the turn of the century, research techniques have developed to such a point that there has been a distinct change in the tone of behavioural sciences. For that matter this improvement in the methodological rigour can be used as a definition for this field of inquiry. Many executives, impressed by the successes of the physical and biological sciences, have turned their hopes and aspirations to behavioural science in expectation that the development of more rigorous and refined techniques will make it possible to inject a degree of professional probity into the "management sciences." Most executives readily accept the notion that probity is measured ultimately by the degree of penetration of science into the activity. In terms of methodological probity, individual psychology comes at the top of the league, especially the fields of psychophysical measurements, intelligence measurement, and learning. Other branches of behavioural science, such as social psychology and industrial psychology, have sought to take over and apply the well-established and well-tried methods of individual psychology to the group and the organization. For example, in social psychology, considerable success has been achieved with both sociometry and attitude measurements.

Many executives, taking the opposite point of view, believe that they already know the essential facts and principles of organizational life—facts and principles which they have learned as the result of practical experience in the world of hard knocks. Not unexpectedly, they feel that any theoretical or scientific knowledge about organizational life is redundant. Unquestionably, it must be accepted that experienced and successful executives have accumulated a great deal of practical know-how about how organizations operate and how they can be manipulated, and by any pragmatic test their knowledge of organizational life may be adequate to handle many of the day-to-day problems of business. But many of the most successful and intelligent businessmen are only too acutely aware, to judge from their public pronouncements, that the most significant organizational problems of our time still remain unresolved. For example, we still do not know how to set about the dismantling of the demarcation system that impedes our industry from being really efficient; we do not yet know what is the best way to fuse functional and line management to achieve at once the most effective performance and highest morale for the working group; and, as yet, we are unable to create organizations within which existential man can develop and grow in a natural way while contributing to organizational effectiveness.

THE SCIENTIFIC METHOD

What must be understood is that there is an important difference between practical and scientific knowledge about organizational life. The fundamental aim of science is not primarily to control, but to understand and predict. Many executives, understandably, would be content to settle for the former—some system of control which would enable them to structure the behaviour and attitudes of the work group and predict its behaviour. But the behavioural scientist would argue that effective control is the reward of understanding and that accuracy in prediction can be used as a method of checking on understanding.

The new research techniques are of interest to the executive for two reasons: first, it is impossible to make a proper assessment of the meaning and validity of experimental results unless we have some knowledge of the methods employed to collect the data displayed; and second, knowing that a research technique has been used successfully in one context may lead to its use in an entirely different context.

To understand how the behavioural scientists operate, it is necessary to look at the scientific process in some detail. The scientific process is usually triggered off by some discordance—a sense of maladjustment, a feeling that something does not fit. At this juncture, the experienced researcher is acutely aware that a familiar complex situation has arisen in which one particular fact or theory no longer fits with his knowledge of the extant situation, and a compulsive need is felt to try to explain this discordant fact by creating a new theory or modifying an old one. In Figure 5–2 this is referred to as Theory A. Theory A is the theoretical structure which can connect the unexplained fact with other facts or theories. At this stage of the game, it is important to be clear about the definitions which are being employed, the inherent assumptions, and the actual "laws" implicit in the theoretical system. The next stage typically is concerned with the

FIGURE 5-2
THE SCIENTIFIC METHOD

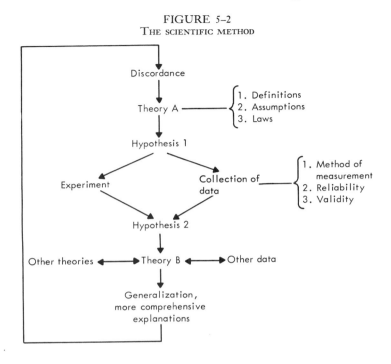

deduction of a hypothesis which can be tested; this usually involves playing around with the theory to ascertain which testable hypotheses are
generated.

Next comes the actual testing of the hypothesis. In the broadest sense,
two routes are available here: the experiment and the collection of data.
An experiment is any investigation that includes two elements, the manipulation or control of one variable by the researcher and the systematic
measurement of and observation of the change in the other. In this context,
when the behavioural scientist refers to measurement, he usually means
something broader than a scale measure such as a temperature reading. The
other route, the collection of data, may be achieved either by interviewing, observation, or by the examination of documents. Here it is most important to specify the method of measurement; for example, to ensure
that controlled observation is used. Likewise, questions of the reliability
and validity of the measure must be considered.

When the process of experimentation or data collection has been gone
through, a hypothesis is either confirmed or denied. It may be possible to
express these conclusions in the form of hypothesis 2. The researcher, at
this point, may engage in some further theorizing and produce Theory B.
Other behavioural scientists, when this work is published, may take
Theory B and relate it to other theoretical work, or to other experimental

data, generalize the results, and produce a more comprehensive theoretical structure.

The object of science is to explain things. But what is a scientific explanation? A behavioural scientist would accept that an observed fact is explained by a theory when it is possible to predict this fact under particular circumstances from the examination of the theory. In science, there are two different kinds of statements: (1) descriptive statements, which record observations or summarize observations; and (2) explanatory statements, which meet a need for intellectual coherence and intelligibility and enable the behavioural scientist to predict behaviour in different circumstances.

THE CASE STUDY

Classifying research studies according to method shows that they can be divided into three types—exploratory, descriptive, and hypothesis-testing. The exploratory study is probably the most appropriate at the beginning of a research project, to enable the researcher to gain some familiarity with the problem and develop some insight into organizational dimensions. Descriptive studies serve to define, in a standard uniform way, the characteristics of the organization, to determine the frequency of their occurrence, and to measure their association with one another. The hypothesis-testing study is more critical and sets out to ascertain whether a particular hypothesis is valid and to define the circumstances of the relation.

One particular example of the descriptive study warrants closer examination. This is the case study. In ideal circumstances, the case study intensively examines many characteristics of one particular organization over a period of time. The aim of the case study is "to learn all about" the particular organization being studied. A case study might be concerned with giving an account of how an organization grew and developed and then became involved, say, in a take-over bid. The major advantage of this method is that it enables the reporter to collect and present detailed information about an organization over a long period of time, and to formulate his ideas in regard to the nature and cause of particular organizational events.

The case study has been most heavily criticized because the results are based on a sample of one, so the degree of generality can never be known. The critical question here is, "Would another company, with the same resources and problems and in the same culture, respond in the same way?" Again the case study has been criticized because it is subject to the *post hoc, ergo propter hoc* fallacy; a control group is not employed nor is the effect of the researcher guarded against. While case studies rarely prove anything, they are frequently rich in clues and perceptive insights about organization life which trigger off useful investigations.

Their supreme value, of course, lies in their use as teaching material; but here their value is founded not in the accuracy or the validity of the material but in the fact that the case study presents an organizational stimulus which triggers off discussion for a group of executives. The credibility of the case study among executives may be gauged from the curious fact that many executives refuse to believe that there is no "staff solution." This widely accepted view of the authenticity of the case study points to the need for executives to be more critical about data collecting procedures. In any case, woe betide the management teacher who expresses a "couldn't care less" attitude as to the correct solution. Unfortunately many executives and even a good number of behavioural scientists still regard the case study as their principal source of information about organizational behaviour. In a curious way behavioural science seems to be recapitulating the early history of psychology, including many of its faults. Organizational psychology has been widely criticized because of the extensive use made of anecdotalism as a method. No conclusions can be drawn from such a method, either because there are no checks on the reliability and validity of the observation or because a large number of observations in a number of firms in different industries would be required before a valid conclusion could be drawn. Most case studies are in fact anecdotes; yet many behavioural scientists and managers continue to use them as foolproof sources of theoretical principles about organizational life.

DATA COLLECTING METHODS

It is also possible to classify research procedures according to the technique employed in the collection of data. Fundamentally the methods of gathering information about people are three: by watching them, by questioning them, and by examining their written records; and the corresponding categories of research in the behavioural sciences are observation, interviewing, and examination of documents. These are the "methods of research" most frequently indicated in the systems model used throughout this text.

Observation

Turning first to the technique of observation, this operation may be structured or unstructured. In unstructured observation, the observer tries to keep as complete a record as possible of all the different behaviours of the members of the group that are being studied. The unstructured technique was utilized in the Hawthorne experiment in the bank wiring room. In general terms, there has been a movement away from unstructured observation, which requires an exhaustive recording of all behaviour, toward the use of structured methods, where particular aspects of behaviour are defined and recorded. Structured observations may be broken down into three types: self-recording, continuous recording, and activity sampling.

In observational studies the key question is, "Who collects what?" In this context "who" may refer to either a member of the organization being studied or an outside observer who has spent enough time within the organization to guarantee his acceptability. "What" refers to the segment of behavioural data but gives no guidance as to the method of collection. This may vary from observations which have been carefully checked for reliability and validity, requiring careful and clear definition of the terms, to the crudest of methods, where the observations are entirely impressionistic and uncontrolled. Summing up, the types of observation are:

1. Structured:
   a. Self-recording.
   b. Continuous recording.
   c. Activity sampling.
2. Unstructured.

Interviewing

Interviewing, too, may be structured or unstructured and may be direct or indirect. For example, the direct unstructured interview is exemplified by the psychoanalytical interview of the motivation researcher talking for the first time to a consumer. This is the technique used by the researcher at the beginning of the research, before the aim has been defined. A great deal of the research carried out at the Glacier Metal Company was carried out by social scientists using this technique. It is sometimes referred to as the process of "working through." It essentially involves the application of psychoanalytical ideas to the methods of social research. In this method the consultant will not enter the organization until he has been invited to do so by the client. Very often the analogy of a sick person calling in his doctor is evoked. This procedure is particularly useful for diagnosing and identifying some of the less obvious factors affecting organizational behaviour. The consultant tries to encourage the members of a work group to accept the responsibility of examining their own behaviour and attitudes, trying to reach some conclusion as to the nature of the forces (external and internal) influencing their behaviour. It is claimed, with some justification, that the groups will thus acquire a better capacity to tolerate the painful process of gaining insight into their own personal dynamics and the dynamics of the work group.

The advantages of this approach include the fact that it emphasizes the importance of negotiating entry into organizations. Secondly, it has considerable diagnostic value, in the sense that it frequently enables the researcher to catalogue in a systematic manner the forces operating at the individual, the group, and the organizational levels. Thirdly, both executives and operators who take part in this procedure frequently report that they find the experience stimulating and refreshing.

Coming now to the disadvantages of "working through," its critics have claimed that "working through" is justified by the aphorism "when all is known, all will be well." This they regard as an overoptimistic oversimplification. Secondly, it is an essentially therapeutic technique, and no real effort is expended in the direction of reliability and validity testing. Another major criticism of this procedure is that it is ascriptive of motive. Through the technique of interpretation it has been argued that the consultant may project his own anxieties and hostilities onto the solution of the problem. It also has been criticized on the grounds that it approximates a psychoanalytical interview. These criticisms relate to the fact that material collected is rarely used for predictive purposes and that relationships between a consultant and a client are confidential and thus cannot be checked. Finally, the material produced by this method is usually presented in the form of a case study. If this is accepted at face value, then all the criticisms appropriate to the case study are appropriate here.

Other forms of interviewing are often used as parts of other techniques and in various kinds of organizational studies. One form of structured interview is the use of questionnaires. In summary form, the types of interviews are:

1. Structured:
    a. Direct.
    b. Indirect.
2. Unstructured:
    a. Direct.
    b. Indirect.

Examination of documents

The simplest technique for getting thoroughly objective data about organizations is to examine the documents relating to that particular organization. The documentary examination may be unstructured, as when the researcher considers organization charts, policy documents, abstracts of accounts, and other documents relating to the company. In this case, the documents are sometimes used in an impressionistic way similar to the methods of the historian, and a picture of the organization may be built up in this manner.

A more structured investigation may be made of company documents by using some technique of content analysis in order to establish the frequency with which given themes occur. Katz and Kahn, for example, were able to use company records as a means for defining which work groups had high productivity records and which had low productivity records. In general terms, insufficient use has been made of documentary evidence in organizational research as a means of furnishing the investigator with precise and definitive information about the organization. This technique can be considered as having two types:

1. Unstructured (impressionistic; e.g., using organization charts, policy statements, annual financial statements).
2. Structured (systematic investigation; e.g., using production and maintenance records, detailed accounting figures, minutes of meetings).

Reliability of data

In describing the above research procedures, it is frequently assumed that reports by observers correspond closely or exactly with the way in which the events described occurred. This may not be the case; there may be a number of uncontrolled and even unacknowledged sources of error. One major source of error is the observer's perceptual slant. This has often been demonstrated in social psychology, particularly in experiments relating to the reliability of testimony. If a self-recording technique is used, it may well be that the executive completes his diary retrospectively and may be unable or unwilling to recall what in fact happened. A considerable degree of elaboration and attenuation may take place in the account that is given of a particular episode. A significant source of error may be the reluctance of the executive to record his true impression of what happened. Many executives consciously or unconsciously distort accounts of events or relationships, in case the information, divulged, leaks back into the organization and may lead to some form of retaliation or disturb the executive's relationships. Again, the executive may be unwilling to verbalize about a particular event because he may find even the process disturbing. Another factor, sometimes known as the Hawthorne effect, is the effect the observer may have on the process which he is supposed to be studying. The same factors may affect interviewing; and even documents may have been distorted when produced at the broad levels of policy, explanation, justification of procedures, and the like.

SIMULATING ORGANIZATIONS

Behavioural scientists have revealed a diabolical genius in designing bizarre experiments. Psychologists and their students have convincingly demonstrated that if a sane person gets himself labelled insane and committed to a mental hospital, it is the label that becomes the reality and determines the treatment. Organizational experiments have been carried out in mental hospitals with staff and patients trading places, and—to demonstrate the power of socialization—the "patients" were soon displaying typical psychopathic symptoms (uncontrollable weeping, incessant pacing, depression, and hostility) and the "staff" started to boss the "patients."

A psychologist at Stanford University, Professor Philip G. Zimbardo, conducted a research project in which a group of male students was split into two sections in a random fashion, with one section playing guards and the other prisoners. Soon the "guards" were bullying and humiliating the "prisoners," who apparently rapidly became cowed and dependent. So effective was the experience that some "prisoners" had to be released after a couple of days; one developed a psychosomatic rash over his entire body. Apparently an autocratic apparatus with all the typical behavioural and role paraphernalia emerged very swiftly and turned the "guards" into thugs who insulted the "prisoners," threatened them, and used night sticks and fire extinguishers to keep them in line. To add horror to horrors, apparently the "prisoners" who could cope best were those who scored highest on a test to measure authoritarianism. The project seemed to result in a gradual Kafkaesque transformation of good into evil, all by the development of a particular organizational arrangement with a completely asymmetrical distribution of power.

The whole matter of simulated organization experiments is a fascinating one; they can produce dramatic practical results. If the obvious dangers can be eliminated or controlled, there would appear to be a strong case for exploiting this kind of research design as a means of exploring the effects of different organization designs.

MODELS AND THEORIES

When behavioural scientists are trying to conceptualize a problem, they frequently make use of a model. Models are simplifying systems which represent a problem in terms of its structure but not its content. The purpose of a model is to show important relationships in such a way that the model builder is encouraged to play around with the variables depicted in the model. More specifically, the aim of a model is to depict how the phenomenon under consideration functions and operates. It provides a structure or set of operating rules for controlling or manipulating the phenomenon.

The main objective of a model is to develop something simpler than the phenomenon being explored so that a model builder can bring order out of chaos. Both researchers and executives like playing with models which provide descriptive, explanatory, and ultimately predictive guidelines for controlling phenomena. There is an interesting relation between a theory and a model. A theory is a respected and respectable, well-established model which has been raised to the peerage after critical examination by the top scholars of that particular discipline, who have carefully examined its empirical foundation; pored over its definitions, hypotheses, and laws; and checked them against other well-established theories. A theory is a model which has been admitted to a respected club of other well-established theories. A model is just a model—a debutante theory which lacks complete empirical reference but has some local value in manipulating a particular phenomenon. A model has limited usefulness in explaining some phenomenon, is easy to understand and make, encourages people to take liberties with it, doesn't expect to live forever, and tries to have a good time by being useful while it is there.

Thus, it is useful to summarize the relation between a theory and a model as the comparison between a well-established, respectable matron who has a gourmet taste for a limited type of facts and a young fly-by-night who has a gourmand taste for any kind of facts. The better class, more useful model which can do lots of interesting things but is careful about its ancestry (in terms of assumptions, data gathering, and relations with established theories) may make it into becoming an established theory.

Putting the distinctions more explicitly, a theory is a set of explanatory or descriptive propositions which other people can understand and which allows us to make predictions about events. Models are simplifying analogies of phenomena which, while having limited empirical reference, encourage people to play with them so that they can develop a better insight into the relations and functions of the problem under review. We can compare the characteristics of the two as follows:

Theories are:	*Models are:*
Explanatory	Simplifying analogies
Codified	Manipulable
Communicable	Not established as valid
Public	Easy to construct
Predictive	Highly subject to
Empirically sound	obsolescence
Fairly long-lived	

In working with models it is important to keep the following in mind:

1. They are abstractions from reality, and reality should be revisited fairly frequently.
2. Their assumptions must always be made explicit.
3. Models ultimately are analogies, and analogies are not expected to be completely accurate.
4. Most models have a short life expectation.

The throwaway model

If in the affluent society you can have disposable diapers, throwaway plates, and dispensable organizations, you can likewise have temporary, easy-to-build theories which you can throw away when you are finished with them. These throwaway theories, models, were invented to make up for the fact there are not enough Einsteins, Webers, Freuds, and Keyneses around to dream up watertight theories which will cover all the exciting explanatory options that keep coming at us. The odd thing about behavioural science is that so much progress has been made since 1920, considering that many of the greats were dead by then or had stopped producing dramatic new theories. Yet more pedestrian, less spectacular minds have made steady advances by inventing models to explain and exploit the concepts of role, group dynamics, change, organization, conflict, and so on.

A recent example is Eric Berne's *Games People Play*, which was built on the model that people have a need for dramatic routines (transactions) which throw others into bad-guy roles and give themselves better ones. For example, in the game of "courtroom," a husband (prosecutor) accuses his wife (defendant) of some outrageous peccadillo in the presence of a guest (judge or jury). The guest is supposed to listen to the evidence calmly, objectively, and above all quietly while the husband and wife hack away at their roles. "Putting him on" or "putting him down"—whatever the game, it involves putting people into roles. In developing transactional analysis, Berne described three basic roles or ego states: the Parent (the respectable, authoritarian, not OK subsystem), the Adult (the OK reality-oriented data processing and decision subsystem), and the Child (the insecure, not OK, but also creative, spontaneous, innovative, and joyful subsystem). Further developing these three roles and their functioning in transactions, Thomas Harris in *I'm OK—You're OK* set out the rules for trading with the enemy, both internal and external. With the Adult in control of both Parent and Child, people can overcome the need for destructive "games."

Some model advice

This brief glance at the concept of behavioural models is meant to be a semantic aperitif for the fuller treatment of particular models in the rest of the text. As the description of organizational behaviour winds its way forward, the way stations can be recognized from the different models that appear before the reader. We are going to look at different structural models for personality, role, group, and organization; we are going to "invent" and elaborate process models for motivation, decision making, conflict management, and change. In the chapter on the future, we are going to look at a computer simulation of the world. Why is model building so important for the student of organizational behaviour?

What is important about all this model building is that making models is a kind of game where a person plays Einstein or Freud and, letting his imagination run riot, comes up with some kind of diagram which gives the impression that it will imitate the behaviour he is studying. Put another way, the model is the poor man's theory, and the whole object of this exercise is to get people thinking about theories. The student should be ready to reach into his mental bag and whip out a scenario, a model, a paradigm, a game, a subroutine, a heuristic, and (as they say in the land where a man must earn his age in kilo dollars) "pump the other guy through his paradigm."

CONCLUSION

This brief review of research methods suggests certain conclusions for two different parties, the student and the potential research man. The student should recognize that the findings of organizational research projects are only as good as the methods used to establish these findings. How you look at a subject determines what you see. Sometimes what you see is determined by just the fact that you're looking. It is not only lovers who are put off by a voyeur but also research subjects, who may in the laboratory react in a way which is significantly a function of being observed.

The critical activity in research is asking the right question and then employing the right method, one which will allow the researcher to answer the question with confidence. Then he has got at the truth of the situation. The student should consciously remind himself that every method has its own particular problems as well as its strong points. For example, he should look at laboratory experiments rather carefully and ask himself to what extent the findings are a function of the "laboratory culture" before attempting to extrapolate such findings into the real world of organizational actualities. We shall return to the examination of these laboratory cultures, which is one of the central functions of behavioural technology. The important point to make for the moment is the need to evaluate the validity of the extrapolation.

The student should also keep in mind that it is not sufficient to establish predictions (given X, we can forecast Y), but it is also necessary to supply an explanation of the actual process (why does X lead to Y?). A telling example of prediction without explanation is the brilliant research work of F. E. Fiedler of the University of Washington, who showed that psychologically distant (remote, task-oriented) managers were effective in some circumstances but not in others. A carefully established prediction —but why is it so? Not only do we not know why in regard to the relation, but we are also uncertain what psychological distance is in behavioural terms. This lack of understanding has significantly held up both the development of Fiedler's theory and its application.

The student should always be aware of the "spread versus depth" dilemma. Is he going for a large sample, say, in an observational study, so that he will know very little about each individual but his results will satisfy certain canons of statistics in regard to sampling? In regard to questionnaire studies, the student should bear in mind that he is primarily dealing with expressions of values and attitudes which may or may not correlate with behaviour. Sampling the attitudes of managers and shop floor operatives about a foreman will give us two sets of perceptions; and both have to be contrasted with the actual behaviour of the foreman.

For the potential research man, the important point is to keep in mind that a wide variety of research methods are available, each with its own particular perspective; each method allows the researcher to see his subject in a particular light, from a specific angle which inevitably excludes other important angles. For the research man, the vital act is to search the journal literature for the specific instruments that have been used before, adapt them to his purpose, and then try the instruments out in pilot experiments. If the instruments look promising (i.e., tell him something he didn't know before), he should then set out to check their reliability (do they measure the same thing in the same way on different occasions?) and validity (do they measure what they claim to measure?).

This section should help the student to keep his critical faculties alive when examining research findings, by suggesting to him particular questions:

1. What methods were used—interviewing, observation, or examination of documents? What are the pros and cons of each method? Was the sample size right?
2. Was the case study method used? To what extent does the study have an anecdotal ring about it?
3. Have the research findings been set out as a list of hypotheses to give the study a scientific ambience, when in fact what the researcher did was more of an exploratory study?
4. Did the researcher ask the right questions in formulating his research focus?
5. Does his research answer the questions which he set out as his problem?
6. If his answers disagree with other answers, does the researcher offer an explanation?
7. Do the research findings give you a "so what" feeling?
8. Does the research suggest further lines of inquiry or possible applications to actual organizational operations?

TOPIC 2
Action research in organizations

Kurt Lewin was the first behavioural scientist to realize in a systematic way that the laboratory was an extremely limiting place for studying complex real social events, and that the better strategy was to go out and study the real world by trying to change it. Lewin's approach, which was essentially pragmatic and in some cases somewhat manipulative, consisted of using a whole battery of tactics as a means of effecting change through studying behaviour. Lewin might begin his work by identifying a gatekeeper in the target system, such as a company president or personnel director, and establishing some contact with him.

In his approach to the problem, Lewin was very much aware of the problems of values and power. For Lewin, an organization did not achieve a state of stationary equilibrium but rather a kind of quasi-stationary equilibrium. His theory of change, with its three stages of unfreezing, changing, and refreezing, recognized that a group could be seen in terms of the kinetic theory of gases, with the group being made up of a whole bunch of atoms full of energy. The group as a Gestalt of atoms (or roles) rearranged themselves in peculiar ways according to the rules (e.g., inferiors cannot readily initiate contacts with superiors) and relations (e.g., one man, one boss). The group is bounded by the perceptual periphery of its members, but somehow the group must respond to its environment. When the group is ready for the change process, the group's efforts are no longer appropriate to the mandates of the environment. Internal frustration is building up. The first phase of the Lewin change metaphor requires the increasing of this tension to break down the old rules, roles, and relations.

What Lewin was first to realize in an explicit way was that the group was a Gestalt with structure, process, and values organized in a particular way that gave the group coherence, stability, and credibility. And these last three factors produce a gigantic inertia which takes a considerable burst of energy to overcome. Somehow the frustration of the group has to be mobilized, canalized, and exploited to break this stability. In the 1940s, only social science consultants of Lewin's stature had the combination of nerve, insight, and personal élan needed to carry off this change strategy. Nowadays it is a commonplace, and behavioural scientists can walk into work groups and say, "I'm going to change you," and explain to their clients what change process paradigm they are going to use. The arousal, the anxiety, the conflict which is provoked in the client can be focused to reveal the group dynamics of the situation. But the beauty of the change effort is that to the experienced behaviour scientist, who has lived through this kind of applied action research before, the actual process has clearly identifiable elements.

Lewin's seminal contribution was of two kinds, one theoretical, the other practical. In theoretical terms, he set out a model of personality, $B = f(P, E)$, which recognized that man's behaviour was a function of both his personality and the forces in the environment. The individual could be seen as a self-propelled, electrically charged particle which was being monitored by the field force of the environment. The field forces in the environment were generated to a considerable extent by other electrically charged, self-propelled particles. How these particles fitted together in a set was the whole subject of group dynamics.

Lewin gave the subject of group dynamics, which had been an intellectual displaced person, a new identity. On both sides of the Atlantic, Lewin's ideas of group dynamics—with mathematical vectors as forces on individuals and the electrical field analogy which could "explain" attraction, repulsion, clustering, polarization, and semipermeable membranes—were seen as catalysts which spawned all sorts of interesting experiments with groups. On the American side, the Center for Group Dynamics was developed at Ann Arbor, with the focus on the individual and group process but with strong connections with experimental psychology. On the British side, the Tavistock Institute of Human Relations developed an approach which achieved the difficult feat of fusing Freud's psychoanalysis and Lewin's field theory and somehow applied this peculiar optic to solving organizational and social problems.

On the practical side, Lewin had the knack of thinking up new ways of studying groups. For example, he was once involved in a study of community interrelations which involved whites talking to blacks in a conference setting, and his use of observers to study the dynamics of the discussion was more interesting to the participants than the discussion itself. From such an apparently unimportant and relatively trivial beginning came the idea of T groups, where people come together, without an agenda, to rediscover the wheel of group dynamics by observing themselves forming a group, with all the trials and tribulations involved.

Lewin did not bring about all these dramatic new insights and revolutionary training techniques by himself. For example, L. P. Bradford, K. D. Benne, and R. Lippitt originated T groups at Bethel, Maine, in 1947—bringing together an apparently unstructured bunch of strangers to form, grow, and dissolve as a group, all in two weeks. But they were guided and inspired by Lewin's work. Given the task they had set themselves and their inevitable lack of experience, the success of these early group ventures (especially considering the risks of such encounters) is to be wondered at. Perhaps the feat was possible only because the risks, and thus the anxieties, arousals, and energy mobilization, were so high. And anyway, the groups were not in fact unstructured, as soon became obvious to the early trainers of T groups, who proceeded to write the definitive texts and research papers which set out what phases groups go through, what roles are to be filled, what crises must be met, and so on.

T groups, in the first instance, were essentially for the participant's self-insight. It was only later that social science consultants realized what a powerful technological tool T groups could be for trying to get somewhere in a task sense. Then, in time, T groups went out of fashion—scorned as, perhaps, "a bunch of strangers sitting around trying to figure out who they are." More seriously, it was seen that T groups are, or can be, dangerous. Some of the danger derives from the fact that many neurotic people are attracted by the potential of the T group. It was an old rule working again. Psychoanalysis was discovered by studying neurotic patients, but it has turned out to be most therapeutic for those who need it least—the raging normals with a few minor neurotic traits who learn how to exploit their disabilities. Likewise with T groups. They were designed to help people understand themselves, but became powerful tools for affecting organizational change; and the principal beneficiaries were well-organized, successful businesses with few faults which learned how to function much more efficiently by becoming the patient on the couch.

The most brilliant, or at least the most comprehensive, exploitation of T group technology is the work of R. R. Blake and J. S. Mouton. They designed the "managerial grid," with two axes, one to measure concern for production and the other concern for people. The full Blake programme has six phases: (*a*) laboratory training for small group face-to-face exchanges on people-versus-production values, (*b*) team training, (*c*) intergroup problem solving, (*d*) goal-setting and change implications, (*e*) support for goal realization, and (*f*) stabilization. The Blake programme can be easily understood as a sophisticated interpretation of Lewin's unfreezing-changing-refreezing strategy:

UNFREEZING—*Team training*—CHANGING—*Goal setting*—REFREEZING
Laboratory   *Intergroup*   *Support,*
training   *training*   *stabilization*

PLANNED CHANGE

In the 1960s a whole theory of planned change was evolved to help social science consultants and their client businesses to function more effectively. Fundamental to this theory is the relationship between consultant and client: the consultant tries to change the client, and the client tries to understand the consultant (and, in both cases, vice versa). What makes this relationship so important to understand is that an increasing number of organizational relationships, such as that between system analyst and user, are of this type. How such a relationship begins, how it can be encouraged and terminated, and what both parties' expectations are, are typical of the questions that corporate people puzzle over.

In capsule form, change agents seek out gate-keepers in client organizations, who have usually been alerted to the potential of a particular consultant by the grapevine or through attending a seminar or T group. The gate-keeper signals the change agent in and pilots him through the corporate mine field into the inner sanctum of the top group.

Now the big question is: Who is conning whom? Is the consultant there to practise applied behavioural science and help the organization to achieve its goals more effectively while helping individual members to realize their personal destinies through self-actualization? Or is it that someone in the client group is sponsoring this behavioural exercise to introduce a "scientific" ally to further his own cause?

Both consultant and client are usually sharp and alerted to such issues. But corporate executives are frequently sharper at organizational politics in their own backyards than behavioural scientists (who typically spend perhaps 20 days a year with the client). Further, it is difficult to say who is using whom and who the prime beneficiary is—especially when it is kept in mind that the behavioural scientist writes up the report for publication. Only those who have been on the inside of major behaviour science projects know what really happened, and sometimes they "ain't saying."

Then there is the major social science industry of revisiting the sites of famous experiments and doing a debunking job. Such debunkers should tread warily, for many of the "greats" in applied behavioural science are still alive and kicking.

THE CONSULTANT

The social science consultant who knows his job will make sure that his role is properly defined and his terms of reference clear. A small number of consultants do most of the business of acting as change agents. Why a small number? Because the change agent cannot be effective unless he charges very large fees, which set the level of expectations for his client—who then sets out to get value for his money. But the change agent cannot set large fees without a successful track record. Only the brightest and the bravest break into this cycle, and when they do their charisma travels ahead of them. Like legendary heroes, they live dangerously and sail into the wind time after time—and mostly seem to pull it off. The essence of their strategy is easy to set out. They create a collaborative relation with their clients and then proceed to show up the client's failings. Apparently the whole exercise is carried through with so much élan and dash that the client finds the process not only fascinating in an educational sense but entertaining to boot. How is it done? Nobody really knows! The books that have been published on these change strategies mostly contain catalogues of steps which tell the neophyte nothing (and the expert, not much).

Perhaps a better insight into the process is provided by speculating about the consultant and trying to figure out what he brings to the change game. One of the most outstanding and effective consultants is Edgar H. Schein of the M.I.T. School of Management, who apparently began his career in the early 1950s by getting involved in the study of American prisoners who were repatriated from Korea. By an exercise in detective work, Schein was able to reconstruct in a sensible and rational way what happened to these prisoners and to explain such bizarre matters as brainwashing in clear, straightforward behavioural science terms. Schein showed that the Chinese technique was basically similar to Lewin's three-stage process. Another major step in Schein's career was his interest in laboratory groups, which helped him to fashion a number of tools for studying groups. A question that puzzled Schein was how people negotiate access to work groups. Out of this enquiry emerged a whole series of studies in socialization which are concerned with how newcomers are taught the ropes, learn the group's values and norms, and acquire roles.

Schein's most recent efforts have been in process consultancy, a change strategy which concentrates on the process as a means of helping the client to solve his problems. Schein is not the only behavioural scientist using process consultancy, but he is one of the most sought after. What is the secret of his success? Is it the process, the person, the place, or the time? Or is it the client? The important point is surely that sets of didactic rules, spelling out how to do it in terms of action research, are almost bound to be misleading. Consider some of the real dilemmas of this type of behavioural technology, for example:

1. Collaboration versus confrontation.
2. The need for public debate versus the need for privacy of feelings.
3. The consultant as manipulator versus the consultant as political ally.
4. Creating conflict versus creating supportive relations.
5. The need for organizational effectiveness versus the need for individual self-actualization.
6. Consultancy versus research.
7. Publication versus client confidentiality.

Only top-notch behavioural scientists can presently walk the tight-rope among these dilemmas.

One of the major aims of studying organizational behaviour is to provide cognitive maps, appropriate concepts, research findings, and above all learnable and effective techniques which practitioners in this field can acquire and utilize. But before proceeding with that large topic which is concerned with the realities of personality and motivation, group dynamics, leadership, and the nature of organizations, it is perhaps as well to say a word about the client. The customer has to play "client" if the behavioural scientist is to play "consultant." As we will develop in the Chapter 8 discussion of role playing, both parties in an interaction must fulfill their roles simultaneously and supportively if they are to mobilize, monitor, and maximize each other's perceptions, emotions, and behaviour. No one can play "doctor" unless someone plays "patient," or "parent" unless someone plays "child." It takes two to make a consultation; the client has a major role.

THE CLIENT AS PHILOSOPHER-KING

It is one thing to dream up an ideal solution to an organizational problem, but it is another thing to put your solution into practice. When Plato faced this problem in writing *The Republic*, his conception of the ideal government of the state, he got around the problem by imagining the emergence of the philosopher-king—a king who follows his philosophy, not vice versa. In terms of making behavioural science a living actuality in organizations, the client as a philosopher-king has played a critical part in almost all modern major organizational research projects. These contemporary philosopher-kings usually have some knowledge and experience of behavioural science, which they may have derived from having been in a successful psychotherapeutic relation or through participating in a productive T group or managerial grid session. Occasionally they have formal and significant training in behavioural science itself.

Having recognized the potential of the behavioural sciences, the philosopher-king tentatively decides to get his feet wet by inviting a psychologist or sociologist to carry out an action-oriented research project in his company. If this first venture is successful—if it appears to solve the actual problem and the researcher can package the research findings in such a way as to titillate the interests of both the business and academic world—the way forward for both the philosopher-king and his behavioural scientist is clear. A happy, life-long symbiotic relation may well be established that produces dramatic dividends for both. The behavioural scientist typically establishes himself as the company's social scientist, available for consultation to all employees, and has in return the finest field laboratory for actual studies; the client is able to mobilize considerable social-scientific talent to help solve his organizational problems, while at the same time guaranteeing himself a place in the hall of fame for organizational philosopher-kings.

Two organizational philosopher-kings of modern times are Alfred J. Marrow and Wilfred Brown, the former American and the latter British. A. J. Marrow is not only president of Harwood Manufacturing Company but also the holder of a Ph.D. degree in psychology. When Kurt Lewin, a world-famous German psychologist, resigned from the University of Berlin in the 1930s and accepted an appointment at Cornell University, Marrow quickly established a good working relation with him which not only influenced Marrow's doctoral studies but also proved to be decisive in the actual behavioural research projects which were carried out at Harwood, a plant in the clothing industry. These studies have been going on for more than 30 years and have been mainly concerned with determining the effect of participation on decision making when introducing technological and operational changes. In a sentence, what the studies have shown is that participation leads not only to higher productivity but also to higher morale and job satisfaction all round.

If this is true and participation is the decisive factor, both academics and executives had better pay attention and try to figure out what actually happened at Harwood. No one for a moment could challenge the credentials of the distinguished psychologists who collaborated in the Harwood studies. The list reads like a page from the behavioural scientists' "who's who" and includes Kurt Lewin, Alex Bavelas, Rensis Likert, John R.P. French, Stanley Seashore, David Bowes, and Edward E. Lawler. Many of the Harwood psychologists have been associated with the University of Michigan's Institute for Social Research. Thus Marrow drew on the University of Michigan, while Wilfred Brown and the Glacier Metal Company drew on the Tavistock Institute of Human Relations—which, it so happens, has a very happy and felicitous relationship with the Michigan Institute. Many of the techniques developed at Tavistock have been used at the Institute for Social Research, and vice versa.

TAVISTOCK AND THE GLACIER STUDIES

In Britain the Tavistock Institute of Human Relations has provided the necessary theoretical constructs and empirical research to enable action research to develop effectively. Therefore, it might be considered relevant to specify the contributions of this famous research institute to the work of behavioural scientists in industry. The Tavistock Institute of Human Relations developed from the Tavistock Clinic, which from its inception had a pervasive interest in the psychoanalytical approach to psychotherapy. As well as drawing its basic concepts from psychoanalysis, many of the behavioural models have developed from the holistic approach to organizational behaviour—Gestalt psychology, Lewin's field theory, functional anthropology, open systems theory, and lately the idea of sociotechnical systems.

Fundamental to this approach is the acceptance of the complexity of interacting forces operative in any human situation. This complex of forces may involve personal, social, and historical factors. Integral to this technique of analysis is a reluctance to accept chance as a significant factor causing an individual, group, or institution to develop according to a particular mode. The required approach is dynamic rather than static. This may seem "old hat" now, but in the 1940s it represented a revolution in traditional thinking about human behaviour. The effectiveness of the Tavistock approach derives from the ability of its members to operate from diverse points of view; for example, the ability to integrate apparently contradictory theoretical systems of psychoanalysis and field theory. Psychoanalysis presumes that the past, which is assumed to be almost exclusively sexual, is of paramount importance; whereas field theory derives its strength from the mapping of contemporaneous forces operating on the individual. Tavistock's supremacy in applying social science to business behaviour is derived from the elegant and valuable concepts which represent a kind of synthesis between the apparent paradox composed of the thesis (psychoanalysis) and its antithesis (field theory).

Even a casual glance at the professions from which Tavistock behavioural scientists are drawn shows that they accept that organizational problems rarely manifest themselves neatly parcelled according to academic function. Thus, in Tavistock, you will find medical psychiatrists, clinical psychologists, sociologists, statisticians, and economists working in teams.

We have discussed the key influence of Lewin on the concept of group dynamics. To develop his ideas on this subject in terms of vectors, he introduced the concept of life space, which refers to the whole system of the group and its environment; this includes not only the real aspects of members' personalities (their physical environment, their concepts of one another) but also the unreal elements (their aspirations, expectations, fears, ambitions, etc.). Integral to this approach is the belief that members have goals which they desire to achieve; and by moving towards these goals,

Box 5.1: The Glacier system of management

By any standards, the Glacier studies must be regarded as a tremendous contribution to management knowledge because of their scope, significance, and design. These studies, which began in 1948, arose largely from the collaboration of two men, Wilfred Brown (one-time chairman of Glacier, who is "an industrial philosopher-king") and Elliott Jaques (a psychiatrist who has fused psychoanalysis and field theory to provide a new orientation).

The Glacier Metal Company, which is probably the most studied, best documented, and most heavily dissected organization, is a successful public company, employing 4,500 people in six locations. It is the largest manufacturer of plain bearings in Europe and occupies a special position in the esteem of those who study organization theory. In scope, length, theoretical significance, and general impact, the Glacier studies merit comparison with the Hawthorne investigations. In fact, the Glacier research started in the human relations period and was at first largely concerned with making committees effective.

In Glacier, the essentially human relations view is in turn giving way to Brown's conception of "task management," whose flavour and economy may be gathered from two propositions, one positive and the other negative. In task management, optimal organization is a function of the work to be done (task) and the resources available to do it (personnel, technical, and economic); personality plays no part.

THE FACTORY IS THE STATE "WRIT SMALL"

The most comprehensive exposition of the Glacier system has been provided by Brown in *Exploration in Management*. In the policy document for the company there are outlined four systems of organization: the legislative system, the executive system, the representative system, and the appeals system.

The function of the legislative system is to make policy for the whole organization. In May, 1949, the managing director introduced a revolutionary change in the Works Council. He proposed that the Council should become a policy-making body for the company so that "every major policy decision would become a matter for consultation with the entire Works Council." The managing director rightly argued that there were two stages in management: policy making and executive action. He further argued that the Works Council should be responsible for policy, and management for executive action.

The executive system represents a network of roles for carrying out the day-to-day work of the company within the framework of the company policy.

J. Kelly, *Is Scientific Management Possible?* (London: Faber & Faber, Ltd., 1968).

they may gain release from tension. Another key concept is that a group is viewed as a field of forces which are in a state of equilibrium.

GLACIER

Elliott Jaques, a brilliant Canadian psychiatrist, gained significant experience with the Tavistock Institute during World War II. The Institute

THE GLACIER SYSTEM

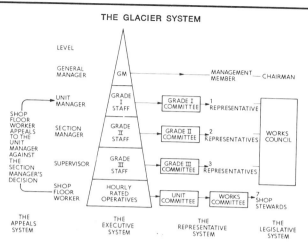

In the company there are three grades of staff, as well as hourly rated members. Each staff grade elects representatives to serve on the appropriate staff committees, and the operatives have a Works Committee, where all the stewards can meet and decide shop floor policy. The appeals system enables the decision of a superior to be challenged.

An adequate understanding of the Glacier system requires viewing it in broad perspective. What is important to understand is that the theory and practice of administration labelled "Glacier" are in a state of flux and still in the process of development. The Glacier project may be regarded as a well-documented capsule account of the contemporary history of organization theory, which starts with the classical theory of organization, followed by the human relations schools, and then the task approach. A curious symbiotic relationship exists between Glacier and Tavistock which has produced correlated theoretical changes in both. Thus, from Tavistock, Glacier adopted the following ideas:

1. That the individual's behaviour can be explained through the analysis of the complex of forces acting on him. These forces can involve personal, social, and historical factors. Some may be unconscious.
2. Making these forces explicit is the technique of "working through." Inherent in this approach is the optimistic view that chance factors are of minimal significance.
3. When all is known (by working through), then all will be well.
4. The socio-technical systems approach provides the basis of task management.

pioneered such dramatic behavioural science inventions as group selection procedures for officers, which were later used to select saboteurs and parachutists, and which eventually formed the basis of the assessment centre. After the war, Jaques led a team of behavioural scientists from Tavistock in an investigation of the Glacier Metal Company. Box 5.1 contains an earlier (1968) description of the collaboration of Jaques, who brought with him an outstanding reputation for fusing Lewin's theory and Freudian psychoanalysis, and Wilfred Brown, who joined and became managing director of the firm in the 1930s.

In the on-going process of transforming Glacier into a democratic organization, "clocking on" was abolished, foremen were transformed into section managers, and piecework was abandoned. As the organization has moved towards the systems approach, the human relations approach of the elected works council has been retained. When a large sum of money became available to the company by way of profits, the problem of its distribution was settled by democratic means. The function of the legislative system, making policy, is largely carried out by the works council. In the council, proposals must be passed unanimously before they are accepted; thus representatives at all levels have veto power. The executive, representative, and appeals systems also function as described in Box 5.1 in this beautiful, elegant, and comprehensive organization.

THE TECHNIQUE OF WORKING THROUGH

Based on his experience both with the military in World War II selecting officers and with group therapy at the Tavistock Clinic, W. R. Bion developed a psychodynamic approach known as "working through." Elliott Jaques applied the technique of "working through a problem" to gain insights into the attitudes and beliefs of employees of the Glacier Metal Company which he reported in *Changing Culture of a Factory*. When a group is brought together, it goes through a phase of confusion and disturbance before it settles down to the actual task. Its success in solving the problem is a function of the group's sophistication. With a sophisticated and mature group, the members will deal with the realities of the situation and "work through" to a solution. Less sophisticated groups are likely to respond emotionally to stress. According to Bion, they may respond by fight or flight reaction, by dependency, or by pairing.

Earlier in this chapter (see the section on "Interviewing" under Topic 1) we noted many criticisms made of this technique, and the disadvantages it may have. However, Jaques was able to utilize it in the Glacier studies as an excellent diagnostic tool in identifying organizational forces, many of them unconscious. In particular, he was able to identify various organizational defence mechanisms such as adaptive segregation (where a worker would choose to ignore, for example, matters of joint consultation which had no immediate relevance for him) and multiple role holding (where a manager who was both managing director and general manager would oscillate between these roles, depending on the circumstances).

HARWOOD: PARTICIPATION AND PERFORMANCE

The wide circulation given to *The Failure of Success*, by Alfred J. Marrow, has given added publicity to the unusual story of the Harwood

Manufacturing Company which began in 1937 when Marrow, then fresh from receiving a doctorate in psychology, was appointed president of the family firm. With his academic background and ownership position, Marrow was in an especially favourable position to apply behavioural science concepts; and the operating problems of the textile manufacturing concern he headed were sufficiently serious to justify a major departure from previous managerial practice.

Working initially with the distinguished German psychologist, Kurt Lewin, Harwood rapidly adopted "participative management" as the major strategy for improving organizational performance. What is "participative management"? In Marrow's view it is not a particular technique but an overall attitude which encourages employees to share in setting goals, making decisions, and solving problems. It is based on the well-proven psychological principle that an individual is more strongly motivated towards goals which he himself has helped to establish than those which are set for him by others. Its practicality is supported by the scope it provides for the full utilization of the talents of each member of the organization. The principles of participation established at Harwood aimed at giving the employee a piece—"just a piece"—of the action in the decision-making process. They did not attempt to get everyone to participate in all decisions but restricted participation to those with knowledge relevant to the particular question at hand and with enough time available to play a meaningful role. The extent of participation varied considerably: at times the employees were fully empowered to make the decision, at other times their consent to a decision was sought, and at still other times their advice was requested but not necessarily followed.

The behavioural consequences of successfully applied participative management are highly rewarding from both a psychological and financial point of view. Although managers find that their jobs are tougher, the quality of decisions is improved and the increased motivation of employees is reflected in a better quality and higher quantity of production, increased job satisfaction, reduced turnover, and greater flexibility in responding to change. Employees suffer less from tension, have better health, and are away less frequently. The existence of these benefits has been confirmed by over 30 years of independent testing at Harwood Manufacturing, in what must be the longest continuous analysis of any firm by behavioural scientists. The payoff for adopting participative management being so high, what prevents immediate general adoption of the system? There appear to be two areas of difficulty:

1. How much participation is enough? As indicated above, Harwood did not get all employees involved all the time. However, the degree of participation must be high enough to generate a significant change in the attitude of employees. The amount required is affected by individual attitudes, existing organizational relationships, and the history of the organization. There do not appear to be any scales to predict how much change in

managerial practice is needed to convince employees that participative management exists. However, the attitude surveys developed by Rensis Likert are a powerful tool for indicating when the proper mood has, in fact, been achieved.

2. How can management overcome suspicion and distrust by employees and reluctance within its own ranks to actually change from an authoritarian to a participative system? The means used by Harwood Manufacturing to accomplish this goal are discussed in the paragraphs below.

THE BEGINNING

Shortly before A. J. Marrow took over as president, Harwood moved its manufacturing operations from New England to the rural community of Marion, Virginia. The low productivity rates and high turnover of employees being experienced at the new plant threatened the very existence of the company and presented the first challenge for the application of behavioural science. After conventional methods failed to unearth the cause of the problem, Marrow invited Kurt Lewin to visit the plant.

Lewin quickly identified the cause of the high turnover as fear of failure on the part of apprentice operators who were striving to reach a production rate of 60 units per hour. Many who approached this rate, but despaired of attaining it, left the company. The quitting rate actually increased as the operators' productivity went up, with a rate of 96 per cent among operators at the 55-unit-per-hour level. By providing short-range targets in small increments, Lewin was able to give new operators frequent opportunity for achievement; within a year the quitting rate was down by half. The application of behavioural science at Harwood Manufacturing was on its way.

During the association of a number of distinguished academics with Harwood over the years, the main thrust of their programme was toward highly practical goals. Marrow and Lewin agreed at the beginning that there should be "no action without research," but they likewise insisted that there should be no research without action. The standards used to measure success in applying participative management were generally economic, for example unit production cost, production volume, absenteeism, and turnover rate. Although Likert scales were used to measure shifts in workers' attitudes, no project was considered a success simply because employee opinion had shifted in the desired direction. Demonstrable contribution to the profit goals of the company appears to have been sought after more than "happy" employees.

This practical outlook is demonstrated in the techniques used to implement participative management at Harwood. Dr. John French, who spent many years as a consulting psychologist to the company, initiated a programme for giving foremen leadership training. Little lecturing or reading was involved; instead the emphasis was on role playing of real-life situations, with open mutual criticism and feedback. The supervisor's increased skill in handling people as well as the technical aspects of the job was reflected in higher production and better co-operation. The techniques used by Dr. French in these sessions were the precursor of the sensitivity training programme offered by the National Training Laboratories.

Another demonstration of the pragmatic participation practiced at Harwood was the manner in which prejudices in the staff against the hiring of older women were broken down. By having the staff themselves establish the criteria and collect data on the performance of older women already in the company, it was possible to prove that productivity, turnover, absenteeism, and speed of learning were at least as good as for younger workers. More important, those who took part in the study had full confidence in the results and persuaded other supervisors in group meetings that accepting older workers was a good idea.

Harwood operated at piecework rates and, being in the apparel business, had frequent need to modify styles and production methods. These changes were strongly resented by the workers and caused sharp declines in both morale and productivity. To deal with this problem, group meetings were set up to explain the need for change and to invite suggestions for cost reduction or job improvement from the employees. The results were highly gratifying: the participative group regained its former level of productivity within two days and exceeded it by 14 per cent after three weeks, while a control group with no participation restricted production, saw productivity fall 35 per cent, and had low morale and high turnover. This group was disbanded but later reassembled and, using participative methods, handled similar changes with considerable success. Later, Harwood used similar principles to accomplish a major modernization programme involving fundamental changes in piecework rates. Because the employees had full understanding of the reasons for the change and were able to take part in planning it, suspicions of a speed-up were not aroused and there was no absenteeism or rate restriction in retaliation.

MAJOR CHANGE

The largest participative management project attempted by the Harwood organization came when the company took over its major competitor, Weldon Manufacturing. This case has received wide attention in organizational literature and only certain salient points will be noted here. The reader who wishes a fuller description should refer to *Management by Participation*, by Marrow, David Bowers, and Stanley Seashore.

Weldon's operations were quite similar to Harwood's, with the important exception that Harwood had much higher productivity and consequently was much more profitable. Management decided that Weldon's authoritarian management style was responsible for its high costs and set out to introduce participative management on a major scale.

The project started with sensitivity training sessions, team-building and problem-solving meetings for all levels, and attempts to delegate influence and authority downward. There was considerable scepticism among employees accustomed to authoritarian methods, and progress was so slow that the company's financial position was threatened. After seven months, the following more drastic measures were adopted:

1. Sensitivity training sessions to work out antagonisms and develop collaboration were held, starting with top management.
2. "Family groups" of employees who worked together were arranged and attendance was compulsory.
3. The sessions were held away from the plant on an intensive basis, lasting two to four days. A psychologist attended each session.

Although the meetings were unstructured, in the sense that an agenda was not followed, the pattern that established itself consisted of (1) problem census and discussion, (2) personal relationships, and (3) assessment of the participants' own behaviour and desire for change.

The more intensive programme produced the desired changes in behaviour, and considerable improvement in motivation, co-ordination, and co-operation was achieved. As the programme was spread down to lower levels in the organization over a period of 18 months, the employees began to develop team spirit and morale and to accept responsibility for their own production goals. The dramatic turn-around in profitability and other performance indices is shown in Table 5–1

Of equal significance to the gains achieved is the fact that a study by Seashore and Bowers four and a half years after the intensive programme ended indicated that the benefits continued to be realized and that no retrogression to previous managerial patterns was evident. The study concludes that participative management is attractive to employees who will resist any attempt to reassert authoritarian measures.

TABLE 5–1
INDICATORS OF ORGANIZATION EFFICIENCY IN PRODUCTION

Area of Performance	Weldon		Harwood	
	1962	*1964*	*1962*	*1964*
Return on capital invested	−15%	+17%	+17.00%	+21.00%
Make-up pay	12	4	2.00	2.00
Production efficiency	−11	+14	6.00	16.00
Earnings above minimum (piece-rate and other incentive employees only)	−0−	16	17.00	22.00
Operator turnover rates (monthly basis)	10	4	0.75	0.75
Absences from work (daily rate, production employees only)	6	3	3.00	3.00

WHY IT WORKED

It may be useful to summarize briefly the reasons why the Harwood experience with participative management was so successful:

1. The fact that the head of the company was a trained psychologist committed to and involved in the programme appears to be of paramount importance. Marrow's security of tenure, based on his ownership position, gave him the freedom to try new methods; and the fact that he was an enthusiastic participant, rather than a critical bystander, must have given the whole programme great weight with all employees. Indeed, in the Weldon case at least, it is obvious that managers were under considerable pressure to introduce participative measures.

2. The involvement of trained psychologists on a continuing basis appears to have provided considerable confidence that the organization knew what it was doing. In addition, the use of sound research principles gave the results achieved considerable credibility and enabled new projects to build on facts proven to have validity in the Harwood context.

3. The use of highly practical goals and measures of achievement gave the programme legitimacy even in the eyes of old-style task-oriented managers. The "new-fangled" methods obviously produced results that were laudable even by old-fashioned bookkeeping standards. The fact that both Harwood and Weldon were originally in economic difficulties facilitated the introduction of new management methods, since the failure of the old ones to cope with the situation was obvious.

Not every company has an environment similar to that of Harwood Manufacturing and not every attempt to introduce participative management has been a success. However, the Harwood story provides long-run proof that participative methods can produce highly desirable practical and psychological results.

HARWOOD AND GLACIER: THE PUZZLE OF PARTICIPATION

The most striking common characteristic of the Harwood and Glacier companies was that both made use of participation and both made it a success by the conventional corporate standards of earnings, productivity, pay and morale. Exactly what constitutes participation is not all clear; it has been a continuing puzzle to behavioural scientists.

The most important conclusion about the studies at Harwood and Glacier is that we cannot be certain about the reasons why participation in decision making was successful. While at Harwood the participation was most frequently carried through with shop floor workers and supervisors, and occasionally with executive groups using the T group approach, participation at Glacier was more formalized and used the work council as its forum.

It is impossible to escape the conclusion that a great deal of success at both Harwood and Glacier must be attributed to that particular blend of genius provided by the powerful combination of a philosopher-king and an outstanding behavioural scientist. How such a combination operates—who provides what in terms of perspective, process, and function—is not at all clear and is really the basic puzzle in participative management, which rarely seems to work without such a symbiotic, synergistic, combination. Perhaps this is the reason why so much attention in the contemporary literature of organizational development is devoted to the definition of the relation between the consultant and the client.

In brief, in participation it is not what you do but how you do it, and perhaps even more importantly whom you do it with, that counts. Perhaps the good behavioural consultant is worth his fee—but only if he is intuitively sound in selecting clients. Participation is still an enigma, and we still do not know what problems, work groups, technologies, cultural backgrounds, stages, organizational levels, and environments, both social and economic, favour or disfavour its use. At least we can be certain that participation is no panacea, valid in all circumstances.

TOPIC 3
The integration of behavioural science and behavioural technology

The study of organizational behaviour has become a major vehicle for integrating the social sciences. Anthropology, social psychology, sociology, and sometimes political science and economics, have converged in studies of organizations which have integrated material from all these sources in order to produce change.

The two streams called behavioural science and behavioural technology also converge in the field of organizational behaviour; in fact, as noted in the discussion of action research, it is often difficult to separate the two. The technologist, concerned with engineering choice to achieve a desired behaviour, must have the results of scientific research and analysis as a guide. The scientist often needs a problem-solving orientation as an inoculation against the disease of analytic decomposition. As he attacks a specific problem, he will confront the need for technological techniques.

Looking back at Figure 5–1 and the opening discussion in this chapter will remind us of this interrelatedness and interdependence as we review the subject of behavioural science in preparation for moving on to concentrate on behavioural technology in the next chapter. As that discussion will emphasize, the technologist is essentially concerned with knowing what will happen when he intervenes in an organization to produce change. Before he embarks on efforts to control and manipulate, he needs to ask himself: What goals or ethical principles should guide my actions? What effects will my intervention have on this organization? On behavioural theory? On my personal growth? Who is likely to be helped —and who may be hurt—by this intervention? What terms of reference will achieve a "good" solution?

Not easy questions to answer; some may not be capable of being answered some or all of the time. Nevertheless, what answers exist are likely to be found in a solid grounding in behavioural science. To review, and perhaps shed some new light on, the material in this chapter, we can pick up our systems model and see what behavioural science looks like considered as a system in itself.

SCIENCE AS A SYSTEM

Modeling behavioural science as a system in Figure 5–3 illustrates, first of all, its critical dimensions. The structure indicates its interdisciplinary approach, which, besides the basic academic fields, may call on mathematicians, psychiatrists, information scientists, philologists—or practically anyone with a fact to contribute. Frequently the focus of research is a topic which falls at the boundaries of two or more traditional disciplines.

The process is likely to be the theory-hypothesis-theory method illustrated in Figure 5–2. Careful attention is paid in this method to conceptual parsimony: only the minimum number of hypotheses needed for adequate analysis of the organizational actuality should be developed. There may be a need for reanalysis of previous investigations to uncover implications hidden or missed the first time around.

The process might equally be the use of models. This does not include a structural model such as an organization chart, which is static. Process models are dynamic; they are to be played with. They encourage speculation, identify variables, facilitate dialogue, promote innovation and creativity. They are a credit card for almost unlimited excursions into the realms of theory. Models reflect life, and so they include the unobvious things always going on behind the scenes and under the tables—a certain *je ne sais quoi* spice of the unconscious, the informal, the hidden aspects of organizations. As we develop models throughout this text, the variables are often characterized as input-transformation-output variables. The transformation process may well be a "black box," so that while we know the causal sequence we do not know everything that happens. Models nearly always include means of feedback, so that results can be weighed and perhaps new variables used or a new model constructed. Of course, a model is only a model, not reality—as everybody knows, but sometimes forgets in the process of playing around.

The value system of behavioural science is objective and positive, not normative. It is concerned with what is, not what ought to be. Science should echo the famous phrase of "Dragnet"—"all we want are the facts, ma'am." As far as possible, it should be quantitative, empirical, and clinical. Research should be capable of replication by others to be of the most value. Here the social scientist is often caught between the need to be empirical and the adamant irrationality and unpredictability—that is, humanness—of his raw material. Lord Kelvin said, "When you cannot measure it, when you cannot express it in numbers, your knowledge is of a meagre and unsatisfactory kind"; to which Jacob Viner pithily retorted, "When you can measure it, when you can express it in numbers, your knowledge is still of a meagre and unsatisfactory kind." One cannot add

FIGURE 5–3

BEHAVIOURAL SCIENCE AS A SYSTEM

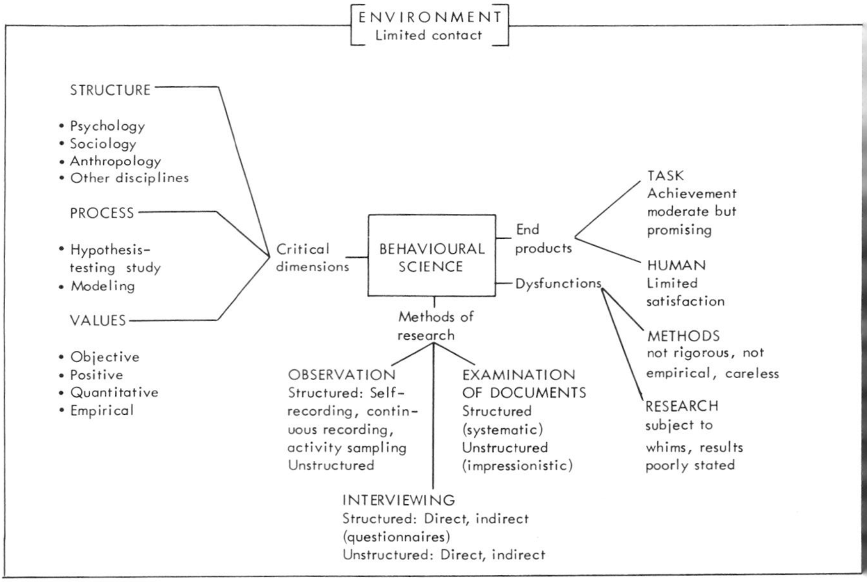

much, except perhaps Kurt Vonnegut's, "And so it goes." The dilemma is not likely to be resolved.

Hence the end products of our system are designated somewhat wryly in Figure 5–3. Behavioural science moves on despite its handicaps; and at optimistic times it is indeed promising and the satisfaction of pursuing it even heady. Objectivity requires balancing those moments against the bad days.

The methods of research are obviously of critical importance in this particular system. They are summarized here by the three fundamental data collecting procedures; but many qualifications must be noted. The behavioural unit must be defined, the measuring instruments specified, the data checked for reliability. The scientist needs a knowledge of statistics

and surveying techniques; questions such as sample type (random, strati-
fied, quota), sample size, and experiment design must be settled before an
investigation starts. Typically a carefully defined problem is attacked on a
very narrow front.

For example, a behavioural scientist setting out to investigate a communication process might ask himself such questions as:

1. What is the purpose of the communication process?
   a. What is the nature of the task?
   b. How complex is it?
   c. Does it involve innovation?
   d. Is there a creative element in the task?
2. Is the communication designed to produce changes of attitude?
3. What is the shape of the communications network?
   a. How many persons must the message pass through?
   b. Does it pass vertically, horizontally, or both?
4. What is the cultural setting of the process?

The answers to such questions enable the behavioural scientist to ascertain
what kind of research is appropriate and to define what kind of study will
be most effective, under what circumstances.

As with most systems, behavioural science must admit to dysfunctions.
It is sometimes accused of using a sledge-hammer to confirm a cliché. The
need for rigorous methods is compared to the number of conflicting
theories still in circulation. Research is subject to whims of fashion. (What
happened to the human relations experts of the 1940s? Are they the systems theorists of the 1970s?) Research findings are often couched in language indecipherable to other social scientists, not to mention laymen
(before this text ends the reader will have encountered such terms as
adhocracy, synectics, mobicentric, proxemics, anti-hospital, ratomorphic,
and similar coinings not locatable in standard dictionaries; an effort is
made not to use a term without clarifying). Finally, it must be admitted
that some behavioural scientists have not been scrupulous in respecting
such human rights as privacy.

With this survey of behavioural science, we are ready to proceed with
our scientist Dr. Jekyll as he transforms himself into technologist Hyde—
or, we may hope, a skilled and productive manipulator and controller of
organizational behaviour towards the betterment of individuals, groups,
organizations, and society.

REVIEW AND RESEARCH

1. What is behavioural science? What are the arguments for and against this
   approach to the study of human behaviour?
2. Why do subjects in psychology experiments behave differently in university
   laboratories from the way they behave in the outside world?

3. Design an experiment to study how people walk on the sidewalk in your city. Some tentative issues include:
   a. What is the average size of a group?
   b. How do they pass each other?
   c. How do they queue up at the lights?
   d. What is their average speed?
   e. How does the traffic of pedestrians vary from hour to hour?
   What research techniques would you use? Consider an experimental design using video-tape recording equipment.

4. Develop an interviewing form to assess the public's attitudes to one of the following issues: (1) working for a woman, (2) employing men with shoulder-length hair.

5. Your company is considering bringing in a behavioural scientist as a consultant. Draw up a brief, listing the issues which management ought to consider in making the decision. Some suggested headings are: terms of reference, suitable problems, methods of introduction, time span, measurement of performance, payment, sources of advice.

6. Why does participation produce better performance and morale? How can your business school or firm introduce more participative management?

7. Why are clients who are philosopher-kings so important in organizational research?

GLOSSARY

Action research. The application of behavioural science techniques to an organizational problem as a means of solving it; introducing changes as a means of understanding a system. Action research is usually a subtle process involving matters of values and power, usually requires a social science consultant to work with a "philosopher-king" who has corporate control.

Behavioural science. The field of inquiry dedicated to the study of human behaviour through sophisticated but rigourous methods. The emphasis is on theoretically significant empirical research which avoids the trivial. It includes such disciplines as anthropology, psychology, and sociology, but also maintains a watching brief on other relevent disciplines such as psychiatry, ethology, and econometrics.

Case study. A study which intensively examines many characteristics of one organization over a period of time to "learn all about" that organization.

Descriptive study. Studies which serve to define, in a standard uniform way, the characterisctics of the organization, to determine the frequency of their occurrence, and to measure their association with one another.

Exploratory study. The study which is probably most appropriate at the beginning of a research project, to enable the researcher to gain some familiarity with the problem and develop some insight into organizational dimensions.

Face validity. The concept that the content of a test should be considered reasonable and relevant by the persons taking the test and by the persons evaluating the test.

Hypothesis. A tentative statement, not yet verified, that states a relationship among empirical or theoretical variables; usually takes the form of "if *X*, then *Y*." The object of research is to try to prove or disprove the relation through examining the facts.

Hypothesis-testing study. A more critical study than the descriptive or exploratory which sets out to ascertain whether a particular hypothesis is valid and to define the circumstances of the relation.

Model. A simplified representation which often takes the form of a set of hypotheses—of a system under study. The purpose of a model is to enable the experimenter to manipulate variables and to examine relationships without disturbing the real system.

Parsimony. The general principle that the explanation of theory with the smaller number of assumptions is to be preferred.

Participative management. Management not by a particular technique but by an overall attitude which encourages employees to share in the setting of goals, making of decisions, and solution of problems; based on the psychological principle that an individual is more strongly motivated towards goals which he himself has helped to establish than those which are set for him by others.

Reliability. The degree of consistency of a measure of a variable when that variable is measured a number of times; the trustworthiness of the measure irrespective of what it measures.

Sample survey. The collection of data from a limited number of units which are assumed to be randomly distributed and to be representative of the whole group.

Test. A measuring technique used for evaluating an ability, character trait, knowledge of a particular subject, etc.

Theory. A description of a set of phenomena which can be used for making predictions about these phenomena.

Validity. The validity of a psychological test or interview may be generally defined as the extent to which it measures what it claims to measure; of a number of measures of validity, the most important is predictive validity, which is established statistically through correlation and gives a prediction of future performance of employees.

Working through. A diagnostic problem-solving technique developed by social scientists at the Tavistock Institute of Human Relations. A social science consultant, experienced in group dynamics, helps a work group to examine through interpretive comments its structure, process and value system. The work group can thus gain painful insights into phenomena such as scapegoating, rivalry, and dependency. In time the work group can· develop the ability to deal effectively with difficult reality problems.

6

Behavioural
technology

How can you get people to believe, feel, and act as you want them to? The modern answer is behavioural technology, the new applied science of behaviour control. It is based on the research of psychologists, pharmacologists, psychiatrists, and sociologists, fleshed out by the experiences of corporate officials, the practical expertise of the interrogator who uses brainwashing techniques, and the mystical insights of the new wave of organizational development (O.D.) consultants.

Quite rightly, many people have lurid ideas about behavioural technology, which is seen as Faustian—with the behavioural scientist having sold his soul to the devil for the power to manipulate other men's minds. The modern Machiavellis of the behavioural sciences have been busy developing new techniques which go well beyond such well-established methods as brainwashing and hypnosis; they have now come up with an exciting new repertoire including genetic engineering and electrical and chemical stimulation of the brain (ESB and CSB, respectively). Some behavioural scientists—influenced no doubt by the superior performance of drugs over any other form of psychotherapy in dramatically shortening the duration of the average stay in mental hospitals in the 1960s—are looking for a "peace pill" to control the aggression of corporate and political leaders.

Figure 6–1 provides an overview of the various levels of behavioural technology—the ways in which behavioural scientists try to affect men, and the concept or model of man which they have in mind as they do so.

One of the many methods of control we will look at in this chapter

FIGURE 6–1
LEVELS OF BEHAVIOURAL TECHNOLOGY AND MODELS OF MAN

	Technology	*Model of man*
Individuals	Genetic engineering	A complex of DNA molecules
	Electrical and chemical stimulation of the brain (ESB, CSB)	A cluster of neurons
	Stimulus-response (S-R)	A vending machine
	Stimulus-organism-response (S-O-R)	A dynamic integration of values, attitudes, needs, expectations, self-concept, and perception
	Path-goal (P-G)	An internal cognitive map helps him measure utility and probability of paths (means) and goals (ends)
Groups	T groups	The world is a microcosm of the group and vice versa
Organizations	Organizational development (O.D.)	Man is an element in the system
	Organizational Gestalt	Fusion of the system and existential man

(under the Skinner S-R concept) is behavioural modification, which regulates behaviour through the use of rewards and punishments. For example, it is possible to modify deviant sexual behaviour such as fetishism, homosexuality, and transvestism through the contiguous pairing of a primary aversive stimulus (such as an electric shock) with a stimulus eliciting the undesirable response or symptom. Behaviour modification can be used effectively with groups as well as individuals, and it has been used in the form of the "token economy" to regulate the behaviour of an entire ward of psychiatric patients. Patients who did such things as taking care of their personal needs, attending scheduled activities, and helping in the ward were rewarded with tokens which could be used to get cigarettes, money, and passes for watching television; patients who did not do things "right" were punished with fines (removal of tokens).

It may strike the reader that behavioural modification sounds like the "plain ordinary work situation," where you get paid for doing what the boss wants. In fact, a great deal of the experimentation carried out in the behavioural sciences uses a paradigm which in effect creates an employment relation between the experimenter and his subjects. In "Some Unintended Consequences of Rigorous Research," Chris Argyris argues that a good deal of behavioural research creates a Theory X (old fashioned master-servant) relationship between the researcher and his subject, with predictable consequences for the latter's behaviour.

Thus, according to its critics, psychology seems to be compounding a felony; when psychologists are not experimenting with rats and coming up with irrelevant answers for human behaviour, they are carrying out experiments with human beings which frequently involve deception, are often unethical, and generate payoffs in research findings that are inexcusably low. The question has been raised and is worth examining in some detail whether behavioural science is in fact a giant hoax. Perhaps that's how behavioural technology works—by exploiting this hoax.

MAKING PEOPLE DO WHAT YOU WANT THEM TO DO

Behavioural technology consists of the application of behavioural science concepts, research findings, and methods to control peoples' responses, emotions, and perceptions. What can be achieved by this new approach? Almost anything.

For example, in one behaviour laboratory subjects (people) seemed prepared to administer large electric shocks to other subjects (people) even when the victims screamed to be let off. If properly cued, lab subjects (usually students paid $2 to $3 an hour) are apparently prepared to say preposterous things, spend long hours playing childish games, and even sleep for a week at a time with equipment attached to their heads which can be used to stop them from dreaming. Many are prepared to tell stories about ink blots. Others exist for days on end in sensory-deprived environments, apparently until they are driven completely "bonkers"—or so some psychologists would have us believe. Many can be persuaded to learn endless lists of nonsense syllables. Lie detector tests are a commonplace. A few have had sexual intercourse under observation. Using exotic technologies derived from group psychotherapy, behavioural technologists have gotten people to tell all in the T group, fight each other in the encounter group, and stay in one room with 10 other men and women for up to 24 hours in the marathon.

Does this litany of activities remind you of anything—such as work? If the answer is yes, the advantages of behavioural technology for work situations are obvious. The boss plays the behavioural scientist and the worker plays the subject; and if subjects will do all those things for $2 or $3 an hour, what will they do for real money—say, $6 or $7 an hour?

A curious thing about much of the laboratory research is that it puts the subject in a bind and elicits behaviour which in fact is abnormal for him as he tries to placate the experimenter. The laboratory atmosphere apparently scares the subject and easily throws him into a subordinate (master-servant) role, which then structures his responses.

Behavioural technology began on a large scale during World War II, when it was used to study and influence civilian reaction to bombing and to select and train pilots, saboteurs, and officers. A fairly typical use was the "country house scene," where broken-up air crews from the bombing

Box 6.1: Getting maximum effort via L.M.F.

There are many ways in which the life history of an aircrew can be charted. There would be a simple graph of the odds that an insurance company would offer. The chances on this one began low—the first three trips were five times as dangerous as the average. But as skills and experience mounted so the chances of survival for each trip became better. Another graph, thirty trips with a five-per-cent casualty rate, would be a simple straight line: a mathematical proposition in which each trip held equal danger and the line ended at trip number twenty. There was yet another graph that could be drawn, a morale line charted by psychiatrists. Its curves recorded the effect of stress as men were asked to face repeatedly the mathematical probability of death. This graph —unlike the others—began at the highest point. Granted courage by ignorance and the inhibitory effect that curiosity has upon fear their morale was high for the first five operations, after which the line descended until a crack-up point was reached by the eleventh or twelfth trip. Perhaps it was the relief of surviving the thirteenth operation that made the graph turn upwards after it. Men had seen death at close quarters and were shocked to discover their own fear of it. But recognizing the same shameful fears in the eyes of their friends helped their morale, and after a slight recovery it remained constant until about the twenty-second trip, after which it sloped downwards without recovery.

The eleventh trip was not marked by crews asking to be taken off flying, getting drunk or running sobbing through the Mess. In fact few men asked to be grounded, and their reluctance was fortified by the RAF authorities who would stamp the words "lack of moral fibre" across the man's documents, strip him of rank and brevet and send him away in disgrace with the bright unfaded blue patch of tunic proclaiming him an officially recognized coward.

No, the eleventh trip was marked by more subtle defensive changes in the crew: a fatalism, a brutalizing, a callousness about the deaths of friends and a marked change in demeanour. Noisy men became quiet and reflective while the shy ones often became clamorous. This was the time at which the case histories of ulcers, deafness, and other stress-induced nervous diseases that were to follow the survivors through their later years, actually began. The crew of Joe for King were on their eleventh trip.

Len Deighton, *Bomber* (London: Pan Books, Ltd., 1970).

offensive over Germany were allowed to go for a limited stay so that new, self-selected crews could emerge. Self-selected crews became operational quicker. The effectiveness of bombing went up sharply when an automatic camera took a picture of the target when the bombs were released.

Sometimes systems could do terrible things (see Box 6.1). For example, it was well known that night bombers often bombed short out of fear and anxiety to get away from the flak at the target. To counteract this "human error," path-finder bombers dropped markers a little beyond the target, so that bombing short was actually spot on. But what happened when conditions changed, and enemy flak was light? A good deal of the damage done in the infamous Dresden raid resulted from this phenomenon. Behavioural technology is always potentially dangerous.

A surprising number of both American and European senior corporate managers are familiar with basic behavioural science ideas. The success of

magazines such as *Psychology Today* and *New Society* is to a large extent
a reflection of this interest. Other magazines such as *Time, Newsweek,* and
Playboy devote a significant amount of space to behaviour. Many books
and movies also cater to this interest. An excellent example of a film of
this genre is "A Clockwork Orange," directed by Stanley Kubrick of "Dr.
Strangelove" fame ("How I learned to stop worrying and love the
bomb"). Based on Anthony Burgess's book, the story portrays a young
punk (Alex) who is given to a sadistic satyriasis which is triggered off by
the music of Beethoven. He lands in gaol, the behavioural technologists do
their thing, and Alex is cured both of his violent excesses and his love of
Beethoven, but in the process turned into a robot. Although his slavishly
conditioned aversion to violence renders him unfit to survive in the chill-
ing society Burgess sees just over the horizon, he is "saved" when he returns to his previous savage self. What interests the executive in such
movies is this ability of behavioural technology to dramatically transform
behaviour and attitudes.

While genetic engineering and ESB and CSB are rapidly developing
technologies which in the long run will have significant effects on organization life, the immediate interest for the executive lies in the use of
behavioural technology. Before discussing each of the technologies listed
in Figure 6–1 in detail, as we will do in this chapter, it is a good idea to
take a look at how they link to the three principal theories already examined. A theory is only as good as its assumptions, and it is important to
examine the assumptions the three theories of organization make about
people. The linkage can be summarized as follows:

Theory	Model of man	Principal variables
Classical (scientific management)	Stimulus-response (S-R)	Money as stimulus
Human relations	Stimulus-organism-response (S-O-R)	Values, attitudes, needs, expectations
Systems (task)	Path-goals (P-G)	Utilities and probabilities

CLASSICAL THEORY

With regard to one strand of classical theory, scientific management, it
is important to note that aside from the Calvinist work ethic and an
emphasis on monetary inducements, the presumption is made that if man is
given additional substantive financial rewards as a stimulus, he will respond
with increased effort. The basic personality assumption underlying scientific management is the doctrine of rational-economic man, who operates
on the principle of hedonism—he seeks to maximize pleasure and minimize
pain. This philosophy presumes a society of two classes; a small, sophisticated, intelligent élite dedicated to managing the many; and a large class of
somewhat passive, unambitious, and lazy individuals who need to be led.

In this industrial world of "the officers and the men," money in the form of pay is regarded as a generalized conditioning stimulus which because of its repeated pairings with the good things of life can always elicit the right work responses. In the Tayloristic model, work gets done by getting the workers into highly structured routines designed by work study engineers; the worker is rewarded with money when he gives the right responses. What goes on inside his head or heart is presumed to be irrelevant. Basically, scientific management treats the worker as a stimulus-response (S-R) organism in much the same way as B. F. Skinner, the contemporary behaviourist, gets rats in his laboratory at Harvard to press levers to get a pellet of food.

The S-R model of man, which represents main-line North American psychological respectability, is the basis of both aversion therapy and behaviour modification. Aversion therapy modifies behaviour through the use of an aversive (unpleasant) stimulus. This treating of symptoms, contrary to established psychoanalytical practice, has turned out to be an effective means of removing the symptoms. Behaviour modification treats the subject like a Pavlovian dog, encouraged with a reward every time he gives the right response.

HUMAN RELATIONS

The human relations school rejects the S-R view of man because it fails to recognize that man is full of cognitions, feelings, and motives. In positive terms, the presumption in the human relations school is that people react to organizations on the basis of their perceptions, and that their perceptions are based on values, attitudes, needs, and expectations (VANE). Therefore to change organizations it is necessary to change perceptions and, as the Hawthorne experiment demonstrated, the best vehicle to do that is the group. Since man is responsive to the forces of his peer group, the way forward for management is through participation. The hope is that group discussion will lead to the establishment of consensus.

Thus human relations behavioural technology employs the stimulus-organism-response (S-O-R) model and sets out to change the organism's (man's) VANE. Instead of approaching the subject with the frontal assault of aversion therapy or behaviour modification, it comes at him tangentially. The rationale for this tactic is that a direct approach will make the subject defensive and resistant to change.

SYSTEMS THEORY

Corresponding with the emergence of the task or systems approach is the emergence of path-goals (P-G) man, who can look at the options open to him and select the one that most meets his interest. This model is derived from Victor Vroom's work on motivation of the worker, which uses as essential concepts (1) expectancy (estimating probabilities such as the likelihood of being able to do a particular job and being rewarded for it; (2) utilities (what it's worth to him in real psychic terms); and (3) instrumentalities (for some people high production causes loss of group membership, for others it is instrumental in increasing income). Vroom has argued that performance is a function of an individual's perceptions of the abilities required to do a job, the degree to which he perceives that he has these abilities, and the extent to which he values the possession of such abilities. Thus a person performs effectively when effective performance is consistent with his self-concept. L. W. Porter and E. E. Lawler, who have further developed and modified the Vroom model, put forward the view that managerial performance is a function of the perceived value of the reward (its utility), the probability that the effort will bring the reward (its expectancy), and the accuracy of role perceptions. The P-G model of man basically presumes that man can make choices on the basis of his perceived idea of these utilities and probabilities. Thus, the P-G man model has a natural affinity with systems theory, which contains the decision-making sequences integral to organizational choice. J. G. March and H. A. Simon (one-time colleagues of Vroom at the Carnegie-Mellon School of Industrial Administration and major architects of the theory of organizational decision making) use expressions such as "the perceived consequence of evoked alternatives" and "the expected value of reward."

STRUCTURE OF CHAPTER 6

Topic 1 deals with S-R technology or Skinnerism. It briefly reviews behaviourism, the school of psychology which simply defines psychology as the science of behaviour. Behaviourism leads naturally to the consideration of behaviour modification, which is being increasingly used as a practical tool for changing behaviour and attitudes.

Our second topic is S-O-R technology, which deals with the VANE model. To get a better understanding of how an individual's VANE can be changed, this topic includes several change strategies, including Schein's model of unfreezing-changing-refreezing.

Topic 3 deals with the strategies suggested by the P-G (path-goal) model of man, which is particularly important for the light it throws on job design and performance.

Our fourth topic is learning and the new training technology. The principles of learning are linked to such new training technologies as computer-assisted learning and programmed learning.

To bring this chapter to a close, Topic 5 is a critical review of behavioural technology which attempts to assess the contributions and limitations of these new change strategies.

TOPIC 1
S-R technology: Skinnerism

Stimulus-response technology is a science of control that aims to change human behaviour by applying principles discovered in the psychology laboratory to real-life situations. The major exponent of this point of view is Burrhus Frederic Skinner, professor of psychology at Harvard and one of the most influential of living American psychologists. Central to his approach is a technique of conditioning which has been used with great success in training laboratory animals, particularly rats and pigeons. Skinner believes that the same techniques can be applied to humans. In his famous didactic novel, *Walden Two*, Skinner has described utopia where control of the environment enables human behaviour to be predicted and shaped exactly as if it were a chemical reaction. Such a proposition is of great interest to both managers and organization theorists; if such a model is possible, organizational control comes within their grasp. Even if few managers believe this, many behavioural psychologists do, and it is in the interest of managers to understand the intellectual infra-structure of the scientists who may be coming to "help" them and their organizations.

Skinner's presumption is that behaviour is determined not from within but from without. The basic argument is that by arranging effective rewards, such as feeding a pigeon only if its turns clockwise, behaviour can be directed. In brief, rewards or sanctions determine whether a particular behaviour becomes habitual. For Skinner the reward contingency system is the way. Reinforcing the right responses produces what society wants. What society wants is another argument—which leaves Skinner open to the charge of being undemocratic.

Skinner was greatly influenced by John B. Watson, the father of behaviourism, who believed that if he were given "a dozen healthy infants and required to select one at random, he could train him to be anything irrespective of his talents and predilections." It is something of a curiosity that Watson drew on the work of the great Russian physiologist Ivan Pavlov, and that Soviet psychological interrogation and reeducation procedures are direct outcomes of the control of reinforcements and sanctions in the conditioning process. Behaviour control, if not thought control, has been established through the conditioning process which has emerged from Skinner's work with pigeons, which have been taught such bizarre behaviours as walking figure eights, dancing with each other, and even playing ping-pong.

Even though "pigeons aren't people," Skinner's ideas have been applied in schools, to produce teaching machines which programme learning; in mental hospitals, to get patients to come to the dining room on time; and in business firms, to reward good behaviour with compliments. Behaviour control through strategies of contingent reinforcement have been codified in the school of psychology known as behaviourism.

BEHAVIOURISM

Behaviourism is a school of psychology which defines psychology as the positive science of behaviour. For the behaviourist, psychology should be "purely objective" and should exclude consideration of intelligence, thinking, purpose, and personality as unscientific topics. Skinner believes

FIGURE 6-2
THE BASIC PARADIGM OF THE CONDITIONED REFLEX

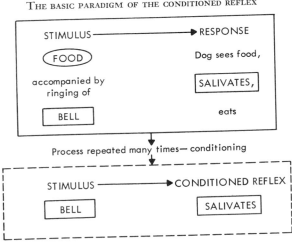

that the study of behaviour can be turned into an exact science. His most significant contribution has been the clarification of the role of reinforcement in the learning process. This follows directly on the tradition of Pavlov, who discovered the conditioned reflex. Figure 6-2 diagrams the way a dog could be trained to salivate on the ringing of a bell, provided the dog had been conditioned by having the two stimuli, the food and the ringing of the bell, presented at the same time.

Behaviourism, or S-R psychology, concentrates on the study of the linkage between the stimulus and the response elicited. The goal is the control and prediction of behaviour. Skinner says in *Walden Two:*

> I've had only one idea in my life—a true *idée fixe*. To put it as bluntly
> as possible—the idea of having my own way. "Control" expresses it. The
> control of human behavior. In my early experimental days it was a fren
> zied, selfish desire to dominate. I remember the rage I used to feel when a

prediction went awry. I could have shouted at the subjects of my experiments, "Behave, damn you! Behave as you ought!"

By experimenting with positive and negative reinforcements on animals, particularly pigeons, Skinner learned to predict and control their behaviour. To achieve control, he developed an "operant conditioning apparatus" which contains a food dispenser activated by a lever. Animals in this apparatus gradually learn to control their environment by pressing the lever and thus receiving a pellet of food. Over the years, more complex equipment has enabled him to teach rats, pigeons, and monkeys fairly complex skills.

Central to Skinner's approach is his belief that human behaviour can be predicted exactly as if it were a chemical reaction, because behaviour is determined from without rather than from within. Thus the control of the environment becomes the critical factor in determining what people will do and become. For example, to the behaviourist neurosis is just a bad habit, learned in the same way as Pavlov's dogs learned to salivate on the ringing of the bell. Presumably, what has been learned can be unlearned. The unlearning technique, known as "systematic desensitization," uses gradual methods of confronting neurotic behaviour to overcome anxiety. For this method to be effective, the triggers or stimuli which switch on the anxiety have to be identified; and the patient is gradually exposed to each of these triggers, starting with the least frightening. A related technique is aversion therapy, where desired behaviours are rewarded and the undesired punished.

THE RATOMORPHIC FALLACY

Behaviour therapy has been criticized both because it lacks an underlying theory to explain human personality and because it treats human beings as objects. Skinner answers such criticism by arguing that freedom and free will are illusions. Skinner has been accused by Arthur Koestler of the "ratomorphic" fallacy—of attributing to man processes that have been demonstrated only in lower animals. Berkeley Rice's article in *The New York Times* magazine reported:

> Skinner scoffs at such criticism. "It's not a question of getting people to subject themselves to proper laboratory conditions. The world at large is a laboratory. Take the people in Las Vegas, pulling levers on slot machines. They are in a laboratory situation, and very willingly. The slot machines simply use a schedule of conditioning and reinforcement similar to those we use in the laboratory—with money dropping down the chute instead of food. Of course, pigeons aren't people, but it's only a matter of complexity, and we're learning the differences now."
> "But can you prove that the contingencies of reinforcement work in society the same way they do in your laboratory?" I asked.

"Well, we have used them successfully with mental patients and programmed instruction," Skinner replied, "but you don't have to prove all this. If you've studied contingencies long enough in the laboratory, you get to the point that you can see them operating in society. You don't need proof. Just as the physical scientist doesn't need proof of the theories of trajectory, elasticity and gravity each time he sees a tennis ball bouncing."

"Have you run experiments on human beings in which you also had control groups who were not conditioned?"

"Well, with the teaching machines we've been able to compare their effect with the performance of similar classes who have not used them, but the whole idea of control groups is silly in research like this. You don't need them. The success of such experiments is immediately obvious. When you get a new washing machine, you don't wash the clothes by hand every other week as a control test on the efficiency of the washer, do you?"

In *Walden Two*, Skinner says that scientific control of behaviour would lead to a society where men and women could live in a state of equality and harmony, without anxiety. Communal ownership would permit people to devote themselves to art, music, and literature. In this utopian environment, according to Skinner, we could no longer afford freedom, but men and women would be able to live and work together in harmony. For many, the price would be too great.

Though the reinforcement techniques (which work well in some circumstances) are widely recognized, many critics reject Skinner's essentially ratomorphic view of man and argue that what gives man his unique dignity is his capacity for choice. Many of the critics of behavioural technology reject behaviourism out of hand as being trivial and naive, because of its failure to treat of such vital matters as consciousness, mind imagination, personality, and purpose.

Humanistic psychology, on the other hand, follows the theorizing of such existential psychoanalysts as Rollo May and Carl Rogers and give central importance to man's capacity for self-determination and self actualization. Such existential theories of personality are considered in some detail in Chapter 7.

BEHAVIOUR MODIFICATION

In spite of the criticisms of behaviourism, there is a growing interest among social scientists (and to a lesser extent among executives) in development in behaviour modification or behaviour therapy, in the hope that this new approach may provide a practical tool for shaping, improving and directing the behaviour and attitudes of organizational members. We have noted that behaviour modification, which is based ultimately on the Skinnerian principles of conditioning, has been used extensively both in the treatment of mental patients and for the behavioural control of schoo children. Now behavioural scientists are considering its application to other populations, both in a training context and for actual operating situations.

Behavioural modification, in its simplest form, aims to change the individual's responses by changing his environment, essentially by changing the reinforcement contingencies. The actual process requires systematic reinforcement of positive behaviour and ignoring undesired behaviour or exercising negative reinforcements (punishments or sanctions). Therefore this technique focuses on overt behaviour and not on the underlying causes. During the 1960s there were tremendous developments in behaviour modification programmes, which have now spread far beyond their original use into broader settings such as industry and the military.

F. Luthans and D. D. White, Jr., have suggested ways and means of applying behaviour modification to the work situation. In "Behaviour Modification: Application to Manpower Management," they give several examples of how this technique can be used in business organizations:

> Another example could apply to white collar employees. An objective of the sales department is to increase the volume of sales. In terms of manpower management, the individual salesman becomes the critical variable in obtaining this objective. Each salesman might be given a book in which he records only the amount of his monetary commission and/or points toward a desirable bonus gift. The entry would be made *immediately* following each sale. In order to assure that the instructions are being carried out in practice, the district manager would communicate to his salesmen that the record book would be examined first on a continuous (perhaps daily) basis and later intermittently. The reinforcement that the examination provides will cause the salesman to make entries immediately after each sale and not at a later time. Recording the monetary commission in the record book will directly reinforce each sale that is made, and each sale would, in turn, serve as a stimulus for each subsequent selling situation. Finally, his recognition that sales are increasing will motivate him to continue making entries and would become a self-generating reward. This example is significantly different from incentive programs currently used by many sales organizations. The commission that is recorded reinforces the sale, not the act of making the entry. The desired benefit of commission or bonus systems is often lost when the reward becomes "just another entry" on a daily or weekly sales report.

> Application of the principle of reinforcement is not restricted to individual task performance. An aircraft company used an innovative technique in the final assembly hangar of a repair and overhaul operation. A large sign visible to all was placed on the wall. This sign indicated the number of planes that had passed final inspection and the number which still remained unfinished. When word was released that a plane had passed the final inspection phase, bells rang throughout the plant. All work temporarily stopped while employees observed the numerical changes which were made on the wall sign. The workers were observed to turn to one another to nudge or voice approval concerning their accomplishment. In

this case the reward served to reinforce participation in the final product and enabled the employee to see himself as a contributor to overall organizational objectives.

A. Bandura has also set out how behaviour modification can be applied to the training situation. But applying this technique to training problems requires a very rigorous definition of the training objectives, in terms of both the specific desired behaviours and the specific behaviour variables that are open to manipulation and change. After the behaviour has been modified, the whole personality system must be made self-regulating through some process of integrating the new behaviour with the old.

This synthesis of the old and new behaviours is usually achieved in fact by some process other than conditioning, such as appealing to the subject's imagination, some form of exhortation, or supplying the subject with suitable rationalizations for the proposed change in his cognitive map. In other words, in spite of the yearnings of the behaviourist for a simple and automatic theory of behaviour, it is necessary to recognize that the S-R model is ultimately focused on only one element of the human condition. More useful change strategies also recognize that people are full of values, attitudes, needs, and expectations; that they carry cognitive maps around in their heads; and that they act as if they believe they are members of a wider social fabric.

TOPIC 2
S-O-R technology: The VANE model

The concepts, research methods, formulations, and methods of presentation of traditional North American psychology all too often leave the student stone cold, unimpressed, and frustrated. Many people are quickly turned off by the apparent triviality and artificiality of the so-called scientific material about behaviour which is presented to them. They are fed up with accounts of rats running mazes and pigeons pressing levers; they are bored with learning lists of nonsense syllables and playing "prisoner's dilemma" games. But they are vitally concerned about what is going on inside their own heads and what gives with the other guy. In a nutshell, they want to know what makes us all tick.

What this means in conceptual terms is that the discussion has to be moved from consideration of the S-R model to an explanation of the S-O-R (stimulus-organism-response) model. This model is essentially similar to the input-transformation-output model. But what is the "transformation" process in the organism? How does it process the stimulus into the reaction? Classical psychology has always treated the psychological process in three distinct but interacting steps, namely:

Cognitive	Perceptual (e.g., see the enemy)
Affective	Emotional (e.g., experience fear)
Conative	Behavioural (e.g., decide on fight or flight)

This conception presumes that the organism becomes aware of some stimulus in the environment. It experiences some emotion, makes some decision, gets mobilized to act, and does something (or nothing) in response. Some of the steps in this sequence may be different (e.g., the emotion may follow the decision). In any case, it involves a complex set of psychic events. A more complex model of an information-processing S-O-R system is shown in Figure 6–3. This model can be linked to the concept of

FIGURE 6–3
An S-O-R model

STIMULUS	ORGANISM	
	Activities	*Specific activities*
Perceptual	Searching for and receiving information	Detects, inspects, observes, reads, receives, scans, surveys.
	Identifying problems, options, incoming strikes	Discriminates, identifies, locates.
Mediational	Information processing	Categorizes, calculates, codes, computes, interpolates, itemizes, tabulates, translates.
	Problem solving and decision making	Analyzes, calculates, chooses, compares, computes, estimates, plans.
Emotional	Anxiety generated	Low: mobilizes. Medium: disorganizes. High: immobilizes.
Communicative	Transmits information	Advises, answers, directs, indicates, informs, instructs, requests, transmits.
RESPONSE		
	Simple–discrete	Activates, closes, connects, disconnects, joins, moves, presses, sets.
	Complex–continuous	Adjusts, aligns, regulates, synchronizes, tracks.

Adapted from a behaviour classification system originally proposed by J. Berliner, as modified by G. F. Rabideau, presented in K. B. De Green (ed.), *Systems Psychology* (New York: McGraw-Hill Book Co., 1970).

the personality of the organism as the transformation step of the input-output model. This is illustrated in Figure 6–4.

Now, how can these somewhat complex information models be used as a means of studying the human condition? One possible answer is to consider a simpler model.

THE VANE MODEL

The S-O-R model of man improves on the S-R model by adding the organism to the picture. The organism—the person—has values, attitudes,

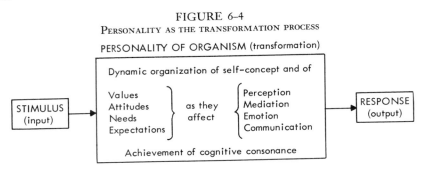

FIGURE 6–4
PERSONALITY AS THE TRANSFORMATION PROCESS

needs, and expectations, which we symbolize as his VANE. The VANE affects how people feel, perceive, and behave (as indicated in Figure 6–4).

A telling illustration of how a person's VANE affects his perception of the world is revealed by some of the reports of flying saucers, which are still being "seen" all over the globe. Although the U.S. Air Force, after examining 12,618 sightings over a period of 22 years, gave up, people still see UFO's (unidentified flying objects) of all kinds, form organizations about them, and claim to have met strange occupants of (and taken jaunts in) them. The *New York Times* of June 25, 1972, reported:

> Even though the thousands of reports in the files of the Aerial Phenomenon Research Organization have not been thoroughly analyzed, a pattern of sorts can be established by reading them. Reports of U.F.O.'s that have been examined from close range say they have portholes or windows in the outer rim of the ring. This rim spins when the disk moves, the portholes giving the impression that the U.F.O. is surrounded by a ring of spinning lights. When the U.F.O. lifts, bright white lights streams from grids on the bottom of the craft.

Which goes to show that even unworldly things are seen in worldly terms. UFO's have become astral Rorschach ink blots, perhaps resembling H. G. Wells' spaceships. What is interesting about this example is that it highlights the relationships between perception and attitudes; whatever it is that people see in the sky, they tend to interpret it in terms of their social, interpersonal, political, and cosmic attitudes.

Every marketing man is a keen student of perception and attitudes; and anyone who ever took even a "baby" course on consumer psychology has heard of subliminal perception—the idea that movie-goers will buy more popcorn if "eat popcorn" messages of extremely brief exposure are periodically flashed on the screen, although they are not consciously aware of being exposed to the message. Perception research of this genre was begun during World War II to train antiaircraft gunners in aircraft identification. Using a tachistoscope, which allows a picture to be thrown on a screen for an extremely brief period (so brief that few subjects consciously see it), an instructor would first present a series of pictures of aircraft silhouettes. The gunners were asked to note down the types of aircraft shown. On the first showing, the response was poor. Then a second series would be shown which included a subliminal pin-up girl. This series inevitably produced a bunch of cat calls, hoots, and whistles. Thus, playing the visual tom-toms of sex, the gunners' perceptual modification had begun. Although use of this technique has run into road-blocks, it is a dramatic example of what behavioural technology may hold in store.

A major problem in organizational behaviourism is to try to get a handle on the dimensions of the VANE. In this section, we begin this process by looking at values and attitudes. Needs and expectations are discussed partially in Topic 3 (P–G man) and more fully in Chapter 7.

VALUES

The value system of classical, traditional organization theory represents an individualistic, rational approach to life which sets the highest values as achievement, aggression, and affluence. Historically derived from Calvinism, this "Protestant ethic" system presumes that a man is predestined to either heaven or hell and that the ticket is made out according to how well he manages his stewardship of the worldly goods that come his way. Hard work and thrift are intrinsic goods; good works which benefit the less fortunate are to be practised in moderation lest "you sap their diminishing will to work." With a philosophy of "work or want," of producing more than you consume to pile up inherited wealth, and of "God helps those who help themselves," unregulated capitalism bestrode the industrial world of the late 19th and early 20th centuries. It combined an economic faith and a social ethic which required society to be structured in a particular way. For example, it required a large working class. Automatically suspect as to their virtue, members of this less "blessed" class were driven to be clean, respectable, sober, and tidy; to feel guilty if they couldn't work; and to respect authority, be patriotic, know their place, and otherwise strive for sanctity.

It was a pervasive value system, seeping into every aspect of life, defining sexual habits and attitudes (the ideal wife was "a madonna with a whore inside her"), attitudes towards alcohol (in Scotland, the favourite drinking night for the working classes was Friday, so that there was the least chance of upsetting the working week), and attitudes towards everything else—especially anything that smacked of enjoyment. Even the name "Protestant ethic" is misleading, for the value system pervaded every religious and ethnic culture to some extent. The past tense may also be misleading; it has not vanished utterly, though under attack.

If the traditional value system no longer pervades, the finger cannot be pointed at any one replacement. Contemporary society exhibits a melange of value systems, "new" coexisting with "old." This was perhaps inevitable

in a world which took Freud seriously; where children were fed o
demand, à la Spock; where the taboo was taken out of sex by the birth
control pill; where consumption had to exceed productivity to keep th
GNP growing; where democratic leadership was a must (to be some
times enforced at gun-point); where push-button nuclear war nearly pu
paid to the need for infantrymen; where instant communications via T
satellites landed us in the global village after supper in our dining room
where no human being could devise a system that would let everybod
work at once; and where the women's movement turned the nuclea
family inside out. With the notion that God was dead came the realiza
tion that most people may have been only half alive. As the membershi
of the traditional religions of the West began to decline, increasing nun
bers of people turned to the newly "discovered" religions of the East an
to instantly invented religion in such forms as the human potential move
ment. What the "new" religion promised was mysticism, mystery, an
the magic of transcendental experiences that gave meaning to a life robbe
of time by time study, reduced to a few simple therbligs by method study
and consumed with anxiety and guilt in the rat race of career trajectorie

The curious feature of this new movement was that management wa
an accomplice to the whole thing by encouraging the development c
T groups, democratic leadership styles, job enlargement, management b
objectives, and Theory Y managerial styles. Businessmen helped to set th
scene for the rejection of traditional work roles, and inevitably the crunc
came first of all in traditional industries like railways, shipyards, publi
utilities (including the police, garbage collectors, and teachers), and th
automobile industry. Though money is still an issue, it is the basic indig
nity of having to do the same thing day in and day out for 40 years tha
cannot be forgotten and forgiven. Hence the success of Toffler's *Futur
Shock* (the future cannot be faced), Reich's *The Greening of Americ*
(there is no hope of structural change, consciousness-raising is the onl
way forward), and Puzo's *The Godfather* ("I'll make him an offer h
can't refuse"). The dialogue has broken down; the legitimacy of authorit
relations, which depends on a moral consensus, has gone, to be replace
by power relations.

To establish a new dialogue based on awareness and authenticity, a
existential approach is required where people stop talking at each othe
and begin to act in good faith, recognising the basic validity of the othe
man's optic. Such a dialogue would try to reach, not compromises tha
reflect the extant power situation, but rather a meeting of the minds tha
will lead to a good society where man can find his dignity again.

ATTITUDES

Attitude may be defined as the predisposition or tendency of a perso
to evaluate some symbol, person, place, or thing in a favourable or un

favourable manner. His opinion constitutes the verbal expression of an attitude. In essence, an attitude is a state of mind which the individual carries around in his head, through which he focuses on particular objects in his environment such as foreigners, Communists, pornography, the unions, women, students, or professors.

In "The Functional Approach to the Study of Attitudes," Daniel Katz has set out the four functions which attitudes perform for the personality:

1. The *instrumental, adjustive, or utilitarian function* upon which Jeremy Bentham and the utilitarians constructed their model of man. A modern expression of this approach can be found in behavioristic learning theory.
2. *The ego-defensive function* in which the person protects himself from acknowledging the basic truths about himself or the harsh realities in his external world. Freudian psychology and neo-Freudian thinking have been preoccupied with this type of motivation and its outcomes.
3. *The value-expressive function* in which the individual derives satisfactions from expressing attitudes appropriate to his personal values and to his concept of himself. This function is central to doctrines of ego psychology which stress the importance of self-expression, self-development, and self-realization.
4. *The knowledge function* based upon the individual's need to give adequate structure to his universe. The search for meaning, the need to understand, the trend toward better organization of perceptions and beliefs to provide clarity and consistency for the individual, are other descriptions of this function. The development of principles about perceptual and cognitive structure have been the contribution of Gestalt psychology.

Attitudes are made up of three elements, the cognitive, affective, and conative steps discussed earlire in this topic. The dimensions of an attitude are presumed to follow a particular sequence, such as (1) cognition ("I see the Communists as a threat to the stability of the free world"), (2) emotion ("I feel strongly about the Red threat"), and (3) behaviour ("I would rather be dead than Red"). This sequence or train of cognition, emotion, and behaviour may be followed in some circumstances but not in all; the three elements interlock and interact. For example, by changing a person's behaviour it is possible to change his attitudes also.

CHANGING AND INTEGRATING THE VANE

A number of methods have been invented for changing the VANE. Four are suggested by the model of personality shown in Figure 6–5:

1. Restructure the stimulus, which depends upon the kind of information, its ambiguity, the order of presentation, and the credibility of the communicator.

FIGURE 6–5
STRATEGIES FOR CHANGING THE VANE

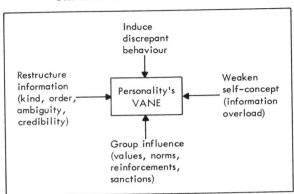

2. Weaken the self-concept by subjecting the person to an information overload, which increases the noise in his data processing system.
3. Induce discrepant behaviour, which places the person "on the spot"; he now has to shift his VANE to accommodate his new behaviour.
4. Facilitate group influence; for example, a group of peers, through a values-norms-reinforcements-sanctions nexus may change the person's role and relationships and thus his attitudes.

Typically, attempts to change individuals use all four strategies, mixed in varying degrees. The important point to note at this juncture is the fact that our model is a dynamic balance model, where a change in one element will produce change in other elements. This is precisely the model of change adopted by both the Chinese Communists in dealing with United Nations prisoners in Korea and by organizational development specialists who use T group technology. Integral to this approach is the idea of changing the individual's self-concept or identity, through some process of self-alienation, and then moving the self-concept in the desired direction, usually through exposure to a peer group who have the "right" attitudes. Such approaches employ a theory of balance (unbalance one element and other elements will also change to some degree) or a theory of cognitive dissonance (an individual will strive to reduce the lack of fit between one element and another by changing his VANE).

A caution is required at this point in regard to the notion that an attitude change necessarily implies a behavioural change. In general, behavioural scientists have oversimplified this attitude-behaviour change train by assuming a simple cause-and-effect relation between change in attitude and change in behaviour. In fact, an individual may change his attitude in general without changing it in regard to a particular person. For example, a training programme for supervisors may succeed in changing their attitudes in general towards trade unionists without changing their specific attitudes to the shop stewards with whom they have to interact in their work situation. The general conclusion of research in changing attitudes and behaviours is that not only should the training seek to change attitudes, but a new repertoire of behaviours must be induced.

Any attempt to directly explore or change a person's behaviour is unlikely to succeed unless the reward-sanction system is particularly strong, as for example in a prison. The reason for this resistance is that an individual's personality is structured and organized to limit the amount of damage that can be done to it; and normally he also holds himself in good esteem. The individual's self-concept has to fit with his VANE, even if the real world has to be changed a little to fit this model.

When an individual feels threatened, he acts defensively. He reduces the amount of information by restructuring the stimulus (changing his perception), thus restructuring his response to a stereotype which may only give faint clues as to what his real VANE is. As Freud discovered, if you want to get to know an individual's personality (his VANE), he must be placed in a nonthreatening environment where he can feel free to express himself; and this is exactly what psychoanalysis does.

It is possible to flesh out the VANE model in various ways. Values may be classified as traditional or existential. Attitudes might be characterized as autocratic versus democratic or liberal versus conservative (with any such term rated on a scale from weak to strong). Needs may be ego needs, social needs, self-actualization needs, or physiological needs (such as safety). Expectations may be high or low, and of several kinds. The model will be examined in more detail in Chapter 7.

Given only the framework of the model, we can see what may happen when the individual feels threatened. As an example, suppose that a low-income worker receives the information that members of a disadvantaged minority are being recruited and trained to do the kind of work that is his employment. His value system may respond, "You can't count on anybody but yourself" (traditional), or "Everyone deserves a chance, but what about me?" (existential). His attitudes may be such expressions as, "Society is coming apart at the seams. Even the TV is full of 'them'" (autocratic), or "I'm not against change, there's just too much of it" (conservative). He may feel anxious about social needs—"My neighbors won't respect me if this happens"; very basic physiological needs—"I need the money; I've got my family to think about"; or ego needs he can scarcely express himself—the unconscious need to be better than somebody else (the threatening "them"). He may expect the "best" or the "worst" to happen. All of these and many other tangential workings of his VANE may produce, to the observer, only some stereotype response: "I'm against this," or "Who needs this? Haven't I got enough troubles?"

Examination of such examples suggests certain general principles:

1. Not all elements in the system can be fitted together.
2. People have a high need to avoid cognitive dissonance.
3. Some elements in the system will have to be changed to be made to fit. The threat can be increased; the examination of values can be suppressed; expectations can be changed.
4. The effect of achieving a fit can only be realized by applying pressure to the elements, which inevitably generates tension.

SOME MODELS OF CHANGE

How can change be achieved and then integrated? One answer is by going at the problem indirectly or tangentially. This was the most significant finding that emerged from the counselling programme at Hawthorne. Instead of approaching the workers directly through a structured interview, which might satisfy the VANE of the interviewer, the employee was encouraged to talk about what was important to him. The interviewer adopted a generally supportive, nonstructuring attitude, and much useful intelligence about employee attitudes was collected, which turned out to be invaluable in training programmes for supervisors. The employee achieved catharsis or release of emotional tension through talking things out (in many cases, matters quite unconnected with his work).

The important theoretical point is that a person, in revealing his VANE in this supportive context, can release some of his tension by:

1. Realizing he is not unique.
2. Putting elements of his VANE together in a different way.
3. Identifying elements that require further work.

At the same time as the Hawthorne studies, a similar technique was being developed by Carl Rogers. In his client-centered therapy, the counsellor adopted a permissive, supportive, nondirective role where the interviewee could set his own goal and direction of change. People were helped to change themselves by developing a collaborative relation between the changer and the changee.

The first person to exploit this new change ethos in a commercial way was Dale Carnegie. His *How To Win Friends and Influence People* implicitly recognizes that to effect changes in the other person it is first necessary to change his VANE, and that this can be achieved by developing a relationship valuable to the other person and then using the relationship as a lever to effect the desired change. While it was always fashionable to ridicule the Carnegie approach, the transactional analysis approach of "stroking" takes up where Carnegie leaves off. Hence the recent success of Eric Berne's *Games People Play* and Thomas Harris's *I'm OK—You're OK*: one "hooks" and "strokes" the other's not-OK VANE in order to bring out his OK elements. More scientifically, such approaches use the theory of cognitive dissonance and balance illustrated in Figure 6–6.

Edgar H. Schein from the Massachusetts Institute of Technology has come up with an excellent model for changing values, attitudes, needs, and expectations. For nearly 20 years, Schein has been preoccupied with the question of how attitudes are transformed, even when in the first instance the subject may be most unwilling. Schein developed his conceptual model from his studies of the Chinese Communist techniques for controlling civilian and military prisoners during and after the Korean war. He based it on Kurt Lewin's unfreezing-changing-refreezing model, which looks deceptively simple. Putting it in the framework of this chapter, the change agent shakes up the changee's VANE, changes it, and then integrates it again. Change will not occur unless the changee is motivated and

FIGURE 6–6
THEORY OF BALANCE MODEL

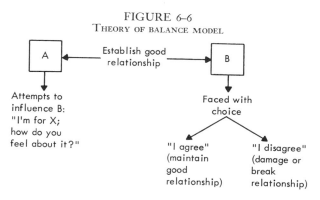

ready to change. Since the individual's VANE is usually highly structured and integrated, mere exhortation or intellectual explanation will not be sufficient. In "Management Development as a Process of Influence," Schein describes the three steps as follows:

1. *Unfreezing:* an alteration of the forces acting on the individual, such that his stable equilibrium is disturbed sufficiently to motivate him and to make him ready to change; this can be accomplished either by increasing the pressure to change or by reducing some of the threats or resistances to change.
2. *Changing:* the presentation of a direction of change and the actual process of learning new attitudes. This process occurs basically by one of two mechanisms: *(a) identification*—the person learns new attitudes by identifying with and emulating some other person who holds those attitudes or *(b) internalization*—the person learns new attitudes by being placed in a situation in which new attitudes are demanded of him as a way of solving problems which confront him and which he can-

not avoid; he discovers the new attitudes essentially for himself, though the situation may guide him or make it probable that he will discover only those attitudes which the influencing agent wishes him to discover.

3. *Refreezing:* the integration of the changed attitudes into the rest of the personality and/or into ongoing significant emotional relationships.

This is just what the Chinese Communists did in what came to be known as "brainwashing" prisoners. By manipulating the overall situation —in particular by destroying the authority system, systematically separating the officers and NCO's from the enlisted men, and breaking up the informal groups—they began the process of unfreezing. Such devices as fixing confessions, selective delivery of mail, and offering prizes of fruit or cigarettes were used to manipulate in a systematic way the values and attitudes of the captives. As the prisoners' groups disintegrated, so did their values and norms. As their "old" values broke up, the captors applied considerable pressure to the prisoners to go through the motions of expressing values and attitudes supportive of the Chinese position. A key element in this process, as Schein points out, was that at the critical moment the Chinese would help the prisoner with rationalizations to help him in redrawing his cognitive map.

In the West, similar techniques are, of course, utilized in prisons and mental hospitals as a means of changing attitudes. Management development uses a rather similar model. In the management development context, unfreezing is facilitated by isolating students in a remote resort hotel and utilizing dramatic, gimmicky training devices which have a sure-fire capacity to break up the students' preconceptions. Of course, the whole operation has the seal of senior management approval. The unfreezing is followed by the actual changes which the training specialists have planned. To facilitate the refreezing process, which is usually completed after the student returns to work, the participants are given a chance to express themselves in an evaluation of the programme.

Schein's model of unfreezing, changing, and refreezing has considerable explanatory value and can be used to illuminate what happens when a neophyte joins an organization. The process of assimilating a new member of an organization is technically known as socialization. In the process of socialization, the new man's VANE is first unscrambled through some technique of information overload and then changed by forcing him to join a primary work group which demands value consonance from him; and finally his new VANE is fixed by institutionalization.

We will keep the VANE model in mind as we proceed to Topic 3, since its NE—needs and expectations—are what path-goal theory is all about. These two elements are also discussed more fully in Chapter 7, which deals with personality.

TOPIC 3
P-G man: The path-goal model

The more hard-headed North American organizational psychologists, who put great weight on the empirical end of the proposition that behavioural scientists should engage in "theoretically relevant empirical research," have come up with the extremely important concept of path-goal (P-G) man. The underlying idea is that modern man in our contemporary organizational society can make choices that reflect his preferences in terms of his utilities. The concept of P-G man received its initial thrust from the work of Victor Vroom, an organizational psychologist at the Carnegie-Mellon School of Industrial Administration, where H. A. Simon, the famous management polymath who made information and decision-making central concepts in organization theory, also works. Vroom argues that performance is a multiplicative function of motivation and ability:

$$Performance = f(M,A)$$

Motivation to perform a task can be assumed to vary with (1) the utilities of outcomes associated with the performance of that particular task and (2) the instrumentality (belief that performance and outcome are linked) of performance for achievement or avoidance of particular outcomes. In *Work and Motivation*, Vroom defines motivation as "a process governing choices, made by persons or lower organisms, among alternative forms of voluntary activity." This theory of motivation is complex and difficult to grasp and its fuller consideration is postponed until Chapter 7; but what is important to understand at this juncture is that it is a theory of decision making which is essentially outward looking. The presumption is that a man can make intelligent and rational estimates about the consequences of particular choices and how such consequences will affect his interests. Thus the theory presupposes that man can estimate expectancies (in terms of probabilities that range from 0 to 1) in regard to both whether he can carry through a particular task and the likelihood that his boss will notice his effort and reward him accordingly. It is further assumed that man can arrange his preferences in a hierarchy of particular outcomes; that is, he has a set of utilities on which he can base his choices. The theory claims that employees, both superiors and subordinates, are aware, at least intuitively, of the logical train presented in Figure 6–7.

Why is this theory so important? Perhaps the best answer in the first instance is that it avoids the general error of the human relations approach, which puts the cart before the horse by arguing that enhancing human satisfaction always leads to improved task performance. P-G theory gets the horse and cart in the right order by arguing that getting the task right

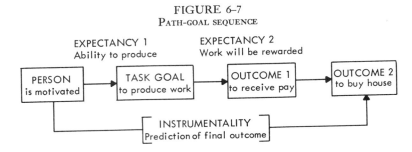

FIGURE 6–7
PATH-GOAL SEQUENCE

determines human satisfaction. This last point can be illustrated by considering some of the advantages of P-G theory in terms of its ability to explain findings which had previously seemed contradictory.

For example, P-G theory can explain why job enrichment programmes are not uniformly successful. Apparently many city workers have a preference for work which is routine and nonchallenging but well paid; they do not want to become overinvolved in the work situation and they believe that overproducing will put them out of court with other members of their work group. Workers from small towns, on the other hand, respond well to job enrichment; they appear to welcome challenging work which promises better pay and the prospect of promotion—which reflects their value identification with the middle classes and presumably with their bosses. What these empirical facts show is that these two groups of workers have different concepts of instrumentality and utility. These same concepts affect attitudes towards pay and performance among managers and professionals, many of whom apparently believe that rewards are unrelated to effort and largely reflect academic qualification and salary at the time of joining the organization.

If such empirical findings are true, management is compelled to adopt a different strategy from that suggested by the soft-centred human relations approach, where the answer is presumed to lie in making the implicit explicit, in getting the facts on the table and getting people to face up to them. A very different approach is suggested by P-G theory, where the emphasis must be on doing carefully thought-out empirical work to determine what employees' expectancies, utilities, and instrumentalities are; and then, presumably, setting out to change the structure of the situation to get what management and the workers want.

JOB DESIGN AND EXPECTANCY THEORY

In the continuous campaign to motivate employees to more effective performance, the changing of job design through techniques such as job enlargement or enrichment has often been advocated. E. E. Lawler makes use of expectancy theory to analyse the effects of such changes and the conditions which determine how they should be applied. (See Box 6.2.)

ox 6.2: P-G attitudes and job performance

Employee attitude surveys are an important tool for measuring the internal state of an organization. However, E. E. Lawler argues that their effectiveness in predicting absenteeism and turnover rates is not matched by their ability to predict job behaviour. What most surveys ignore, says Lawler, is the path-goal attitudes of the employees; that is, the type of behaviour they feel provides a path to the rewards that they value.

As an example, Lawler cites a survey which he conducted and which showed that the importance of money to managers has virtually no relationship to how hard they work. Only those managers who placed a high value on money and also felt that high performance was instrumental in obtaining it were prepared to exert greater effort for monetary reward. If pay was felt to be based on factors other than performance (such as education, for instance), even a satisfactory level of compensation failed to provide a strong motivating effect.

The importance of path-goal or reward expectancy attitudes is further illustrated in another study by Lawler ("Job Design and Employee Motivation"). The employees of an organization were quite dissatisfied with the promotion opportunities it offered despite the fact that a number of people had in fact been promoted. Investigation revealed that the promotions were not perceived to be based on good performance, so that other employees continued to have a low reward expectancy for good performance.

Lawler suggests that measurement of path-goal attitudes become the chief criterion for measuring the effectiveness of pay and promotion programs. By emphasizing the paths to rewards, leaders can increase motivation without necessarily raising the reward levels. Consistent administration of performance rewards and clear explanations to employees of how decisions are made is necessary to produce positive path-goal attitudes. It is suggested that a consensus of the subordinate's peers should be obtained before performance is rewarded, to insure that there is agreement on what is considered appropriate behaviour.

E. E. Lawler, "Attitude Surveys and Job Performance," *Personnel Administration*, September-tober, 1967, pp. 485–87.

Lawler contends that job design mainly affects the instrumentality of good performance, by clarifying and increasing the rewards. It is less relevant in changing the worker's expectancy concerning the amount of effort required to achieve "good" performance. The most powerfully motivating rewards are those which are internally mediated and thus available immediately when the worker feels that his performance has been good. They appeal to high-order needs such as self-esteem, self-actualization, and the use of valued abilities. Externally mediated rewards, such as recognition or pay, require that achievement be noticed and evaluated by other people and there is generally some perceptual distortion that makes the worker feel a discrepancy between his achievement and the outcome.

The content of the job will determine the extent to which employees will be able to derive feelings of accomplishment from good performance. Lawler lists three critical characteristics:

1. The employee must be provided with meaningful feedback on his performance.

2. Valued abilities must be utilized in performing the job effectively.
3. The individual must feel he has a high degree of control over the setting of goals and the paths to their attainment.

In changing job design to incorporate these characteristics, consideration must be given to both the horizontal and vertical dimensions. The horizontal dimension includes the number and variety of the operations an individual performs on the job. The vertical dimension includes the degree to which the jobholder controls the planning and execution of his job and participates in the setting of organization policies. Horizontal enlargement is desirable mainly to provide the worker with feedback through the production of something approximating a finished product, while vertical enlargement provides him with some control over his work environment. However, this control is most effective if it relates directly to the work process rather than to general company goals. Neither vertical nor horizontal enlargement ensures that employees will be able to utilize valued abilities. This and the possession of high-order needs are variables which may be quite different in any given situation.

Lawler points out that since the motivational effects of job enlargement are largely based on intrinsic factors, it is reasonable to expect that the worker's increased effort will be mainly directed toward achieving higher quality production. It may also be necessary to reduce the division of labour and the degree to which machinery can be utilized. It is not surprising, then, that heightened motivation does not manifest itself in greater quantity of output but rather in better quality and increased job satisfaction.

Not only has progress been made in terms of an individual theory of motivation, but a giant step forward has been taken by Robert House of the University of Toronto's School of Management. House has taken the P-G theory of motivation as modified by Cummings, Lawler, and others and developed a path-goal contingency theory which has considerable explanatory value. This theory will be considered in some detail in Chapter 9, on leadership.

The P-G contingency theory of leadership could not have come at a more opportune moment, for it arrived at a moment when F. E. Fiedler's leadership theory, which has held the field for almost 20 years, is coming under serious attack from two separate but related optics, one theoretical and the other statistical. Fiedler's genius had its origins in his concept of psychological distance, which can be thought of in terms of the ability to accept or reject subordinates on the basis of performance, and the concept that psychological distance is related to effectiveness. The relationship is contingent upon the nature of the task, the group atmosphere, and the amount of power the superior possesses. Thus Fiedler's theory is a contingency model which predicts a set of relations whose nature varies according to the situation. Now serious empirical findings are coming forward which do not fit the predictions of Fiedler's model; and many of Fiedler's sample populations are too small to allow firm conclusions about the relations between psychological distance and effectiveness. The other major criticism of Fiedler's model relates to the theoretical meaning of psychological distance: both academics and executives are in a quandary trying to figure out what the concept means.

It may well be asked why it is considered relevant to introduce the P-G concept of man at this stage and then drop it before exploring Fiedler's and House's theories. The answer, which takes a P-G form itself, is that much of what lies ahead is a necessary preamble to both understanding and evaluating the two contingency theories of leadership. We have introduced P-G man because he, like the S-R and S-O-R models of man, represents one way in which a response is connected to a stimulus. The question inevitably arises as to whether there are any generalized rules above this process of connection. This is exactly what learning theory is about, and it is to this topic we now turn.

TOPIC 4
Learning and the new training technology

All theories of organizational behaviour exploit or depend on the basic principles of human learning. Learning is such a common phenomenon that most executives take it for granted; yet modern experimental psychologists devote more time and resources to research on learning than any other topic in psychology. In the broadest terms learning refers to the development and modification of the tendencies that govern psychological functions. Such a definition avoids specific formulations of how learning in fact happens. In most basic learning situations it is possible to think of the learning process in terms of the linking of a particular stimulus to a particular response.

Our earlier discussion of stimulus-response models traced this concept back to Pavlov's Nobel prize-winning studies on the conditioned reflex. Pavlov introduced a number of terms of considerable explanatory value for the psychology of learning which have gained very wide currency. One such concept is the notion of reinforcement. Reinforcement is the reward or punishment which follows a particular response. Positive reinforcement refers to rewarding, and negative reinforcement to punishing, conditions. A reinforcer may be thought of as any object or event that has the effect of increasing the strength of the response.

FACTORS AFFECTING LEARNING

MOTIVATION

It is widely assumed that learning does not take place in the absence of motivation. Many experiments in the psychology of learning are being directed at determining the effects of different motives on the degree rate, or amount of learning. Skinner coined the term "operant condition-ing" to refer to the process of how the organism operates on the environ ment in order to get a reward. The word "operant" emphasizes the idea that the behaviour operates on the environment to produce consequences Skinner has carried out a large number of experiments with pigeons which have been trained to carry out fairly complex tasks using some form o operant conditioning. Such operant conditioning usually depends on some kind of reinforcement, which in the case of these animals usually takes the form of the reward of a small piece of food.

Most of the experimental work has been carried out with animals and i is difficult, if not impossible, to apply these findings to human learning. The law of effect (which states that rewarded behaviour is retained and punished behaviour is dropped) has achieved very wide currency and i widely used in explaining human learning, in the following way. If the person is striving to modify his behaviour and makes what is regarded as a positive adjustment, he is given positive feedback or a reinforcement which facilitates learning; if he makes a negative adjustment, he may be denied positive feedback and may well receive some form of negative feedback which inhibits further performance of that maladjustive act.

Knowledge of results is an important factor in the learning process, and the timing of the feedback of information is extremely important if the learning is to be made more effective. For example, an infantryman learn ing to shoot has to know immediately after he fires where his shot fell in the target area. Given this kind of feedback data, he is in a better position to modify his behaviour accordingly.

Knowledge of results also plays an important part in social learning For example, E. E. Smith and S. S. Knight in "Effects of Feedback on Insight and Problem-Solving Efficiency in Training Groups" report tha management trainees who met on a daily basis in small syndicates and re veiwed each other's managerial style showed a greater increase in self insight regarding their roles as leaders, and they also apparently improved in problem solving to a greater extent than their colleagues in the same training program who received no such daily feedback. It goes withou saying that individuals differ in their ability to cope with this kind of feed back. There is some evidence to support the view that persons who have high levels of aspiration, a marked need for accurate evaluation, and a strong desire for self-esteem positively welcome such feedback. In train ing, feedback is more acceptable if it is clear, relevant, and represents the shared and considered view of the group rather than the judgement of a single person. Perhaps it is just as well to point out at this stage that knowl edge of results is the most common, probably the most important, single source of reinforcement for the human learner.

Closely linked to the law of effect is the law of exercise, which argue that the more frequently one is placed in a learning situation the more effective the learning will be.

RELATIVE ECONOMY

Starting from the assumption that the subject is well motivated, the question then arises as to what the best procedures for developing efficiency are. For example, how should a person distribute his effort in learning? Should he practise steadily until he has mastered the skill or should he distribute his practice period, taking breaks in between? The burden of modern evidence suggests that over a wide range of situations, distributed practice is more effective than massed practice. A certain amount of caution is required in interpretation of this finding. For example, while this proposition is true in the question of motor skills, when the material to be studied is brief and relatively easy massed practice has some advantage. Again, with complex tasks a varied strategy may well prove more effective.

WHOLE VERSUS PART

A great deal of work has been done in the psychology of learning to decide whether learning the whole job is superior to breaking the job into parts and learning the parts. In parts learning, the individual is not only required to learn each individual part but he must be able to combine the separate parts so that the whole performance can be accomplished. No simple overall conclusion has been reached in this field.

R. S. Woodworth and H. Schlosberg in *Experimental Psychology* have observed:

> The net result of all the studies of whole and part learning seems to be something like this: the parts are easier to learn and the learner is often happier and better adjusted to the problem when beginning with the parts. . . . But he finds that putting together the parts is a serious problem requiring much further work. In the end he may have saved time and energy by commencing with the parts—or he may not—much depending on the size and difficulty of the total task and on the learner's poise and technique. In a practical situation it is probably best to start with the whole method while feeling free to concentrate at any time on a part where something special is to be learned.

LEARNING CURVES

An extremely useful concept for understanding the phenomenon of learning which is valid for a wide range of learning situations is the notion of the learning curve, as illustrated in Figure 6–8. The learning curve gives a diagrammatic presentation of the amount learned in relation to time. A typical learning curve will show on the y axis the amount learned and on the x axis the passage of time. Figure 6–8 represents a generalized learning curve and shows the extent to which the rate of learning increases or decreases with practice.

FIGURE 6-8
DIAGRAM OF A GENERALIZED LEARNING CURVE

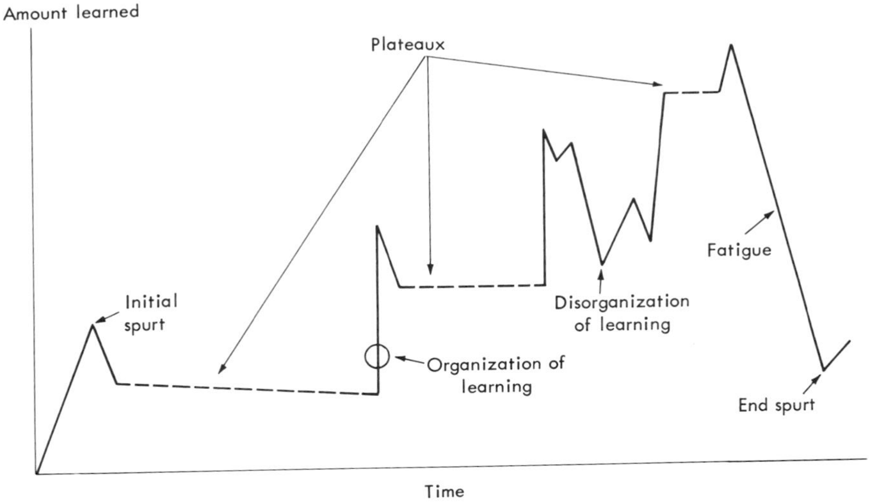

There are certain general characteristics of learning curves. For example, at the beginning the rate of learning frequently shows a spurt. Usually the graph levels off at some stage, indicating that maximum performance has been achieved. Apparently at the beginning of the learning process, the subject is very highly motivated and seems to exhibit a significant surge of effort. Many experienced trainers exploit this initial spurt by selecting the most important items to be communicated and presenting them as a package to the students at the beginning of the training unit. In many ways it is possible to exemplify the initial spurt with the aphorism "the first step is the best step."

Plateaux

Another extremely common characteristic of learning curves is the phenomenon of learning plateaux. At some point in the learning process there is usually a flattening off in terms of improvement, a plateau. Frequently the process of learning is marked by discontinuities and involves escalating from one plateau to another. Most subjects in the learning situation are only too aware of the experience of finding themselves on a plateau, which manifests itself in the feeling that they are never going to get anywhere. It is perhaps just as well to point out at this juncture that Figure 6-8 represents a purely hypothetical presentation and that actual learning curves show a considerable degree of irregularity. Nevertheless, examination of such learning curves reveals plateaux in which no learning appears to be taking place.

The escalation from one plateau to another is usually described as organization of learning. Organization of learning is achieved when a new and more effective way is discovered by the subject for performing particular tasks. For example, in learning to drive a car the escalation from one plateau to another is achieved when the trainee discovers that he can locate the gear shift by kinæsthetic feedback rather than by visually searching for the actual shift stick. Much the same escalation takes place with more academic subjects—when, for example, in the case of mathematics the student learns to apply calculus in dealing with the problem of simple harmonic motion.

Besides the organization of learning, we also have disorganization of learning, where there is an actual fall-off in performance. This fall-off or disorganization very frequently arises when the subject has to choose (frequently he is not consciously aware of the choice) between alternative methods of tackling the task. At the early stage of such a choice, the relative advantage of the more effective method over the less may only be marginal. The disorganization of learning inevitably produces emotional correlates in the behaviour of the subjects concerned and can lead to the generation of considerable frustration, anxiety, and even guilt. Very highly planned training programmes for the acquisition of operator skills have managed successfully to eliminate this feature of disorganization of learning, but with more complex skills and learning situations the student can expect considerable disorganization in the learning process, with appropriate emotional correlates.

The end spurt

Yet another aspect of the generalized learning curve is the phenomenon of fatigue. If the subject has experienced long exposure to the learning situation, the presumption is that there will be a fall-off in performance with time. This phenomenon of fatigue is not equally valid for all learning situations; it has more relevance to the question of motor skills but less relevance for the performance of simple clerical tasks such as adding or subtracting groups of digits. One other feature of the learning curve is the end spurt, which refers to the fact that when the subject knows the training session is coming to an end there appears to be a brief resurgence of interest and effort. As is well known, the more effective after-dinner speaker exploits this by prefacing the last quarter of his speech with the remark "finally" followed in the next minute by "to sum up," then "lastly" followed by "my penultimate point is . . ." and then "Before I sit down."

Many very effective speakers seem to be aware intuitively of the characteristics of the learning curve and to exploit them systematically, thus ensuring a very high standard of presentation. It is possible to combine the idea of a learning curve with the concept of Gestalt psychology that "the whole is more than the sum of its parts" to produce very slick aphorisms to describe how lectures should be structured. A good example of such an aphorism is "tell them what you are going to tell them, tell them, and then tell them what you've told them."

THE NEW TRAINING TECHNOLOGY

A revolution is coming in education as college campuses begin to absorb new technologies such as programmed learning (PL), computer-assisted learning (CAL), and video-tape recording (VTR). The Carnegie Commission on Higher Education estimates that within the next three decades between 10 and 20 per cent of campus instruction and 50 per cent of off-campus education will be carried out by television, PL, CAL, and the use of cassettes and other electronic devices. This dramatic use of electronic resources for education has. been termed "the fourth revolution." The first revolution was the shift from home instruction to education in the school; the second was the adoption of the written word as an education tool; the third was the exploitation of printing and the use of books. The fourth revolution is essentially electronic in character; and it allows the student to play the same lesson over and over again. It should become possible to define as the criterion of performance for a course that 80 per cent of participants will score more than 90 per cent. The reason for this fantastically high level of performance is that each student will be able to learn at his own rate, with feedback about his performance built into each educational event.

Three examples of the new training technology were described in the *New York Times* on April 6, 1972:

> A student in a special campus laboratory sits at a computerized typewriter with a Russian keyboard and, as he receives instructions through his earphones, he types sentences in Russian. The voice on the earphones prods and corrects.
> Students in a classroom absorb a history lesson from a professor seen on a television screen and register their responses through a transmitter that keeps the instructor informed of their progress and permits him to change the topic, if necessary, by remote control.
> A student in his dormitory room slips a cassette into a machine and listens to a play or a panel discussion as part of a course.

Already the hardware, the actual technology, exists, and educationalists are preparing the tapes which form the software of this electronic revolution. The advantages of the new training technology include:

1. Students can learn at their own pace, on their own.
2. "Disadvantaged learners" can engage in overexposure by increasing their frequency of learning.
3. Central institutions can prepare tapes which smaller colleges can use, thus widening their offerings.
4. Professors will not need to repeat courses ad infinitum and ad nauseam.

This fourth revolution in education will require a new breed of teacher who can programme computers, who has an advanced knowledge of learning theory and behaviour technology, and who knows how to use the expertise of the expert. There is one disadvantage—the new training technology will reduce further the contact the student has with a "live" teacher. For those who do not immediately perceive this as a disadvantage, it must be said that a good teacher, if he has the teaching programme (the step-by-step analysis of the particular lesson), can teach as effectively as any machine and may well have a better personality. Certainly neither student nor teacher can lose if the drill work and the sardine-can lecture hall where hundreds of students listen to a monotonous drone can be replaced. Just as certainly, both have much to gain if the replacement leads to creative use of the time gained for small discussion groups, seminars, and the kind of human interaction that can never be replaced in the learning process—and which gives it its flavor, its fun, its kicks.

TOPIC 5
A critical review of behavioural technology

SOME ACHIEVEMENTS

What can behavioural technology do? Almost everything. Figure 6–9 lists some of its aspects which we have discussed or will take up in later chapters. A good subject to consider is motivation. Some 20 years ago Ernst Dichter showed what a knowledge of motivation research could do when applied to the marketing of automobiles. He showed that men regard cars not only as a means of transportation but also as status, power, and sex objects. As every driver knows, "Hit my car, hit me." The car is an extension of the driver's personality, and the connection between his foot and the gas pedal becomes an extension of his being. With these not unreasonable assumptions, it is easy to believe that some male drivers see convertibles (especially the red variety) as the steed struggling at the bit to take them to their mistresses, real or imaginary. But most men buy family saloons in spite of their male chauvinist pig aspirations. Thus the powerful, low-slung convertible (Cougar, Dart, XK 140) is put in the window of the showroom to lure the family man in to buy his standard sedan, which has the outward signs of his fantasies but the inward graces of the family buggy.

Not a very telling example. Old hat. And so it is, compared with the modern techniques of motivation modeling, which can turn insipid, boring, lacklustre executives into go-getter tigers who will hustle to get the job done on schedule. To examine this behavioural alchemy, we have to turn to the work of Frederick Herzberg and David C. McClelland.

FIGURE 6–9
BEHAVIOURAL TECHNOLOGIES

Level	Technology	Basic strategy	Location
Individual	Aversion therapy	Modifying deviant behaviour through use of an aversive stimulus to discourage undesirable responses.	Chapter 6
	Behaviour modification	Controlling strategy of reinforcements.	Chapter 6
	Motive acquisition	Developing the need to achieve.	Chapter 7
	Attitude changing	Changing people's attitudes in terms of good performances.	Chapter 6
Group	T group	Used as a means of studying group dynamics to facilitate team management.	Chapter 16
	Synectics	Developed as a means of making groups more creative.	Chapter 11
	Brainstorming	Developed to get work groups to find unusual solutions.	Chapter 15
Organization	Organizational development	To train the system; to get organizations to move from one stage to another.	Chapter 16
	Process consultancy	To induce new existential life styles into work groups through change strategy— unfreezing, changing, refreezing.	Chapter 16
	Intervention strategy	To intervene in an organization to confront executives with the actualities of their own behaviour.	Chapter 16
	Action research	To encourage participative management (the Glacier and Harwood research projects).	Chapter 5
	Conflict management	To arouse, mobilize, direct, and dissipate conflict.	Chapter 14

Herzberg's theory of motivation, based on evidence which respected psychologists suspect is a function of the experimental design employed, swept North America in the 1960s and (like the 1918 flu in reverse) is percolating into Europe in the 1970s. Herzberg "proved" that people work best when they are given recognition, achievement, and personal growth and claimed that things like money, interpersonal relations, and company policy get them only to the zero point on the job satisfaction scale. In spite of the scientific evidence to the contrary, executives (especially ones on the way up) love this theory and it is almost impossible to get it out of the system as it wanders round like solar debris. It seems to be the opposite number of the saying, "Truth will not tolerate error." Perhaps the important conclusion to draw from this "Herzberg heresy" is that both the research method and the executive "motivation theory" preferences should be examined (as they are in our next chapter) in a nitty-gritty fashion.

More formidable from a scientific point of view is the work of David C. McClelland of Harvard University, who has spent a lifetime studying the need to achieve (*n Ach*) and has come up with the conclusion that the colder countries like the United States, Norway, Sweden, and Canada are full of people who are high in *n Ach* and the hotter countries are low in such people. But, fortunately, *n Ach* can be taught. If you are a black, a Mexican, or an Indian, you can be put through a 10-day course which builds up this need, as a muscle which has lain dormant too long can be given a suitable regime of calisthenics. The evidence is too strong and convincing to discard McClelland's claims as just another example of American imperialism or the Calvinist gospel (of course, there is an implicit assumption that *n Ach* is a good thing).

If the other guy's motivation is up for grabs, what about his perceptions, emotions, behaviours? The answer is that they can all be changed. The problem is identifying the conditions that favour the desired change. As an example, psychologists have shown a diabolical genius for making and breaking conflict at will. You can take your neurosis along to your psychologist and trade it in for something less offensive or frightening. There appears to be no limit to the kinds of changes that can be produced.

Psychologists must accept a major slice of the glory and the blame for the new value systems that are emerging in the swing from the three A's of aggression, achievement, and affluence to the contemporary values of authenticity, actualization, and awareness. These new values take cognizance of complexity, interdependence, uncertainty. Figure 6–10 illustrates how behavioural technology can be used to achieve value changes.

FIGURE 6–10
CHANGING TRADITIONAL VALUES TO EXISTENTIAL ONES

UNFREEZING
Traditional values: Achievement—"Making it"   Self-control—"Watch it!"   Independence—"I did it my way"   Endurance—"Grin and bear it"
CHANGING   Behavioural technology techniques
REFREEZING
Existential values: Self-actualization—"What I can be, I must"   Self-expression—"Do your own thing"   Interdependence—"Let's all pull together"   Capacity for joy—"Right on!"

A CAUTION

Behavioural technology as a branch of applied psychology is dependent on pure psychology as a source of theory, concept, method, and data. The surprising thing is that with the number of psychologists increasing at the present rate, the discipline of psychology is not equal to the needs of society in terms of generating relevant theory and research.

Psychology, a remarkable diverse subject, is torn with dissension and often seems at odds with both itself and such cognate disciplines as sociology and psychiatry. Internecine warfare has long been the order of the day within psychology: clinical therapist against behaviourist, "brass instrument" man against personologist, "rat man" against "shrink." At one time it was fashionable to believe that this conflict was merely the growing pains inevitable in such a complex field as human behaviour and that eventually a stable, eclectic science would emerge. In fact, it has not worked out like that. In such subject areas as organizational behaviour, both executives and academics are hung up because adequate theoretical constructs are just not available.

A major criticism of psychological theory and method relates to the fact that so much of it is based on experiments with the albino variety of the brown rat. To many executives, and to a good number of psychologists, this type of research seems irrelevant and out of touch with real human needs. Critics of the approach argue that the albino rat is an atypical organism on which to base generalizations about human behaviour. Even more dangerous is the fact that research on the social behaviour of animals in captivity has produced particularly misleading results; it is now recognized that zoos drive apes psycho. In "Primate Behaviour," I. Devore persuasively points out:

> From the perspective of modern field studies, the conclusions based on the behaviour of primates in captivity bore as little relation to the behaviour of free-ranging groups as would a monograph on middle-class society based solely on a study of inmates in a maximum-security prison

At the level of using human subjects in experiments, psychologists typically take the bodies or minds which are handiest, namely first-year students in psychology classes. Not surprisingly, students come into laboratories with behaviour and attitudes which are not always matched outside the laboratory. C. I. Hovland has shown that in the laboratory up to half the subjects show attitude changes, whereas in the field the proportion is only 1 in 20. Apparently the students who take part in such experiments work on the assumption that there exists a laboratory culture with one rule: "Go along with the researcher, no matter how crazy, absurd, ridiculous, or unethical his experiments seem."

Another unfortunate aspect is that psychologists select problems, usually on the basis of reading professional journals, rather than having to dea with the problems that people worry most about. In "Will Psychologists Study Human Problems?" N. Sanford argues that psychology "is fragmented, overspecialized, method-centered, and dull" and that psychologists write primarily for academic journals; these "journals do not tempt the reader and tend to be cluttered with inflated jargon rather than with psychological insights." The research findings are not integrated; many cannot be. In spite of sophisticated design and data handling, much of the research is irrelevant and dull. Worse still, too many psychologists are reluctant to tackle real live problems.

Unlike their brothers in the physical sciences and technology, psychologists have shown little ability (except in times of great crisis, such as a world war) in translating laboratory research into an operational setting. For example, in 1962, some 30 per cent of the space in psychology journals (60 percent in the *Journal of Experimental Psychology*) was devoted to reports on learning research. Curiously, both academic and applied psychologists agree that only a very limited percentage of learning research has had any practical value. It can come as no surprise to executives to learn that there are communication problems among psychologists themselves because of technical jargon.

Not all of the social sciences have made equal progress. Kenneth Boulding believes that economics has produced some notable successes, especially through Keynesian methods. Unfortunately the human sciences have not made the same progress, although organizational studies had some striking successes in the 1950s and 1960s, especially the work of H. A. Simon. All social sciences have great problems in application; we need not look far to see what political and social pressures do to economic models in the existential situation. What has happened in our own field is even more severe: a new focus of study has been identified, namely, the organization; but as yet the empirical study of the organization per se has been limited, fragmented, and simplistic.

In spite of—and because of—all these problems, there has been a dramatic and significant change in the zeitgeist of behavioural science in the last decade. Most scientists—including a great number of behavioural scientists—believe that science is mainly concerned with the "facts," facts being "objective truths" about the world. Now this perspective—what Liam Hudson, professor of educational sciences at Edinburgh University, calls the *Cult of the Fact*—is being challenged, for much of what behavioural scientists have produced by way of research is trivial and occasionally malign. At the heart of Hudson's criticism lies the application of Werner Heisenberg's principle of uncertainty ("the very process of measurement interferes with what is being measured") as it applies to the behavioural sciences.

Behavioural science students, turned off by the sterility and triviality of the superficial approaches of some psychologists, are turning to R. D. Laing, Erich Fromm, and Rollo May to find out about their complicated

Organizational behaviour

and convoluted inner feelings, their doubts and apprehensions, their aspirations, values, and hopes. R. D. Laing, for example, has had a tremendous effect on the minds of American and British students in the last five years, essentially because he has been concerned with the process of how one person becomes acquainted with another. In Laing one does not find the "detached" observer of classical science or, for that matter, the traditional psychiatrist, but a human being trying to help people who are struggling in the midst of the existential miasma to understand what is happening to them and to give meaning to their lives. To understand this new approach to behaviour, it is useful to think of man as an information-processing and image-making system. To get inside his inner experiences, it is necessary to develop a more complex model of man which recognizes his values, attitudes, needs, and expectations and how such elements often reveal contradictions when they are fitted together in his self-concept. This new model essentially involves an existential systems approach to personality.

AN EVALUATION

Behavioural technologists believe, correctly in my opinion, that there are myriad ways in which man's behaviour can be controlled. The wide variety of techniques varies from the relatively simple operant conditioning through which children learn multiplication tables to the complex strategies of the T group trainer and the military brainwasher, who can get people to tell all, to let it all hang out, and to experience conversion. Newer and more dramatic techniques are constantly being developed. José Delgado, a Yale professor of medicine, has demonstrated the technique known as ESB (electrical stimulation of the brain) by doctoring a bull before it entered the ring, placing in its brain electrodes which could be activated by radio signals. When the bull charged, Delgado (who was no matador) literally switched it off. He has used similar techniques with human beings, for example to help patients suffering from epilepsy. The implications of such research are indeed awesome.

Behavioural technology has been called "Faustian power" and is frequently seen as the machinations of the devil himself, as reflected in the myths of Prometheus, Icarus, and Dr. Faustus. "Those who have explicitly avowed an interest in control have been roughly treated by history," notes B. F. Skinner in "Some Issues Concerning the Control of Human Behaviour" (Rogers and Skinner). "Machiavelli is the great prototype. As Macaulay said of him, 'Out of his surname they coined an epithet for a knave and out of his Christian name a synonym for the devil.'" But how potent is behavioural technology? Are there any limits or constraints on its development?

One constraint is contained in the fact that man's behaviour is a function of both heredity and environment. It is a curiosity of modern social science that anyone taking up the heredity function is regarded as a fascist, a social wrecker, a criminal, a person to be despised. So much abuse has been hurled at the heads of those who emphasize the role of heredity as opposed to environment in explaining human behaviour that a group of psychologists and geneticists from several countries jointly signed a resolution noted in *The (London) Times* on August 20, 1972:

> "Suppression, censure, punishment and defamation" are being applied against hereditarian scientists, the Resolution says. "Published positions are often misquoted and misrepresented: emotional appeals replace scientific reasoning; arguments are directed against the man rather than the evidence, e.g., a scientist is called a 'Fascist,' and his arguments are ignored."
>
> In academic circles, the Resolution goes on, "it is virtually heresy to express a hereditarian view, or to recommend further study of the biological bases of behaviour. A kind of orthodox environmentalism dominates the liberal academy."

This strongly worded resolution, signed by Nobel laureates Francis Crick and John Kendrew and psychologist H. J. Eysenck among others, is part of the fall-out from a controversy triggered off in the early 1970s by a paper by Arthur Jensen of the University of California, who argued that intelligence quotients are largely determined by heredity and that the gap in the I.Q.'s of whites and blacks in the United States might be partly due to heredity.

The important point to note in our discussion is that behaviour is a function of both heredity and environment, and thus the existence of heredity may be a sizable constraint on the kind of behavioural change that is possible. For example, most psychologists who specialize in mental measurement believe that intelligence is about 75 to 80 per cent determined by heredity (which leaves considerable latitude for determining differences in I.Q. between whites and blacks in environmental terms, to comment further on "the Jensen affair"—leaving aside the question of whether I.Q. tests have anything to do with intelligence).

Thus the ultimate step in behaviour control, going beyond even such techniques as ESB, is to change the person's heredity by changing his genes. This takes us into the realm of genetic engineering, which is where the action is in biology since the subject was changed from a descriptive to an analytical science by the research of James Watson and F. H. C. Crick, who discovered the structure of DNA and started molecular biology.

Attempting to portray behavioural technology as a sytem (see Figure 6–11) thus reminds us of many flaws and dysfunctions. The structure—the models of man as an individual and in groups—has not been defined as satisfactorily as could be wished. Many of the processes—the techniques—work spectacularly well; but the value system employing them is badly in need of scrutiny by both specialists in the field and society in gen-

FIGURE 6–11
BEHAVIOURAL TECHNOLOGY AS A SYSTEM

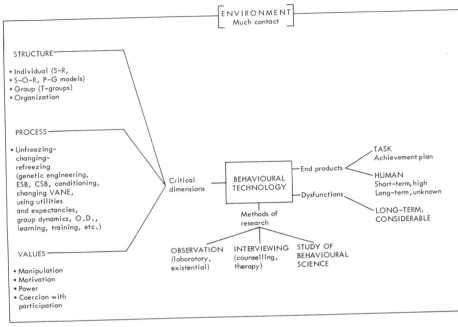

eral. Some of the techniques are as potentially explosive as "the bomb" (genetic engineering, ESB and CSB); will they likewise simply be developed in the lab and used as expedient, with evaluation and control only peripheral or by hindsight?

As we have noted, the methods of research are perhaps the most unsatisfactory element of this system. Laboratory methods are largely sterile and irrelevant. Interviewing, counselling, and study at the individual level has been fragmented and lacking in cohesion. At the group level, some progress has been made, but not as much as might have been made if social psychologists would study real groups doing real things. It was George Homans who reminded his students of Nelson's advice to his captains before Trafalgar, "If in doubt about what to do, lay alongside the enemy"; and Homans added his own advice that much the same could be said about the study of groups.

The most important development in group dynamics related to behavior control has been the work in T group technology. This study has mapped out the anatomy and physiology of how groups explore groups but it had only limited value until the T group became the handmaiden of organizational development (O.D.). And the criticism par excellence of O.D. is that it is largely concerned with changing the ideology of the work group, which leaves the corporate executive on his own. Thus the captain of applied behavioural technology often tries a little of Dale Carnegie, splashes in a little of Hawthorne, takes a dash of Herzberg, and fills up the rest of his glass with Theory X carrots and sticks topped off with a layer of Theory Y.

Management has always been the business of getting results through people, usually whether they like it or not. Thus, perforce, managers have been ready to step into the field of behaviour control; their very willingness has often been the unstated premise of the human relations school. But with such behaviour control, all is not completely predictable. "You can't win them all" reflects a policy preference as well as a consequence of limited ability to predict. For perfect prediction predicates persons unpersoned. Human beings, being human, prefer to err as proof of their humanity. Perhaps the resultant element of the existential bizarre cannot be removed from the equation; but the attempt must be made to exert some control over chaotic reality.

We have now completed Part One of our presentation, which has discussed organization theories, methods, and technologies. The theories set out the big pictures or scenarios of organizational life, which vary all the way from the organization as administrative machine to the idea of the organization as an information-processing system which is trying to grow, adapt, survive, and learn. The methods tell us how "the facts" are collected and the technologies tell us how to change the facts. Now that we have set out the larger structure, we can turn to look at the basic concepts of organizational behaviour.

REVIEW AND RESEARCH

1. Why are executives attracted to behavioural technology?
2. What is behaviourism? What are the arguments for and against this approach to human behaviour?
3. How can behaviour modification be used in industry?
4. What developments in technology will favour the development of behavioural technology? In your answer consider developments in computers, lie detectors (including ECG and EEG machines), sleep technology, programmed learning, and computer-assisted learning.
5. What are the advantages of the VANE model?
6. Why is T group technology so widely used today?
7. Who is P-G man? How does he operate at work?
8. Describe an experience where you have either manipulated somebody or been manipulated yourself. Consider the following headings: trick used, relation established, power factor, information control, feelings afterward.
9. What is learning? How can you make your own learning more effective?
10. How can the new training technologies be applied in business organizations?
11. Critically evaluate behavioural technology.

GLOSSARY

Attitude. A predisposition to evaluate an object or idea in a favourable or un favourable manner. Attitudes describe mental states of readiness for emo tional arousal and have four functions: instrumental (used to get some where), ego-defensive (staying "together"), value-expressive (life style) an cognitive (make knowledge meaningful).

Behavioural technology. An emerging science of control that aims to chang human behaviour by applying principles discovered through behavioural sci ence research to real-life situations.

Behaviourism. The school of psychology which defines psychology as the posi tive science of behaviour. Behaviourism, which uses S-R psychology, concen trates on the study of the linkage between the stimulus and the respons elicited.

Behaviour modification. A form of training developed by psychologists wh follow B. F. Skinner's approach and who set out to change behaviour syste matically by regulating the use of rewards and punishments as reinforce ments. Behavior modification, which exploits S-R psychology, aims to chang individual responses by changing the subject's environment.

Conditioned response. A response that has been imprinted through repeate presentation of a stimulus reinforcement.

ESB and CSB. Electrical and chemical stimulation of the brain as a means o controlling behaviour; have been used with both animals and humans and ar likely to be a major area of future development in organizational behaviou

Law of exercise. The principal that the more frequently one is placed in learning situation, the more effective the learning will be.

Learning. The development and modification of the tendencies that gover psychological functions. In its simplest form it is the development of th ability to link a particular stimulus to a particular response.

Learning curve. A diagrammatic presentation of the amount learned in rela tion to time. A typical learning curve will show on the y axis the amoun learned and on the x axis the passage of time.

Operant conditioning. A term coined by B. F. Skinner which refers to th process of the organism operating on its environment in order to get a reward

Ratomorphic fallacy. A coined description of the fallacy of attributing to ma the processes that have been demonstrated only in lower animals.

Reinforcement. Strengthening behavioural conditioning through the reward o punishment following a particular response.

T *Group technology.* A decisive turning point in the search for change strate gies which management could exploit to make things happen the way the wanted in business. Group dynamics exploits the rules, roles, and relation ships that emerge in an unstructured group situation with guidance (no direction) from a trained resource person.

VANE *model.* A further explication of the S-O-R model, where 0 stands fo the organism. The organism contains values, attitudes, needs, and expecta tions which affect perceptions and thus behaviour. Attempts to directly ex plore or change behaviour are resisted by the VANE unless they can b organized into the person's self-concept.

Part two

Basic concepts: Individuals, groups, and organizations

The theme of this section is examining basic concepts which concern the individual, the group, and the organization. Looking first at the personality and motivation of the individual leads into the subject of his role in the group. Group dynamics are at work as the individual is socialized into the larger structure, the organization. Leadership is a pivotal subject as the individual moves into his group role and into the organizational environment, culminating in the process by which leaders of organizations make decisions.

CHAPTER 7: PERSONALITY AND MOTIVATION

Chapter 7 is concerned with both the executive personality and the need for the executive to understand personality theory. Existential man has values, attitudes, needs, and expectations which affect his perception of the world as he struggles for identity. Man as an information-processing system searches for meaning. As part of his search he needs the kind of map of his own unconscious processes provided by the great psychologist Sigmund Freud. "What makes Johnny run," his motivation, includes his hierarchy of needs and expectations. The topics in this chapter are:

1. Personality as an open system.
2. The existential concept of personality.
3. The structure of personality.
4. The Freudian concept.
5. Motivation.
6. The executive personality.

CHAPTER 8: GROUP DYNAMICS

The chapter on group dynamics is concerned with a larger Gestalt, and it examines how the group shapes personality into roles. How a role is shaped and then shapes other roles through the norm of reciprocity and the ascription of status leads naturally to the subject of conformity, without which groups would fall apart. The topic of socialization emphasizes the theories of Edgar Schein and H. C. Kellman about how people are influenced. All of the theories about groups are, finally, related to the primary working group. The topics of Chapter 8 are:

1. Structure, process, and values of groups.
2. Role and status.
3. Conformity.
4. Socialization.
5. The primary working group.

CHAPTER 9: LEADERSHIP

Chapter 9 begins with the question of whether there is a leader type whose traits can be identified and measured. What are the situational roles? Is it better to be task-oriented or human relations–oriented? The answer depends on the contingencies. F. E. Fiedler's contingency theory and Robert House's path-goal contingency theory are discussed in detail. The assessment of leadership potential includes that critical moment for the would-be executive, the interview. If he passes such hurdles, the organizational leader will need help in developing his strategies. The chapter topics are:

1. Trait approach and group approach.
2. Fiedler's contingency theory.
3. House's path-goal theory.
4. Identifying leadership potential.
5. Strategies of organizational leadership.

CHAPTER 10: THE ORGANIZATION AND ITS ENVIRONMENT

Chapter 10 deals with the organization's immediate (economic) and more remote environments. We take the approach that the organization's environment is a flow of information, and that it can range from placid to turbulent. What the climate is, is one subject; how it is perceived by managers is another. The topics of this chapter are:

1. The economic environment.
2. The environment as a flow of information.
3. Organizational climate: The environment perceived.

CHAPTER 11: THE DECISION PROCESS

The environment as a flow of information obviously affects decision making, which is the subject of Chapter 11. The decision process includes the collection, processing, and distribution of information. What are the dynamics of decision making? Who are the deciders, and how do they decide? These are the questions which our review of the decision subsystem attempts to answer. The chapter topics are:

1. Search and decide.
2. The dynamics of decision making.
3. Review of the decision subsystem.

7

Personality and motivation

It is impossible to give a full and comprehensive account of executive behaviour without raising questions of why. For example, Why do effective executives spend so much time on personnel matters? Why don't they concentrate their efforts on production? When we ask such questions regarding executive behaviour, we are trying to explore questions of motivation. Motivation is concerned with the study of the direction and persistence of action. Personality is the organizing centre around which the motives of man form a unified and integrated system. In particular, the aim of this chapter is to present an organized summary of some of the contemporary theories of personality that may be of interest to the executive. We hope to present a guide to each theory and to indicate its relevance for the thoughtful executive. But before we proceed, it might be as well to say why a knowledge of personality theory is important.

UNDERSTANDING PERSONALITY THEORY

Why does the executive need to know about personality theory? A variety of answers can be given to this question. First of all, having some knowledge and insight into his own personality dynamics may help him if not to avoid a neurosis, at least to mitigate its effects. Second, being in a position to understand and explain some of his own anxieties and motives may assist him in dealing with other executives and subordinates and enable him to exploit his interpersonal relationships more effectively. Third, a knowledge of personality theory and research findings may

242

prove extremely important in developing an efficient executive selection procedure and development programme. Finally, in our culture, sophisticated and educated people make extensive use of the language of personality.

THE NATURE OF HUMAN NATURE

At the bottom of every problem in management are people, and you can't make much headway until you have some idea of what makes them tick. Exploring "what makes us tick" has become a vast and vigorous industry, which is complex, convoluted, and partisan. At the root of the issue is the concept of personality. A whole series of arguments has grown up around the nature-nurture controversy. Is man a servant of his instincts, ultimately impelled by his libido (psychic energy)? Or (following B. F. Skinner, who denies the usefulness of both inner states and personality) is he a slave to his environment? Is he just a glorified computer which can reproduce itself? Or perhaps just a naked ape? How behavioural scientists attempt to solve the heredity-environment problem introduces the other great issue in psychology, which is whether the answer is to be found in the study of abnormality, through psychoanalysis and psychiatry, or in the study of normal successful people and what makes them healthy and effective, as A. H. Maslow and Carl Rogers have suggested.

Neither avenue can be left unexplored. The approach pursued in this chapter is try to marry the psychoanalytical and the existential. On the one hand are the seminal research of Sigmund Freud (particularly his ideas of the unconscious and the defence mechanisms) and, to a lesser extent, of his one-time disciples Carl Jung (especially his idea of extraversion and introversion) and Alfred Adler (who gave us the term "inferiority complex"). On the other hand are the works of Rogers (client-centred therapy) and Maslow (with his idea of "self-actualization"). It was drawing such ideas together that gave Eric Berne and Thomas A. Harris the basic ideas that led to transactional analysis, which is a most useful and valuable way forward in understanding interpersonal relations. It has the supreme virtue that most people can understand, and better still use, their model.

For those who see heredity as the major cause of human behaviour, the ultimate explanation is to be found in the molecular biology of the enzymes in the genes, located in the chromosomes. In fact, much of the early work in personality could be subsumed under the series: heredity is transmitted through the genes; the genes determine the hormone balance; hormone balance determines physique; and physique shapes personality. As recently as 20 years ago it was still believed (based on the theory of a German psychiatrist, E. Kretschmer) that small, fat, rotund men succumbed to the manic-depressive psychosis and tall, thin men were more prone to schizophrenia—that there was a relationship between physique and personality. When an American study by W. H. Sheldon (which was "loaded" by its experimental design) overestimated the size of the relation in normals, the way forward looked clear. But further research demonstrated beyond all reasonable doubt that personality type could not be settled by a measurement tape.

There is growing evidence that schizophrenia moves biologically from generation to generation, and now research evidence is coming in to suggest that manic-depressive psychosis may be due to a twisted enzyme in the gene. The tremendous successes of drug therapies in treating mental illness in the 1960s points up the idea that at the root of the problem is a chemical disturbance which was built into the germ plasm with which the patient began his existence.

Turning to the environment side of the equation, most management students can quickly recognize the value of viewing personality as an existential information-processing system with an image. Focusing on the informational aspects does not pit nurture against nature, environment against heredity. For what James Watson's and F. H. C. Crick's work on the molecular structure of DNA (the building blocks of heredity) showed was that the DNA molecule carries in its double helix a programme of instructions (with one cell carrying the complete programme) from which a person can be "constructed." Thus schizophrenia could be understood as a metabolic disease where the patient went into information overload rather easily.

The modern approach to personality begins with perception—how the person sees the world or searches for and processes stimuli in his environment, and how he stabilizes his world by adjusting both his perceptions and his intellectual infra-structure of values, attitudes, needs, and expectations. The integration of perception and the VANE has become the essence of personality study.

The word "existential" was used as one of our approaches to personality, for man is searching both the world and himself for the meaning which will allow him to live fully and joyously. Thus a major focus of modern personality study is the work of Maslow, Rogers, and Erik H. Erikson, who see man in the process of "becoming" and trying to maintain his centre in an often hostile environment. Such studies of the growth of self-concept—how man moves from one identity crisis to another, with moratoria in between—is based largely on the work of Erikson, who in turn draws heavily on the greatest psychologist of all time, Sigmund Freud. This chapter's brief review of the Freudian structure of the mind is intended to illuminate the great psychic processes of repression and transference, an understanding of which is integral to executive life. As every executive knows, there is an inherent polarity in human nature, a built-in opposition between the rational and the irrational parts of our psyches. Freud unfolds the rules governing the irrational as he mines the depths of the unconscious, mapping out the defence mechanisms which save us from facing the darker sides of our natures.

Irrespective of the probity of all this probing of the depths of man's being, personality can still be measured on the scales of extraversion-introversion and neuroticism-normality. These are what most personality questionnaires set out to answer, by presenting the subject with questions such as "Do you often feel just plain miserable?" to which he is allowed to respond by ringing one of three responses, yes, no or maybe. A wider range of answers is expected from the projective test, where the subject is presented with an ambiguous, inchoate, ill-defined stimulus such as an ink blot and invited to tell what he sees.

MOTIVATION

If personality describes the structure or anatomy of the person, motivation sets out the process of what makes him do things. In talking about motivation, both heredity and environment are still relevant. Both physiological needs (such as hunger, thirst, and sex), which are largely determined by innate factors, and psychogenic needs (such as self-actualization), which are greatly influenced by the nature of the social environment, have to be considered. Frederick Herzberg bases his theory of motivation on the idea that man has two sets of needs. The first set is related to the need to avoid pain and seek pleasure; the second set is such factors as achievement, recognition, and growth. While Herzberg's theory is now regarded as passé by the more rigorous academic psychologists because of its lack of scientific validity, it is still immensely attractive to executives, who like its simplicity and utility and are not overconcerned about empiricism.

A more sophisticated approach to motivation is provided by the work of Victor Vroom, J. W. Atkinson, and D. C. McClelland. This approach is essentially concerned with cognitive maps made up of expectations, utilities, probabilities, and outcomes (payoffs), primary and secondary. This view of motivation is more complex and complicated, but it is apparently the road forward in this field. The empirical results emerging from the new expectancy theories make the intellectual efforts involved in understanding them worth-while.

STRUCTURE OF CHAPTER 7

Six topics are discussed in Chapter 7. Topic 1, personality as an open system, is based on Gordon Allport's well-known definition of personality and examines the relation between perception and personality. Personality is always in the process of becoming, and perception is the process by which a person becomes aware of the world. Perception is initially an act of categorization, which is a function of personality.

Consideration of perception leads naturally to the development of the existential concept of personality, our second topic, which is winning increasing recognition in North America among both academics and executives. The existential approach emphasizes choice, awareness, authenticity, and good faith, which are all integral to executive life.

Topic 3 deals with the structure of personality. The two major dimensions called extraversion and anxiety are examined in some detail.

Consideration of anxiety leads directly to the Freudian concept of personality (Topic 4), where the role of the unconscious and the nature of defence mechanisms are presented.

Topic 5, dealing with motivation, begins with Maslow's classification and covers Herzberg's motivation-hygiene theory before turning to motivation via payoffs and probabilities. The expectancy models, including Vroom's theory, and money as a motivator are also discussed.

Topic 6 summarizes what we know about the executive personality, based on behavioural studies of executives.

TOPIC 1
Personality as an open system

Gordon W. Allport, in *Personality: A Psychological Interpretation*, introduces his definitive account of the subject by noting:

> The term "personality" expresses admirably this interest of the psychologist, and yet it is a perilous one for him to use unless he is aware of its many meanings. Since it is remarkably elastic, its use in any context seldom is challenged. Books and periodicals carry it in their titles for no apparent reason other than its cadence, its general attractiveness, and everlasting interest. Both writer and reader lose their way in its ineffectual vagueness, and matters are made much worse by the depreciation of the word in the hands of journalists, beauty doctors and peddlers of gold bricks labeled "self-improvement."
>
> "Personality" is one of the most abstract words in our language, and like any abstract word suffering from excessive use, its connotative significance is very broad, its denotative significance negligible. Scarcely any word is more versatile.
>
> Let us take a word such as Person. Nothing can be more abstract. It is neither male nor female, neither young nor old. As a noun, it is hardly more than what "to be" is as a verb. In French it may even come to mean nobody.

Allport, after examining a mass of different definitions, produced the neatest, most penetrating, and most frequently cited definition: "Personality is the dynamic organization within an individual of those psychophysical systems that determine his unique adjustments to his environment."

For Allport, personality is dynamic and describes something which is always in the process of becoming. Personality is seen as an expanding system seeking new and better levels of order and transaction. Thus his definition emphasizes the idea of organization, of how the individual pulls himself together by trying to integrate his values, attitudes, needs, expectations, and abilities to give his life meaning. Implicit in his definition is the belief that a person achieves this integration by a particular life style which is unique to him. This personal style is stamped on everything that comes in contact with a particular individual and thus determines the form of his adjustment. The idea of adjustment to the environment is included in the definition, for personality has the functional value of facilitating survival and the evolution of behaviour. Environment describes the field of forces, the culture, the roles and interaction set—the situational context in which the individual finds himself.

For Allport, personality is seen as an open system which is engaged in an extensive transactional commerce with its environment. Information in the form of stimuli is absorbed and transformed, and responses are generated. Personality stands between the stimulus and the response and tries to achieve some "good order and military discipline" between the input of the stimulus and the output of the response. This good order is not a static framework but an evolving one which, in the case of the healthy person, over time can handle more complexity by becoming not only more differentiated but also more integrated. Thus personality as an open system has to achieve not only stability, but also growth.

The modern approach to personality stresses a cognitive approach where information and meaning are key concepts. How the individual deals with the problem of reducing uncertainty through coding inputs has become the natural point of departure in studying personality. What is being studied here is how perception, or the process of coding, structures the stimulus so that the person sees the world in terms which are meaningful for him. Thus the modern student of personality begins his work by enquiring what effect values, attitudes, needs, and expectations (the VANE) have on perception; and, following Allport's idea of becoming, how the environment (the stimuli outside and inside the person) affects the VANE.

The reader will recognize the VANE concept developed in the stimulus-organism-response (S-O-R) model of man in Chapter 6. Personality as a system seeks to organize the person's VANE and abilities into a meaningful pattern to facilitate his adaptation and growth.

The healthy individual makes a significant effort to respond to the environment as a whole. For example, when a person is put under pressure, he will bring into action a variety of defences which, as the pressure increases, utilize a great variety of subsystems. When a person is placed in an environment where he receives too many informational inputs or when inputs from the environment are too incongruous with the information already stored and coded, he tends to withdraw. Again, as Leon Festinger has shown, when a person is presented with information dissonant with his beliefs or expectations, he tends to discredit either the incoming information or the source. Individuals develop a whole repertoire of defence mechanisms to keep their personalities intact, though the adaptation may be suboptimal.

PERCEPTION

Perception describes the process whereby an individual becomes aware of the outside world and himself. It is necessary to begin by putting aside the commonsensical view that perception simply registers what is "out there." A fundamental assumption of the modern psychology of perception is that an individual distorts his perceptions of the outside world to make it congruent with his set of beliefs and attitudes.

The common-sense view of perception (that the eye is a camera and the mind a film which can completely and minutely examine itself) presumes that all the information gathered by our senses actually reaches the mind. Common sense argues that reality is mirrored in the mind. But the new look in perception—structuralism, as it has been called—has produced the insight that knowledge about the world enters the mind not as raw data but in already highly abstracted form—structures. The structure is known in psychology as a Gestalt, which is the German word for configuration or shape. In the preconscious process of converting raw data into structures, information is inevitably lost. The creation of structures—the establishment of Gestalts—is nothing less than the selective destruction of information to facilitate the recognition of patterns which have meaning for the perceiver. Therefore, without all the raw data, "the mirror of reality" thesis of perception fails. Instead, for the perceiver reality is a set of structural transformations of primary data taken from the world.

The new look in perception has been pioneered by Jerome S. Brunner of Harvard, who argues that "Perception involves an act of categorization." Brunner is saying that when we perceive something we try to fit it into a classification system or frame of reference, and a trading process goes on between the perceived qualities of the thing and the hole in the classification system where we think it should fit. In the process some of the qualities of the object are derived from the classification system and tried on the object for size. Perceptual readiness refers to the relative accessibility of the category system to the kinds of stimulus information being input. The frame of reference includes subjective elements such as values, attitudes, needs, and expectations. Figure 7–1 illustrates this transactional classification as the organism responding to the stimulus by filtering sense data though the frame of reference.

SELECTION AND ORGANIZATION

The modern approach to perception presumes that each person behaves in a way consistent with his perceptual field, the somewhat fluid

FIGURE 7–1
STIMULUS AND ORGANISM'S PERCEPTION

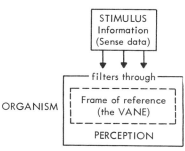

nd dynamic organization of personal meanings which a person carries around in his head. This "little world" in which a person lives has also been called his psychological field, or life-space or phenomenal field. The last term is derived from the Greek *phainesthai*, which means "to appear." As D. E. Hamachek has pointed out, a phenomenon is "that which is known through the senses and immediate experience rather than through deductions." Thus for the perceiver, reality lies not in the event but in the phenomenon, or his perception of the event. If a person is reacting to something as real, then that phenomenon is real for that person.

Since a person is constantly bombarded by sensory stimulation, there must be processes of selection and organization to make this glut of data meaningful for him. Thus perception is, first of all, a selective or screening process which ensures that some information is processed and some is not. This selective process requires categorizing stimuli into two kinds; those of which a person is aware and which he can recognize fairly readily after selection, and those which may be below his threshold of awareness.

The second component of perception is organization. A person "sees" his environment in such a way that it has personal meaning for him. The sensory data that is processed must be ordered or classified in some way that allows him to ascribe meaning to the stimulus data. An individual does not rest content with a mass of unorganized data, but devises and perceives what psychologists call a good Gestalt, or meaningful and satisfying shape or form. Thus the perceptual world is organized in ways that are mandated not only by the construction of the central nervous system but also in accordance with the values, attitudes, needs, expectations, and self-concept which each of us brings to our perception of "reality."

PERCEPTUAL STYLE

What factors affect what a person perceives? A large number of factors have been identified. The first factor is response disposition: a person tends

to perceive familiar stimuli more readily than unfamiliar ones. Secondl
an individual more quickly perceives things about which he has stror
rather than neutral feelings. Thirdly, there is the factor of respon:
salience, which refers to the structuring effect of motivation on perce}
tion. Perceptual style is also related to personality.

Salience

Common observation makes us realize that people see the world di
ferently. Different things stand out for different people, and the san
thing means different things to the same person depending on time an
circumstance. In order to explain the differential meaning of concep
from moment to moment, we use the term salience to refer to the degre
of presence of a particular concept in a person's awareness at a particul;
time. Three factors influence the degree of salience of a particular thin;
The first factor is the amount of learning or experience with a given cor
cept. If a manager is used to viewing organizations in terms of hierarchic
levels, spans of control, line-staff relationships, and so on, and this mod
has worked well for him, then such concepts will be highly salient fc
him. They will remain salient for him until he is not only exposed to
new model of organization, for example the information-processing sy.
tem approach, but also given training in using the new concepts.

The second salience factor depends on the stimulus situation at a give
time. If the manager is given classroom training in using new system cor
cepts and still uses such statements as "A must delegate to B the respons
bility for a specific assignment" in the work situation, he reveals that h
mind still works in the classical mode in the employment context, wit
the systems concepts reserved for the university seminar.

The third determinant of salience is motivation. The primary way i
which needs and expectations influence salience is the basis of the patl
goal approach to motivation. What an effective manager does in the patl
goal approach is to ascertain the utilities and probabilities of particula
tasks and play with the salience of particular trains of behaviours an
outcomes so that he can achieve his objective by structuring perceptior
(making the "right" things salient) for his subordinates.

In other words, what a person sees in the outer world is related to hov
he feels about his inner self. People develop perceptual attitudes—"the wa
I see things"—irrespective of the physical reality of external things.

Two different types of individuals who see the world in different way
have been identified by behavioural scientists. One type of person, th
field-independent, is unable to change his mental set (mind) even whe
presented with new information. The field-dependent individual allow
information from the field to influence him too much. Hamachek says i
Encounters with the Self:

> Now let us look at the personalities of the field-dependent—those wh
> are strongly influenced and controlled by the situation in which they fin

themselves. Witkin and his associates found that adults who were field-dependent were inclined to be passive and submissive to authority, to be afraid of their sexual and aggressive impulses, and to have low self-esteem and self-acceptance. In general, they are people who are very dependent on environmental supports. Field-independent people, on the other hand, tended to be independent in their social behavior, rather accepting of their hostile and sexual impulses, and better able to control them. They were generally less anxious, more self-confident, and more accepting. Other research reviewed by Elliott indicated that field-dependent people tend to rate high on gregariousness and conventionality, whereas field-independent people tend to rate high on measures of inter-personal hostility, creativeness, and originality. People who are field-dependent tend to be rigid in their perceptual style and to be somewhat prejudiced against minority groups.

H. H. Kelley, in his study of the warm-cold variable effect on the impression of others, has shown that the majority of students who were told a visiting lecturer was a "warm" person participated in the class discussion, whereas only a minority of those who received a "cold" description participated.

PERCEIVING PEOPLE

A critical activity for executives is sifting the impressions which they have of others. As one would expect, the perception of persons is a more complex matter than the perception of physical objects. For starters, the perceiver not only takes in data about the subject but also allows the background to affect his perceptions. Management consultants typically exploit this relation by meeting clients in exclusive business clubs, where the setting will enhance their stimulus impact. As Box 7.1 illustrates, because of the pressure from the category system or "apperception masses," perceivers are often quite willing to make a neat, tidy job of assessment by reaching "firm" conclusions on the basis of a fairly limited sample of the other person's behaviour. Most people seem to carry stereotypes in their heads of what "foreigners" look like.

PERCEPTUAL CONSTANCY

Psychological evidence suggests that people strive to maintain unity and consistency in their perceptions of both their own behaviour and that of others. We frequently detect more consistency in the behaviour of others. In fact, our expectation of behavioural consistency in others is so strong that we treat others as if they were of one piece; and if they are not, we react negatively to them. In general terms our social perceptions tend to be fairly stable; once we have labelled a person as friendly or aggressive or whatever, we are reluctant to give up that perception. Further, we will go to considerable lengths to distort or reject information which challenge stereotypes we have formed about particular people.

Box 7.1: Influence of beliefs

By and large, people tend to behave in a manner which is consistent with what th
believe to be true. In this sense, seeing is not only believing; seeing is behaving! A fa
is not what is; a fact is what one believes to be true. When man believed that the ea
was flat he avoided its edges; when he believed that blood-letting would drain out t
evil spirits and cure a patient he persisted in this practice despite the fact that peo
died before his very eyes. When man believed that phrenology could help him, he h
his head examined (literally). There is even evidence to suggest that when a research
believes that his hypothesis is true, he is more apt to find evidence supporting th
hypothesis than if he didn't believe it was true. And so it goes.

Our beliefs influence our perceptions, nurture our assumptions, and to a large exte
determine our behaviour. We do not easily give up that which we believe to be true. T
church of our youth and the first political party to which we gave our allegiance usua
continue to be our choices. Perceptions of one person by another person can be
varied as the assumptions on which the perceptions are based. An interesting examp
of how different beliefs can influence different perceptions was reported by Stachr
and Ulrich in a paper in which they described the divergent perceptions of Barry Go
water by psychiatrists after he received the 1964 Republican nomination for Preside
Fact magazine sent a questionnaire to all 12,356 psychiatrists registered in the Americ
Medical Association asking, "Do you believe Barry Goldwater is psychologically fit
serve as President of the United States?" Not all answered, but of the 2,417 who c
reply, 571 said they did not know enough about him to answer, 657 said they thouc
him psychologically fit, and 1,189 said he was not. Consider some examples of he
dramatically the perceptions of Goldwater differed. One psychiatrist said, "I not or
believe Barry Goldwater is psychologically fit to serve as President, but I believe he
a very mature person." On the same subject, however, another psychiatrist observe
"I believe Mr. Goldwater is basically immature . . . He has little understanding of hims
or why he does the things he does." It is also interesting to note that diametrica

---

Don E. Hamachek, *Encounters with the Self* (New York: Holt, Rinehart & Winston, 1971).

The stability of our personal perceptions makes us feel more comfortable and allows us to make predictions about future behavioural events. The
term stereotyping is widely used to describe bias in perceiving others
particularly people of other ethnic groups. Another example of perceptua
constancy or unity is the so-called halo effect, whereby an assessor o
another person takes his own halo off and puts it on the other person anc
rates him highly not only on one personality trait but on a whole spectrun
of traits. Figure 7–2 illustrates how a manager may unconsciously be
affected by the halo effect in making an assessment of a subordinate.

Sheldon Zalkind and T. W. Costello have provided us with a succinc
summary of the literature on the halo effect:

> Bruner and Taguiri suggest that it is likely to be most extreme whe
> we are forming impressions of traits that provide minimal cues in the
> individual's behaviour, when the traits have normal overtones, or whe
> the perceiver must judge traits with which he has had little experience
> A somewhat different aspect of the halo effect is suggested by the re

opposing views regarding Goldwater's fitness were defended with rock-like conviction. For example, a Connecticut psychiatrist concluded:

> I believe Goldwater is grossly psychotic . . . he is a mass murderer at heart and a suicide. He is amoral and immoral, a dangerous lunatic. Any psychiatrist who does not agree with the above is himself psychologically unfit to be a psychiatrist.

A Georgia psychiatrist was just as adamant, but had a different belief about Goldwater:

> I value my reputation as a psychiatrist, but I am willing to stake it on the opinion that Barry Goldwater is eminently qualified—psychologically and in every other way—to serve as President of the United States.

The authors suggested, tongue-in-cheek(?), that among other things "A Republican seeking psychiatric counsel should be sure to see a Republican psychiatrist since this apparently enhances the probability of receiving a favorable diagnosis. . . ."

Beliefs are difficult to change. This is even more true for persons who have strong prejudices, which, after all, are nothing more than beliefs which have become so fixed as to become permanent props in one's personality structure. Perhaps the point that beliefs change slowly can be illustrated by the yarn about the man who believed he was dead. His psychiatrist, after hearing his story, suggested that during the next week he repeat thrice daily, "Dead men don't bleed." When the man returned the next week the psychiatrist asked the man if he had followed his advice. Assured that he had, the psychiatrist took a needle and pricked the man's finger and squeezed out a drop of blood. "Well," said the psychiatrist, "What do you thing about that?" The man regarded his finger with some care, looked up at the psychiatrist with a puzzled expression and answered, "I'll be darned. Dead men *do* bleed!"

search of Grove and Kerr. They found that knowledge that the company was in receivership caused employees to devalue the higher pay and otherwise superior working conditions of their company as compared to those in a financially secure firm.

Psychologists have noted a tendency in perceivers to link certain traits. They assume, for example, that when a person is aggressive he will also have high energy, or that when a person is "warm" he will also be generous and have a good sense of humor. The logical error, as it has been called, is a special form of the halo effect and is best illustrated in the research of Asch. In his study the addition of one trait to a list of traits produced a major change in the impression formed. Knowing that a person was intelligent, skillful, industrious, determined, practical, cautious, and warm led a group to judge him to be also wise, humorous, popular, and imaginative. When warm was replaced by cold, a radically different impression (beyond the difference between warm and cold) was formed. Kelley's research illustrated the same type of error. This tendency is not indiscriminate; with the pair "polite-blunt," less change was found than with the more central traits of "warm-cold."

In evaluating the effect of halo on perceptual distortion, we may take comfort from the work of Wishner, which showed that those traits that

FIGURE 7–2
RATING SCALE SHOWING THE HALO EFFECT

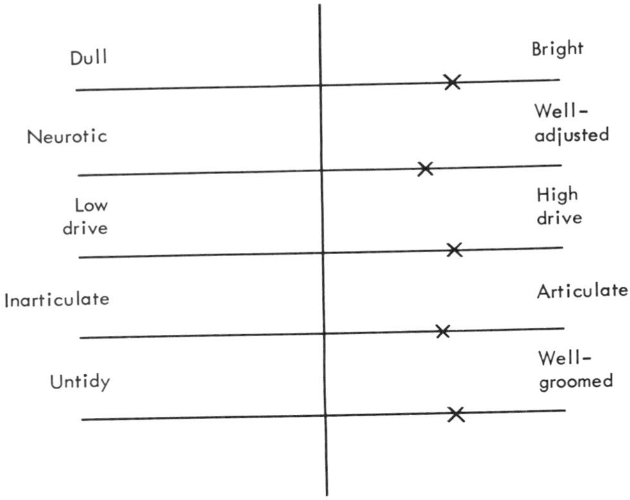

correlate more highly with each other are more likely to lead to a halo effect than those that are unrelated.

In judging other people we commonly use ourselves as the norm, and the better we know and accept ourselves the more accurate will be our perceptions of the other. If you are status-conscious yourself, you are more likely to interpret the other man's behaviour in terms of keeping up with the Joneses. Organizational neophytes are frequently disturbed by the paranoid outbursts of organizational veterans, who see in small nuances (such as who was invited to a particular meeting) some dramatic, deep signal of power mania.

The perceiver is limited in his ability to judge others by his own values, attitudes, needs, and expectations; and it is as well for practical purposes to accept that accuracy in perceiving others is not a single skill.

A MODEL OF PERSONALITY

From Gordon Allport's definition, it is possible to build up a model of personality which will facilitate discussion. Figure 7–3 completes the S-O-R model of Figure 7–1, showing that within the organism there is a dynamic structure of perception, self-concept, values, attitudes, needs, and expectations.

To develop the model, it was necessary to begin by considering the relation between perception and personality. Figure 7–1 showed that personality (in the form of the VANE—values, attitudes, needs, and expectations) affects perception, and therefore behaviour. But how a person thinks

FIGURE 7–3
S-O-R MODEL OF PERSONALITY

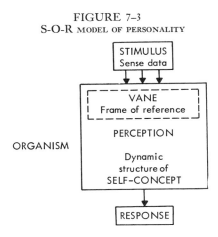

of himself also affects both personality and perception. Thus it also is necessary to examine the psychological entity called self-concept.

The study of the self-concept, or identity, leads naturally to the question of how people in the process of growing up change their identities. Using the model in Figure 7–3, topic 2 moves on to formulate an existential, systems definition and model of personality. Further consideration of needs and expectations is taken up in our discussion of motivation, Topic 5.

TOPIC 2
The existential concept of personality

Existentialism has turned out to be an extremely useful source of ideas for contemporary psychologists. Existentialism, as a philosophy which has practical utility, caught on in a dramatic way during World War II in occupied France, when people like Jean Paul Sartre and Albert Camus were fighting for their lives in desperate circumstances. What existentialism demands is that man must face up to the decisions that confront him. As Sartre puts it—and every executive worth his salt would agree—man is condemned to freedom. For many existentialists, God is dead and the responsibility for individual choice is thrust upon the individual. In other words, it is no longer possible to pass the buck to "the guy up there" or "the system." A total personal response is called for, and nobody can opt out. There are no innocent bystanders. This recognition of being alone, yet free, and thus totally responsible is inevitably accompanied by feelings of dread, anguish, and angst. As every executive knows, each day has to be faced anew. As the existentialist puts it, "If I was a hero yesterday, there is no guarantee I'll be a hero today." Everything has to be chosen afresh every time.

Existential ideas have also been adapted to philosophies which recog nize religious or moral order and purpose. American psychologists hav been reviewing existentialism as a means of dealing with the identity crise which characterize our time. Many behavioural scientists see in the worl of Rollo May, Carl Rogers, and Abraham Maslow a return to the grea American tradition begun by William James and John Dewey, who base so much of their work and writings on the analysis of the "here and now.

PERSONALITY—FUSION OF EXISTENTIALISM AND SYSTEMS THEORY

An extremely fruitful approach to personality theory is provided by synthesis of systems theory and existentialism. In formulating such theory, certain guidelines can be identified.

1. Personality is seen as an open system trading with its environment.
2. Perception, which involves an act of categorization, requires searchin the environment for information.
   a. Each person has an optimal capacity for handling informatior arousal, novelty, and conflict.
   b. Some of the characteristics of the stimulus are inferred from th category system.
   c. The category system (or set) is greatly influenced by the individual' VANE.
   d. People strive for perceptual simplicity—they see "things" as Gestalt.
3. Decision making is central to existentialism. To act unfree continually i to run the risk of becoming neurotic.
4. In terms of behaviour, individuals struggle to be authentic, to give thei lives meaning, to achieve some kind of identity.
5. The personality process is unknowable, which leads to the use of th black box concept as a means of controlling and limiting our need to control and to understand.
6. The systems approach by itself is insufficient because the system o personality has the unique characteristic of being self-conscious (i.e. aware of itself). This produces echo systems which interact with the originating system.
7. Man represents the fusion of two great trends, both present in anima evolution from the lowest to the highest forms, which have reachec their fullest development in man. These two trends are:
   a. A decrease in the instinctive determination of behaviour.
   b. An increase in the size and complexity of the brain (man is capable of symbol formation and language) and an increase in self-awareness and self-control.

With these guidelines, it is now possible to formulate an existentia model of personality. This model of personality is based on a concept of perception which rejects the simplistic view of stimulus-response theorists and emphasizes the Gestalt approach that perception is organized according to the laws of proximity, similarity, and closure. In essence, perception as an information-gathering process is not a purely mechanical, routine, physiological process but a transactional process with one's environment which is highly subjective and arbitrary, and as such is capable of change.

Figure 7–4 represents a potentially useful model for discussing the dynamics of personality change. This model is based on the notion that while personality represents a moderating variable between the stimulus

FIGURE 7–4
EXISTENTIAL MODEL OF PERSONALITY

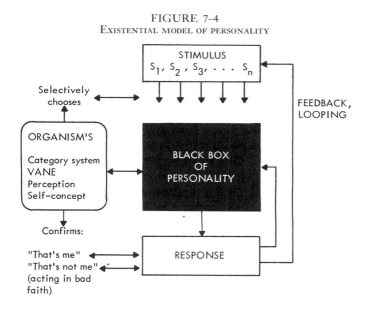

and the response, the process cannot be known and hence is a "black box." The personality variables and the interacting processes are therefore only indicated outside the box. Research reveals that the determinants of perceptual organization are needs and cultural values. This new look in perception forces consideration of the nature of distortion generated by defensive attitudes and prejudices (particularly unexplored and dysfunctional value systems). Hence, one assumption in the model is that personality does not respond to the whole environment but selectively to those stimuli which are appropriate to the individual's needs, previous experience, and present partial information.

Perceptions of behaviour or events involve an act of categorization. Everyman is a walking taxonomy. Perceptions formed in this mode generate action or a tendency to action. But they are perceptions derived from transactions with the environment, not reactions to the environment.

Thus we have added the variable "category system" to our previous models of personality, referring to the fact that a person has a set of categories which contains arbitrary elements for structuring perceptions, reflecting needs and cognitions.

Many people, if not most, behave in a manner indicating an underlying pattern. Frequently, when it is pointed out to the person concerned that his behaviour is predictable and stereotyped (e.g., he may hold the view that he will never employ a black person as a manager), he will respond by saying "That's me" and give a rationale for this assertion of "unfreedom.' Once this situation is analyzed, using the model in Figure 7–4 and the existentialist's concept of bad faith (i.e., he is choosing to act unfree), the stage is set for change. This is frequently indicated by the reversed response, "That's not me." If he chooses to act unfree he can loop the circuit again, but such looping is largely regarded as neurotic. The vital point is to gain acceptance of the notion that his category system contains significant arbitrary elements.

If arbitrariness is admitted, change is facilitated. This diagnostic technique confronts a person with his stereotype—forces a choice between the person and his ghost. This induction of an identity crisis is the key mechanism in sensitivity training. But our society may not have a set of socially approved stereotypes with whom the young person may feel satisfied to identify. The contemporary heroes of our youth often seem to be anti-heroes, or at least anti-establishment figures (e.g., Ralph Nader). So the efficacy of the model is limited by sociological factors such as the supply of suitable stereotypes in our society.

In this approach, the black box of personality is accepted as containing arbitrary elements but is also seen as capable of change and growth; the important point is to make the actual choices of categories more meaningful and less arbitrary for the individual. Such a model has value in so far as it encourages managers to formulate more sophisticated systems for examining personal behaviour. It is not definitive, but a basis for further and more meaningful and relevant models.

IDENTITY: THE SELF-CONCEPT

Man has been concerned since the beginning of time with the issue of his identity, of defining who he is. This preoccupation is reflected in the time-honoured dictum "Know thyself." Man has struggled to understand himself, for how he thinks of himself will influence both what he chooses to do and what he expects from life. Knowing his identity connects him both with his past and the potentiality of his future.

Identity and self-evaluation are closely linked. How should a man value himself? How he values himself—the respect in which he holds himself—is a major determinant of how he values or respects others. There is ultimately a conflict between man's self-concept and society. In such a conflict history, or at least literature, is on the side of man's self-respect. As Shakespeare has Polonius say in *Hamlet*, ". . . to thine own self be true; and it must follow as the night the day, thou canst not then be false to any man." But Polonius's advice is constantly being challenged by modern personality psychologists, who see the need to be able to change one's identity by some process of self-alienation. Weakening the bonds which hold the personality system together facilitates change.

What is meant by the concept of "self"? Are we discussing the subject pronoun "I" (the self as knower) or the object pronoun "me" (the self as known)? William James got around this difficulty by talking about the stream of consciousness, in which images, ideas, feelings, and sentiments flowed. For James, "I" and "me" were to be considered discriminated aspects of the same phenomenon. James also provided some guidance on the age-old issue of "How many selves are there?" James answered this question by saying that "there are as many different selves as there are groups that you belong to." K. T. Gergen in *The Concept of Self* reviewed a number of different concepts and came up with a useful definition:

> The notion of self can be defined first as process and then as structure. On the former level we shall be concerned with *that process by which the person conceptualizes (or categorizes) his behavior—both his external conduct and his internal states.* On a structural level, our concern is with *the system of concepts available to the person attempting to define himself.*

Ultimately, every person (and every executive) is faced with three questions: Who am I? Where am I going? Why? Each of these questions, in its own way, deals with our concept of self—our values, attitudes, needs, expectations, and beliefs—and ultimately with our life style. Each of us is struggling in some way, sometimes in a terrible way, with the problem of identity: with giving meaning to our lives through some form of self-concept. Yet some individuals never seem to confront themselves with the issue of identity.

REASONS FOR RESISTING PERSONAL GROWTH

Some of us resent finding out more about ourselves for fear of having to give up an identity with which we have grown comfortable. Developing into the next phases in our life cycles may be too threatening. Ultimately, people fear maturity because they are unwilling to accept the demands for autonomy, interdependence, and self-discipline that such a state requires.

People not only fear failure; they fear success, too, because success defines a higher standard of performance which is both frightening and disturbing. Possibly this is why Bernard Cornfield, when he was selecting salesmen to sell mutual funds, asked them, "Do you sincerely want to be rich?" The executive who sincerely fears success may take solace from Lawrence Peter's "Peter principle"—that "a man is promoted to his own level of incompetence." The executive is constantly bewildered by the prospect and possibility that he won't be able to grow to meet the challenge of tomorrow. Abraham Maslow has commented on this fear of doing one's best, explaining it in terms of "fear of one's greatness" or "evasion of one's destiny" or "running away from one's best talents."

To compound matters, man comes to desire what he fears. In modern times, Rollo May, the existentialist psychologist, has drawn our attention to this paradox. This inspiration came to Rollo May some 20 years ago when he was lying in a tuberculosis hospital fighting for life. At the time, he was searching for the meaning of anxiety.

Two books which significantly influenced May were *The Problem of Anxiety* by Freud and *The Concept of Dread* by Soren Kierkegaard. From Freud he took the idea that anxiety is either the reemergence of repressed libido or the ego's reaction to the threat of loss of the loved object, and from Kierkegaard the idea of anxiety as the struggle of the living being against nonbeing. Kierkegaard's notion of anxiety was very clear to May in his tubercular condition, and he readily recognized the validity of Kierkegaard's definition, "Anxiety is the desire for what one dreads." This was precisely what May and his fellow patients were going through.

What Rollo May recognized, then, was that man has a need for certain values (typical of which are prestige, power, tenderness, and love) which on occasion is greater than his need for pleasure or even for survival itself. An increasing number of American psychologists are recognizing the force of this argument and giving preeminence to a theory of personality that puts the greatest value on recognizing the individual's unique pattern of potentiality. This is central to Abraham Maslow's notion of making self-actualization the core of personality, with more basic needs such as psychological and safety needs, social needs, and ego needs occupying lower levels of the pyramid. Existential psychologists such as May recognize that the neurotic personality of our time springs not from the fear of libidinal satisfaction or security, but rather from the person's fear of his own powers and the conflicts generated by that fear.

There are many illustrations of this principle that people desire what they fear in organizational life. For example, it is not uncommon for executives to opt for being fired when they find themselves in a tight bind where the situation they face is not sharply defined and considerable anxiety has been developed. In such circumstances, many choose a solution such as the acceptance of being fired because it is cognitively simple and allays that part of their anxiety generated by choice. Considerations of the effect of choice on behaviour compel us to consider the impact of existentialism on modern personality theory.

Developing ever more complex models of personality requires a quantum of energy to make the leap in level of organization and complexity. This is precisely what self-conscious personal growth requires of us. In effect, healthy growth requires a person to be able to jump from one identity to another when the moment is ripe. What a prospect! To hold the co-ordinates of identity to some trajectory of life cycle becomes life itself. To achieve this trajectory of growth, it is necessary to have some kind of ground plan. Freudian psychoanalysis is largely concerned with tracing out the ground plan as the infant moves through the oral phase, then the anal, phallic, and latency phases, and then through the stage of puberty into the adult part of life.

Especially important for the student of organizational behaviour are the problems of adolescence, as the student struggles through role confusion to find his occupational career path, and the problem of the executive in his forties and fifties, working his way through middle age, wondering if he chose correctly and arguing with himself whether he should resign himself to his fate. On such problems of personal growth and identity, Erik H. Erikson in *Identity, Youth and Crisis* has provided some guidelines. What happens in the in-between period, when people are in transition between one identity and another? People "in between" ask for and need a moratorium. Erikson is particularly helpful in his definition of moratorium—how society allows people a substantial period while they change identities.

EXISTENTIAL MAN

A picture of existential man can be drawn from the work of Carl Rogers and A. H. Maslow, two American psychologists who have made a significant and sustained effort to introduce existential psychology to American academics. Rogers, who regards the self as a nuclear concept in his theory of personality, has developed from his many years as a practising clinician some ideas of what it means to be a fully functioning person. Maslow's unique contribution emerges from his preoccupation with healthy people rather than neurotic ones. Maslow felt that too much effort in psychology had been directed at the study of man's frailty and not enough towards his strength. Maslow, who developed a psychology that recognized man's need for love, compassion, gaiety, zest, and excitement, made a special study of what makes healthy people healthy and great people great. Out of this research emerged a description of what self-actualizing people are like. The composite picture of existential man that emerges from the work of Rogers and Maslow has the following characteristics.

Existential man is realistically oriented and carries in his head a model which recognizes the interaction between his VANE and his perception of the world. Not only can he accept himself as he is, but he can also accept other people more or less as they are. "More or less," because existential man recognizes the improbability of quickly changing the other person's VANE. In any case, since existential man is empathetic, he is capable of putting himself in another person's shoes and thus catching a glimmering of why the other person sees the world as he does.

Existential man is spontaneous in his thinking, emotions, and behaviour, partly because he is interested in "seeing what he is going to do" and partly because he places a high value on personal growth. But existential man is not always interacting with others, for he values highly the opportunity for privacy, to "get himself together" again, to recapitulate and reorganize his experiences.

For the existentialist, man, as man, supersedes the sum of his parts. Man is a human Gestalt who can only be understood "ultimately" by fitting together the parts of a dynamic system which is continually growing, and thus is always incomplete and striving to reach another level of development. He has a tremendous need for integration. While he tends to integrate experiences into a pattern which is consistent with his self-concept, he knows that to some extent it is a self-defeating process because his self-concept is continuously growing. Existential man can then tolerate a fair amount of inconsistency among his responses to the multiplexity of social life. Existential man can accept a degree of self-alienation.

Kenneth J. Gergen, in *The Concept of Self*, has neatly spelled out the relationship between the multiplexity of social life and self-alienation:

> What does this increased multiplexity of social life have to do with self-alienation? With each new relationship, new behavioral demands are placed on the person; each new relationship requires a unique form of adaptation. Under these conditions the likelihood of engaging in behavior inconsistent with major ways of viewing self, behavior that violates identity aspirations, and behavior that is unrelated to major conceptions of self is maximal. When a wife, children, car-pool cronies, secretary, boss, subordinates, office messenger, colleagues of equal rank, business and personal acquaintances who visit or call, bartender, waiter, newsstand manager, barber, drop-in or back-fence neighbors, in-laws, Vladimir Nabokov, and Johnny Carson must all be catered to, grappled with, confronted, cajoled, influenced, loved, punished, taught, or escaped within one day, maintaining an integral sense of identity is a laborious task at best. In essence, multiplex demands and expectations constitute a generating milieu for self-alienation.
>
> One peculiar paradox follows from this analysis. To be maximally adaptive in a multiplex social environment is to be maximally vulnerable to experiences of self-alienation. In order to relate successfully over a wide range of relationships, it is virtually impossible to bind our behavior to a limited set of self-conceptions. Self-alienation, then may be viewed as a necessary by-product of successful adaptation in a complex social world. Whether self-alienation is worth the price is a matter of personal decision.

Given the problems of personal growth, integration, development of identity, and self-alienation, it is not surprising that existential man intuitively recognizes the need for moratoria in his life. He has the ability to develop a behavioural mix of work and pseudo nonwork (existential man is working all the time at "becoming") which gives him a nearly optimal mix of arousal, anxiety, and energy.

Existential man is intentional; he places high value on choice, particularly in regard to his own identity. Like Ibsen, he is constantly trying to ascertain where his destiny is. "What I can be, I must be" is a directing principle which helps him to achieve self-actualization—a movement from the self he is not, towards the self that he really is.

In formulating his ethical position, existential man somehow allows the "is propositions" to interact with the "ought propositions"—to facilitate the marriage of the behavioural and ethical sciences. The naturalism of John Steinbeck, Ernest Hemingway, and John Updike seems natural to him. He is essentially inner-directed and suits himself, with minimal disregard of the interests of others. He views himself as a person in the process of becoming. Life becomes a process rather than a striving for an end state. He wants to live joyously and has the capacity "to stand in awe again and again of the basic goods of life, a sunset, a flower, a baby, a melody, a person." He has frequent "mystic" or "oceanic" experiences, not necessarily religious in character. He has intimate relations with a few specially chosen people.

Existential man has a full life trying to understand his self, coming to terms with it, keeping his perceptions of reality accurate, and trying to divine his own destiny and understand the other fellow on the same terms. He is searching for an image of himself that is accurate enough to be workable yet acceptable to him; that will allow him to live his life with joy and zest.

Having looked at what existential psychologists, who are considered somewhat soft-centred scientifically, have to say about personality, we turn to the structure of personality, which is essentially the domain of the more hard-headed scientific psychologists.

TOPIC 3
The structure of personality

In modern respectable, scientific, hard-headed behavioural science a major effort has been made to describe personality structure in terms of its principal dimensions and to measure these dimensions. To develop these dimensions, psychologists began by drawing up lists of traits. A trait is any enduring characteristic which gives to behavioural acts their typical colour or quality; trait names are adjectives which describe behaviour (mature, timid, loyal, and so on). The trouble with traits, as Allport soon discovered, is that there are too many of them. Allport searched the dictionary and found over 3,000 trait words for describing personality.

Raymond Cattell, while trying to construct a valid test of personality, boiled this list of traits down to 171 by combining synonyms. Then a sample of 100 adults, drawn from many different walks of life, were rated by associates who knew them well on these 171 traits. Intercorrelation of these ratings were obtained and then subjected to a statistical technique, factor analysis, which completes the process of boiling down by extracting the set of communalities that can explain the correlations. Using this technique, Cattell identified 16 factors which he called "the primary source traits of personality." Cattell then constructed a personality test which is called the Sixteen Personality Factor Questionnaire (16 PF Questionnaire). The 16 personality factors, which are bi-polar in nature, are listed in *The Scientific Analysis of Personality* as:

> *Schizothymia* (aloof, cold) v. *Cyclothymia* (warm, sociable); *Dull* (low intellectual capacity) v. *Bright* (intelligent); *Low-Ego Strength* (emotional, unstable) v. *High-Ego Strength* (mature, calm); *Submissiveness* (mild) v. *Dominance* (aggressive); *Desurgency* (glum, silent) v. *Surgency* (enthusiastic, talkative); *Low-Superego Strength* (casual, undependable) v. *High-Superego Strength* (conscientious, persistent); *Threctia* (timid, shy) v. *Parmia* (adventurous, thick-skinned); *Harrion* (tough, realistic) v. *Premsia* (sensitive, effeminate); *Inner Relaxation* (trustful, adaptable) v. *Protension* (suspecting, jealous); *Praxernia* (conventional, practical) v. *Autia* (Bohemian, unconcerned); *Naïveté* (simple, awkward) v. *Shrewdness* (sophisticated, polished); *Confidence* (unshakable) v. *Timidity* (insecure, anxious); *Conservatism* (accepting) v. *Radicalism* (experimenting, critical); *Group Dependence* (imitative) v. *Self-Sufficiency* (resourceful); *Low Integration* (lax, unsure) v. *Self-Sentiment Control* (controlled, exact); *Low-Ergic Tension* (phlegmatic, composed) v. *High-Ergic Tension* (tense, excitable).

J. P. Guilford (10 factors) and H. J. Eysenck (2 factors) have also developed personality tests which measure traits rather similar to those measured by Cattell. Eysenck's two factors are introversion-extraversion and neuroticism-stable. There is an interesting connection between Cattell's work and Eysenck's. In factor analysis, it is possible to examine the factors themselves to see if there is any measure of interconnection. When Cattell carried through this exercise he identified two second-order factors, introversion-extraversion and high anxiety–low anxiety. Thus Cattell's two factors are broadly similar to Eysenck's.

Figure 7–5 shows how a typical population would be distributed on a curve of extraversion-introversion. Few people are at the extremes of these traits; most fall in between.

It is possible to bring these two factors of introversion-extraversion and high anxiety–low anxiety together to define personality types. S. R. Maddi points out in *Personality Theories*:

FIGURE 7-5
DISTRIBUTION OF THE EXTRAVERSION-INTROVERSION TRAIT

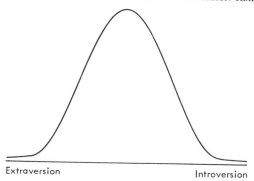

Extraversion   Introversion

These two second-order factors suggest four personality types. The first type, *High-Anxiety–Introversion*, is tense, excitable, insecure, suspecting, jealous, emotional, unstable, lax, unsure, and in addition aloof, cold, glum, silent, timid, shy, Bohemian, unconcerned, and resourceful. The second type, *Low-Anxiety–Introversion*, is phlegmatic, composed, confident, unshakable, trustful, adaptable, mature, calm, and self-sufficient, in addition to being aloof, cold, glum, silent, timid, shy, Bohemian, unconcerned, and resourceful. The third type, *High-Anxiety–Extroversion*, is tense, excitable, insecure, suspecting, jealous, emotional, unstable, lax, unsure, and also warm, sociable, enthusiastic, talkative, adventurous, thick-skinned, conventional, practical, imitative, and dependent. The final type, *Low-Anxiety–Extroversion*, is phlegmatic, composed, confident, unshakable, trustful, adaptable, mature, calm, and self-sufficient, and also warm, sociable, enthusiastic, talkative, adventurous, thick-skinned, conventional, practical, imitative, and dependent.

It will readily be seen that while the broad categories are useful, this kind of empirical research has reached a dead end because such listings are full of undefinable concepts and internal contradictions. If the trait approach were to be useful, it should at least contain verbs as well as adjectives; but, as we will see in Chapter 9, it has largely been discarded as unscientific.

DIMENSIONS OF PERSONALITY

The two broad personality scales that are most widely accepted by psychologists as descriptive of personality structure are the large, ubiquitous, and virtually unavoidable dimensions of extraversion and anxiety. H. J. Eysenck, professor of psychology at London University, has developed the Eysenck Personality Inventory (E.P.I.) which measures these and also has a lie scale. Validation shows that it provides an excellent measure of extraversion but is not as good at measuring anxiety.

A caution is perhaps appropriate at this stage. Experimental psychologists in the field of personality research are apparently unable to reach firm conclusions, convincing and acceptable to other psychologists, as to the nature of extraversion. A good illustration of this difficulty is provided by examination of the literature on extraversion and conditioning, which reveals many contradictory findings that present theory cannot explain. But these two basic dimensions, extraversion and neuroticism, are so widely established in the literature and common parlance that it would be extremely difficult to dispense with them.

EXTRAVERSION

The extravert is oriented towards the outside world. He is characteristically outgoing and spontaneously more concerned with restructuring his environment than with analysing its effects on his "inner being." The extravert seems to have the capacity to suppress negative feedback or criticism. He is strong in drive and zestfully involved in accomplishing things. He is sometimes described by psychologists as a sociophile, i.e., he prefers to be with people. He is assertive—even, on occasions, aggressive.

There is probably a genetic basis to extraversion, in the sense that the extravert seems capable of mobilizing sufficient energy to maintain a high level of drive, which is presumably a function of his basic metabolism. It is possible to argue that there must be neural correlates of the psychological process of suppression, which inhibits negative feedback. Leaving aside this speculation, it is nevertheless possible to assert that an extraverted adolescent seems more able, for example, to ask a question at a public meeting. On the positive side, his assertive temperament enables him to contribute; and his suppression of negative feedback (in this case, people turning to look at him) will facilitate his continuance.

The introvert, the obverse of the extravert, is oriented towards the inner world of the psyche; he tends to be shy, withdrawn, and inhibited in social affairs. The introvert is usually introspective and as such is more interested in the world of ideas than practical affairs. The Bernreuter personality questionnaire results, when analysed, show a strong correlation between neuroticism and introversion. Modern research findings support the view that the extraversion-introversion dichotomy is a far from simple dimension of personality and is in fact made up of a number of components which are organized within the framework of a type.

ANXIETY

Apparently few executives, if any, escape the feeling of anxiety which seems to be the dominant theme of modern life. A great number of people including many executives, seem to suffer from a kind of cosmic hypochondria, marked by a diffuse anxiety neurosis and frequently couple with a vague sense of futility.

Anxiety is characterized by diffusion of emotion in the sense that the cause may be difficult to specify and the choice of focus open. This leads to a situation where psychologists are inclined to treat individuals as if they have a "free floating pool of anxiety" which is continually searching for a focus. In *The Meaning of Anxiety*, Rollo May has defined anxiety as "the apprehension cued off by a threat to some value which the individual holds essential to his existence as a personality."

Although at one time it was customary for clinical psychologists to view any form of anxiety as unhealthy, the contemporary attitude is a little different and is based on the notion that a low level of anxiety may have some utility. However, it is usual to treat neurotic anxiety as irrational, in the sense that even a logical explanation of a subject's anxieties may not necessarily lead to their alleviation.

TABLE 7–1
EFFECTS OF ANXIETY

Slight anxiety	Moderate anxiety	Severe anxiety
General alerting	Less spontaneity	Organization of behaviour breaks down
Increased sensitivity to out-outside events	Rigidity, reliance on "safe" habitual responses	Inability to distinguish between safe and harmful stimuli
Physiological mobilization	Reduced ability to improvise	
Effective integration of behavior	More effort needed to maintain adequate behavior	Stereotyped, unadaptive, random-appearing patterns
Increase in ability for productive behavior	Narrowing and distortion of perception	Irritability, distractability
		Impaired learning, thinking

These generalizations are drawn from many studies including Cannon, 1939; Liddell, 1944; Combs, 1952; Ausubel and others, 1954; Basowitz and others, 1955.

Source: J. C. Coleman, *Personality Dynamics and Effective Behavior* (Chicago: Scott, Foresman & Co., 1960).

It is not uncommon in modern experiments on anxiety to allocate subjects into the three categories described in Table 7–1. Research with soldiers going into combat and patients going for surgery supports the proposition that those who admit to moderate and high levels of anxiety face stress less well than those who admit only slight anxiety. For example, both soldiers engaged in combat and patients after surgical operations appear to make a more effective adjustment to the difficult circumstances in which they find themselves if they admit to a low level of anxiety. Apparently a low level of anxiety enables the subject to mobilize his resources more effectively. Much the same can be said about the performance of university students. There is some evidence from British research work to support the belief that slightly neurotic but highly intelligent students seem to have a certain advantage over their better adjusted but equally intelligent fellows. Box 7.2 comments on some experiments dealing with anxiety.

Box 7.2: Real anxiety: Parachuting

A recent series of studies on volunteer free-fall parachute jumpers has incorporated interference and reported responses as well, on a time scale reckoned in minutes. The advantages of parachuting as a stress stimulus are many. The subjects may be carefully selected and examined, the requirements of jumping do not preclude carrying heavy telemetry packs, and the emotional high points of the experience can be precisely located in time within one second: jump, chute opening, and landing. Furthermore, there is a highly organized and traditional social surround to sport parachuting that remains constant over many trials and for many individuals; and finally, no matter how much experimental procedure and paraphernalia are introduced, there is not the slightest doubt in the subjects' minds that the experimental jumps are as dangerous as ever. While easily subject to scientific monitoring, the jumpers are obviously beyond the range of the scientist's intervention. For these reasons, several independent groups studying stress have selected sport parachuting as their experimental object.

Shane and Slinde have determined heart rate on a continuous basis during free-fall parachuting, using a 3½-pound telemetry pack on experienced jumpers. Heart rates for all jumpers were astonishingly high during the jump—twice normal levels at exit and higher yet at chute opening. They were lower at landing than at chute opening and decreased steadily once the jumper reached the ground. The jumps were consistently stressful, even for experienced jumpers. Peak heart rates were associated with a violent somatic tremor, which hindered motor coordination, and tumbling during free-fall caused nystagmus and G-force visual deficits that impaired sensory perception.

Fenz has conducted a wide series of reported and interference experiments on novice parachutists before and during their first three jumps. The parachutists demonstrated increased auditory thresholds to tones on the day of their first jump; this increase was most severe following presentation of words relevant to jumping. The effect became more pronounced as the moment for the jump approached. Correct perception of words related to parachute jumping was not impaired, but such "anxiety" words as *killed, panic,* and *accident* were consistently misperceived the day of the jump. Many other autonomic and perceptual changes were shown to be related to the proximity of a jump and the experience of a jumper. Paradoxically, the stress-induced deficits were more severe in those with some experience than in those with none at all. Apparently the stress of jumping is not reduced by repeated exposure to it, and only those with much experience of it at all can maintain their composure in the minutes before leaving the airplane.

Fenz' work with parachutists also had led to one of the few studies on record quantifying the stress of apprehension and anticipation. Certain physiological arousal patterns were observed to be a function of the time interval remaining before an impending jump. The highly ritualized and consistent emotional characteristics of a series of parachute jumps undoubtedly contributed to the success of these experiments.

Kenyon B. DeGreene (ed.), *Systems Psychology* (New York: McGraw-Hill Book Co., 1970).

These findings in regard to the functional significance of a low level of anxiety are congruent with the research of F. E. Fiedler in regard to the superiority of the psychologically distant executive in certain circumstances. Apparently executives also function better with a modest level of anxiety.

Guilt and anxiety are intimately related; anxiety is characterized by a sense of dread—a feeling that something ominous is going to happen.

When people talk about their feelings of guilt, they describe feelings of anxiety, in this case arising from infringement of moral rules or the value system and accompanied by the feeling that they ought to be punished. Guilt becomes a source of frustration because it blocks our need for self-esteem. Most normal people, in the process of growing up, experience a need for rules of behaviour within which they can operate and exercise discretion.

Brainwashing in part depends upon the exploitation of this feeling of guilt. This technique of persuasion apparently works best when the subject is left on his own to mull over his "sins." If he is denied the support of his primary group to resist, he may well come up with the desired formulas. This may lead to the experience of conversion. The primary working group (see Chapter 8, Topic 5) plays a key part both in work and in combat situations. Breaking up this primary work group seems to be an integral part of the brainwashing process, Communist self-criticism groups, and T groups. To many disinterested parties, there are remarkable similarities.

TOPIC 4
The Freudian concept

There are two fruitful starting points for the executive looking at Sigmund Freud's contribution to psychology, one linguistic and the other emotional. Considering first a strictly emotional appeal, it may be convincing to remember that many people, when the going is good, "bubble over like little kids." To take a military example, it is reported that Nazi General Rommel used to break into Swabian, a local German dialect, when the battle was going his way. Much the same kind of hilariousness, which psychoanalysts describe as regression, may be observed in executives when the tide begins to move in their favour. In other words, "true happiness can only be realized by the indulgence of certain infantile needs." While "true happiness" is certainly an overstatement, how is it possible to explain the change of accent, the coarsening of speech, the enrichment of expletives usually associated with a general feeling of euphoria experienced by managers when "things start to go their way." This emotional experience is so common among executives that many of them regard themselves (wrongly, in the vast majority of cases) as manic-depressives, the depressive phase being an inevitable product of the anxiety and guilt—partly warranted but to some extent irrational—which inevitably follow the euphoria induced by success.

Regression presupposes going from a higher to a lower state. What is this evolutionary trail along which it is apparently possible to return? Freud in his theory of psychosexual genesis provides a rough kind of map to mark out some of the stages that most Western persons go through.

Like all maps, it has a particular legend which has somehow or other been absorbed into the *lingua franca* of the professional and executive and it is a language of sophistication and considerable explanatory value.

For example, how could the educated person get by without the term ambivalence? Ambivalence is having two apparently contradictory attitudes towards a person or event—love-hate, plus-minus, for-against. The world of executive life is suffused with conflict, ambiguity, and change. Ambivalence is the rule rather than the exception. The coming of age for most managers is the recognition that relations are inevitably complex, almost certainly ambivalent, and always imperfect to a degree. It can be reassuring to a manager to discover that there is nothing necessarily unusual about him and that his relations with others will always be imperfect.

The most dramatic and significant discovery by Freud was the mapping out of the role and function of the unconscious. People very often find themselves doing things again and again for reasons they are either totally or partially unaware of. Freud introduced the idea of the unconscious as the repository for ideas of this type, which cause a person to behave in odd ways which he cannot justify or whose justification makes him wonder what is going on. Freud gives many examples of this sort of apparently contradictory behaviour, such as a normally grumpy and discourteous middle-aged father surprising everybody by leaping up to hold a chair for an attractive young girl taking her place at the table. Freud was his own best publicist and by his brilliant, extremely witty, and urbane writing did much to awaken the generations of the 1920s and 1930s to the implications of the unconscious, especially to the notion that it was the apparently hidden source of man's animal nature. Freud's final view was that man was driven by two basic or fundamental instincts, Eros (sexual instincts) and Thanatos (aggression or death wish). The conflicts between them can be expressed as sex versus aggression, love versus hate, life versus death, and so on.

Figure 7–6 may help to explain Freud's concept of the unconscious. In this concept, a Complex *I* which was troubling the patient could be repressed during hypnosis, but the unconscious would find a method of returning *I* to consciousness. Freud thought that real emotional problems were deeply embedded in the unconscious, and he developed techniques such as dream analysis and free association to locate them.

FIGURE 7–6
FREUDIAN CONCEPT OF THE UNCONSCIOUS

Repressed during hypnosis — Unconscious / I / Conscious

Reappears in consciousness in a disguised form

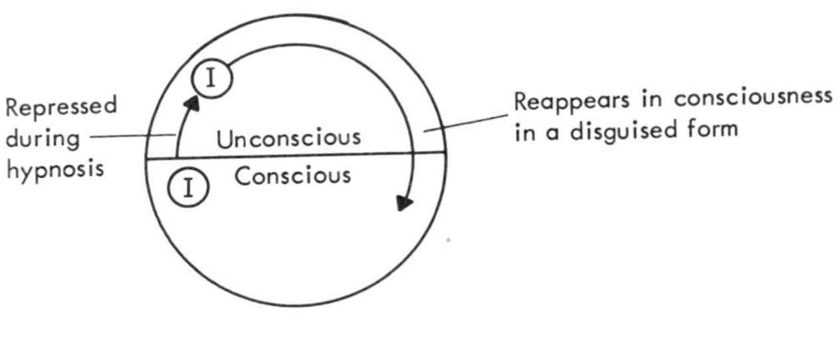

Freud developed a model of personality based on three psychic systems, the id, ego, and superego. The id is the source of energy for both the libido and the ego (libido being the biological drives, the "instincts" seeking gratification). Freud characterized the basic drives as being sexual, but he included much more in the term "sexual" than others. At any rate, the id can be thought of as what the person wants and goes after; it is in closer touch with the body and its processes than with the external world. It operates on the principle of maximizing pleasure and minimizing pain. The id is the foundation on which the personality is built. It is infantile and recognizes nothing external to itself.

The ego may be briefly described as consciousness, or how the person goes about getting what he (the id) wants. The ego is in contact with reality; it has to mediate between the desires of the id, the strictures of the superego, and reality.

The superego is basically a censor mechanism. When it is conscious, it represents conscience. The identifications upon which the superego is based are those of idealized and omnipotent parents. As the ego sets out to get what the id wants, the superego dictates what the permissible methods and strategies are. While it represents the moral values of parents, authority figures, and society, the superego should be recognized as internalized—it is the person's own value system, what he has taken in and made his own, even if in part unconsciously.

The Oedipus complex is so named from the play by Sophocles wherein the son unwittingly kills his father and marries his mother. Freud believed the Oedipal stage of childhood to be basic and fundamental to all human relationships. He defines the Oedipal situation as, "the boy craves exclusive sexual possession of the mother and feels antagonistic towards the father." More generally, each person feels a rivalry with the parent of his own sex for the love of the parent of the opposite sex. According to Freud, the solution to these psychological equations determines the fundamental basis of an individual's personality.

N. Walker, in *A Short History of Psychotherapy*, assesses the important assumptions of Freud's psychology as follows:

> In the first place it is deterministic. *It looks for a cause for every human change in the present state—mental or physical—of that human being.... Its implications, however, are not as materialistic* as the Edwardian Christians feared. . . . It is also what I call "egalitarian," *in the sense that it pays as little attention as possible to hereditary differences between one person and another. . . . It is also what I call "optimistic."*

THE DEFENCE MECHANISMS

When an executive suffers severe or prolonged frustration, his failure to achieve his goal may cause a considerable increase of pressure on his ego. The ego comes under pressure from three sources: the id (pressure for gratification), the environment (the source of "real" threats), and the superego (with its desire to censor the ego). To meet these pressures, Freud developed the idea of the defence mechanism. Examples of defence mechanisms include:

Regression: relapsing into an earlier stage of psychosexual genesis as a consequence of frustration. A frequently cited example of regression to the oral phase is thumb sucking. A good illustration of regression is the behaviour of the managing director who has for months strained every nerve to carry through an important negotiation with shop stewards and union officials only to have the whole process brought to a halt by some trivial matter on which the stewards refuse to compromise. Suddenly, as a result of this frustration, the managing director begins to pound the table and starts to repeat "I just won't have it; it isn't good enough. I'll have their guts for garters."

Rationalization: developing untrue but creditable motives instead of facing up to true motives, especially if they are unconscious or unpleasant. Rationalization, which requires the invention of "plausible" reasons to account for some behaviour which leaves the individual open to criticism, does not necessarily represent a deliberate act of lying. Rationalization is most obviously used to explain failures when job hunting, as in the case of the applicant for a broadcast announcer's job who explained, "they w-w-wouldn't h-hire m-me because I'm a C-C-Catholic."

Projection: ascribing one's own defect or motive to another when one will not admit it in oneself. For example, the puritanical, sexually frustrated spinster regards most other women as promiscuous. A good example of projection is the executive in a crisis who keeps muttering to his personal assistants, "Don't panic, don't panic, don't panic." Using projection, an executive is able to redefine the situation by assigning his own undesirable traits to others.

Sublimation: channelling sexual energy into a socially more acceptable direction. It is often alleged by experienced production managers that in the early days of personnel management, some of the do-gooders who entered this field were obviously sublimating more primitive emotions.

Repression: subjecting frustrated motives and anxieties to forces which make them less accessible to consciousness. Sexual and aggressive motives frequently have to be repressed because of social values and taboos. An executive who is unable to admit his need for affection and security because he sees this kind of behaviour as a sign of weakness may display a very tough aggressive exterior.

Reaction formation: acting in a manner opposite to one's true feelings or motives as a consequence of the repression of anxiety. An executive who is noted for his hostility may display excessive friendliness towards his colleagues because of anxieties which his hostility has generated in the past.

Identification: assuming the characteristics, attitudes, mannerisms, or eccentricities of another person. Many managers' social learning is greatly facilitated by the technique of identification.

Freud placed great emphasis on dreams as one way the unconscious thrusts repressed anxieties back towards the conscious mind. Remembering and correctly analysing dreams is central to his psychoanalysis. Modern research lends support for this emphasis. Psychologists have demonstrated that when people dream, rapid eye movements (R.E.M.) take place. In experiments, subjects wakened during periods of R.E.M. report that they have been dreaming; those wakened while still-eyed do not. All the subjects studied dreamed every night (on an average, four to five times a night). People who were denied the opportunity to dream by being awakened whenever R.E.M. took place apparently became anxious and upset, while those awakened at non-R.E.M. times were not. One subject in the experiment who was denied the opportunity to dream left the study in apparent panic. Most executives will readily understand the role of dreaming in alleviating anxiety and mitigating guilt. Some psychologists believe that if dream deprivation is continued long enough, a serious disruption of personality may ensue.

WHY EXECUTIVES SHOULD KNOW ABOUT PSYCHOANALYSIS

It is obvious to teachers of human relations that executives who take such courses are not unaware that psychoanalysis has been heavily criticized by psychologists such as H. J. Eysenck. The principal criticism directed at psychoanalysis is that it lacks curative value; or, more precisely, examination of available data shows that psychoanalysis is not more effective than, say, spontaneous remission. In any case, most executives' interest in psychoanalysis is not in its value as a therapeutic agent for the mentally ill, but rather in the possibility of shoring up their own egos and explaining their own behaviour and attitudes.

Executive life, being what it is, demands considerable strength of ego. In business, problems do not present themselves in such a fashion that an executive can make a decision which is certainly correct. Usually many options will be open to the executive; none will be absolutely free of risk or disadvantage. He must make a decision which inevitably will only reduce the degree of uncertainty, not eliminate it. In many, if not most, cases, it will be impossible to say whether he was right (or to measure the extent to which his decision was suboptimal). Given this problem of objective verification, most managers opt for the "best decision" and hope for consensus from superiors and colleagues. The need to rationalize decisions is only too painfully obvious to the executive of the 1970s. The executive act is iterative; i.e., you can't solve the equations involved exactly but can only get approximate solutions which you then resubstitute in your original equations to improve the accuracy of the decision-making process.

The modern justification of psychoanalysis assumes that the object of treatment is not to cure patients in the traditional sense—i.e., free them completely from neurotic traits or anxiety—but rather to give a semantic explanation of the patient's behaviour and attitudes which makes sense to the patient. Most executives taking management courses, in my experi ence, readily accept and welcome the idea that for most people there is no hope of being fully integrated, completely mature, free from neurotic anxiety and guilt. Most accept the idea that their mental health will be suboptimal.

Thus arose the idea that psychoanalysis is basically a biological theory of meaning which will help a person to reconcile himself to his basic in stinctual needs—"to each his own delusional system" might be a good slogan. Further, the idea that psychoanalysis offers the patient the oppor tunity to establish a relationship of a fruitful kind with another person i one which most executives can appreciate and exploit.

TOPIC 5
Motivation

Modern organization theorists have found the concept of personality natural and fruitful starting point for looking at business behaviour. Inher

FIGURE 7–7

cause	generate	to reach	lead to

NEEDS – – – ►DRIVES – – – ►BEHAVIOUR – – ►GOALS – – – –►REDUCTION OR RELEASE OF TENSIC

ent in this approach is the notion that personality can be thought of as system of organized drives and that the parts of personality hold togethe because a change in one part of personality produces a change in othe parts.

Central to the concept of personality is the idea of motivation (i.e. behaviour instigated by needs and directed towards the goals that can satisfy these needs). Figure 7–7 illustrates the motivation sequence. It i widely believed that when a person is motivated, he is in a state of tension and this generates energy. He feels impelled to take some kind of action Motivation selectively organizes an individual's perception so that hi learning is structured in a certain direction.

Basically there are two categories of needs:

1. *Physiological needs* are the needs associated with hunger, thirst warmth, cold, sleep, sex, pain. It is generally assumed that the body regulates its activities in some cybernetic manner to achieve some kind of homeostasis where action can be taken to correct any imbalance of physiological needs (e.g., if a person is deprived of salt, then offered choice of two foods, he will automatically opt for the food with the greater amount of salt).

2. *Psychogenic needs* are needs learned by the individual through his association with other people. They include: (*a*) the need for association (the need to belong), (*b*) the need for achievement, and (*c*) the need for power (the need to control and dominate others).

Maslow in his motivation theory of sequential development has classified human needs into five categories:

1. Physiological needs; e.g., thirst, hunger, sex.
2. Safety needs; e.g., security and order.
3. The need to belong; e.g., identification and love.
4. Esteem needs; e.g., success, self-respect.
5. Need for self-actualization; i.e., need for identity and self-fulfilment.

Maslow's theory of human motivation is the most widely taught view of motivation in North American business schools and provides the theoretical framework for much organization theory. He takes the view that a 'lower need must be filled before the next higher need can emerge." Once the "lower" need has been filled, it occupies a less important role.

THE MOTIVATION-HYGIENE THEORY

Frederick Herzberg, an American psychologist, produced in the 1960s a new and exciting theory of motivation which attracted a great deal of attention among both executives and academics. In his widely read and very well-written *Work and the Nature of Man*, Herzberg starts from the proposition that business is the dominant institution of contemporary society and goes on to set out his concept of man's basic needs in his now famous motivation-hygiene (M-H) theory. The two basic and fundamental propositions of M-H theory are:

1. The factors producing job satisfaction are separate and distinct from those that lead to job dissatisfaction.

2. (*a*) The factors that lead to job satisfaction (the motivators) are achievement, recognition, work itself, responsibility, and advancement. (*b*) The dissatisfiers (hygiene factors) such as company policy and administration, supervision, interpersonal relations, working conditions, and salary contribute very little to job satisfaction.

In brief, according to Herzberg, employees feel good about their work when it provides the opportunity for psychological growth within which they can meet the fulfilment of self-actualizing needs. A "hygienic" environment, on the other hand, reduces or prevents discontent. As Herzberg points out in *Work and the Nature of Man:*

> To reiterate, mankind has two sets of needs. Think about man twice:
> once about events that cause him pain, and, secondly, about events that
> make him happy. Those who seek only to gratify the needs of their
> animal natures are doomed to live in dreadful anticipation of pain and
> suffering. This is the fate of those human beings who want to satisfy

only their biological needs. But some men have become aware of the advantage humans have over their animal brothers. In addition to the compulsion to avoid pain, the human being has been blessed with the potentiality to achieve happiness. And, as I hope I have demonstrated man can be happy only by seeking to satisfy both his animal need to avoid pain and his human need to grow psychologically.

Table 7–2 shows how Herzberg's factors can be compared to those of Maslow and to D. McGregor's Theory X and Theory Y.

HERZBERG'S RESEARCH METHOD

Herzberg's research technique is based on the critical incident technique and uses interviewing as its method. The findings could be graphed

TABLE 7–2

Maslow	*Herzberg*	*McGregor*
Physiological needs . . . . Safety needs	Hygiene factors	Theory X
The need to belong . . . . Esteem needs . . . . The need for self-actualization	Motivators	Theory Y

as shown in Figure 7–8. Herzberg's patterned interview technique can be gauged from the introductory paragraph which he uses to start his interviewing, as described in Herzberg *et al., The Motivation to Work:*

> Think of a time when you felt exceptionally good or exceptionally bad about your job, either your present job or any other job you have had. This can be either the "long-range" or the "short-range" kind of situation, as I have just described it. Tell me what happened.
> 1. How long ago did this happen?
> 2. How long did the feeling last? Can you describe specifically what made the change of feelings begin? When did it end?
> 3. (For obviously SR sequences.) Was what happened typical of what was going on at the time?
> 4. Can you tell me more precisely why you felt the way you did at the time?
> 5. What did these events mean to you?
> 6. Did these feelings affect the way you did your job? How long did this go on?
> 7. Can you give me a specific example of the way in which your performance on the job was affected? (For productivity effect when the effect information was vague.) How long?
> 8. Did what happened affect you personally in any way? How long? Did it change the way you got along with people in general or your

FIGURE 7-8
COMPARISON OF SATISFIERS AND DISSATISFIERS

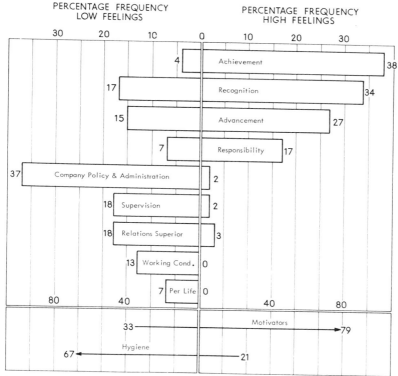

PERCENTAGE FREQUENCY LOW FEELINGS — PERCENTAGE FREQUENCY HIGH FEELINGS

Achievement 4 / 38
Recognition 17 / 34
Advancement 15 / 27
Responsibility 7 / 17
Company Policy & Administration 37 / 2
Supervision 18 / 2
Relations Superior 18 / 3
Working Cond. 13 / 0
Per Life 7 / 0

Motivators 33 / 79
Hygiene 67 / 21

Data on a survey of Pittsburgh accountants from F. Herzberg *et al., The Motivation to Work.* (New York: John Wiley & Sons, Inc., 1959).

family? Did it affect your sleep, appetite, digestion, general health? and so on.

Both the research technique and M-H theory as a whole have been severely criticized (see Box 7.3). The concept of self-actualization is not an entirely happy one: for the shop floor operative it is almost meaningless and for top management almost an act of faith. It is always as well to bear in mind that academics, who place considerable value on autonomy and inner direction, have an obsession about making work meaningful. The notion that it is possible to realize man's true nature through creative work which is its own reward is an exceedingly attractive proposition to the learned don which is rarely fully shared by his wife. What is certain from research using Herzberg's scale is that management is much more highly motivated in the growth, recognition, and achievement sense than are supervisors who, in turn, are more highly motivated than shop floor operatives.

Box 7.3: The façade of the dual-factor theory

Robert J. House and Lawrence A. Wigdor, both of the Bernard M. Baruch College of the City University of New York, have reviewed the evidence on the validity of Herzberg's "dual-factor" theory of job satisfaction and motivation.

They review approximately 40 studies which criticize the theory on three grounds. The first is that the theory is methodologically bound. The critical incident method which was used by Herzberg recounts extremely satisfying and dissatisfying job events. When things are going well people tend to take the credit, but they protect their self-images when things go poorly by blaming failures on the environment. As long as the critical incident method is employed, the results will be an artifact of the method. The second criticism is also related to research methodology. The respondent's description of his previous behaviour was evaluated by a rater, which required an uncontrolled evaluation on the part of the rater. Rater contamination of the dimensions derived could easily have occurred.

A third criticism is that no measure of overall satisfaction was employed in the research on which the theory is based. A person may dislike a part of his job yet still think the job is acceptable. A fourth major criticism is the inconsistency of the theory with previous research. Situational variables seem to play an important role in any relationship between satisfaction and productivity. Further research is needed to be able to predict in what situations worker satisfaction will produce greater productivity.

In a secondary analysis of Herzberg's data, House and Wigdor show results contradictory to the results presented by Herzberg in *Work and the Nature of Man*. It is shown that, in fact, achievement and recognition are more frequently identified as dissatisfiers than working conditions and relations with the superior. Studies directly testing the Herzberg theory are summarized. These studies yield results that for the most part fail to support the theory. Since the data concerning the first proposition does not support the two-dimension theory, the second proposition (that satisfiers have more motivational force than dissatisfiers) appears highly suspect. The voluminous number of studies cited show that one factor can cause job satisfaction for one person and job dissatisfaction for another. This result can occur even in the same sample. Also, these studies show that intrinsic job factors are more important to both satisfying and dissatisfying job events. These conclusions led House and Wigdor to conclude that the two-factor theory is an oversimplification of the relationship between motivation and satisfaction and the sources of job satisfaction and dissatisfaction.

R. J. House (with Lawrence A. Wigdor), "Herzberg's Dual-Factor Theory of Job Satisfaction Motivation: A Review of the Evidence and a Criticism," *Personnel Psychology*, Vol. 20, No. 1 (Winter 1967), pp. 369–89.

The idea of self-actualization implies that it is possible to design organizations that are not only compatible with the human personality but which by their very design will allow the complete flowering of individual talent. To my mind, this optimistic approach frequently induces a reaction of despair in supervisory groups who are being led through the mysteries of Maslow, Herzberg, and McGregor. This is particularly true of female supervisors and older male supervisors, the former on account of the male dominance of executive posts and the latter because the educational ladder as a means of "actualization" is less readily available.

In general, it would seem that the concept of self-actualization must be thought of as more an ethical concept than a psychological reality. This multilevel approach to organizational motivation which commands wide support in business schools seems unlikely to survive scrupulous examination in its present form.

MOTIVATION VIA PAYOFFS AND PROBABILITIES

Motivation has to do with the forces that maintain and alter the direction, quality, and intensity of behaviour. The motivation of a person has three aspects:

1. The direction of his behaviour—what he chooses to do when presented with a number of options.
2. The intensity, amplitude, or strength of his response once the choice has been made.
3. The persistence of the behaviour—how long he is able to maintain an effort.

What does it mean when you say you are motivated? It means perhaps that you are all set to go. There is something out there which you are going to do, or at least going to have a good go at. You know what's in it for you if you do, or perhaps if you don't. You are mobilized. In your innocence, you wonder if you'll run out of adrenalin before getting started. If there is a hang-up in getting started, you wonder, "Why the hell am I doing this? There must be easier ways of doing things." Then you think, "I'm not backing off. I'm going through with this." And, luckily for you, the perceptual astigmatism of motivation comes into play and you get tunnel vision about what you are going to do. The alternatives are out of the way—rightly or wrongly, you're off.

Afterward, when round one is over, you feel somewhat tired. It possibly didn't turn out quite as you expected. You feel a little drained and you wonder. Motivation seems to work like a Gestalt completion test; a bit of a circle is missing and you feel you can pull, say, task T together:

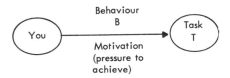

Put another way, your motivation causes you to behave (B) in a way that will achieve the task and get the payoff, P, which can be extrinsic (salary, promotion) or intrinsic (satisfaction of a job well done):

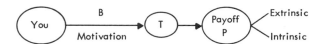

All this may work for you, but how do you motivate or energize the guy who works with you? What are his values, attitudes, needs, and expectations that you can stimulate (manipulate)?

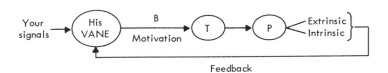

Feedback

How can you get him going (trigger his circuits) and keep him going? What can the behavioural scientist tell you about this process that will help to make both of you more effective? How can you structure his perceptions? Some of the issues that we will be exploring are:

1. How big is the buck for him?
2. Does he want recognition?
3. Is a word at the right moment all he needs?
4. Does he need to be reassured that he is on the team?
5. Does he just need a chance to sound off?

What about his unconscious motivations? Is his life a rerun of his World War II adventures? Is he playing out the Oedipal stage you think he should have worked out in growing up? Basically, you need to figure out what his model of the world is and act accordingly.

ATKINSON EXPECTANCY MODEL

Recognizing the complexity of motivation, J. W. Atkinson has developed and extended the theory of motivation to include the concept of expectancy. Basic to the expectancy model are the notions that people have expectations concerning the outcomes that are likely to occur as the result of what they do and that they have preferences among outcomes. The assumption is that an individual has some insight about the possible consequences of his acts and makes conscious choices among consequences according to the probabilities of their occurring and their value to him.

Atkinson postulates the existence of a class of motives whose end result is the minimization of pain. This particular motive Atkinson terms fear of failure. He proposes essentially an expectancy–valence model of motivation which has three elements:

1. The strength of the motive.
2. The incentive value which arouses the motive.
3. The individual's expectancy that his behaviour will lead to the reward or incentive.

As Figure 7–9 illustrates, the individual has a tendency to approach a task (T) with the intention of performing successfully (T_s) in a multiplicative function of the type:

$$T_s = M_s \times P_s \times I_s$$

where M_s is the strength of the achievement motive, P_s the subjective probability of success, and I_s the valence of the incentive value of success. Likewise:

$$T_f = M_f \times P_f \times I_f$$

where T_f is the intention to avoid failure and the motive strength, probability, and incentive value are stated in terms of avoiding failure by avoiding the task. For any given task, the observed behaviour tendency is the resultant of T_s and T_f.

FIGURE 7–9
ATKINSON MOTIVATION MODEL

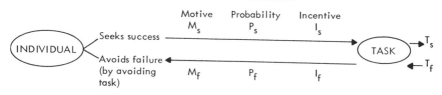

The Atkinson model was developed to explain behaviour and performance related to the need for achievement (*n Ach*), the need for power (*n Pow*) and the need for affiliation (*n Aff*). The need for achievement is the need to excel in relation to competitive or internalized standards; the need for power is the need to influence, monitor, control, and manipulate others as an end in itself; and the need for affiliation is the need to belong, to be loved, and to have warm and friendly relations.

MEASURING NEEDS

A projection test, where a person projects meaning while perceiving something, is a rather useful way of gaining insight into personality. The method involves presenting a person with an unstructured, incomplete, or ambiguous stimulus such as an ink blot or a picture and asking him what he sees. Presented with a stimulus which has no definite, fixed, or correct meaning, he may attempt to infer the nature of the object from the category systems which structure his perceptions and thus reveal, at least in part, something of his values, attitudes, needs, and expectations.

A little thought will show that almost any kind of stimulus material may be the basis for a projection test. H. A. Murray devised an extremely useful projection test called the Thematic Apperception Test (TAT) which consists of 20 pictures which are presented to the subject, one at a time. The person is asked to tell a story which can explain the events in the picture. The instructions for the TAT include:

> This is a test of imagination, one form of intelligence. I am going to show you some pictures, one at a time; and your task will be to make up as dramatic a story as you can for each. Tell what has led up to the event shown in the picture, describe what is happening at the moment, what the characters are feeling and thinking; and then give the outcome. Speak your thoughts as they come to your mind. Do you understand? Since you have fifty minutes for ten pictures, you can devote about five minutes to each story. Here is the first picture.

Using the TAT, Murray identified about 20 basic needs including the need for achievement, the need for affiliation, and the need for power.

Both David McClelland and J. W. Atkinson have built on Murray's work, refining and intensively investigating these three needs, which we will discuss in the next sections.

THE NEED FOR ACHIEVEMENT

The achievement motive may be defined as the need to master or overcome difficulties. The motive is presumed not to operate until it is brought on or aroused by certain situational cues or incentives which signal the individual that certain behaviours will lead to feelings of achievement. Atkinson has argued that a particular motive—whether it be achievement, affiliation, or power—is actually a label for a class of incentives which, when they are activated, produce essentially the same result. When they are activated you experience a sense of satisfaction and pride in accomplishment, or a sense of belonging, or a feeling of being in command, which correspond respectively to *n Ach, n Aff,* and *n Pow.*

Since achievement motivation is learned, it should be possible to specify the conditions of development which lead to its establishment. McClelland has described persons high in achievement as "independent in action as well as thought; their independence appears almost to be a consistent 'way of life' which either originates or is reflected in their relationship to their parents." Box 7.4 summarizes more of his achievement theory. McClelland argues that the general level of achievement motivation in a given society is connected with economic growth. After careful examination of a wide variety of evidence, he concludes that a relationship exists between the general level of achievement motivation and cycles of increased productivity and industrialization.

If an executive spends a great deal of time thinking about his job and about how he can achieve excellence and thus advance his career, such an executive has a high need for achievement. Some of the elements of this

7.4: The need to achieve

avid C. McClelland, chairman of the department of social relations at Harvard, has roduced one of the most interesting modern theories on motivation. This theory states at a person's desire to do things better is due to a very specific motive, namely the eed for achievement or *n Ach* motive, and that the *n Ach* motive is acquired rather an genetic.

Persons who exhibit the following characteristics are said to possess the *n Ach* otive:

. They "set moderately difficult, but potentially achievable goals for themselves."

. They "prefer to work at a problem rather than leave the outcome to chance or to others." That is, "they are concerned with personal achievement rather than with the rewards for success per se."

. They have "a strong preference for work situations in which they get concrete feedback on how well they are doing."

The strength of the *n Ach* motive is measured by "taking samples of a man's spontaneous thought [such as making up a story about a picture he has been shown] and ounting the frequency with which he mentions doing things better."

Research has shown that not all people who are considered great achievers score igh in *n Ach,* because success in the various professions depends on other motives as vell as personality characteristics. It has been found, however, that business executives end to score high in *n Ach* and that companies which have a significant number of xecutives high in *n Ach* tend to grow faster.

Analysis of the evidence also indicates that the *n Ach* motive can be acquired hrough training, by teaching a person to think and behave in *n Ach* terms. Such training has been given to American, Mexican, and Indian business executives and to underchieving high school boys. "In every instance save one [the Mexican case], it was ossible to demonstrate statistically, some two years later, that the men who took the ourse had done better [made more money, got promoted faster, expanded their businesses faster] than comparable men who did not take the course or who took some ther management course." In the group of high school boys it was found that "the oys from the middle class improved steadily in grades in school over a two-year period, ut boys from the lower class showed an improvement after the first year followed by a rop back to their beginning low grade average." This result may indicate that the environment in which a person lives helps to encourage the expression of the motive.

McClelland is somewhat cautious about his findings but nonetheless optimistic, and e takes the view that this approach to the motivation to work could be very useful in elping underdeveloped groups and countries to help themselves.

). C. McClelland, "That Urge to Achieve," *Think* (published by IBM), Vol. 32, No. 6 (November-ember, 1966), pp. 19–23.

need are revealed by study of this kind of executive. He actively seeks to take responsibility for finding solutions to problems. The achieving executive gets a charge, not from the payoff, but from managing the situations that generate the payoff. Research findings suggest that the achieving executive is not interested in gambling games, where the outcome is mainly determined by chance. He is interested in decision making which involves risk if his efforts are a significant factor in determining the outcome. But in setting the level of risk, the high achiever sets moderate goals and takes calculated risks.

The achieving executive, having set his goals, is capable of evolving a set of alternatives which will let him reach his goals. He is then able to evaluate each of these alternatives against a set of criteria and make an intelligent selection. Having selected an alternative, he can spot blockages impeding his intention and develop tactics to circumvent or remove them. The achieving executive has a strong need for feedback to monitor his efforts and to give him satisfaction as he moves towards his goal.

THE NEED FOR POWER

The executive who spends his time thinking about how he can influence, control, and manipulate others as an end in itself has, of course, a strong need for power. The power-hungry executive desires to possess people, to punish them, to bend them to his will, and to make them give way in argument. Bedevilled by a compulsive need to influence others, those with a high power need are frequently fans of both Dale Carnegie and Niccolo Machiavelli.

This need to dominate others often manifests itself in an argumentative, polemical, verbally fluent life style. Typically others see power needers as forceful and outspoken, but also hard-headed and demanding, others feel they have to respond to them.

From an occupational optic, people with a strong need for power enjoy persuasion, cajoling, and "seduction" as means of influencing others, and they are strongly attracted to roles such as teaching and public speaking. Motivation studies of managers reveal that while entrepreneurs and managers have significant needs for achievement, the man who makes it to the top in business is usually strongly motivated by the need for power.

But the need for power does not guarantee a place at the top of the pecking hierarchy, and even when the *n Pow* man arrives, what he does is influenced by other needs.

THE NEED FOR AFFILIATION

The man who gives up his days and nights to thinking about how he can get other men to love him has a strong need for affiliation. Such *n Aff* men are more alert to the feelings and needs of colleagues, and they seek roles which offer opportunities for friendly interactions. In corporate affairs, they are attracted to the human relations type of personnel appointments. The curious thing is that *n Aff* does not seem to be important for effective executive effort and performance and may even be detrimental. But it is widely believed, at least by psychoanalytically inspired organizational psychologists, that superior executive performance requires a basic affiliative attitude. At least, executives who are short on *n Aff* can be made to feel guilty unless they achieve considerable interpersonal competence. Much of such comment appears naive and has little contact with reality. Common experience produces a wealth of examples of high-powered corporate officials who got to the top by delivering "the cookies" and in the process were not overly scrupulous or careful about whose toes they stepped on. Such superior performers frequently are more complex mentally than their colleagues, and attempts by the less able to interpret their behaviour are often misleading. The high performer would argue that "less complex systems cannot control or understand more complex systems" (as every budding student of operations research knows). The less powerful may not have a counterargument—but at least they can make the high-powered feel guilty.

NEEDS AND JOB DESIGN

Atkinson has developed a projection test (similar to the TAT) which can be used as a means of identifying aroused motivations. When this test is used with a group of people of similar backgrounds and experiences, differences of scores can be indicative of variations in the strength of basic motives. Such tests are often of considerable value in training situations as a means of alerting managers to their own particular motivation structure. The scoring instructions are both complex and complicated. Nevertheless, such tests have been integrated into programmes developed to teach the need to achieve.

What is more important for the busy executive is to be aware of these different motives and to take them into consideration when designing jobs and selecting people for them. The effective executive will have a growing and consuming interest in monitoring the motivation processes of colleagues after selective signalling which he hopes will trigger off or maintain patterns of appropriate (whatever this term means) behaviour. He must selectively arouse, satisfy, and reinforce other peoples' motivation tracks. To do this, he must understand the other fellow's expectancies and incentives: how he gets his kicks, how certain he is of them, what constitutes challenge for him, what he wants out of work, and what the score really is.

All these matters are integral to the path-goal theory of motivation, to which we are going to turn in a moment. What is important in n Ach, n Pow, and n Aff motivation theory is not the substantive research findings, interesting as they may be, but the actual path-goal process which such a theory needs to make sense of its findings. To end on a negative note, when somebody challenges your motives, the answer is not to deny his allegations (which he cannot make stick without your confession) but rather to try to peer behind the challenge to understand the process model which he is using. Motivation theory too often involves a mechanical analogy, usually with valves, pumps, reservoirs, and work and energy transactions. Such hydrostatic models of motivation, usually dreamt up by psychological plumbers, tie the whole discussion of the meaning of life to the workings of simple water closet models. The importance of a model is to suggest new ways of looking at problems which facilitate collecting and organizing new data in different ways. The path-goal model has fewer moving theoretical parts, has not broken down yet on test, and is a general-purpose theory which has turned out to be at home in the leadership field.

VROOM'S MODEL OF MOTIVATION

A new theory of motivation has been developed by Victor Vroom, professor of industrial administration and psychology at the Carnegie-Mellon School of Industrial Administration in Pittsburgh. Vroom's theory, which is much more difficult to grasp then Herzberg's, has considerable scientific validity and has generated a considerable amount of empirical activity since it was published in 1964.

A good way of getting into Vroom's theory is to consider the path-goal hypothesis, which essentially opposes the widespread but unsubstantiated human relations view that improving a worker's satisfaction increases productivity. Reacting against this human relations view, A. H. Brayfield and W. H. Crockett in "Employee Attitudes and Employee Performance" suggest a different relation between productivity and satisfaction:

> It makes sense to us to assume that individuals are motivated to achieve certain environmental goals and that the achievement of these goals results in satisfaction. Productivity is seldom a goal in itself but is more commonly a means to goal attainment. Therefore . . . we might expect high satisfaction and high productivity to occur together when productivity is perceived as a path to certain important goals and when these goals are achieved.

B. S. Georgopoulos, G. M. Mahoney, and N. W. Jones, in "A Path-Goal Approach to Productivity," added some empirical flesh to the path-goal hypothesis by trying to determine why only some workers turn out to be high producers. They define the path-goal hypothesis as:

> *If a worker sees high productivity as a path leading to the attainment of one or more of his personal goals, he will tend to be a high producer. Conversely, if he sees low productivity as a path to the achievement of his goals, he will tend to be a low producer.*

and point out:

> This approach is based on the following assumptions: Individual productivity is, among other things, a function of one's motivation to produce at a given level; in turn, such motivation depends upon (a) the particular needs of the individual as reflected in the goals toward which he is moving, and (b) his perception regarding the relative usefulness of

productivity behavior as an instrumentality, or as a path to the attainment of these goals.

In other words, for a person to be motivated, the task must evoke some of his needs and the successful completion of the task must be instrumental in reaching his goals.

Vroom has taken up the idea of the path-goal hypothesis and developed it into a full-blown expectancy theory of motivation. In *Work and Motivation*, he defines motivation as:

> A process governing choices, made by persons or lower organisms, among alternative forms of voluntary activity.

Vroom's process theory utilizes the concept of instrumentality. Implicit in his theory is the notion that behaviour is perceived as instrumental for the achievement of some outcomes and the evaluation of the outcomes. Fig-

FIGURE 7–10
VROOM'S MODEL OF MOTIVATION

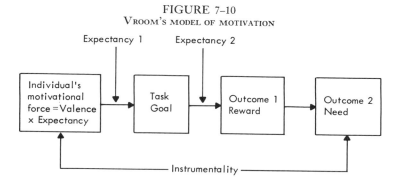

ure 7–10 illustrates Vroom's theory. The expectancies are the probabilities the person sees, first of accomplishing the task goal, and second of being rewarded for this achievement. Task accomplishment may be high, medium, or low productivity. The first (reward) level of outcomes includes such things as pay, promotion, good working conditions, and job security. The second-level outcomes are the individual's needs, physical (food, shelter), ego (status, fulfilment), and so on. Vroom's model uses two unusual concepts, valence and instrumentality.

The valence is the strength of an individual's preference for a particular outcome and is related to his concept of utility—how he values a particular outcome. The instrumentality is the individual's perception of the relationship between first-level outcomes (rewards or incentives) and second-level outcomes (needs). He has the second-level outcome in mind (predicts it) from the outset. For example a highly productive worker may see high productivity as a means of increasing his income (first-level outcome), which in turn is instrumental in achieving improved status (second-level outcome), perhaps by facilitating home improvements. An-

Box 7.5: Empirical tests of Vroom's model

Vroom has already shown how his model can integrate many of the empirical findings in the literature on motivation in organizations. However, because it is a relatively recent development, empirical tests of the model itself are jus† beginning to appear. Here we shall consider four such investigations.

In the first study, Vroom is concerned with predicting the organizational choices of graduating college students on the basis of their instrumentality-goal index scores. These scores reflect the extent to which membership in an organization was perceived by the student as being related to the acquisition of desired goals. According to the theory, the chosen organization should be the one with the highest instrumentality-goal index. Ratings were used to obtain preferences for 15 different goals and the extent to which these goals could be attained through membership in three different organizations. These two ratings were thus measures of the valences of second-level outcomes and the instrumentality of organizational membership for attainment of these outcomes, respectively. The instrumentality-goal index was the correlation between these two measures. But Vroom's theory also involves consideration of expectancy, i.e., how probable is it that the student can become a member of a particular organization. The choice is not his alone but depends upon whether he is acceptable to the organization. A rough measure of expectancy in this study was whether or not the student had received an offer by the organization. If he had received an offer, expectancy would be high; if not, it would be low. The results show that, considering only organizations from which offers of employment were actually received, 76 percent of the students chose the organization with the highest instrumentality-goal index score. The evidence thus strongly supports Vroom's theory.

The next study, by Galbraith and Cummings, utilizes the model to predict the productivity of operative workers. Graphic rating scales were used to measure the instrumentality of performance for five goals—money, fringe benefits, promotion, supervisor's support, and group acceptance. Similar ratings were used for measuring the desirability of each of the goals for the worker. The authors anticipated that a worker's expectation that he could produce at a high level would have a probability of one because the jobs were independent and productivity was a function of the worker's own effort independent of other human or machine pacing. [The following diagram] outlines the research design.

Multiple regression analysis showed that productivity was significantly related positively to the instrumentality-goal interactions for supervisor support and money, and there was an almost significant ($p < .10$) relationship with group acceptance. The other factors did not approach significance and the authors explain this lack of significance in terms of the situational context. That is, fringe benefits were dependent not so much on productivity as on a union/management contract, and promotion was based primarily on seniority. Thus the instrumentality of productivity for the attainment of these

J. G. Hunt and J. W. Hill, "The New Look in Motivational Theory for Organizational Resear⟨ *Human Organization,* Vol. 28 (Summer, 1969), pp. 100–109.

other worker may be quite happy with his pay and see medium productivity as leading to a first-level outcome of group acceptance, which meets his need to belong, a second-level outcome. Box 7.5 explains all of these concepts in more detail.

Valence is measured by asking workers to rate important personal goals, such as promotion, pay, and pleasant working conditions, in the

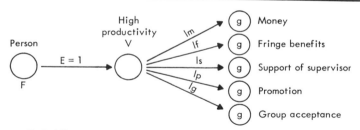

g = Desirability of a particular outcome (rating)
I = Instrumentality of production for particular outcomes (rating of relationship)
E = Expectancy (= 1 here because worker sets own pace and is assumed to be capable of high productivity)
V = (Valence) the sum of the cross products of instrumentality and g
F = (Force) expectancy times the valence of productivity
Productivity = Objective measures of amount of production in relation to the production standard

goals was low and the model would predict no relationship. The Galbraith and Cummings study thus supports Vroom's contention that motivation is related to productivity in those situations where the acquisition of desired goals is dependent upon the individual's production and not when desired outcomes are contingent on other factors.

A third study is that of Hill relating a model similar to Vroom's to behavior in a utility company. Hill's model is based upon Edward's subjective expected utility maximization theory of decision making. Here one given a choice between alternatives A and/or B will select that alternative which maximizes his subjective expected utility or expected value. If the outcomes associated with action A are more desirable than those associated with B, and their probability of occurrence is greater than or equal to those associated with B, then an individual will choose behavior A over behavior B. The basic concepts are subjective expectation and subjective utility or valence. Expectation and utility are multiplicatively related and can be measured by the same techniques used to test Vroom's theory. Where a relationship is found between Subjective Expected Utility S.E.U.) and overt behavior, it can be interpreted as support for Vroom.

The behavior considered in Hill's study is that of job bidding. This behavior is encountered in organizations that post descriptions of job openings on employee bulletin boards and encourage qualified employees to "bid" (apply) for them. Here records were kept of the number of bids made over a three-year period by groups of semi-skilled electrical repairmen matched in learning ability, seniority in grade, and age. The men were asked about the consequences of bidding and not bidding on the next higher

order of their desirability. Instrumentality is measured by asking employees to state the relation and direction between a first-level outcome (e.g., pay) and a second-level outcome (e.g., acceptance by the work group).

According to Vroom, instrumentality, like the coefficient of correlation, varies between +1 and −1. What this means is that when the instrumentality is +1, a first-level outcome is seen as always leading to a particular second-level outcome, and when the instrumentality is −1, as never

grade job, and rated the consequence on a seven-point scale of desirability and a similar scale of probability of occurrence. Bidders were those who had bid three or more times during that time.

Fourteen different S.E.U. indices were computed from interview data to determine the relative validity of each in predicting bidding behavior. Typical of these indices were: (1) the sums of the cross products of expectation and utility for the positive consequences of bidding ($\overset{+}{\Sigma}$ S.E.U.); (2) the same score for the negative consequences of bidding ($\overset{-}{\Sigma}$ S.E.U.) and (3) the cross products of the *mean* expectation and utility scores for positive and negative consequences $\left(\dfrac{\overset{+}{\Sigma} \text{S.E.U.}}{N}, \dfrac{\overset{-}{\Sigma} \text{S.E.U.}}{N} \right)$. In addition to these S.E.U. indices, two traditional attitudinal and motivational measures were used. Semantic Differential scales measured each subject's respective evaluation of bidding and the next higher grade job and each subject's Need for Achievement was obtained.

It was hypothesized that: (1) there would be a positive correlation between the S.E.U. indices and bidding; and (2) the S.E.U. indices would be more highly related to bidding behavior than the traditional measures.

We do not discuss relationships for all of the indices here but do consider results for one of the more comprehensive indices and those from multiple regression analysis. This index is the algebraic sum of the cross products of the positive and negative consequences of bidding minus the same score for not bidding for each individual. The correlation of this index with bidding was .26, $p < .05$ for a one-tailed test. The correlations between the two Semantic Differential scales and bidding were $-.09$ and $-.25$ respectively. Neither of these is significant for a one-tailed test predicting a positive correlation. The correlation between Need for Achievement and bidding was a nonsignificant .17. A multiple regression analysis determined the relative contribution of the S.E.U. indices to the prediction of bidding. A variable was selected for analysis on the basis of its relationship to the criterion and its intercorrelation with the other predictors. The multiple correlation for bidding and seven selected variables was .61 $p < .05$. This correlation included four S.E.U. indices, all of which had higher beta weights than the Semantic Differentials or Need for Achievement. Thus, these variables accounted for more variance in the criterion than did the traditional attitudinal and motivational measures. Both hypotheses were therefore confirmed. This study adds support to the usefulness of this type of model in the study of motivation.

Finally, Lawler and Porter report a study that attempts to relate managerial attitudes to job performance rankings by superiors and peers. In it, 154 managers from five different organizations completed questionnaires concerning seven kinds of rewards, and

leading to a particular second-level outcome. Vroom (*Work and Motivation*) defines the valence of the first-level outcome as:

> A montonically increasing function of an algebraic sum of the products of the valences of all [second-level] outcomes and his conceptions of its instrumentality for the attainment of the [second-level] outcomes.

The expectancy aspect of Vroom's theory is based on the notion that people have expectations concerning the outcomes that are likely to arise

their expectations that different kinds of behavior would lead to these rewards. The expectations and the ratings of the importance of instrumentality and valence, respectively, were combined multiplicatively to yield multiple correlations which were significantly related to supervisor and peer rankings of the manager's effort to perform his job well. The correlations were higher in the effort to perform then with the rankings of job performance. Lawler and Porter predicted this result because they reasoned that job performance is influenced by variables other than motivation—e.g., by ability and role perceptions. Of course, Vroom's model is not a behavioral theory but one of motivation only. Motivation is not going to improve performance if ability is low or role perceptions are inaccurate. Vroom's model explains how goals influence effort and that is exactly the relationship found by Lawler and Porter.

CONCLUSION

Taken together, the four studies discussed in the previous section seem to show that Vroom's model holds great promise for predicting behavior in organizations. There still remain some unanswered questions. We do not know all of the goals that have positive valence in a work situation. We do not know how much of a difference in force is necessary before one kind of outcome is chosen over another. Nor do we know what combination of measures yields the best prediction in a given situation. The answers to these and other questions await further research.

One more point should perhaps be made concerning the four studies and their measurement of Vroom's concepts. While it is true that all of them used subjective measures, the model can in fact be tested with more objective devices. Instrumentality can be inferred from organization practices, expectations can be manipulated by instructions, and goals can be inferred from observed approach and avoidance behaviors. Of course, all of these techniques require assumptions concerning their relationship to the worker's subjective perceptions of the situation; but the model is certainly not bound to the methods of measurement used so far. In fact, Vroom specifies in considerable detail the different kinds of techniques that might be used to test his model.

More work must be done before we can make any statements concerning the overall validity of Vroom's model. But the vigor of his formulation, the relative ease of making the concepts operational, and the model's emphasis on individual differences show considerable promise. We are also encouraged by the results of relatively sophisticated studies testing the theory. We believe it is time for those interested in organizational behavior to take a more thoroughly scientific look at this very complex subject of industrial motivation, and Vroom's model seems a big step in that direction.

as a result of what they do. Expectancy can vary between 0 (no expectation of relation) and 1 (expectation is certain). Expectancy can thus be expressed as a subjective probability ranging from 0 to 1 (note that it is the subject's perception of probability that is used, not the objective probability).

In this theory of motivation, it is useful to distinguish between two types of expectancies. The first (expectancy I in Figure 7–10) measures the subjective probability of an employee accomplishing a particular task goal.

Basically, it reflects an employee's assessment of his own skills in regard to the task in hand. Expectancy II describes an employee's expectation as to whether the accomplishment of a particular goal will lead to a particular first-level goal. In his theory of motivation, Vroom ties valence and expectations together by arguing that the force on an individual (his motivation) to exert a given amount of effort is a monotonically increasing function of the algebraic sum of the products of the valence of all first-level outcomes and the strength of his expectancies that each level of performance will be attained by that amount of effort.

FIGURE 7–11
HYBRID MODEL OF MOTIVATION

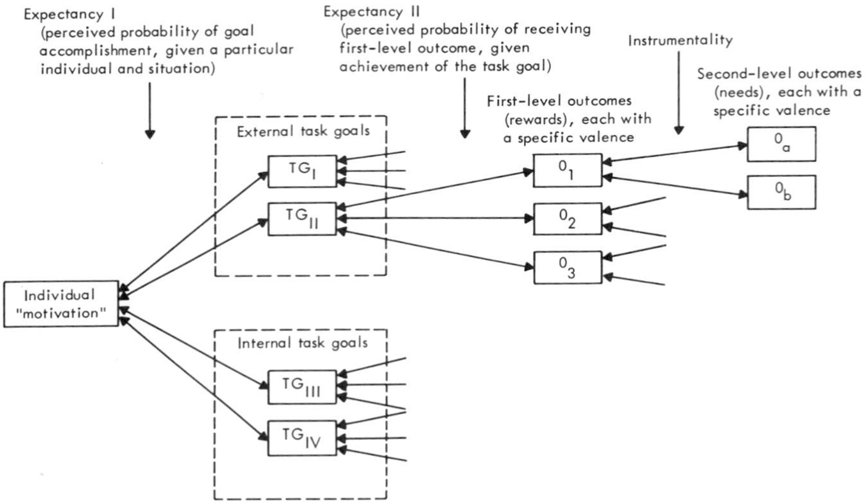

Campbell *et al.*, in *Managerial Behavior, Performance, and Effectiveness*, have developed a hybrid model of motivation to facilitate the absorption of the empirical data emerging from their researches to validate Vroom's model, reproduced here as Figure 7–11. It outlines the determinants of the direction, amplitude, and persistence of individual effort.

MONEY AS A MOTIVATOR

Despite widespread recognition of the psychological and social needs fulfilled by working, money continues to be the main tool used in industry to reward and motivate behaviour. A review by Robert Opsahl and Marvin Dunnette indicates that despite this central role of money, and a great deal of literature about compensation, there is very little theoretical or empirical knowledge about how money affects behaviour or how it interacts with other variables in the motivation process. In this context, the function of money is studied only in terms of its effect on behaviour on the job and not on how it may be instrumental in attracting or holding workers to the organization.

THEORETICAL ROLE OF MONEY

There are a number of theories about the basic psychology underlying the motivating power of money. One theory is that it is a generalized conditioned reinforcer, effective because there is almost always some need for which it is appropriate. A different view is that the repeated use of money to satisfy primary needs (hunger, thirst, shelter) leads people to develop a need for money itself. This need may manifest itself as anxiety in the absence of money. While all of these theories have some intuitive appeal, their empirical base rests on rather unrelated animal experiments, none of which can be regarded as conclusive.

Herzberg advanced the idea that money is a "hygiene factor" whose perceived inadequacy or inequitable distribution could cause dissatisfaction (and presumably inhibit performance) but which could not produce positive motivation. However his evidence is based entirely on subjective, anecdotal reports and is thus open to considerable distortion. There is also some question as to whether the actual data support the inferences Herzberg made from them. A significant number of respondents indicated long-term satisfaction related to salary.

Vroom's expectancy model does not deal specifically with money, but it is implied that money can provide positive motivation. The strength of this motivation will depend on the subject's expectancy that a certain level of effort is required to obtain a specific amount of money and his perception of the instrumentality of money in satisfying basic needs. S. W. Gellerman has noted that the instrumentality of money is a factor of an individual's training, history, financial status, and outlook and is thus highly variable between different persons and over time.

Obviously the role of money is far from clear and it would appear that it may be different in various circumstances. To understand its motivational effect we should examine the major task and subject variables that have been identified through various studies.

JOB AND TASK VARIABLES

Opsahl and Dunnette identify the schedule of payment, secrecy about pay, and pay curves as variables which account for significant variation in job behaviour.

Incentive pay schedules are based on performance by the employee rather than his training or experience. Among the most common forms of incentives are piece work and commission selling, but the "merit increases" common to most salary systems are also performance-related to a certain extent. The historical evidence indicates that incentive systems do increase productivity—suggesting that money does motivate. As Opsahl and Dunnette point out, however, the new pay techniques are usually introduced in conjunction with other organizational improvements which may be the factors actually responsible for the volume increases achieved. There is also a considerable body of evidence concerning resistance to incentive schemes through various forms of rate restriction. D. J. Hickson has identified four causal categories for rate restriction: (1) uncertainty about the continuance of the "effort-bargain" between workers and management, (2) uncertainty about the continuance of employment, (3) desire to retain control over one's own behaviour, and (4) fear of losing the respect and friendship of one's workmates—which is often heightened by the co-operation involved in applying restriction. For more consistent success in instituting incentive schemes, we need to find means of avoiding the frequent conflict between the worker's interest in money and his desire for satisfactory relationships with his co-workers.

One of the traditional taboos in the compensation of salaried workers in private industry has been against any public disclosure of the salaries paid to workers in the organization. Research by E. E. Lawler has indicated some serious dysfunctions of this secrecy: managers were found to overestimate the pay of subordinates and peers, to underestimate the pay of their superiors, to feel underpaid in relation to all three groups, and to underestimate the financial rewards of promotion. It is obvious that this misinformation seriously impairs the motivating power of money. However it is equally obvious that there would have to be wide consensus in the organization that actual pay levels were properly related to the performance of various individuals before public disclosure could be made. Otherwise the employees would perceive no relationship between performance and reward and would not be motivated by pay.

Several factors provide a rationale for the periodic increases granted to most employees:

1. Compensation for inflation.
2. Reward for meritorious performance.
3. Acquisition of additional job skills.

The manner in which these factors are evaluated and administered determines the shape of the individual's historic pay curve. According to Elliott Jaques, these pay curves are negatively accelerated with younger employees experiencing the greatest rate of growth. Jaques relates the pay curve to the growth in the employee's "time-span of discretion," which is the maximum period of time during which he is required to exercise initiative and judgement without review by his supervisor. This span usually increases fastest during the earlier years in the organization, hence the negative growth curve; although, for employees who later rise to senior executive positions, the curve may take a positive inflection.

The shape of the curve may be varied to reflect the employees' estimated potential and actual achievements and also the competitive situation in the employment market. Relatively little is known about the effects of pay curves on motivation, although it has been found that raises have an inconsistent effect on employees' expectations. Some employees consider pay more important after they get an increase, while others become less interested in it.

Subject variables

We noted above the evidence of Gellerman and Vroom suggesting that the effect of money on motivation is a highly individualistic variable. Some of the determinants of this variable are reviewed below.

A prime factor is the worker's expectancy about the effort-reward relationship. The worker must feel that he can perform well if he makes the effort and he must also feel that reward will be obtained if, and only if, he achieves the performance goal. There is considerable evidence that employees do not see these relationships clearly. Incentive schemes, particularly in large units, often fail because employees do not perceive increased effort as the path to higher pay. Lawler's study of 600 managers showed that many felt their training and experience were more important than performance in determining pay.

Incentive pay systems can relieve boredom on the job by providing a meaningful goal and greater individual control over work pace. The evidence is that they work best for jobs which the employee enjoys and is good at. This suggests that the incentive is not the money but an increase in the intrinsic valence of the job. As a matter of fact, E. L. Deci has found that in laboratory experiments, monetary reward may reduce intrinsic satisfaction; but in an industrial setting the extra attention focused on the skilful employee by an incentive plan is likely to increase intrinsic valence despite the "cheapening" effect of the money.

The studies reviewed by Opsahl and Dunnette indicate that employees do not generally rank pay as the most important factor in job satisfaction. However the authors comment that the use of self-reports introduces biases caused by the subject's desire to give socially acceptable responses in reporting the extent of his satisfaction with his current pay level. Their conclusion is that we do not have reliable measures for the relationship between pay and such other job outcomes as security or advancement.

Despite what has been said regarding the effectiveness of incentive pay schemes, several studies show that most people prefer a straight salary. Considerable investigation is required into the apparent discrepancy between those factors which satisfy workers and those which persuade them to work harder. This also applies to fringe benefits, whose ability to motivate on the job (as opposed to persuading employees to accept jobs or remain in the firm's employ) has not been demonstrated, despite the fact that they are popular with workers.

The concept that employees seek equity in the outcomes they obtain from their jobs has important implications for financial compensation. A number of authors have described the manner in which employees compare themselves to others and what perceptions cause inequity. In "Inequity in Social Exchanges," J. S. Adams defined inequity as:

> Inequity exists for Person whenever he perceives that the ratio of his outcomes to inputs and the ratio of Other's outcomes to Other's inputs are unequal, either (*a*) when he and Other are in a direct exchange or (*b*) when both are in an exchange relationship with a third party and Person compares himself to Other.

Inequity can be the result of overreward as well as underreward, and the outcomes of a job may include factors other than pay, such as security, satisfaction, good social relationships, and prestige. However pay is the easiest outcome to quantify and has, therefore, been the principal subject of study by equity researchers. Inherent in the theory is the prediction that a person will try to resolve any strong feelings of inequity, although there may be many modes of resolution.

Adams conducted a number of experiments using students doing proofreading or interviewing tasks and being made to feel over- or underpaid by experimental manipulation of the supposed qualifications of the job. Overpaid workers were found to work harder when they were paid on an hourly basis in order to "earn" their money; but at piece-work rates they reduced the quantity of their output and tried to do a better quality job. It was found that job security did not affect the manner in which the inequity was resolved. Workers who felt overpaid but secure increased their output as much as those who felt overpaid and in danger of being fired.

Adams' results have been contradicted by K. E. Weick and others who found that it was underpaid workers who worked harder and who, incidentally, enjoyed their jobs more. Despite the appeal that this will undoubtedly have for the cost-conscious manager, it must be noted that there is considerable variation in the manner in which different people choose to resolve inequity, and that principles of general validity are not yet available. In the article cited above, Adams has advanced some tentative hypotheses:

1. Person will maximize positively valent outcomes and the valence of outcomes.
2. He will minimize increasing inputs that are effortful and costly to change.

3. He will resist real and cognitive changes in inputs that are central to his self-concept and self-esteem.
4. He will be more resistant to changing cognitions about his own outcomes and inputs than to changing his cognitions about Other's outcomes and inputs.
5. Leaving the field will be resorted to only when the magnitude of inequity is high and other means of reducing it are unavailable.

The highly complex and variable effects of money on motivation described above suggest that any simplistic "answer" to compensation problems should be viewed with scepticism. We need reliable empirical answers to some of the questions posed by Opsahl and Dunnette: How can the needs that money fills for an individual be measured? What schedule of payment best reinforces the value of money? How much money is enough to be an incentive? How can employees achieve maximum reward, fairness of reward, and group acceptance simultaneously and, if they can't, what determines which goal will be sacrificed? Answers to these questions will not come quickly but, in the meantime, an awareness of the complexity of the situation can be of help in making real-life decisions.

SUMMARY

Some general statements have been put forward by those who have studied motivation. In *Work and Motivation*, Vroom found a negative relationship between job satisfaction and the probabilities of resignation, absences, and accidents. He found no simple relationship between satisfaction and performance, but did state some clues to the relationship: (1) Level of performance seems to vary directly with the strength of need for achievement, particularly when the task is presented as difficult and challenging. (2) Workers paid on an hourly basis perform at a higher level if they believe they are being overcompensated. (3) Workers perform better if they believe the task requires abilities which they value or believe that they possess. (4) Workers given feedback about their performance, or who are given an opportunity to participate in making decisions which will affect them, perform at a higher level.

In relation to the motivation of managers, Vroom's "Motivation in Management" points out that managers have high achievement and power motivations and are very highly motivated by economic and status considerations.

Other findings on managerial motivation can be gleaned from the studies of M. S. Myers. Motivation is highest among top managers, and when the executive is realizing his potential. It is strongly related to the style of the immediate boss; highly motivated managers describe their bosses as open-minded, approachable, Theory Y types. Motivation depends on the existence of appropriate management systems and the opportunity to work for meaningful goals. The executive needs helpful systems for setting and achieving goals, and must be able to relate his personal goals to the organization's goals so that he will be ready to respond favourably to them.

TOPIC 6
The executive personality

We began by saying that the executive needs to understand theories about personality. Figure 7–12, modeling personality as a system, sum-

FIGURE 7–12
PERSONALITY AS A SYSTEM

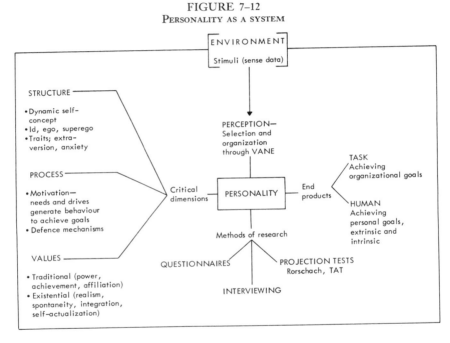

marizes many of the concepts about personality we have discussed. Learning about these theories not only helps the manager understand other people; it provides him with many clues about himself. What do we know about him from studies of the behaviour of executives?

MOTIVATION

For starters, managers have more powerful achievement imagery than nonmanagers, as measured by the TAT. Managers have a fixation about achieving. They rate "having an interesting job" higher, and score higher on initiative tests, than the general population. Not unexpectedly, they have a significant need for power. How do they exercise this need? Managers often obtain exceedingly high scores on scales measuring persuasiveness.

It would be wrong to assume that the same characteristics hold for all managers. For example, Japanese executive decision processes are so different from those of North America that it would be idle to expect similar executive profiles in the two areas. In terms of areas of specialization, one is not surprised to discover that personnel managers tend to have interest profiles rather similar to members of other people-oriented professions such as YMCA secretaries and social science teachers, who all score high in humanitarian interests. And presidents of companies are a unique bunch, quite different from other occupational groups. It is also possible to separate the effective from the ineffective executive. The effective executive:

1. Has a lifetime pattern of high achievement, power, and economic motivations.
2. Is more dominant.
3. Scores higher on the political and economic scales of the Allport-Vernon Scale.
4. Is more interested in directing others, prefers independent activities, enjoys a measured risk, rejects regimentation, and enjoys interactions.
5. Had a high need to achieve before he became a manager, not the other way around.

The higher level manager places greater emphasis on self-actualization and autonomy needs and opportunities for personal growth; he puts a high value on participation in goal setting.

BEHAVIOUR

From behavioural studies of executives, we can be convinced beyond all reasonable doubt that managers feel compelled to work excessive hours at an unrelenting pace, with few opportunities for breaks or recreation. This critical executive fetish becomes more pronounced as we ascend the hierarchy and must be regarded as a function of the kicks, rewards, and challenges which more senior executives get out of their jobs. The manager's life is suffused with brief contacts and fleeting interactions; it is highly fragmented, with a fair level of noise. Managers appear to operate at several levels, if not simultaneously, at least in rapid succession.

Managers apparently spend most of their time communicating, mostly by the spoken word and mostly at meetings. For most, writing letters is not a major activity. Managers have a preference for the immediate, the concrete, the specific problems which they immediately proceed to simplify further through some model. The scheduled meeting is the mainstay of their days.

Box 7.6: The mobile manager

When a valued man cleans out his desk and heads for the door, most corporations fin his departure hard to face. He has in effect "fired" his employer. Others often an inspired to follow his lead. The corporate ego is directly challenged. Instinctively, lo alists rally to shore up the company's image of itself, and, as in a divorce, the re reasons for the break often are obscured by bitterness, disappointment, or, at bes ritual good wishes. The company loses not only a good man but a chance to understan a major new phenomenon of American corporate life—*the mobile manager.*

One recently concluded study of 1,500 managers and executives in 500 large co porations, a 16-year project of Professor Eugene E. Jennings of Michigan State Un versity, shows that turnover has risen fivefold since the Korean war years. By 197 Jennings expects, nearly every corporate president in the United States will hav changed companies at least once, and 60 per cent of them twice.

Corporations faced with a heavy talent drain typically try one of two strategies—an here is where the bad news gets worse. Some believe the answer lies in careful rejecting all applicants whose personal traits appear to correspond with those employees who have previously resigned.

The opposite strategy is to build fences around the corporate talent pool, usin super-rapid promotions, enticing career plans, fat salaries, frequent raises, and lus stock options to win and hold loyalty. But if the fences are high enough to corral me of exceptional value for a time, they are almost certain to lock-in mediocre men for lif Soon second-raters clog the channels of advancement. Blocked, the abler men belo them start polishing up their resumés. Some are coaxed into swallowing their frustra tion and settle for less demanding jobs than they feel able to handle. The spirit ar drive that made them highly prized slowly corrode.

New Values	*Old Values*
1. Accepts independence and detachment.	1. Accepts loyalty to corporation.
2. Prefers maximum choice and mobility.	2. Accepts all assignments.
3. Develops a gourmet attitude to problems.	3. Accepts that executive mobility basically bad.

Robert C. Albrook, "Why It Is Harder To Keep Good Executives," *Fortune*, November, 1968. listing of values paraphrases parts of Albrook's article.)

ROLES

Based on a sustained and thorough review of the literature, H. Mintzberg came up with the idea of the 10 working roles listed below. These roles are interrelated and are performed by all managers.

Interpersonal roles:
　　Figurehead—symbol
　　Leader—defines interpersonal relations
　　Liaison—makes external contacts
Informational roles:
　　Monitor—searches out information
　　Disseminator—transmits information
　　Spokesman—represents firm
Decisional roles:
　　Entrepreneur—initiates
　　Disturbance handler—manages conflict
　　Resource allocator—controls
　　Negotiator—sorts out

4. Principal motivation—"get a new job, master it, and move on."
5. Accepts "strengths travel better than weaknesses."
6. Places loyalty to his career first; values a spell in government service or university business school or academy company.
7. Believes that managerial style is related to speed of movement.
8. Accepts a correlation between executive turnover and corporate effectiveness.
9. Accepts assignments that give him high visibility.
10. Avoids "defensive clutch" and welcomes growth conflict on strategic issues.

4. Expects the new M.B.A.'s will soon settle down.
5. Believes executive turnover can be contained by "paying over the odds" without necessarily exploiting managerial talent.
6. Views mergers and acquisitions as real dangers.
7. Fears "the Young Turks."
8. Is disturbed by the mobile manager.
9. Regards executive recruiting expenses as a total waste.
10. Cannot understand the notion of task-oriented, psychologically distant executive who rejects conventional human relations as a universal panacea.

A triumph of the individual

For the foreseeable future, organizational loyalty in its old form plainly is dead, and it is not likely to be revived in a generation in which the sweet juices of self-development and self-renewal are flowing faster and faster. But the human energies that economic advancement and scientific discovery have loosed from the bondage of depression and corporate authoritarianism can fuel even greater corporate progress than the old system produced. Properly distinguished from its unhealthy variants, the mobility drive of today's and tomorrow's executive represents the emerging triumph of the individual over the conformism and feudal fealty still demanded by too many corporations. But it can also mean a triumph for the companies that have the nerve and imagination to build their fortunes on this new force.

STYLE

Curiously enough we do not know at this time what style is appropriate in which circumstances. (See Box 7.6 for one particular managerial style.) It seems safe to assume that the more effective supervisor is concerned with both getting tasks accomplished and human relations, and that he gets both productivity and satisfaction from his workers. Workers apparently have a strong need for a human relations approach, although this proposition is not true for all work groups studied. House's work with middle managers and professionals suggests that effective managers must be concerned about task effectiveness, but their human relations skills do not affect productivity or satisfaction. Can it be that middle managers prefer good human resource planning even if a little anxiety is generated in the process? Top management seem to live in an entirely different world, if we are to believe a philosopher-king like Wilfred Brown, who argues that optimal organization is not a function of personality.

The research findings indicate that top managers have higher verbal skills and are less "masculine" (perhaps this just means they know more "female" words, or that they mobilize less opposition) than engineers. Perhaps it is these same verbal skills that allow managers to get into risk syndication and consensus formation as techniques in participation which derive their virtue, not from their democratic value, but rather as a feedback model (makes sure the men have the information) and as a motivational model (men feel it is right).

We will pursue these and related topics further in Chapter 9, on leadership.

REVIEW AND RESEARCH

1. What is perception? What are the factors which determine how people are perceived?
2. Do you agree that adolescence is a growth stage particularly liable to the identity crisis? Describe the dilemmas of this stage.
3. Why do individuals fear personal growth?
4. List the main subsystems of any system and show how they can be applied to human personality.
5. Make a list of defence mechanisms and give examples of each from your own experience.
6. Why are executives attracted to Freud's theory of personality?
7. Compare and contrast the extravert and introvert personality types. What occupations are suitable for each type?
8. Why is an optimal level of anxiety necessary for survival and growth?
9. What is Herzberg's motivation-hygiene theory? What are the arguments for and against this theory? Why are executives reluctant to give up this theory in spite of the evidence against it?
10. Why is the theory of achievement motivation so attractive in North America? Outline a training programme to develop the individual's need to achieve.
11. Explain the expectancy theory of motivation. Consider a decision problem which you face today and analyse your choices in terms of primary and secondary outcomes.
12. Why are managers more highly motivated at work than shop floor operatives?
13. Define your VANE (1) before you came to business school and (2) now.
14. How does a manager identify the VANE of his subordinates? What problems may arise from the actions he takes to identify these factors? How may he use this knowledge profitably?

GLOSSARY OF TERMS

Anxiety. The apprehension caused by a threat to some value which the individual holds essential to his existence as a personality (Rollo May).

Anxiety is characterized by diffusion of emotion in the sense that the cause may be difficult to specify and the choice of focus open.

Achievement motive. The need to master or overcome difficulties. The motive is presumed not to operate until it is brought on or aroused by certain situational cues or incentives which signal the individual that certain behaviours will lead to feelings of achievement.

Ego. That part of personality whereby the individual becomes aware of external reality and himself, i.e., consciousness and self-concept. In psychoanalysis, the part of the psyche which is an outcome of reality testing and which mediates among the id, superego, and reality.

Expectancy theory. Motivation model based on the notion that individuals have expectations concerning the outcomes likely to occur as the result of what they do and that they have preferences among outcomes. Vroom's model incorporates expectancies (probabilities of outcomes), valence (strength of preference for a particular outcome), and instrumentality (prediction that "reward" outcomes will lead to "need-fulfilling" outcomes).

Extravert. person oriented towards the outside world, characteristically outgoing and spontaneously more concerned with restructuring his environment than analysing its effects on his "inner being." The extravert seems to have the capacity to supress negative feedback or criticism. He is strong in drive and is zestfully involved in accomplishing things.

Id. The source of psychic energy; principally the person's pleasure-oriented drives striving for gratification or release. The function of the id is to provide for the immediate discharge of energy or tension.

Identification. The process whereby a person assumes the characteristics, attitudes, mannerisms, or eccentricities of another person.

Instrumentality. See expectancy theory.

Introvert. The obverse of the extravert; a person oriented towards the inner world of the psyche; he tends to be shy, withdrawn, inhibited in social affairs, and more interested in the world of ideas than practical affairs.

Motivation. Process whereby needs instigate behaviour directed towards the goals that can satisfy those needs. Motivation has three aspects: (*a*) direction of behaviour (choice among options); (*b*) intensity, amplitude, or strength of response; and (*c*) persistence of the behaviour.

Perception. The process whereby an individual becomes aware of the outside world and himself. Sense data are filtered by a frame of reference, and a trading process goes on between the perceived qualities of the thing and the individual's classification system.

Perceptual readiness. The relative accessibility of the category system to the kinds of stimulus information being input. The frame of reference includes subjective elements such as values, attitudes, needs, and expectations.

Personality. The organizing centre around which the motives of man form a unified and integrated system. "Personality is the dynamic organization within an individual of those psycho-physical systems that determine his unique adjustments to his environment" (Allport).

Projection. The ascription of one's defect or motive when one will not admit it in one's self.

Rationalization. The development of plausible motives for behaviour to avoid recognizing the true motives.

Reaction formation. Producing, because of repression and anxiety, behaviour directly opposite to what might be expected.

Regression. Relapsing into an earlier stage of psychosexual genesis as a consequence of frustration.

Repression. The process whereby an individual's frustrated motives and anxieties are subjected to forces which make them less accessible to consciousness.

Role. A standardized pattern of behaviour which is expected of everyone in a particular position, irrespective of who he is.

Self-actualization. The need to realize who one is; need for self-fulfilment.

Sensitivity. The capacity to predict what an individual will feel, say, and do. Sensitivity is not a single and global trait but is made up of a number of relatively independent components.

Sentiment. An enduring emotional disposition centred around the ideal of an object.

Sublimation. The channelling of sexual energy into a socially acceptable direction. Often used loosely of any substitution of a higher satisfaction for a lower one.

Superego. A censor mechanism reflecting values inculcated by parents and authority figures. When it is conscious, it represents conscience.

Unconscious. That part of the mind which holds ideas and feelings which are not readily recalled and which require a special technique to facilitate recall. The preconscious is that part of the mind from which ideas can be summoned more readily than from the unconscious.

8

Group
dynamics

The new social science approach to business behaviour optimistically assumes that the modern executive has a grounding in social psychology and its most important subdivision, group dynamics. The origins of group dynamics are to be found in the work of Kurt Lewin. Research in group x atmosphere and styles of leadership produced empirical evidence to support the concept of "democratic" leadership. Now the "democratic" leadership of the 1930s and 1940s has given way to a more positive direct form of leadership.

Psychology is a shocking subject, in the sense that it hands out traumas like placebos. The general public had just begun to realize the advantages of the central Freudian thesis "that all men are cads" and to master the intricacies of the Oedipus complex, when along came group dynamics, with its insistence that true understanding can come only from knowing how the group works.

What is group dynamics? Malcolm Bradbury in "The Institutional Joneses" has produced an amusing, if somewhat cynical, definition:

> . . . It is simply: You know how you feel uncomfortable at parties when you haven't fastened your flies? Well, that's Group Dynamics. Just as Americans think they can overcome war by abolishing it, they think they can get rid of any abrasions in any situation by understanding an explanation. Group Dynamics is a way of getting people out of toilets without anyone hearing the flush. In larger situations it is called "How to Keep People Waiting Four Days in a Fog and Make Them Like It." The implication is that all the hostilities that exist in society

can be solved given goodwill—and sociologists to explain them. Group Dynamics is based on the discovery that the reason why people disagree with one another is that they are different and they have perceived a simple solution which will abolish all conflict: you simply make all people the same.

The term has gained considerable popularity but, unfortunately, with its increasing circulation there has been a certain loss of precision. According to one view, group dynamics describes the way in which groups should be organized; great stress is laid on democratic leadership, group members participating in decisions and, above all, the value of co-operative activities in groups. A second view emphasizes the techniques of group dynamics, such as role playing, brain-storming, buzz groups, and leaderless groups; these techniques are all used to give training in human relations, especially for managers. According to a third view, group dynamics is concerned with gaining knowledge about the nature of groups, how they develop, and their effect on individual members, other groups, and larger institutions.

A more formal but extremely useful definition defines a group as two or more people who bear an explicit psychological relationship to one another. Integral to this approach is the notion that groups are bounded by the perceptual periphery of their members. This idea of a boundary is fundamental to the modern group concept. The implication is that members of a group act as if they believe "some cocoon of ether" separates them from other parts of the social environment. The modern idea would be to replace the "cocoon of ether" with a field of force similar in character to the field generated by a magnet or gravitation. Using this analogy, it is easy to understand why people refer to the feelings of being attracted to one group and repelled by another group. Likewise, when tension is generated in a group, it is not uncommon to say that the "atmosphere could have been cut with a knife."

The concept of a group which is implied here can be illustrated in Figure 8–1. From this map of the social forces in a group, it will be seen that the group is fairly stable, with the lines of rejection pointing out of the group; this, at the same time, makes the group more cohesive. Only one member has a positive force "pulling him out of the group"; the same person is also shown as being involved in a measure of internal conflict. Nevertheless, it is a fairly well-integrated group with a relatively low level of internal friction or conflict.

The lines of force, which theoretically have magnitude and direction, structure the behaviour and attitudes of group members so that roles are created. Executives who have been trained in physics or chemistry will recognize that the idea of treating a group as a complex of ions in a dilute electrolyte is an extremely useful analogy. When two plates connected by a wire are placed in a dilute electrolyte, the solution is then polarized; positive ions go to one plate and negative ions to the other. Give an un-

FIGURE 8–1
LINES OF FORCE IN A GROUP

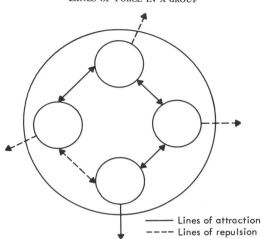

——— Lines of attraction
– – – Lines of repulsion

structured group a problem and in some circumstances the group's attitudes will polarize: some will take one view, some the opposite. Hence
such expressions as polarization of sentiment and opinion.

What is vital about the modern view of group theory is to consider the
idea that people live and work in a microcosm composed of groups, and in
a group the member is both a captive of the structure and a captor in so
far as he creates ånd maintains its structure. It is useful to think of a group
as a network of relations within which roles emerge. Thus, a group member is compelled, or at least experiences pressure him, to act in a particular
way ("it may go against the grain"); and he compels or tries to compel
others to behave in particular ways ("I wasn't going to let him get away
with that"). It is as well to remember that physical proximity does not
necessarily create a group.

Groups consist of two or more people who meet requirements of interdependence and also share an ideology. The members are interdependent,
which is but to say that each person's behaviour influences the behaviour
of the other members of the group. Inevitably, on account of their interdependence (which after a time becomes institutionalized) the members
develop an ideology, which implies that they have a common set of values,
beliefs, and norms which regulates their behaviour and attitudes. This
group ideology is developed as the group works on particular tasks and
may become peculiar to the group. In this approach "leadership" may be
defined as the ability to influence others in the group. If this is so, everyone in the group has a degree of leadership. The amount of influence the
leader has on the group depends on the amount of influence the other
members of the group have on the leader.

The question arises as to how groups can be recognized and identified. Basically there are two ways: by asking and observing. Asking people, in technical terms, is usually described as investigating perceptions and cognitions of individuals. Ultimately this comes down to asking people questions such as, "Who would like to work with whom?" Observing requires actual behaviouristic studies. One might, for example, study people in an informal situation, observing how they group themselves for lunch.

Having some notion of what is meant by the concept of "groups," it is necessary now to turn to the concept of "dynamics." By dynamics we mean adjustive changes in the group structure as a whole produced by changes in any part of the group. In general terms these changes tend to be self-distributive (analagous to the electric charge in a field producing a variation throughout the whole field); any change goes through the whole group. There is a tendency for any action to be balanced by a counter-reaction. These two general principles, self-distribution and reaction, mean that the change in groups is relatively slow.

Two dangers of group dynamics study must always be borne in mind: (1) the "group mind" concept and (2) forgetting that a group is made up of individuals. The group mind fiction has a corollary in the "institutional fiction"—the belief that the organization exists in a superordinate way. While organizations do have synergistic aspects, they are composed of people and are never infallible, inevitable, or unchangeable. Pitfalls of this sort lead to "pluralistic ignorance," the wry situation in which each group member believes he alone has covert disbeliefs in group assumptions or norms.

STRUCTURE OF CHAPTER 8

Topic 1 deals with the structure, process, and values of groups. The three R's (rules, roles, and relations) of groups are introduced. This topic previews some of the concepts of group dynamics which are important enough to consider as separate topics later on as it sets forth the basic anatomy, activities, and attitudes that prevail in groups.

Topic 2 turns to the pivotal problem of role and its attendant concept of status. The concepts of role, role set, and role sending are examined to see what light they can throw on the organizational web of relations. Next we turn to role playing and reciprocity, including the idea of the role trap. The scene has now, we hope, been set for the subject of role conflict and strain. The question is raised whether roles pick personalities or personalities pick roles. This topic concludes with a brief look at the concepts of status and status symbols.

Topic 3 takes up the matter of conformity, or how the rules are enforced. Why do people conform in groups? To try to answer this question, three processes of social influence—compliance, identification, and internalization—are discussed. Next we turn to the matter of engineering conformity, paying particular attention to the roles of the eccentric, the conformist, and the nonconformist. To get a reading on the roles of the cosmopolitan, the local, and the chancer requires an understanding of the concept of reference groups.

Topic 4 is socialization, which is the process of getting people into roles. This section draws heavily on our discussion of conformity and on Schein's seminal work on the brainwashing techniques used by the Chinese Communists on American prisoners during the Korean war.

The chapter concludes with Topic 5, the psychology of the primary working group. All of the principles of group dynamics ultimately focus on this essential nucleus of the organization.

TOPIC 1
Structure, process, and values of groups

We have already defined a group as two or more people who come together to achieve particular goals. How do groups—in particular, work groups—operate? To get a better insight into why some groups are more productive; why some resist change; why some disintegrate under pressure: it is necessary to look at the structure, process, and value system of the group.

STRUCTURE

One characteristic we would want to know about a group is its size. It must have at least two people; and theoretically there is no upper limit. The smallest group consists of just two people—doctor and patient, husband and wife. When the group increases in size, its potential complexity rises rapidly. If we assume that two people have two relationships going (A's to B and B's to A), a triad has six. A group of four has 12 relationships, and so on according to the $n (n - 1)$ formula; so that a group of 10 people has 90 interpersonal balls juggling.

In practice, when a group gets above a certain size, it tends to splinter into subgroups. This breaking up is usually anticipated by the formation of cliques which are nearer to the optimum size for the particular group's psychological economy. This is also potentially very complex; even a triad can arrange itself into five different groupings competing for roles, status, and payoffs.

Where the subgroups are interlocked and connected, an organization has emerged. In a way, an organization is a group of groups; and society subsumes all of these levels:

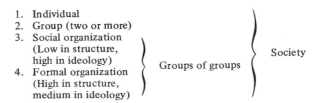

1. Individual
2. Group (two or more)
3. Social organization (Low in structure, high in ideology)
4. Formal organization (High in structure, medium in ideology)

Groups of groups

Society

Every society includes all of these levels. The concept of social organization is one we have not encountered before; we can define it as a specific grouping of people characterized by possession of the following (with illustrative examples for doctors in parentheses):

1. Cultural products—buildings, uniforms, magic formulas, songs (hospitals, white coats, prescriptions).
2. Collective name or symbol (doctor, M.D., G.P.).
3. Distinctive action pattern (putting a thermometer in your mouth).
4. Common belief system (the Hippocratic oath).
5. Enforcing agents or techniques (American Medical Association).

The medical illustration may remind us that we frequently liken structure to anatomy. In groups the basic framework is the three R's: rules, roles, and relations. These have the effect of creating a boundary, a perceptual periphery, for group members. The members interact with each other in such a way that the behaviour of one influences the behaviour of the others. People take up roles within the group; the group sanctions that role within specific rules; and relations are established that keep each person within his role. The intent of the structure is to accomplish the groups's tasks and achieve its goals.

The relations and interactions of a group build up, in time, a web of expectations. If this web becomes too rigid, overwhelming, and unresponsive to changes in the environment, the members, trapped and trapping, may be unable to meet either their own or the group's needs. They may even be destroyed, to no more purpose than the World War II Japanese kamikaze pilot attacking a technologically sophisticated task force. But usually a compromise is worked out between the web of expectations and reality (in the form of goals); even the Japanese suicide pilots were sometimes picked up from the sea "unconsciously" swimming.

Group structure can also be described as the network along which information flows to influence the perceptions, emotions, and behaviour of members. This reminds us of our concept of information-processing systems; a group is such a system.

Structure essentially describes the complex of roles and how they are fitted together. Structure is a function (f) of role (R) and status (S):

$$\text{Structure} = f(R, S)$$

When role and status have been defined, the communication pattern has been defined.

The concept of role is so important that Topic 2 of this chapter is devoted to expanding on it. At this point, it is useful to get enough of an idea of roles to help us understand structure. Figure 8–2 diagrams a typical work group and the kind of roles likely to emerge in it. The figure indicates that the group aims to accomplish tasks and reach goals. However, it is important to keep in mind that a group is composed of individuals. The people in the group have their own purposes and needs; and the group will not satisfy its aims unless it fulfills theirs. These needs of the individual also influence and shape the kind of role he takes up.

The first role we will look at in Figure 8–2 is that of the task specialist (*T*). He focuses on the group task by attempting to structure the perceptions of members, mobilize their anxieties, and direct them. His mind is preoccupied with productivity, profitability, and performance. He has a

FIGURE 8–2
DIAGRAM OF A GROUP SHOWING ROLES AND RELATIONS

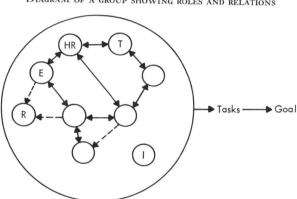

high need for power, and he tries to monitor the behaviour of the group by ensuring that a good deal of the verbal communication is channeled through him. To locate the task specialist, look for the person who uses such phrases as, "Let's zero in on the problem," and, "Let's bear down on the subject." The task specialist does not hesitate to exploit the others' needs for achievement or affiliation, so he inevitably does quite a bit of psychic damage. He gets away with it because he is more feared than loved, and because our next character is usually rushing up with some psychic blood plasma to repair the behavioural wounds.

The human relations specialist (*HR* in Figure 8–2) tries to spread balm and relieve anxiety and tension. He is essentially concerned with people, and usually has a strong need for affiliation. His verbal style is placatory: "How do all of you feel about this?" "This is kinda interesting, isn't it?" To function properly, the group needs a coalition of the task specialist and the human relations specialist—a formidable combination. In the family, great feats of socialization are achieved when father and mother combine these roles against, but for, the children. It is difficult to combine the two at the same time in the same person (which is what behavioural science has often demanded of the executive); but common sense and common experience suggest that groups can work out effective kinds of role specialization.

The eccentric (E in Figure 8–2) is the group member who is allowed and encouraged to break group norms. It is a curious fact that while most members are required to obey the rules, a few are required to break them. Some nonconforming behaviour is encouraged, because it gives the group important options when it wishes. Eccentrics have their uses; if they did not exist the group would have to invent them. The group neophyte may be in hot water if he attacks this "odd fellow" before he has completed his initiation; for the eccentric usually has friends in high places.

Then there is the scapegoat or rejectee (R in Figure 8–2), the person in the group who becomes the focus of hostility. Groups balance the emotional economy by selecting individuals for this role. Whom does the group pick on? Who's the fall guy? Does he welcome the role? The U.S. Watergate scandal in 1973 furnished fascinating examples of former team members scrambling to avoid the scapegoat role (John Dean), "toughing it out" (John Mitchell), or marching off, tight-lipped, to prison (Gordon Liddy).

There are many other roles. Figure 8–2 includes an isolate (I), someone who is technically part of the group but is not really involved in it. He may be simply a loner, or he may be the group voyeur who likes the role of scientifically detached spectator. Other roles might be called father figure, arbitrator, and so on. Then there are several roles that are concerned with communication between groups—go-between, external representative, gate-keeper. The gate-keeper is often of critical importance, as we mentioned in describing how research teams gain access to work groups; he selects, edits, routes, recycles, and evaluates information coming into the group.

PROCESS

Structure defines the network of expectations and communication, but it says nothing about what is communicated along the channels. Research in group dynamics has a great deal to tell us about group process.

Studies of T groups reveal that groups in the process of development go through certain phases which include:

1. Independence-dependence:
    a. Tendency to stand off or run away because of anxiety.
    b. Splitting into warring factions.
    c. Resolution through catharsis.
2. Interdependence:

a. Enchantment with the group.
b. Disenchantment.
c. Consensual validation.

While these are T group phases, most groups go through similar struggles on their way to maturity, and mature members are able to weather the storms.

One of the major reasons people have for joining groups is to define their performance, function, status, and role with regard to their fellows, especially those whose judgement they value. This need to establish consensual validation helps the individual to work through the phases, and it helps the group to establish itself as a functioning unit.

Group processes are the rituals and rubrics the group develops for handling different behavioural phenomena. Chapter 1 described the process phases of clarification, evaluation, and decision (they are included in this chapter's glossary for memory refreshment). Other processes will be discussed at length in the further topics of this chapter. They include initiation and socialization—how the price of admission is levied from the neophyte and how he is taught the ropes. A major activity is processing people into conformity—engineering their behaviour through group influence. As the group develops, it creates a matrix of values, norms, reinforcements, and sanctions, which we will discuss in the following section on "Values." Influence by rewards and sanctions is a process.

In dealing with processes, it is important to remember that groups have two sets of them, a public agenda and a hidden agenda. The public agenda is the visible, stated set of tasks and goals. The hidden agenda deals with all the undercover processes and is apparently perverse, pathological, and irrational (but only at first sight). Its purpose is to deal with the irrational emotions which are inevitably present. It processes such emotions, giving the group member his due or his come-uppance, putting people in their places. It involves complex calculations of effectiveness and equity. Again, the Watergate scandal provided excellent illustrations, as a group's dynamics were laid bare in televised hearings—a case study of a "hidden agenda" not only in terms of illicit activities but also in terms of undercurrents of emotion and relationship among group members.

A theory with considerable explanatory value of both the public and private processes of groups is exchange theory.

EXCHANGE THEORY

Exchange theory sets out to explain group behaviour in terms of rewards exchanged and costs incurred in the interaction. Four concepts are fundamental to exchange theory; reward, cost, outcome, and comparison level. Rewards are the payoffs which emerge from the interaction; any behaviour that adds to the gratification of a person's needs constitutes a reward as far as that person is concerned. Similarly the term "cost" is a very broad concept and encompasses not only factors such as fatigue, anxiety, loss of status, and punishment, but also the value of rewards which the members miss by not participating in other exchanges. An outcome is defined as rewards minus costs; if positive, the interaction is said to yield a profit; if negative, a loss. The fact that a person profits from an interaction does not necessarily mean that he likes his partner in the interaction. For attraction to develop, it is necessary for the outcome to exceed some minimal level of expectation. Level of comparison describes the process whereby a person evaluates the outcome of a particular interaction against the profit which he is forgoing elsewhere.

Exchange theory explains why particular individuals with particular idiosyncrasies receive more than their proportionate share of choices and why one person distinguished by a particular trait selects others with different traits. For example, an effective executive is capable of widening the field of participation for his colleagues by structuring relations and activities; so that, say, if a lunch is arranged to introduce a visiting dignitary, he arranges to have his associates introduced, initiates topics of conversation which allow his fellows to participate in a rewarding manner, and generally fosters a feeling of tolerance among his associates.

The effective executive is also able to manage his emotional economy in such a way as to minimize the cost to his fellows, by monitoring his moods so that he does not inflict his anxieties and depressions on them. "Tolerably well" becomes the minimal score to describe his condition. In essence, effective group members possess traits that increase the rewards and minimize the costs to their fellows. Those who are rejected are those who raise the costs to their fellows by being hostile, domineering, and inconsiderate.

VALUES

A group develops its own particular ideology or complex of values. These are expressed in a set of norms or standards for group behaviour. Conformity to the norm is rewarded (reinforcement) and nonconformity is punished (sanctions).

Since values vary according to the group, it is impossible to specify them beyond some basic norms; but they are indicated and can be observed by studying groups in terms of such measures as member satisfaction and morale.

Before taking up those subjects, an illustration of a shop floor matrix of values, norms, reinforcements, and sanctions will help to understand how this system operates. Suppose a group of workers (perhaps goaded by a traditional, Tayloristic management structure) comes up with an overriding value such as "Management is the enemy; they're trying to screw us and we'll show 'em they can't get away with it." The value may be emotional and somewhat unclear; but it produces a precisely defined, specific norm: production will be restricted to a fixed number of units within a time period. The group then develops a set of rules to maintain the norm (the value), with the reinforcement of group approval and such sanctions as intimidation, sending a member to Coventry, or spoiling excess production. Communication may be by jokes and double-edged statements, or it may be explicit. The group often employs one person, usually an older, nonthreatening type, to break in new members; he will help the neophyte with his work and explain the norm until the value is inculcated. If he fails, a younger and tougher worker may begin to intimidate him with sanctions; or perhaps the group eccentric is brought into play. The techniques do not always work; a rate-buster will break the norm if he has a different, strong value (and perhaps a low need for affiliation).

RECIPROCITY

One norm which is basic to all groups is reciprocity, which is no more than the common idea of equity expressed in such clichés as "tit for tat" or "you scratch my back and I'll scratch yours." More formally, this norm expresses the value judgement that when A exercises a right at some cost to B he thereby incurs the obligation to allow B to exercise a right at some cost to him. The norm of reciprocity binds the group together in a mutuality of rights, obligations, and gratifications.

Alvin Gouldner has argued that the norm of reciprocity is universal in the form of "(1) people should help those who help them and (2) people should not injure those who have helped them." This group dynamics version of the Golden Rule regulates exchange patterns and thus gives the group its stability. The process is always incomplete; the balance of rights and obligations is never perfect. This lack of perfection (something is always owed), coupled with the goodwill of previous exchanges and possible future transactions, keeps the group going (sometimes, as "old boy" class and regimental reunions illustrate, long after the original group functions have been completed).

The establishment of bonds of reciprocity is never unconditional, but depends on the principle of comparative advantage—which is the essence of exchange theory.

MEMBER SATISFACTION

Studying and analysing the mass of data that emerges from research into group behaviour is one way of determining common group values. The satisfaction of group members indicates individual and group values and needs which the group has successfully met.

Richard Heslin and Dexter Dunphy of Harvard University have developed a computerized technique for collating such data. After researching the literature and collecting detailed abstracts of 450 small group studies, they concluded that three variables account for most of the variance in member satisfaction: status consensus, perception of progress toward group goals, and perceived freedom to participate.

Status consensus. Heslin and Dunphy noted that consensus about the status of the task specialist has a significant influence on member satisfaction. Considerable disagreement on this subject leads to factionalism and dissatisfaction. High status consensus, and thus high satisfaction, is more likely to be achieved in groups where two complementary and mutually supportive roles emerge—the task specialist and the human relations specialist.

Perception of progress towards group goals. A number of the collated studies showed quite clearly that progress towards the group goal was a significant factor in satisfaction. For example, a number of psychological experiments have been conducted where groups were asked to solve insoluble problems. Two types of reaction were observed: the development of factions and the emergence of intermember aggression.

Perceived freedom to participate. To most people, the ability to participate in an exercise is a major factor determining the amount of satisfaction they get in that activity. The "I'll take my ball and go home" type of comment is usually taken as indicative that the owner has not been given sufficient opportunities to participate. The most rigorous research in this area has been a study of communication networks. In these studies it is necessary to distinguish between high centrality and low centrality. High centrality describes a situation where the subject may communicate with and receive messages from all the other members of the network. Low centrality, in its extreme form, is the situation where a subject is in two-way communication with only one other person. Centrality affects not only the amount of communication which the subject receives but his ability to structure the reactions of others, as well as his feeling of belonging. Analysis of communication studies shows that groups with asymmetrical participation among members have a low level of satisfaction. For example, it was found that the morale of the most central person was considerably higher than that of the peripheral person. The average satisfaction decreased in moving from the circle (where everyone communicated with two other persons) to the wheel (where four members communicated with only one member, who communicated with them all).

MORALE

Studying the morale of groups again indicates that values are crucial to satisfaction. Such indicators as orderliness, high production, and lack of conflict may confirm that the structure and process of the group are functioning, and yet group morale may be low. A highly structured group like an army platoon may look very smart and have low morale.

Towards the end of World War II, German work units were actually increasing productivity as German morale caved in under aerial bombardment and Allied land triumphs. Lack of tension is not a good morale indicator; the modern attitude is that a healthy degree of tension and conflict is necessary to facilitate group adaptation and foster creativity.

There have been various attempts to define group morale more precisely than by such general terms as *esprit de corps* or unity of the group. D. Krech and R. S. Crutchfield in *Theory and Problems of Social Psychology* have defined the criteria of high and low morale.

High morale, usually characterized by an optimistic "we're going to win" attitude, or at least "what we are doing, we've got to do," can sometimes be clear to even an untrained observer. The dimensions of high morale can be measured from the following criteria:

1. The group is held together through internal cohesiveness rather than external pressures. The members feel a strong need to maintain the identity and integrity of the group; the members believe and act as if they believe their group constitutes an élite.

2. A minimal level of divisive frictions—usually characterized by statements such as, "we can sort this out ourselves"—marks the behaviour of the group.

3. The adaptability to change is such as to enable the group itself to handle inner conflicts and to produce the necessary readjustments of an interpersonal nature. Adaptability facilitates the group's development and growth while achieving effectiveness.

4. Substantial amounts of positive attraction and goodwill exist between people (sometimes characterized as the "in-group feeling").

5. A community of goals exists among the members. In other words, there is a shared consensus of goals and values.

6. The positive attitude of group members concerning their objectives and the style of leadership allows and structures the flow of interaction appropriate to their mission.

7. The desire of members to retain the group is so strong that they regard its continued existence as of positive value (hence "old boy" reunions).

Low morale is revealed by the following factors:

1. Under pressure, the group is likely to disintegrate and splinter into antagonistic subgroups. This kind of internecine strife stifles the group's mission.

2. Internal strife arises from mutual distrust and destructive criticism.

3. The group cannot resolve its problems when anxieties are generated.

4. The absence of friendly emotional currents among the members makes it difficult for the group to innovate, improvise, and create the "new" solutions which it needs to survive.

5. There is a lack of consensus in regard to group objectives and values, and the aims of individual members are at variance with group objectives.

6. Members have negative attitudes towards group purposes.

7. Members lack a sense of identification with the group; the feeling of not belonging indicates a short life expectation for the group.

TRADING VALUES ACROSS GROUPS

One of the most interesting, least studied, yet crucial aspects of value systems is the trading process that goes on between interacting groups. An excellent illustration of this value overlap has been provided by Albert J. Reiss, Jr., a sociologist from Yale University. Reiss led a team of researchers who investigated how the police operate in 5,360 meetings between 579 policemen and 11,255 citizens. This study destroys a number of myths.

FIGURE 8–3
OTHER GROUP VALUES IMPINGE ON POLICE VALUES

The most important finding was that—contrary to the widely held belief that corruption is confined to a "few rotten apples"—in fact, one in five of the policemen observed was in criminal violation of the law. Corrupt practices included taking money and property from deviants, stealing from previously burglarized premises, not giving traffic tickets in exchange for bribes, accepting both money and goods from merchants, and accepting money to alter sworn testimony. Drinking on duty, ridiculing citizens, and acting in an authoritarian manner were not uncommon.

Why does this corruption happen? The answer lies in the fact that policemen as a group are caught between their own values and those of many other groups who have a high influence on them, as shown in Figure 8–3. One dilemma for the police is that while they are charged with fighting crime, their efforts are undermined by other forces in our society. Reiss says, in *The Police and the Public:*

> The judgments of the police and others in the legal system are intricately balanced in a commitment to justice. If, on the average, the officer's

sense of justice is not confirmed, or his moral commitments are not sustained by others, he loses his own moral commitment to the system. Where moral commitment is lost, subcultural practices take over.

Techniques like plea bargaining, the condescending manner of judges and prosecutors, punitive treatment handed out by his superiors, political interference, and public apathy all serve to force the policeman into role conflict. The point here is not whether "going on the take" is justified; the point is understanding that a group, like an individual, needs reinforcement and support from other groups. A web of conflicting and confusing expectations can threaten its very survival.

TOPIC 2
Role and status

Getting people to do what you want them to do requires building up their expectations in the direction in which you wish to proceed. The expectation thesis—"England expects every man will do his duty," to quote Admiral Nelson before the battle of Trafalgar—is a critical ingredient of organizational behaviour.

Every normal person carries around inside him sets of expectations which are organized in particular ways. The expectations, which involve perceptions, attitudes, feelings, and behaviour, can be organized in various ways. When a person plays a role, he "reads from one of these sets of expectations."

The concept of role is of critical importance to the student of organizational behaviour, as it represents a sort of theoretical point of intersection between psychology and sociology. The concept of role is "the largest possible research unit in psychology and the smallest possible within sociology," according to R. Rommitreit in *Social Norms and Roles*. Given this pivotal position as a theoretical construct, the concept of role has turned out to be of tremendous productive value in the organizational sciences.

Until recently the concept of role occupied a rather secondary position in the minds of behavioural scientists because of its abstract nature and the fact that it dealt with normative (ought) considerations, which (they felt) should be excluded from a science which claimed to deal exclusively with behavioural facts. But an individual's behaviours frequently have a pattern or regularity about them which is a function of his position or job. This is perceived by him and those with whom he interacts as a pattern of stereotyped behaviour and attitudes which he justifies by saying, "I'm just doing my job." This "taking of one's place" has turned out to be a major source of explanation for understanding what people say, do, and believe in organizational settings.

The arrival of the systems approach has made the study of the concept of role mandatory as a bridge between the individual personality and the organization. The personality takes on a role as it goes into a group; the group, fitted with other groups, becomes an organization. As Daniel Katz and R. L. Kahn point out in *The Social Psychology of Organizations*, the role is

> the major means for linking the individual and organizational levels of research and theory; it is at once the building block of social systems and the summation of the requirements with which such systems confront their members as individuals.

How is role defined? Let us begin by defining a role as a set or litany of behaviours or attitudes appropriate to a particular position in an organization, irrespective of who occupies it. The word "litany" is used to convey the inference that role behaviours have a "sacred" or "holy" aspect. Thus it is not uncommon to find that when someone assumes a role, especially for the first time, some kind of quasi-religious procedure is gone through. Doctors take the Hippocratic oath, British officers swear allegiance to the Queen, and Presidents are sworn in. Thus it is not sufficient to describe a role as a set of duties or obligations with a corresponding set of privileges. Somehow a role not only encompasses duties and privileges but takes on a mystique which both diminishes and enriches personality.

An organization may be thought of as a giant molecule with roles for atoms. The interlocking complex of roles achieves functional specialization by being populated with people who are expected to behave in particular ways which are functional for the organization. Since the system is interlocked, the roles are connected by a set of rules (which make behaviours legitimate) and relations (which hold the roles in their correct psychological spatial co-ordinates). The three R's are also held together by the principle of complementarity (reciprocity).

Personality shapes and is shaped by role. As an individual takes up his role, his personality moves into a role configuration which structures his perception of the world, moves his self-concept towards his stereotype of the role, and attenuates his behavioural choices as he responds to the signal of the role senders in his group. Figure 8–4 very simply diagrams a role

FIGURE 8–4
A ROLE SET

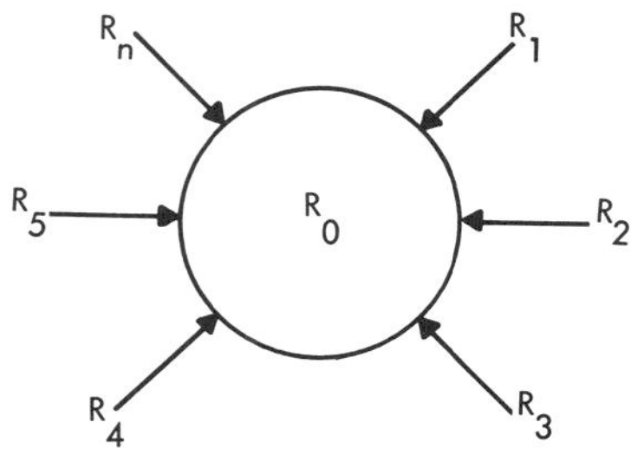

set where R_0 is trying to restructure his VANE, perceptions, and dynamic self-concept to fit his group role. R_1 through R_n are role senders—the other members of the group, who want to monitor R_0's behaviour to fit the group's values and norms through the use of reinforcements and sanctions. The role senders commonly try to influence the focal person by sending him signals (arrows in Figure 8–4) containing their expectations. The integration of the role senders' expectations will significantly affect the focal person's stereotype of his role, so we can say that role is a function of these expectations (E):

$$\text{Role} = f\ (E)$$

The principle of complementarity states that pairs of roles tend to be grouped around a set of complementary rights and duties. This is, of course, an aspect of the norm of reciprocity. Complementarity means essentially that a role cannot be defined in isolation—that it can be only defined in terms of other roles.

For example, consider the doctor-patient relation. Suppose you have been on the town the night before and you come to in the morning feeling a little off and your wife decides to call your physician. When he shows up in the afternoon, you, while still in bed, by now feel bright and breezy. The conversation might go like this:

YOU: Hi, Doc!
M.D.: Hello.
YOU: Nice day, Doc.
M.D.: Open the top of your pyjamas.
YOU: Doc, my wife. . . .
M.D.: Put this in your mouth.
YOU: Uh, uh. . . .

In other words, the doctor-patient relationship represents a conspiracy in which you have to play patient so that he can play doctor, and vice versa.

Complementarity can be illustrated in relation to organizational life as in Figure 8–5. Suppose that a manager has been duly initiated into his role with appropriate title, status, access to information, and key to the executive washroom. He will find that he has also gained a set of obligations corresponding to his set of rights.

ROLE PLAYING

When a person takes up a role, he is acting, albeit in most cases unconsciously. As the late Tyrone Guthrie's *On Acting* says:

> Have you noticed how often in "real life" people react to events, to real events, in an almost unbelievably "ham" way? I was a bystander once at a motor smash. The behaviour of the spectators, no doubt including myself, could have been reproduced as a Hideous Example of Bad Acting.

FIGURE 8-5
COMPLEMENTARY ASPECTS OF THE MANAGER ROLE

MANAGER	
Rights	*Obligations*
1. Gate-keeper prerogatives (to determine group membership by hiring and firing; to accept or reject material, information, energy inputs)	1. Accessibility to and honouring rights of others (subordinates, superiors, clients)
2. Delegation of authority and allocation of activities	2. Responsibility for all activity under his direction
3. Reviewing and rewarding performance of others	3. Allowing his activities and decisions to be reviewed
4. Conflict management when jurisdictional problems occur	4. Operating within company policy
5. Access to factors that keep him tuned in to the system	5. Adapting to role and company values and processes

One person pressed the back of his hand against his forehead in token of grief or horror: another pressed his hands forward, palms outwards, as if to avert danger: I caught myself in a sort of crouching position, knees bent, uttering the deathless line, "Oh no!"

Much the same sort of acting is apparently witnessed in bank stick-ups and airliner hijackings; the participants play out their roles using a kind of "hamming" or stereotyped acting. The interesting question is, Where do they learn their roles? Probably the answer is that they learn from movies, books, and plays. The learning is frequently quite complete and includes standard clichés, facial gestures, and body postures.

Many a pleasant hour can be passed with executives discussing what they learned from the 1930s film "The Big House," in which Edward G. Robinson (the tough-minded warden) goes into the prison yard to confront Humphrey Bogart (leader of rioting prisoners). Apparently this squaring off has been used as a paradigm for conflict between the formal leader and his informal opposite number. Of course, both film and executive were rooted in the good old days of classical theory. A decade or two later, the manager could model himself on Gregory Peck as "The Man in the Grey Flannel Suit," pondering his conflicts between work and family. In the 1970s, the middle-aged manager has to play the heavy and learn to handle the would-be Dustin Hoffmans trained by "The Graduate."

The question arises, "Why is the process of role assimilation so complete?" The answer seems to be that the needs of the situation are so demanding that both parties must convince each other they are absolutely authentic and sincere in their respective roles. The bank robber means business and the teller means to comply. So life imitates art in reaching for authenticity.

The same sort of thing applies to the executive role. Apparently effective executives learn from other effective executives. But, perhaps more important, they also have the ability to learn from other, nonexecutive experiences and events. In fact, effective executives rarely seem to step out of role whether they are at a funeral, a cocktail party, or an executive board meeting. They seem always to be training for events that lie ahead. Apparently trivial speech patterns, dress styles, and phasing or sequencing of events matter much to them.

GETTING UPSTAGE—THE EXECUTIVE AS ENTERTAINER

When thinking about the concept of role, it is useful to keep in mind such theatrical ideas as the script (let's see how we are going to play this one), the size of parts (stars, supporting cast, walk-on parts), props, how to get off and on stage, how to get the drama in and out, and so on. Most of what we will have to say about status is concerned with this aspect of role.

Why do people play these roles? To entertain others? Yes, but only in the full sense in which an effective actor entertains: reaching out to his audience, establishing rapport, focusing their attention, stopping them from nervous diversions such as coughing and fidgeting, and passing a "message" to them. But an old show business line says, "If you're going to send a message, use Western Union." So it is not an ordinary telegraphic message you get from Edward Albee or Harold Pinter. It is a message like an artistic Rorschach ink blot—full of promise, but promises that vary from optic to optic.

The executive sets out to entertain in the same way as the actor. His entrances are carefully timed; he chooses his dialogue with care; he exits on cue. He captures and captivates his audience and he has too much to do to send all of his messages by Western Union. So he must signal, some of the time, by ink blot. All of this can't be learned from a textbook on management; so the fledgling manager grasps every clue he can find on how to "make like an executive." Constant practice and careful imitation, coupled with brilliant imagination—and reinforced by trips to the right movies and plays—can produce virtuoso performances.

Reciprocity is one purpose of all this role playing. As we said earlier, each person must play his role fully to allow other persons to play theirs. The executive must transmit signals which reflect both the objectives he is shooting for and the inevitable conflicts between them.

What makes the whole exercise of role playing so intriguing is that the metaphor of conventional theory is quite inappropriate to modern times. Roles, plays, props, time spans, and audience preferences are constantly changing. New dramatic forms such as guerilla theatre, the theatre of the absurd, or even the theatre of cruelty may be more appropriate. With the invention of the adhocracy, task management, and matrix management, roles shift like musical chairs. The adhocracy may well be a one-night stand. In the face of all this—and of pitfalls like the role trap—the show must go on.

THE ROLE TRAP

One of the curiosities of life is why a person will adopt behaviour that is inconsistent with his own personality and carry on with it even when it is apparently dysfunctional. The answer lies in the fact that his role senders keep him in a fixed orbit. U.S. Vice Presidents are frequent examples, since they have so few functions except to take up the role of alter ego to the President, who can use them to send up trial balloons and cater to the more extreme ideologies a President eschews in favor of "statesmanship." Seldom is the behavioural contrast made so painfully obvious as in Vice President Spiro Agnew's championship of "law and order" ending in 1973 in exposure of his unlawful activities; but aside from that, his tenure in office is most illustrative of the role trap. Official and party role senders had a vested interest in his appeal to the super-patriot and anti-intellectual portions of public opinion; his attacks on news media absorbed both him and the media in spiraling role expectations; audiences cheered his provocative stances; and the 1972 campaign demonstrated how useful a surrogate can be in taking on almost the entire political role so that the presidential role can be maintained as "above all that."

Much the same thing happens in the business executive role, where the experience is remarkably common of being boxed into a particular role, whether it is the task specialist (9, 1 on the Blake managerial grid), the human relations specialist (1, 9), the funny guy (the eccentric), the "start-up genius," the company's "ace fire fighter," or the hatchet man when things go awry. Experienced executives make a considerable effort not to get type-cast, and thus keep their options open. But usually this is extremely difficult, as the role set typically bands together in different coalitions to ensure that particular functions are distributed in a particular way that freezes roles.

While the position of the executive in a particular role, or of any person caught in a role trap, is of interest, it is thus important to remember that the role set—the whole group of role senders—is composed of individuals playing out their own roles and perhaps caught in their own traps. "You play your part so I can play mine" reciprocity is not confined to two-way situations but functions throughout groups and organizations. Role analysis could be carried out, say, for the entire senior management set of a large corporation. The difficulty in providing concrete illustration is that, unlike the days of the colorful entrepreneur (Henry Ford, John D. Rockefeller), corporate management has receded into gray anonymity (how many people, for example, could tell you even the name of the president of General Motors or Standard Oil of New Jersey?). In a general sense, we can point out that the "statesman" president needs the "hatchet-man" personnel manager, who needs the "human relations" vice president, and so on throughout all the roles we have mentioned and many more—all interacting and interdependent.

When the role set in any particular group has developed, it often takes on the enduringly fixed nature of the solar system or a particular molecular structure. To unfreeze and try to change an intrarole set at such a point requires a powerful process, such as T group technology.

A striking example of the role set, and of the process of changing it, is provided by the groups called Al Anon and Alateen. While most people are aware of the tremendous work Alcoholics Anonymous has done (through a form of group dynamics), the auxiliary groups for family members are at first glance less understandable. Probably a common reaction of spouses and children is, "Why should I join a group? I'm not the one with a drinking problem." But a group like Al Anon not only provides group support ("We're all in the same boat") but also functions with a shrewd awareness that the family is a role set. By changing the dynamics—by altering the role expectations and signals—it is often possible to help not only the family members but "the one with the problem."

Although the role set can come to be a powerful psychic engine that effectively defines who's who, we have already indicated that the web of expectations can generate both confusion and conflict. A given role player may not know who's who in his group to such an extent that he doesn't know who he is either. His problem is known as role conflict.

ROLE CONFLICT

In any organization, considerable role conflict is inevitable. This conflict stems from the supreme advantage of the concept of role: that it represents the fusion of a variety of expectation signals, some of which inevitably must be contradictory, and thus allows an organization to move towards multiple contradictory goals. Thus the focal role holder is expected not only to read the incoming signals but also to compute their relevance for the organization's strategy at that particular moment. An organization prospers by continually redefining its goals after the event, and it presumes that its members will have the "savvy" or initiative to guess how to respond to its needs. Needless to say, the advantages do not all lie with role clarity and simplicity. Most managers are fairly adept at clarifying their terms of reference in a manner which facilitates meeting their needs.

Two types of role conflict have been identified, intrarole and interrole. Intrarole conflict results from the perception of conflicting expectation signals from role senders—for example, when a manager receives a signal from the head office to increase production and suboptimize on quality and a signal from his subordinates that they are professionals who are unwilling to put out faulty work.

Interrole conflict arises when an individual occupies more than one role. A not uncommon example is the person who is both general manager (*GM*) of a factory and a manager of one of its departments (*DM*), as shown in Figure 8–6. Interrole conflict of this type can be very difficult for the section managers (*SM*) in the department; when they try to pin down their superior, the department manager, to get him to define department policy, they may find him "changing hats" and answering them as general manager. Such a situation is extremely dysfunctional. The person holding two roles may experience considerable anxiety and guilt, for his varying role senders will try to monitor his behaviour according to their different needs.

Organizational roles vary in their vulnerability to conflict. Typically, roles close to the boundary of the organization (particularly where the

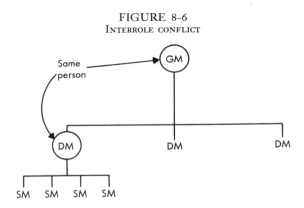

FIGURE 8–6
INTERROLE CONFLICT

role holder has to engage in a large number of interactions with a wide variety of other roles) experience greater conflict. To cope with such conflict demands adjustment not only in terms of organizational structure, process, and values but also in terms of personality variables. R. L. Kahn and his research colleagues, in *Organizational Stress: Studies in Role Conflict and Ambiguity*, have challenged the traditional wisdom of industrial psychology by showing the crucial functions of personality dispositions as moderators between formal requirements and individual outcomes. The research team showed by comparing six organizational levels that the tension created by role strain increased as one ascended in the hierarchy. Since role conflict affects mental health, executive positions may be more difficult than many academics had previously believed.

ROLE AND PERSONALITY: THE UNEQUAL CONTEST

An intriguing relation exists between the concepts of role and personality. For the naive and unsophisticated, role is the cell within which personality does its time, tied to a regime of subroutines that hones personality down to the bone. "Bureaucratized" for the individual and "institutionalized" for the patient are terms which describe the process of role encompassing personality. But this is typically a pathological reaction reported by a victim who can't get service because of the red tape that some official is generating. The possibility is excluded that the official is deliberately being officious, deliberately choosing a bureaucratically rigid role, a narrow interpretation of the rules, and a depersonalized response. Many sociologists prefer to believe that the role dominates personality.

Alternatively a person may be seen as exercising his personality in selecting his role behaviour. After all, roles are socially ordained and fit webs of expectations; behaviour meeting such expectations conforms to probabilities and is thus credible and understandable. A skilled role player can send messages within this web of expectations and probabilities. An excellent illustration is the poker gambit, "play it by the rules while signalling on the second circuit," illustrated by Bobby Fischer at Reykjavik. The *New York Times* for August 20, 1972, reported as follows the dual role playing Fischer used in winning the world chess championship from Boris Spassky:

> At the board Fischer exerts a fearsome aura. He scares his opponents, although his over-the-board behavior is impeccable. For whatever his behavior away from the game itself, Fischer is a sportsman while he is playing. Like Spassky, he has a poker face. He never squirms when he is losing, never exults while he is winning. Those familiar with his mannerisms know when he has the game under control. There is the faintest flicker of triumph in his face, the flicker that comes to the eyes of a high-stake poker player who connects with the case ace in a stud game. But for the most part Fischer, while playing, observes the amenities as carefully as does Spassky. Spassky almost never looks at Fischer. Every once in a while Fischer will look for a few long moments at Spassky, especially when he knows he has a winning position. It is an expressionless yet calculating look, bleak yet scary. So Achilles must have looked at Hector. In chess, Fischer is a killer, and his opponents know it. As he has said in the past, he likes "to see 'em squirm."
>
> Spassky is a cultured gentleman. Fischer has scant consideration for anybody else. Men like Spassky are ill-equipped to deal with the combination of sadism and savagery that is Bobby Fischer. And, despite his being able to achieve a draw in the 15th game last Thursday and Friday, it is telling on Spassky. For chess is not played in a vacuum. It is a direct confrontation between two brains, and psychological elements play as much a part as pure logic and a knowledge of the openings. In this match Spassky has not only been outplayed. He has been psychologically pistol-whipped.

Thus the man in command of himself, like a film star, picks his roles with care, selecting those that are consonant with his personality configuration, public image, and career trajectory. Once he has taken up the role, he plays within the norms—but with a somewhat elastic quality. Without such reneging on norms, change would be impossible and the original social contract would dominate events, so that life would have the quality of a rerun late movie. But things change, and people fail to fulfill the expectations of roles: troops surrender though they have written orders to fight on signed by the Emperor to whom they have sworn allegiance; meek "inferiors" become fire-eating militants; R. C. priests marry; heroes display clay feet; and leaders explain that their love of peace compels them to make war.

Roles can be turned upside down by the knowing and the known, but only with the connivance of the less powerful. There is a special breed of person who opts to become a legend among his peers (and sometimes undergoes a life of existential hell in the process) as he conceals his true self behind veils of flamboyant posturing. Such is the fate of the General George Pattons, who never seem to be off-stage but always playing the scene for those who will some day chronicle their genius. Sometimes the role assimilation is so complete that it in fact becomes the individual's personality. Such theatrical role interpretation does not necessarily involve hypocrisy or bad faith, but probably represents unconscious choices of functional role plays which in turn become fully blown parts, welded to the spectator's expectations.

Good executives, like good actors, execute their parts with a mastery of nuance and gesture that overwhelms the audience. This acting allows the skilful executive to meet a wide repertoire of needs (which only a psychopathologist could recognize as a syndrome) and be entertaining to boot. The QED of the virtuoso performance, which never comes cheap, is the applause signal from the audience: "You've got to hand it to him."

Thus much that is made of the disjunction between the organization (that socializes people into roles—"nonpersons unperson persons") and personality (inviolate centre of man's sacred human nature) is so much poppycock. When it comes to a show-down between the organization and man, man may just take the hemlock and bring the house down. Academics who invoke anomie, alienation, and apathy at the drop of a hat see these conditions everywhere, much more than the red-blooded executives and Archie Bunkers of this world who are supposed to cause and suffer from them. The answer is often that the Archie Bunkers archie bunker through life blissfully unaware that they ought to be miserable, with the connivance of both friend and foe.

The conspiracy theory of organizational life—that people pick their parts according to their own destinies rather than the needs of the organization—is true. But it is a giant conspiracy with all conniving—the main stars, the supporting cast, the walk-on people, and the two-bit players. The organization writes a script of role expectations, and the actors interpret and improvise out of their own needs and abilities. Whether they get it together into a format that works for the clients, which is what the formal organization is meant to do, is taken up in Topic 4, "Socialization."

STATUS

Status is the rank held by a person and the value of that individual as measured by a group or class of persons; this estimate of rank is based ultimately on the extent to which his traits or attributes are seen as contributing to the commonly held needs and values of the group or class (see Box 8.1). Status is usually legitimated through certain value propositions which provide criteria of status achievement. Inevitably the search for value measures is so demanding that they tend to be applied in a somewhat relentless manner; this, of course, underscores the need that people have to achieve some kind of status definition. Not only aristocrats require a *Who's Who;* everybody requires some definition of rank that is visible, uniform, acceptable, useful, and if possible, reasonable. This need produces such criteria as "publish or perish" for university professors. Closer examination of the premises of such a criterion reveals the essence of what is involved in most status judgements.

In a university, as in other institutions, some measure of status is necessary but hard to get. Much of the complexity flows from the nature of specialization, which makes it difficult for colleagues to assess the performance of their peers. But the act of publication in a learned journal requires submission of the author's work to an editor, usually a distinguished academic, who rates the article in the first instance and then, if he is favourably impressed, submits the article for further consideration to referees distinguished in this field. In this way, an evaluation which is based on the judgement of one's peers is ultimately achieved. In much the same way are postgraduate students assessed for higher degrees. A similar type of mechanism, requiring assessment by peers or near peers, is carried out in the military in regard to officers who are seeking promotion.

There are several bases for status including:

1. The ability of the individual to reward those with whom he interacts; but only provided his rewards are a scarce commodity. Taking a negative example, the praise of a person lacking power has negative value for the recipient.
2. The extent to which he is perceived as receiving rewards which other members of the group value. For example, an academic who engaged in consultancy purely for cash would be downgraded, whereas an academic publishing in learned journals would be upgraded.
3. The costs he incurs, in terms of effort and risk involved, must be considerable. If an academic's research requires continuous and arduous observation, this will be seen as a status-conferring labour.
4. His investments, including considerations of seniority. For example, how long has he worked in the field?

Box 8.1: A contemporary study of social class

In this classic study of social stratification, Harold M. Hodges identified five socia classes.

1. The lower-lower (LL) class

One out of every six Peninsula families inhabits this class. Occupationally, the ma is an unskilled lower blue-collar worker. He is the last to be hired and first to be fired.

The LL lives in cramped quarters. He is perennially in debt. He seems especiall fearful of venturing beyond the familiar confines of the family group. Almost half of a LL's—in comparison to 1 in 10 middle-class Peninsulan People—claim relatives livin within a four-block radius of their own dwellings.

The LL readily concurs that "the wife's place is in the home"; that the husban should "run the show"; and that the child is ideally obedient, quiet, and even servile 1 parental dictates. For many LL's, the way of coping with life appears to be a reactic blended of apathy and resignation. His is a fatalistic, what-can-I-do-about-it, why-both universe. He belongs to few or no organizations.

2. The upper-lower (UL) class

The UL has a semiskilled or skilled occupational status. He is like the LL in his pr clivity for authoritarian, anomic, misanthropic, and patriarchal values; he is often open intolerant of Mexican-Americans, Oriental-Americans, blacks, and Jews (although suc prejudice is present in every class).

In contrast to the LL, the UL seems infinitely more confident and ebullient; he is le concerned with his self-image among strangers and rates himself as aggressive ar friendly. He describes himse:f as "strong and silent," "tough-minded," and "manly."

The UL is plagued by "status concern"—"raising one's social position." Neighbo hood status competition is also of disproportionate concern to the UL. Four in five his closest friends are classified as UL's.

3. The lower-middle (LM) class

The LM represents the "typical" American—salesman, clerical worker, foreman, e One in three Peninsula-dwellers is a member of this class. His traits include a hig school diploma and a home in the suburbs. An apt description of the LM is, "one wh is extremely or excessively strict in matters of morals and religion." Sex is a naugh word to many a LM. The characteristic LM believes that hard work, frugality, ar saving for a rainy day are virtues.

Harold M. Hodges, Jr., "Peninsular People: Social Stratification in a Metropolitan Complex, Clayton Lane (ed.), *Permanence and Change* (Cambridge, Mass.: Schenkman, 1969), pp. 5–36.

Basic to the notion of status is the process of comparison. G. C. Homans has persuasively argued that responses to such comparisons can be given meaning in terms of two principles: distributive justice and status congruence. Distributive justice is achieved when the profits of each person (i.e., rewards minus costs) are in direct proportion to his investments. Status congruence, which flows from the concept of distributive justice, assumes that an individual's rank is consonant with his achievements and aspirations. In other words members of a group strive to balance role status with role competence. Striking such a balance reduces the uncertainty associated with positions in a group or organization and enables members to

The LM belongs to many clubs. He is a baseball aficionado. No one is more of a homebody than the LM. He spends time at the family dinner table, on family vacations, weekend auto trips, etc.

He is this era's "forgotten man." His is the only level where the value of the "real" dollar has actually shrunk. He had to work longer hours in the 1960s than he did in the 1950s.

4. The upper-middle (UM) class

This class depicts the American of tomorrow. Scarcely one subject in seven, characteristically the professional, semiprofessional, or independent businessman or corporate employee belongs to the UM level. No one word describes the distinctive qualities of the UM, but the words flexible, trusting, democratic, tolerant, and non-dogmatic come most quickly to mind.

Almost three fifths of the UM's were "upward-mobile," and the key to their mobility was the college diploma. "Education" and "career" may be said to be the most focal UM concerns.

At this level, "organization process" most emphatically prevails. They are frequently elected to the presidencies of their organizations. The UM is not very religious. However, the broken-marriage rate is lowest of all at the UM level, less than 1 in 10. The UM's enjoy fine arts, and rarely attend motion pictures or view television. They read more books.

5. The upper (U) class

Less than 1 in every 500 Peninsula families belong to the ranks of the upper class. The U is heavily addicted to a seemingly unending chain of parties, charity balls, first nights at the theatre; he makes frequent sorties to resort homes and has box seats for the baseball games. He drinks more frequently, but is less given to smoking. He likes formal dress; white tie social affairs and, at work, dark or banker's gray suits with vests. His wife often prefers simple ("basic black") dress styles. The U is likeliest of all to live in the city. His educational attainment is equal to that of the UM.

The U is in many ways more akin to the lower than to the middle class. Like the L, he is tradition-oriented; and like the L's in general, he claims to be tougher-minded, more introverted, and more in accord with the idea that husband and parents should be dominant. He seems to be the most nonconforming and individualistic of all Pensulans.

structure the response of others towards them, especially in the future; thus status has an element of insurance about it in regard to future interpersonal transactions. It follows that where there is a lack of status congruence, interpersonal conflict is more likely to arise.

STATUS AND COMMUNICATION

The relation between status and communication has been investigated in a large number of studies. The findings of these investigations may be summarized in three propositions:

1. Communication is likely to be directed towards high-status members. For example, on balance, nurses prefer to talk to doctors.

2. Communication is likely to be directed towards individuals of equal status. If doctors are not available or "open" for communication, nurses prefer to talk to nurses.
3. Where equality of status is uncertain, communication will tend to be avoided. If two nurses are competing for promotion and there is a marginal difference in qualifications, seniority, and so on, contact will be avoided.

Such propositions refer to probabilities and represent, on balance, preferences. Many executives apparently regard with some distaste the fact that it is possible through statistical aggregates to illustrate status preferences in communication patterns. The admission of such preferences implies a self-structuring of behaviour to further self-interest, which most relatively unsophisticated executives find offensive. On account of this reluctance to admit a structuring of communication by status, many executives when they are first promoted experience considerable disturbance before they adjust to the situation.

For example, in a university, staff members prefer to communicate with the head of department, albeit there is usually considerable filtering of information to provide a favourable picture of the communicating subordinate. If this upward communication is not possible, the horizontal dimension of communication (contact with peers) is preferred. Much of this horizontal activity is subject to a degree of censoring, but not to the same degree as the vertically upward; a great deal of it is concerned with validating and confirming one's role and status in the group. The third option is communication downward, if possible with junior members of the department—frequently for the purposes of testing for deference. A strategy of last resort is communication with students (outside of the statutory requirements for lectures, seminars, supervision of research). The vital point is that students constitute a relatively minor part of the academic's reference group; in other words, they rarely contribute much towards defining his role. Academic apartheid is necessary for excellence in terms of research, which is the touchstone for promotion, but engenders a sense of anomie in the student. But if you wish excellence, it implies a long totem (or status hierarchy) with impediments of communication among the strata of statuses; ultimately a status gradient implies a hiatus in communication.

STATUS SYMBOLS

In "Status Race," a penetrating and intriguing analysis, J. Forster starts by observing:

> The battle for status symbols in British industry is fierce, expensive, and immensely time-consuming. "The giving and receiving of status symbols causes us more trouble than any other single thing," the personnel

boss of a big light-engineering firm told me not long ago. "Let status symbols get out of hand and you're in dead trouble," said another personnel boss.

If an organization is to function effectively, roles must be created; some roles must be superior to others in terms of authority and power; and the superior roles must be attractive. The way to make such roles sufficiently attractive is to confer on them a higher status; and we noted earlier that status must be visible. Hence the status symbol.

For example, in British hospitals, it is common for young newly qualified doctors to carry stethoscopes to indicate their status. Nurses wear an elaborate but archaic uniform which indicates their rank. Junior doctors wear white laboratory coats, but so do medical auxiliaries such as X-ray technicians. The problem becomes acute in the case of female doctors. Fortunately, the female auxiliaries keep their coats fastened and usually wear a coloured belt, which detracts only slightly from their professional status by adding a note of female flamboyance. Female doctors keep their coats open and, of course, don't wear coloured belts. The complexity of the status system is further revealed by the fact that many senior doctors do not wear white coats and are addressed as Mr.

Forster in "Status Race" presents some very intriguing evidence about the totemistic milieux of modern management. For example:

> The sheer volume of office real estate a man gets is an important status indicator, though not everybody parcels it out as rigidly as the Civil Service. There, a Permanent Secretary is allowed up to 550 square feet, a Deputy Secretary up to 450, an Under-Secretary up to 350, and so on right down to the typist, who gets 60. . . .
>
> The size of a man's desk can be a crucial measuring-rod. Directors are generally allowed to choose their own, at a cost that may reach £350; few of them—except for the megalomaniac fringe—exceed an eight-foot spread. An "overhang" is strongly favoured, so that subordinates can gather round comfortably; and a really good desk will often have a secret shelf just below the top, so that loose papers can quickly be swept off to preserve an appearance of dignity and leisure.
>
> In companies where these things are tightly regulated, only directors choose their own desks à la carte, and according to the buyer at one of the best-known suppliers of office furniture "people generally drop about a foot in size for each rank down." Junior managers seldom get more than a five-footer, which might cost £40.

The boss of one large firm of office furnishers said:

> Other rough rules of décor are widely observed. Directors often have conference tables, but they very rarely have filing-cabinets in their own rooms. They also tend to personalise their offices freely—perhaps with an odd golf-club in the corner or an old army dagger on the wall. Managers, on the other hand, often have to live with their filing-cabinets, and even have to put up with metal desks.

Said one management consultant:

A secretary provides the equivalent of the estate agent's "secluded setting." She shuts her boss away from intrusions and trivia—and, don't forget, her loyalty is to him and not to the company. There are refinements in the relationship. The setting his position entitles him to put her in enhances both his status and hers. Can the boss, to begin with, give his secretary her own room? Directors and senior managers, I was told, usually can; in other cases, the girl and the filing-cabinets are in with the boss.

Most sophisticated executives have come to terms with the concept of status symbols, recognize their necessity, and try to avoid their proliferation by sensible regulation.

Some companies claim to get by quite effectively by pursuing a policy of conspicuous democracy, but where this apparent absence of a status gradient pervades, there is a tendency for senior executives to achieve some kind of isolation or executive apartheid by, for example, timing their lunch to an hour when the mass of the shop floor people have already eaten.

What is needed is conscious and explicit recognition of the function of status in regard to the proper discharge of the executive role; blank refusal to recognize the need for a status gradient with appropriate symbols usually leads to covert activities, involving devious arrangements and conspiracies which are resented, time-consuming, and expensive.

TOPIC 3
Conformity

A subject of consuming interest to executives is conformity—the influence which the group exerts on the individual to get him into a role, keep him in it, make him follow group norms, and in general meet the group's expectations. Groups cannot survive without most of their expectations being realized. For a sufficient number of role holders to default on their payments, in terms of meeting expectations, would lead to a break-down of the basic processes of the group.

What the member must conform to is the group's norms—the specifications of its values. A norm may be defined as a verbal statement that many members believe is a valuable guide to behaviour. A norm is thus a behavioural rule accepted by several (usually a majority of) members of the group. As the comics say, "It's all in the head." Once norms have been specified and codified, group life becomes easier, since recourse to either power or ingratiation will diminish because of lack of necessity. Norms are thus behavioural inventions to facilitate group life.

Why do group members conform? For starters, conformity to group norms is rewarded and lack of conformity punished. Reinforcements include approval, acceptance, recognition, and positive feedback. Sanctions include denial of membership, rejection, isolation, and negative feedback. Conformity thus offers an inducement to the individual. Higher status also influences a member to make his attitudes and behaviour conform to the norms of the group. For example, army officers have greater faith in the avowed aims of the army than enlisted men.

Complete conformity indicates that a member depends entirely on the norms of the group. As Figure 8–7 indicates, utter conformity is not as healthy a situation for the individual as a measure of nonconformity which allows him some options. The anticonformist does the exact opposite of

FIGURE 8–7
AXES OF CONFORMITY AND NONCONFORMITY

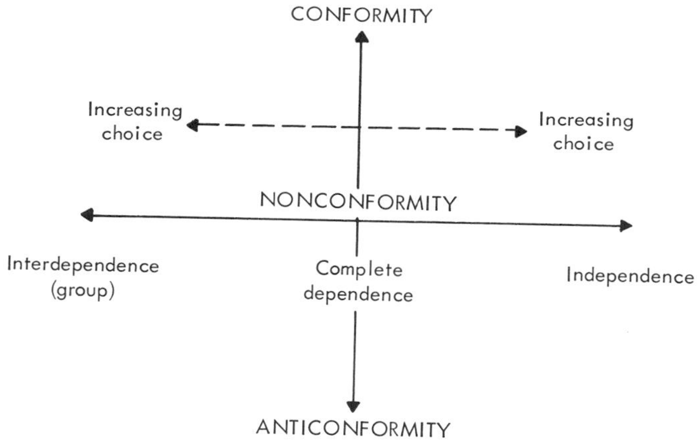

what group norms demand, and thus is as much a "slave" to the situation as the conformist.

COMPLIANCE, IDENTIFICATION, AND INTERNALIZATION

People may conform overtly without accepting the party line. For example, many POW's in North Korea went through the motions of ideological conversion to communism to survive, without in fact privately changing their political beliefs. Herbert C. Kelman was puzzled by this problem of public conformity without private acceptance. In exploring this problem further, Kelman was led to distinguish three processes of social influence—compliance, identification, and internalization.

Compliance occurs when an individual accepts influence from another, hoping to achieve a favourable response from him. "Making the right noises," saying and doing the right things to stay in somebody's "good books," constitutes compliance. Compliance lacks conviction and manifests itself only when the person is under observation.

Identification occurs when a person adopts the behaviour or attitudes of another for the purposes of keeping in good standing with the other person. An example would be an executive imitating his boss in terms of accent, dress, style, and so on. Identification is similar to compliance in the sense that the conforming person is under the influence of another; it differs in the sense that the individual acts voluntarily, out of admiration rather than compulsion (unlike the state of compliance, he does not behave differently in private).

Finally, internalization occurs when an individual is not merely influenced by another's (the group's) values, but incorporates them into his own value system. The three processes indicate an increasing level of conformity, from behaviour that is only an appearance to a restructuring of attitudes within the self-concept.

ENGINEERING CONFORMITY

One of the most widely established findings in group dynamics is the fact that opinions converge when individuals become members of a group. The classical research in engineering conformity was conducted by M. Sherif, who set his subjects the task of estimating the extent of movement of a single point of light in a completely dark room. The light, though stationary, will be seen to move; and further, the movements are perceived as being erratic. This phenomenon is known as the autokinetic effect.

Individual judgements made in private were compared with estimates made by the same individual as a member of a group. The effect of convening the group was to make the estimates converge. On matters of this type, where there is no objective actuality, consensus may be essential because consensus is the only reality. Hence the executive expression "validity by consensus."

Apparently group members experience considerable pressure to conform with peer estimates even when such estimates clearly run contrary to the facts. This particular proposition has been demonstrated in an extremely influential series of experiments by S. E. Asch. In experiments matching the length of a given vertical line with three other lines, Asch has shown that a subject, after hearing phoney "evidence" which contradicts the evidence of his senses, will go along with the phoney consensus. The importance of communication in avoiding this sort of pluralistic ignorance is obvious.

Given the social psychologists' ability to engineer consensus, management training and sensitivity training in particular become a cinch. By carefully selecting group members and organizing "experiences"—both their nature and sequence—it is apparently possible to get managers to agree to anything (see Box 8.2).

Group pressures to uniformity are substantial and are based on such considerations as:

1. If uniformity of opinion is held to be important for the group, the group will try to bring this state about to maintain its reality. For example, in management training, "We are here for a week; let's give it a try—let's not pack everything in the first hour of the first day."

2. Groups have a variety of rewards which they can give for conformity—especially indications of esteem and acceptance.

3. Groups usually can exercise sanctions for failure to conform—"binging" in the Hawthorne experiment.

THE NONCONFORMIST

Though deviance in groups tends to be punished, and considerable pressure is usually applied to induce conformity, some nonconformity is tolerated and understood as helpful. If the eccentric is properly received in the group, his bizarre behaviour will be welcomed, but at a price. He is expected to undertake both the comic and scapegoat roles from time to time to facilitate the discharge of group tensions. But if outsiders attack the eccentric, his peers will rush to his defence. The nonconformist has two other important roles for the group. Taking the less important first, he confers glamour on the group by making it more interesting and tolerant. Second, he facilitates group change by holding a set of opinions which, though differing from group norms, can be called up for consideration, and which allow the more conservative in the group to consider unusual and new courses of action. The ability to explore such propositions is a necessary first step to change. The well-established nonconformist is recognized by the group as a useful and necessary role, as long as his behaviour is not too extreme and as long as he contributes to and interacts with the group.

Unfortunately the role of the nonconformist is not widely understood; many aspirants for this interesting role fail the casting test because they imagine that the first and only behaviour required is breaching group norms. Proving acceptability, whether by achievement, ability to maintain a dissonant position, or proof of loyalty is a necessary correlate of nonconformity if it is going to be accepted.

In brief, the nonconformist is needed so that the others can conform while he provides a reserve of change options. He also has the reserve roles of comic and scapegoat. Curiously, other members of the group often make their roles more conservative to facilitate the work of the nonconformist. Willingness to be type-cast is usually a condition, if not a proof, of group membership.

THE CONFORMIST

Among executives, the problem of their own uniformity has become a foremost topic. Our era has frequently been described as the age of con-

Box 8.2: Obedience to authority

If X tells Y to hurt Z, under what conditions will Y obey? Stanley Milgram of Yale Un versity investigated this problem, using adult males from a wide variety of occupation Each subject became the teacher in a learning experiment and was told by the exper menter to shock the learner when he made a mistake. The teacher sat in front of shock machine with 30 levers ranging from 15 to 450 volts, and verbal designation ranging from "Slight Shock" to "Danger: Severe Shock." The teacher was given a 4 volt shock to convince him of the authenticity of the machine. The learner sat in a "electric chair."

Since the learner made many mistakes, the teacher had to administer a higher lev of shock with each mistake. In the pilot studies, the victim could be dimly seen by th teacher through silvered glass. In spite of the verbal designations on the machine, a subjects blithely obeyed the experimenter. Then studies were conducted with verba protests: at 75 volts the victim "grunts and moans"; at 150, "demands to be let out"; 180, "can no longer stand the pain"; and at 300, "refuses to answer."

"IT'S ALL RIGHT IF YOU SHUT YOUR EYES"

Even though the subjects were worried about the victim—that he might have a hea condition, or be killed by the shock—most of them nevertheless obeyed. Subjec frequently averted their eyes from the person they were shocking, often turning the heads in an awkward and conspicuous manner. One subject explained: "I didn't wa to see the consequences of what I had done."

The proximity of the victim was found to be important. Four "psychological" di tances were used: (1) victim in another room, cannot be seen or heard, but does poun on the wall at 300 volts and silence at higher levels; (2) voice feedback from anoth room; (3) voice and visual cues from a distance of 1½ feet; (4) the teacher had to plac the victim's hand on the shockplate.

The proportion of subjects who refused to obey to the 450 level of shock increas from 34 percent to 70 percent as the proximity increased. Since the subjects attribute the same amount of pain in all conditions, these results cannot be explained by a increased awareness of the pain the teacher is causing. Milgram suggests that oth mechanisms may be involved—increased empathic cues, greater difficulty in ignorin the victim, the "discomfort" of being watched by the victim, increased awareness of th direct relation between pressing the lever and hurting the victim. Incipient group form tion may also be important—the teacher can ally himself either with the experimen or the victim, but alliance with the victim is easier if he is close to the teacher.

IF THE COMMAND COMES FROM A LEGITIMATE AUTHORITY . . . .

Even more important than the closeness of the victim was the closeness of authori

Stanley Milgram, "Some Conditions of Obedience and Disobedience to Authority," *Human Ɩ tions*, Vol. 18 (1965), pp. 57–75.

formity. Neither the high degree of uniformity in values and practice nor sheer conventionality can be simply equated with conformity. Thus, for a man to wear trousers in our society does not leave him open to the charge of conformity. Conventions represent the ready-made rules of society, which, if followed, minimize conflict.

Conformity, in this context, is the act of conceding to group pressures. Conformity must be judged against the perspective of a conflict between

(the experimenter). Obedience dropped sharply if the experimenter left the laboratory and gave orders by telephone. Teachers also began to "cheat," giving the victim the lowest possible level of shock while telling the experimenter they were increasing the shock levels.

The subjects were exposed to a distressing conflict situation when they had to choose between the demands of the experimenter and increasing pressure from the victim to stop; they were observed to sweat, tremble, stutter, and groan, yet many continued to obey. Several had nervous laughing fits due to the tension.

Here is a transcript from an obedient subject. He began the experiment calmly, but became increasingly tense as the experiment proceeded. After administering the 150-volt shock, he began to address the experimenter in agitated tones:

> 150 volts delivered. You want me to keep going?
> 165 volts delivered. That guy is hollering in there. There's a lot of them here. He's liable to have a heart condition. You want me to go on? 180 volts delivered. He can't stand it! I'm not going to kill that man in there! You hear him hollering? He's hollering. He can't stand it. What if something happens to him? . . . I'm not going to get that man sick in there. He's hollering in there. You know what I mean? I mean I refuse to take responsibility. He's getting hurt in there. He's in there hollering. Too many left here. Geez, if he gets them wrong. There's too many of them left. I mean, who is going to take responsibility if anything happens to that gentleman? [The experimenter accepts responsibility.] All right.
> 195 volts delivered. You see he's hollering. Hear that. Gee, I don't know. [The experimenter says: "The experiment requires that you go on."] I know it does, sir, but I mean—hugh—he don't know what he's in for. He's up to 195 volts. 210 volts delivered. 225 volts delivered. 240 volts delivered. Aw, no. You mean I've got to keep going up with the scale? No sir. I'm not going to kill that man! I'm not going to give him 450 volts! [The experimenter says: "The experiment requires that you go on."] I know it does, but that man is hollering in there, sir. . . .

There are probably two different kinds of forces at work: (1) a personality factor enabling the subject to transfer responsibility to authority; and (2) the structural properties of the social situation.

If we can generalize from Milgram's work and apply his conclusions to our own society, who is guilty? What do his findings say about the Nuremberg judgements? Are judgements of culpability impossible to sustain in organizations?

what the individual (free from group pressures) knows to be correct or right and what the group tries to impose upon him. (See Box 8.2.)

C. N. Crutchfield has developed a technique for measuring conformity. Five subjects are seated side by side in separate screened booths. Each booth has a set of numbered switches to enable the subject to signal his judgements and a display panel showing the answers given by the others. In fact, the subjects are "fed" a "bogus consensus" to impose group pressure on the subjects' judgement.

This experimental procedure has been used to demonstrate that a substantial amount of yielding to the phoney group consensus takes place. One item included in this test consisted of the presentation of two figures, a circle and a star, with the circle being one-third larger in area. The subject was asked to name which figure had the greater area. In a sample of 50 military officers, 46 per cent of the testees agreed with the phoney group consensus that the star was larger.

Personality descriptions of uniformity have been built up by research. Compared with nonconformists, conformists have been shown to be less intelligent, lower in ego strength, inclined towards pronounced feelings of personal inferiority and inadequacy, lacking in self-confidence, and preoccupied with other people. They also express more conventional attitudes regarding morals, often coupled with a low tolerance for ambiguity.

Crutchfield presented personality descriptions of highly independent and highly conforming military officers. The nonconformist was described as:

1. An effective leader.
2. Taking an ascendant role in his relations with others.
3. Persuasive; tends to win other people over to his point of view.
4. Turned to for advice and reassurance.
5. Efficient, capable, able to mobilize resources easily and effectively.
6. Active, vigorous, expressive, ebullient.
7. Seeking and enjoying aesthetic and sensuous impressions.
8. Natural, free from pretence, unaffected.
9. Self-reliant, independent in judgement, able to think for himself.

The Conformist was described as:

1. With respect to authority, submissive, compliant, overly accepting.
2. Tending to do the things that are prescribed.
3. Having a narrow range of interests.
4. Overcontrolling impulses; inhibited; needlessly delaying or denying gratification.
5. Unable to make decisions without vacillation or delay.
6. Confused, disorganized, and unadaptive under stress.
7. Lacking insight into his own motives and behaviour.
8. Suggestible, overly responsive to other people's evaluations rather than his own.

REFERENCE GROUPS

It has been suggested that a major reason why some people do not conform is that they are "marching to a different drum." The nonconformist is marching to the tune of his reference group.

A reference group is any group, real or imaginary, which has significantly affected a person's expectations of life by planting its values, norms, reinforcements, and sanctions nexus in his consciousness. It may be a group in his past, present, or (he hopes) future.

Aware of the importance of reference groups, some organizations (such as prisons and other total institutions) seek to remove all evidence of their existence by purification rituals; other organizations deliberately seek out members with compatible reference groups. For example, the English military and foreign service prefer candidates from public (private) schools and Oxbridge, mainly because reference group congruence makes organizational life so much more predictable (if somewhat boring) and removes from it the danger of upstarts who have innovative ideas. In the United States, similar arrangements prevail between top business schools (Harvard, M.I.T., Stanford) and top corporations (IBM, ITT, Ford) to maintain congruence of reference groups. Not a bad arrangement, in the main—and fortunately, the system is sufficiently inefficient to produce a Ralph Nader or Daniel Ellsberg from time to time.

The concept of the reference group has thus become one of the most important analytical tools for the organizational psychologist. The group serves as a point of reference in evaluating what is happening to a person at a particular time. A person uses the perspective of his reference group to gauge how well he is performing or how well he is being treated in his present group. The reference group is thus a standard which an actor invokes as a means of forming his estimate of other groups' structure, process, and value systems.

An executive who has recently graduated with an M.B.A. may well view the problem-solving style of his work group in a derisory way because it falls far short of the style which he learned at business school. He has absorbed certain values and norms at school which have become anchor points in structuring his perceptual field. Figure 8–8 shows some of the most important groups that may serve as reference groups.

Reference groups arise through the internalization of norms, setting a perspective or perceptual frame of reference for comparing the new expectations of the new audience for whom one organizes one's behaviour and attitudes. Many organizations (for example, prisons, officer cadet schools, some hospitals) develop stripping processes to "purify" new members of their old frames of reference by attempting to destroy connections with their previous lives. Reference groups also explain the behaviour of the rate-buster (who cannot accept the norms of his primary working group but derives the meaning for his behaviour from some other group) and the eccentric.

COSMOPOLITAN, LOCAL, AND CHANCER ROLES

The concept of reference group provides a very useful concept for getting at the difference between two interesting roles: the cosmopolitan and the local. The cosmopolitan, as the name implies, is the mobile, sophis-

FIGURE 8–8
IMPORTANT POTENTIAL REFERENCE GROUPS

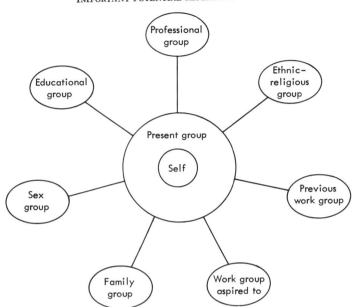

ticated expert who takes his reference from his professional group. Locals are organization men who take their reference from their present organizations. They can be compared in terms of:

	Loyalty to work group	Professional skill	Reference group
Cosmopolitan	Low	High	Outside work group
Locals	High	Low	Inside work group

A commonly cited illustration relates to university departments, where the cosmopolitan is the copious publisher who derives his reference from academic peers in his specialty elsewhere and pays scant heed to what is going on in his own department. The local keeps the department going—teaching, administering, and maintaining community relations—and is frequently uncertain as to what is happening at the frontiers of knowledge in his discipline. In most universities, cosmopolitans have the highest prestige and salaries while rendering the least service to undergraduate students.

In business, cosmopolitans were traditionally found among the staff experts in personnel, finance, and engineering and locals were the line managers. But now, with management emerging as a profession, a new breed of cosmopolitan managers is emerging. This new, mobile manager follows a different career path: graduate school to get his M.B.A.; a consultancy firm for a high base salary and rapid experience in a wide variety of industries; a spell in a company like Proctor & Gamble or IBM to get corporate planning experience; the second-top position in some company which is fighting to get into the *Fortune* 500 league; then, depending on chance, the top slot somewhere. By the age of 45, he may also have served in government, been on the faculty of some business school, or retired to private consultancy to live on his stock options. With this kind of cosmopolitan career path, his reference group has to be somewhere other than his temporary resting places of employment.

The chancer is another role holder, this time one who uses his reference group as his guide with primary group members, and vice versa. Marshall Pugh in his book *The Chancer* describes a person who had been seconded to the Commandos (an elite combat unit), who wore his line infantry officer's uniform when with the Commando unit, but his Commando battle gear when with his line infantry unit. The same kind of hypocrisy is frequently witnessed in other organizations. The intent is to impress each group or to excuse mediocrity ("I'm only here by chance, but I do as well as most of you 'regulars' anyway"). Another example is the married woman who accepts a low-status position but "identifies" with the higher status of her husband or her social class (taking care to let her job associates know about these reference groups).

CONCLUSION

Without conformity, groups could not survive. But modern research shows that conformity is more complex than was first thought. There is virtue in conformity, and the group rewards the member who pays the price of admission and does not renege on his obligations to meet group norms. But nonconformity also has its virtues. An interesting question here is, why isn't the eccentric rejected by the group? Just as the individual must decide his balance in terms of dependence-independence, the group apparently must strike a balance in how hard it exerts influence on members to comply and identify with it.

What a person is, does, and believes is to a large extent dependent on the features of the reference groups to which he has belonged, belongs, or aspires to belong. Thus his behaviour is unlikely to be completely determined by membership in any single group. A reference group is a primary source of perspective, providing a person with premises for action.

If a group is to be effective it must have some processes of socialization to get new members to assimilate its values and norms. Somehow or other, established members of a group are aware of this need for socialization, which accounts for the "song-and-dance" rituals new members are led through.

TOPIC 4
Socialization

Organizations process not only material, energy, and information but also people. The "new boy" entering the organization has to be taught the ropes before he can acquire the three R's (rules, roles, and relations) of the game. To achieve this personal transformation, the rookie—the trainee, the cadet, the new patient—has to be socialized. Figure 8–9 is an overview of this process.

The process of socialization is the assimilation of the values and behaviours required to survive and prosper in the organization. It begins even before the organization gets its hooks into the victim to be processed.

FIGURE 8–9
SOCIALIZATION

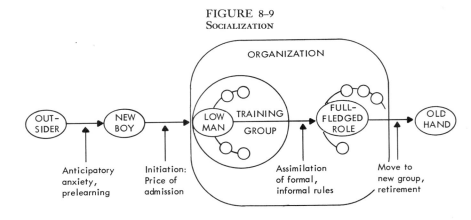

Crack institutions such as the Harvard Business School, the Marines, the paratroopers, IBM, the Mayo Clinic, and Sing Sing have a distinct reputation which gives off an ambience, a cultural odour which alerts and preconditions the new boy for what lies ahead of him—"It's going to be tough." Nobody can really tell him what lies ahead, not even the people who have been through the hoop. Sometimes the process is so dramatic (something like electroshock therapy, which has been compared to facing the patient with the crisis of simulated death) that amnesia is introduced, and the destruction of one identity is achieved and another created. At the very least, anxiety is generated.

As one preliminary, the victim has to be sold the organization so that he will step on the conveyor system from which there is little chance of escape. This may be involuntary (prison), but ideally it is a free choice where he values and esteems what lies ahead, where he sees himself as a member of an élite which has a coveted, distinctive status. For a pilot's wings or a company president's eight-foot desk, there must be a price of admission which few can pay while many are left out in the cold.

The prelearning process will make some effort to break down and replace previous reference groups. At the extreme—in a mental hospital, a religious order, a prison, or an officer cadet school—the old self is symbolically destroyed by a process of stripping which may include removal of clothes, previous status symbols, reference to previous achievements, and even, in some circumstances, hair. New names and titles, such as "cadet" and "management trainee," are conferred. This process of purification prepares the acolyte by altering his previous role and status. He is now ready to be kitted out afresh.

INITIATION: THE PRICE OF ADMISSION

The new boy becomes the low man on the group totem pole. He, and others like him, form a training squad or work group where the process of role assimilation begins. At this stage his group is assigned problems (cases to do, floors to polish, litter to pick up, technical information to acquire) which are well beyond their individual capabilities. Considerable anxiety is generated; fear of failure and the possibility of rejection are always there. The squad bosses (NCO's, professors, psychiatrists, training managers) become the focus of a love-hate relation. To survive, the group forms informal structures, processes, and values, and this peer group takes over the job of indoctrinating other new boys. Such primary groups typically begin with a high level of tension, which reaches a maximum just before the mid-point of the training period. Just when the new man is weighing the advantages of quitting, there is usually a slight letting up to let him get through to the second half. From then on in, it's cheaper to stay in than quit.

ASSIMILATION

The assimilation of the new role, identity, and value systems is now developed further by taking the neophyte into his first operational assignment. From a socialization point of view, the object of this part of the exercise is to introduce the neophyte to the complexities and dilemmas of a sector of the organization where the cozy feeling of being inside the training group, with its peer support, is now somewhat diminished. The first assignment introduces him to a novel world of fiefdoms, each with its own territory, mandate, values, and norms—all operative, but mostly hazy and somewhat difficult to pick up. Again he will have to endure the humiliations of initiation, the learning of new passwords and prayers, until his eventual absorption into the new apparatus.

Soon the critical first assignment will be coming—which to his mind is designed "to make or break him." Much depends on the accidents of history in technology; the assignment may be solvable or not, depending on the guy upstairs or the support of peers, who may also be going through this trial by fire. In any case, the structure of a career path will slowly reveal its clues. Of the neophytes, a few will be nudged to the exits; most will be sent to relatively routine assignments and the gradual career escalator; a few will be directed to the fast escalator, with accelerated challenges, status, and rewards built in.

As our organization man frees himself from his neophyte status and moves into the heartland of the institution, he will have to learn new roles and styles, which only the right kind of exposure and visibility will ensure. Much depends on the sort of assignments he picks up and the people he lands with "accidentally."

Frequently the organization cannot provide sufficient experience to ensure accelerated growth, and elaborate training rituals in the form of T groups, the Blake managerial grid, and other simulated problem-solving exercises have to be gone through. The contemporary exaggerations of change make continual demands for further role developments. In the future, changes in the external environment are likely to outpace and defeat the strategy of concentrating on assimilation of a particular organization's specific role. The emergence of the mobile manager, the rapid development of computer firms, the mushrooming of consultancy, the slowing down of the aerospace and electronics business, women's liberation, human liberation in terms of the hip existential culture, and a multitude of other factors may make single-role assimilation a distinct hazard.

In any case, our corporate official as he enters middle age may well find himself in a real crisis. Beset by anxieties as to whether he has made the right career choice, fearful of reduced physical and sexual vigour coupled with a changing appearance, and facing career and salary levelling-off plateaux, his situation is indeed another adolescence. So far, our culture has provided him mostly with the option of succumbing to apathy and anomie and, like the old soldier, "just fading away." Yet many persons have provided clues to another choice: "second (or third) careers," development into new life styles, and ways of making the term "golden age" more than a mockery. Increasing mobility and personal freedom may contribute. Certainly the individual who experiments with many roles rather than putting all his eggs in one basket is in a better position to move on—or out—with self-confidence.

REHABILITATION

To survive outside the organization, its roles and values must be unlearned or environments found which will allow the transfer of the role skills. Where socialization has been institutionalization, as for military officers, prison inmates, long-term hospital patients, or prisoners of war, special programmes staffed by psychiatrists and psychologists are needed to

facilitate the process of decompression. Business organizations are responding to this problem by laying on courses to familiarize older executives
with the problems and possibilities of retirement. Much more needs to be
done to increase the options for the aging and aged.

SOCIALIZATION PROCESSES

One of the most powerful demonstrations of behavioural techniques in
recent times has been the brainwashing techniques used by the Chinese
Communists on American prisoners during the Korean war. Edgar Schein
has used an analysis of the Chinese techniques to demonstrate the relationships among communication, group solidarity, influence and tractability.
These relationships have important implications for the manner in which
individuals are socialized into organizations. We have described Schein's
unfreezing-changing-refreezing model earlier; a deeper look at it is in
order here.

Schein points out that interpersonal communication, both verbal and
nonverbal, expresses how people feel about each other as well as giving
information relevant to task performance. The central theme of his argument is that the expression of proper mutual regard and the stability of
social relationships and roles is necessary not only for the maintenance of
group solidarity and organized activity but also for personal identity and
security. Interpersonal communication is therefore necessary for both social and personal integration.

Our opinions, beliefs, and fundamental values are formulated and reinforced through contact with those whom we regard and trust. The disruption of interpersonal communication can lead, therefore, to social
alienation and a search for new relationships. This "unfreezing" of the
personality makes the individual highly susceptible to external influences,
particularly those which promise to allow him to regain his psychological
stability. A person's ability to restructure his self-concept is increased
when contact with those to whom he normally looks for guidance is cut
off. The extent to which he will be influenced will depend, says Schein, on
the degree to which he has been alienated, the degree of pressure to
change, and the availability of new values and beliefs which he can accept.
The Chinese showed remarkable understanding of how to make the process
work. However, providing a manual on brainwashing is not our purpose,
so only a brief summary of their methods is presented here.

Alienation was achieved by depriving the prisoners of any organized
activity in which they could share information and affirm their solidarity.
Constant spying made the men suspicious of each other and individuals
were forced into co-operation with the enemy in order to protect fellow
prisoners or get urgently needed food and medicine. Even slight acts of
co-operation were then shown to other prisoners as evidence that one of
their number had sold out, and this created great mistrust as well as en-

couragement to others to "go with the trend." Mail was censored so that a prisoner would only get bad news and be made to feel that people at home cared for neither him nor the war effort. This manipulation of the communication channels proved more effective than total disruption through solitary confinement.

Schein comments that the POW's, although they became lonely and withdrawn, did not become as thoroughly broken as those civilian political prisoners who were subjected to much greater pressure for change. This pressure was applied by placing prisoners in groups whose members' degree of "advancement" in thought reform varied. The progress of the group towards less stringent conditions of imprisonment was made contingent on the extent to which the least "advanced" member could be brought along. This man was subject to the strongest group pressure to admit his "crimes," often being reduced to subhuman treatment and made to feel completely worthless. If he confessed, his alienation was completed by forcing him to implicate others in his confession.

In Schein's opinion, no human can live for long in this alienated condition. The individual will seek a new role and self-image that can be confirmed through interaction with others. The Chinese provided many opportunities for the prisoners to form relationships with guards and others who would provide new sets of values consistent with Communist aims. Those who showed progress in accepting these values were given numerous rewards, the greatest of which was the information that they were once again individuals worthy of respect and regard. The prisoners were also given many rationales for collaborating; for example, that it was less harmful than getting your comrades shot. By saturating the information system with the Chinese version of the "truth" and depriving the prisoners of contact with trusted officers or comrades with whom they could evaluate new moral standards for the many novel situations they faced, it was possible to exert considerable influence on the prisoners and to effect considerable change in their behaviour and beliefs.

Schein's research is not of merely historical interest. Major social institutions, including business enterprises, must exert some degree of influence on their members if they are to accomplish their aims. Some already use, perhaps unwittingly, some of the techniques of alienation, pressure, and influence employed by the Chinese. Knowing how such techniques are used in an organizational environment is important to understanding socialization.

EFFECTS OF VARIOUS TYPES OF INFLUENCE

An organization wants to instill in its members attitudes that are conducive to goal-directed activity. The theoretical and empirical observations of H. C. Kellman provide considerable enlightenment on the operation of this process.

Kellman argues that the manner in which communications are perceived will affect the type of conformity that they elicit and the conditions under which they will continue to influence the subject's attitudes. The type of influence that will result from any given communication will depend on how the subject feels he is being approached. An essentially similar line of argument can result in compliance, identification, or internalization, depending strictly on the way the information is presented. If the influencing agent uses control and power, the elicited response will be compliance. If the agent is attractive, the subject will tend to accept the argument because of identification with the agent. If the authority of the agent is based on credibility as an expert, the respondent will tend to internalize the arguments.

The impatient executive may well ask at this point what difference the whole thing makes as long as the subject can be influenced to accept the desired attitudes. The traditional short-cut method to achieve this has been the use of organizational power to enforce compliance. However, Kellman's analysis of the consequences of the influence process must also be considered:

1. Compliance can be relied on to produce the desired effects only as long as the subject continues to be under surveillance.
2. Identification will affect behaviour as long as the relationship between the attitudes in question and the group to which the subject wishes to belong remains salient.
3. Internalization will continue to affect the subject's behaviour as long as the issue seems relevant, whether he is observed or not.

So it makes good sense to try to influence subjects by appealing to their basic values; the attitudes thus instilled can be relied on to produce the most long-term effects and require the least reinforcement.

Kellman tested his theory in an experiment which measured the attitudes of black college freshmen on a race-related issue. Four communicators presented essentially the same message—one which most of the students originally disagreed with—but the four were represented as having different power bases. One was presented as having considerable control over the financing of the subject's school and as intolerant of dissenting views. The second appealed to the students as a spokesman for student organizations, presenting a consensus of members' opinions. The third adopted the role of an unbiased and highly knowledgeable expert. A fourth communication, used for control purposes, was presented by an "ordinary citizen" who was made to appear both unattractive and ill-informed on the topic. Attitude measures were taken by three kinds of questionnaires: (1) a "surveillance" questionnaire, where the student was identified and his answers were purportedly shown to the communicator; (2) a "salience" questionnaire, with answers given in confidence immediately after the communication; and (3) a "relevance" questionnaire administered about two weeks after the communication, when the issue could be expected to have faded somewhat. The results confirmed Kellman's hypotheses:

1. When the basis of the power was means control, the degree of influence was reduced as soon as the subject felt he was no longer under observation. This supports the thesis that compliance must be enforced by surveillance to be effective.
2. Identification with an attractive communicator faded as an attitude-determining force as the relationship between the agent and the message lost its salience over time.
3. Internalized attitudes did not change even when surveillance was dropped and salience decreased.

Kellman concluded that the existence of "favourable" attitudes may not have significant behavioural consequences unless we look further to determine whether these attitudes were formed by compliance, identification, or internalization. This will determine how the individuals act in different circumstances and what kind of process is required to modify their attitudes.

UNFREEZING AND CHANGING

The process of organizational socialization takes place each time a person enters a new environment such as a school, business firm, or even a new department within a company. From his work with the Chinese techniques, Schein identified basic elements applicable to general organizational behaviour:

1. The basic *goals* of the organization.
2. The preferred *means* by which those goals should be attained.
3. The basic *responsibilities* of the member in the role which is being granted to him by the organization.
4. The *behaviour patterns* which are required for effective performance in the role.
5. A set of rules or principles which pertain to the *maintenance of the identity and integrity* of the organization.

Learning these values and norms may require considerable shifts in the attitudes of the new member. Schein uses the POW analogy to postulate that this learning can be best accomplished by "unfreezing" the initiate's personality—showing him that his present self is worthless and must be redefined in terms of his new role. In schools the unfreezing may be accomplished by initiation rites or by piling an impossible work load on the students. In business enterprises the new man can be given impossibly difficult (or, conversely, utterly trivial) tasks to perform or simply assigned to watching others do work. These techniques indicate to the newcomer that he isn't as smart as he thought he was and that he can't be trusted with any meaningful job. This creates a powerful drive to absorb the learning which will enable the person to prove himself and become accepted by the new group. Obviously, the amount of pressure exerted has to take into consideration the motivation of the newcomer to join the organization and the extent to which he can be held in the organization until his socialization is complete. The Chinese had advantages over American businessmen in this respect, but Schein points out that pension plans, stock options, and other financial incentives, as well as the inevitability of the process in any new organization, provide a strong argument to stay and see the thing through.

The organization has considerable power to influence attitudes through compliance and identification as well as the internal changes described above. Training programmes, procedure manuals, performance appraisal, salary administration, promotion, demotion, and informal counselling by more experienced members can all be used to instruct a new man in the standards he is expected to comply with. Of course, rate restriction, featherbedding, and theft may also be taught as norms of behaviour by those peers who are not greatly committed to the goals of the organization.

Identification can be achieved by showing interest in the man's welfare, flattering him with attention from superiors, stressing the company's loyalty to good workers, and giving him generous pay and benefits. The desire to identify with such a fine company can cause a man to accept its value system without question. Schein observes that he may feel guilty if he can't repay the investment the company makes in him by working hard and acting in the manner expected of him.

Schein also draws an interesting parallel between the behavioural commitment demanded by the Communists, who forced confessing prisoners to implicate others, and the use of promotions to force rebellious employees to accept the company value system. He notes that a commitment to very general goals such as "work for the good of the company" can be translated into compliance with a wide array of distasteful or boring tasks because they are necessary for the corporate welfare.

The conclusion of the socialization process comes when the man has acquired the necessary value system and is provided with titles and status to reflect his position of trust and importance in the firm. Unfortunately, not all of the learning process has a positive effect. Schein points out that some employees rebel against the value system and tend to engage in behaviour that is destructive of corporate aims. Total conformity, on the other hand, can stifle the organization's ability to respond to changes in its environment. Schein feels that "creative individualism"—which accepts key values but lets the individual determine his own standards on other issues—is the attitude most consistent with long-term organizational health.

TOPIC 5
The primary working group

Socialization assimilates the new man into the primary group, which may be defined as a group in which every member interacts directly, and frequently with every other member, usually on a face-to-face basis. The term "primary group" was introduced to the literature of sociology by Charles H. Cooley in 1909 with his book *Social Organization*, where he noted:

> By primary groups I mean those characterized by intimate face-to-face association and co-operation. They are primary in several senses, but chiefly in that they are fundamental in forming the social nature and ideals of the individual. The result of intimate association, psychologically, is a certain fusion of individualities in a common whole, so that one's very self, for many purposes at least, is the common life and purpose of the group.

The primary group, with its face-to-face interaction, is the nucleus of all organizations and represents the molecular structure (with roles for atoms) from which all social structure is built. The peer group represents an organized but informal group which protects the organized from the organizers. Of necessity, peer groups must be factional. At one time they were regarded as pathological, perverse, and dysfunctional, now they are regarded as a *sine qua non* of a healthy organization.

Functions of primary work groups include:

1. Providing emotional support for group members.
2. Facilitating horizontal communication.
3. Defining standards of performance.
4. Allowing role specialization.
5. Creating value systems, i.e., generating a calculus of aims which members more or less accept.
6. Specifying acceptable norms, i.e., limiting and defining the means which are acceptable to group members.
7. Specifying sanctions for breaches of 3, 4, 5, and 6 above.
8. Exhibiting functional autonomy, i.e., after the original reason for the creation of the group has passed, the group will create new needs to exploit the social capital that the membership has generated.

All of the concepts covered in this chapter apply to the primary working group. In order to review them, understand them as a system, and relate them specifically to the working group, Figure 8–10 applies the system model developed in Chapter 1 to the group (and to the organization conceived as a group of groups). Although dysfunctions are not specified in this model, it should be noted that they exist in relation to

FIGURE 8–10
THE GROUP AS A SYSTEM

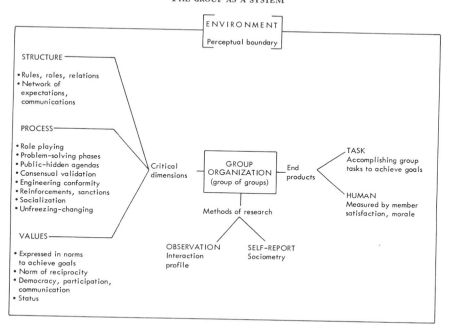

many of the key concepts and should also be reviewed. There are too many kinds of groups to specify particular values or end products, except to point out in a general way what should be looked at and measured in studying a particular group. Technology will have varying influences on group styles, too.

One part of the model we have not touched on is methods of research. When we have gotten an understanding of the group system concepts and set out to study a particular group, how do we go about it?

METHODS OF STUDYING GROUPS

Fundamentally, there are two methods for studying group behaviour: observational methods and self-report methods.

OBSERVATION

The most celebrated method of observation is that set forth by Professor R. F. Bales, whose brilliant and authoritative work in the field of group dynamics has been conducted in the laboratory of social relations at Harvard University. He has developed an extremely useful 12-category system (see Table 8–1) for classifying group behaviour; comprehensive

TABLE 8–1
THE BALES SYSTEM

HUMAN RELATIONS	+	{	1. Shows solidarity 2. Shows tension 3. Agrees
TASK	+	{	4. Gives suggestion 5. Gives opinion 6. Gives orientation
TASK	–	{	7. Asks for orientation 8. Asks for opinion 9. Asks for suggestion
HUMAN RELATIONS	–	{	10. Disagrees 11. Shows tension 12. Shows antagonism

and exhaustive, it is easy to use and can be applied in a large number of situations. He has also provided us with a number of perceptive insights into how groups function, and particularly how discussion groups operate, making his work of great interest to both business executives and academics.

Basic to Bales's approach is the idea that all behaviour can be classified as either task-oriented or human relations–oriented, and that each of these can be either positive or negative. His research put together experimental groups and set them to solving problems by the clarification, evaluation, and decision process. Bales observed these groups and analysed them according to "the interaction profile."

The patterns which emerged in these profiles showed that, on the average, the groups spent about a quarter of the time on positive human relations activity and only about 10 per cent on negative human relations activity; negative task behaviour took 5 per cent of the time and positive task behaviour about 50 per cent. In other words, a relatively small proportion of the time, about 5 per cent, was taken up by people asking for suggestion, opinion, and orientation; attempted answers—i.e., giving orientation, opinion, and suggestion—took up about half the time. On the human relations side of the discussion, positive responses, showing tension release and solidarity, were twice as common as negative reactions. If the human relations balance was not of this order, the group would probably disintegrate. Thus a central notion to emerge from Bales's research was the idea of equilibrium in small groups.

Group structure—the three R's—can often be revealed by asking questions: Who are you? Where did you come from? What are you doing? Who said you could? Bales, in observing his groups, built up matrices based on such a question: Who speaks to whom? The matrix included who spoke, for how long, to whom, and thus delineated participation by individual members. Of course the groups varied; for example, leaderless groups distributed participation more than those with leaders.

Analysis of the who-to-whom matrices showed that each member received back approximately half as much as he put out. It was found that high-ranking people (those who spoke most) spoke more to the group as a whole than to individuals, whereas low-ranking people spoke more to individuals and less to the group.

Individuals were rated according to their "basic initiating rank," which is related to the total amount of participation by each. After the experiment, members were asked to rank each other as to productivity—who had the best ideas and who did most to guide the discussion. Bales showed quite clearly that basic initiating rank was related to both productivity and ability to guide the group.

Bales's interaction process analysis is a very powerful technique and has been used for the study of both therapeutic groups and labour-management disputes. This technique is high in reliability, validity, and utility. It has the supreme advantage of being relatively simple to use. A great deal of scientific research in the social sciences consists of applying a well-established method to a new area. The really elegant development, on the other hand, takes place when a method is evolved which has been custom-built for a problem chosen because of its crucial nature. The best research sets out to answer questions, or at least to see if they can be answered. Bales's work is outstanding precisely because it answers the question, What happens in a discussion group? His compelling and complete answers have a certain consonance with common sense.

Self-report

To define, analyse, and record the exceedingly complex network of interrelationships that exist within even simple groups requires some systematic method. For this purpose, J. L. Moreno developed a sociometric method. The objective of this method is to establish the pattern of acceptance and rejection, like and dislike, in a group. Moreno argues that the most significant social groupings are based on such feelings rather than on formal organization. The understanding of group life, in Moreno's view, can best be accomplished through a study of these "spontaneous" groupings and the way in which they harmonize or conflict with the formal group structure that is imposed externally.

The sociometric method involves asking each member to specify (privately) which other members he likes or wishes to work or eat or live beside, and which ones he dislikes or wishes to avoid. Such data obtained from all group members enables the researcher to build up a diagram which portrays for the group the patterns of mutual like, dislike, and indifference. In this way the investigator can see the interpersonal structure of a group—the cliques, the social isolates, the scapegoats, the leaders, and those who are just popular.

REVIEW AND RESEARCH

1. Select a group known to you through experience and:
   a. Define its structure. Include samples of behaviour to specify particular roles.
   b. Describe the process of how the group developed. List the different stages of development.
   c. Specify the values, norms, reinforcements, and sanctions of the group.
   d. Decide (setting out the evidence) whether your group was high or low in cohesion.

2. Define the terms "group" and "dynamics." Work out the analogy between group dynamics and eletcrolytic action.

3. Compare and contrast a group, a social organization (such as a political party), and a formal organization.

4. How do small groups link the individual to the organization?

5. Why is the concept of role critical in linking social psychology and sociology?

6. "Status symbols are inevitable in any organization." Argue the case for this proposition. How should status symbols be controlled in an organization?

7. Define status and role and show how they are linked.

8. Define the role of a dean in a business school. Describe his role set. Give examples of role and personality conflict as applied to the office of the dean.

9. How are roles learned? To develop your answer, consider some episode in your life such as your experience in the military, at work, or in some leisure group. Alternatively, consider how you learned a family role (e.g.. father, son, daughter, brother).

10. How can Bales's analysis of interaction in small groups help in running effective discussion groups? What does sociometry tell us about group roles and boundaries?

11. Why do all effective groups have initiation rites?

12. If man is basically conflictive, why does he co-operate in groups?

GLOSSARY

Clarification. First of three phases of group problem solving (see also *Evalua- tion, Decision*); definition by group members of the facts about the problem and the assumptions needed to solve it.

Compliance. Acceptance of influence in which the individual gives the appear- ance of conforming while he is being observed, but in fact lacks inner con- viction and behaves differently in private. (See also *Identification, Internal- ization.*)

Conformity. Adherence to the norms and expected behaviour of the group. Conformity may range from partial to complete dependence on group standards; anticonformity (invariably acting against group standards) also indicates dependence.

Decision. Third phase of group problem solving (after clarification and evaluation); specification of solutions and structuring behaviour of the group to choose and carry out the best alternative.

Evaluation. Second phase of group problem solving; attempt by members of the group to establish a consensus of value judgements, spelling out their feelings about the facts and assumptions produced by clarification before proceeding to the decision phase.

Exchange theory. Explanation of organizational behaviour in terms of rewards exchanged, costs incurred, outcomes (rewards minus costs, yielding positive or negative result), and level of comparison (evaluating the outcome of a particular exchange in comparison to other possible exchanges).

Group. Assembly of two or more people who bear an explicit psychological relationship to one another; who are interdependent and interact to produce a common ideology; and who form a network of communication and of expectations in order to influence the behaviour of group members.

Group dynamics. Adjustive changes in the group structure produced by changes in any part of the group. The study of group dynamics is concerned with learning the nature of groups, how they develop, and their effect on individual members, other groups, and larger institutions.

Human relations specialist. The group role whose holder is primarily concerned with the feelings of persons, trying to placate, relieve anxieties, and release tensions; this role is complementary to that of the task specialist.

Identification. Acceptance of influence in which the individual adopts the behaviour and attitudes of another because of admiration for him; differs from compliance in that the influenced person does not behave differently in private; differs from internalization in that he imitates behaviour without adopting internally the values from which it springs.

Internalization. Acceptance of influence in which the individual makes the influencing values, attitudes, and behaviour his own, incorporating them into his self-concept.

Member satisfaction. An indication of group values in terms of status consensus, perception of progress towards group goals, and perceived freedom to participate.

Morale. An indication of group values in terms of cohesiveness, ability to resolve conflict, community of goals, positive attitudes, mutual goodwill, and so on.

Nonconformity. Independence from group influence which ranges from rejection of the group to acceptance of interdependence within the group. The group accepts nonconformity within limits, because it provides the options necessary for change and growth; it accepts individual nonconformists because of proven ability and the healthy contributions they are perceived to offer.

Reciprocity. A universal norm in groups which embodies the ideas of equity, give and take, rights and obligations. The fact that the balance of favours is never perfect gives the group stability.

Reference group. The group (real or imaginary) an individual uses as a standard for evaluating the standards and behaviours of other groups; usually a crucial group in his development such as his family or school.

Roles. The function which group members serve; the parts which grou actors play. In addition to the two most basic and important roles of tas specialist and human relations specialist, common roles include the eccentri the scapegoat, the isolate, the detached observer, the gate-keeper, the cosm politan, the local, etc.

Role conflict. Anxiety generated in a role holder in one or two ways: intraro conflict arising from the perception of contradictory expectations by variou role senders; or interrole conflict arising from the occupancy of multip roles.

Socialization. The process by which a new person entering a group or organ zation is initiated and assimilated so that he acquires the values and behaviou patterns of the group.

Status. The rank held by a group member, indicating the value which th group places on his contributions and achievements; usually made visible t status symbols.

Task specialist. The group role whose holder concentrates on achieving grou tasks, chiefly through mobilizing the anxieties of members and directir them; this role is complementary to that of the human relations speciali

9

Leadership

Most managers and many social psychologists have an obsessive interest
eadership, which they believe to be the critical factor determining or-
izational outcomes. This perceptual astigmatism dates from a time in
1930s when little significant work had been done on such topics as the
ure of authority and power, each of which is essentially concerned with
v the perception of the other is changed; the nature of conflict, which
ically deals with the problem of the clash of wills, values, and styles;
such other vital matters as sharing out the spoils of corporate war.
vertheless, the subject of leadership still continues to fascinate its de-
ees, precisely because it provides both a a set of insights about that
ional extra called leadership and because its study provides a useful
mework within which corporate events can be seen more clearly.
The natural starting point for looking at leadership is the leader. The
ividual approach essentially begins by asking whether leadership is best
lerstood as referring to a particular type (General de Gaulle, Joseph
lin, Winston Churchill, Napoleon, Adolph Hitler, Presidents Franklin
osevelt and Dwight Eisenhower, Harold Geneen—what do they all
e in common?) or a list of traits (able, active, adept, affected, agree-
e, aggressive, amiable, ardent, asinine, attractive, august, average, awe-
ie—to list some of the traits that begin with the first letter of the alpha-
). While most executives have their own pet lists of traits or a particu-
historical, political, or military figure in mind when they talk about
lership, science is not on their side. Increasingly behavioural scientists
focusing on the systems of rules, roles, and relations that characterize

the microsocial world of the group rather than researching the leade▮ attributes and actions.

The group approach to leadership is concerned with mapping out t▮ *roles* in the group which the leaders can fill; the *relations* that facilita▮ the exercise of initiative and influence; the *rules* in terms of subroutin▮ and rituals; and the values and norms which are a sine qua non of grou▮ life. Accordingly, the structure, process, and value system of the grou▮ determines which particular leadership style is appropriate. A major issu▮ is the relation between the style, structure, and setting of organization▮ leadership. Presumably leaders pick their styles not only in the light ▮ the VANEs of the led but also in terms of the structure and setting with▮ which the leaders and the led interact to achieve particular goals.

What is leadership style? Edwin P. Hollander, professor of psycholog▮ at the State University of New York at Buffalo and long-time theoretici▮ and researcher in the field of leadership, catches the subtlety of style wh▮ he notes, "In a broader sense, however, style may involve the interacti▮ characteristics of the leader's personality, which stamp his relationshi▮ with followers, particularly in terms of the role expectancies which th▮ hold."

The situational approach to leadership is the belief that style, structur▮ and setting are interlocking variables. This optic introduces an element ▮ behavioural science relativity by proclaiming the view that there are ▮ absolute leaders, arguing rather that leadership is a process which can ▮ its very nature require different group members to take command at di▮ ferent times. Only then can the group achieve the diversity of goals th▮ normally makes groups superior to individuals in performance.

THE EFFECTIVE EXECUTIVE

The efficiency of executive management is probably the most impo▮ tant single factor influencing the productivity of the work group. In spi▮ of this, very little is known about the effectiveness of executives. Whi▮ managers confidently discuss the characteristics of the successful manage▮ and while many executives boast of their prowess in selecting good leade▮ on the basis of a brief interview, most modern social psychologists ha▮ accepted the fact that research has failed to provide a description of t▮ effective leader in terms of the personality trait approach. A rather diffe▮ ent approach suggests that the ways in which effective managers wo▮ should be explored. The leaders of effective groups have been found ▮ maintain greater "psychological distance" between themselves and oth▮ people than do leaders of less effective groups.

Both approaches to this problem converge if it is accepted that t▮ group has two contrasting functions: the achievement of some speci▮ object and the maintenance or improvement of the social and emotior▮ climate. These functions are sometimes known as the work and nonwo▮ functions, and leaders who specialize in these areas as the task specia▮

and the human relations specialist, respectively. The psychologically distant executive is essentially a task specialist who achieves his results by systematically varying his relationship with other members of the work group. In contradistinction to this view, experiments such as the Hawthorne experiment in the 1930s stressed the executive as a human relations specialist. Contemporary thinking suggests that this apparent antithesis may be explained to some extent as a reflection of the needs of different societies, and that a synthesis can be achieved through role specialization in the group.

STRUCTURE OF CHAPTER 9

Our first topic, after examining some definitions of leadership, reviews the validity of the trait approach. The trait approach, which is an essentially individualistic view of leadership, has largely given way to the group approach, which draws on the findings of group dynamics. Two basic group activities are the task and human relation functions, which have suggested two basic dimensions of leadership: initiating structure and consideration. An extended review of these two dimensions as they affect productivity and satisfaction is included. The scientific validity of these two dimensions as descriptions of leadership behaviour is examined in some detail.

In Topic 2 we turn to F. E. Fiedler's contingency theory of leadership, examining the role of psychological distance in producing group effectiveness. Fiedler's theory, which utilizes a situational approach, requires three dimensions to define the group context; leader-member relations, task structure, and position power. Fiedler predicts different leadership styles for different combinations of these dimensions. A number of studies evaluating this model are reviewed.

Topic 3 is concerned with R. J. House's path-goal theory of leadership, which is based on Victor Vroom's theory of motivation. An attempt is made to give an interim evaluation of this theory.

Topic 4 is concerned with identifying leadership potential and deals mainly with the group approach to selection via the assessment centre.

Finally, Topic 5 considers the strategies of organizational leadership. Leadership is seen as the capacity to manage the structure, processes, and values of an organization; the themes of the chapter are drawn together by modeling leadership as a system.

TOPIC 1
Trait approach and group approach

Various approaches to the idea of leadership are suggested by the many ways it has been defined. Some definitions, because they have been formulated in a language which psychologists are reluctant to use, have been considered mainly because of their literary worth. A modern example of this type of definition is taken from Bertrand Russell's *Power, A New Social Analysis*, where he comments, "To acquire the position of leader he (the individual) must excel in the qualities of authority, self-confidence quick decision and skill in deciding the right measures."

A formidable number of definitions have flowed in recent years from psychological sources. It might be profitable to sink a few critical shafts into this mass of definitions so that we may look at the term from various elevations. Much of the earlier work identified leadership with dominance in *Handbook of Social Psychology*, K. Young argued that "Leadership then, is but one form of dominance, in which the followers more or less willingly accept direction and control by another." Very early on, a distinction was drawn between leadership and dominance, and stress placed on the importance of the integrative aspect. According to P. J. W. Pigors in *Leadership or Domination*, "Leadership is a process of mutual stimulation which, by the effective interplay of relevant differences, guides human energy, in the pursuit of a common cause. Domination is a process of control in which by the assumption of superiority a person or a group of persons regulate the activities of others for the purposes of his own choosing."

The literature of social psychology refers to a variety of different things when the term leader is used. In general, Mapheus Smith's classification of leadership appears to have sifted out the essential distinctions that have been made. As described in A. W. Gouldner's *Studies in Leadership*, Smith found that three formulations include the most typical usages of leadership. These are that leaders are those: (1) whose attainments, in terms of set goals, are considered high; (2) whose status is recognized as superior to others engaged in the same activities; and (3) who emit stimuli that are responded to integratively by other people. As Helen Hall Jennings, one of the earliest behavioural scientists to use sociometric techniques, points out in "Leadership and sociometric Choice," "Leadership phenomena happen in a human setting where people get into interaction on the basis of feeling (or tele)." J. L. Moreno, who produced the original idea of the sociogram (or map of the social forces in a group), demonstrates that the "tele" process of attraction and repulsion must be considered dependent upon both individuals in a relationship (even though the flow of feeling on the part of one individual may be unknown by the second), since its direction is not random but depends upon the second person.

In general terms, the earlier discussion of leadership and its relation to other psychological variables fluctuated between an analysis of specific traits descriptive of leaders and a synthesis organized around the notion of biopsychological types. Since these approaches have been found unsatisfactory by most researchers in this field, we will only summarize this earlier work. The principal theoretical objections have been raised by those behavioural scientists who have acknowledged the preeminence of Gestalt psychology and argued that "personality is more than the sum of its constituent parts." More specifically, Gouldner's *Studies in Leadership* trenchantly criticized the trait approach on the basis that "most trait studies flowing from the empiricist tradition have approached the study of personality atomistically and with little regard for personality as an organized whole. Not being orientated to any systematic theory of personality, they have pursued the facts of personality only to find that empiricism can be just as treacherous a guide as the most speculative of theoretical systems." If this basic limitation is accepted, then it must be realized that a wide range of approaches must be exploited if we are to understand leadership. As G. Murphy, L. B. Murphy, and T. M. Newcomb point out in *Experimental Social Psychology*, "Personality study is necessary, sociometry is necessary, analysis of the kind of leadership permitted and included is necessary before the trait of leadership can be defined."

THE TRAIT APPROACH

The classic study relating physique and leadership was that of E. B. Gowin, who found certain executives whom we would probably nowadays classify as institutional heads to be taller and heavier than the average of the groups they controlled. Of more importance to us are the various studies of intellectual and emotional traits. Many of the earlier books dealing with leadership include lists of the psychological characteristics which are essential to leadership, e.g., G. W. Allport—19 traits; L. L. Bernard—31 traits; Ordway Tead—10 traits. The most frequently noted were intelligence, noted by 10 studies; initiative (6); extraversion and sense of humor (5); enthusiasm, fairness, sympathy, and self-confidence (4). E. D. Partridge's study of Boy Scouts showed a high positive correlation between a rating of leadership and specific traits. Rating of leadership correlated with: intelligence 0.87, athletic prowess 0.62, dependability 0.87, acceptable and pleasant voice 0.54, appearance 0.81. Perhaps it is as well to keep in mind that general ratings of leadership are likely to be consciously or unconsciously based on physique, appearance, and the like, so that such high correlations with specific traits may be somewhat spurious.

Many studies have been undertaken to ascertain the personality traits of the leader. For example, it has been reported that the leader tends to be bigger and brighter than the rest of the group but only marginally so. Whatever social psychologists think of such studies, most managers, including many personnel managers, still believe that they have the ability to select good leaders on the basis of a brief interview. This optimistic if somewhat naive attitude springs from the belief that a manager is a person who has some of the following characteristics (which and how many depends upon the prejudices of the individual making the selection): analytical, intelligent, not too bright, keen, enthusiastic, aggressive, capable of maintaining smooth interpersonal relationships, persuasive, dominant, personally acceptable, tactful, extraverted, well-balanced, needing to succeed, ambitious, etc. Different selectors combine such lists of personality traits in their own ways, according to their own biases. A fairly typical example of the use of the trait approach was provided by Clive Bradley in "New Men at the Personnel Desk":

> The qualities that make a good negotiator—possibly the most exciting part of the job—may be very different from those of a person who is good at selecting future top managers, of a good management development man. It is almost impossible to define what the qualities of a good negotiator are: they include toughness, experience, detailed knowledge of existing conditions of employment, a clear idea of what has to be achieved, ability to explain what he is trying to get, ability to divine the intentions and flexibility of the other side—and an honest face, if nothing more.
>
> By contrast, the man who is good at selecting personnel for promotion is likely to have a fairly detailed knowledge of psychology, and to be aware at the same time that a little knowledge in this field can be highly dangerous. Selection these days has become a highly specialist function, often involving detailed scientifically based tests, a series of interviews, and considerable penetration into how a man's mind works, including while under stress. Many candidates for top jobs have to undergo "hot and cold" treatment, designed to bring out their best qualities and to shake their confidence.

Why has the trait approach failed? One explanation that has already been suggested is that neither personality nor personality traits are clearly understood or capable of accurate measurement. Efforts to isolate traits that would distinguish leaders from others proved disappointing and full of contradictory results. C. A. Gibb, in "Leadership," states, "reviews such as that by Stodgill reveal that numerous studies of the personalities of leaders have failed to find any consistent pattern of traits which characterizes leaders." Many social psychologists hold the view that leadership traits may exist, but if they do, they have not been recognized.

But no study is ever completely fruitless. From the failure of individual trait studies alone, F. E. Fiedler suggested that it might be important to ascertain how the executive position was achieved. Executive appointments may be made on the basis of managerial potential, but they may also be made on the basis of technical competence, seniority, kinship, lack of managerial potential, or membership in a particular educational, military, or religious organization. Working from this basis, Fiedler moved to the study of leadership effectiveness. His important research and theorizing is described in Topic 2 of this chapter.

Research findings produced other, important pointers to the idea that leadership is situational. In general, results indicated that while certain minimal abilities are required of all leaders, these traits are also distributed among other members of the group according to a normal distribution curve. The inference was that a more fruitful line of inquiry would be an investigation based on the theory that there are various leader roles in the group. In essence, the results indicated that an approach based on the individual should be replaced by the group approach to the problem of leadership.

THE GROUP APPROACH

Following the failure of the trait approach, social psychologists turned hopefully to examine the structure and function of groups. In the group approach, the psychologist is not concerned with identifying certain invariant leader traits but takes the wider view that leadership is the performance of acts which assist the group in achieving certain ends. The nub of the matter is that leadership in these circumstances may be performed by one or many members of the group; leadership is regarded as a quantitative variable, not as something which is found in some people and not in others.

Inevitably whenever two or more people get together, one will dominate and leadership emerges. But the form of leadership in a group depends on group members, the task, and the group ideology. Study of executive leadership has become a very important and major activity in all advanced industrial societies. In the most general terms leadership can be defined by observation or by exploration of the perceptions of group members. For example, officer selection could be made by setting a number of soldiers a problem and watching for leaders to emerge as they try to solve the problem, or by asking for nominations.

A very simple but extremely useful definition of leadership is: the ability to influence others in the group. The supreme virtue of this apparently simple definition is that it allows for the possibility that all group members may exhibit a degree of leadership; the leader in the conventional sense is the one whose influence predominates. In this context leadership is regarded as an interpersonal behavioural event; this means, for example, that by communicating their fears, anxieties, etc. to the leader, followers can influence him. For that matter, the official leader of a group may have no influence; formal leadership need not coincide with informal.

As has already been noted, what kind of leadership emerges depends on the task, the situation and the group. Obviously complex tasks require a hierarchy of leaders, as is the case in modern business organizations. In crises a simpler form of leadership is required. In moments of high drama and tension, choice is not made logically but on the basis of charismatic qualities attributed to the leader (e.g., Churchill during the Battle of Britain). It can come as no surprise to learn that leaders emerge more easily in unstable situations, precisely because the structure of the group is loosened due to some change in one of the major constraints—a change in the nature of the task, a new person joining the group, a powerful person leaving, or a change in the ideological climate.

LEADERSHIP FUNCTIONS

There are two basic types of group functions: the first, the task function, is concerned with the achievement of some specific goal; the second, the human function, is concerned with the maintenance or strengthening of the group itself. Examples of task behaviour are "stressing the importance of the object of the exercise," "focusing attention on production," and "reviewing the quality of the work done." Examples of human relations behaviour are "keeping the group happy," "settling disputes," "providing encouragement," and "giving the minority a chance to be heard."

A. W. Halpin and B. J. Winer, who studied leadership in air crews, found it useful to analyse leaders' behaviour according to two dimensions, "initiating and directing" and "consideration." Leaders high in initiating and directing make sure not only that their role is understood by the group but also that official procedures are followed; they try out new ideas on members. This type of structuring leadership is of especial value when the group faces a task problem. On the other hand leaders who are high in consideration are group-oriented; they reward good work and invite participation in the setting of group goals.

Of course, in many cases social behaviour cannot be classified under either the task or the human relations headings, but there is a tendency for specialists in these functions to emerge. For example, experiments in group dynamics concerned with analysis of discussion-leading procedures show that there almost always appear in any group the task specialist and the human relations specialist. This duality of group functions is indicated in our systems model for this text. The end products of organizational behaviour systems can be measured by such task indices as productivity, profitability, and innovation, and by such human indices as satisfaction and morale (or, negatively, absenteeism and labour turnover).

Ever since R. F. Bales came up with the basic idea of these two functions, organizational psychologists have proliferated the labels by which they are known. For example:

	Task	*Human*
Rensis Likert	Job-centred	Employee-centred
R. R. Blake and J. S. Mouton	Production-oriented	People-oriented
R. Lippitt and R. K. White	Autocratic	Democratic
E. A. Fleishman	Initiating structure	Consideration

From a factor analysis based on the description of 100 International Harvester foremen, E. A. Fleishman and D. A. Peters in "Interpersonal Values, Leadership Attitudes and Managerial Success" came up with the following descriptions:

> *Initiating Structure* (S): Reflects the extent to which an individual is likely to define and structure his role and those of his subordinates toward goal attainment. A high score on this dimension characterizes individuals who play a more active role in directing group activities through planning, communicating information, scheduling, trying out new ideas, etc.
>
> *Consideration* (C): Reflects the extent to which an individual is likely to have job relationships characterized by mutual trust, respect for subordinates' ideas, and consideration of their feelings. A high score is indicative of a climate of good rapport and two-way communication. A low score indicates the supervisor is likely to be more impersonal in his relations with group members.

Fleishman developed two separate questionnaires to measure these factors. The leadership opinion questionnaire (LOQ) measures how the supervisor thinks he should behave in his leadership role and the leader behaviour description questionnaire (LBDQ) measures a subordinate's perception of his supervisor's behaviour.

Figure 9–1 summarizes overall results of leadership behaviours. An Ohio State University leadership group found that leaders high on initiating structure (i.e., those who make specific work assignments, spell out deadlines, evaluate the quality of work, and establish well-defined work patterns and procedure) were highly rated by their superiors and generated high performance in terms of productivity, and avoidance of scrap and cost. Researchers at the University of Southern California reported, using

FIGURE 9–1
LEADERSHIP BEHAVIOURS AND RESULTS

Supervisors high in:	Behaviours	Results
Initiating structure	Make specific work assignments; emphasize deadlines; evaluate quality; define work patterns	Superiors satisfied. High productivity, low costs and scrap. High turnover and grievances. Subordinates dissatisfied.
Consideration	Consider subordinates' needs; be understanding, warm, supportive, friendly.	Superiors dissatisfied. Productivity low. Intragroup co-operation. Low turnover and grievances. Subordinates satisfied.
Both	Combination of above.	Superiors satisfied. High productivity, low costs and scrap. Low turnover and grievances. Subordinates satisfied.

a similar scale which measured advance planning and organizing skill, that high scorers were described by their subordinates as well organized and by their bosses as highly productive. But, perhaps not too surprisingly, there is some evidence to support the proposition that high-production supervisors (high in initiating structure) had higher rates of grievance and labour turnover than their low-scoring colleagues.

The Ohio State leadership group also found that supervisors scoring high on consideration (i.e., those who were supportive, willing to explain their actions, warm, and friendly) had more satisfied subordinates who displayed more intragroup harmony and lower levels of grievance and turnover. The essence of the situation appears to be that superiors and subordinates view the leadership behaviour of supervisors from different perspectives. Superiors evidently prefer supervisors who are structuring and thus effective from a task point of view, whereas shop floor employees prefer a supervisor who is considerate and not overly concerned with production. And, of course, as Fleishman and E. F. Harris found out, production supervisors high on both dimensions could get the production out without increasing either the rate of grievances or labour turnover.

It should be noted that Figure 9–1 and this discussion relate to specific findings and in particular to the supervisory level. They are not necessarily true at other managerial and professional levels.

In "Relation of Leader Consideration and Initiating Structure to R. and D. Subordinate Satisfaction," R. J. House, A. C. Filley, and S. Kerr were surprised to find a generally positive relationship between initiating structure and role satisfaction. As a result of their research, House and his associates concluded:

> One might speculate about the relationships between the dimensions of leader behavior and satisfaction under various conditions of organizational formalization and occupational level or intrinsic job interest. The above interpretations of the findings suggest a two-by-two matrix which yields four combinations of formalization and occupational level. This matrix is . . . :

	High formalization	Low formalization
High occupational level	1	2
Low occupational level	3	4

> If the degree of formalization serves as a constraint on the magnitude of the relationship between leader behavior and role satisfaction, and if the occupational level or intrinsic satisfaction associated with the job determines the sign of the relationship between structure and role satisfaction, then one could predict differential relationships between the two dimensions of leader behavior and role satisfaction, depending on the cell in which the respondent is located. Specifically, it is predicted that

in cell number one there would be low positive relationships between the two dimensions of leader behavior and role satisfaction. Here initiating structure would serve to reduce role ambiguity, and consideration would serve to increase the pleasantness of the environment of the respondent. However, the effect of both leader dimensions would be limited by the high degree of formalization.

Under conditions of low formalization and high occupational level, cell two, positive relationships between both dimensions of leader behavior and role satisfaction are predicted, and the magnitudes of these relationships would be higher than those of cell number one, where formalization is high. Under conditions of cell three, high formalization–low occupational level, a low negative relationship between structure and role satisfaction and a low positive relationship between consideration and role satisfaction is predicted. That is, at low occupational levels, structure would be perceived as a form of external control, and consideration would be seen as a form of supportive supervision. However, since in cell three organizational formalization is high, the effects of leader behavior would be restricted, and therefore the magnitude of relationships between the dimensions of leader behavior and role satisfaction would be low. Under conditions of low formalization and low occupational level, cell four, the same relationships as predicted for cell three are predicted, but with higher magnitudes. The higher magnitudes would be a function of the low amount of formalization which permits the leader to have more discretionary control and greater effect on the behavior and role satisfaction of his subordinates.

Korman's caution

Rarely have psychological concepts been developed after more exhaustive research than was performed at Ohio State University to identify consideration and initiating structure as the two basic dimensions of leadership behaviour. However, a review by Abraham Korman of the substantial literature dealing with these dimensions comes to the conclusion that we know very little about how they may affect work group performance and that we cannot use them to predict leadership effectiveness.

Korman summarized all of the available studies dealing with consideration, initiating structure, and a variety of effectiveness criteria (for example, grievance rate, turnover, popularity, morale, technical competence, overall ability). Many of the studies failed to find a significant relationship between the dimensions and the effectiveness criteria used; and other correlations, though significant, were nevertheless very low. Korman notes that even these are open to question because, in most cases, the same people made both the predictor and criterion ratings, thus raising the possibility that one or the other is distorted in order to attain a more balanced cognition. There appear to have been no experimental manipulations to prove that consideration or initiating structure affected the outcomes, rather than the latter determining how the former were rated.

Korman also notes the dearth of research on how situational variables such as unit size, organizational climate, or subordinate attitudes might affect the type of leadership behaviour that would be most appropriate. Most studies recognize that these may have an effect, but then make no attempt to either measure or manipulate them to establish a hypothesis about the relationship.

While the scientific validity of consideration and initiating structure as descriptors of leadership behaviour is in no way impugned, it is apparent that practical application of the concepts requires considerable elaboration of how they predict work group effectiveness and in what type of situation each would be most appropriate.

TOPIC 2
Fiedler's contingency theory

Professor F. E. Fiedler, of the University of Washington, has shown that the leaders of more effective groups, when evaluating subordinates, indicate that they maintain greater psychological distance between themselves and their subordinates than do leaders of less effective groups. The explanation for this appears to be that a manager cannot properly control and discipline subordinates if he is too close to them emotionally. Likewise if a manager is emotionally dependent on a subordinate, he cannot afford to alienate him in case he loses his support.

An ingenious technique has been developed for measuring psychological distance. The manager is asked to rate his most preferred and least preferred subordinates on various psychological traits. The greater the difference between these two ratings, the more psychologically distant the manager is considered to be. Thus the psychologically distant manager (P.D.M.) rejects those with whom he cannot work easily, while the psychologically closer manager (P.C.M.) is more tolerant of his subordinates —or he accepts or rejects subordinates on some criterion other than his ability to work with them. It has been suggested that the P.D.M. "has many acquaintances, but few friends; he likes to be with others but he does not want to become emotionally dependent on them." Fiedler has shown in his study of the management of small consumer co-operatives that the P.D.M. is a task specialist.

Two distinctly different portraits emerge from Fiedler's studies. The P.D.M. is more efficient and has the following characteristics:

1. He tends to formalize role relationships both with his superiors and his subordinates.
2. He tends to be somewhat reserved and withdrawn in his relationships within the firm.
3. He has a preference for formal staff consultation rather than seeking opinions informally.

4. He accepts and rejects subordinates on the basis of performance.
5. Though he is reserved, he is still sufficiently skilled to ensure smooth interpersonal relationships.
6. He does not develop deep friendships with his colleagues.
7. He demands and gets considerable freedom of action from his superiors.
8. He expects his subordinates to make mistakes and plans accordingly.
9. He prefers ambitious subordinates.

The P.C.M. is relatively inefficient compared with the P.D.M. and has the following characteristics:

1. He does not seek to formalize role relationships.
2. His behaviour is concerned with ensuring good human relationships within his organization, often at the expense of efficiency.
3. He prefers informal discussion with his subordinates to regular staff meetings.
4. He is inclined to select his friends from colleagues and subordinates in the firm.
5. He is inclined to dominate and possess subordinates.
6. He will only delegate on relatively minor matters, and insists on frequent individual consultation.

In a sentence, the P.D.M. is a task specialist and the P.C.M. is a human relations specialist. Fiedler suggests the explanation for this is that "psychologically closer and warmer relations make it difficult for the manager to criticize his subordinates and that a tendency to become emotionally dependent on one or two group members encourages rivalries and the charge of favouritism." These comments comparing the P.D.M. and the P.C.M. are fully consonant with the view that too much emphasis on maintaining friendly relationships within the working group can reduce the group's goal of achieving efficiency.

The P.D. leader is effective in achieving greater productivity only when he is informally accepted by the members of the group. If this condition is not met, then the group will not "listen to" him, and he cannot influence their behaviour. Subject to this qualification, P.D.M.'s are more efficient on task problems and, in contradistinction to P.C.M.'s, they tend to formalize role relations.

In "The Leader's Psychological Distance and Group Effectiveness," Fiedler illustrates this emphasis on the task and the formalizing of the role:

> . . . by the experience of one air force officer in command of an air base who systematically varied his psychological distance from his chief subordinates. When he had very close relations with these officers, they seemed to feel secure; and they did not worry overly about the efficiency of their units. As soon as he became more reserved and role-oriented, his subcommanders began to worry whether anything had gone awry; they became less secure of their standing in the organization, and channelled their anxieties into paying more attention to their work. As a result, there was a noticeable increase in the efficiency of the base.

THE THREE DIMENSIONS OF THE WORK SITUATION

The research work of Professor Fiedler is of great interest to executives mainly because he developed a contingency model to facilitate the analysis of leadership effectiveness. Fiedler's findings put him on the side of those executives who believe in reality-centred leadership. His seminal work represents an attempt to deal with "the critical, directive, autocratic, task-oriented versus the democratic, permissive, considerate, person-oriented type of leadership."

With a considerable body of empirical evidence behind him, Fiedler developed a theoretical model which set out to define the conditions under which each particular kind of leadership is more effective. Both the beauty and the relevance of Fiedler's empirical works rest on the measurement of psychological distance. In one study, Fiedler invited leaders to rank (on eight-point bipolar adjective scales similar to Osgood's semantic differential) the person he liked working with best and the person with whom he could work least well. The strength of Fiedler's work rests on its diversity, accuracy, and extent. Some notion of the extent of his work may be gained from the fact that he experimented with this measure of psychological distance in studies of high school basketball teams, civil engineering teams, smelter foremen, and managers of co-operatives.

On account of the difficulties he encountered trying to reconcile some of his findings, Fiedler has been compelled to develop a more complex model. He starts with the rather simple proposition that leadership is essentially concerned with the problem of exercising influence and power. To facilitate his analysis he postulates three important dimensions of the total situation which structure the leader's role:

1. *Leader-member relations* refers to the extent to which the leader enjoys the confidence and loyalty of his men and is regarded as personally attractive by them. This aspect is usually measured by a sociometric index.

2. *Task structure* refers to the extent to which the task represents an order "from above." The presumption here is that if a foreman issues a direct order to a subordinate, say, to wear his safety glasses, he can expect the support of his departmental leader if the operator is unwilling to comply. Task structure can be operationally defined by:

a. The extent to which the decision is capable of being verified.

b. The extent of goal clarity, i.e., the degree to which the task requirements are known to members of the group.

c. The multiplicity of goal paths—the variety of means available (whether there are many or few procedures for solving the task).

d. The solution specificity—whether there is one or a large number of correct solutions.

3. *Position power* refers to the power inherent in the position of the leader and includes the rewards and punishments which are traditionally at his disposal, his official authority, and the organizational support on which he can depend.

Fiedler has been able to classify groups on the basis of these three dimensions and he has presented this classification system in the form of the cube shown in Figure 9–2. As each group is high or low in each of the three dimensions, it will fall into one of the eight cells.

FIGURE 9–2
Fiedler's cube

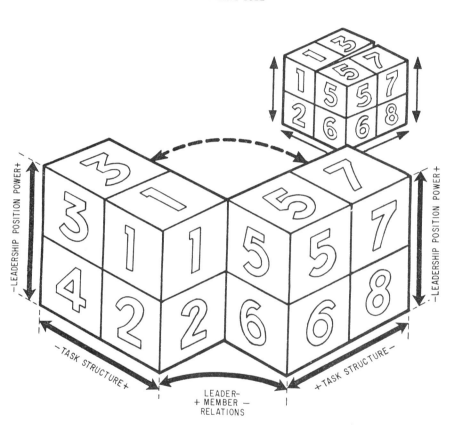

By first sorting the eight cells according to leader-member relations, then task structures, and finally leader position power, Fiedler arranges these cells according to the favourableness of the environment for the leader as shown in Figure 9–3.

LEADERSHIP STYLE

In evaluating leadership style in his contingency model, Fiedler uses as a predictor measure the least preferred co-worker (L.P.C.) score. To obtain this score, an individual is asked to think of all the co-workers he has ever had. He is then asked to describe on a semantic differential scale the

FIGURE 9–3
FIEDLER'S PREDICTION OF LEADERSHIP STYLES

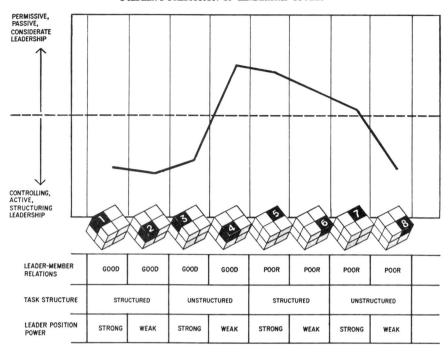

LEADER-MEMBER RELATIONS	GOOD	GOOD	GOOD	GOOD	POOR	POOR	POOR	POOR
TASK STRUCTURE	STRUCTURED		UNSTRUCTURED		STRUCTURED		UNSTRUCTURED	
LEADER POSITION POWER	STRONG	WEAK	STRONG	WEAK	STRONG	WEAK	STRONG	WEAK

one person he has been least able to work with. The assessment is made by rating that person on eight-point bipolar adjective scales like these:

friendly :——:——:——:——:——:——:——:——: unfriendly
           8   7   6   5   4   3   2   1

cooperative :——:——:——:——:——:——:——:——: uncooperative
              8   7   6   5   4   3   2   1

The L.P.C. scale usually contains 16 to 24 such items. The L.P.C. score is obtained by averaging the item values of one to eight. Thus, a high score (Fiedler suggests an average item value of five on the eight-point scale) indicates that the subject views his least preferred co-worker in relatively favourable terms. A low score (say, an average of two) means that the least preferred co-worker is described in a very negative, rejecting manner.

The L.P.C. score is somewhat difficult to interpret. At first Fiedler interpreted it as meaning that lower scores indicated greater task orientation and higher scores greater human relations orientation. Fiedler now regards this interpretation as somewhat misleading. According to Fiedler, the low-scoring person describes his least preferred co-worker in a uniform and thus undifferentiated or stereotyped manner, whereas the high scorer spreads his scores on different items over a wider part of the scale (greater item variance). The argument is that the labels "relationship-oriented" versus "task-oriented" for high versus low scores are only valid in situations characterized by anxiety and stress, where the leader has little control. T. R. Mitchell in "Leader Complexity and Leadership Style" reports some evidence in support of the proposition that leaders with high L.P.C. scores tend to be more cognitively complex in their manner of thinking about groups, while low scorers tend to be more stereotyped in their thinking. But precisely what the L.P.C. scale measures is impossible to say, and this has turned out to be a major difficulty of Fiedler's theory (a subject to which we shall return).

LEADER STYLES AND THE WORK SITUATION

Using his three-dimensional model, Fiedler has been able to examine his earlier empirical work on leadership and produce a more sophisticated and convincing explanation of the nature of effective leadership:

> Considerate, permissive, accepting leaders obtain optimal group performance under situations intermediate in favorableness. These are situations in which (a) the task is structured, but the leader is disliked and must, therefore, be diplomatic; (b) the liked leader has an abiguous, unstructured task and must, therefore, draw upon the creativity and cooperation of his members. Here we obtain positive correlations between L.P.C. and group performance scores. Where the task is highly structured and the leader is well-liked, non-directive behaviour or permissive attitude (such as asking how the group ought to proceed with a missile count-down) is neither appropriate nor beneficial. Where the situation is quite unfavorable, e.g., where the disliked chairman of a volunteer group faces an ambiguous task, the leader might as well be autocratic and directive since a positive, non-directive leadership style under these conditions might result in complete inactivity on the part of the group. This model, thus, tends to shed some light on the apparent inconsistencies in our own data as well as in data obtained by other investigators.

To test the relevance of his new thinking, Fiedler carried out an experiment based on the contingency model with Belgian naval forces and found results which seemed to be supportive of his thesis. Fiedler's contingency model, mainly on account of its flexibility, represents an improvement over much of the earlier, more naive work in the leadership field and provides a useful theoretical framework for further research.

For the hard-pressed executive the vital point to emerge from Fiedler's work is the realistic view that business can utilize a fairly broad spectrum of individuals in executive positions. One of the most difficult criticisms to meet on any previous theoretical description of a leader was the question, "How many executives do you know who are like that or operate in that manner?"

Box 9.1: Leadership and decision making

One of the most persistent and controversial issues in the study of management concerns participation of subordinates in decision-making. Traditional models of the managerial process have been autocratic in nature. The manager makes decisions on matters within his area of freedom, issues orders or directives to his subordinates, and monitors their performance to insure conformity with these directives. Scientific management, from its early developments in time and motion study to its contemporary manifestations in linear and heuristic programming, has contributed to this centralization of decision-making in organizations by focusing on the development of methods by which managers can make more rational decisions, substituting objective measurements and empirically validated methods for casual judgments.

Most social psychologists and other behavioral scientists who have turned their attention toward the implications of psychological and social processes for the practice of management have called for greater participation by subordinates in the problem solving, decision-making process. Pointing to evidence of restriction of output and lack of involvement under traditional managerial systems, they have argued for greater influence in decision-making on the part of those held responsible for executing the decisions.

Empirical evidence provides some, but not overwhelming, support for belief in the efficacy of participative management. One of us has previously described field studies and experiments the results of which both support and question the usefulness of participation. Reconciliation of these discrepant findings is not an easy task. It is made complex by different empirical interpretations of the term "participation" and by great differences in the situations in which it is applied. It appears highly likely that an increase in participation of subordinates in decision-making may increase productivity under some circumstances but decrease productivity under other circumstances.

The conclusion appears inescapable that participation in decision-making has consequences which vary from one situation to another. Given the potential importance of this conclusion for the study of leadership and its significance to the process of management, we think it critical that social scientists begin to develop some definitions of the circumstances under which participation in decision-making may contribute to or hinder organizational effectiveness. These could then be translated into guidelines of potential value to managers in choosing leadership styles to fit the demands of the situations which they encounter.

In this article we will describe one approach to dealing with this important problem. A normative model is developed which is consistent with existing empirical evidence concerning the consequences of participation; it purports to specify a set of rules which *should* be followed in determining the form and amount of participation in decision-making by subordinates to be used in different classes of situations.

V. H. Vroom and P. W. Yetton, *Leadership and Decision-making* (Pittsburgh: University of Pittsburgh, 1973).

As many managers know, the real problem falls in the area of placement and training. The nub of the matter is that executives have to be taught both to recognize their own styles and to accept assignments in work areas where their particular style is relevant.

Another interesting practical tip to emerge from Fiedler's work is that it may well lie within the power of the executives to decide whether to give structured or relatively unstructured instructions and that this ought

The model serves to regulate choices among alternative processes for translating roblems into solutions. The alternative processes are defined in terms of amount and orm of participation by subordinates and are shown in [the following table].

TABLE
DECISION METHODS FOR GROUP PROBLEMS

AI   You solve problem or make decision yourself using information available to you at that time.

AII   You obtain necessary information from subordinate(s), then decide on solution to problem yourself. You may or may not tell subordinates what the problem is in getting the information from them. The role played by your subordinates in making the decision is clearly one of providing the necessary information to you, rather than generating or evaluating alternative solutions.

CI   You share the problem with relevant subordinates individually; getting their ideas and suggestions without bringing them together as a group. Then *you* make the decision which may or may not reflect your subordinates' influence.

CII   You share the problem with your subordinates as a group, collectively obtaining their ideas and suggestions. Then, you make the decision which may or may not reflect your subordinates' influence.

GII   You share problem with your subordinates as a group. Together you generate and evaluate alternatives and attempt to reach agreement (consensus) on a solution.

ONCEPTUAL AND EMPIRICAL BASIS OF THE MODEL

A model designed to regulate, in some rational way, choices among the leadership yles shown in [the table] should be based on sound empirical evidence concerning the ely consequences of the styles. In this paper, we will restrict ourselves to presentaon of a model concerned only with group problems. A comparable model for individual oblems has been developed but will not be presented here.

To aid in understanding the conceptual basis of the model, it is important to distinguish three aspects of the ultimate effectiveness of decisions:

1) the quality or rationality of the decision;

2) the acceptance or commitment on the part of subordinates to execute the decision effectively;

3) the amount of time required to make the decision.

One of us has reviewed the evidence regarding the effects of participation on each these aspects and concluded:

The results suggest that allocating problem-solving and decision-making tasks to entire groups, as compared with the leader or manager in charge of the groups, requires a greater investment of man-hours but produces higher acceptance of decisions and a higher probability that the decision will be executed efficiently. Differences between these two methods in quality of decisions and in

to be decided in the light of the situation. Along these lines, as described in Box 9.1, Victor Vroom and P.W. Yetton have given us some very practical advice for deciding how much participation is optimal. Fiedler also makes the rather interesting point that:

The model also throws new light on phenomena which were rather difficult to fit into our usual ideas about measurement in social psychology. Why, for example, should groups differ so markedly in their performance on nearly parallel tasks? The model—and our data—show that the situation becomes easier for the leader as the group moves from

elapsed time are inconclusive and probably highly variable . . . The critics and proponents of participative management would do well to direct their efforts toward identifying the properties of situations in which different decision-making approaches are effective rather than wholesale condemnation or deification of one approach.

Stemming from this review, an attempt has been made to identify these propert of the situation or problem which will be the basic elements in the model. These pro lem attributes are of two types: 1) those which specify the importance for a particu problem of quality and acceptance (see A and E below); and 2) those which, on basis of available evidence, have a high probability of moderating the effects of parti pation on each of these outcomes (see B, C, D, F, G and H below). The following the problem attributes used in the present form of the model:

A. the importance of the quality of the decision;
B. the extent to which the leader possesses sufficient information/expertise to ma a high quality decision by himself;
C. the extent to which subordinates collectively have the necessary information generate a high quality decision;
D. the extent to which the problem is structured;
E. the extent to which acceptance or commitment on the part of subordinates critical to the effective implementation of the decision;
F. the prior probability that the leader's autocratic decision will receive acceptan by subordinates;
G. the extent to which subordinates are motivated to attain the organizational go as represented in the objectives explicit in the statement of the problem;
H. the extent to which subordinates are likely to be in conflict over preferi solutions.

[The following flow chart] shows the normative model for group problems express in the form of a decision tree. The problem attributes are arranged along the top of figure expressed in less technical language and in Yes-No form. To apply the model a particular problem one starts at the left-hand side and works toward the right, aski oneself the question immediately above any box encountered. When a terminal node reached, the prescribed decision-making process from [the above table] (AI, AII, CII and GII) is specified.

LOGIC UNDERLYING THE MODEL

What is the logic underlying the model's behavior? The model begins with the a sumption that any of the decision processes may be feasible in a given situation. proceeds by examining the status of problem attributes for that problem and emplo

the novel to the already known group-task situations. The leaders who excel under relatively novel and therefore more difficult conditions are not necessarily those who excel under those which are more routine, or better known and therefore more favorable. Likewise, we find that different types of task structure require different types of leader behavior. Thus, in a research project's early phases the project director tends to be democratic and permissive; everyone is urged to contribute to the plan and to criticize all aspects of the design. This situation changes radically in the more structured phase when the research design is frozen and the experiment is underway. Here the research director tends to become

DECISION PROCESS FLOW CHART

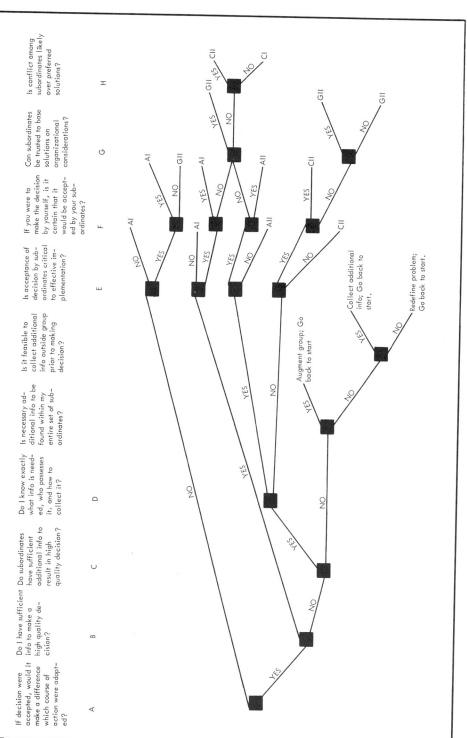

A — If decision were accepted, would it make a difference which course of action were adopted?

B — Do I have sufficient info to make a high quality decision?

C — Do subordinates have sufficient additional info to result in high quality decision?

D — Do I know exactly what info is needed, who possesses it, and how to collect it?

E — Is acceptance of decision by subordinates critical to effective implementation?

F — If you were to make the decision by yourself, is it certain that it would be accepted by your subordinates?

G — Can subordinates be trusted to base solutions on organizational considerations?

H — Is conflict among subordinates likely over preferred solutions?

Is necessary additional info to be found within my entire set of subordinates?

Is it feasible to collect additional info outside group prior to making decision?

Augment group; Go back to start

Collect additional info; Go back to start.

Redefine problem; Go back to start.

a set of seven implicit rules which progressively limit the feasible paths by searching for combinations of problem characteristics which contra-indicate particular processes. The rules are intended to protect both the quality and the acceptance of the decision.

The decision tree enables examination of the nature of the problem and its context and generates a feasible set of methods by eliminating any method which risks the quality or acceptance of the decision. When more than one method remains in the feasible set after applying all of the rules, a number of alternative decision rules can be applied. The one underlying the methods prescribed in [the decision tree] chooses that method which requires the least investment in man-hours in making the decision. This is assumed to be the method closest to the autocratic end of the scale. Thus, this decision rule acts to minimize man-hours, subject to quality and acceptance constraints.

APPLICATION OF THE MODEL

To illustrate application of the model in actual administrative situations, we will present two cases and analyze them by the model. Following the description of each case, we will present our analysis, indicated by the model shown in [the flow chart]. While an attempt has been made to describe these cases as completely as is necessary for the reader to make the judgments required by the model, some room for subjectivity may remain. The reader may wish to analyze the case himself using the model, and compare his analysis with ours.

Case I: Your divisional vice president has authorized you to take two of your subordinates to a marketing conference on Wednesday of next week. This conference will take place at the Hilton Hotel downtown and has a deserved reputation for providing an excellent lunch and other refreshments.

The company will pay the $25 fee, and the conference is considered one of the best of a number of fringe benefits which are shared out between your six subordinates. Selection means little in terms of opportunities to make useful contacts, and has not in the past been used as a mechanism for rewarding good performance. It is obvious that all of your subordinates would like to go.

ANALYSIS
Questions—A (Quality?) = No.
E (Acceptance?) = No.
Feasible Set—AI, AII, CI, CII, GII.
Minimum Man-Hours Solution [flow chart]—AI

Case II: You are the head of a staff unit reporting to the vice president in charge of finance. He has asked you to provide a report on the firm's current portfolio to include recommendations for changes in the selection criteria. Doubts have been raised about the efficiency of the existing system under current market conditions, and there is considerable dissatisfaction with prevailing rates of return.

managing, controlling, and highly autocratic and woe betide the assistant who attempts to be creative in giving instructions to subjects, or in his timing of tests. A similar situation is often found in business organizations where the routine operation tends to be well structured and calls for a managing, directive leadership. The situation becomes suddenly unstructured when a crisis occurs. Under these conditions the number of discussions, meetings, and conferences increases sharply, so as to give everyone an opportunity to express his views.

Your own specialty is in the bond market, but four of your team specialize in the equity market. They are young, eager and conscientious and among them have the knowledge and talent which this task requires.

ANALYSIS

Questions—A (Quality?) = Yes.
B (Manager's Information?) = No.
C (Subordinates' Information?) = Yes.
D (Structured?) = No.
E (Acceptance?) = No.

Feasible Set—CII, GII

Minimum Man-Hours Solution [flow chart]—CII

SHORT- VERSUS LONG-TERM MODELS

The model shown [here] seeks to insure, if relevant, the quality of the decision, to create any necessary acceptance of the decision, and to expend the least number of man-hours in the process. In view of its attention to conditions surrounding the making and implementation of a particular decision rather than any long-term considerations, it could be termed a short-term model.

It seems likely, however, that leadership methods optimal for short-term results may be different from those best for long-term results. Consider a leader who has been uniformly pursuing an autocratic style (AI or AII) and, perhaps as a consequence, has subordinates who cannot be trusted to pursue organizational goals (attribute G), and who have little additional knowledge or experience to bring to bear on the decisions to be made (attribute C), An examination of the structure of the model shown in [the flow chart] reveals that with few exceptions, the leader would be instructed by the model to continue his present autocratic style.

It appears likely, however, that the use of more participative methods would, in time, change the status of these problem attributes (i.e., creating greater loyalty and greater competence in making decisions on the part of the subordinates) so as to develop ultimately a more effective problem-solving system. In the example given above, an autocratic approach would be indicated to maximize short-run benefits, but a higher degree of participation might maximize performance aggregated over a longer period.

A promising approach to the development of a long-term model is one which places less weight on man-hours as the basis for choice. Given a long-term orientation, one would be interested in the trade-off between man-hours and team development, both of which increase with participation. Viewed in these terms, the model shown in [the chart] places maximum relative weight on man-hours and no weight on development, and hence chooses the style closest to the top [of the table] within the feasible set. A model which places no weight on man-hours and maximum weight on development would, we think, choose the style closest to the bottom within the feasible set.

EXTENSION OF THE CONTINGENCY THEORY

Fiedler's theory of leadership has attracted the interest of a great number of behavioural scientists who have tested his theory with a wide variety of work groups in a variety of milieux. In attempting to integrate these findings into his theory, Fiedler differentiates between interacting and coacting groups.

In an interacting group, as the name suggests, the members are required by the task to act co-operatively and interdependently to achieve their common task. For example, in a tug-of-war team, the contribution of individual team members is difficult to isolate and for this reason members are rewarded or penalized as a group. Another example of an interacting group would be an assembly team of 20 operators putting voltmeters together, where one operator's work must be completed before the next begins.

In a coacting group (for example, a bowling team) members carry out their tasks relatively independently of one another. Typical examples of coactive work groups include work teams on piece work, telephone operators, and management trainees who are going to be assessed individually.

In order to classify the studies which he was trying to integrate into his theory, Fiedler invited four independent judges to review the kinds of work groups reported in different studies, to classify the studies as dealing with interacting or coacting work groups, and to decide in which octant the groups should be placed. Fiedler further classified the studies to be reviewed in two categories, field studies and laboratory studies, depending on where the data were collected.

A FIELD STUDY

One of the first studies to test the contingency model was carried out by J. G. Hunt, who studied three different organizations: a large physical science laboratory, a chain of supermarkets, and a heavy machinery shop. Hunt's study is of particular interest because it was made in on-going business settings rather than in ad hoc groups and applied the theory to groups performing relatively independent (coacting) tasks as well as interacting groups. Of the three business organizations, Company X was a research firm in the atomic energy field, Company Y was a grocery chain, and Company Z manufactured farm implements. Data were obtained from 18 teams of research chemists and 11 groups of shop craftsmen in X, 21 meat and 24 grocery departments in Y, and 15 superintendent-foreman teams in Z.

Measurement of variables

Leader-member relations were measured by "group atmosphere" ratings completed by the leader and split into "good" and "moderately poor" categories at the median for each firm. The leader's position power was rated by independent company officials and was considered high in all groups.

Task structure was rated on an 11-point Thurstone interval scale by a panel of company judges and then verified by an independent panel using job descriptions. The two sets of ratings were pooled and the division between "high" and "low" task structure made at a score of six on the scale. The production foremen and those research groups doing pure research had low task structure, while the other groups, including those in "service research," had high task structure.

Hunt was able to establish reasonably objective criteria for measuring performance in all three companies. The foremen in Company Z were rated by the performance of their crews against time-study standards for three six-month periods. The meat and grocery departments were measured on sales per man-hour, which were recorded for 22 periods of 28 days each. The shop craft supervisors in Company X were rated by three company officials who ranked them on (1) output quality and quantity of their crews, (2) attitudes of the crew members, and (3) the rater's overall impression. Hunt's solution to the difficult problem of quantifying the performance of research chemists is interesting: (1) Five objectives of the division were listed and weighted, with "advancing chemical knowledge for the least money possible in areas of interest to the Atomic Energy Commission" given the greatest weight. (2) The six most important activities were then delineated and weighted according to their contributions towards the objectives. (3) Each group's performance on each activity was rated. The overall performance was the sum of the weighted averages for each activity and objective.

After discussion with company officials, Hunt classed the shop craftsmen in Company X and the grocery departments in Company Y as coacting groups. Despite some reservations about the basis used, the other groups were considered to be interdependent.

As in most empirical tests of the contingency theory, the situations studied did not produce data for all eight octants. In this case the fact that all leaders had high position power eliminated octants 2, 4, 6, and 8 from consideration. A summary of the Spearman rank-order correlation between leader L.P.C. scores and group task effectiveness is given in Table 9–1.

The correlations are generally in the direction predicted by Fiedler except for the research chemists in octant 3, for whom a negative correlation would be predicted. In Hunt's view the equal but opposite correlations in octant 7 approximate the zero result predicted by Fiedler. Although the individual correlations are not statistically significant at the .05 level, Hunt established that a combined test of significance was supported for both interacting and coacting groups. The model appears to be applicable in both types of situations and, by combining the samples in each octant, Hunt was able to demonstrate statistical significance for the results in octants 1 and 5.

Hunt examined the effects of the situational variables separately and concluded that, in this study at least, only leader-member relations appeared to be related to the leader's L.P.C. score. Task structure did not correlate with L.P.C., and going from high- to low-structure groups did not affect the L.P.C.–effectiveness relationship.

TABLE 9–1
HUNT'S CORRELATIONS

Octant	1		3		5		7		Type of Group
Leader-member relations	Good		Good		Mod. poor		Mod. poor		
Task structure	High		Low		High		Low		I–Interac
Position power	High		High		High		High		C–Coact
	N	Rho	N	Rho	N	Rho	N	Rho	
Company X:									
Research chemists	7	−.64	6	.60			5	.30	I
Shop craftsmen	6	−.48			5	.80			C
Company Y:									
Meat department	10	−.51			11	.21			I
Grocery department	13	−.06			11	.49			C
Company Z:									
Foremen			5	−.80			5	−.30	I

Conclusions

Hunt notes that his finding of support for the model in coacting groups is at variance with earlier research done by Fiedler himself. This variance may be due to the fact that Fiedler's study dealt with groups doing tension-arousing, creative tasks while Hunt's samples performed more routine, structured jobs of a production nature. Hunt expresses the need for better understanding of the interaction between group member inter-dependence and other variables in the leadership setting. He suggests that a more precise reflection of the variability of group interaction in occu-pational settings would extend the applicability of the contingency model.

In the group task situation, position power and task structure are clearly independent variables external to the leader. Leader-member relations are, however, affected by both the leader's behaviour and his perceptions since, in most studies, the variable is measured by the leader's rating of the group atmosphere. Hunt comments that "the theory is conceptually different depending on how we conceive leader-member relations" and calls for further research into the effects of measuring leader-member relations by the members' rather than the leader's rating.

Hunt concludes with a discussion of some of the implications of the model for organizational change. Present studies only predict the L.P.C.-performance relationship within each situational octant and do not indi-cate how absolute performance would change if the situation varied. For example, would a leader with a low L.P.C. score get better absolute results if he moved from an intermediate octant such as 5 to an unfavourable octant such as 8? Hunt's interpretation, supported by some of Fiedler's studies, is that performance does not decrease when the situation becomes less favourable but more appropriate to the leader's L.P.C. style. This startling conclusion suggests that organizational change in terms of clearer job descriptions, more delegation of authority, and better human relations may be ineffective, if not actually harmful, unless the new situation produced is appropriate to the L.P.C. characteristics of the organization's leaders.

A LABORATORY STUDY

A crucial laboratory investigation was the Belgian Navy study carried out by Fiedler, where 288 petty officers and recruits (selected on the basis of pretest measures from among 546 stationed at St. Croix-Burger Naval Training Centre) were allocated to 96 three-man teams. These teams were experimentally assembled so that 48 teams would be made up of members all speaking one language (French or Dutch) and 48 teams would be bilingual (the leader from one language sector and the members from the other).

The groups were given four different tasks, but in the final analysis only two of these tasks were included. The structured task required the group to find the shortest route for a ship that must visit a given number of ports, given the restraints that the ship had a limited range and had to stick to certain required sea lanes. The unstructured task required the group to compose a recruiting letter for the Belgian Navy. Perhaps it is worth-while to point out at this juncture that there is some argument in the literature as to the relative degree of "structuredness" of these tasks.

In this particular study, Fiedler has been criticized for exercising too much direction in allocating different work groups to different cells in his model. Fiedler had four additional variables to deal with: (a) language group of the members, (b) language group of the leaders, (c) verbal intelligence, and (d) task sequence; and the way he took these variables into consideration in allocating work groups to octants must have significantly affected outcomes in terms of correlations between L.P.C. scores and effectiveness. Further, the actual size of the correlation coefficients has been challenged, and Fiedler seems to be open to the charge that he allowed himself a measure of statistical leniency. As G. Graen et al. point out in reviewing the Belgian Navy study in "Contingency Model of Leadership Effectiveness: Antecedent and Evidential Results":

> Calculating the correlations between the leader's LPC and performance within each of the 16 cells for each of the three tasks separately showed that only 2 of the 48 rank-order correlations ($N = 6$) were significant ($p < .05$). However, the apparent criterion of reliable relationships for the contingency model merely requires that the observed correlations approximate those predicted at least in terms of direction. For example, in discussing the results of a church-leadership study, Fiedler stated: "While only one of the sixteen [sic] correlations was significant, only one of the eight correlations, namely, .03, was not in the hypothesized

direction". . . . This was followed by an interpretation of the correlations that were not significant but were in the hypothesized direction. Thus, the correspondence of correlations to the hypothesized direction (sign of the correlation) has been employed as an alternative criterion of reliable results.

FIELD VERSUS LABORATORY STUDIES

Fiedler has summarized the field and laboratory studies testing the contingency theory as shown in Table 9–2. Summarizing the results from a large number of studies with both interacting and coacting groups, using both field and laboratory data, Fiedler concluded that his model predicts leadership performance in field situations but not completely in laboratory

TABLE 9–2

SUMMARY OF FIELD AND LABORATORY STUDIES TESTING THE CONTINGENCY MODEL

Study	Octants							
	I	II	III	IV	V	VI	VII	
Field studies								
Hunt (1967)	−.64		−.80		.21		.30	
	−.51		.60				−.30	
Hill (1969)[a]		−.10	−.29			−.24	.62	
Fiedler et al. (1969)		−.21		.00		.67*		
O'Brien et al. (1969)		−.46		.47		−.45		
Laboratory experiments								
Belgian Navy	−.72	.37	−.16	.08	.16	.07	.26	
	−.77	.50	−.54	.13	.03	.14	−.27	
Shima (1968)[a]		−.26		.71*				
Mitchell (1969)		.24		.43				
		.17		.38				
		.34		.51				
Fiedler exec.								
Skrzypek[a]	−.43	−.32	.10	.35	.28	.13	.08	
Median								
All studies	−.64	.17	−.22	.38	.22	.10	.26	
Field studies	−.57	−.21	−.29	.23	.21	−.24	.30	
Laboratory experiments	−.72	.24	−.16	.38	.16	.13	.08	
Median correlations of Fiedler's original studies (1964)	−.52	−.58	−.33	.47	.42		.05	

Note.—Number of correlations in the expected direction (exclusive of Octant VI, for which no predictio been made) = 34; number of correlations opposite to expected direction = 11; p by binomial test = .01.
  [a] Studies not conducted by the writer or his associates.
  * $p < .05$.
  Source: Reprinted by permission of the publisher from F. E. Fiedler, "Validation and Extension of the C gency Model of Leadership Effectiveness," *Psychological Bulletin*, Vol. 76, No. 2 (1971), pp. 128–48.

situations. But then, as Fiedler points out, leadership in an organizational setting is a different kettle of fish from leadership in a laboratory setting. Fiedler further suggests that leadership research should differentiate between coacting groups and training groups, which should lead to a more insightful understanding of executive performance in task and training organizations. On the failure of research to support a relation between leadership training and effectiveness, Fiedler argues in "Validation and Extension of the Contingency Model of Leadership Effectiveness: A review of Empirical Findings":

> These disappointing results can be deduced from the contingency model. Specifically, we can interpret leadership experience and training as improving situational favorableness (e.g., human relations training is supposed to improve leader-member relations; technical training would make the task appear more structured). Training and experience should then differentially affect the performance of high and low LPC leaders. The contingency model would then predict that training for intermediate situations will improve the performance of high LPC leaders—but *decrease* that of low LPC leaders. Likewise, training and experience for favorable and unfavorable situations will improve performance of low LPC leaders—but *decrease* performance of high LPC leaders. These results have now been obtained in several studies and further support the contingency model.

A CRITICAL REVIEW OF FIEDLER'S THEORY

In the early 1970s, a number of critical reviews of Fiedler's contingency theory of leadership appeared in the literature which challenged his model on empirical, methodological, and theoretical grounds. Ahmed Ashour has argued that the cumulative empirical evidence indicates that the major hypothesis of the model—that situational favourableness and the leader's L.P.C. score are related—has not been established. In "Organizational Behavior and Human Performance," after reviewing the correlations shown in Table 9–2 for the field and laboratory studies, Ashour concluded:

> An examination of the correlations [in Table 9–2] reveals that out of the 51 correlations included, only two were statistically significant and 14 correlations had either zero value or were not in the predicted directions. Field data, on which Fiedler claims support for his model, had only one statistically significant correlation out of the 19 correlations included! Furthermore, correlations not in the predicted directions or of zero value appear in octants III, IV, VI, VII, and VIII. Clearly, and contrary to Fiedler's conclusions, the empirical evidence does not provide conclusive support for the contingency model.

What both Ashour and Graen argue is that Fiedler merely accepts correlations obtained in the predicted direction, regardless of whether or not these correlations are statistically significant.

Box 9.2: An evaluation of Fiedler's contingency model

Fiedler's contingency model could be evaluated from three perspectives: (1) empirical validity, (2) methodological rigor, and (3) theoretical adequacy. The empirical validity of the model, judged by the results of individual studies testing the model and by the cumulative evidence of these studies, is questionable. Most of the correlations obtained from individual studies lack statistical significance. The cumulative evidence [in the table below], based on combining correlations obtained from different studies, shows that only for octants I and IV were the composite correlations significant. Most of the proportions of variance corresponding to these correlations are too small to be of practical value. It is interesting to note that these cumulative results are based on data that Fiedler used to claim empirical support for his model. The cumulative evidence shows, contrary to Fiedler's claim, that the model is not empirically valid and that the predictions it offers are trivial for the most part.

Octants	I	II	III	IV	V	VI	VII	VIII
Composite correlations	−.59*	.02	−.16	.40*	.19	.08	.19	−.26
Proportions of variance explained	.35	.00	.03	.16	.04	.01	.04	.07

* Significant at the .01 level

The lack of empirical validity of Fiedler's model seems to be rooted in the methodology of its research and in the underlying theory. The measurements and the sampling procedure have serious flaws. Consider for example the LPC measure. In addition to the reliability problems of that measure (some test-retest reliabilities were .59, .47, .31 and .41), it is doubtful that the measure is systematically related to leadership style or behavior. Similarly, evidence is lacking to support Fiedler's contention that the sit-

Ahmed S. Ashour, "The Contingency Model of Leadership Effectiveness: An Evaluation," *Organizational Behavior and Human Performance*, Vol. 9, No. 3 (June, 1973).

In terms of methodology, the process for assimilating negative findings into the model has been criticized by Graen *et al.* in the article cited above:

> A second and equally important difficulty is that this procedure insulates the model from the possible correcting influences of disconfirming empirical results by trapping the theorist within the data-proof confines of his model: Results of empirical studies are forced by the procedure into a form that cannot present negative feedback to the theorist. Thus, the model is rendered insensitive to the correctional influences of negative results. The theorist can change the model only by expanding it to include more variables; however, he is usually not in a position to doubt the essence of the central model. Therefore, the model cannot develop through symbiotic interaction between ideas and empirical results. The model has lost the capability of directing meaningful research.

Part of the objection is that Fiedler adapts and reclassifies other researchers' findings so that they have an enhanced probability of fitting his original model.

uational classification represents levels of situational favorableness. Furthermore, the use of small samples obtained from heterogeneous populations in the original studies (from which the model was inferred) probably added sampling error, and hence, compounded the methodological problems of the results.

On theoretical grounds, the model fails to provide meaningful explanations for the predictions it proposes for each octant. It does not specify leader and group behaviors that link leader's and group characteristics to performance outcomes. In this sense it ignores the many behavioral linkages that intervene between a trait variable such as LPC and group productivity, and ignores also the possibility that situational variables could have differential effects on each of these linkages. Thus, having no knowledge about the critical behaviors of leaders and members in different situations makes it extremely difficult to assign any behavioral meaning to the correlations Fiedler proposes. The model is a simple *empiric generalization* that is not fully supported by empirical results; it *is not a theory.* Not only does a theory have to offer valid and nontrivial predictions, but it also has to provide meaningful explanations of the predictions it proposes. Fiedler's model fails to fulfill any of these requirements.

Fiedler's model is deficient in two other respects. First, it proposes static connections between variables. It fails to account for the dynamic aspects of leadership and group behavior exemplified by the long-run effects of the group on the leader, and of the situation on leader and group behaviors. Second, the model omits the important dependent variable of members' satisfaction. Being concerned only with productivity makes it a classical model.

The evaluation of Fiedler's contingency model suggests that the key to constructing a valid and meaningful leadership theory lies in examining and monitoring critical leader and group behaviors in different situations in the short and long runs. These behaviors should be linked to productivity and satisfaction variables on the one hand, and to predictors of behavior on the other hand. Particular attention should be given to the measurement and sampling procedure in future research.

Fiedler has also been criticized for employing rather small samples, which is almost inevitable given the large number of different cells his model requires. Most of the studies reported by Fiedler used sample sizes under 10. Further, few of the studies investigated the full range of the situational types simultaneously.

Fiedler's model has also been criticized on theoretical grounds. For example, Korman has criticized the model as being static and ignoring the long-range influence of the situation on the leader and the group. Ashour (see Box 9.2) has suggested that the contingency model be revised and, to facilitate this revision, that new directions be pursued to provide data that will help in devising an improved model. In the first instance, larger samples should be used to clarify the problem of statistical significance. More data should be collected on leader and group behaviour using the critical incident technique. More information, especially of a cognitive and motivational character, is needed in regard to what the L.P.C. score actually measures. More variables, such as size and homogeneity of the group, must be introduced to define the situational characteristic more fully. Finally, longitudinal studies are required to see how the different variables interact over a period of time.

The major criticism of Fiedler's model—raised by executives who are exposed to his ideas—is that the model is essentially academic, and that no significant effort has been made to apply the findings to actual management operations as a means of improving organizational or group performance. What some of these managers have in mind is the success which R. R. Blake and J. S. Mouton achieved in the late 1950s and early 1960s by taking the findings of group dynamics of those days, synthesizing them into the managerial grid, and using T group technology to train a generation of managers. Perhaps the crucial difference is that Blake and Mouton used a two-dimensional model (a *tour de force* for its day) which raised the level of discussion of managers by a quantum leap; whereas Fiedler's contingency model is basically a three-dimensional model, with all sorts of complexities built in. The ultimate criticism of Fiedler is that he has revealed his genius twice; firstly in devising the model, which stands like calculus to arithmetic compared with previous leadership models; and secondly, more dangerously, in his ability to integrate new findings into his model. Why should an ugly fact destroy a beautiful model?

TOPIC 3
House's path-goal theory

Puzzled by a number of contradictory findings in leadership research, Robert J. House of the University of Toronto's business school has come forward with an exciting new theory of leadership which is based on Vroom's theory of motivation, with its concepts of expectancy, outcomes, utilities, and instrumentalities (see Box 9.3).

What started House off was the fact that research in the 1950s—dealing with first-line supervisors and measuring the factors of initiating structure and consideration—revealed that leaders who initiate structure for subordinates generally get higher performance ratings from superiors and have more productive work groups, while leaders who are considerate of subordinates have more satisfied subordinates. But other evidence revealed that initiating structure for unskilled and semiskilled workers causes dissatisfaction, and that employees in large groups apparently either prefer initiating structure more or dislike it less than employees in small groups. From his own more recent research work on roles at a different occupational level, House found that with high-level employees, initiating structure is related to role conflict and ambiguity.

To explain these apparent contradictions in research findings, House has developed a path-goal theory of leadership which has already attracted considerable attention among both academics and executives. Using this theory, House has been able to reconcile apparently conflicting results of previous research concerning the relations between initiating structure and consideration and performance and employee satisfaction. For example, a study by E. A. Fleishman and E. F. Harris had indicated the following results of initiating structure:

Managers, professionals . . . . Satisfaction, performance, perception of organizational effectiveness
Workers . . . . Performance, dissatisfaction

But a study of salaried employees by House *et al.* found the following relations of consideration and satisfaction to initiating structure:

Independent variable: Occupational level (structure)	Moderating variable: Consideration	Dependent variable: Subordinate satisfaction
Supervisors	{ High . . . . . . , .	High
	{ Low	Low
Salaried professionals and administrators.	{ High	High
	{ Low	High

House explains these findings (in "A Path-Goal Theory of Leader Effectiveness") as follows:

Leader initiating structure can be hypothesized to clarify path-goal relationships for higher occupational level jobs which are frequently ambiguously defined. Such clarification reduces role ambiguity and increases the employee's perceived instrumentality of effort toward goal attainment. That is, it increases his subjective probability estimates that his effort will result in goal attainment. Thus, the path-goal theory advanced here offers an explanation for the positive correlations between leader initiating structure and satisfaction among the high occupational level groups studied by House *et al.* (1970, 1971a, 1971b). The theory also explains the negative relationships found at lower occupational levels by Fleishman and Harris (1962). If it can be assumed that lower level jobs are generally more routine, that their path-goal relationships are usually self-evident, and that the job itself is frequently not intrinsically satisfying, then it can be hypothesized that leader initiating structure would be viewed by subordinates as an imposition of external control that does little to clarify path-goal relationships and is viewed by subordinates as being directed at keeping them working at unsatisfying activities. Although such control is likely to increase productivity by preventing soldiering, work restriction, or slowdowns, it is also a source of dissatisfaction to employees.

Another hypothesis derived from path-goal theory explains the findings concerning the moderating effect of consideration in some studies and not in others. Where the path is not viewed as satisfying, that is, for

Organizational behaviour

Box 9.3: Path-goal theory of leadership

The theory advanced here is derived from the path-goal hypothesis advanced by Georgopoulos *et al.* (1957), and from previous research supporting the broad class of expectancy theory of motivation (Atkinson, 1958; Vroom, 1964; Porter and Lawler, 1967; Galbraith and Cummings, 1967; Graen, 1969; Lawler, 1968). The central concept of expectancy theories is that the force on an individual to engage in a specific behavior is a function of (*1*) his expectations that the behavior will result in a specific outcome; and (*2*) the sum of the valences, that is, personal utilities or satisfactions, that he derives from the outcome. The research findings indicate that the function is a nonlinear, monotonically increasing product of expectations and valences. Thus, according to this theory of motivation, an individual chooses the behaviors he engages in on the basis of (*1*) the valences he perceives to be associated with the outcomes of the behavior under consideration; and (*2*) his subjective estimate of the probability that his behavior will indeed result in the outcomes. Vroom (1964) formalized one perspective of expectancy motivation theory mathematically, and Galbraith and Cummings (1967) extended his formulation by pointing out that some of the valences associated with a specific behavior are intrinsic to the behavior itself and some are the extrinsic consequences of that behavior. To the extent that behavior is intrinsically valent it is also intrinsically motivational because the behavior is highly instrumental to the outcome of satisfaction. A person will be motivated to engage in such behavior because his expectancy that satisfaction will follow is nearly unity. That is, if the outcomes were contingent on an external rewarder—any significant other—the expectancy would be less [than] unity because the behavior might not be observed or recognized by the rewarder. However, when the reward is essentially self-administering, expectancy approaches unity.

The theory may be further extended and broken down into parts that have specific relevance for leadership using the concept of path instrumentality advanced by Evans (1968: 14): "This is the cognition of the degree to which following a particular path (behavior) will lead to a particular outcome, it is akin to (but not identical to) the concept of 'expectancy' introduced by Vroom." Evans (1968) has also advanced an extension of Vroom's (1964) theory and a path-goal theory of leadership. His theory is different from the one presented here in that its predictions are not contingent on situational variables, and it is not an attempt to account for the conflicting findings just reviewed.

Robert J. House, "A Path-Goal Theory of Leader Effectiveness," *Administrative Science Quarterly* Vol. 16, No. 3 (1971), pp. 321–38.

lower level jobs, it can be hypothesized that consideration serves as a source of extrinsic social satisfaction and support to the employee, thus making the path easier to travel. Consequently, for Fleishman and Harris' (1962) blue-collar workers, leader consideration moderated the unsatisfying effects of leader structure; whereas, for higher level jobs, where the path was intrinsically satisfying, the need for such support was lower and consequently consideration would be expected to have little or no moderating effect on the relationship between initiating structure and satisfaction.

To support his theory further, House has carried out a series of experiments with professional and administrative employees, using a measure of structure taken from the Ohio State Leader Behaviour Description Ques-

According to the formulation advanced here, the individual makes probability esti-
ates with respect to two linking points connecting behavior with its outcomes, and
bjectively places values on the outcomes. The magnitude of these probability esti-
ates indicates the degree of path instrumentality of his behavior for work-goal accom-
ishment and valence. This formulation can be expressed in the following formula:

$$M = IV_b + P_1 \left[IV_a + \sum_{i=1}^{n} (P_{2i} EV_i) \right]$$

$$i = 1, \ldots, n.$$

ere:

M = motivation to work;
IV_b = intrinsic valence associated with goal-directed behavior;
IV_a = intrinsic valence associated with work-goal accomplishment;
EV_i = extrinsic valences associated with work-goal accomplishment;
P_1 = path instrumentality of behavior for work-goal attainment;
P_{2i} = path instrumentalities of work goal for extrinsic valences.

In work situations the individual estimates the path instrumentality, P_1, of his behavior
the accomplishment of some work goal. Here he considers such factors as his ability
behave in an appropriate and effective manner as well as the barriers to work-goal
complishment in the environment, and the support he will receive from others to ac-
mplish the work goal. In addition, he estimates the path instrumentality, P_2, of the
rk goal for attaining personal outcomes that have valence for him. For example, he
imates the probability that his superiors will recognize his goal accomplishment and
ard him accordingly. He also considers, and places subjective values on the intrinsic
ence associated with the behavior required to achieve the work goal, IV_b, the
rinsic valence associated with the achievement of the work goal, IV_a, and the extrinsic
ences associated with the personal outcomes that he accrues as a result of achieve-
the work goal, EV_i.
The behavior of the leader is clearly relevant to all of the independent variables in
formulation. The leader, at least in part, determines what extrinsic rewards should

ionnaire and measures of performance, job scope, satisfaction, and role
mbiguity developed specifically developed for his research.

TESTING THE PATH-GOAL THEORY

In its generalized form, House's theory of leader effectiveness encom-
asses such an enormous number of combinations of variables that both
mpirical testing and practical application are highly circumscribed. How-
ver, the theory can be made operational by describing how leader behav-
our can affect the expectancies or outcome valences of subordinates in
ertain specific situations. What will emerge is not a "one best way" in-
truction manual but a range of possible actions, some with conflicting re-
lts, from which the leader must select those most appropriate to his par-
cular situation.

be associated with work-goal accomplishment, EV_i. For example, he has some influer over the extent to which work-goal accomplishment will be recognized as a contribut and whether it will be rewarded with financial increases, promotion, assignment of m interesting tasks or opportunities for personal growth and development. Consequen he influences the magnitude of the sum of the personal outcomes available. Second, leader, through his interaction with the subordinate, can increase the subordinate's p instrumentality concerning the rewards forthcoming as a result of work-goal accompli ment, P_2. If he is consistent in his decision making with respect to recognizing a rewarding work-goal achievement, he will clarify the linkage between work-goal achie ment and rewards. Thus, if he consistently rewards achievement, this will most proba increase the subordinate's path instrumentality, P_2, for valent personal outcomes. Thi through his own behavior he can provide support for the subordinate's efforts a thereby influence the probability that this effort will result in work-goal achieveme that is P_1. Fourth, the leader influences the intrinsic valences associated with g accomplishment, IV_a, by the way he delegates and assigns tasks to subordinates, wh determines the amount of influence the subordinate has in goal setting and the amo of control he is allowed in the task-directed effort. The greater the subordinate's opp tunity to influence the goal and exercise control, the more intrinsically valent work-goal accomplishment. Finally, the leader can increase the net intrinsic vale associated with goal-directed behavior, IV_b, by reducing frustrating barriers, being s portive in times of stress, permitting involvement in a wide variety of tasks, and be considerate of subordinate's needs.

PROPOSITIONS

The above interpretation of motivation theory as applied to leadership suggests following general propositions:

1. The motivation functions of a leader are to increase the net positive valen associated with work-goal attainment, attainment, increase the net positive valences sociated with the path—behavior—to work-goal attainment, and increase the s ordordinate's path instrumentality with respect to work-goal attainment for perso outcomes and the behavior required for work-goal attainment. This statement assur that when the subordinate is working under ambiguous path-goal relationships subjective probability estimates that his behavior will affect the valences he receives

House has begun to study the correlates of leader behaviour with th motivation of subordinates through a test of eight hypotheses applied in three different business organizations. The behavioural dimensions studie were initiating structure (I.S.) and consideration (C.S.), but they wer treated as personality traits of the leader rather than as measures of specifi behaviour. While this simplification is necessary to permit the gathering of data, it should be noted that the path-goal theory applies to specific be haviours and not to general personal characteristics.

STUDY 1

This study tested three hypotheses on a sample of office employees in a heavy equipment manufacturing firm.

less than the objective probabilities that his behavior will affect the valences he receives. When this assumption does not hold, that is, when under conditions of role ambiguity, his subjective probability estimates exceed the objective probabilities, then clarification of path-goal relationships will result in reduced motivation.

Stated less formally, the motivational functions of the leader consist of increasing personal pay-offs to subordinates for work-goal attainment, and making the path to these pay-offs easier to travel by clarifying it, reducing road blocks and pitfalls, and increasing the opportunities for personal satisfaction en route. The function of making the path easier and more satisfying to follow has been dealt with only implicitly in the leadership literature and, as will be shown, his significant implications for leader's behavior.

2. In increasing path instrumentality by clarifying path-goal relationships, the leader's behavior will have positive motivational effects to the extent that it reduces role ambiguity or makes possible the exercise of externally imposed controls. Reduction of role ambiguity results in increased motivation because role ambiguity is both negatively valent to subordinates (Rizzo *et al.*, 1970), and because it is usually associated with low path instrumentality. Externally imposed controls are motivational because they make possible the allocation of valences contingent on desirable behavior. Externally imposed control results in improved performance only to the extent that the rewards that are under the control of the leader are positively valent to the subordinates; punishments that are under the control of the leader are negatively valent to the subordinates; rewards and punishments are contingent on performance; and the contingency is clearly perceived by the subordinates. Whether performance motivated by external controls is satisfying to the subordinate, depends on his unconscious needs, conscious values, and perceptions of equity in the exchange of effort for rewards.

3. Where leader attempts to clarify path-goal relationships are redundant with existing conditions, that is, where path-goal relationships are apparent because of the routine of the tasks or objective system-fixed controls, attempts by the leader to clarify path-goal relationships will result in increased externally imposed control and will be seen by subordinates as redundant. Although such control may increase performance, it will also result in decreased satisfaction.

4. Leader behavior directed at need satisfaction of subordinates will result in increased performance to the extent that such satisfaction increases the net positive valence associated with goal-directed effort.

Hypothesis 1. Leader I.S. will be positively related to subordinate satisfaction.

Hypothesis 2. Leader I.S. will be negatively related to subordinate role ambiguity.

Hypothesis 3. The variance in role ambiguity will account for the relationship between I.S. and subordinate satisfaction.

All of these hypotheses were based on the assumption that the sample subjects were doing ambiguously defined tasks for which a directive leader could clarify path-goal relationships and increase satisfaction. The calculations shown in Table 9–3 provide support for the hypotheses, but House notes that the lack of control on task characteristics, which resulted in many routine tasks being included, prevents a clear conclusion about the effects of leader I.S. in reducing role ambiguity.

TABLE 9-3
CORRELATIONS BETWEEN LEADER I.S. AND SUBORDINATE SATISFACTION

Variables	Zero-order correlations	Correlations with role ambiguity held constant
Satisfaction with:		
Advancement opportunity	.20**	.09
Job autonomy	.10	−.05
Intrinsic job rewards	.17*	.03
Job security	.03	−.06
Pay	.05	−.01
Recognition	.16*	−.06
Social environment	.21**	.04
Role ambiguity	−.41**	

* $p < .05$.
** $p < .01$.

STUDY 2

The following hypotheses were tested on 192 nontechnical office employees.

Hypothesis 1. For autonomous (and presumably ambiguous) jobs, leader I.S. will increase satisfaction.

Hypothesis 2. Performance, as opposed to satisfaction, will be increased more by leader I.S. when the job lacks autonomy (and interest) and control is necessary to ensure continued effort.

Hypothesis 3. Leader consideration will increase satisfaction more when the job is nonautonomous.

Hypothesis 4. Leader consideration will also increase performance more when the job is nonautonomous.

Hypotheses 3 and 4 assume that autonomous jobs are intrinsically satisfying and consequently leader behaviour will be less relevant to the needs or performance of subordinates than when the path is hard to travel.

Hypothesis 5. Job scope will reduce the correlation between C.S. and subordinate satisfaction and performance, because a wider range of tasks is more likely to substitute intrinsic satisfaction for the support provided by the leader.

Measures were taken of I.S. and C.S., the employees' attitudes toward the company, their satisfaction with role expectations, multitrait and multirater ratings of individual performance and job scope, and task autonomy. An abbreviated summary of the results is given in Table 9–4.

It should be pointed out again that I.S. and C.S. are treated here as leader traits—it is not the demonstration of considerate behaviour that reduces

TABLE 9–4
CORRELATION OF I.S. AND C.S. WITH JOB AUTONOMY AND SCOPE

	Average satisfaction	Average performance
Correlation of leader I.S. with job autonomy:		
Low	.19	.47
Medium	.21	.18
High	.33	.18
Correlation of leader C.S. with job autonomy:		
Low	.37	.42*
Medium	.30	.11
High	.23	.08
Correlation of leader C.S. with job scope:		
Low	.36*	.52
Medium	.30	.02
High	.30	.09

* $p < .01$.

erformance as tasks become more autonomous, but the failure of the elations-oriented supervisor to take the necessary steps to structure the ob so as to clarify the goal path for his subordinates.

The average correlations shown in Table 9–4 are all in the predicted irection. House's analysis of the statistical significance of the correlations with individual factors indicates that strong support, though not empirical roof, has been demonstrated for hypotheses 1 to 4. For hypothesis 5, the elationship between C.S. and satisfaction as moderated by job scope is ot supported, although job scope did significantly affect the C.S.–performance relationship.

STUDY 3

Hypotheses 3, 4, and 5 of Study 2 were replicated in a sample of 122 mployees of a chemical plant which included all groups but had a preonderance (99) of hourly workers. The classification of job scope and utonomy as low, medium, and high was on the basis of the average scores the study itself. Thus, given the sample used, even the relatively more autonomous" jobs were, on an absolute basis, rather routine.

Perhaps for this reason, no support was found for hypothesis 4, and ypothesis 3 was only supported to the extent that intrinsic job satisfaction creased for high-consideration leaders when the tasks became less aunomous. The other measures of job satisfaction did not change with job utonomy in the predicted direction. On the other hand, the moderating effect of job scope expressed in hypothesis 5 was supported more strongly than in the previous study.

CONCLUSIONS

House recognizes the limitations of inferring theoretical constructs such as intrinsic task satisfaction and ambiguity of role demands from situational measures of task autonomy, job scope, or occupational characteristics. It is also recognized that the causal relationships between leader behaviour and the variables affecting the motivation of subordinates have not been demonstrated by his correlational studies. However, he feels that "moderate to strong support for seven of the eight hypotheses tested . . . suggests that the theory holds promise and warrants further testing with more direct measurement of the theoretical constructs using experiment as well as correlational methods."

FURTHER DEVELOPMENTS OF THE PATH-GOAL THEORY

House has now revised and extended his theory to include both environmental variables and individual difference variables. His basic thesis is that a critical function of the executive is to enrich and enhance the psychological status of subordinates in order to increase motivation to perform (task effectiveness) and satisfaction (human factor). Thus, the path-goal theory of leadership focuses the efforts of the executive on the following elements:

1. Recognizing and mobilizing group members' needs for outcomes over which the leader has some control.
2. Making a more active effort to link personal payoffs for subordinates with actual work-goal achievement.
3. Making a detailed and careful analysis of the paths to these payoffs and making it easier for subordinates to travel these paths by coaching and direction.
4. Interacting with team members to help them to clarify their expectancies, so that they will have a better grasp of the probabilities of particular relations and outcomes. ("If I do this and get there, what are the chances: (*a*) That you will recognize it? (*b*) Reward it?")
5. Reducing frustrating barriers; for example, making sure executives are not held up by lack of computer resources or secretarial assistance.
6. Increasing the opportunities for personal satisfaction, contingent on effective performance.

In stating his theory this way, House has linked in a dramatic, stark, and clear way how performance and payoffs (extrinsic and intrinsic) are locked in a subtle web of subjective probabilities or expectancies which the effective executive is being taught how to monitor. House takes the whole subject of executive leadership out of the age of Aquarius into the age of cost benefit analysis, where utility and probability become the aces. To get the show on the road, the executive has to be able to figure out these networks of utilities and probabilities; he must also come up with the necessary coaching and guidance for the problem, but only when it is appropriate. As a leader accomplishes these functions, his behaviour will increase the motivation of his subordinates.

House recognizes that individual differences among subordinates will affect their perception and interpretation of leader behaviour. For example, subordinates with high needs for affiliation would obviously prefer leaders high on consideration; on the other hand, those with high needs for achievement prefer more structured leadership styles that clarify path-goal relations, generate goal-oriented feedback, and generally facilitate goal achievement. Subordinates with high needs for extrinsic rewards would obviously prefer leader behaviour that helps them gain recognition, promotion, and salary increases. Another individual factor is the subordinate's perception of his own ability with respect to the assigned tasks. This recognition of the factor of individual difference clearly ties House's work into established VIE (valence, instrumentality, expectation) motivation theory.

House has also sought to look at the effect of the environment on the work group. Unfortunately, path-goal theory is somewhat limited in coping with environmental factors such as the formal authority system, the primary working group, and the cultural environment. Indeed, the major difficulty of path-goal theorists is their inability to escape from the one-on-one optic. Nevertheless, path-goal relations can be thought out and monitored by task structures, group norms, and system constraints.

AN INTERIM EVALUATION

It is too early to make anything but a preliminary assessment of House's path-goal theory of leadership, mainly because there is so little research data to go on and the findings that are available are based exclusively on the research efforts of House and his research associates. Unfortunately, they have not used the variables of the path-goal theory, but I have made use of variables developed for a different approach. But it is useful to try to evaluate this new point of departure in leadership study in terms of theory, methodology, and practical relevance.

In terms of theory, House's contingency theory comes at a very opportune moment. It has arrived in the professional journals just at a moment when its great rival, Fiedler's contingency theory, appears to be on the decline. That decline occurred mainly because more careful analysis of his empirical data failed to support his predicted relations, but also because Fiedler's theory lacks a proper explanatory rationale. And it is just in terms of logical infra-structure that House's theory has a distinct and significant advantage. House built his leadership theory on the solid and well-established motivation theory of expectancy, valence (or utility), and instrumentality developed by Vroom, Cummings, and Lawler; and this theory not only makes good sense in terms of explaining human behaviour at work but also has a substantial body of empirical evidence to support it. A fair number of research reports show that the Herzberg two-factor theory of motivation lacks empirical foundation, but no behavioural scientist has yet come forward with data to challenge the expectancy theory of motivation. Thus in building on expectancy theory, House built on a solid theoretical foundation which allowed him to think out the consequences of leader initiating structure and consideration as they affect the individual's motivation. In essence, what House has done is to propose a proper theory of leadership (in terms of path-goals) and motivation (in terms of utilities) which could explain a variety of behavioural data which were previously in conflict.

As for methodology, House's theory represents a triumph for the attritional empirical behavioural scientist who is dedicated to the research logic of building a model with explicit assumptions, deriving testable hypotheses with measurable variables, and collecting data from a critical population which can disprove the relations asserted in the hypotheses. Aside from his brilliant decision to build on the expectancy theory of motivation, House derived significant advantage from using only measures which had been properly checked for reliability and validity. And how House fitted these variables together in a particular logical train will prove useful to other researchers who wish to test this theory. The basic variables are of the three types:

Independent variable	Moderating variable	Dependent variable
E.g., role ambiguity	E.g., structure	E.g., performance

The moderating variable works on the independent variable to affect the dependent variable; in our example, structuring by the leader reduces role ambiguity in order to increase performance.

Finally, what are the implications of path-goal theory for management practice? The first point for the practising manager to note is that the kind of leadership style needed varies according to the situation; in particular, that what is valid for supervisors is not necessarily valid for middle managers. The path-goal theory appears to reinforce the point that while shop floor personnel prefer human relations–oriented supervisors, middle managers and professionals work better with good human resources planning—even if a little angst is generated in the process.

In the immediate future, it seems reasonable to expect a great number of empirical research projects, both to replicate and to extend the path-goal theory of leadership. If the theory survives this kind of critical empirical examination, an important new point of departure in organizational behaviour will have been established which should have dramatic and useful consequences in terms of both management practice and training. On the latter point, if the path-goal theory is valid, we can expect a revolution in management training, with close and careful research to establish the effects of structure and consideration and to measure expectancies and utilities before a management team is actually trained. It does not seem unreasonable to believe that some academic entrepreneur will generate just such a package; for management training truly abhors a vacuum. And essentially at this time it is a vacuum, at least in terms of structure if not in terms of process.

But perhaps it is wise in closing this enthusiastic evaluation of the path-goal theory of leadership effectiveness to note that the model presented by House is a contingency model which has been validated by correlation tests in a cross-sectional survey research. This research strategy, as House

FIGURE 9–4
LEADERSHIP STYLES INTERACT

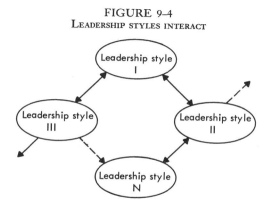

has pointed out, can rule out invalid hypotheses but cannot establish causal relationships among the variables. Finally, it is also wise not to expect too much from leadership research; for after all, the leader and his subordinates are trapped in the web of relations, activities, and beliefs that make up the structure, process, and values of an organization.

It does not seem unreasonable to believe that different leadership styles will be required for different occupational groups, depending on their function and level. It may well turn out that different groups who make up the environment of the target group to be studied may have a signif-icant effect on the leadership style revealed. Just as in Chapter 8 we pic-tured group members interacting along lines of attraction and repulsion, and pictured the various groups whose values impinge on a central group like the police, we can (as in Figure 9–4) suppose that the situational lead-ership styles in groups are an interacting set. In brief, what is needed is not only a contingency theory of leadership but also a contingency theory of organizations.

TOPIC 4
Identifying leadership potential

One of the most interesting and dramatic developments in executive selection has been the emergence of the assessment centre, where management—using T group technology—can "objectively" evaluate the aspiring executive's managerial potential. In the assessment centre, it is claimed, management can get an excellent gut feeling for whether a new man will fit, where, and how he ought to adapt to meet the challenge of organizational life as he steps up the career ladder.

So much for the official picture (based on the conventional wisdom of traditional industrial psychology) of the assessment centre. A quite different picture emerges when the assessment centre is seen as a presocialization device where candidates, under the rubric of scientific selection, are run through a set of behavioural routines which collectively constitute a scientifically selected sample of the behavioural repertoire that constitutes the executive role. The assessment process becomes a rehearsal of role learning, and the selectors and inventors of the assessment centre have devised a wonderful training exercise for themselves in the process. In the good old days in the military it was the TEWT—tactical exercise without troops. Now the assessment centre has become a TEWA—tactical exercise with assessees.

Disappointed not only with the low reliability and validity of the traditional interview but also with the lack of faith employees have shown in its fairness, companies are now exploring the assessment centre as a means of identifying management talent. About 20 major companies including the American Telephone and Telegraph Company, Sears Roebuck, J. C. Penney, National Cash Register, and the Cummins Engine Company have successfully used this technique for selecting promotables (see Box 9.4).

The assessment centre, which utilizes a relatively new situational technique for identifying management potential and determining individual development needs, requires bringing together assessees (usually candidates for supervisory positions) and assessors (usually line managers of actual supervisors). The assessees are required to work together on a series of specially selected exercises so that their executive potential can be evaluated.

GROUP SELECTION PROCEDURE

In Britain, group selection procedure was introduced early in World War II to choose candidates for officer training after the supply from the public schools (such as Eton and Harrow) had largely dried up. In essence the procedure required a group of candidates, usually about eight, to perform a variety of tasks together under observation by a panel which in-

4: A selection programme in harmony with line and staff

Douglas W. Bray, director of personnel research at the American Telephone and
egraph Company, directed an extensive and penetrating study into "the factors
ch determine the progress of young men in management," which has generated a
/ interesting personnel assessment programme. This procedure *aids* line super-
rs, who have the final responsibility for making promotions, by supplying them with
rmation which is usually difficult to obtain in the job setting. What follows is a brief
cription of the programme:

The men who are under consideration for a particular promotion are asked to par-
ate in the personnel assessment programme. If they agree, they are sent to the
sonnel Assessment Center, where they undergo extensive testing for 20 factors which
considered relevant to success in management. These factors include oral com-
ication skills, leadership skills, and scholastic aptitude. The measures on these
ors are obtained by the following tests and techniques:
aper and pencil tests which include "The School and College Ability Test," "The
ritical Thinking on Social Science Test," "The Abstract Reasoning Test," "The
ontemporary Affairs Test," and "The Organizing a Report Test."
roup performance tests which include "The Manufacturing Problem" (a group
iscussion of a business problem in a small enterprise), a leaderless group discus-
ion, and a case discussion of a union-management problem.
work situation test in the form of the "In-Basket Test."
n extensive interview.

he actual evaluation of the candidates is done by six supervisors who are at least
levels above the people who are being assessed (in order to eliminate conflict of
rest) and who have been trained in the various selection techniques prior to the
uation session. Each assessor first evaluates each candidate on the various man-
ment variables and then makes a final rating of each candidate's overall management
ntial. Once the decisions have been reached independently, the six assessors meet
discuss any divergent results. A summary of the ratings and the group discussion
assed on to the line supervisor.
his selection programme represents a welcome development, since it combines the
wledge and ability of both the line supervisors and the personnel men, who, in many
panies, tend to be foes rather than friends. Much further work is needed in this
to work out the optimal balance of tests, group exercises such as the leaderless
up, and interviewing techniques. Many of new techniques developed in T group labs
prove relevant both in terms of reliability and validity. The vital point is the need
urther experimentation.

N. Bray, "The Identification of Executive Ability," *Business Review*, May, 1967, pp. 140–47.

uded psychologists and a psychiatrist. The selection process usually
sted three days, during which time the candidates, to give the whole
ercise an atmosphere of anonymity and fairness, were clad in coveralls
d distinguished by number plates.

There are four elements in the selection process: (1) intelligence and
titude tests; (2) group exercises over an obstacle course in leaderless and
d groups; (3) group discussions, some with appointed leaders and others
ithout; and (4) interviews by a board of psychiatrists and other per-
nnel selection officers.

The introduction of this selection procedure, officially known as the War Office Selection Board (WOSB, or, more familiarly, WOSBie) led to an increase in applications for commissions and a reduction in the failure rate at officer training schools. A somewhat similar technique was used in the British Civil Service and called the CISBie. This process was known to candidates as the "country house" or "knife and fork" test. It is widely used in the civil service as a means of picking candidates for the administrative grade. Group selection has been extensively used in industry.

The American Office of Strategic Services (O.S.S.) began experimenting with group selection procedure in 1943, when it rented a 118-acre area outside Washington, installed its now legendary Area S, and began the process of selecting agents and saboteurs for wartime missions. While the success of the WOSBie and O.S.S. procedures was publicized after the war, it was not until the mid-1950s that industry began to experiment with the idea.

What happens in the assessment centre? In the presence of a group of trained assessors, the candidates go through an evaluating procedure consisting of six to eight "management games" which simulate real executive problems which the successful candidate will face when he is promoted. The tasks include in-basket exercises, discussions, and interviews.

THE PROCESS

The assessment centre process was rediscovered in the 1950s when management began to realize the futility of using batteries of selection tests or the traditional interview as a means of selecting supervisory and managerial personnel. In order to slow down the Peter principle, which insists that "a man is promoted to his own level of incompetence," something more effective in the selection context is needed. Perhaps the assessment centre is one of the answers, or at least part of the answer.

The process begins when top management—after being made aware of the company's need for effective managers and after being given the data on managers who have asked or had to be demoted and on the talented who quit because they couldn't wait for the system to discover them— decides it has a problem on its hands. This stage of "discovering the problem, its costs, and opportunities lost" by top management is the most important one in the whole exercise. Nothing can happen in any significant way unless top management is prepared to commit itself to recognizing and solving the problem.

DIMENSIONS OF THE ROLE

When the problem has been discovered, a group of managers (who should be two levels above the people occupying the posts to be filled get together and draw up a list of dimensions descriptive of the actual managers' job to be filled. The personnel specialist, either a company behavioural scientist or a consultant, takes the list and knocks it into shape by removing redundancies and consolidating categories. At the next meeting, our first group of managers (the bosses of the bosses of the role to be filled) get together with the next lower level of managers (the actual bosses of the role to be filled) and they all have a go at revising the dimensions of the role. One possible criticism of such lists—which typically include dimensions such as ability to communicate orally, capacity for planning, decision making ability, technical competence, and knowledge of company policies—is that they could be dug out of any good textbook on management. This criticism is offset by the fact that top and middle management have collectively and intuitively decided what they are looking for. An alternative and more scientific way to proceed is to collect critical incident data on the actual roles to be filled. This can be done by studying in a systematic way how these jobs are in fact being carried out in the company.

SELECTING THE EXERCISES

The next stage involves a variant of the critical incident technique in which the superordinate manager group decides what particular incidents, cases, or exercises will be used to measure performance on particular role dimensions. Typically, short cases and a major in-basket exercise are developed which are specific to the company milieu.

THE FUNCTION OF THE INTERVIEW

The function of the various interviews to be included in the assessment process is then reviewed. It is important here to ensure that the information which is already available on the candidate (such as personal data, work history, absence record, educational achievements) is not collected again. Rather, the interview should focus on such issues as: What is your most significant achievement to date? What areas of your potential managerial role need further development? What have been your significant executive learning experiences? What problems do you generate for those who have to work with you? How do you learn? What motivates you? How do you motivate others? What is your critical disability?

The problem now passes to the personnel administration people who have to develop the various cases, the vital in-basket exercise, the interview forms, and the rating scales for the various projects. Further careful administration is required in regard both to developing a timetable to cover the two to three days the candidates will be at the assessment centre and to working up sets of administrative instructions for candidates and assessors, to control the whole assessment process.

ACTION, DECISION, IMPLEMENTATION

The actual exercise begins when, say, 10 candidates and 5 assessors mee
at the assessment centre, which is typically located in a resort hotel wel
removed from the hurly-burly of business. In this monastic setting, lubri
cated by the bar in the evenings and sustained by four-star hotel meals
the two groups come to grips as the candidates get down to work on th
group problems. Shades of the T group—but a T group with a difference
for the participants are playing for real. When the candidates leave afte
their strenuous three days of playing managers on "almost the real thing,
the assessors stay behind for a further two days. Their job is to argue ou
who among the candidates is ready for what. Three decisions are possible

1. Candidate is ready for immediate appointment as a manager.
2. Candidate is not ready immediately, but will be ready within, say, on
   year, provided specific training or development is given.
3. Candidate is unsuitable for a management position.

Typically a third of the candidates are allocated to each category.

The next stage in the assessment process requires the bringing togethe
of the assessors (the bosses' bosses) and the actual superiors of the candi
dates to evolve an actual decision in each case. Finally the personnel ad
ministrator who has staged this whole assessment process organizes th
data, in regard to each candidate. Armed with this data, he has a "con
frontation meeting" with the candidate, informing him about the decisio
and the specific data on which it is based.

The whole process is invalidated unless the company is prepared to ac
on the decisions that emerge from the assessment centres, both by makin
the actual appointments and by providing the specific training and devel
opment that particular candidates need. Three further problems must b
addressed. The process must be made objective and realistic by designin
and redesigning exercises which in fact constitute a mini-variation of th
actual role to be filled. Secondly, the process must not only be operate
fairly but be seen to be operated fairly. A significant way of achievin
fairness is to allow failed candidates to go through the process again i
they so wish. Thirdly, some form of statistical control must be introduce
to measure the validity of the process and to reconcile the numbers of suc
cessful candidates with the company's needs, both present and future.

ARE THE ASSESSMENTS VALID?

"In brief—yes, they can be," is the opinion of William C. Byham, wh
has had considerable experience in running and researching assessmen
centres. Byham refers to a research carried out by Douglas Bray an
Richard Campbell at A.T.&T. in which the ratings of the new salesme
were withheld from their managers. Commenting on their findings (show

in Table 9–5), Byham noted, in "Assessment Centers for Spotting Future Managers":

All these men were subsequently hired as salesmen, and six months later their performance in the field was evaluated by trained observers who accompanied them on their calls. The results of both the original assessments and the performance review are shown in [Table 9–5]. This exhibit shows, for example, that of the 32 salesmen assessed as "acceptable" at the center, 19 were still judged "acceptable" when their field performance was reviewed.

In this study, the correlation between assessment ratings and performance is .51. Interestingly, when these men's performance in the field was compared with the ratings of the men made by their supervisors, no significant correlation emerged. Similarly, no significant cor-

TABLE 9–5
VALIDITY STUDY OF ASSESSMENT OF SALES REPRESENTATIVES

| Findings | Number of candidates | | |
	Original assessment	Field review	Validity of assessment
More than acceptable.	9	9	100%
Acceptable.	32	19	60
Less than acceptable	16	7	44
Unacceptable	21	2	10

Source. Douglas W. Bray and Richard J. Campbell, "Selection of Salesmen by Means of Assessment Center," *Journal of Applied Psychology,* Vol. 52, No. 1 (1968), p. 38.

relation was found between their field performance and the ratings given them by training personnel who worked with them in a sales training program.

One curiosity of the findings in Table 9–5 is that the validity of assessment (agreement between original assessment and field review) is 100 per cent for the top category and 10 per cent for the lower category, which offers the interesting possibility of controlling the effectiveness of such procedures by moving the cut-off line up. In this particular example, if the cut-off line were moved up so that only the "more than acceptable" were accepted, the process would be 100 per cent effective. Or would it? Figure 9–5 diagrams the cut-off points for the Bray-Campbell data in Table 9–5. Assuming just the figures given in that table, since 28 of the "accept" ratings proved valid, apparently 13 failed. Moving the cut-off line to the "more than acceptable" rating would be 100 per cent valid, but would locate and utilize only 9 of the potential managers in the field of 78. Moving it to the entire "accept" group would be 68 per cent valid and

FIGURE 9–5
CUT-OFF POINTS FOR DATA IN TABLE 9–5

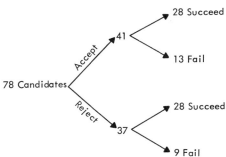

locate 28 talents. But, looking at the 37 "rejects," since only 9 in fact failed, apparently the same number (28) of "successes" would be lost by moving the cut-off line. It is apparent that simply moving the cut-off line is not "effective" for the overall purpose of locating and using all available talent. Research into the reasons for rejecting potential successes (as well as accepting potential failures) is necessary to improve genuine effectiveness.

It may well be that 51 per cent (or 68 per cent in the total "accept" group) validity for assessment procedures is better than would otherwise be achieved. In the same article, Byham notes:

> Reports have proved to be remarkably valid. Longitudinal studies of thousand of employees assessed over the last few years indicate that this assessment method is much more accurate than traditional appraisal procedures, and these seem to be the reasons:
>
> The exercises used are designed to bring out the specific skills and aptitudes needed in the position(s) for which a group of candidates is being assessed.
>
> Since the exercises are standardized, assessors evaluate the candidates under relatively constant conditions and thus are able to make valid comparative judgments.
>
> The assessors usually do not know the candidates personally; so, being emotionally disengaged, they are unbiased.
>
> The assessors are shielded from the many interruptions of normal working conditions and can pay full attention to the candidates' behavior in the exercises.
>
> The procedures focus their attention on the primary kinds of behavior they ought to observe in evaluating a promotion candidate.
>
> They have been trained to observe and evaluate these kinds of behavior.

P. E. Vernon and J. B. Parry have listed the main advantages of group selection as: (1) it presents a large sample of a candidate's behaviour on which to base an assessment; (2) it enables the selection staff to observe the candidates engaging in social interplay with one another; and (3) high in face validity, the assessment centre appears to applicants and employers to be a good test of the real thing, whether or not it is scientifically valid.

Vernon, who carried out research to determine the validity of the CISB, found a correlation of 0.5 to 0.6, which must be regarded as reasonably high when the difficulties of getting a reliable criterion of performance are considered.

H. J. Eysenck describes an experiment with the WOSB type of selection in which a batch of candidates was split at random. Twenty-three per cent of one-half of the batch were deemed successful by one board and 48 per cent of the other half successful by another board. It is extremely improbable that such a difference in the percentages of successes could result from chance distribution of the candidates; it is more likely that the different boards had different standards. Eysenck concluded from the results of researches in this field that the use of intelligence tests and objective personality tests was more discriminating than holistic methods, i.e., those calculated to assess total personality. Research evidence suggests that executives on selection boards find it difficult to differentiate between intellectual ability and social skill in the candidate. There is also evidence to suggest that the strength of this selection process is not necessarily its validity as a selection device.

In a British Institute of Management survey of selection methods in British industry publilshed in 1963, it was claimed that nearly one in five of the companies studied regularly used group selection methods. The technique was mainly used to select management trainees, salesmen, and graduates. This survey referred to one company where the selection process lasted more than two weeks.

To evaluate group selection, it is useful to start from the point that although the method may not be high in scientific validity, it *is* high in face validity. This stimulates recruitment. The fact that candidates think that this method is closely related to the real thing may suggest that the procedure has a training function. In the army many candidates learned at WOSBie the desirability of "showing initiative," "getting organized," "bashing on," and "being nonchalant at all times." Behaving this way helped them greatly to be a success in their role as officers. Again, many candidates regard group selection as a very tough exercise. Some aspiring executives see it as a kind of initiation rite which must be passed before joining the "big boys" in the executive club. The group selection procedure, therefore, derives much of its strength from its recruitment, training, and initiation functions. But evaluation also means looking at some of the issues still in need of research. For example:

1. Should the exercises relate to general management problems or problems particular to the company?
2. What attributes of management should be assessed—oral communication skill, planning, decision making, personal acceptability?
3. Who are the major beneficiaries? The candidates, who get an insight

into the nature of the job that lies ahead? The assessors, who get to know the "ins and outs" of their subordinates' roles? The personnel people, who get experience with a new training and selection technique?
4. Is the assessment centre the answer to the U.S. Supreme Court decision which stated that job requirements and testing must have a demonstrable relationship to job performance? In *Griggs* v. *Duke Power Company* the Court ruled, moreover, that the burden of proof for showing a connection between the screening process and the position is on the employer.
5. Can the assessment centres be kept honest? The reports are not meant to be "go or no-go" documents which decide the fate of the candidate forever in his company. But the reports are carefully filed.

THE BIG ISSUE: VALUES

The most telling issue in regard to assessment centres relates to the question of whether in fact their major function lies in their ability to act as a socialization agency which preconditions a man for his new role. This socialization function undoubtedly exists and is important. The critical issue is, Whose values are being assimilated?

Perhaps a useful lesson can be drawn from the British experience with the WOSB, which worked well in the war years but not so well after the war, when the military dropped both the psychologists and the psychiatrist from the boards. In the early 1950s, when the British government changed the conscription rules, it was discovered that if you drew a line from The Wash to the Bristol Channel, 90 per cent of the junior officers for the reserve units north of this line were living south of the line. And so began a national scandal.

What had happened was that the military had institutionalized a "scientific procedure" as an agency of maintaining the traditional class structure of British officers. Where, before, candidates who spoke like the Beatles had to learn a Southern English drawl before they could be commissioned, now, by moving the cut-off point, virtually only those who had been "born" with the accent (i.e., attended an English private school) were commissioned.

Much the same kind of phenomenon can be observed in executive selection for the British Foreign Service, the American State Department, the Marines, or the Guards—institutions in which high status is largely reserved for members of the establishment. A leavening of members of the "lower orders" is usually admitted to keep the social arithmetic right and to introduce some genuinely talented persons who overcompensate by working harder, being twice as brave, and so on.

All of the issues raised thus focus into a central issue: whether candidates are actually being fairly assessed on the basis of ability to fill particular roles (a difficult task in itself), or whether the assessment procedure is gummed up by extraneous considerations of class, skin color, sex, ethnic origin, physical handicaps (including age), and other organizational "values" hidden beneath the surface. Research to improve the structure and process first needs the clarifying question: What are the values that count here?

TOPIC 5
Strategies of organizational leadership

To facilitate the analysis of strategies of organizational leadership, it is useful to distinguish consideration of leadership as (1) an individual phenomenon, (2) a group manifestation, and (3) an organizational requirement.

AN INDIVIDUAL PHENOMENON

The first and most primitive approach to the problem of leadership is predicated on certain assumptions which are no longer relevant to the modern corporate environment. Nevertheless, they require restatement because so many executives still believe they are valid. The central proposition of the individual approach is the presumption that there is one leader and a number of followers. The leader is seen as a kind of charismatic figure who is virtually omnipotent, omniscient, and omnipresent. Thus leadership is seen as an exclusive property of an élite, a property that can be defined with a catalogue of traits. This naive and simplistic view is unsupported by any careful examination of the empirical evidence. Nevertheless, it continues to be a source of surprise (and occasional entertainment) that so many executives still accept the individual and trait approach as gospel—the view that there exists a particular leader who can walk on water and who can be recognized by the cut of his jib.

A GROUP MANIFESTATION

It is possible to get a more penetrating and realistic insight into leadership by studying it as a group manifestation. An essential prerequisite of the group approach is acceptance of the notion that leadership is the ability to influence others. The supreme virtue of this simple definition lies in the fact that within it the "follower" can influence the leader, perhaps by denying him the positive feedback he so earnestly craves. To get into the group approach to leadership presupposes a knowledge of group dynamics; so a very brief review here of our Chapter 8 discussion of the group's structure, process, and values is in order.

Group structure is the network of information flows that determines lines of authority, power, and influence, and is most obviously characterized by the presence of the task specialist, the human relations specialist, the eccentric, the exemplar, the scapegoat, the gate-keeper, the father figure, and other interacting leadership roles. A great deal is known about such roles, and experienced work groups can existentially accept various members' taking up the roles appropriate to their aspirations and life styles.

In terms of process, the group optic facilitates the understanding of the different stages groups go through in their growth. For example, we have discussed the process of clarification, evaluation, and decision as the phases through which a discussion group goes in trying to solve a problem. In Chapter 12, which treats the topics of authority and power, we shall go into the process of influence in considerable detail and deal with such matters as consensus formation and risk syndication within the zone of indifference of subordinates.

Values are also of critical importance in determining how groups operate. Perhaps it is sufficient to say at this time that obviously work groups develop values appropriate to their technology, structure, process, and goals, and to recall that the way different work groups interact can significantly affect the value systems of the groups concerned. For example, police work groups share some of the values of the criminal gangs that their role requires them to interact with. How else can the police communicate with and control the criminal, unless their value systems overlap? Thus, to understand leadership it is necessary to escape from a fixation with the primary working group and to look at how groups interact— which is the essence of the organizational approach.

Most of the research in leadership at the group level has concentrated on the two factors of initiating structure and consideration. The main finding to emerge from this research is that supervisors who are high in structure generate productivity (and the approval of their superiors) but also produce grievances and turnover (and the disapproval of their subordinates); and supervisors high in consideration keep the grievances and turnover low but fail to generate productivity. To get the best of both worlds, both productivity and subordinate satisfaction, requires supervision high in both initiating structure and consideration. But apparently not all research studies support this conclusion. Another research indication is that as you ascend a hierarchy, initiating structure is the vital factor. But apparently even this finding has to be taken with some reservation, for the factors of individual differences and the environment obviously affect such relations.

What's good about this type of research is that it allows the investigation of specific leadership factors, which can be measured with a considerable degree of rigour by questionnaire and related to factors like productivity and job satisfaction. What is bad about this kind of research is that researchers rarely make any effort to get into the actual group process. The issue is not whether a leader should exhibit initiating structure or consideration, but rather what particular blend of these factors each member of the work group in fact manifests. A group is made up of a mélange of the task specialist (high in structure), the human relations specialist (high in consideration), the eccentric, the exemplar, and so on. The problem in group leadership is to get the optimal mix of needed roles, and the goal is to help the members to live in an existential world where they can recognize the efficacies and tolerate the dysfunctions, not only of their own roles but of other roles as well.

At least the studies of group dynamics and leadership have gotten us away from the cosy view that democratic leadership is always to be preferred. Perhaps even more shattering is learning that effective leadership probably only accounts for a 15 per cent advantage in terms of productivity. The problem with the group approach is that when the matter of primary work group leadership has been settled, there still remains the whole issue of how one primary work group interacts with another. We are again led to the conclusion that close examination of intergroup matters is the essence of the organizational approach to leadership.

AN ORGANIZATIONAL REQUIREMENT

To pursue the discussion of leadership more effectively, it is useful to think of leadership as the capacity to manage the structure-process-value matrix, which has to be activated in mysterious ways to generate organizational effectiveness. To-day, a dramatic, new and different view of organizational leadership has emerged which draws its inspiration from the fields of information theory, psychology, and economics. In this particular optic, power, legality versus legitimacy, and information are the critical factors. Figure 9–6 draws together the key concepts of this chapter as they relate to organizational leadership and gives us an idea how they might constitute a systems model from this new viewpoint.

This dramatic new perspective gives crucial importance to power and is predicated on the notion that the leader can only be effective in so far as he has power. Power means that he commands not only scarce resources like secretarial support and computer time but also the logistics of information, path-goal utilities and valences, and influence in terms of task and role structuring. D. C. Pelz has produced abundant evidence to show that executives low on the organizational totem (lacking real power) reduce morale by handing out praise and approval. Power is a critical variable in Fiedler's contingency theory; but Fiedler fails to supply any kind (never mind a convincing kind) of picture of why one particular executive style is effective in one set of circumstances but not in another. This criticism in regard to lack of process information may be remedied in time, as House's path-goal theory of leadership generates more research on how executives structure the perceptions of subordinates in regard to payoffs and probabilities by playing around with task structure and other variables.

Some interesting research of this kind has been done by Tom Burns, who observed the necessity of managing the interaction of the cliques and cabals formed within an organization. According to Burns, a "clique" is likely to be formed of the older men in a firm who believe they have little chance for further promotion. It is a mutual defence system which gives

FIGURE 9–6
ORGANIZATIONAL LEADERSHIP AS A SYSTEM

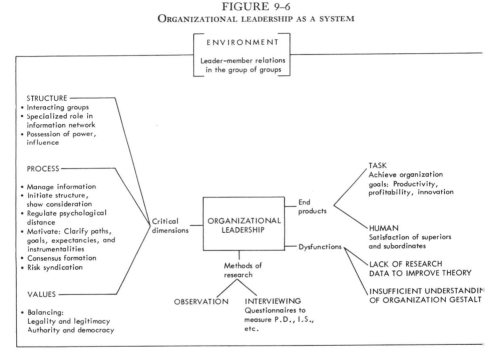

play to the comic role in ridiculing the firm's efforts. A "cabal" Burns describes as a group of upwardly mobile people who try to restructure the situation to suit their own interests. One ploy is "capturing" powerful organization members to support their group.

On the practicalities of leadership, both House and Fiedler fail to mobilize the interest of middle and top executives who feel that both theories are remote from the kinds of reality Burns describes. For the tycoon who begins each day by dipping his pen in his own blood and with a few sharp sentences settling the fate not only of his subordinates but also of governments and the valuations of national currencies, and for the aspiring neophytes at his heels, the conventional wisdom of academic behavioural science culled from management journals has scant relevance.

To the hard-pressed executive of modern times, matters of power are a continuous preoccupation best understood in the value conflict between legality (going by the book) and legitimacy (going by what's morally right). Perhaps the most brilliant insight into how legality and legitimacy interact has been provided by Wilfrid Brown, who came up with the four systems: legislative, executive, representative, and appeals. While Brown's Glacier Company laid these four systems out formally, all organizations evolve them either explicitly or implicitly.

A dramatic and highly documented case study of how failure to resolve the dilemma of legality versus legitimacy can blow an organization apart was revealed in the 1973 Watergate inquiry. While we shall deal with the matter of authority more fully in Chapter 12, it is perhaps sufficient to note at this time that the Constitution developed in the United States emerged as a reaction to the divine rights of kings which had been the lot of luckless Europeans. It regulated power in the checks-and-balances division among legislative, executive, and judicial functions. But in time, Congress allowed critical powers to fall into the hands of the President. Thus the wheel of power envisioned in the Constitution went off-centre, increasingly offering (through two or three decades) opportunities for illegitimacy to mask itself as legality.

What happened in the office of the President in the 1970s illustrates in a signal way how the three elements of organizational leadership (power, legality versus legitimacy, and information management) were exploited in a peculiar way which led to bizarre, baffling, and dysfunctional consequences. An administrative apparatus was created which duplicated many of the functions of the executive departments of government but which was the President's own thing. Organizational *real-politik* was played out in a new, dramatic way, where power was derived from controlling both the informational flow to and personal access to the President. The President, who read no "ordinary" newspapers and viewed no "ordinary" TV, received daily a "complete" synopsis of the news prepared by his staffers.

It was not for nothing that Nixon's aides in the White House, the so-called Orange County boys (most, like Nixon, were from California) were in large part men who had earned their spurs and livings as information massagers in advertising or public relations. They had grasped the ad-man fact that people live by perceptions of reality, not reality; and perceptions can be restructured by rearranging the perspective, the backdrop, or the sequencing of presentations without changing the central idea, person, or thing to be sold. They mastered the developing art of political image-selling—of a candidate, as in 1968; or of an incumbent officeholder, so that in 1972 the image of "the President" was the candidate rather than Mr. Nixon (the Committee to Reelect the President).

Information managing by the government in relation to the "sovereign" electorate, with attendant credibility gaps, had also been a long-term process now reaching dramatic new proportions. The control of information, its collection (legal and illegal), abbreviation, destruction ("deep-sixing"), recycling, dissemination, and denial (making original statements "inoperative") were more than ever critical managerial activities. The organization world had become a life of calculated leaks and power had become manifestly a matter of "arranging" to the utmost possible degree the perceptions of all the players so that illegitimate realities could be swept under rugs of legality.

What makes the whole thing so fascinating is that all organizations have some of the Watergate manifestations, although with wide variations in the number and degree. Everywhere lists of enemies are drawn up, patronage is dispensed, departments of dirty tricks are set up, counter-intelligence and sabotage are employed. Opponents are discredited—hopefully by their own hands. But there is hope—and there are broad lessons—in the fact that ultimately, the Watergate message massagers underestimated the power of the press to do investigative work and to "publish and be damned"; the dormant but not dead power of Congress and the courts to call to account the executive branch; and the lust of people for an insight into the dynamics of the power game. Nixon's apparatchiks failed ultimately because they did not understand the realities of organizational politics; they did not understand the concept of separation of powers; they did not understand the balance of power, privilege, and prudence and how the system of checks and balances must be managed; but above all they did not understand that single-virtue philosophies must always ultimately fail. (What the massagees learned about manipulation remains to be seen, but the lessons are there.)

What Watergate specifically underscored was that officials driven exclusively by upward loyalties and using mechanical problem-solving algorithms must always fail, for they cannot cope with the complexity of the modern corporate world. Executives are paid to use their initiative, which means they must accept prescriptions only when they are understood and can be fitted in within policies which are frequently at variance with the intention of the prescription. Thus, executives operate in an environment of the double bind, suffused with conflict and ambivalence. Experienced executives who realize that simple instructions taken literally can lead to disaster use what psychotherapists call paradoxical instruction. This ability to talk in two-sided messages or Rorschach ink blots demands a skill in paradoxical communication which most executives somehow intuitively learn.

INFORMATIONAL STRATEGIES OF LEADERSHIP

A major problem in organizational behaviour is to find the connective tissue that holds the different topics that we choose to study together. Leadership is an integrating topic whose consideration should help to pull together findings and concepts in the fields of authority and power, communications, and conflict, and perhaps reveal why different research strategies come up with different answers.

Leadership research enables us to pull together a number of disparate findings from different topics whose connection might not have been so obvious otherwise. For example, one odd finding to emerge from Tom Burns's self-recorded data on the behaviour of his departmental work group was the fact that frequently when the boss thought he was giving orders or instructions, his subordinates took it that they were being given advice.

The present author has been pursuing research in organizational development (O.D.) mainly with government executives in both the United States and Canada but also with corporate executives in Canada and

FIGURE 9-7
EXECUTIVE BIFOCALS

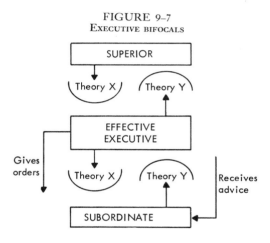

Britain. This research requires managers to describe their best boss, the problems they generate for other people, and their concepts of functional specialists and clients. An interesting model emerges, in which the subjects of the research seem to use bifocals with Theory Y lenses to look up to their bosses and Theory X lenses to look down on their subordinates (theory Y being, we recall, human relations–oriented and theory X task–oriented). As illustrated in Figure 9-7, this could account for Burns's order-advice perceptions. It also sheds light on Fiedler's finding that bosses' perceptions of subordinates had to do with differential establishment of psychological distance; while D. Katz and R. L. Kahn found that subordinates had differential perceptions of bosses in terms of democracy and participation. Executives seem to live in a schizophrenic world where superiors are seen as nonthreatening and most problems are generated by subordinates who are not quick enough to grasp what is required of them. In the O.D. model, the functional specialist is seen as giving advice which the executive is free to accept or reject.

Semantic alchemies that transform orders into advice are ultimately based on the strategy and tactics of information processing, which is essentially what the executive process is all about. As we will see in Chapter 12, in exercising such informational strategies as consensus formation and risk syndication, the executive finds himself increasingly cast in the role of resource person or consultant. His prime functions are to produce superior information and give professional judgements where information is limited; to act as the upward link to the rest of the system, and as such to fight for the biggest share of resources he can get; and, *in extremis*, to give a first opinion on "who's right" in conflicts in his group. To get him into this new role of resource person, new techniques in O.D. have been invented which utilize T group technology to unfreeze the executive's role structure, change it, and refreeze it in quite a different mould. Such psychic surgery is best carried out with teams of executives who represent a diagonal slice of their organization.

There is abundant evidence—from both rigorous experiments in group dynamics with communication nets and analysis of contemporary political events such as the Cuban missile crisis—to make it clear that searching for, processing, and disseminating information is a critical, if not the decisive, factor in organizational leadership. But information does not tell the whole story.

For example, careful and scrupulous examination of the Gulf of Tonkin incident—where it was alleged that North Vietnamese torpedo boats attacked American destroyers on routine patrol, which led to the escalation of the war and won over Congress to the side of the hawks—reveals that no American warship was hit and that no definite evidence of hostile fire was available. Yet President Johnson and his advisers responded to this incident with an escalation in the war from which there was no turning back. Why? Because they were evil men? Nonsense. They escalated because they wouldn't back off and leave themselves open to the charge of appeasing the communists as Britain had appeased Hitler in the 1930s; because they overestimated U.S. military power, particularly air power; because they thought in the last and worst military analysis it would end up like Korea; because they believed. . . . "Because they believed" propositions are to be found everywhere in organizational leadership, whether the object of the exercise is waging war, buying computers, or designing research projects.

Such value propositions cut right across the whole organizational scene determining what information is collected, how it is sorted, and the destinations to which it is sent. Knowing that values affect perceptions, a student of organizational behaviour should have no difficulty in understanding how credibility gaps develop; for as information moves up and down the organization, it passes through a whole series of filters. Figure 9–8 illustrates the difficulty top management would have in speaking unambiguously to all members of the organization. Instead information must travel (often in tortuous circuits rather than our simple diagram) through layers of trend setters and influential opinion formers; and each layer has its own value set and its "invisible college" of experts who contribute to the evaluation of intelligence.

In the light of the above analysis of information flows, it seems puerile to suggest that the leader "tell the whole truth and nothing but the truth." The leader's responsibility is to achieve the organization's goals (multiple and varying in priority); by the exercise of power (restructuring peoples' perceptions) through the collection of intelligence (loaded according to the values of the collector); leading to decisions (further corroded by the need to achieve consensus and risk syndication) which frequently have to be implemented by uncommitted disaffected dissidents. The process must, of course, produce superior performance that keeps the business in busi-

FIGURE 9–8

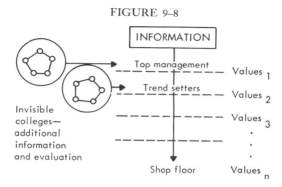

ness and puts a chicken in every pot and a second car in every driveway— and throws in a Christmas bonus.

The proposition that all would go well if organizational members were put on a truth serum is as inappropriate as having a plumber's model of the human body or believing that the earth is flat. Organizations have their own peculiar logic and can only be understood in terms of a set of propositions that are peculiar to organizations. And to get further into organizations, we turn in Chapter 10 to the subject of the organizational environment, which can be thought of as a flow of information.

REVIEW AND RESEARCH

1. Why has the trait approach to leadership failed? Why, then, do most managers still believe in the trait approach?

2. What are the leadership functions that have to be exercised in a work group?

3. What are the problems associated with making the informal group leader the appointed leader?

4. Define influence. Why does the boss whom subordinates can influence have considerable influence himself?

5. Reconcile the psychologically distant, task-oriented leadership of Fiedler with the employee-centred democratic leadership of Katz and Kahn.

6. List all the techniques you are familiar with for increasing psychological distance. Consider the following headings: exchange of salutations, spatial layout, access systems, methods of communication.

7. Describe Fiedler's contingency theory of leadership.

8. How does "Catch 22" work in a business setting?

9. Devise an experiment to test the path-goal theory of leadership.

10. Consider a restaurant where the highest priced meal costs $5, with seating accomodation for 50, and design a work team which sets out the rules, roles, and relations that govern the executive and the supervisory group.

11. Explain why initiating structure as a leadership strategy produces effectiveness and satisfaction for middle-level executives but ineffectiveness and dissatisfaction for shop floor workers. Try to tie in your answers with the expectations of (*a*) shop floor workers for human relations and (*b*) managers for good human resource planning.

12. Develop a contingency theory of leadership that integrates Fiedler's and House's work.

GLOSSARY OF TERMS

Assessment centre. A place in which candidates for leadership positions are gathered, tested, and evaluated in an attempt to prejudge their abilities and potential; the group selection procedure used is a presocialization device.

Consideration. The quality exhibited by a leader in showing respect for subordinates' ideas, concern for their feelings, concern for group rapport and communication, and all human relations (nontask) functions. The leader with high consideration is likely to satisfy his subordinates, less likely to satisfy superiors because he is not as concerned or productive in the task area.

Initiating structure. The quality exhibited by a leader in concentrating on task functions such as planning, scheduling, and production, principally by structuring his own role and those of subordinates toward goal attainment. The leader high in initiating structure is likely to satisfy his superiors, less likely to satisfy subordinates because he is impersonal and maintains his psychological distance from them.

Leader. A person who is willing or eager to accept publicly the responsibility for his own and other people's behaviour and attitudes; the person who has the most influence in a given situation.

Leadership. In a simple sense, the ability to influence others; in fact a complex social skill requiring flexibility and adaptability to varying circumstances. Reality-centred leadership is the ability to select the most appropriate pattern for organizational behaviour at any given time in any existential situation.

Leadership style. The stamp of the leader's personality on his relationships with followers in group interactions, particularly in terms of role expectancies.

Leader-member relations. Interactions of group members, especially the extent to which the leader enjoys the confidence and loyalty of followers and is regarded as personally attractive (usually measured by a sociometric index).

Least preferred co-worker (L.P.C.) score. A measure used by Fiedler to predict and evaluate leadership style, employing bipolar trait ratings of the subject's co-workers; the rating gives some indication of leaders' cognitive complexity and task orientation, but its usefulness and validity remain unclear.

Path-goal leadership theory. The theory developed by Robert House incorporating Victor Vroom's path-goal model of man. The leader uses the concepts of expectancies and instrumentality in motivating followers by clarifying the paths to rewards, structuring roles to avoid ambiguity, reducing road-blocks in the way of goal achievement, helping associates relate their positive valences and needs to organization goals, and in general both making clear the paths which are needed and making the paths easier and more attractive to follow.

Position power. The power inherent in the leader's position, including such traditional manifestations as official authority, ability to reward and punish, and so on; more importantly, his ability to manage and control information flows and to structure role, path-goal, and task perceptions.

Psychological distance. The manner in which the executive varies his relationships with others in order to keep task and role functions predominant in dealing with subordinates and to achieve considerable freedom from his superiors. The psychologically distant manager sees himself as a professional administrator, in contrast to the psychologically close manager who gives prime importance to human relationships and close informal group interactions.

Sociometry. The study of the dynamic interrelationships of individuals within a social group. Sociometric tests, which are essentially action tests, measure the feelings individauls have towards others in the group; to be effective, the criteria of the test must have explicit meaning for the individual and offer him specific opportunities to give information which can be of help in restructuring his social situation.

Task structure. The manner in which organization tasks are defined by leaders to their subordinates, in which it is important that decisions are verifiable (and supported by higher echelons), requirements for reaching goals are made clear, possible goal paths (procedures) are outlined, and solutions specificity (whether there can be only one or many correct solutions) is defined.

Trait. An individual characteristic or adjectival description of personality such as "authoritarian," "persuasive," "aggressive," etc. The approach of assessing potential leaders by such (usually intuitive) descriptions has little empirical support but is still used by many "seat of the pants" managers.

10

The organization
and its environment

We are now about to embark on an escalation in our study of organizational behaviour from which there is no way back, and the road forward is not at all clear. We have looked at the individual, hopefully grasped something of the complexities of personality, and puzzled over the mysteries of VIE (valence-instrumentality-expectancy) theory. We have tried to get our heads clear on the primary working group, that web of structure, process, and values that is a microcosm on its own. But our study of leadership made it clear that there are worlds of groups outside the primary working group and that the way the intra- and intergroup *realpolitik* is managed is the essence of the organizational approach to leadership.

Now all of these escalations, from the individual to the primary working group and from the group to the organization as a group of groups, serve mainly as stepping stones for the final escalation. To take this last step, it is necessary to accept that there is something outside the organization called the environment; that the organization and the environment interact; and that the environment is made up of other organizations.

Now we know a good deal about how organizations work in terms of the management of groups as cliques, cabals, and coalitions. We know how they work by rules of satisficing—taking just a little more than they need, enough to keep stockholders and boards of directors happy, but not the maximum which would bring down the wrath of the government and consumers. We know how side payments are arranged for the groups that lose out ("you never know you might need them again"). We know something (not as much as we would like) about how internecine strife is regulated. But what is rather unclear is how the organization manages its environment. To get into this subject, let's look at the economic environment.

What role do profits play? Traditional economic theory has it that profits are the carrots that induce entrepreneurs to endure uncertainty and engage in dynamic innovation—new products, new marketing concepts, and new technology. Tradition also says that competition should keep corporate giants like International Business Machines, Xerox, and General Motors from monopolizing the market. But the modern approach, as expounded by J. K. Galbraith, sees economics as a branch of politics—the "dismal science" is nothing less than the study of corporate *real-politik*. The great corporations develop their own peculiar purposes, which they impose on lesser corporations. But being too successful in terms of profitability, share of the market, and return on investment can be extremely dangerous. Most large American corporations have learned this lesson and have shown a strong desire for the monopolist's or oligopolist's "quiet life." Not IBM; and a short case study of its environmental interactions is a good scene-setter for this chapter.

IBM AND THE WORLD

International Business Machines is an organization whose environment is literally the world. The $9.5 billion per year operations of this corporate giant make it easily the biggest company in the computer business, and one of the biggest in any kind of business. Even its detractors admit that IBM has been the major force in the invention, development, and promotion of information processing. But it is not primarily its technological excellence (excellent as that may be) that IBM is noted for; its marketing genius has made it what it is and also mobilized and armed its critics. IBM approaches information processing not as an equipment-and-parts business but as a complex total systems business that locks the supplier (IBM) and the customer together. IBM is the consultant providing solutions to corporate problems, with the customer as client.

In 1973 IBM was involved in seven antitrust actions, four of which it considered major. The company was being challenged by the U.S. government, Control Data Corporation, and Telex Corporation, among others. The government has alleged that IBM has monopolized the general-purpose computer market by combining the prices of hardware, software, and support services; by arranging prices of new computers at unusually low levels of profit; by "announcing new models" to ruin the competition (knowing it could not deliver on the announced schedule); and by granting discriminatory price discounts to educational institutions. The question is, How big is too big? and the issue is whether IBM should be broken up.

An interesting part of the environmental interplay, because of its David versus Goliath aspects, has been Telex Corporation's antitrust action against IBM. The original court decision in 1973 ruled that IBM pay Telex $325.5 million in damages, enjoined specific marketing and pricing practices, and instructed IBM to release to competitors information on certain products. While the litigation was far from over (unlike old soldiers, industrial titans do not quietly or easily fade away), it was striking that Telex, a small Tulsa-based manufacturer of peripheral equipment, mounted as successful a challenge as it did of perhaps the most successful corporate enterprise the world has ever seen. One of the major consequences of the 1973 decision was that capital will almost certainly begin to flow to the smaller efficient computer companies, mainly because IBM's ability to dominate the plug-compatible peripherals market has been challenged. What was established in this case was that monopoly power is the economic ability to charge unreasonable prices and to exclude competition.

In reaching this decision, Judge A. Christensen reviewed the records of IBM's management committee, which, in February 1970, designated peripherals as a "key corporate strategic issue." At a meeting of the management review committee in April, 1971, IBM's chief executive, T. J. Watson, Jr., formulated IBM's basic policy on peripherals, which required the company to swallow whatever financial pills it had to in the short term in order to insure growth in the long run. To achieve this, IBM set up a management group it called a "blue ribbon task force" to deal with the plug-compatible competition. Judge Christensen found that IBM had engaged in "sophisticated, refined, highly organized, and methodically processed" efforts to force Telex out of the peripherals market.

It should be noted that the court found that Telex, for its part, was far from blameless. Adjustments of the original decision and further litigation were based on countercharges that Telex had hired away IBM employees with a specific view to obtaining IBM technical and trade secrets, and had been able to achieve lower prices by copying IBM designs as closely as possible. Which points up the fact that environmental interchanges are seldom simple fables of Davids and Goliaths, or good guys and bad guys.

IBM faces pressures abroad as well as at home. In Europe, IBM has some 60 per cent of a multibillion-dollar market, and the European computer firms (who sometimes call themselves "the Seven Dwarfs") see IBM as a Snow White who has run off with the handsome prince—in this case, this large market. Now the Seven Dwarfs are forming coalitions, if not to worry Snow White to death, at least to trim her figure. West Germany's Siemens and France's Compagnie Internationale pour L'Informatique (CII) are organizing together to market a unified line of computers that will be compatible with IBM equipment. Likewise Britain's International Computers Ltd. and Germany's AEG–Telefunken and Nixdorf Computer companies (all make equipment incompatible with IBM's) are getting together. And, of course, the European Economic Community and the various European governments are pushing such coalitions very hard.

All of which brings us to the gist of the matter. We have said earlier, and can well repeat in introducing this chapter: organizations are open systems which trade with their environments—importing materials, energy, information, and people; transforming them; and exporting them into the environment with value added. But unless we can relate such a statement to the tough, complex realities; unless we can get a handle on the environmental forces—political, economic, legal, technological, and ecological—that impinge on an organization; then something vital will have been left out of our analysis.

THE CHARACTERISTICS OF THE ENVIRONMENT

A major theoretical exercise—at the moment a somewhat baffling one —in organizational behaviour is to find a category system to define the characteristics of the environment. It is usual to begin this analysis by differentiating between the internal and external environments, as shown in Figure 10–1. The internal environment is the organization's programming,

FIGURE 10–1
THE ORGANIZATION'S INTERNAL AND EXTERNAL ENVIRONMENTS

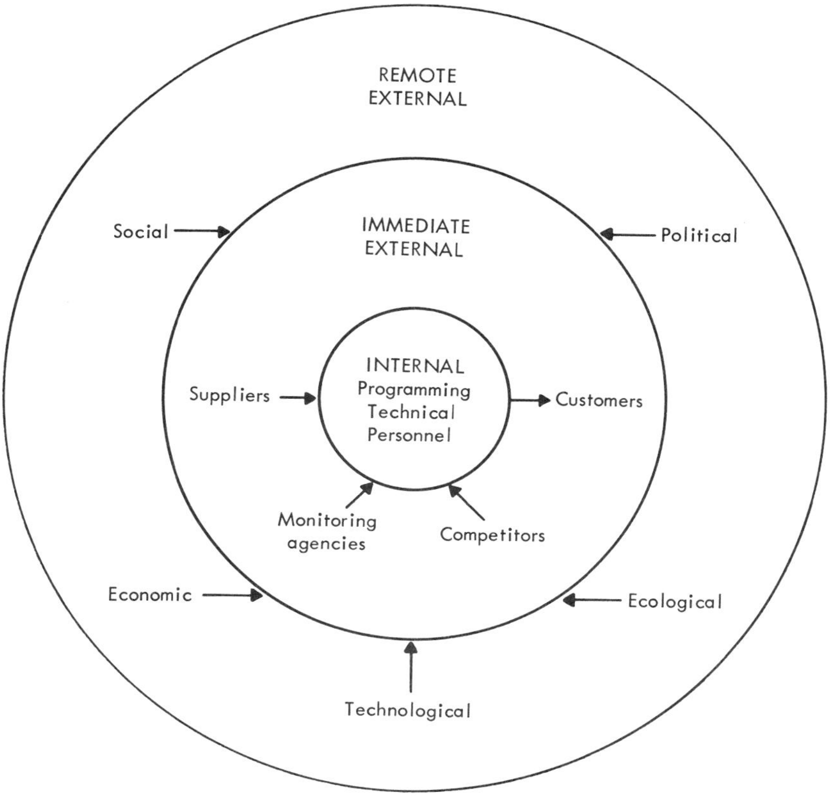

technical, and personnel forces affecting decision making. The external environment has two elements, the immediate and the remote. The immediate element consists of forces arising from interactions with customers, suppliers (material, equipment, cash, capital, energy, people, and information), competitors, and monitoring agencies (trade unions, professional associations, trade associations, consumer groups, political and religious groups, government agencies, the Mafia, and so on). The remote, which may be the more important, consists of the social, economic, political, technological, and ecological forces that affect or may affect the organization.

The difficulty of categorizing the remote external component can be illuminated by considering the North American automobile industry. This industry in the 1970s is trying to meet competition from foreign-manufactured small cars built with less expensive labour, while at the same time coming under pressure from government regulations requiring higher standards on both exhaust emission controls and safety devices for new cars. To add uncertainty to uncertainty, these external forces are hitting the companies at a time when their work forces are absorbing the hippie-existential culture (which is not only "out-a-sight" but has its origins out of site), causing internal pressures of no small dimensions.

From a technical point of view, the environment is best considered as an information flow. The management of the environment is essentially the management of information: searching for factors, weighing them, allocating probabilities, preparing contingency plans. For example, Paul Lawrence and J. W. Lorsch, whose theory is described in Topic 2, deal with organizational uncertainty by identifying three information components:

1. Lack of clarity of information.
2. The long time span of definitive feedback.
3. The general uncertainty of causal relations.

The virtues of their analysis become immediately obvious when applied to decision making in the auto industry, when a comparison is made between how uncomfortably structured this industrial environment was in the late 1960s and the relative comfort it enjoyed in 1972 when it had been brought under at least a measure of control (both by lobbying with the government and by coming up with technological advances in emission control and vehicle safety).

How do executives perceive the uncertainty of the environment? Robert B. Duncan, in "Characteristics of Organizational Environments and Perceived Environmental Uncertainty," provides one answer:

> Although there was difficulty in the preliminary research in getting respondents to verbalize their views of uncertainty, there was a remarkable degree of similarity in the way in which the concept was ultimately defined. Three components of uncertainty were mentioned by some or all of the eighteen individuals who gave a definition: (1) the

lack of information regarding the environmental factors associated with a given decision-making situation, (2) not knowing the outcome of a specific decision in terms of how much the organization would lose if the decision were incorrect, and (3) inability to assign probabilities with any degree of confidence with regard to how environmental factors are going to affect the success or failure of the decision unit in performing its function.

STRUCTURE OF CHAPTER 10

The first topic in this chapter, the organization and its economic environment, sets out to examine the general economic and technological environment of the firm and how this interaction affects investment, long-range planning, managerial values, and organizational structure.

Topic 2, on the environment as a flow of information, begins by considering the Lawrence and Lorsch contingency theory of organization, where environmental uncertainty is the major independent variable. Their empirical evidence, which is based on the study of 10 firms in three different industries, is reviewed. We then turn to consider the causal texture of the organizational environment as proposed by F. E. Emery and E. L. Trist, who have identified four different kinds of environment ranging from the placid to the turbulent. The question is posed as to how firms cope with the uncertainties of a turbulent environment. To try to answer this question, a number of strategies are briefly reviewed, including co-operation (legal and illegal) and co-optation.

Topic 3 takes a quick look at organizational climate, or how managers perceive the environment. The elements of environment modeled as a system are discussed. Finally, to come to grips with organizational Gestalt, Rensis Likert's four systems provide an interesting view of the climate.

TOPIC 1
The economic environment

While other economic systems (socialist and communist) may be of interest, for North Americans the economic environment is the modified capitalism which has developed and evolved on our continent. This topic considers, first, this environment in terms of its structure, process, and value elements; and second, the kinds of firms that exist in and interact with it.

THE ENVIRONMENT

The outstanding paradox in the Western economic environment is the failure of success which the capitalist system has illustrated in producing growth, but only at a tremendous price. As John Kenneth Galbraith pointed out in *The Affluent Society*, it was growth via production for private affluence that brought public squalor. Too many cars, too much tobacco, too much dog food, too much booze, too much steak, too much deodorant; and not enough fresh air, fresh water, health care, decent housing, and safe streets. How did it all come about? According to Galbraith, such undesirable consequences arise directly from the fact that the corporate oligarchs who run both private and public bureaucracies are now the decisive game players in the economic and political life of a nation. The technostructure, to use Galbraith's name for the corporate oligarch, runs its organizations neither in obedience to the market nor in response to social need, but in accordance with the rules of bureaucratic politics. For the lawyers, accountants, advertising men, economists, and engineers who are members of the technostructure, their primary loyalty is to their team; and what's good for their team may not necessarily be good for the country. To pursue this question further—how the parochial interests of the technostructure took precedence over the interests of most North Americans (more so in Canada than in the United States, because of the branch plant economy mentality)—it is necessary to examine the changes in the structure of the economy, its processes, and the values by which it is governed.

STRUCTURE

The structure of the American economy consists of a relatively small number of extremely large organizations and a very large number of extremely small ones. The large firms account for a disproportionate share of employment, output, and investment; in many industries one or a few large firms completely dominate. In 1968, the 200 biggest held 60 per cent of manufacturing assets, which is up from 45 per cent at the end of World War II. The "Manhattan argument" (named after the Manhattan Project, which brought us the atomic bomb on order at short notice) for the big corporation was that the imperatives of technology required organizations big and powerful enough to plan the future, to control suppliers, and to create and manipulate markets. The argument was that, dangerous as it may be, the large corporation is a *sine qua non* of modern life.

But no longer are economists like Galbraith prepared to accept this argument, which leaves large corporations free to prey on the public. The extraordinary advantages enjoyed by the mature corporations through their control over technology, finance, markets, and men's minds enables them to function like modern Greek city-states who can defy governments at their whim. Usually, in fact, the mature corporation operates through influence in government rather than directly through the marketplace. The point is that mature corporations function like governments. To understand this last point better, it is necessary to look further into the subject of economics.

Economics comes in two sizes, macro and micro. Macro economics is all about national income, investment, savings, and interest rate changes, and it should be able to make predictions about the size of the gross national product and its component elements. As often as not such predictions are seriously in error. Why? Because micro-economics, which is mainly about how firms fix prices and make a buck, has little to do with the dismal science of economics but everything to do with politics and the psychology of power.

As Adam Smith, the economist for all seasons, pointed out in 1776 in his *Wealth of Nations*: "People of the same trade seldom meet together, even for merriment and diversion, but the conversation ends in a conspiracy against the public, or in some contrivance to raise prices." Galbraith has carried Adam Smith's line of argument into modern times to show how planning of prices, production, and preferences is built into the mature corporation's psyche, forcing it into illicit relations with all sorts of strange economic bedfellows.

Galbraith has shrewdly demonstrated in *Economics and the Public Purpose* how the top executives of the great corporations develop their own particular purposes which they impress on others; and predictably, production for private affluence has brought not only public squalor but produced a ruination of classical macro-economic theory in the process.

Thirty years ago Harvard economist Joseph A. Schumpeter pronounced large firms to be more innovative than small firms. Professor Schumpeter argued that profits are the juices behind the corporate process of dynamic innovation, and that some degree of monopoly was an inevitable consequence of modern technology and mass production. But John M. Blair's *Economic Concentration*, based on his scholarly study of non-competition in United States extracted from 44 volumes of Senate Anti-Trust Subcommittee hearings, argues against the simplistic notion that the large-scale enterprise is more efficient and more innovative. As often as not, large corporations seem to have a positive genius for killing innovation. The motives behind this stifling of invention can be better understood through the study of corporate *real-politik*, which is what micro-economics is concerned with.

Corporate officials are concerned with one thing only—the success of corporate officials. Their potential enemies include stockholders, regulatory commissions, tax collectors, creditors, labour unions, and customers. Given such a formidable list of enemies, corporate officials don't try to maximize profits but merely satisfice—provide something (not too much) for everybody, just enough to keep stockholders and directors happy without bringing down the wrath of the regulatory agencies, consumer groups, or business competition upon them. Corporate officials have a passion for secrecy and make a gigantic effort to protect their books and bailiwicks from the prying eyes of outsiders (a category which includes the firm's "owners," the stockholders). For corporate executives know that controlling information is the key to exercising power.

The primary affirmative purpose of the technostructure, following Galbraith, is the growth of the firm. In fact, growth is the *sine qua non* of capitalism. This hunger for growth has produced an accumulation of power whereby a few hundred firms exploit the world's economy for their own purposes. Large multinational firms such as IBM, Exxon, Fiat, Caterpiller Tractor, Imperial Chemical Industry, and the like, produce about $450 billion of the gross world product (estimated at $3 trillion); are growing at the rate of 10 per cent a year; and threaten the whole idea of the nation-state. The net result of all this economic concentration and consequent noncompetition is to make a mockery of macro economics which follows the conventional wisdom of believing that the customer is sovereign and that the corporation is subject to the state. For example, on the last point, as a firm saturates a market or comes under restrictive legislation, it broadens its horizons and seeks new markets in other countries.

The mature corporations which, to use Galbraith's phrase, "completed the euthanasia of stockholder power" are very difficult for governments and economists to deal with because they can plan and operate on a global scale which has undercut the U.S. (and destroyed the British) government's ability to control fiscal events.

The growth of the technostructure has had important implications for the economic system. A. A. Berle notes that "the capital is there and so is capitalism. The waning figure is the capitalist." The well-documented separation of ownership and management in many large corporations has led to the development of motivations which are quite different from those of the entrepreneur. These will be discussed below.

PROCESS

Classical economics emphasized the manner in which competition allocated resources in an objective and efficient manner. Free enterprise has been a mainstay of our social and economic thought, and much political and economic exhortation has been delivered against any interference with free competition. However, unfettered competition led to such violent fluctuations in business activity that the ability of the firm to carry out technological development was seriously impaired, as was the reputation of the capitalist system. This has led to an acceptance of planning as a valid alternative to the free play of short-term market forces. Shonfield outlines how macro-economic planning is carried out in different countries with varying levels of government participation and influence. Although in the United States, government planning is still not consciously accepted, its development and the development of private corporate planning has reached a very high stage. It is curious—and unfortunate—that this fact has largely escaped general notice, so that a great deal of rhetoric is still couched in archaic "free enterprise" terms. The economic literacy of vast numbers of Americans remains at the "lemonade-stand" level in the midst of space-age technology.

Galbraith describes the main function of planning as the replacement of unreliable market forces. This can involve vertical integration to assure supply of customers, control over the market by virtue of relative size, long-term contracts, and the use of advertising and marketing policies to ensure suitable levels of demand. Essential to this approach is the use of a pricing policy which, unlike classical ones, is not concerned with profit maximization but with long-term stability and growth. A.D. Kaplan and others lend support to the theory that pricing is based more on a firm's cost structure and production goals than on market forces. Prices should be low enough to attract new customers but high enough to generate reasonable profits. Stability, discouragement of competitors, and social acceptability are also important factors. While it is true that the market is an information system registering customers' tastes and ability to spend, it is also an open system into which the firm can make inputs that will significantly affect the outcomes.

The existence of substantial depreciation allowances has provided companies with most of the funds required for new investment. This has facilitated the orderly arrangement of new facilities, but has supplanted the classical market considerations of alternative rates of return as factors in the financing of new business. In short, it can be said that the prime factors in economic life—prices, rates of technological change, and rates of capital investment—have become institutionally determined by the corporate technostructure.

The substantial costs and risks involved in new technology provide a strong incentive for attempting to get government support in the form of subsidies or guaranteed markets. J.-J. Servan-Schreiber notes (with envy) the substantial U.S. government aid provided to the aerospace, atomic energy, electronics, automotive, and chemical industries. Since a large part of consumer demand is now centered on goods other than those required to sustain life, there is considerable potential instability in consumer spending volume. This has been reduced by a growing proportion of government consumption which provides a stable base of activity.

The state also provides the education system, which dutifully produces the trained manpower needed by the modern corporation. Galbraith emphasizes that the apparent antipathy between business and government is based on outmoded concepts inherited from another era. It is obvious that it has little real effect.

VALUES

The separation of ownership and management has led to significant changes in the motives of business leaders. The drive for maximum profits has diminished as salary payment has become the major means of compensating management. The relative affluence enjoyed by most workers has to some extent reduced the significance of pay as a motivation for work; and, as the level of sophistication of the technostructure has increased and the variety of job opportunities has gone up, the effectiveness of compulsion as a motivating force has diminished.

The corporation has ceased to be the rapacious exploiter of both its employees and the public that it had previously been considered to be. On the other hand, we have only begun to assess the "prices" that both corporate growth and affluent consumption have exacted in ecological pollution, dwindling natural resources, and similar areas. The current interest in subjects like overpopulation signals at least an examination of values such as "growth is always good"; and the gathering clouds of "energy crises" indicate that our economic values may have to change from those of children turned loose in the candy store.

The technostructure has diffused power and lent new importance to the utilization of each individual's abilities. This has required adaptation of corporate goals to identify with those of its individual members as well as that of society in general. The concern for efficiency has made it an article of faith to permit the expert to do his job with a minimum of interference. In Servan-Schreiber's words, "this wager on man is the origin of America's new dynamism." He contrasts the American willingness to trust human nature with the French fear of delegation and remarks on the debilitating effect on economic effort of his country's centralized controls.

The desire of managers in the technostructure to do their jobs to the best of their ability without interference affects the economic goals which are set. Stable and growing profits are sought to avoid confrontations with shareholders, while restraint in pricing is practised to avoid public conflict and the threat of government interference.

THE FIRM

Our discussion of the economic environment has suggested that changing technology and structure has increased the need for most business firms to operate as open systems, interacting with their environment and modifying their strategies and structure to fit particular needs. We have also described the tendency of the managerial technostructure to plan for an orderly growth of the organization. A brief outline of how this is done by firms in different circumstances would now be useful.

James Thompson has identified three types of technology:

1. *Long-link*—involving a series of interdependent actions, as in an auto assembly line.
2. *Mediating*—linking of clients who wish to become interdependent, like the savers and borrowers in a bank.
3. *Intensive*—selection, combination, and application of techniques based on feedback from the object itself; for example, a hospital.

Each of these types of organization will try to reduce the uncertainty in its environment by different means. Firms with a long-link technology will attempt vertical integration to ensure that the supplies and markets required by the core technology are available. Steel mills, aluminum companies, and auto makers offer examples of this type of activity.

A good example of vertical integration is provided in a study of the petroleum industry in the United States, which is dominated by 18 large firms (the "majors") which produce about 70 per cent of the domestic crude oil, control some 80 per cent of the refinery capacity, and market about 72 per cent of the gasoline sold in the United States. Vertical integration, which is standard for the "majors," means that the company operates in every phase of the business, including exploration and production, transportation, refining, distribution, and marketing. Not content with the gigantic advantage of vertical integration, most of the majors work hand in glove with each other—where one is marginal in one function (say refining crude) or one area, another major will carry the function for a favour elsewhere. The fuel shortage beginning in late 1973 may well have been engineered by the majors before the Arab countries got into the act. The suspicion of the Federal Trade Commission is that some of the majors did conspire to maintain and reinforce a noncompetitive market structure in the refining of crude oil into petroleum products.

Thompson notes that there are limits to integration based on the extent to which the factors surrounding the main mission fan out. The producer of a widely used raw material (such as steel or many basic chemicals) cannot capture a significant part of the market and put it under its control. The use of long-term sales contracts is a method for dealing with such uncertainties.

Firms with a mediating technology try to reduce uncertainty by increasing the population which they serve. The enormous growth in chain stores and bank branches indicates the widespread desire of the competing firms to ensure that they will not run into difficulties by being overly dependent on one section of the market.

McDonald's, a good example of mediating technology, has shown the way forward in market penetration in the fast-food industry. Using a computerized, standardized, premeasured, superclean operation, McDonald's has turned the hamburger business into a cybernetic food-eating dream. A major feature of the McDonald idea is the use of franchises which require the franchise holders to attend McDonald's "Hamburger University" in Illinois. The game of doing it the McDonald way only begins at this university. After graduating, the franchise holder's performance in everything from the cleanliness of the floors to the quality of the hamburgers and the temperature of the frying fat is relentlessly watched by roving inspectors. Given its scale of operations (with sales of $1.03 billion in 1973); rate of expansion (adding one new store every day to the existing 2,500), and tidy financial, training, and merchandizing routine, McDonald's has enough clout through mass buying power to line up steady supplies at stable prices (it purchases 1 per cent of all U.S. wholesale beef). Thus is the environment controlled for McDonald's. McDonald gives a virtual license to print money to its franchise holders, who are required to "do it the McDonald way." Many apply; economies of scale become possible; and soon the environment is munificent.

Firms with intensive technology will try to incorporate the object worked on into their domain. Perhaps the most typical example of this is the "military-industrial complex" in the United States, where the lines between supplier and customer become very blurred. A high level of uncertainty was introduced into the environment of Boeing and General Dynamics by the decision of Robert McNamara to reinstitute open competition for a new fighter plane contract. The ability of Lockheed to incorporate national prestige and welfare into its own business aims enabled it to obtain the support required to survive after the bankruptcy of Rolls Royce (although it proved a near thing and aroused much controversy).

Companies also try to reduce uncertainty by less legitimate means. The great scandal over collusion in the electrical industry served to indicate that certain methods of market control are not acceptable even if they do not result in higher mark-ups than are achieved in other, less unruly, competitive environments, by quieter methods.

Growth and diversification are also fostered for reasons other than protection for the core technology. First, they provide financial strength to withstand unexpected problems and stabilize earnings by increasing the range of markets served. Second, they provide an outlet for increases in capacity or technological capability resulting from changes in the environment for the firm's basic activity. A. D. Chandler describes how the growth of DuPont into a chemical giant was to a considerable extent the result of a desire to use surplus plant capacity or to apply research discoveries made in an unrelated field.

The growth of business enterprise and the increasing variety of activities undertaken by some firms has increased interest in the study of appropriate organizational structures.

Companies with highly interdependent parts operating unified technologies will find the centralized organization structure to be most appropriate. Vertical integration leads to units whose operations are different in many respects but touch at those points where the outputs of one unit become the inputs of the other. Such firms can decentralize management, but each unit must adhere carefully to plan which integrates all of the input-output variables. Those companies whose technologies are highly diversified and independent of each other have a problem maintaining a valid basis of organizational control, which accounts for some waning in the enthusiasm for conglomerates. It is obvious that central management in such firms cannot assume the passive role thrust upon most shareholders to-day, since the rationale for the existence of the organization would then be more questionable. The development of task teams of specialists to provide expertise to the different parts of the organization may be a way of utilizing the resources of the larger organization.

The growing complexity of the organization structure, the need for frequent interaction with many levels of the environment, the continuous need for technical innovation, and the sophistication and high educational level of the technostructure are creating a need for administrative procedures that are different from the old standardized bureaucracy. Information—its collection, processing, distribution, and suppression—lies behind these new procedures and is becoming a critically important aspect of the successful operation of business organizations.

TOPIC 2
The environment as a flow of information

All organizations are open to environmental influences, though obviously some are more open than others. And, of course, some degree of closedness in terms of boundary maintenance (usually maintained by gate-keepers, who are agents of the system's power structure) is necessary to maintain the system's identity. While early theorists treated organizations as closed systems, where the prime problem was the transformation of inputs into outputs, the modern approach is to treat the organization as an open system which interacts with its environment. An excellent example of the modern approach is the Lawrence and Lorsch contingency theory of organization, in which environmental uncertainty is the major independent variable.

The open systems theorist conceptualizes the environment in informational terms and sees the environment as a source of both threats and opportunities arising from the interactions of other organizations. This interconnectedness is what Emery and Trist call the "causal texture of organizational environment," which almost invariably turns out to be enormously complex. To bring some good order and discipline into the organization's environment, it is necessary to treat the environment as a flow of information; and since the environment contains a surfeit of information, the organization's objective is to search for, collect, process, and disseminate only as much of it as it needs to maintain its viability.

The organization as a system, with the information-processing subsystems we have already described, operates in such a manner as to keep itself informed at the right cost, on time. Organizations, of necessity, evoke elaborate, complex, complicated informational strategies for bringing the data about their environments under control. Elaborate intelligence apparatuses are created to engage not only in such systematic "rifle" techniques as market research, technological forecasting, analysis of government action, and evaluation of competitors' performance, but also in such "shotgun" techniques as reading newspapers, journals, and competitors' advertising; attending conventions; and even on occasion indulging in a little industrial espionage.

The curious aspect of the whole intelligence operation is that the effectiveness of the total process is only as good as the top executives are in evaluating what is presented to them. Thus the critical limitation on understanding the environment is not the timeliness, reliability, and validity of the intelligence collected and assimilated by staff officers, but the sophistication, relevance, and accessibility of the minds of top management. What top management allows itself to believe is the decisive factor in its understanding of the environment.

LAWRENCE AND LORSCH: THE INFORMATION NEXUS

With increasing recognition of the fact that organizations are organic systems in continuous interaction with their environment has come a growing interest in analysis of the environmental variables which are critical for the effective functioning of the organization. Paul R. Lawrence and Jay W. Lorsch, who are among the leading theoreticians in this field, have recently aligned their concepts with those of James D. Thompson, who has also published major studies of the ecology of organizations.

Early in the history of industrial organizations it was perceived that the variety of tasks to be performed demanded a segmentation of functions into major task areas, each dealing with a particular subenvironment of the firm such as the market or the technoeconomic or scientific subenvironment.

Lawrence and Lorsch identify degrees of certainty and uncertainty in each subenvironment by measuring three major dimensions:

1. Rate of change of information.
2. Time span of feedback.
3. Certainty of information at any one time.

It is possible for a firm to enjoy a high degree of certainty in one subenvironment and face great uncertainty in another. The extent to which the different parts of the environment are similar determines whether the total environment is diverse or homogenous. The greater the diversity, the greater the need for differentiation of the organization into different units dealing with various parts of the environment.

A second critical characteristic of the environment identified by Lawrence and Lorsch is the dominant competitive issue. Their examples vary considerably among industries, ranging from efficient scheduling of production facilities to a need for continuous product innovation.

The third major environmental characteristic is the pattern and degree of interdependence required between units. Thompson has identified three types of interdependence:

1. *Pooled*: each part renders a discrete contribution to the whole and each is supported by the whole, but no direct interaction is required between the units of the organization. Examples are branch banking or the stores in a supermarket chain.
2. *Sequential*: "direct interdependence can be pinpointed between them [the units] and the order of the interdependence can be specified." This interdependence is not symmetrical. The classic illustration of this type is to be found in the various units comprising the automotive division of General Motors.
3. *Reciprocal*: "the outputs of each [unit] become the inputs for the others . . . under conditions of reciprocal interdependence each unit involved is penetrated by the others." Thompson uses the modern hospital as an example of this type of interdependence.

Some organizations do not need the tightness of interdependence required in others; and while simple organizations may deal with just pooled interdependence, all three types may be present in more complex firms.

The fact that the various units of an organization depend on each other for success and even survival is no guarantee that proper integrating or co-ordinating strategies will actually be found. In the study discussed below, Lawrence and Lorsch found that some firms—with the same environment as the rest of the industry—achieved above-average results through more effective integration of their subfunctions. This cannot be achieved by a standardized formula but must reflect the conditions in the particular industry. Thompson suggests that where pooled interdependence is typical, standardized procedures can be used to co-ordinate. Where sequential interdependence is the norm, co-ordination can be achieved by plans and schedules which will guide each unit for a considerable length of time. Reciprocal interdependence requires much more frequent interaction between the units to work out mutual adjustments to issues.

EMPIRICAL EVIDENCE

Lawrence and Lorsch derived their original theories from a study of 10 firms in the container, plastics, and food processing industries. They incorporated Thompson's formulations into their model after the study was complete, so the empirical support for his theories is indirect. A summary of their findings is shown in Table 10–1, which, it should be noted, shows data for the effective firms only. The authors' more detailed reports clearly indicate that the less effective firms had significantly less suitable organization arrangements for their respective environments.

Some amplification of the data summarized in Table 10–1 is required. The environment of the plastics firm was considered diverse because the scientific subenvironment was very certain while the production environment was relatively certain. Accordingly, the functional units were highly

TABLE 10–1
ENVIRONMENTAL FACTORS AND ORGANIZATIONAL INTEGRATION

	Industry		
	Plastics	*Food*	*Container*
Environment density	High	Moderate	Low
Dominant type of interdependence	Reciprocal	Reciprocal	Pooled-sequential
Actual differentiation	High	Moderate	Low
Integration devices	Teams, roles, departments, hierarchy, plans, procedures	Roles, plans, hierarchy, procedures	Hierarchy, plans, procedures
Special integrating personnel as a percentage of total management.	22%*	17%*	0
Interaction pattern	Team	One-to-one peers	One-to-one superior-subordinate
Hierarchical influence	Evenly distributed	Evenly distributed	Top, high; bottom, low
Unit having high influence	Integrating unit	Sales and research	Sales

* This proportion was constant for the high and low performers within these industries.

differentiated and a great deal of integrative effort was required. Sales opportunities and research discoveries of new types of plastic affected the direction pursued by both marketing and research departments, which were reciprocally interdependent. Thompson's prediction that mutual adjustment would be the dominant co-ordinating technique was supported by the frequency of team action, the high status of the unit formally responsible for integration, and the wide dispersal of influence, as nearly everyone had to have a say in arriving at acceptable decisions.

In the food organization the differentiation of the various units was not as pronounced and, while reciprocal interdependence between product development and marketing was a dominant force, there was less need for a formal integrating unit. It appeared possible for individual co-ordinators to meet with the different specialists on a one-to-one basis and help them reach a mutually satisfactory accommodation.

The container industry was much less differentiated and, because it was enjoying a seller's market, the competitive issue was the straightforward scheduling of the production units to meet sales. Pooled interdependence between branch plants and sequential interdependence between production and sales were the dominant types, and communication could be handled by a standardized routine. The environment was simple enough to permit top management to make almost all decisions, and there was little influence in the lower levels of the hierarchy.

Lawrence and Lorsch emphasize that even a good understanding of the environment and its implications for organizational strategy is not sufficient to guarantee success. They observed that identical organization structures in identical environments had significantly different rates of effectiveness. Particularly when standard procedures or plans could not be followed, the process of arriving at mutual adjustments acceptable to all units required considerable interpersonal skills and a willingness to handle conflict by open confrontation.

FOUR ENVIRONMENTS

Emery and Trist have provided one of the most useful concepts of environment in describing it as a "causal texture." Their descriptions of four types of environments under this heading are reproduced here in Box 10.1 —which, in this case, is required rather than optional reading for an understanding of this section.

Producing a blueprint of a business enterprise is complicated by the fact that it is not a physical object which interacts only to a slight extent with its environment but a complex of processes and interactions embedded in a cultural environment which places a system of constraints or limits on its development. The traffic of effects between organizations and society is a two-way affair. Thus, it is necessary to accept that no organization can be isolated from its cultural background. Secondly, a business organization may develop its own peculiar culture or organizational climate— patterns of communication and behaviour developed within the context of the larger culture pattern. But which cultural factors are relevant in the study of organizations? In the ecology of administration, historical, economic, technological, and theoretical forces are of major importance

There is a growing recognition that simple statements of the enterprise's objectives are no longer possible. The proposition that a firm exists simply to make a profit is no longer generally accepted. The enterprise has a number of tasks, including social and personal objectives, even if these only exist as limitations and constraints. The term "mission" has been suggested as a single name for this complex of tasks. To develop this argument further, at the British Tavistock Institute of Human Relations, workers have developed the concept of the sociotechnical system. E. L. Trist and K. W. Bamforth, as a result of their study of the introduction of the mechanized long-wall system of mining, did the early work in the development of sociotechnical theory. A sociotechnical system is concerned with the interaction between the technical and social aspects of the problem. A. K. Rice, in *Productivity and Social Organization*, says more generally:

Box 10.1: Four organizational environments

A main problem in the study of organizational change is that the environmental contexts in which organizations exist are themselves changing, at an increasing rate and towards increasing complexity. This point, in itself, scarcely needs labouring. Nevertheless, the characteristics of organizational environments demand consideration for their own sake, if there is to be an advancement of understanding in the behavioural sciences of a great deal that is taking place under the impact of technological change, especially at the present time.

. . . We may now state the following general proposition: that a comprehensive understanding of organizational behaviour requires some knowledge of each member of the following set, where L indicates some potentially lawful connection, and the suffix 1 refers to the organization and the suffix 2 to the environment:

$$L_{11}, L_{12}$$
$$L_{21}, L_{22}$$

L_{11} here refers to processes within the organization—the area of internal interdependencies; L_{12} and L_{21} to exchanges between the organization and its environment—the area of transactional interdependencies from either direction; and L_{22} to processes through which parts of the environment became related to each other—i.e., its causal texture—the area of interdependencies that belong within the environment itself.

FOUR TYPES OF CAUSAL TEXTURE

1. Placid, randomized environment

The simplest type of environmental texture is that in which goals and noxiants ("goods" and "bads") are relatively unchanging in themselves and randomly distributed. This may be called the *placid, randomized environment*. It corresponds to Simon's ideas of a surface over which an organism can locomote: most of this is bare, but at isolated, widely scattered points there are little heaps of food.

A critical property of organizational response under random conditions has been stated by Schutzenberger: that there is no distinction between tactics and strategy,

F. E. Emery and E. L. Trist, "The Causal Texture of Organizational Environments," *Human Retions*, Vol. 18, No. 1 (1965), pp. 21–32.

The concept of a production system as a socio-technical system designates a general field of study concerned with the interrelations of the technical and socio-psychological organization of industrial production systems. . . . The concept of a socio-technical system arose from the consideration that any production system requires both a technological organization—equipment and process layout—and a work organization relating to each other those who carry out the necessary tasks. The technological demands place limits on the type of work organization possible. But a work organization has social and psychological properties of its own that are independent of technology. . . . A socio-technical system must also satisfy the financial conditions of the industry of which it is a part. It must have economic dimensions, all of which are interdependent but all of which have independent values of their own.

It has been further argued that a more comprehensive picture of an enterprise will be gained by viewing it as an open sociotechnical system.

"optimal strategy is just the simple tactic of attempting to do one's best on a purely local basis."

2. Placid, clustered environment

More complicated, but still a placid environment, is that which can be characterized in terms of clustering: goals and noxiants are not randomly distributed but hang together in certain ways. This may be called the *placid, clustered environment*.

The new feature of organizational response to this kind of environment is the emergence of strategy as distinct from tactics. Survival becomes critically linked with what an organization knows of its environment. To pursue a goal under its nose may lead it into parts of the field fraught with danger, while avoidance of an immediately difficult issue may lead it away from potentially rewarding areas.

3. Disturbed-reactive environment

The next level of causal texturing we have called the *disturbed-reactive environment*. It may be compared with Ashby's ultra-stable system or the economist's oligopolic market. It is a type 2 environment in which there is more than one organization of the same kind; indeed, the existence of a number of similar organizations now becomes the dominant characteristic of the environmental field. Each organization does not simply have to take account of the others when they meet at random, but has also to consider that what it knows can also be known by the others. The part of the environment to which it wishes to move itself in the long run is also the part to which the others seek to move. Knowing this, each will wish to improve its own chances by hindering the others, and each will know that the others must not only wish to do likewise, but also know that each knows this. The presence of similar others creates an imbrication of some of the causal strands in the environment.

4. Turbulent fields

Yet more complex are the environments we have called *turbulent fields*. In these dynamic processes, which create significant variances for the component organizations,

This assumes that an organization both operates on the environment and is influenced by the environment.

Coping with the uncertainties of a turbulent environment

An important question to address is how organizations cope with the uncertainties of the turbulent environment of modern times. As Emery and Trist point out (see Box 10.1), in the turbulent environment the dynamic processes arise from the field itself. Turbulence is characterized by complexity, which is largely generated by interactions of other organizations which may not directly interact with the organization most disturbed.

Emery and Trist illustrate the operation of a turbulent environment by citing the example of a company which for many years had maintained a steady 65 per cent share of the market for its principal product, a canned vegetable. The company had made a massive investment in automated

arise from the field itself. Like type 3 and unlike the static types 1 and 2, they a
dynamic. Unlike type 3, the dynamic properties arise not simply from the interaction
the component organizations, but also from the field itself. The "ground" is in motion.

Values and relevant uncertainty. Social values are here regarded as coping mec
anisms that make it possible to deal with persisting areas of relevant uncertainty. Unab
to trace out the consequences of their actions as these are amplified and resonate
through their extended social fields, men in all societies have sought rules, sometim
categorical such as the ten commandments to provide them with a guide and rea
calculus. Values are not strategies or tactics; as Lewin has pointed out, they have t
conceptual character of "power fields" and act as injunctions. . . .

From organization to institution. Turbulent fields demand some overall form of org
nization that is essentially different from the hierarchically structured forms to which v
are accustomed.

A main problem in the study of organizational change is that the environmental cc
texts in which organizations exist are themselves changing—at an increasing ra
under the impact of technological change. This means that they demand considerati
for their own sake. Towards this end a redefinition is offered, at a social level of analys
of the causal texture of the environment. . . .

The strategic objective . . . could no longer be stated simply in terms of optimal loc
tion (as in type 2) or capabilities (as in type 3). It must now rather be formulated
terms of *institutionalization.* According to Selznick organizations become institutio
through the embodiment of organizational values which relate them to the wider socie
As Selznick has stated in his analysis of leadership in the modern American corpo
tion, "the default of leadership shows itself in an acute form when organization
achievement of survival is confounded with *institutional* success . . ." ". . . the exec
tive becomes a statesman as he makes the transition from administrative manageme
to institutional leadership."

---

plants to can this product, but was caught out by changes in postwar government controls that facilitated the manufacture of cheaper cans; in the
availability of alternative products; in quick-freeze technology that put
the staple in packets; and in marketing, with the emergence of supermarkets which (1) placed bulk orders with small firms to can the product
under supermarket brand names and (2) offered a wider range of similar
products to a consumer who was widening his area of choice with increasing affluence. In brief, governmental, technological, and marketing forces
impinged on this company's operation, and these environmental forces to
some extent were at least one step removed from the immediate environment of the firm.

Following Emery and Trist's classification of organizational interactions
(see Box 10.1), the firm in this example—like far too many firms—paid
insufficient attention to L_{22} (interorganizational) relations. Typically,
such firms think and act in terms of the simple input-transformation-out-

FIGURE 10–2
CLOSED SYSTEM WITH SIMPLE ENVIRONMENTAL EFFECTS

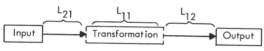

put model shown in Figure 10–2, dealing only with L_{11}, L_{12}, and L_{21} interactions, with fixed system boundaries (solid lines) which are permeable (broken lines) only at the input and output points. The management of the canned vegetable company treated their firm as this kind of relatively closed system instead of realizing that it was in fact part of a turbulent environment (see Figure 10–3), affected by the L_{22} changes in the social context.

The fact is that almost no firm, in these complex times, is an island; organizational environments are such that externally induced changes are going to be more significant than internally induced changes for virtually every organization. The critical issue, then, is how an organization can deal with L_{22} changes. The levels of complexity and uncertainty induced by the accelerating rate of change make long-range predictions of the

FIGURE 10–3
MODEL OF FIRMS IN A TURBULENT ENVIRONMENT

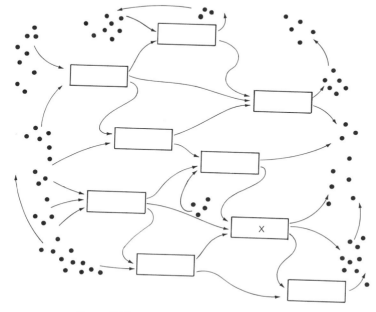

Source: Shirley Terreberry, "The Evolution of Organizational Environments," *Administrative Science Quarterly,* Vol. 12 (March, 1968), pp. 590–613.

future, based on extrapolation from a noncomparable past, subject to considerable error. Given the emergence of turbulent environments, organizations can only cope with change by developing a pragmatic flexibility where the emphasis is on the process of short-run adaptive reaction.

A useful lead for dealing with this problem has been suggested by William Evan, who has put forward the idea that the organization be treated as a "social actor" and the idea that the "organization set" (which is similar in structure to R. K. Merton's role set) be utilized as a means of studying L_{12} and L_{21} relations in a turbulent environment.

What emerges from this discussion of the turbulence of contemporary environments is first of all the difficulty of making predictions, which in turn compels management to proceed by satisficing rather than optimizing; to accept bounded rationality; to keep some of its options open by allowing a plurality of coalitions with various objectives within its system; to review continuously the spectrum of goals; to seek regulated competition; to favour bargaining, co-optation, and coalition strategies— and above all to recognize that organizational survival and growth is a function of the ability of the system to learn and perform according to changes in the environment. To achieve this level of adaptation, organizations are required to devote more effort to information processing than to production and maintenance activities. The development of such information strategies has been greatly facilitated by the rapid improvement of the information-processing capacities of computers and has led to the transformation of the subject of organizational behaviour, where systematic efforts are being made to write out definitions, concepts, and findings in information and transactional terms.

STRATEGIES FOR MANAGING THE ENVIRONMENT

How do organizations manage their environments and make them more munificent? Essentially by managing their external dependencies. To achieve the measure of certainty necessary for survival, organizations attempt a number of strategies, including co-operation, the use of long-term contracts, the exploitation of illegal collaboration (price-fixing cartels and conspiracies), lobbying the various levels of government, and, last but not least, through merger and acquisition activity.

For example, co-optation is widely used by government agencies, universities, banks, business and religious organizations, hospitals, prisons, and many other organizations as an accommodating mechanism. This process of selective alliances allows representatives of powerful groups in the environment a say in setting goals and selecting means in return for information of what their parent organizations are going to do. Co-optation, which essentially involves exploitation of the "old boy" net, is somewhat hazardous. The wrong external groups or group representatives may be selected or the structure of representation may not reflect the realities of the en-

ironment; or the conflict of interests involved may impair the judgements
f the parties involved, who are unable to navigate the shoals marked
collusion" and "conspiracy" by the map makers from government anti-
ust agencies.

Long-term contracts are useful but can be dangerous, as the aerospace
ompanies have discovered in their dealings with government procure-
ient agencies. An excellent illustration of this problem at a different level
'as the contract negotiated between Lockheed and Rolls-Royce for the
ipply of the jet engines for the Tri-star jet airliner, which was the largest
xport order Britain had ever received and which eventually brought
olls-Royce to bankruptcy and nearly finished off Lockheed as well. The
ritical decision was Rolls-Royce's, and concerned the price which Lock-
eed had to pay for each engine. The formula was: $P = P_0 F$, where P is
ie actual price, P_0 the base price, and F a factor to measure the inflation-
y costs of labour and materials. In fact F was estimated correctly by a
omplicated calculation, but P_0 was hopelessly wrong, being much too
w. Management had failed to anticipate the gigantic technological diffi-
ilties that Rolls would have in engineering the carbon blades (which
ere selected, among other characteristics, for lightness) of the fan of the
t engine. The net result was the Rolls bankruptcy (with the British
overnment's credibility challenged in the process) and Lockheed's near-
ınkruptcy (with the American government, which guaranteed the loan
o keep Lockheed going, accused of undermining the free enterprise sys-
m). The moral of the story, for students of the environment, is that
ver a period of 30 years fighter aircraft costs had risen by a factor of
000 and development costs by such a large factor that a single wrong
ecision of the Rolls-Royce magnitude could destroy an extremely large,
omplex, sophisticated technological organization.

With such dire consequences a distinct possibility, merger and acquisi-
on become prime routes to achieve environmental control. This is pre-
sely what has been happening to the aerospace companies in both Eu-
ope and North America, which has resulted in a situation with a very
nall number of airframe manufacturers and an even smaller number of
ngine builders. And, contrary to widely held public opinions, govern-
ients in both Europe and North America have imposed contract terms
their dealings with aerospace firms that on occasion have had the firms
sing extremely large sums on every aircraft built.

Fortunately, better data are now becoming available as a means of eval-
iting options open to organizations for managing their environments. For
tample, Jeffrey Pfeffer of the University of Illinois has some useful
iings to say for managers in "Merger as a Response to Organizational
iterdependence," and we can expect further useful contributions in the
meral area of the organization and its environment. The subject is now
ceiving increasing attention, not only from economists interested in
icro economics, but also from organization theorists.

TOPIC 3
Organizational climate: The environment perceived

Every organization has a corporate zeitgeist and is characterized by a particular, distinctive ambience. How this ambience is perceived—how this bundle of "vibes" is organized into a Gestalt—is termed organizational climate. Climate is usually easy to recognize. In many organizations, it

FIGURE 10–4

THE PERCEIVED ENVIRONMENT AS A SYSTEM

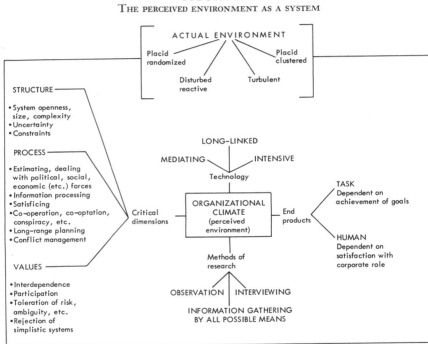

hits you as you walk through the front door. The House of Commons reeks of pomp, persuasion, and power. The U.S. Marine Corps has "can do" written all over it, in crew cuts, ramrod backs, and machismo. The hippie commune smells of permissiveness, passion, pot, and patter. The question is not whether climate exists, but how to get a handle on it.

One way is to pick up our systems model, as in Figure 10–4, and attempt to model the organizational climate. Climate may be thought of as the perception of the characteristics of an organization. Since the actual environment is well described by Emery and Trist's classifications, and we have opted for the idea that the turbulent environment is the one most firms must deal with, the model in Figure 10–4 deals with the idea of these perceptions. Here the structure, process, and value dimensions and other system elements are the aspects of organizations that individuals will look at in assessing their distinctive climates—which have to do with both internal environment and the way the organization deals with external environments.

Structurally, organizations will be judged in terms of complexity and such constraints as roles, regulations, and red tape. Is there an official organization chart and how slavishly do people stick to channels? Organizational climate, like air conditioning, can be switched not only on and off but also up and down. "Getting into role" is normally preceded by a standard set of signals. Size and structure are closely linked. Usually bigness is associated with more impersonal relations, centralization, more absenteeism, lower morale. As we noted in Chapter 2, technology and structure are closely related. The atmosphere of the automobile assembly line is driving the new crop of workers, who are better educated and less compliant than their parents, loony. This weariness of the spirit, which has hit the auto plants hardest, is related to job boredom—which in turn is generating both poor workmanship and absenteeism. To meet this problem Chrysler Corporation, for example, has asked plant managements to consult the workers and to keep four principles in mind:

. Fix responsibility as far down the line as possible.
. Give enough authority to go with it.
. Make workers aware of the concrete results of their suggestions.
. Create a climate which encourages change.

Such proposals acknowledge that it is not sufficient to change specific job characteristics such as wages, schedules, and job designs; it is vital to establish a different climate.

Climate is concerned with the perception not only of structure but also of organization processes. As we would expect, the handling of information is a critical factor determining climate. Information can be communicated internally in an autocratic, benevolent, consultative, or participative climate. External and overall information management includes the researching and gathering of all possible data and the evaluation of all the impinging societal forces. Management of conflict is another process factor. The extent to which conflict is perceived as being confronted and not suppressed varies widely from organization to organization. Since we shall deal with this topic in considerable detail in Chapter 14, perhaps it is sufficient to say that the processes and value systems developed to cope with conflict can decisively affect the climate of work. Our Chapter 9 discussion of the Watergate scandals indicated what happens when an authoritarian, "Berlin wall" atmosphere designates all conflict as "disloyalty" and all dissent as "enemy" action to be suppressed. Such a climate of power relations erodes and destroys informed judgement and withers the flower

of legitimacy which is a prerequisite of proper authority relations. Ulti
mately, climate is concerned with the reading of other people's minds an
the unscrambling of their motivations and values.

The perception of other people's values is an integral element in de
termining the climate of an organization. A good climate exhibits suc
values as recognition of complexities, uncertainties, mutualities, and inter
actions, and hence a tolerance for the necessary boat-rockings and adapta
tions. Again referring back to Watergate, any simplistic, single-virtu
value system that posits a world of black and white with no delicate shade
of grey should signal to the perceiver an organization that, if not alread
in the soup, is headed for it. Values are tied up with life styles and dea
not only with authority and power relations but also such matters as un
derlying attitudes towards innovation and scientific and technological de
velopment. For example, IBM used to foster a particular life style for it
executives which required them to appear in dark business suits with whit
shirts. Many IBM executives believed they would be sent home if the
came to work dressed otherwise. But to IBM, it was meant to be an out
ward sign of inner graces—seriousness and dedication to problem solving

RESEARCHING THE CLIMATE

Much of the organizational literature uses the term "climate" as inter
changeable with "environment" and, as we have been doing, seeks t
identify the perceived characteristics that make up the climate. Researcher
have identified (often through the use of questionnaires and rating scales
many significant areas of organizational members' perceptions, including

1. Structure: perception of constraints such as rules, regulations, re
   tape, closeness of supervision and direction, tightness of budget
   "You've got to recite the history of the alphabet here before you ca
   get a pencil out of the store."
2. Autonomy: feelings of setting one's own pace, running one's ow
   show. "You're on your own here as long as you produce. Nobod
   breathes down your neck every time you turn around."
3. Reward structure: share of the payoffs, psychic and financial; promo
   tion-and-achievement, profit-and-sales orientations. "You get a fai
   shake around here if you can deliver the goods."
4. Warmth, support, consideration: an ambience of good fellowship an
   helpfulness. "They're nearly all good eggs."
5. Tolerance of conflict: the extent to which conflict is confronted an
   not suppressed. "They like everything, and I mean everything, righ
   out in the open."
6. Need for innovation: technological and managerial rate of change. "I
   something has been operational here for 24 months and hasn't bee
   declared obsolescent for 23, somebody's been slipping."

Campbell *et al.*, who have summarized the empirical work on environmental variation and managerial effectiveness in *Managerial Behavior, Performance, and Effectiveness*, point out that:

> At the empirical level things have not progressed very far, but perhaps a few inferences can be made. The simulation studies by Frederiksen and Litwin and Stringer strongly suggest a number of beneficial effects for organizations which maintain a consistent climate. They further suggest that if individual differences are not taken into account, there is little reason to expect *mean* differences in performance under different climate conditions. One thing these studies do not do is suggest how the influence of climate differs for different tasks. Studies of climate should take a cue from a laboratory experiment by Roby, Nicol, and Farrell which showed that a decentralized structure was best if the task required cooperative effort but that a centralized structure was best if individuals (students in this case) worked independently toward a common goal.

Climate, since it represents the perceived environment, is a bridging concept between people and the organizations in which they work. Climate is thus an individual's perception of structure, process, and values as they relate to his task achievement and human satisfaction in the particular organization to which he belongs. For example, it has been found that there is a relationship between job satisfaction and climate. G. Litwin and R. Stringer found that satisfaction was highest in "affiliation-induced" climates, relatively high in "achievement-induced" climates, and low in "power-induced" climates.

SEARCHING FOR THE ORGANIZATIONAL GESTALT: LIKERT'S SYSTEMS

A major preoccupation of sophisticated executives is to find a Gestalt or configuration or frame of reference or climate which will enable them to synthesize the multitude of concepts and findings which are rolling out of research and practice. Useful theories have the same obsolescence characteristics as modern jet fighters and date themselves as they emerge from the drawing boards of organization theorists. Such theories should be judged both in terms of validity and utility.

One of the most significant reasons why theories cannot keep up with events is that events won't stand still. A useful model for getting a reading on this rapid rate of organizational change has been provided by the seminal work of Rensis Likert, who has proposed the model of changes in organizational climate shown in Figure 10–5. The model illustrates that as the technological mandate changes, human needs expand and different organizational climates emerge. Examples of organizations and their places in such a spectrum are given in Table 10–2, and the following sections describe Likert's four systems more fully.

FIGURE 10–5
LIKERT'S MODEL OF CHANGES IN CLIMATE

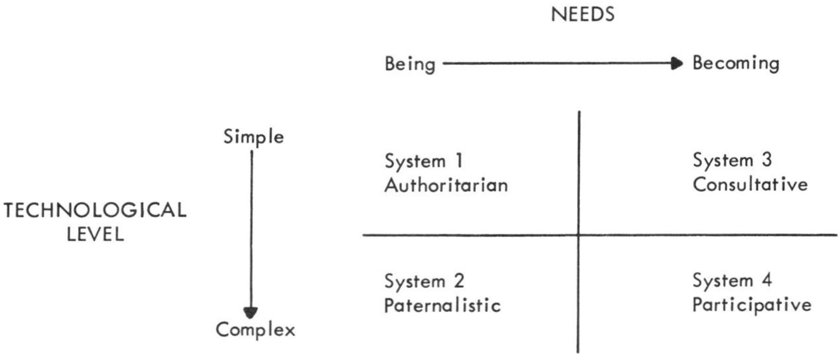

NEEDS

Being ──────────────▶ Becoming

	Simple	System 1 Authoritarian	System 3 Consultative
TECHNOLOGICAL LEVEL			
	Complex	System 2 Paternalistic	System 4 Participative

SYSTEM 1

There are many examples of System 1 still around today—organization
which are run with Draconian efficiency, in a completely autocrati
manner, with virtually total indifference to the feelings, beliefs, and senti
ments of the less powerful.

A good deal of the agricultural work which employs casual or transien
labour uses System 1 management. For example, in picking potatoes, th
potato-digging machine (dragged by a tractor) brings the potatoes to th
surface and the labourer gathers them up in a basket. The efficiency o
mechanical farming turns on the speed with which the farmer drives th
tractor. The workers, who are poorly paid and rarely unionized, ar
sullen, apathetic, and dispirited. The machine determines the pace not only
on the farm but also in many assembly line operations and larger mechan
ized offices. System 1 also prevails in officer cadet schools, maximum secur
ity prisons, and custodial mental hospitals.

Modern times still need System 1; only the techniques have changed
As Jessica Mitford points out in *Kind and Usual Punishment*, in U.S
prisons (with a population of 1.33 million) psychological degradation ha

TABLE 10–2

Plant	Technology	Needs	Climate
Small knitting factory in the West of Ireland	Simple	Being (survival)	Authoritarian- paternalistic
Quaker chocolate factory in England	Moderately complex	Being to becoming	Paternalistic- consultative
Car plant in Detroit	Complex	Being to becoming	Paternalistic- consultative
Apollo space project	Highly complex	Becoming (self-actualizing)	Participative

been added to physical degradation, and "diagnosis" and "evaluation" are the "Catch 22" of modern prison life. A "cure" is pronounced, Mitford suspects, when a "poor/young/brown/black captive appears to have capitulated to his middle-class/white/middle-aged captor." And further, System 1 to-day is going to be maintained by behaviour modification, aversion therapy, and adjustment centres—and not only in prisons. The behaviourists are blooming, and "criminals, deviates, oddballs, queers," rate-busters, and eccentrics of all kinds can now be brainwashed.

SYSTEM 2

Many organizations make System 1 into System 2. A good example of System 2 is the small pharmaceutical manufacturing plant which is a commonplace in both North America and Europe. The packing houses are where the costs are generated, with usually two thirds of the employees counting pills, putting them in bottles, labelling bottles, inserting bottles in boxes, and packing boxes in cartons (to say nothing of all the activity that goes on checking and stamping batch numbers and checkers' numbers on labels). Looking into a packing house, you would see a platoon of women in white smocks, with their hair tied up, working alongside an assembly line belt. It is all highly mechanized, with counting machines, labels, packing machines, and so on.

In many ways, it is rather similar to the sewing rooms of the old-fashioned needle trade, but there is a difference. The women are cosy and comfortable; conversation flies back and forth, products are handled carefully (pharmaceutical firms measure their efficiency, among other ways, by the length of time that has elapsed since they killed someone); the whole atmosphere is different. Coffee breaks, rest rooms, good training facilities, education for employees, factory clubs, and social unions are all encouraged. Supervision is supportive, helpful, and thoughtful. The women think of themselves as nurses on life-saving missions. In the sterile rooms, where products are packed by women wearing special masks and gloves working in glass cases to avoid contamination, the workers can't touch their faces while they work. To them it is life or death work—like an operating theatre. They respond to national crises with determination.

In short, System 2 organizations are human relations–oriented. They include schools, mental hospitals, and most larger department stores.

SYSTEM 3

In System 3, there is a distinct and significant effort to get beyond benevolence via consultation. The Glacier project (see Chapter 5) is the best example of System 3 I know. Many idealistic people were attracted to the Glacier Metal Company because of its distinctive culture. Elliott Jaques, in his 1950 book entitled *Changing Culture of a Factory*, described the transition of the company to System 3, where consultation in the form of work councils became the natural way to manage. The whole thing worked pretty well except for one thing, the vagaries of the British economy. Glacier, a manufacturer of bearings which are used in the assembly of automobile engines, was vulnerable to the stop-and-go character of the British economy. The internal climate was knocked sideways by the external environment. My own research of Glacier was carried out at their Scottish plant, which was greatly affected by another kind of environment, the peculiar Presbyterian-Catholic character of Ayrshire which is a mixture of machismo, Marx, Mass and the Manse—too much for any sensible, scientific system.

Systems 3 and 4 are now fairly standard in most manufacturing units in North America and Europe. The American way is not through work councils, but they are widely used in the United Kingdom, West Germany, and Sweden. For example, co-determination legislation passed in the early 1950s in West Germany (arranged by the United States and Britain to keep the Germans democratic, i.e., "nonfascist") is known as *Mitbestimmung*. This system gives labour and capital equality on company "supervisory boards" (similar to boards of directors). Progressive companies such as Monsanto, Corning Glass, Eaton, Texas Instruments, Syntex, General Foods, and Procter & Gamble in the United States and Steinbergs in Canada have taken a different road to get to industrial democracy. We call it participation—System 4.

SYSTEM 4

The Harwood Project, which we discussed in some detail in Chapter 5, is the best example of System 4. System 4 is a North American way of life which is highly suitable to a society which believes itself to be more open, less class-oriented, more mobile, and better educated (whether it is or not is neither here nor there) than its European cousins. System 4 means participation in planning change, job enrichment à la Herzberg (even though scientifically disproved, it still changes the climate), team management à la the managerial grid, and assessment centres. One of Likert's concepts is that of the "linking pin," the group member who is, for example, a supervisor in one group and a subordinate in a group at the next higher level of the organization. Group interrelation in this manner achieves vertical integration in the organization as well participation and supportiveness from one group to the next.

System 4 is (or can be) somewhat gimmicky; it means lots of work for managers and behavioural scientists. Yet somehow it works. All the behavioural exercises, regardless of their scientific validity, do help to change the climate. But so far only a tiny minority of companies have a System 4 climate, which we might call industrial democracy.

Several serious attempts have been made to get the industrial democracy debate going in the United States, especially in view of the kinds of problems we have mentioned in regard to the auto assembly lines. Why don't we have industrial democracy? Even the phrase is resented. Some blame the unions, which have too often gone after the buck and ignored matters of organizational climate. Others blames the brutality of the economic system, which makes shut-downs and layoffs such on-going realities that no one thinks about climate. A great number of Americans and Canadians think of "going back to school" as the answer to bad working conditions. "Ethnics" and blacks have picked up a disproportionate share of the dirty work in both industry and the military, and there is intransigent resistance to democracy in that respect. There is also the emergence of the Archie Bunkers, "Joes," and "hard hats" who have created a political climate of right-wing reaction—partly because our universities went too far (or seemed to) in introducing participation. An excess (and abuse) of System 4 in one sector of society produces System 1 in another sector.

CLIMATE CLIMAXED

In summary, climate is a second-order subjective variable which describes how people perceive organizations (essentially, how they see the elements of our model—structure, process, and so on). But climate after a while achieves a somewhat separate existence, a kind of functional autonomy. What life style does for the individual and morale for the group, climate does for the organization. Now climate, culture, ideology, mythology, call it what you may, is not a completely rational thing. It inevitably contains elements that cannot be reconciled. Establishing the right climate is a vital executive activity and an area where behavioural scientists can play a significant part, even though the instruments they use are imperfect.

Three points should be stressed. First, climate is an atmosphere, an ambience, an *esprit de corps*, a corporate zeitgeist. Second, while climate may be difficult to measure, people are usually immediately alerted to it; it comes on as a corporate aura, odour, echo, flavour. It can be intoxicating, soporific, aphrodisiac, enervating, apathy-inducing, stimulating, hysteria-producing. Third—and above all—climate affects judgement, which is what Watergate told us about the 1972 presidential campaign. The climate of "can do," total delegation by (and isolation of) the President, business (not political) efficiency, boy scoutery, complete loyalty, football symbolism, and the paranoia of black-and-white issues led to poor judgement and bad decision making.

Decision making is the ultimate product of the organizational environment. Chapter 11 ends Part 2 by considering how the organization leader makes decisions—preferably, good ones.

REVIEW AND RESEARCH

1. Explain the concept of satisficing. Why don't General Motors and Ford combine to knock out Chrysler and American Motors?
2. Define the internal and external environments of a firm with which you are familiar.
3. What are the organizational arguments that favour the survival of capitalism?
4. Explain how aerospace firms cope with the uncertainties of the environment.
5. Describe the Lawrence and Lorsch concept of the environment. From their empirical studies, explain how they related environmental factors and organizational integration.
6. List the factors of organizational climate. Assess your business school or organization on these factors.
7. Why are Emery and Trist's four environments so complicated? List some of the factors that make environments turbulent.
8. Consider an L_{22} change such as the invention of a relatively inexpensive domestic machine combining computer, copying machine, television, and video-tape recording functions. How would the introduction of such a machine affect work and leisure?

GLOSSARY

Climate. Often used interchangeably with "environment"; more usefully thought of as the environment as it is perceived; a corporate ambience or aura typifying an organization's style.

Environment. All of the surrounding elements and factors with which an organization interacts and trades. The organization's internal environment consists of programming, technical, and personnel factors; its immediate external environment includes suppliers, competitiors, customers, and monitoring agencies; its remote external environment includes all of the political, social, economic, technological, and ecological factors which impinge on its activities.

Emery and Trist describe environment as a causal texture which can be classified as (1) placid, random; (2) placid, clustered; (3) disturbed-reactive and (4) turbulent. The turbulent environment, which affects most organizations, is highly complex and characterized by dynamic processes.

Lawrence and Lorsch conceptualize the environment according to three factors: (1) uncertainty; information measured by its rate of change, time span of feedback, and certainty at any one time; (2) dominant competitive issues; and (3) interdependence, which is of three types—pooled, sequential and reciprocal.

Likert's System 4. Rensis Likert described organizational style or internal environment as an evolution through four systems along axes of changing human needs and technological levels: System 1, authoritarian; System 2 paternalistic; System 3, consultative; and System 4, participative. System is most appropriate in a complex, technologically advanced industry; it fulfills human needs for industrial democracy.

Sociotechnical system. An industrial production organization with high technical and social interrelations, interacting with its environment (an open system).

11

The decision
process

To the beleaguered executive of contemporary times, life is an uphill struggle—a process of continuous decision making, an excruciating process of deciding what to do today, what can be safely postponed, whether to buy or sell, whether to fire a troublesome subordinate or remonstrate with him, whether to send a memo increasing controls or call a conference to talk the problem out, whether to order the new computer system or get the current one sorted out. Traditionally many executives have solved the endless multitude of problems coming their way by intuition. But it is a cardinal principle of decision theory that intuition alone is not sufficient to meet the complexities of modern life.

Modern decision theory presumes that the executive cannot master all the information available to him and that he calculates the odds in favour or against, not in terms of mathematical probabilities but rather in terms of his will to win. It presumes that the executive operates under bounded rationality and tries to accommodate the elusive facts of value and utility within a framework of probability. To get the best out of modern decision theory, the executive must understand the decision process and grasp the difference between programmable and nonprogrammable decisions. He must be able to categorize his environment as to whether he is dealing with outcomes that can be specified in terms of certainty, risk, or uncertainty. We begin this chapter by defining some of these terms of the decision process.

TYPES OF DECISION MAKING

A theoretical model of decision making must distinguish among several different types of problem solving which basically can be subsumed under two main headings: programmable and nonprogrammable decisions. The programmable problem, leading to the "computational" decision—which presumes an agreed desired goal and the existence of calculable technological means to achieve it—is an essential characteristic of classical theory. Strategy sets out the goal and tactics are invented to produce means to get there; all problems can be solved via the algorithm. Nonprogrammable problems, which involve the use of heuristics, are much more judgmental in character, make limited or no use of computers, and frequently put tactics before strategy. As the name suggests, the actual decision process is not sequential but is usually sporadic and fragmented. Nonprogram-

FIGURE 11-1

Decision type	Process	Examples
Programmable	Routine; computable by algorithm	1. Factory load meeting to schedule production
		2. Clarkson's portfolio selection model
Nonprogrammable:		
1. Creative	Limited heuristic	Technological forecasting group to select new product
2. Negotiated	Noncomputable; conflict technology	Management-labour union bargaining

mable decisions can be further classified as creative or negotiated. Examples of these three types of decisions are given in Figure 11-1.

What is very clear from both consideration of the literature and common observation is that management is paid to engage in all three types of decision making, but that most of their problems arise because of their inability to recognize that different decisions require different processes. In particular, operations research problem-solving techniques are only appropriate for relatively small-scale problem solving, where the number of variables to be considered is small and the value problems restricted. The traditional, classical theory of decision making assumes some such process as statement of the objective, definition of constraints, evaluation of means, selection of strategy, and invention of tactics; but such processes are largely reserved for generals and statesmen as a means of writing historic memoirs where everything can be put in neat tidy categories. Such reactive accounts of decision making are only useful for active decision making if you can be guaranteed that history will repeat itself.

Unprogrammed decision making is greatly dependent on information processing, which involves searching for intelligence, setting up options, making choices, implementation, evaluation, and then beginning the whole process again.

All decisions have varying degrees of risk and uncertainty, depending on the environment in which the decision maker operates.

Certainty is a state of knowledge in which the decision maker knows before the event the specific outcomes that will result from each alternative course of action.

Risk is a state of knowledge in which the decision maker can specify outcomes of each alternative course of action and assign probabilities to the likelihood of each outcome. Risk represents measurable uncertainty.

Uncertainty is a state of knowledge in which the decision maker may be able to specify the outcomes for each particular course of action but is unable to assign probabilities.

Certainty presupposes situational omniscience and the idea of decision making under conditions of certainty is utopian. Decision making under risk is applicable to the tactical problems of middle management. Decision making under uncertainty applies to situations where there is no basis in past experience for estimating the probabilities to be assigned to particular outcomes.

In weighing which course of action to follow, it would seem reasonable to assume that a decision maker, as well as estimating the probabilities of particular outcomes, would also attempt to gauge or measure the *utility* of each outcome—that is, how much he receives in payoffs, no matter how he measures these payoffs. It usually is possible to rank payoffs. Obviously, many men act in a way that indicates that they are not completely rational in measuring utilities. How else can you explain the fact that many men gamble at casinos when they know that the odds are loaded in favour of the house?

The utility of a payoff in a particular commodity is related to how much of that particular commodity that you are holding at that time. For example, the value of an additional dollar depends on the size of your present fortune. As Daniel Bernoulli pointed out, if ΔU represents the increase in utility and X your holdings, then:

$$\Delta U = \frac{\Delta X}{X}$$

and if ΔX is \$1, then:

$$\Delta U = \frac{\$1}{X}$$

if it assumed that U and X are continuous variables, it is possible to say, in terms of differentials,

$$dU = \frac{dX}{X}$$

This last equation implies that U is a logarithmic function of X. What this means is that a useful way of measuring the utility of an increase in income is to calculate the logarithms of both salaries, the new and the old, and then measure the ratio of utilities by the ratio of the logarithms.

STRUCTURE OF CHAPTER 11

Topic 1, search and decide, spells out the steps in the decision process as perceiving the problem, formulating alternatives, setting up decision rules, selecting the alternative, implementation, and evaluation. A critical part of this process is getting the facts straight. How organizational members select and distort the information collection process is examined in some detail.

Our second topic, the dynamics of decision making, is concerned with how executives generate alternatives and actually make decisions. Particularly important here is the fact that to-day most executive decision making is made in a group context. The question is posed as to how the group affects individual decision making. To try to answer this question, we critically examine the proposition that discussion leads group members to prefer more risky decisions than they would have selected as individuals. We then turn to the creative element in decision making and look at the corporate technique of synectics, which helps to make executives more creative. Having reviewed the process and its dynamics, we then turn to the deciders.

Topic 3 is a review of the decision subsystem. In it, Russell Ackoff's excellent advice on how to classify decision making according to the availability of models is introduced, and decision making is modeled as a system in itself.

TOPIC 1
Search and decide

As H. A. Simon has pointed out, organizations are made up of three layers: an underlying system of physical processes, a layer of programmed decision processes, and a top layer of nonprogrammed decision processes. Top management makes the critical decisions which middle management absorb into their plans, which in turn monitor the physical processes at the bottom layer.

The decision-making process, according to Simon, consists of three steps:

1. The sensor subsystem searches the environment for conditions calling for a decision. This is essentially an intelligence activity. The aim of this two-way process is to capture data about events impinging on the organization and its immediate environment.
2. The data processing subsystem manipulates and is manipulated by these data.
3. The decision-making subsystem enables a particular course of action to be selected.

The modern approach to decision making in organizations treats the organization as a coalition of individuals or groups who formulate goals through formal and informal bargaining, coupled with searching the environment for suitable opportunistic problems to solve.

FIGURE 11–2
COALITIONS BARGAIN TO ACHIEVE GOALS

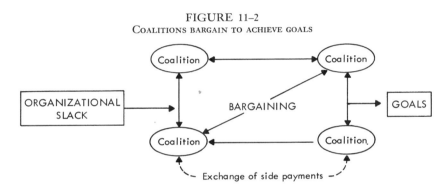

R. M. Cyert and J. G. March have identified five major goals for modern organizations: production, sales, inventory, market share, and profit. Organizations also usually have a certain amount of organizational slack, which constitutes a kind of reserve which by effective management can be committed to new battles. Organizational slack arises when the rewards (financial or psychic) exceed the amount needed to obtain members' contributions. (For example, organizational slack is presumably taken up when the decision by the consultant to fire 20 per cent of the personnel is implemented.) Figure 11–2 illustrates how coalitions within the organization employ this organizational slack in a bargaining process whose aim is the satisfaction of some varying combination of the five major goals.

THE SEARCH PROCESS

Organizational members are continuously searching the environment to find either means of meeting goals better or solvable problems that will induce new goals for the organization. Figure 11–3 shows how the decision cycle then begins to operate.

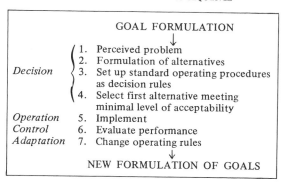

FIGURE 11–3
A POSSIBLE DECISION PROCESS SEQUENCE

GOAL FORMULATION
↓

Decision
1. Perceived problem
2. Formulation of alternatives
3. Set up standard operating procedures as decision rules
4. Select first alternative meeting minimal level of acceptability

Operation   5. Implement
Control   6. Evaluate performance
Adaptation   7. Change operating rules
↓
NEW FORMULATION OF GOALS

The quality, quantity, reliability, relevance, and presentation of information gathered is a function of members' satisfactions and the amount of organizational slack available. Choice arises as a response to a perceived problem. A typical decision cycle begins with a search of the environment to select a suitable problem which is tested for relevance against organizational goals (present or future). Then standard operating procedures (rules of thumb) are applied to solve the problem. In the process various alternatives are formulated and evaluated. Normally the first alternative which meets the minimum level of acceptability on the complete range of standards is selected. Afterwards the strategy selected is evaluated, and in this process organizational learning takes place. Adaptation is based on past performance evaluated against both expectations and the performance of other comparable organizations. Adaptation focuses the perceptions of members on salient elements of the environment. Thus the search process produces information which is biased in particular ways.

The amount of data provided by an organizational member is a function of his level in the organization, his area of operations, what his superiors desire, what will get him a favourable decision, how easy the data are to collect, and what he will be held accountable for collecting later. Inevitably, considerable bias is introduced in the process.

A study titled "The Behavioral Theory of the Firm and Top Level Corporate Decision" concerned an expanding organization whose main business was providing computer equipment and professional services to many governmental, commercial, and educational organizations. In this article, E. Eugene Carter, as a result of his research, argued for a more complex view of the decision process:

> Major additional criteria suggested as of major importance in the framework of an extended Cyert and March approach are: the impact of multiple organizational levels on decisions; the bilateral bargaining between project proponents and those managers responsible for review

of proposals; the influence of technology and general uncertainty in the environment upon criteria for project evaluation; the nature of an active stimulus for search induced by corporate strategy rather than the more passive, crisis-induced stimulus suggested by Cyert and March; the concept of a threshold-level system by which projects quickly are rated or evaluated on multiple attributes; and the Pollyanna-Nietzsche effect, by which ex post uncertainty absorption can be used by firm members to induce a positive-thinking approach to subsequent performance.

GETTING THE FACTS STRAIGHT

The beauty of the systems approach lies in its ability to control, regulate, and direct the executive's appetite for facts. The contemporary executive suffers from intellectual obesity because of his insatiable appetite for information—rather like some people's inability to resist just one more peanut. Systems theory essentially is an attempt to persuade the executive to eat intelligence à la carte instead of table d'hôte. The aim should be to search with a gourmet eye for problems which he can sample as hors d'œuvres to find out what is feasible and edible (but healthy) before beginning the main dish. The meal should provide a substantial, well-balanced diet of routine staples, meat he can get his teeth into, and some trimmings to give him a whiff of more exotic foods.

How is the executive to avoid devouring the indigestible plethora of detail which his systems people are going to send his way? The first thing he must do is draw up a model of his organization as an information-processing system which reveals the system of decision making, including the interconnections between decisions. Having mapped out the positive world of the "is," he must tackle the normative world of the "ought." What are the goals of the organization? What are these decisions meant to achieve? From this second exercise, he should be able to identify both the critical decision variables and their interrelations and interactions. Unless he is in an organization which dominates its environment, it will be clear to him that the organization makes progress by optimizing one particular critical decision variable at a time and allowing other variables to be suboptimal. Therefore his next question is, What measure of suboptimality can be tolerated in different variables?

Other questions that suggest themselves are, How often should such data be collected and reviewed? What variables must be inspected hourly, daily, weekly, monthly, quarterly, and annually? Under what conditions is this model valid? As the executive proceeds with this kind of sensitivity analysis, he will come up with the information requirements of his role (see Box 11.1).

But inevitably he will be pushed into considering the individuals or coalitions who manage the particular decision variables and conjecturing about the nature of their administrative and personal convenience, i.e., how much organizational slack they command and how they manage it. For inevitably his "extra" efforts must be resourced and refueled from this slack. How much suboptimality can they stand? Excellence and equity become competing modes, each of which optimizes by suboptimizing the other.

Thus the executive is compelled to search for information that defines the constituencies of other executives and clients and to carefully review his own constituency. Such intelligence is not to be found in computer print-outs, but must be mined from the mire of "the continuous serene dialogue" that constitutes human interactions in business.

There is a third source of intelligence—more difficult to specify, less accessible, and generally inchoate, ill-defined, and ambiguous, but nevertheless potentially the most important—to which the executive must respond, for he cannot order it. This is the intelligence of future shock and the doomsday syndrome which is to be found at every street-corner book store.

Having said something about the structure of decision making, we now turn to the process, or dynamics, of decision making.

TOPIC 2
The dynamics of decision making

Most of the standard books on management and operations research contain analyses of the decision-making process which are largely algorithmic in character. While these descriptions of the decision-making process are supposedly positive, as opposed to normative, they have a distinctly theological ring about them. Such decision theories are strongly reminiscent of the traditional military analysis of problem solving which every junior military officer learns, like an acolyte saying his prayers, but forgets as soon as he is involved in active operations.

Essentially such an analysis takes the form of an algorithm. As shown in Figure 11–4, the assumption is that the factors affecting the problem

FIGURE 11–4
ALGORITHMIC DECISION PROCESS

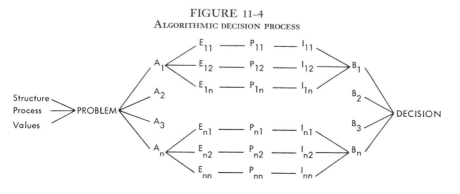

Box 11.1: Assessing the effectiveness of organizational performance—A new approach

Stanley E. Seashore and Ephraim Yuchtman of the Institute for Social Research, Ann Arbor, have applied the technique of factorial analysis in an effort "to seek some order and perhaps simplicity, in the numerous and miscellaneous variables used by managers researchers and the general public in defining and evaluating the performance of an organization."

They confined their research to the insurance field, choosing "75 independently owned and managed life insurance sales agencies located in different communitie throughout the United States" whose annual performance they examined over an 11 year period. Their scheme takes into account the fact that "organizational performance fluctuates with time and that few variables, if any, can be expected to reveal much constancy over time, even though the network may have stable features." With this in mind, they set about to isolate from over 200 variables those which appeared to form some related pattern.

To date, researches have concentrated on the concept of "goal" as the yardstick by which to assess organizational performance. Seashore and Yuchtman felt that because "goals" are so numerous and varied, preoccupation with this concept leads to a dis ordered accumulation of data which cannot be meaningfully structured.

They chose instead to explore the infrastructure of the concept of "goal" and to tease out the underlying dimensions of goal achievement. They were thus able to isolate a common denominator characteristic of all goals—the on-going process of acquiring scarce and valued resources with which to achieve the traditional goals. In this research context, the following 10 factors were given meaningful identification:

1. Business volume:
   This factor comprises the various aspects of agency size, such as the number of lives insured.
2. Production cost:
   Average cost per sale, per $1,000 insurance, and per $100 premium.
3. New member productivity:
   Average volume of sales per new agent as well as relative performance of established agents.
4. Youthfulness of members:

S. E. Seashore and E. Yuchtman, "Factorial Analysis of Organizational Performance," *Adm* *trative Science Quarterly*, Vol. 12, No. 3 (December, 1967), pp. 377–95.

can be analysed in terms of structure (Who is he? What is it? How does it fit?), process (Is it on-going? How did we become aware of it?), and values (What dilemmas and conflicts are involved?). From this analysis, alternatives (A) emerge; the effects (E) of each alternative can be weighed in terms of probability (P) and importance (I); decision factors (B) emerge, and from them a decision is made. This is a tidy scheme; but it is not decision making as it happens in fact. The organizational psychologists' approach is somewhat different. (See Box 11.1.)

SYSTEMS APPROACH

Since the system is not completely knowable, decision making requires a heuristic, rather than algorithmic, model. As A. C. Filley and R. J. House point out in *Managerial Process and Organizational Behavior:*

Ratio of young to old agents as well as ratio of young to old performance as an indicator of viability.
5. Business mix:
   The choice of strategy—selling many policies of relatively low unit value as against selling few policies of high unit value.
6. Manpower growth:
   Absolute and relative increases in sales force.
7. Management emphasis:
   The choice of the individual manager between selling and administration.
8. Maintenance cost:
   Collection costs—total and per $100 premium.
9. Member productivity:
   New business per agent.
10. Market penetration:
    Insurance per capita and lives per 1,000 insurable.

Each of these factors involves competition among firms for the necessary resources which, because of their scarcity, are valuable to the achievement of a firm's visible goals. The degree to which a firm is able to exploit its environment in the acquisition of these resources will then determine its effectiveness, subject to two qualifications: (a) a recognition of differing degrees of environmental potential; (b) an optimization concept which recognizes that successful exploitation is not synonymous with maximum short-run exploitative ability. Such a perspective runs the dangers of environment destruction in so far as it destroys favourable long-run transaction potential; an optimization approach, on the other hand, seeks to balance strategies—for example, increasing the degree of market penetration (long run) at the expense of higher production costs (short run).

Seashore and Yuchtman do not claim that these 10 factors constitute a universal set; they recognize "that while several of them are universal, others may be unique" to the agencies in their study. Because of this they hope that similar procedures will be applied in future studies so that appropriate comparative dimensions can be found.

Hirschman and Lindblom (1962) hold that such sporadic, inconsistent decision making may in the long run produce better results than stable and clearly defined end goals, most of which are only vaguely perceived by the human mind. In their view, progress may actually be impeded by the kind of centralized and rational decision making that classical theory precribes. Thus they criticize traditional theory not only on the ground that it does not adequately describe what actually takes place when a decision is made, but also because it assumes that once a state of imbalance has been resolved by an appropriate decision, the question is settled once and for all. In like manner, Cyert and March (1963) view quasi rather than complete resolution of conflict as characteristic of most organizational decision making. According to these views, the classical model does not allow for change, whether it emerges from developing technology or from the inadequacy of previous procedures.

The modern organizational behaviour approach to decision making is based on the proposition that you do *not* begin by stating what your objectives are and then invent the means and make your selection, but rather that you study the interaction between the process and possible outputs. Since the future is unknown, uncertain, and impossibly complex to figure out completely, the best strategy is to start playing about with the bits you can handle, even if they are apparently tangential, and hope creative synergy will take over at some point.

What is being argued here is a systems approach to decision making. If decision making is remedial (putting out fires), fragmented (deals with one problem partially at a time), and serial, then the system is bound to get unbalanced. But this is exactly what a system is designed to cope with. As one subsystem gets out of balance the other subsystems push and pull to bring the whole system back into line somewhere further forward. As Lenin would say, "One step forward, two steps back."

FIGURE 11–5
Two problems

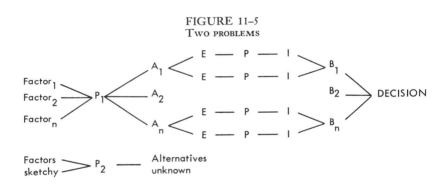

Decision making is more likely to go wrong because of selecting the wrong problem than because of faulty analysis of the problem. Figure 11–5 illustrates two problems, the first easily solvable according to the algorithmic process (Figure 11–4) and the second difficult to solve in any way. Problem P_1 may be easy to define and capable of efficient solution, but P_2 may be the more important problem. As Peter Drucker puts it, "Efficiency is doing things right; effectiveness is doing the right thing." Ideally a manager does the right things right.

What it amounts to is if you take any problem too seriously you have to pay elsewhere. For example, if you become convinced (as Allied planners did in World War II) that if you lose the convoy battle against the U-boat in the North Atlantic you are going to lose the war—an essentially correct conclusion—then there is a distinct danger you may so overkill the U-boat problem in the North Atlantic that the U-boats decide to go somewhere else like the Caribbean or the Indian Ocean and screw up Allied efforts there. Thus the principle of suboptimization was born. If you overkill on production, maintenance and quality will suffer. If you are too thorough on quality, little or nothing will get out the gate.

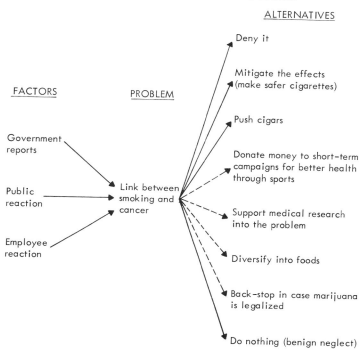

FIGURE 11-6
EXTENDING CIGARETTE MANUFACTURERS' OPTIONS

ALTERNATIVES

Deny it

Mitigate the effects
(make safer cigarettes)

FACTORS   PROBLEM

Push cigars

Government
reports

Donate money to short-term
campaigns for better health
through sports

Public   Link between
reaction   smoking and
                cancer

Support medical research
into the problem

Employee
reaction

Diversify into foods

Back-stop in case marijuana
is legalized

Do nothing (benign neglect)

For example, an automobile manufacturer will operate more effectively at one period by allocating some cash to franchised dealers to repair cars under a warranty than by applying this cash to improving quality standards on the production line. Changing the warranty to a five-year guarantee for the engine and power train, as Chrysler was first to do, may have had a decisive effect on its share of the market. Once you have established a better share of the market, it may be more effective overall, for you, to reduce your guarantee to 12 months and concentrate on production, removing faults that will show up in this shorter period, and to raise your prices less than your competitors. The essential point is that you select your package of options to maintain your overall position and keep your total system viable.

Effective decision making is facilitated by refusing to accept the spectrum of alternatives that appears at first sight. Figure 11–6 illustrates both the readily apparent (solid lines) alternatives that cigarette manufacturers may have come up with when their industry was charged with contributing to lung cancer and a few of the less obvious ones (broken lines) that might be developed with further thought, synectics sessions, asking for suggestions, and so forth.

GROUP-INDUCED SHIFT TOWARDS RISK

In the last decade, considerable evidence has become available to suggest that group discussion leads group members to prefer more risky decisions than they had advocated as individuals. Studies initiated by James A. F. Stoner and given great impetus by M. A. Wallach and N. Kogan have demonstrated this group-induced shift towards risk. The phenomenon arises where subjects in experiments are asked to act as advisers to hypothetical persons who are facing a dilemma such as a move from a secure, moderately paid job to a challenging, well-paid assignment with no assurance of long-range security.

The subject is of great interest to students of organizational behaviour, who have a consuming interest in any process which will commit people to higher risks and thus commit them to greater effort to bring the exercise to a fruitful conclusion. Managers are intuitively aware of the actual process and are not unnaturally curious to find out what behavioural scientists have to say about the process.

Much of this research has utilized a set of 12 life-situation problems developed by Wallach and Kogan. Stoner adopted this instrument to test the hypothesis that groups are more cautious than individuals. He found that group decisions were significantly more risky than the mean of the individual group members' prior decisions. In "Risky and Cautious Shifts in Group Decisions: The Influence of Widely Held Values," Stoner gives this "typical life-situation item":

> Mr. B is about to board a plane at the airport at the beginning of his overseas vacation. Although he has been looking forward to this trip for some time, he is troubled because he awoke in the morning with a severe abdominal pain. Because he has never flown before, he thinks that the pain may simply be an upset stomach brought on by anticipation of the flight. Although he is not far from a hospital where he knows he will obtain quick attention, he realizes that a visit to the hospital will cause him to miss his flight which in turn will seriously disrupt his vacation plans. The pain has gotten more severe in the last few minutes.
>
> Imagine that you are advising Mr. B. Listed below are several probabilities or odds that Mr. B's abdominal pains will *not* become more severe during his trip. Please check the *lowest* probability that you would consider acceptable for him to board the plane.

Subjects are given odds ranging from 0 in 10 to 10 in 10 and required, separately, to choose their recommendation in terms of the minimum odds they would consider acceptable for Mr. B to board the plane. The experimental design then requires that the subjects after making their recommendations on a whole series of such items, get together in a discussion group, thrash out the dilemma, and again make recommendations for each item:

Before	Discussion	After
Make recommendations in terms of probabilities.	Learn of other recommendations and reasons for decisions.	Make recommendations again in terms of probabilities.

Analysis of the results of these experiments reveals that on the average, subjects shift towards greater risk. This group-induced shift has been observed in a large number of different kinds of groups, including groups of senior executives.

The most curious thing about the group-induced shift is that it runs contrary to what one would expect from the theory and findings of group dynamics research. Such research suggests that group members tend to exert the most influence on those members who occupy extreme positions in a discussion, and the effect of this effort is to pull such extreme opinions to the mean. Research on conformity illustrates this conservative effect of group membership. The question then arises as to how the group-induced shift towards risk can be explained.

An extensive and thorough review of this literature has been carried through by Russell D. Clark III, who has identified four different explanations: the familiarization hypothesis, the leadership hypothesis, the diffusion-of-responsibility hypothesis, and the risk-as-a-value hypothesis. The first hypothesis is that as a group through discussion familiarizes itself with the risk involved, the members will feel more confident in taking risky positions on the issue. Secondly, risk takers are perceived as leaders and thus influence those who are initially more inclined to take less risky positions. In this context, Yeshayahu Rim has suggested that high risk takers are the members who are disposed to leadership and influence and who are high in such personality traits as extraversion, machiavellianism, need for achievement, tolerance of ambiguity, and radicalism, and such interpersonal values as leadership and recognition (see Box 11.2). The diffusion-of-responsibility hypothesis argues that the effect of the discussion is to produce emotional bonds between members which save the individual from full responsibility for his later decision. The risk-as-a-value hypothesis argues that in our society, moderate risk is a stronger cultural value than caution.

In terms of R. F. Bales' analysis of discussion leading in small groups, the process seems to follow the following sequence:

1. Individual step:
   Make recommendations individually.
2. Group step:
   a. Process:
      Clarification—familiarization; get. the facts, isolate the issue, collect opinions.
      Evaluation—probe for feelings, establish bonds with other members.
      Decision—engage in consensus formation and risk syndication.

Box 11.2: Influencing others to take risks

Contrary to the belief that committees are cautious and compromising and opt for th conservative alternative, research has revealed that group decisions are more ris oriented than those made by individuals. The evidence is that it is group discussio not the implied safety of a group decision, that leads to increased risk taking. In th discussion, the influence of the riskier members appears to be stronger and affects th private convictions of other group members. Yeshayahu Rim reports on a number studies designed to reveal the characteristics of these more influential members.

Rim had over 750 subjects in groups of three to five answer a series of question individually and through unanimous group decision, and then obtained a private pos decision opinion. The most influential subjects were designated as those whose init score was closest to the group's final score. Various psychometric measures were the made of their characteristics and those of individuals who were most influenced by th group discussion.

Extraverted subjects were found to be both riskier and more influential than othe while those who scored high on neuroticism were least influential. High rating on nee achievement scores was also positively related to risk-taking and group influence. Fr a rating of the basic personality interests—theoretical, economic, aesthetic, social, p litical, and religious—it was found that individuals with high theoretical, above-avera economic, and low social interests were those who were riskier and most influenti Other personal characteristics which were found to be correlated with high risk takir and group influence include: high tolerance for ambiguity, high scores in both co sideration and initiating structure, inner-directedness, above-average scores on th radicalism-conservatism continuum, and above-average rating on tender-mindedne: In this context inner-directedness was defined as a reliance on inner values as oppos to tradition-directedness, which relies on the values of one's forebears, and othe directedness, which indicates dependence on the wishes of others.

In terms of interpersonal relationships, high machiavellianism and high values f recognition and leadership were found to be characteristic of the risky and influent individual.

Although Rim does not draw the conclusion, it seems obvious that the individu: who can influence a group toward taking risks possess all of the personality traits th have been found to be correlated with effective leadership behaviour. It should emphasized that Rim's data do not indicate that these individuals take the greate possible risks, but only that their willingness to take chances is greater than average.

Y. Rim, "Who Are the Risk-Takers in Decision Making?" *Personnel Administration*, March–1966, pp. 485–87.

b. Roles:

Task specialists, who are more extraverted, are prepared to commit the group to risky strategies. Human relations specialists provide support for the change in decision.

3. Second individual step:

Make a riskier recommendation.

What is interesting for the student of organizational behaviour about these experiments is that there has been so little effort to integrate the experimental findings from the laboratory with the data of real, actual decision making. The curious point is that many managers are intuitively aware of this process of the group-induced shift toward risk, and they have developed a body of practical knowledge which helps them to decide such matters as how fully they should poll and inform colleagues on a specific issue before a meeting. They are somewhat knowledgeable about the processes of consensus formation, risk syndication, and operating within the zone of indifference of subordinates. Practitioners and researchers would both profit from becoming aware of each other's positions.

THE CREATIVE ELEMENT IN DECISION MAKING

An executive, like a good physician, begins the problem of decision making by making a diagnosis of the problem to be solved. The diagnosis:

1. Identifies the problem.
2. Specifies the causes.
3. Defines the effects.
4. Helps to clarify the goal to be achieved.

Following the diagnosis, the executive sets out to find possible solutions to the problem. Rarely does he hit on one perfect way to solve it. Instead, as shown in Figure 11–7, he frequently lists the alternatives available to

FIGURE 11–7

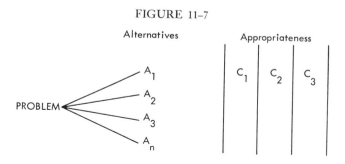

solve the problem and evaluates each against a set of criteria which tests the appropriateness of each solution. If none is completely satisfactory, he looks for further alternatives, hoping to find a better solution. To find other alternatives, he can either draw on his own experience or find out what other executives or companies have done in similar circumstances. Experience in the past has usually turned out to be a good guide to finding solutions to problems, provided allowances are made for changed circumstances. This is increasingly not the case in present circumstances, and novel solutions to novel problems have to be evolved. Figure 11–8 shows some of the stages that may be involved in creative decision making.

In the new industrial state—with the emergence of the new consumer, rapidly changing technology, increasing goernment regulation, rising com-

FIGURE 11-8
STAGES IN THE CREATIVE PROCESS

Process	Stage	Behaviours
Conscious	Preparation	*Saturation.* Investigating the problem in all directions to become fully familiar with it, its setting, causes, and effects.
		Deliberation. Mulling over these ideas, analysing and challenging them, viewing them from different optics.
Unconscious	Latent period	*Incubation.* Relaxing, switching off and turning the problem over to the unconscious mind.
		Illumination. Emerging with possible answers— dramatic, perhaps off-beat, but fresh and new.
Conscious	Presentation	*Verification.* Clarifying and fleshing out the idea, testing it against the criteria of appropriateness.
		Accommodation. Trying the solution out on other people and other problems.

petition, and new value systems—the conservative solutions of yesterday are less relevant to today's problems.

The automobile manufacturers, beset by the difficulties of designing cars which are safe to ride in, trying to keep the pollution of exhaust emission down to a safe level, and under the gun from foreign competition, can no longer rely on past experience as a guide to solving their current problems. With the electric car just around the corner and the Wankel rotary engine a distinct possibility, they are jammed into an entirely new set of problems, which cannot be solved by styling changes. The typical car owner is looking for safety, economy, and reliability, which make the tail fins and hooded lights of the 1960s quite irrelevant. What is needed is fresh, imaginative, and distinctive thinking to develop new cars which are relevant to contemporary needs.

What is creativity? P. E. Vernon in *Creativity* argues that it "involves novel combinations or unusual associations of ideas which must have theoretical or social value or make an emotional impact on other people." Yet surprisingly little systematic study has been given to the creative process. One technique for improving creativity is synectics.

SYNECTICS

Synectics is a creative problem-solving technique developed by William J. J. Gordon which means different things to different people. One view emphasizes the idea of bringing together people with different perspectives, skills, and information and locking them in a room until they come up with a novel solution to a problem. The word synectics, like many new, jazzy organization words, is derived from the Greek and means fitting together different and irrelevant elements. And this is just what synectics sets out to do: to provide a venue and a vehicle where apparently different and irrelevant elements of a situation are integrated to formulate new solutions to problems.

Synectics argues that the creative process can be taught. The synectics paradigm involves two paradoxical steps: making the strange familiar, and making the familiar strange. Ideas are rated on a scale of 0 to 100. And the trick is to get participants to recognize that no idea is useless and that they should build on ideas to move them towards the 100 side of the continuum.

The presumption is that everyone has creativity and the issue is how this creativity can be realized. Modern psychological research has shown that creative people are less anxious and more autonomous, dynamic, and integrated; they see themselves as being different from less creative people. They are less authoritarian, more achievement-oriented, and more accepting of their inner impulses. They appear to have better psychological well-being.

In essence, creative individuals seem to respond well to a moderate level of conflict. They apparently can cope better with their own wild, psychopathic fantasies, which they somehow channel towards solving problems. The aim in synectics is to facilitate the process of "letting go" so that the participants' imagination can run riot.

GETTING GOING IN SYNECTICS

To get a synectics session going, a group of heterogeneous, highly competent people with a wide variety of information should be brought together under the direction of a synectics guru who has a successful record of running such groups. This leader (or consultant, or perhaps catalyst) should explain the ground rules, which include:

1. Participants should explore with the entire group all ideas, no matter how intuitively or primordially formed, which bear on the problem.
2. The process must be characterized by spontaneous communication, not necessarily directed to the leader.
3. Evaluation of ideas must be postponed.
4. Members must exercise considerable listening skills.
5. Members should be prepared to paraphrase the ideas of the previous speaker before making their own contributions.
6. Members should begin their efforts with expressions such as, "What I like about your idea is. . . ."
7. Members should make copious notes which summarize other people's efforts.
8. Members should accentuate the positive and minimize the negative.
9. Questions should not be loaded to put down the other guy.
10. Questions should take the form of requests for information.

11. Meetings should be held in environments which are relaxed and non-stressful.
12. Evaluation should separate the idea from the source.
13. Nobody should be punished for coming up with a ridiculous idea.
14. Consensus should be the objective, with a willingness *in extremis* to settle for majority rule.

In spite of synectics, for many executives the creative process is mysterious and unanalysable; but to the psychologist, creative thinking is a process which is capable of analysis.

COGNITIVE STYLE OF CREATIVE PEOPLE

Man perceives his environment by an active process of transaction rather than being a passive recipient of the sense data with which his environment bombards him. As was discussed in the section on perception and personality, people receive information in characteristic ways, interpret it idiosyncratically, and store it in "the filing subsystem of their memory banks." As A. J. Cropley puts it in "Creativity":

> Hence, the cognitive approach to creativity asks about the extent to which highly creative people are prepared to take risks in their thinking, about their willingness to take in large quantities of the information the environment has to offer (rather than to restrict themselves to a narrow, but safe, segment of it), about their capacity for quickly changing their point of view, and so on.
>   Clearly, the more a person treats data which look to have nothing to do with each other as though they are related, the more likely he is to make data combinations which are unusual (i.e. to think creatively). The kind of person who codes in this broad way is referred to as a wide categorizer, while the opposite kind of person is called a narrow categorizer. People who make very fine discriminations between bits of input and who require high levels of similarity before they can see relationships (narrow categorizers), are inclined to store information as though it consisted of a large number of relatively unrelated, specific bits, and are thus unlikely to make the kind of cognitive leap involved in creative thinking. On the other hand, willingness to treat data whose connexion with each other is not immediately apparent as roughly equivalent would be particularly favourable to the appearance of creativity. Creative thinking thus looks to be related to width of categorizing.
>   Thus, those people whose cognitive style involves the least censoring of the information in the external world are most likely to be creative thinkers.
>   . . . the fact [is] that the highly creative thinker is, to put it plainly, prepared to think boldly. . . .
>   The creative thinker is, above all, flexible and adaptable in his intellectual functioning. He is not committed to the preservation of an exist-

ing *status quo*, and is prepared to rearrange his thinking. On the other hand, the rigid individual is convinced of the logic and rightness of his existing view of the world. He is unwilling to make rapid or drastic changes in intellectual orientation, perhaps even incapable, and he clings firmly to what he "knows" is right. In this latter kind of person, the intellectual flexibility which characterizes the creative individual is missing, and he functions in a highly convergent manner.

Having said much about the process of decision making, it is time to take a closer look at these creative persons who make the decisions.

THE DECIDERS

In making decisions, managers act as if they hold particular assumptions about the process. These assumptions include:

1. They will have a limited use of information.
2. Their own utility function is unclear, subjective, and subject to variation.
3. They will work under conditions of bounded rationality.
4. They will use simplified models.
5. The system will sort itself out.

Limited use of information

Most experienced managers are only too aware of the fact that information is an economic resource and, like all economic resources, has a value and a cost. They are also aware that information is subject to the phenomenon of declining marginal value: beyond a certain point, increases in information yield a declining marginal value. Many experienced managers, unlike their management science colleagues constructing models, are quite willing to let the physical processess process the product and the information and then decide intuitively what they are going to do.

Manager's utility function is unclear

While management scientists have a great and enduring interest in measuring precisely the value of potential outcomes to decision makers, most managers appear to have a rather unclear notion of what outcomes they really value. Perhaps this is just as well. Since the organization has multiple, changing goals, the apparent fickleness of the manager allows a process of suboptimization, perhaps with the margins wider than they should be. In any case, a manager's utility function, by its very subjective character, may lend some humanity to the organization. Even if managers wanted one, management science has made little real headway, in a practical sense, in coming up with a concept whereby preferences could be ordered cardinally on a scale of utilities.

Bounded rationality

Management science and game theory utilize recognized problem-solving procedures which are formal, systematic, and thorough. Nevertheless, managers work with a bounded rationality in decision making. The operations research (O.R.) models available are usually too complex, time-consuming, and untrustworthy from the manager's point of view.

Bounded rationality refers to the notion that the decision maker does not have a complete picture of the situation. Hence the manager may get a distinct feeling that his hands have slipped from the controls. But he is frequently forced to work with incomplete information and a poorly defined utility function. However, since his opponent has bounded rationality too (presumably), it would be a mistake to assume that he has to play against a completely rational decision maker elsewhere.

Use of simplified models

While operations research experts build complex mathematical models, more experienced managers utilize somewhat simplified models. Managers are only too aware of the experience of "paralysis by analysis," and they have learned to resist obstinately the O.R. scientist who wants to delay until he has developed a more and more comprehensive and valid model of the phenomenon being studied. At the other end of the scale is "extinction by instinct," and managers, by virtue of their weak superegos, are wide open to change and usually can be moved from an oversimplified model. O.R. scientists have to help management move away from closed, stereotyped, dogmatic thinking towards more relevant models.

The system will sort itself out

Most managers explain the lack of sophistication in their approach to models by arguing that the system will sort itself out. This may indicate that managers tend to be optimists; a little constructive pessimism, though, is sometimes a good thing.

TOPIC 3
Review of the decision subsystem

Management should begin its review of the decision-making subsystem by listing the important decisions required by the organization. The relations between these decisions should be specified and flow-charted. Decision-flow analysis will facilitate both an understanding of what decisions are being made by default and deciding how the structure of responsibilities and performance measurement can be linked. In the first instance, the decision analysis should be carried through in broad sweeps, with some-

what coarse analysis, if need be, to ensure that the whole system is reviewed. As Russell Ackoff points out in "Management Misinformation
Systems,"

> It is easier to introduce finer information into an integrated informa-
> tion system than it is to combine fine subsystems into one integrated
> system. . . .
> Managerial decisions can be classified into three types:
> (a) Decisions for which adequate models are available or can be con-
> structed and from which optimal (or near optimal) solutions can be
> derived. In such cases the decision process itself should be incorporated
> into the information system thereby converting it (at least partially) to a
> control system. A decision model identifies what information is re-
> quired and hence what information is relevant.
> (b) Decisions for which adequate models can be constructed but
> from which optimal solutions cannot be extracted. Here some kind of
> heuristic or search procedure should be provided even if it consists of
> no more than computerized trial and error. A simulation of the model
> will, as a minimum, permit comparison of proposed alternative solu-
> tions. Here too the model specifies what information is required.
> (c) Decisions for which adequate models cannot be constructed.
> Research is required here to determine what information is relevant. If
> decision making cannot be delayed for the completion of such research
> or the decision's effect is not large enough to justify the cost of research,
> then judgment must be used to "guess" what information is relevant. It
> may be possible to make explicit the implicit model used by the decision
> maker and treat it as a model of type (b).
> In each of these three types of situation it is necessary to provide
> feedback by comparing actual decision outcomes with those predicted
> by the model or decision maker. Each decision that is made, along with
> its predicted outcome, should be an essential input to a management
> control system.

In designing the organizational structure, decisions with the same or
overlapping informational requirements should be grouped in a particular
manager's role specification. The decision-making system will not be perfect, and the deficiencies must be identified and managed. To make the
decision-making subsystem work, it is necessary for three groups—the
information systems specialists (usually located in the control and memory
subsystem's domains; traditionally they are accountants); the operations
research men (usually housed in the data processing subsystem territory);
and the line managers (invariably to be found pinned down in the furnace
of the process subsystem)—to work together.

Not untypically, these people are just in the process of getting the input, transformation, and output aspects of their organization together
when an earthquake in information terms takes place in "an output of
some other system which will subsequently be an input for their system"
and turns their whole system upside down. It's the environment getting to

FIGURE 11-9
ENVIRONMENT TYPES AND DECISION MODALITY

	SIMPLE	COMPLEX
STATIC	Environment: Placid, randomized Perceived uncertainty: Low Factors Few ⌐ Similar ⌐ Unchanging Decision mode: DMUC	Environment: Disturbed-reactive Perceived uncertainty: Moderately low Factors Many ⌐ Nonsimilar ⌐ Unchanging Decision mode: DMUR
DYNAMIC	Environment: Placid, clustered Perceived uncertainty: Moderately high Factors Few ⌐ Similar ⌐ Changing Decision mode: DMUR	Environment: Turbulent fields Perceived uncertainty: High Factors Many ⌐ Nonsimilar ⌐ Changing Decision mode: DMUU

them. Figure 11-9 links the four environments discussed in Chapter 10 to the conditions of decision making under certainty (*DMUC*), under risk (*DMUR*), and under uncertainty (*DMUU*).

DECISION MAKING AS A SYSTEM

Decision making is one of the six subsystems of any system described in chapter 1, and this chapter has treated it as such. Nevertheless, we can also model this subject as a system in itself, and this is done in Figure 11-10. Using this model as a guide will help draw together the key concepts of this chapter into a format the executive can follow when he must decide to decide.

Since programmable decisions, under certainty or near-certainty, are generally computable and straightforward, the process considerations which are of interest pertain to the heuristic and noncomputable decision modes, as the states of risk and uncertainty present the executive with increasing complexity. He must choose his problem for its importance rather than its ease of solution. He must get used to thinking in terms of suboptimization, where scoring on one critical decision variable must be paid for by suboptimizing other variables. He must decide what is important to him, that is, assign values to particular outcomes in view of ultimate goals. He must not surrender his freedom of choice to the computer, which is only an adjunct of human intelligence. And he must accept that decision making is nearly always sporadic, fragmented, and rarely a matter of solving a complete problem in one continuous effort.

In terms of structure, the executive must decide whether the decision is programmable or nonprogrammable. This involves distinguishing among the states of certainty, risk, and uncertainty, and thus points to the kinds of processes to be used.

FIGURE 11–10
DECISION MAKING AS A SYSTEM

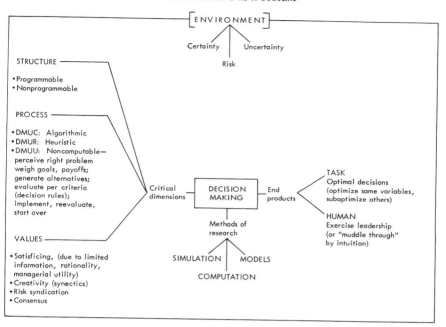

To make all this operational, he must recognize that effective management involves a blend of risk syndication, consensus management, and operating within the zone of indifference of subordinates: that different situations require different executive styles. Thus the executive carefully selects *his* issues. An effective leader relies on an accurate, up-to-date information back-up and is content to have the choice of structuring the sequence of decisions. Individual decisions can be made by consensus as long as he has the significant say in how the series of decisions is sequenced. In other words, other events decide individual events, not the "decision makers" for that particular event.

What this point means in particular is that the executive must seek to understand what is happening in the environment—not only the interactions between the organization and its inputs and outputs, but also the interactions between other organizations whose fusions and fissions may dramatically change the course of history of his outfit. The rates of externally induced change will inevitably make internally induced change into a side show, with the players locked in roles and scripts of yesteryear while the rest of the global village speculates about the course of their impending demise. Thus a vital topic is the turbulent environment of modern times, which refuses to stand still. Consideration of this existential confused complexity is a necessity if we are to avoid the catastrophes predicted by the computer Cassandras of modern times.

REVIEW OF PART TWO

In these five chapters we have examined the three levels of behavioural systems, the individual, the group, and organization—basically the central box of our systems model. How these three systems interact essentially determines organizational behaviour. We began by looking at the individual, his perception, personality, motivation, and learning; we then turned to the interpersonal and social processes within organizations, how people get into roles in groups (structure), learn the rules (process of socialization), and form ideologies (value sets). To flesh out our understanding of the interpersonal process and to convert the group to the organization, we made a detailed examination of leadership structure, process, and values and tried to link these input factors to the output factors, both task and human.

But the leadership literature is limited by its domain, which is essentially that of the group. Getting beyond Fiedler and House, useful and respectable as their researches may be, takes us into the intraorganizational world where J. K. Galbraith, H. A. Simon, and other polymaths rule, not supreme, but as old-fashioned Chinese war lords whose intellectual fiefdoms can be brought down from their dazzling dizziness to grim reality by a little empirical activity. The several dimensions of the intraorganizational environment (including complexity, uncertainty, and modal time of feedback) are reflections of technological, economic, and political realities which in turn are reflected in organizational structure and design, processes and procedures, values and ideologies. Such environments exist, and they are perceived as organizational climates. Climate in turn affects decision making, whose structure, processes, and values we have attempted to delineate.

What is being argued is that there is good evidence that organizational behaviour is the outcome of highly contingent relations and contexts. Such complexity will, we hope, become more comprehensible when examined in the light of our model, and more operational when examined with empirical detail.

REVIEW AND RESEARCH

1. You have been offered an appointment in a large metropolitan city outside your own state as a personal assistant·in charge of corporate planning to the president in a *Fortune* 500 company. (Select a company in the nearest large city outside your state.) Define the conditions (financial, intrinsic to the role), prospects, and other factors which would:

a. Take you to the new job.

b. Keep you in your present job.

Use the decision process sequence to make your decision to quit or stay.

2. Consider a decision (e.g., selection of a person, project, product, etc.) which was recently made in any organization with which you are familiar. List the other decisions that impinged on the focal decision. Identify the spectrum of choice, critical decision rules, quality and quantity of data collected, processes employed. Plot the decision on a yes-no decision tree. How could the quality of the decision be improved?

3. Identify the spectrum of choice, critical decision rules, information collected, processes employed, etc., for one of the following:

   a. The U.S. National Security Council during the Cuban missile crisis.

   b. President Nixon's decision to fire Special Prosecutor Cox in the Watergate case.

   c. The president of IBM's choices in regard to the antitrust suits facing the company (see the introduction to Chapter 10).

4. What is the most important organizational decision in which you have participated? List the search processes employed. Identify the filters in the information process. Construct a process flow chart of the actual decision.

5. Using the typical life situation of Mr. B about to board a plane which is described in the text, arrange for individual members of your class to estimate probabilities. The chances are 0 to 10, 1 in 10, 2 in 10, and so on up to 10 in 10 that Mr. B's abdominal pain will not become more severe during the trip.

Repeat the exercise after the class has discussed the problem. Did the group prefer a more risky decision? Why?

6. Describe the personalities, life styles, and operating procedures of three risk takers you know. Develop a composite portrait. How does it compare with Rim's description?

7. List the rules for creative group decision making. Use these rules either (*a*) to design a new urban rapid transit system, or (*b*) to select teams of students to find full-time jobs as a team after the team graduates.

8. What have you learned about executives as deciders from actual experience? Why *don't* executives follow the book and use the standard decision processes?

9. How is decision making affected by organizational climate? Use Rensis Likert's System 1, 2, 3, and 4 (see Chapter 10) to help you formulate your answer.

GLOSSARY OF TERMS

Certainty. State of knowledge in which the decision maker knows before the event the specific outcomes that will result from each course of action.

Creative process. Decision making under nonprogrammable circumstances, in volving three basic stages: preparation, latent period, presentation. The pre paration stage is conscious and includes the processes of saturation and deliberation; the latent period involves the subconscious processes of incu bation and illumination; the presentation stage (conscious) includes the processes of verification and accommodation (see Figure 11–8).

Decision process. Subject to the limitations of risk and uncertainty, the de cision process follows the basic steps of (1) setting goals and evaluating utilities, (2) perceiving the correct problem, (3) formulating alternatives (4) setting up standard operating procedures as decision rules, (5) selecting the first alternative which meets a minimal level of acceptability, (6) imple menting that alternative, (7) evaluating performance, and, if necessary, (8) changing the operating procedure and formulating new goals (starting the process again).

Decision making. The process of making organizational choices, which may be (1) programmable, (2) nonprogrammable—creative, or (3) nonprogram mable—negotiated, corresponding to conditions of relative certainty, risk and uncertainty, respectively. Programmable decisions presume agreed-upon goals, computational (algorithmic) processes, and predictable outcomes and are characteristic of classical theory. Nonprogrammable decisions as sume conditions of risk or uncertainty in regard to outcomes, demand creative and heuristic processes, are not computable, and are usually sporadic rather than continuous.

Iterative process. A trial-and-error approach to solving problems. It involve making a trial decision and evaluating the outcome of this decision with respect to a desired objective. If the objective has been reached, the proces stops; if not, another decision is made and the process is continued until the objective has been reached.

Risk. A state of knowledge in which the decision maker can specify out comes to each alternative course of action and assign probabilities to the likelihood of each outcome; measurable uncertainty.

Synectics. A group problem-solving technique developed by W. Gordon in which various elements are fitted together to produce novel and creative alternatives with a view to reaching group consensus.

Uncertainty. A state of knowledge in which the decision maker may be able to specify the outcomes for each particular course of action but is unable to assign probabilities.

Utility. The value of an outcome in relation to goals. In weighing which course of action to follow, the decision maker, as well as estimating the probabilities of particular outcomes, also attempts to gauge or measure the utility of each outcome, that is, how much he receives in payoffs (no mat ter how he measures these payoffs).

Part three

Influence

The next four chapters are essentially concerned with the influence process. In discussing influence, three issues are important: (1) its sources —authority and power; (2) the modus operandi; and (3) its consequences in terms of conflict and communication.

CHAPTER 12: AUTHORITY AND POWER

The sources of influence are authority and power, either of which can be defined in terms of the other. Authority, or legitimate power, which operates through consensus and risk syndication, is giving way to illegitimate power relations as the moral consensus in our society breaks down. This crisis of authority and the substitution of coercive power form a major topic. The chapter discusses the topics:

1. Authority.
2. Power.
3. Challenging authority: Marx to Dahrendorf.

CHAPTER 13: STRESS, SPACE, AND THE EXECUTIVE

How is influence exercised? The discussion usually has centred on leadership; but now behavioural scientists are casting their nets wider. In the classical approach to leadership, nothing was said about the consequences of exercising influence—stress and conflict—except the assumption that these were inherently evil and likely to go away when the utopia of good human relations arrived. Zoos drive animals crazy; high-pressure organizations drive men to alcohol, anomie, apathy, and coronaries; stress is a topic that must be dealt with. And, surprisingly, physical space is as important for man as it is for animals. Hence new subjects like proxemics are doing for organizational behaviour what Konrad Lorenz's *On Aggression* and Robert Ardrey's *Territorial Imperative* did for anthropology. Chapter 13 covers the topics:

1. Aggression.
2. Social ecology.
3. Executive stress.
4. Society, stress, and disease.

CHAPTER 14: CONFLICT

The discussion of stress and social ecology sets the scene for the study of conflict. Two models of conflict, the human relations and the realistic, are examined, as well as how conflict operates at different levels. The chapter concludes with the author sticking his neck out to offer some practical advice on taking advantage of this consequence of influence. The topics are:

1. Conflict at the individual, group, and organization levels.
2. Organizational conflict in depth.
3. Making conflict work for you.

CHAPTER 15: COMMUNICATION

Part Three concludes by examining the communication process (how influence is transmitted) and its relation to information theory and cybernetics. Special attention is paid to the roles of perception, personality, and language, and to the *Games People Play*. Chapter 15 considers how and why organizations structure communication flow; its major topics are:

1. Perception, personality, and language.
2. Dyadic communication: A interacts with B.
3. Communication in a group setting.
4. Communication and organizational structure.
5. Managing the organizational interface.

12

Authority and
power

Authority and power are interlocking concepts whose consideration is of central importance to the development of organizational behaviour. For organizations to function properly, some people must be able to influence others. Ultimately, there must be some means of resolving issues where reason is insufficient or intransigence makes it impossible to achieve a decision. Power is needed to direct and control the organization, which by its very nature has been deliberately structured for the achievement of goals.

What is the difference between authority and power? As usual, we must go back to the beginnings of classical theory to begin to work towards to-day's theory. The traditional theorist was more likely to talk about exercising authority within the organization, along the following lines. The need for influence and for making decisions means that A must be able to exercise legitimate authority over B, and B over C, and so on down an asymmetrical distribution (a hierarchy). A is B's superior (and probably, senior); when A instructs B, B's critical faculties are suspended. B is expected to carry out the instruction, which must be within his sphere and his competence—and which also must be within company policy and the law. If these conditions are not met, B will be mobilized in a negative way, and may reject A's authority in order to keep his cognitive balance.

This picture also includes the presumption that there is a shared sense of legitimacy between A and B—that they agree on a set of values and norms. Authority is the relationship between A and B, not an attribute of either individual; it rests on the willing compliance of B. Since it rests on legitimacy, this authority rarely needs to use persuasion or coercion (rewards or sanctions) to achieve compliance.

Authority has been classified in several ways. Max Weber classified it according to the basis of the legitimacy—traditional (e.g., the divine right of kings), charismatic (God-given, e.g., Hitler), and legal (e.g., the military code in the army). Another classification is: structural (position in the hierarchy), sapiential (expertise), moral, charismatic, and personal.

The traditional emphasis is on the structural aspects of power, in terms of hierarchy and the A to B superior-subordinate relationship; much of it is still pertinent to organizational life and will be developed in this chapter. But it takes a simplistic approach to a complex subject. There is abundant evidence from research in organizational behaviour that power or influence does not operate quite so simply in the real situation. For example, Tom Burns has shown in his studies of executive behaviour that frequently an event which a superior regarded as an instruction, his subordinate regarded as advice—two different perceptions of the same behavioural event. My own investigation of this phenomenon led me to the conclusion that an executive looks down in a Theory X (task-oriented) way towards his subordinates and upwards in a Theory Y (human relations–oriented) way towards his superiors. Figure 9–7 illustrated this concept as bifocal vision; Figure 12–1 depicts it as a series of perceptual filters.

So we begin to get clues that the traditional view does not explain much of what actually goes on. Group dynamics introduces the major complication that relations are rarely of the simple A–B type. Usually a group of people is required to make a decision operational, and the terms of reference for the authority relation are incapable of exact specification. In such circumstances, the process becomes more important than the structure.

Thus the single most important clue to our subject that begins to emerge as we get into the processes and value systems is that we need to examine "power" and its relation to "legitimate authority." Is authority the same thing as power? The answer is, yes and no. Power must be understood as having different aspects. For example, power resides simply in the idea of accomplishing tasks and achieving goals. Most organizational members want to get the job done and get the rewards for doing the job; those desires influence their performance and satisfaction. While this chapter focuses on more dynamic power processes, this utilitarian form of power (which is more static, or inherent) is always at work, and should not be discounted.

As we come to understand that authority should be thought of primarily as legitimate power, resting on consensus, we will gain an understanding of the fact that we are living through a crisis of authority. The break-down of the consensus leads to the emergence of what is often called "naked power"; the break-down of legitimacy gives rise to illegitimacy; and more precisely, what we mean by "not-so-nice" power is coercion. Coercive power uses rewards and punishments, control and

FIGURE 12–1
FILTERS TRANSFORM ORDERS INTO ADVICE

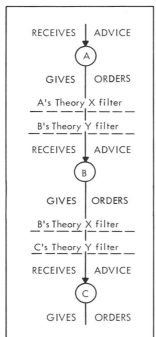

manipulation, and anything else it can get its hands on to "get it done, and get it done my way."

As Figure 12–2 illustrates, power—the ability to make the other fellow do, think, act, or believe as you want him to—can thus be utilitarian, normative, or coercive. Utilitarian power is simply the "carrot" of task payoffs, which A and B will co-operate to get. Normative power (authority) occurs when A and B (individuals, groups, or subunits) are in agreement on group values and norms. When they cannot agree on values and norms, reinforcements and sanctions have to be called into play, and the result is the "stick" of coercive power. As the Godfather would say, "I'll make him an offer he can't refuse."

Inevitably the application of power in organizations produces reactions. Informal groups, cliques, and cabals emerge to try to control the politics and patronage of power.

STRUCTURE OF CHAPTER 12

Topic 1 is authority, or normative power. The structure, process, and value systems are spelled out. The structure of authority is described in terms of its rules (legitimacy), roles (position), and relations (credibility).

FIGURE 12-2
UTILITARIAN, NORMATIVE, AND COERCIVE POWER

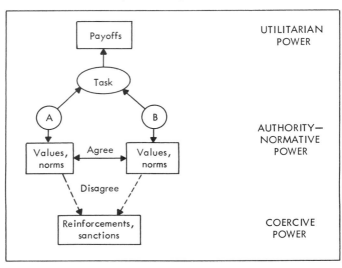

The process develops from an exploration (1) of the nature of the socia
psychological contract of authority and (2) of the achievement of com
mitment through consensus formation. The question is raised whether it i
possible to delegate total responsibility. Authority values are based o
legality, precedent, legitimacy, and due process. Our discussion conclude
with the modern dilemma of authority: the break-down of consensus an
legitimacy from which coercive power relations emerge.

Thus while Topic 2 concerns the full spectrum of power—the whol
process of influence in the organization—it particularly emphasizes th
pragmatic (utilitarian) and coercive aspects. Some executives have
strong need to exercise power, and therefore some attention is paid to th
authoritarian personality. We examine the proposition that power is
function of two variables, information and constituency. Control of infor
mation is the major source of power that flows from the bottom up—th
"lowerarchy." Other issues are the equalization of power and reactions t
the exercise of power, including the possibility of executive unionization
Using our systems model, we review the contrasting aspects of power an
authority in order to examine the modern crisis of legitimate authority
systems.

The question, "How does this massive challenge, this crisis of authority
versus power, sit with our North American preoccupation with democ
racy?" raises the issue of how to make democracy operational in organiza
tional life. Topic 3 reviews the challenge, from Karl Marx to Ral
Dahrendorf, at the level of society as well as of individuals, groups, an
organizations, to see what clues are available to new organizational direc
tions.

TOPIC 1
Authority

When the paralysed man in the New Testament was told, "Arise, take up thy bed, and walk," he did. That was authority being exercised and responded to—some people might say, extraordinary authority. But authority when employed properly, especially selectively, frequently produces extraordinary results. The issue at stake is what constitutes authority. The answer depends upon your point of vantage: authority may be defined by the person holding it or by the person over whom it is held.

The word authority implies the existence of an "author" who makes an instruction legitimate. This source is usually a person, but it can be a document or an abstraction such as "natural law" or "common law" (interpreted by persons). The great plea for civil order (though it ended up guaranteeing the place of the church in the state) was the imperative, "Render therefore unto Caesar the things which are Caesar's, and to God the things that are God's." The first proposition of this double-barreled imperative recognizes the need for some kind of legitimate power in a social system to allow it to function properly. Inherent in this proposition (though unstated) is the idea that there is a hierarchy of decisions which corresponds to the different levels of an organization or society, and that an institution works better when different classes of people address themselves to these different classes of decisions.

This is a traditional, structural optic. For example, in a medium-sized to large business the hierarchy may take the form:

Corporate strategy	Board of directors
Factory policy	General manager
Department programme	Department manager
Section schedule	Foreman
Process	Skilled operative
Task	Operative

Different types of individuals emerge who think and conceptualize in different ways, each with his own particular value system and life style, to manage and operate these different levels. Therefore, an asymmetrical distribution of authority is usually desirable (see Box 12.1).

To try to achieve conceptual clarity about how the term authority is used, it is useful to look at authority from three different optics—structure (rules, roles, and relations); process (how authority is exercised); and values (underlying beliefs and expectations that transcend the particular judgements involved).

THE STRUCTURE OF AUTHORITY

The structural optic is essentially an exercise in moral geometry and looks at authority through the prism of formal position, legitimacy, and

Box 12.1: Power or authority?

Although the myriad definitions of power differ in wording and complexity, the them
conveyed by most centres around the following: power is the ability to cause othe
individuals to adjust their behaviour in conformance with communicated behaviou
patterns (voluntarily or otherwise). The concept of authority is often confused with tha
of power to the extent that the terms are often used synonymously. The best way t
clarify the difference between power and authority is to consider authority a specia
type of power, involving voluntary compliance with legitimate demands and the su:
pension of judgement. Authority is an institutional mechanism designed to defin
relationships between individuals.

H. J. Leavitt offers the following definition:

> Authority is power that enters the two-party relationship through the organiza-
> tion. It is an institutional mechanism that aims to define which of two members of
> a relationship, A or B, will be the superior. Authority is potential extra power,
> given by a third party (the organization) to some of its members in order to guar-
> antee an unequal distribution of power; in order, in other words, to make sure that
> some people are chiefs and others Indians.

This analysis suggests that authority can be assigned or delegated, whereas othe
forms of power, such as expert power, cannot. The delegable forms of power includ
mostly external nonpersonal kinds of power, such as the ability to reward subordinate
with improvements in income or status. Leavitt says further:

H. J. Leavitt, *Managerial Psychology* (2d ed.: University of Chicago Press, 1964).

the rewards and sanctions inherent in the office. In this context, authority
refers to the vertical status relationships between incumbents in formal
positions. The bases of structural authority are these: the rule (legitimacy), the role (the position or office), and the relation (credibility).

RULE: LEGITIMACY

Legitimacy, or ethical sanctification, is the rule for authority. Legitimacy is the presumption that the relation is right and proper in a moral
sense. In its most explicit form, legitimacy takes a legal form when those
in authority have the right to demand obedience and those subject to authority have the duty to obey.

When a relation is perceived as legitimate, there is a suspension of the
critical faculties of the subordinate. This suspension is especially important
when it is difficult or impossible to justify in a rational way the adequacy
of a course of action by the mandates of the situation; here assent may be
achieved, not by rational persuasion, but by appealing to values, attitudes,
needs, and expectations that transcend the particular situation.

Because from his earliest days the child grows up in an aura of law and
order, the exercise of authority is seen as natural and normal, as something
to be expected. What this means in effect is that when one man is in au-

Formal authority is a delegable kind of power. Power to influence behavior may also derive from other sources, largely from the skills, personality, and possessions of the changer. Restrictive authority is seen by managers as a tool for co-ordination and control. It has advantages in simplicity and speed and in personal gratification to powerful changers who feel unsure of themselves. It also helps to establish a minimum level of conformity by all subordinates to the superior's standards.

A major difficulty inherent in restrictive authority is the probability of secondary changes in attitude along with desired changes in act-behavior. Restriction may constitute frustration and may consequently be followed by aggression toward the changer. Restriction may then incur only a minimal amount of the desired behavior change while also incurring significant increases in hostility and decreases in feedback. Restriction may thereby destroy relationships.

Authority, as a restrictive mechanism, seems to be most useful in short-term, specific situations, where B's retaliatory power is minimal, where the change sought is change in specific overt action, and where the restrictions are perceived as depriving rather than frustrating.

The authoritarian view of influence is likely to be motivated in part by needs for order, efficiency, and control. It assumes either that B is less competent than A or that A's role legitimizes A's use of authority on B. And it assumes a kind of B who will accept and live by impersonal rules and social contracts.

thority over another, and the superior orders the subordinate to do something, he does it without asking questions. Authority induces a suspension of the subordinate's critical faculties.

Two reservations are necessary here. The "something" which the subordinate is required to do must be both legal and legitimate. It must be legal in the sense that the order must not run counter either to the law of his country or, in some circumstances such as war, to international agreements to which his country is a signatory. Legitimacy is more difficult to define and is open to a wider range of interpretation, argument, and dispute. In one sense, legitimacy refers to the degree of "OKness" which the instruction has in regard to organizational policies, operating procedures, and standing orders. It may reflect particular informal mores and established personal styles. But legitimacy also can refer to value systems and life styles outside the organization. For example, the dropping of the name Mafia from the script of the movie "The Godfather" was a response to the pressure of a society of Americans of Italian descent. They were able to persuade the film's producers that the name Mafia was no longer "legit."

The verb "orders" is used in this context to make the real meaning of the relation explicit, though in fact it is more probable that in normal operating circumstances words like "please arrange," "it would be useful to," or "to meet our target it is necessary" will be used. When both parties understand the nature of authority, it is not only unnecessary but even undesirable to state too frequently its explicit nature.

ROLE: POSITION

A useful, if not always true, aphorism is that authority inheres in the office, not the person. This proposition can be played either way, to the advantage of either the superior or the subordinate. It all depends. Richard M. Nixon made good use of the separation of person and office to secure his reelection to the presidency, but was then signally unsuccessful in convincing his detractors that in protecting the office of the presidency he was not merely trying to save himself.

What is vital to understand about an office is that a person holding office is expected to behave in a holy way. Hence, the whole mumbo-jumbo about taking up office—inaugurals, taking of oaths, royal (and often religious) rituals, tenure, the issuing of commissions and pardons, the receiving of petitions, the distribution of patronage. A giant conspiracy is entered into which can only be broken from below by some dramatic process such as overthrow or impeachment. And, by God, if you hold the Queen's commission or a presidential warrant, you are going to discharge your solemn duties if it is the last thing you do. To be effective, business organizations have to be able to capture some of this corporate holiness and confer some blessedness on managerial office. Hence the effort that business organizations make to socialize neophytes into managerial roles. But the holiness of the office is not enough; control of rewards and sanctions is also required, although too frequent exercise of either rewards or sanctions weakens authority.

Significant abuse of the holiness of an office leads to a credibility gap, a state of disbelief about the utterances and behaviour of a role holder whose behaviour is seen as injuring the office. President Lyndon Johnson's credibility gap escalated with the Vietnam war, and President Richard Nixon's with the Watergate scandals; in both cases the pragmatic result was the loss of moral and political authority. In any such case, concerned people begin to speculate on the cause—whether it is moral culpability or executive incompetence.

RELATION: CREDIBILITY

Credibility is closely tied to competence, and both are linked to sapiential authority, which is the right to be heard by virtue of knowledge or expertise. Sapiential authority is not limited to formal vertical relations and usually, in fact, cuts right across the organization chart. Both technical competence (know-how) or actual operating experience confer an authority of competence. When people possess authority they have the ability to produce reasons for their orders, if challenged, or at least they are believed to have this capacity. In fact, they are rarely challenged when they possess competence or sapiential authority.

Traditionally, in organizations, two basic types of authority are recognized, line (vertical) and staff (sapiential). Line authority is based on incumbency in an office and staff authority is based on professional competence—and never the two shall meet on an equal footing. The whole invention of line and staff authority (which is, of course, derived from the military) is meant to give the weight to the line—who, after all, when all is said and done, do the fighting, the producing, the flying. To the question, "What does the staff produce?" the line executive would answer "Bumph" (paperwork and the like).

The clash between structural and sapiential authority is endemic to organizations and may be alleviated by invoking the authority of the person. A De Gaulle, a Churchill, a Roosevelt can bring to bear on an issue considerable personal authority. What is it? The literature offers a variety of terms: charisma, élan, leadership, personal magnetism. Personal authority seems to manifest itself in a certain presence, usually with a certain pomp and circumstance. Whether it is charismatic, structural, sapiential, or some combination of these, it all adds up to the same thing—the faculty of winning another man's assent. "Authority" used in this way means the process of securing assent.

THE AUTHORITY PROCESS

For too long now, the main tradition in regard to authority has been structural in its broad assumptions: people ought to do what they are told to do, particularly if told to do so by their lawful superiors; if they disagree, they should do what they are told and complain afterwards. Such structural mandates are incompatible with our moral attitudes and with the actual processes involved in the exercise of authority. A crucial task of organizational behaviour students is to explore the actual process within which authority is exercised.

To travel the vectors of the moral geometry of authority relations requires a grounding in the social contract theory of Jean Jacques Rousseau and Immanuel Kant. Man is born free, and each man has the right to the most extensive basic liberty compatible with a like liberty for others. When authority is exercised, it is exercised in the form of a contract which abridges or constrains this freedom. Both parties should enter freely into that contract. Thus the acceptance and the assumption of authority represent the different ends of a social contract which is integral to the nature of employment relations. This social, and psychological, contract is the agreement on values and norms between A and B in Figure 12–2 which constitutes legitimate authority. E. H. Schein, in *Organizational Psychology*, defines the psychological contract:

> The notion of a psychological contract implies that the individual has a variety of expectations of the organization and that the organization has

a variety of expectations of him. These expectations not only cover how much work is to be performed for how much pay, but also involve the whole pattern of rights, privileges, and obligations between worker and organization.

An employment relation is not slavery nor is it serfdom. This may seem a rather obvious negative proposition to state. But what it means in a positive sense is that the superior uses the minimal authority to achieve the task in hand, and that this must be visible to the party carrying out the order. If the subordinate does not see the contract as legitimate, he feels that he is a victim rather than a sharer, and the process reverts to the legality of coercion.

So far, the discussion has (we hope) proceeded in a reasonable, logical fashion. If the process were so straightforward in practice, books on organizational behaviour would be written by logicians and moral philosophers. But they are usually written by political scientists and behavioural scientists. The reason for this becomes obvious when the question is asked, Why should one man choose to be in authority over another? As Shakespeare said of greatness, "some are born great, some achieve greatness, and some have greatness thrust upon them"; others, we may add, purchase it; some win it by strength, force, or nepotism; and not a few marry into it. Not all learn to love it, but few can resist its trappings.

In any case, when one comes to examine the exercise of authority, it rarely operates within the confines of either logic or morality. There are three main levels of explanation for this divergence. The first relates to individual psychological considerations and treats of such matters as the executive's need to achieve; his need to settle old psychiatric scores (such as balancing his Oedipal equations); his need to test his compulsion for decision making, his irredentist need to expand his role at the other fellow's expense; and his need to vary the pattern of his betting in the organizational poker game.

At the second level, the executive's membership in groups, both primary and reference, plays its part. The three R's of these groups take their toll. A curious illustration of this group force is the enthusiasm with which many executives greet the opportunity to lead groups of their colleagues through the mysteries of the now celebrated managerial grid. In so doing, they freely play out the roles of shaman, shock therapist, and scapegoat. Such are the enigmas of the human relation.

At the organizational and social level, executives play out the class games of the status seekers, acquiring the paraphernalia and knickknacks of upwardly social mobiles. Thus the exercise of authority is bedevilled by all sorts of psychological and sociological forces.

But even within such a framework, managers have intuitively developed practical and pragmatic processes for the exercise of authority. Three different terms, describing different aspects of this process, are currently in use—consensus formation, risk syndication, and working within the subordinate's zone of indifference. They all involve participation.

CONSENSUS FORMATION, RISK SYNDICATION, ZONE OF INDIFFERENCE

Consensus, the present vogue word among managers, is difficult to define. A few strongly react to the term "consensus management," but all use it, including the military. Let us start to define this term by saying what it is *not*. It is not decision making by unanimity nor is it rule by the majority. It is a more subtle matter. In a positive sense, the more powerful clique or minority (usually two or three persons) agree on a solution which in a negative sense the majority agree not to oppose or make unworkable. It is not that top management has had a change of heart and become more democratic in spirit; but the reality of the complexity of the modern organization has gotten to them. Those who yesterday were less powerful to-day derive their power from realities such as the fact that the handful of employees who punch the cards that programme the machines can just as easily help to programme their betters.

C. I. Barnard in *The Functions of the Executive* has underscored the vulnerability of the corporate executive, who to survive must operate within the zone of indifference of his subordinates:

> If a directive communication is accepted by one to whom it is addressed, its authority for him is confirmed or established. It is admitted as the basis of action. Disobedience of such a communication is a denial of its authority for him. Therefore, under this definition the decision as to whether an order has authority or not lies with the persons to whom it is addressed, and does not reside in "persons of authority" or those who issue orders. . . . Our definition of authority . . . no doubt will appear to many whose eyes are fixed only on enduring organizations to be a platform of chaos. And so it is—exactly so in the preponderance of attempted organizations. They fail because they can maintain no authority, that is, they cannot secure sufficient contributions of personal efforts to be effective or cannot induce them on terms that are efficient. In the last analysis the authority fails because the individuals in sufficient numbers regard the burden involved in accepting necessary order as changing the balance of advantage against their interest, and they withdraw or withhold the indispensable contributions.

Reaching the consensus has become a ritual, usually started by top management's formulating contingencies over martinis in the executive dining room, followed by a series of task forces gathering data; then, in turn, the critical meetings begin. As in the "Aha! experience" so beloved of Gestalt psychologists, the chief executive discerns the emergence of a consensus. The various parties have exercised their right to be heard, and the emergent decision incorporates their ideas as far as this is possible.

Commitment has been achieved through risk syndication, which represents the sharing not only of the dangers and penalties inherent in the decision but also of the payoffs. The beauty of risk syndication is that recent research on decision making suggests that groups are prepared to make riskier decisions. The people who complain most about the length of such processes (of the interminable committee meetings) are those who risk least and stand to gain least; but their commitment is vital. This is why, in general, the need to operate within the zone of indifference of subordinates is so important.

Exploiting the myth of total responsibility

All organizations utilize these three processes in making decisions—consensus formation, risk syndication, and operation within subordinates' zone of indifference. Of course, the rituals, routines, and labelling vary from one kind of organization to another.

For example, top military officers have an obvious reaction to this social analysis of decision making which not only reveals their value systems but also throws some light on the whole concept of responsibility and accountability. Military training lays great emphasis on the need to assume command. A neat illustration of the virtue of this argument is provided by a quick look at General Eisenhower's crucial meeting on June 5, 1944, with Field Marshal Montgomery and his meteorologist to decide whether to give the "go" signal for the invasion of Normandy the next day. The weather prediction was somewhat uncertain but hopeful. Montgomery was for going on June 6. After having heard this intelligence and opinion, and knowing that many ships loaded with the first wave of the assault troops were already at sea, Eisenhower weighed the matter and decided to go on June 6. But what if this venture failed? To meet this contingency, the Supreme Commander of the Allied Forces prepared a memo in which he assumed full responsibility for the failure of the invasion.

To the dispassionate organization logician, this might seem to be an unjust allocation of culpability, considering that the operation was central to the overall Allied war policy, which had been decided by the British Prime Minister and the American President and also approved by the joint chiefs of staff. But Eisenhower's assumption of full responsibility freed up his immediate subordinates to assume responsibility for their particular operations. Exactly the same kind of allocation of responsibility takes place in business.

It is not uncommon in business to hear the company president say to the vice president of operations, "I'm holding you totally responsible for the Chicago plant." What can this statement mean? At first sight, it looks as if the vice president is totally responsible, and thus nobody else has any kind of responsibility. What it means in fact is that the V.P. should ask to have his terms of reference clarified in regard to levels of output, profitability, capital resources, market size, presidential support, hire and fire capability, and so on. He is responsible for managing the Chicago plant. His subordinates manage within this responsibility. Nobody is totally responsible.

If nobody is totally responsible, then is everybody equally responsible? As authority is divided asymmetrically, so is accountability. Accountability is normally a function of rank. But where there are disjunctions in the organization allowing a large measure of autonomy, there is the presumption of "total responsibility"—as is the case for captains of ships. In the navy, there is an automatic court martial of the officer who has the con if the ship runs aground. Shades of Admiral Byng, who was hanged by British in 1756 for his failure to relieve Minorea, *"pour encourager les autres."*

Industrial disasters, such as a company heading for bankruptcy, and political disasters, such as currency devaluations require their scapegoats and heads have to roll. One of the more telling arguments against treating business organizations as bureaucracies has been the recent wave of executive firings. Bureaucracies are presumed to be run as meritocracies with guaranteed tenure of employment until retirement. Such was the case for the Catholic Church and the British and American military and civil service; and it was true for the blue chip businesses in both countries until the late 1960s. Suddenly things began to go awry, and executives were being fired right, left, and centre.

What happened was that the turbulence of the environment began to get to the industrial organization. And soon this economic and political tornado struck at Boeing, at Rolls-Royce, at Penn Central, at John Brown's on the Clyde, and at Lockheed everywhere. The tornado was completely democratic and no respecter of rank. This break-down in the idea of treating organizations as bureaucracies has been accompanied by a questioning of the basic concept of authority.

AUTHORITY VALUES

When authority is being exercised properly in regard to matters of any moment, the several parties involved are usually aware of the gravity of the matter under consideration and envelop the occasion with a certain sanctity, if not piety, which is compounded in varying amounts from four separate elements: legality (the law requires it), precedent (it is honoured by time), legitimacy (it is seen as morally appropriate), and due process (proper and tried procedures have removed all reasonable doubt). These values are supremely functional and serve to allow reason, rationality, and reasonableness their full sway. Time is not a factor; there is an absence of duress; cases are to be argued, and argued persuasively if possible; roles (prosecutor, defendant, devil's advocate, etc.) are institutionalized.

When people are exercising authority properly, they experience an emotion which is, at the lower end of the scale, a peculiar amalgam of warm glow, comfortable smugness, boredom, and moral superiority, and at the upper end a heady mixture of hubris, omniscience, and omnipotence like that which took the United States to Vietnam—a quiet glow of moral rectitude and righteous indignation. Now all this augurs well—for the status quo, at least. The mills of authority grind small and exceedingly slowly. The point is that authority is for stability, the establishment, the established; and, if for change at all, for gradual change. Authority is identified in many people's minds, especially young people's, with the forces of repression—hard as this may seem to the established members of our society, many of whom who have fought and worked so hard to establish due process, precedent, and legitimacy in place of arbitrary fiat, unappealable decisions, caprice, personal pleasure, and the convenience of the powerful.

The question is now being raised not only of the legitimacy of authority but of the very concept itself. Many of the young intellectuals of our society see all authority as intrinsically bad. The presumption of societies previous to our own was that authority was built into the very fabric of society. The balancing position between these extremes is that authority relations are consensual—that the several parties to an agreement or contract must agree that in a disagreement there is some civil manner in which the dispute can be resolved (ultimately, by recourse to the courts). When authority is rejected, power relations which are coercive are substituted.

The radical and revolutionary students of the 1960s took this course—choosing coercive power over legitimate authority. Of course, they didn't reject all authority. They didn't argue against the use of traffic lights. Basically, they still accept the authority of learning in such matters as syntax. And they argue the merits of their case using logic.

The generation of workers and managers now entering our businesses have grown up in an affluent society, with Depression- and war-shocked parents determined to shield them from the hard knocks and "give them everything we never had." Brought up with this kind of hedonism and a materialistic view of the good life, such young people came of age with an awareness that there was a great deal of hypocrisy involved (money hadn't, obviously, made the older folks all that happy) and faced with death at an early age in an ugly, undeclared war. Their rejection of the authority of culture, morality, and law, embodied in such statements as "You can't trust anyone over 30" was perhaps not surprising.

This is a crisis of morality which affects not only the school and university but also the government. Most young people and many of their elders have lost confidence in government. And it is not only in the United States that there exists a credibility gap, but also in Britain. Many people in the United States and Canada believe their governments cannot govern because of size, complexity, regionalism, and the economic and technological rate of change. But to a degree there is the same lack of confidence in authority in Britain as well. Britain not only came up with the Beatles but also the skinheads, mods and rockers, swinging London, and Paki-bashers. Even Sweden, which managed a zombie-like social stability with economic growth, is now beginning to experience social tensions. And Communist Eastern Europe feels threatened by the possibility of girls in hot pants emerging in its midst.

The most serious challenge we face in our society is the crisis of authority. It is a challenge between legality and legitimacy. Legality represents decisions and propositions that have usually been reached at an earlier time (when society was structured on different value and power premises) and which are frequently at variance with the legitimacy needed to make such decisions work, in the spirit as well as the letter of the "legal" law. Legality is formal authority; legitimacy, informal authority.

No institution in our society is free from this challenge of authority. The inability of the judge in the Chicago Seven trial to control Bobby Seale sent cold chills running up and down the spines of an older generation, brought up to believe that ultimately what held society together was the law and that the due processes of the law were not only fair but could be shown to be fair.

This lack of confidence is also manifest in universities, where some professors have abdicated their responsibility to formulate the curriculum and to set standards of excellence for their students, to say nothing of their unwillingness to prescribe modes of thought, feeling, and behaviour appropriate to an educated person. What most professors secretly believe, the students openly believe. Sociological studies of class structure demonstrate that the upper middle classes hold the importance of education as a means of upward social mobility as the core element in their value system. But it is education as a means to an end, not as an end in itself; it is education as a meal ticket. And academics have created worlds within worlds— the first step is the diploma curtain, then the master's hurdle, then the Ph.D. rat race, followed by postdoctoral training. The sons and daughters of upper middle class executives and professionals, especially those brought up in a "radical liberal" tradition, recognize the folly and futility of the "university puzzle" that higher education has become. What we need to recognize is that authority has several bases and that appealing only to the legal or structural base may not be sufficient.

AUTHORITY—THE DILEMMA OF INFALLIBILITY VERSUS DEMOCRACY

As we have already noted, for authority to operate in a practical way presupposes the suspension of the critical faculties of the subordinate who is receiving instructions or directives from his superior. Essentially what is involved in the authority relation is a kind of temporary infallibility: that the superior, when he is specifying organizational directives and speaking to subordinates, is not liable to err. What is interesting psychologically about this assumption of authority is that it is a two-way street, where both parties appear to accept the advantages of the relation.

In a curious way, the organization appears to have a requirement for some kind of in-built institutional infallibility. In the Roman Catholic Church there has been the formal assumption of papal infallibility since 1870; in the United States the Supreme Court is required to give rulings which are presumed to be ultimate answers to matters of legal rights under the Constitution; in the 1930s and 1940s Stalin managed the Soviet Union by a kind of infallibility; and more recently General De Gaulle ruled France like a charismatic mediæval despot.

Apparently organizations cannot function properly unless there is the presumption of some kind of infallibility, no matter how restricted, as a presumed attribute of the chief executive's office. Logically, how else is deadlock in decision making to be resolved? The presumption of the need for infallibility does not exclude the need for careful data collection and analysis, for the seeking out of opinions of significant decision makers, for attempting to resolve the problem by consensus following discussion. But ultimately some kind of infallibility, which may rarely if ever be exercised, is required to enable organizations to operate.

Having stated the need for infallibility in the chief executive's office, let's examine what in fact happens when infallibility is invoked. The emergence of democratic institutions in Western Europe was mainly played out in the struggle between the monarch with his divine right to rule and the aspirations of the parliamentarians who wanted rule by committee. What has emerged out of this struggle? In the United States, government is out of the President's office and in Britain, the Prime Minister's office has weakened the role of the cabinet.

But over a longer period, power seems to shift between the office of the chief executive and the legislature. Much the same exchange of power seems to take place in corporate settings. Again, in the Roman Catholic Church, Vatican II introduced the corporate concept of collegiality. As Joseph Roddy, senior editor of *Look* magazine pointed out in its last issue (October 19, 1971):

> It seemed a good place for a miracle—Saint Peter's Basilica in Rome; and in the winter of 1965 after Vatican Council II closed there were many Roman Catholics who thought a miracle of sorts had happened in the vaulting central shrine of their faith. Twenty-four hundred bishops who had gathered there from all over the world, men whose skill at business administration was certain but whose ardor for theological change was faint, had somehow moved an ancient church with medieval ways into the modern world.
>   And it would do an amazing thing to its governing structure: Its popes, instead of carrying on as absolute monarchs long after the age of kings had passed, would share their power with the universal college of

bishops, the same twenty-four hundred very mortal men with their vanities and virtues about them in Saint Peter's. The bishops' new power was called "collegiality," and those who inquired about it were told to regard collegiality as the needed counterbalance to the primacy and infallibility of the pope, attributes of his office that few bishops had even thought to contest.

If the Catholic church is going for collegiality—for a higher measure of participation—then other corporate structures must really be going democratic.

Somehow a trial balance has to be struck. Authority in modern times has managed to survive, aided and abetted by centralized data banks and more comprehensive simulations. Even in authority's intended demise, the authorities programme the schedule or sequence of decision making. Able to invoke the argument of "operational necessity" and retaining the rights to pomp, privilege, and patronage, the authorities soldier on. But coming at them, going strong, is the Pepsi generation—who have never had it so good, who know more about COBOL than English, who understand subversion better than supervision, who know exactly how to pull the plug out of the system, who think the establishment on a good day is a bunch of old hypocritical squares. Given this lack of value consensus and the inability of those in charge to maintain the integrity and relevance of the process for making decisions, why doesn't the system fall apart at the seams? To try to answer this question, it is necessary to be somewhat evasive and change the topic.

THE THEOLOGY OF AUTHORITY AND THE PLEASURE AND PENITENCE OF POWER

Before moving on to Topic 2, let us for a moment recapitulate. We have seen the anatomy of authority in all its structural glory, in terms of legitimacy, position, and competence. We know about the purity of the process, the beauty of the psychological contract. It is good to know about consensus formation, risk syndication, and the zone of indifference of subordinates. And it is interesting to speculate about authority values.

But all of that is not real corporate life, with corpses and coronaries, crash programmes and crises, capitulations and capitalizations, champagne and kippers—just to mention some of the C's of corporate capers. Real corporate life needs the theology of authority to cover the sins of power, and to make the powerful penitent—but only after the power play. Thus having done our duty and looked upon the theological face of influence in the guise of authority, we turn (with the anticipation of pleasures to be stolen) to glimpse the other face, crooked but amiable, sincere but seeking the sinecure, disarming but dissembling . . . the face of influence that is suffused with "buts," called power.

TOPIC 2
Power

Power and authority are in dialectical juxtaposition: power goes beyond legitimate authority; authority is legitimate power. Thus if power represents the interpretation of authority, it shows the same broad characteristics as authority. Therefore, in structural terms, power is a property of a social relation; power is a function of clout, "can do," knowledge, and competence. In process terms, power presumes prediction and control of behaviour through the restructuring of the other person's perceptions. In terms of values, the power ethic is one of coercion, control, and manipulation which challenges and stretches legitimacy.

Continually stretching legitimacy ensures that power has a corrupting element to it. Statesmen and scholars who have shown too much explicit interest in power have been badly treated by history; Machiavelli is the classic example. As the great historian Macaulay observed, "Out of his surname they coined an epithet for a knave, and out of his Christian name a synonym for the devil." This stretching of legitimacy is both a human temptation and an organizational opportunity.

People crave for and play with power in a pathological way that is essential for both personal and organizational effectiveness. But "they" cannot be allowed unbridled power; power must be offset in some way. Hence the need for a balance not only of power but also of prudence. An organization run according to authority (moral and pure, freely contracted) degenerates into the old-fashioned bureaucracy, stale with red tape and stifling the imagination. The illegitimate use of power attracts a particular personality who gets a charge out of "pulling a fast one," taking the mickey," getting things done, making things happen—all by playing the power game. It is the illegitimacy, the bending of the rules, the squaring of the circle that gives the power-hungry his kicks.

It is now possible to set out the basic dilemma of organizational power: corporate health or effectiveness is the ability to mobilize the power centres of an organization to maintain flexibility, growth, and adaptation to the turbulence of the environment; coercive power goes beyond authority and of necessity is somewhat illegitimate, and therefore attracts somewhat pathological people. The issue is how organizational health and personal pathology can work together. The answer is, nicely.

THE POWER MOTIVE

Modern research evidence suggests, as we noted in Chapter 7, that the top man in an organization has a strong need for power. David C. McClelland, who has spent the last 20 years studying the need to achieve, has described his surprise when he discovered that the president of one of the most successful achievement-oriented firms which he had been studying scored exactly zero in need for achievement. McClelland soon realized that it was not the individual top manager who set the pace in an organization but the climate—which, as the reader will recall, is a more complex variable influencing how employees perceive not only the needs for achievement and affiliation but also the need for power.

The need for power, which is characterized by a need if not a compulsion to have influence over others, is regarded in a somewhat negative way by most people in both North America and Western Europe. People perceived as preoccupied with power are seen as harsh, sadistic, machiavellian, autocratic, neurotic, disturbed. The presumption is that such power-hungry types display zealous obedience to a hierarchic superior and require obsequiousness and sycophancy from subordinates, whom they treat in an overbearing and scornful way. Not a very flattering picture of the power-hungry executive; but a useful one. It is precisely this negative aspect of power which is so important to bear in mind. Power is necessary to move organizations, but excessive use (or even display) of power is perceived as threatening and is given a negative connotation. Given this ambivalent context, the powerful can be made to feel guilty. To avoid this consequence, the exercise of power must be made covert, which takes us right back into the double-bind world of R.D. Laing. Knowing this hazard, the sophisticated corporate executive anticipates this reaction and socializes his power.

McClelland became aware of the difference between personalized and socialized power when he was investigating the effect of drinking alcohol on stimulating power thoughts in men; small amounts promote socialized power thoughts and large amounts personalized ones. Socialized power involves the mobilization of energy for useful ends; personalized power is private, pathological, and destructive. People preoccupied with personalized power prattle on about zero sum games ("I win, you lose") and use military metaphors like "move off the beach," "go hull down," and "fire for effect." The opinion of behavioural scientists is that this "law of the jungle" imagery is bad news and should be used sparingly, if at all. In fact, most leaders can move between these two kinds of power pretty freely. Power is two-faced.

From Machiavelli onwards, not only academics but also statesmen have recognized that effective leadership essentially consists of the possession and exercise of power. The power motive—which may be thought of as the desire, if not in fact the compulsion, to establish control over other people so that their behaviour and attitudes can be structured, and so that the powerful can obtain their obedience, compel their actions, orient their thinking, and determine their fate—has enormous significance for understanding the workings of an organization. To be effective, the contemporary executive must be liberally endowed not only with the power motive but also with insight into power structures. Indeed, it is perhaps just as well to remember that on occasion, this craving for power may supersede even the financial motive. Evidence of this craving for power is provided by J. D. Houser, who interviewed a large number of business executives in an effort to uncover their motivation. Houser concluded, in *What the Employee Thinks*, that:

> Frequently the craving of the executive for the exercise of power was actually greater than the desire for financial returns. The desire for self-expression (in executives) is closely related to the desire to obtain and exercise power over others. . . . Power is very often the definite form of expression desired. . . . Their trampling upon other personalities, their hunger for self-expression and their keen joy in using their power constantly produce in workers a bitter resentment.

SOURCES OF POWER

What is power? It is possible to define power as the capacity or ability to secure the dominance of one's values or goals over those of another. The struggle for power within an organization—how power is acquired, transferred, and exercised—is usually referred to as "the power game." Organizational politics—who gets what, when, and how—is endemic to every business organization regardless of size, function, or ownership.

It must be apparent that an executive may exercise power for a variety of reasons. J. R. P. French and B. Raven have identified five different bases of power.

1. *Reward power* is derived from the belief, on the part of the less influential, that they will be rewarded in some way for complying. A considerable segment of an executive's power is derived from his ability to distribute patronage.

2. *Coercive power* has its origin in the belief that noncompliance will result in some form of punishment. This "unless power" becomes increasingly a "strategy of last resort" in our permissive society.

3. *Expert power* refers to the situation when the executive is regarded as having expertise, know-how, special information, or technological skill which has some scarcity value.

4. *Referent power* is held by an executive who is popular or admired, and with whom the less powerful can identify.

5. *Legitimate power* derives from the structural position the executive holds in the organization. In its most common form, a superordinate will "pull rank" on a subordinate.

If leadership is to be effective, it must rely on some basis of power. It is a commonplace to observe that hunger for power brings people to assume the functions of leadership. This is but to say that some people derive satisfaction from "running things." Individuals who are more likely to show initiative in an organizational context are those who are confident of their own views, are high in ego strength, and have a high need for achievement. Likewise in studies of leaderless groups it has been found that the more aggressive, forceful and dominating personalities were more likely to emerge as leaders. The most plausible conclusion is that the emergent leaders possessed a greater need for power, and a leaderless group situation proved an ideal opportunity for gratifying such a need. Nevertheless, it must be recognized that the aggressive, forceful and dominating aspect of executive behaviour is one dimension of organizational leadership. It is necessary to recognize that there is another important dimension, the need to maintain acceptability.

THE AUTHORITARIAN PERSONALITY

Most British executive selectors recognize this paradox in using the cliché "aggressive but clubbable" in job descriptions of aspiring executives. This peculiar combination of aggression and acceptability very often succeeds in producing only the authoritarian personality. Argyris, in *Personality and Organization* has presented convincing evidence that a great proportion of executive behaviour observed in industry was directive, autocratic, and pressure-oriented. Argyris has presented a penetrating and convincing analysis of the authoritarian personality, who compulsively obeys rules and regulations, even when they are irrational and believes that the executive leader is someone who has power, yet somehow is capable of being submissive towards his own boss and dominating towards his subordinates.

How does the authoritarian personality handle the economics of hostility? He represses his hostility towards his superior and by a process of reaction formation develops an uncritical attitude towards his boss while channelling this hostility to his subordinates (see Box 12.2).

Now having reviewed the definition of power, its sources, and its attraction for the authoritarian personality, we turn to how power is exercised.

EXERCISING POWER

Exercising power usually means structuring a situation in a particular way so that behaviour results that would not have occurred if that restructuring had not taken place. Essentially, then, power is the ability to restructure the stimulus qualities of a situation so that the other person's perceptions will be changed in a manner which will facilitate your intention, by reducing his expectations of significantly changing your probability of successfully achieving your objective.

As shown in Figure 12–3, power is a function of two types of variables, information and the constituency represented. The contention of this approach is that high-ranking individuals in organizations have influence

Box 12.2: The authoritarian

Roger Brown has provided an excellent evaluation of *The Authoritarian Personality,* by T. W. Adorno. According to Adorno, the authoritarian personality exhibits a rigid adherence to conventional, middle-class values and believes "obedience and respect for authority are the most important virtues children should learn." For him the businessman and the manufacturer are much more important to society than the artist and the professor. Curiously enough, he reveals a rather submissive attitude to those who command him.

He focuses his hostility on hippies and people who violate conventional values. He believes that "if people would talk less and work more, everybody would be better off." He has a definite bias against the introspective, imaginative, and tender-minded and is as well somewhat superstitious; he tends to think in rigid categories.

Power is extremely important to him. As well as manifesting a generalized hostility, he is inclined to be somewhat cynical. Not too surprisingly, the authoritarian personality believes "that wild and dangerous things are going on in the world." It is predictable that he would believe the underworld has tremendous powers. The authoritarian also enjoys an exaggerated concern with sexual "goings on" and takes a very severe view of sexual perversion. To him, women can be divided into two types—the madonnas (not sexy, but morally good) and the prostitutes (sexy, but morally bad).

Adorno developed the F scale (to measure the tendency to fascism) which revealed the above characteristics of authoritarians, and demonstrated as well that ethnocentrism, anti-Semitism, and potentiality for fascism are closely interrelated.

THE PREJUDICED PERSONALITY

The prejudiced person takes a consistently favourable view of himself. Prejudiced persons say such things as: "I have always tried to live according to His Ten Commandments," or "I think one of my best assets is my poise," or "I've always had a happy disposition, and I've always been honest with my family." From unprejudiced subjects come such appraisals as: "I'm rather shy, don't like competition," or "I don't mean I am in love with my mother, but I have a dependency complex . . . married a woman older than myself."

Roger Brown, *Social Psychology,* Chap. 10 (New York: Free Press, 1965).

because they have access to more information sooner than lower ranking individuals. Further, their information is better; it has higher reliability (consistency) and validity (correspondence to reality), and usually has identifiable sources and rationales. In fact it is possible to define status in terms of information privileges. Thus the source of influence is related to the structure of information and largely corresponds with structural au-

FIGURE 12–3
ROLE AS AN INFORMATION PROCESSING SYSTEM

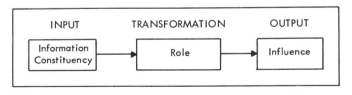

In describing their sexual experiences, for example, prejudiced men boast of their onquests and represent themselves as ideals of masculinity, while women speak of aving "scads of boys friends." By contrast, an unprejudiced woman says: "I'm avoided y the male sex, perhaps because I am heavy"; and a man reports that he has "always een rather inhibited about sex."

Prejudiced subjects say of their fathers: "He is very sincere and very well liked by is friends and employees," and "He is exceptionally good looking, dresses well, has ray hair," and "I've always been very proud to be his son." Of their mothers they say: Most terrific person in the world to me," and "She's friendly with everybody." The rejudiced person does not have a father and a mother for parents; he has Father's Day nd Mother's Day.

Unprejudiced subjects say of their fathers: "Father tries to be rational but is not lways so," and "I think he wanted a boy, so he paid little attention to me." Of their 1others they say: "She is practical and sensible, but she gets too much interested in 1ds," and "She gives me too much advice." Prejudiced subjects were judged to be 1ore rigid and also more intolerant of ambiguity than the unprejudiced.

ROWN'S EVALUATION

What of *The Authoritarian Personality* survives the many devastating criticisms Brown 1akes of its methods? After reviewing the evidence and critiques of this very important tudy, Brown concludes: "On the level of covariation, of one variable correlated with 1other, the findings of *The Authoritarian Personality* seem to me to be quite well estab-shed. Anti-Semitism goes with ethnocentrism goes with anti-intraception goes with lealization of parents and self goes with authoritarian discipline in childhood goes with rigid conception of sex roles, etc. Two of the presumptive correlates are not well stablished: status-concern or marginality, and the cognitive style, characterized by gidity and intolerance of ambiguity."

Brown argues that further research is needed to establish the dynamics of authori-1rianism.

---

thority. To get from structural authority to structural power, an individual should make selective use of the former.

For example, a regional sales manager might elect to telephone a branch manager at 4:30 P.M. on Friday to ask for an explanation of the latest computer print-out on sales which has just come off the computer, a copy of which will be mailed to the branch manager first thing on Monday. Such an action might or might not be justified (legitimate) or capable of being justified (seen to be legitimate). It depends to some extent on the motivation of the people involved, the actual outcome, and the organizational value system. But if the regional sales manager assesses the effect of the initiative as anxiety-provoking and cautions the branch manager on every occasion when they meet with "I'll give you a call on Friday—one of these days. See how you are making out . . . [a pause signals a reference to his original call]. Give my regards to the good lady and the kids"— then authority has been transformed into power.

Secondly, as well as being a function of information influence is also a function of the constituency which the person represents or of which he is a member. Constituency based on influence is very clear in legislatures, trade union negotiations, and international conferences. It is also a source of power for members of a constituency to write to their M.P.'s or congressmen, to the editor of the *New York Times*, or to the president of General Motors.

Exactly the same principle operates in organizations. Membership in a constituency is a source of power. An example of a power interaction among constituencies can be seen in the following dialogue:

COMPUTER OPERATOR: I know I speak for the other operators when I say we can't leave the computer centre to deliver print-outs. We are professionals.

MOVING MAN: It's nothing to do with me. We'll move anything as long as you put your orders through my boss—he'll process the orders.

SECRETARY: We secretaries are paid to do specialized work. We're not "gofers."

BOSS: I'm going to leave you three here till you come up with a solution; if you don't I'll impose one. You're on your own.

Constituency power relates to the notion that a proposition is a requirement of, or an attack on, the value-norm system of the constituency.

Figure 12–4 indicates how role and status are interlocked in this information nexus. Status relates to the possession of certain information privileges. For example, a policeman normally has no more legal authority than other adults in regard to the powers of arrest, except when he is armed with a warrant. The ordinary citizen has the same powers of arrest, which are meant to be exercised in specific circumstances. But what the policeman has is a certain status which gets him faster access to the system; and with it, the presumption that he is probably acting in good faith and, if not, that he can make the whole thing stick.

Thus status has functional value in that the status of a role holder is a kind of credit card which allows him access to an organization's informa-

FIGURE 12–4
CONSTITUENCY INFORMATION NEXUS

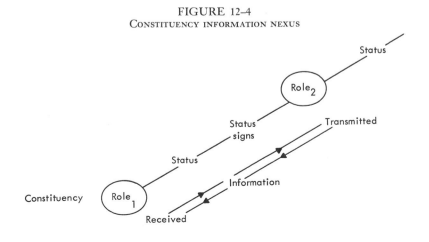

tion system—to input information ("I'll put you on report"), to have information processed ("Schedule the Jones account for credit status"), and to receive information ("Let me have his personnel file"). Through the use of status signs or symbols, a doctor in a hospital or a manager in a plant can quickly tune in or be tuned in to the system. Thus even status symbols have a certain functional value, which is quickly revealed in the young intern with his stethoscope round his neck or the young officer with his binoculars outside his combat jacket. Naturally, there are disadvantages to having to wear status signs. New infantry officers going into combat are warned to put their binoculars inside their combat jackets, but proportionately more officers are still hit, for roles represent sets of obligations which have behavioural implications. In the case of the infantry officer, that means leading; and the led look to the leader, giving his position away.

The led, as members of the "lowerarchy," are usually somewhat skilled in controlling the leader through the monitoring of his information needs. This question of the power of the lowerarchy warrants more careful examination.

POWER OF THE LOWERARCHY

It is not unusual for people at or near the bottom of the hierarchy to exercise considerable power. Power is often attained by executive secretaries, storekeepers, computer programmers, attendants in mental hospitals, guards in buildings, copy machine operators, students in universities, and even prisoners in jail.

As we have already mentioned, power is a function of information received, processed, and dispatched; functions (both critical and routine) performed; and membership in a particular constituency. Taking each in turn and beginning with the relation between power and information, it seems to fit with common sense to accept that a role in an organization has particular informational privileges. But information, like leave in the army, is a privilege, and lowerarchs can influence—indeed may control—the informational inputs of superordinates. A classic illustration of information control was the filtering (in fact, the suppression) of information flows at My Lai in Vietnam during and after the massacre there. More ordinary illustrations are to be found in industry, where lowerarchs report production figures that correspond more with their notion of the quota and rather less with actualities.

Information in this context includes not only knowledge about technological and organizational processes but also the three R's of the primary working group. The lowerarchs control the flow of their data in a cabalistic way, and thus can influence superiors, who can frequently only operate with great difficulty, if at all, without their co-operation.

This argument applies with even greater force to the executive neophyte who takes command of a primary working group. In many process industries, the process operators control the quality of the product by refusing to make the actual adjustments explicit ("When the mix just begins to boil, I spit in the tank and give the stirring control a dirty great kick"). Such fine tunings do not appear in the formal standing orders governing manufacture.

The second source of power for lowerarchs is the function they perform. L. R. Sayles has classified disputes according to the functions which shop floor people carry out. As an example of a critical function, keypunchers can stop punching cards and halt the computers which programme huge car plants. The importance of routine activities is underscored by the fact that hospital attendants, orderlies, drivers, or food servers can bring a large, sophisticated hospital's operations to a grinding halt.

The third source of the lowerarchy's power is membership in constituencies. In his own bailiwick, a person low on the totem pole can claim protection by insisting on conformity with the norms of his work group. The principle being invoked is, "Hit me, hit my group." Superiors have a vested interest in ensuring a measure of consensus as to the rules of the game and the extent, force, and frequency of their application. Alvin Gouldner has pointed out that rules serve as a substitute for surveillance; and since surveillance takes time and effort, is expensive, and mobilizes hostility, rules are to be preferred. Rules facilitate simple screening of violations and legitimize punishment for their violation by making ignorance culpable; finally, the selective ignoring of rules gives the boss power. According to Gouldner, rules are the "chips" to which the company stakes the supervisors, giving them power in playing subordinates. But as David Mechanic points out, rules are "chips" for everybody. The lowerarch has only to "work to rule" to grind the whole place to a standstill. As Captain Queeg in *The Caine Mutiny* put it, "There are four ways of doing a job: the right way, the wrong way, the Navy way, and my way. I want things done my way." Applying the rules his way ended up with a mutiny, a court martial, and Queeg in command of a land ship.

Constituency memberships include groups other than work groups which a person can invoke. Such groups include the Masons, the Knights of Columbus, veterans' associations, professional associations, the Mafia, and many others. Different organizations are influenced by these different constituencies. The military-industrial complex and the university-government-business complex have produced some beautiful "old-boy nets" which keep our pluralistic society functioning by providing connective tissue.

While power for the lowerarchy is a function of information, role and constituency, the weight attached to each factor varies from organization to organization and depends on the personalities involved. In every organization, as we have seen, there is hierarchical power (from the top down) and lowerarchical power (from the bottom up). The need here is to strike a useful balance—to equalize power.

POWER EQUALIZATION

So you have learned to exercise power—to establish dominance by the tone of your voice and the tilt of your head; to command, if not respect, at least compliance; and to send a cold chill running up and down the spine of anyone who would challenge you. Now you have to learn how to achieve power equalization.

We know from studies of mental hospitals that if the system is excessively rigid in terms of bureaucratic control, patients not only do not get personal growth but frequently regress. The continuous exercise of power in our contemporary complex organizations, by the same token, forces members into bureaucratic roles which strangle individual growth and self-development, generating anomie (loss of reference), apathy (indifference), and alienation (rejection of the group's values). All this can be extremely dysfunctional. Complex organizations are dependent upon individual initiative and creativity to flesh out and give meaning to directives coming down the line which cannot be made too specific because of the complexity of the situation. The answer is power equalization.

Power equalization is integral to both the human relations school and the T group approach. Essentially, it requires a reduction in the vertical power-status differential. Power equalization represents a movement against overprogrammed work, rigid hierarchical controls, and excessive job specialization and a movement towards job enrichment, increased delegation, and participation through such techniques as management by objectives and Rensis Likert's System 4.

THE REACTION TO POWER AND AUTHORITY IN ORGANIZATIONS

Undoubtedly the managers of organizations, business or government, military or ecclesiastic, have power and know how to exercise it; they are usually fully aware of the power, privilege, and patronage which they can dispense—usually with considerable pomp. But what about the recipients of such pressures, privileges, and patronage? How do they sort themselves out? Are they willing lieutenants, happy to be on the team? Or do they try to bite off the hand that feeds them?

One of the curiosities of group life is that the "followers" don't band together to depose the "leaders." But in fact, the rank and file are kept in check because the leader usually forms coalitions with some of the stronger "followers" to control the others—at least that's how it sometimes works. Inevitably, there is some reaction; this can be either formal or informal.

The executive's informal behaviour

In an automated society it is going to be the exception rather than the rule for the subordinates of an executive to be operators. In most cases the subordinates will be other executives. It has been argued that with the demise of the democratic leader or human relations specialist and the rise of the task specialist, there is bound to be an increase in anxiety and tension among the group of executives who are subordinate to the task specialist. Then there is likely to be a development of informal organization among these executives to protect their social and economic interests.

While the literature of administration is replete with examples of informal organization among operators, scant attention has been paid to the manifestations of informal organization among executives. Social scientists are slowly becoming aware that management often represents short-term compliance with company standards that may have negative long-term financial consequences for the firm. Some of the language used to describe this informal adjustment is revealing. "Bleeding the line" is one such phrase; it describes the process of sucking all work in progress on an assembly line through the check-point to meet a production goal but denuding the assembly line until it is refilled. Another American expression is "making with a pencil," which refers to adjustments of the records which are not reflected in production changes. Such managerial innovations are certainly not confined to the United States. Studies of Soviet executives have noted the "storming" of production at the end of a quota period at the expense of plant maintenance and the consequent disturbance of production equilibrium.

In Great Britain perceptive insights into the executive's informal behaviour have been provided by Professor Tom Burns, a sociologist at Edinburgh University, who has noted the formation of cabals and cliques in companies (see Chapter 11). Cliques (according to Burns) are made up of older men, passed over by the firm, who tend to make fun of the firm's methods and procedures. Burns concludes, "the clique thus appears as a form of counter-system, a characteristic element in our society in which patterns of behaviour appropriate to dominant positions find their response in countervailing patterns of conduct developed among the least privileged or less powerful positions." Cabals, the younger executives whose objective is to gain further success, are more concerned with power, status, and access to secret information.

Executives react to power not only in informal ways but also in formal ways. The formal way par excellence is the executive union.

The need for executive unions?

Where have they gone, the men in the grey flannel suits of the 1950s, who made dramatic comebacks as mobicentric (mobile) managers in the 1960s? They have gone to join the union—or at least many of them would if such an institution existed. Alienated by computerized management misinformation systems (which leave them as passive readers of print-outs) and rendered thoroughly apathetic by top management's dependence on consensus (not as a means of the best decision making, but as a means of self-protection), the executive of the 1970s is looking for a Godfather.

Looking down the hierarchy with telescope reversed, the executive sees the blue-collar dollar getting bigger and bigger. Turning to those of his brothers who picked the "soft" option of public servant, university professor, or doctor, he realizes there is indeed something to be said for some kind of professional association to keep his slice of the cake growing.

Economic recessions throw into sharp focus the plight of the expendable executive who (denied the advantage of the top quality contract with its built-in golden handshake to sweeten separation) has found himself either in the new style of employment agencies for "aging" (over 40, or even 35) male managers or having to accept a freeze or a cut-back in salary.

Abundant evidence is coming to us from our brave new business schools testifying to the alienation and apathy among middle-rank executives. The 1972 report of the U.S. Department of Health, Education, and Welfare, *Work in America*, points up the fact that organizational blues are not restricted to those who wear blue collars, but that they are biting deeply ino the ranks of managerial technostructures. The more perceptive among academics and top corporate people have already noted the outward signs of inner grace that marked the spread of the hippie existential culture to the guardians of the classical value system. Men at the top were prepared to tolerate moustaches and sideburns, and even to ignore striped shirts; but there is now convincing evidence that these outward signs were manifestations of a deeper malaise, a pervasive and penetrating discontent.

The source of information for these catastrophic facts is none other than the American Management Association. In 1972, the AMA conducted a survey of lower and middle management in 500 companies in the United States which generally revealed a strong sentiment in favor of establishing white-collar unions. Somewhat surprised by these results, the author of this text and D. Bilek conducted a swift preliminary pilot investigation in the city of Montreal. Our findings were in basic agreement with the AMA survey, which in general describes a picture of executive frustration and discontent. A surprising number of managers believe these symptoms would be alleviated by executive unions. Furthermore, a substantial majority of managers endorse the idea of informal company associations for managers and supervisors.

Our Canadian survey was a modest effort, covering only 60 subjects. Their ages ranged from 21 to 50, with a group average of 31.8 years. The salary of respondents ranged from $5,000 a year to more than $20,000 a year; more than 70 per cent claimed a salary of less than $15,000 a year. The most important point of this survey is that it confirms the evistence in Montreal of the same managerial malaise and the surprisingly extensive sympathy for executive unionization found by the much larger AMA survey.

Today's manager possesses fewer opportunities for direct participation in the decision-making process. He has little say about where the corporation is heading, and even less as to where he is going. The long years of expensive and conscientious preparation, job training, and boot polishing have become increasingly less valued and relevant to the more structured, yet stressful, tasks demanded of many middle managers. With the new information technologies, self-actualization has become little more than a pipe dream, and the sense of challenge and dynamism, the feelings of personal reward and achievement, have been replaced by boredom, alienation, and increasing hostility towards upper management. As the H.E.W. report puts it:

> A general feeling of obsolescence appears to overtake middle managers when they reach their late 30's. Their careers appear to have reached a plateau, and they realize that life from here on will be along an inevitable decline. There is a marked increase in the death rate between the ages of 35 and 40 for employed men, apparently as a result of this so-called "mid-life crisis."

Middle managers' attitudes towards upper executives within their respective companies are also somewhat surprising and can be viewed as a further indication of management discontent. When asked how the respondents thought top management would react to the idea of discussing conditions of employment on an informal basis with representatives of middle manager groups, more than half of our Canadian sample predicted that top management would oppose the idea. In fact, only 7 per cent believed that upper executives would welcome the idea. Moreover, 40 per cent of the middle managers rated their superiors as being moderately to very slow to reach decisions and quite resistant to change. Fewer than 9 per cent considered top management to be highly innovative and open-minded, two characteristics traditionally considered essential to the successful functioning of an organization. Actual replies to the question "How would you rate top management in your company?" were:

	Canadian sample	AMA (U.S.) sample
Highly innovative management, outstanding open-mindedness	9%	9%
Reaches decisions and implements change with relative ease.	25	15
Will entertain most suggestions for change, acts reasonably promptly	27	26
Moderately slow at reaching decisions, somewhat resistant to change	34	35
Very slow at reaching decisions, highly resistant to change	5	15

Finally, nearly 63 per cent of Canadians interviewed were afraid that reprisals would thwart attempts to organize informal groups. In the United States, the proportion was 48 per cent.

Middle management's dissatisfaction involves many factors. Traditionally, an executive or managerial position, among other things, signifies a substantial salary, surely above blue-collar wages; to-day, however, with union strength increasing and strike action being used more frequently, the blue-collar unions actually outpace gains of management employees. In 1973, San Francisco city street cleaners, for example, were being paid

$52 per work day. A new university graduate, however, could expect no better than perhaps $35 a day. It is worth noting, however, that while salary and benefit concerns can be found at the top of the list, other non-monetary considerations received more attention with respect to total responses.

How does middle management view the probable effects of unioniza-tion? They do not expect earth-shaking and drastic benefits as a result. Among the nonmonetary considerations, executives agreed that in a world which presently does not offer contracts, and in which a down-swing in the economy could cause their dismissal without prior warning, unioniza-tion could provide a degree of job security.

Moreover, many executives considered that unionization would not only improve their morale but also that the liaison between superiors and sub-ordinates would improve substantially. However, unionization would not aid managers in achieving their higher ego and self-actualization needs; not would it benefit managers' desire to participate more directly in com-pany objective setting or diminish bureaucratic tendencies within large organizations. Perhaps related to the question of reprisals, managers strongly believed that unionized managers would have extreme difficulty advancing to top management positions.

Technology, it appears, is slowly and most effectively replacing the blue-collar worker as the viable "labour force." More surprising, however, are the subtle yet definite inroads technology has made into the once seemingly indestructible bastion of white-collar management. The "ex-pendable" manager is fair game for the quicker, more efficient computer, which doesn't take coffee breaks, doesn't need a vacation, and rarely be-comes ill.

What is the prospect that executive unions will emerge in North Amer-ica? There is abundant evidence from the study of cliques and cabals in managerial groups that executive society has a complex, convoluted, in-formal structure. It is not difficult to construct a scenario which would make executive trade unions a highly probable event.

The prototype of the executive union organizer is Clive Jenkins, an im-peccably dressed automobile and boat enthusiast and man about town— better known in British upper executive circles as a flippant, left-wing trade union leader and among middle managers as an entrepreneurial-type saviour of the white-collar worker. Jenkins, over the past few years, achieved his ambition of unionizing what he terms Britiain's "intelligentsia" into a force of over 120,000 strong, using a whole battery of techniques (which, of course, can be copied).

North America is full of such corporate buccaneers, and we can be only a moment away from the arrival of the new-style executive union organizer, armed with his M.B.A. and hippie life style, who has the necessary zip, panache, chutzpah, and moxie to set up white-collar unions. The "dissident and dissipated" youth of our society, having made their way into business, have brought with them the seeds of anarchy and subversion—all of which they learned chasing university presidents and deans out of their offices. An old-boy net of colleagues throughout the technostructure who are already masters of the picket line should find the organizing of executive trade unions a mere bagatelle.

A SYSTEMS APPROACH

Power as a variable seems very difficult for behavioural scientists to deal with. Part of the reason is confusion between authority and the other forms of power. Since authority is a form of power, the terms are often not separable in practice. We have pointed out some of the distinctions, and Figures 12–5 and 12–6, applying our systems model to both authority and power, serve as a review of the differing processes, values, and results. Of course, there is also a good deal of overlap; for example, controlling the flow of information is important in either system. In Topic 2, we have been dealing primarily with power in its utilitarian and coercive forms. The major differences can be summarized as: (1) Authority presumes a fairly stable environment, not in terms of technology or interaction but in terms of societal consensus and confidence; while coercive power emerges in an atmosphere where those factors are lacking. (2) The chief value of authority is legitimacy, which influences the processes and places more emphasis on human satisfaction; while utilitarian and coercive

FIGURE 12–5
AUTHORITY AS A SYSTEM

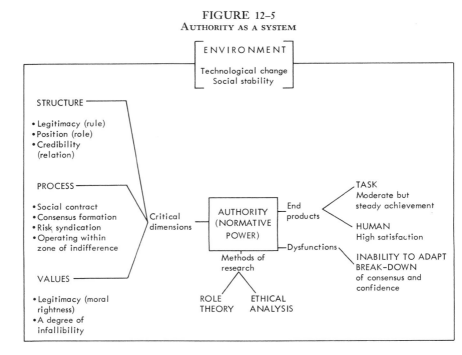

FIGURE 12–6
POWER AS A SYSTEM

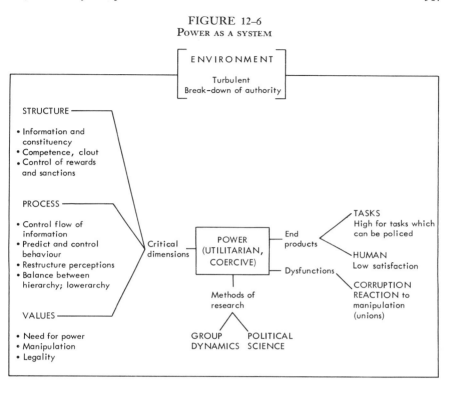

power is more interested in getting the task goals accomplished by any available means which stay within the letter of legality.

The systems approach helps to clarify some of the confusion about the subject. The traditional approach defined power in individual terms, while the modern concept sees it as a property of social relationships. A remaining difficulty is that power is a residual variable not explicitly considered in many analyses of organizational problems. Most interpersonal events can be explained in terms of role, personality, leadership, and so on, without directly touching on the power relationships which are sure to be present—and to be important.

The systems approach to both authority and power emphasizes information as a major factor in determining power. Both role and status can be defined in terms of information privileges. Power is the ability to handle contingencies that may arise, and is therefore a function of information-processing ability. Corporate executives derive power not from control of particular decisions but from controlling the programming of decisions. The effective executive may or may not have the significant say in a given decision; but he is content to have the significant say in some along with the right to decide the timetable of decisions. He is like Marx in desiring to ride the shirt tail of history.

D. J. Hickson *et al.* in "A Strategic Contingencies Theory of Intra-organizational Power" treat power as a characteristic of a subunit of an organization. Power is related to the subunit's (1) capacity to handle uncertainty, (2) substitutability, and (3) centrality, and is manifested in the ability to deal with contingencies. Table 12–1 lists the factors put forward by Hickson and his colleagues as relevant to a discussion of power.

TABLE 12–1
VARIABLES AND OPERATIONALIZABLE SUBVARIABLES

Power (weight, domain, scope)
   Positional power (authority)
   Participation power
   Perceived power
   Preferred power
Uncertainty
   Variability of organizational inputs
   Feedback on subunit performance:
     Speed
     Specificity
   Structuring of subunit activities
Coping with uncertainty, classified as:
   By prevention (forestalling uncertainty)
   By information (forecasting)
   By absorption (action after the event)
Substitutability
   Availablity of alternatives
   Replaceability of personnel
Centrality
   Pervasiveness of workflows
   Immediacy of workflows

AUTHORITY AND POWER—STABILITY AND CHANGE

We have presented the systems models of authority and power at this point in order to set the stage for Topic 3 of this chapter, on challenging authority. Authority and power are crucial topics in an era when we are witnessing—are caught up in—massive crises of authority and thrusts of coercive power.

Authority can only operate in a climate of legitimacy—an undergirding of law and order, equity, due process, a sense of duty among freely contracting members, an atmosphere of credibility. Failing such an environment, an amoral kind of power emerges, concerned only with getting things done—like it or not, no questions asked and none answered. What this usually means is decisive, visible, occasionally diabolical control of the rewards and sanctions. "Diabolical" may be a slight exaggeration—or may not, depending on how far power goes down the route of making clear who's who around here, what the score is, who's calling the shots, and so forth.

The power game attracts a particular kind of personality; the ethics are reminiscent of the textbook description of schizophrenic paranoia. The powerful suffer illusions of grandeur and imagine themselves as Napoleons, Presidents, or King Herods having the heads of their enemies served up on a platter. The powerless suffer that other aspect of paranoia, where even the walls have ears and Big Brother is listening. In such a value system, "restructuring perception" can become thought control; legitimacy is replaced by potency, the office by the person, credibility by capability, contract by bondage, equity by the "fix," and due process by the kangaroo court.

Power and visibility have a peculiar relation. Power has to be made visible from time to time to keep everyone on his toes; but if it is too visible it mobilizes the opposition. Thus power must often be exercised in an ambivalent way involving many features of the double bind. An explicit example of the double bind was furnished by General George Patton when a subordinate indicated his inability to meet orders to advance: "Conform with instructions or nominate your successor." Top corporate executives have the equivalent in, "There is an nth option; you can quit."

In a system of legitimate authority, such "options" would at the most be signaled or used as a last resort. When authority breaks down, the power play becomes bolder and more visible. The high visibility of such breakdowns in the 1960s—the Vietnam war, credibility gaps, politics by assassination, student protest and calls for "revolution" in Europe and both Americas, the overthrow of colonialism in Africa and elsewhere; and in the 1970s—the whole spectrum of Watergate from "dirty tricks" to felony charges against high officials, the Mid-East conflict and the use of oil as a bargaining weapon, the questions of blame and policy involved in energy crises: all of this and much more poses the hardest kinds of questions for countries which value democracy. Where do we go from here? Is legitimate authority a vanishing system? What kind of value system do we want?

These are global kinds of questions. At the level of societies and international affairs, they are beyond our scope—and probably beyond answering. But society is made up of groups and organizations, and each level has profound impacts on the others. Organizations, and their leaders, must shape their own answers—and contributions—to the challenging of authority and use of power.

TOPIC 3
Challenging authority: Marx to Dahrendorf

There has been an erosion of authority in modern times. The evidence is everywhere. In the universities we have student revolution; in the army the refusal of soldiers to obey orders and go into battle, even to save wounded comrades; on the domestic front the urban guerilla, skyjacking, and crime in the streets; in politics the constant threat of civil disobedience; in some high schools armed police patrolling the corridors; in business corporations espionage and sabotage.

The crucial question is whether there is a fundamental, basic cause for this challenging of authority. Dr. Hannah Arendt has argued again and again that the cause is to be found in the unrestrained, "value-free," individualistic secularism of modern times. To modern man, since "God is dead," there can be no moral absolutes; and since modern behavioural science argues that all behaviour can be explained in positive terms ("is" propositions as opposed to "ought" propositions), all positions can be defended. The other person's point of view can always be explained in terms of his ability to rationalize his position.

Authority relations cannot exist in a context which lacks legitimacy. Legitimacy can only exist when both parties agree on the moral assumptions which underlie their choices. The traditional North American philosophy of William James and John Dewey fastens the goodness of an act on the efficacy of its effects, rather than its causes.

Authority relations have increasingly been replaced by coercive relations. In a cultural environment where "the difficult we do today, the impossible tomorrow," moral issues are set aside on the basis that technology can conquer all. The basic issue in Vietnam was that the power of the United States could not be challenged and be shown to be weaker than some small Far Eastern mini-power. The will to dominate, to determine outcomes, becomes the significant factor in coercive power relations.

Most corporate executives recognize that we have begun a revolution in organizational relations which as yet is incomplete. Authority and power were once almost synonymous; it was taken for granted that all power was legitimate, flowing from the top down. Most ordinary employees, and many executives, felt themselves hopelessly dependent on the whim and arbitrary caprice of the invisible men at the top of the oligarchy. Yet we could, from a modern vantage point, almost sigh for the good old days when Karl Marx and "godless Communism" were the only apparent challenge to the orderly way things were.

The real challenges to any system (as Marx shrewdly observed) are likely to come from within. Institutions governed by authority become bastions of the status quo, and can only change slowly and reluctantly without (as they say) "rending the social fabric." Who has ever heard of a cavalry regiment voting to get rid of the horses, or a university department voting itself out of existence? Authority systems can too easily lead to stultifying Mandarinism—to stretching the hierarchy, enveloping roles in rules, embedding processes in myth and mystery, and making the values of the status quo into eternal verities. The stabilizing elements of authority systems are needed; but equally needed are change elements—crucially needed in times when accelerating change is the status quo.

The problem is that authority ("law and order") is invoked to protect the established institutions of yesterday. Authority is suffering from future shock. As Theodore J. Lowi points out in *The Policies of Disorder*, corporate organizations (including trade unions, churches, the military, and other institutions) suffer from an "iron law of decadence," becoming ends in themselves and road-blocks to change. Fixed structures, processes, and values—going through channels, going by the book, fearing to rock the boat—form a self-defeating strategy. Someone has to tell the emperor he has no clothes on; someone has to bell the cat. Someone has to exercise power when a crisis comes; after the crisis, that someone may well have to pay for the privilege, so that authority can be restored, but for a different establishment.

Breaking the contract of authority means the politics of confrontation and conflagration, which gives a role to the executive who marches to a different drummer, whose vision of legitimacy is frequently at right angles to the vectors of the established authority. The new organizational development strategies have made a theatrical fetish out of confrontation and intervention, and most managers love it.

Enlightened managers want to escape from corporate feudalism and capricious capitalism to a system with a high degree of popular participation. They want corporate policies, plans, and practices which allow shop floor employees, supervisors, and middle managers, not to control the conduct of the corporation, but to have a say in the formulation of plans and the ability to contest their application.

Such an outlook is a *real-politik* defence of democracy in the Hobbesian tradition, which argues that both corporate and individual health will be well served by a radical use of democratic values to return corporate power to the people. In turn, the people will demand and create corporations fit for people within and without; which will turn out products, services, and ideas that society needs. As J. K. Galbraith pointed out in *The Affluent Society*, production for private affluence brings public squalor—too much dog food and deodorant, not enough clean food and air. The power to make new products, new markets, and new mergers is based on controlling information. The copying machine and the tape recorder, which can capture information, can be (as the Pentagon papers revealed) great forces on the side of democracy.

The organization has a bad ache which has not been properly diagnosed because the medicine men, academic and executive, have been unable to draw a clear distinction between authority and coercion. In times of tranquility, the theological face of authority appears, nobly structured in lines of legitimacy, sapience, consensus, and credibility. In times of trouble, like the searing crises of the 1960s and 1970s, the coin revolves and the face of power which is pragmatic and cynical appears. Structure becomes a matter of clout, fiefdoms, *capos* and apparatchiks; process becomes a power play of such "teams"; and values take on the win-lose simplicity of the top dog telling everyone else where to get off. Another turn of the coin could bring an evolution to a different authority system rather than revolution into chaos; but reversion to the "good old days" is plainly not in the picture.

DAHRENDORF: POWER HAVE-NOTS

One of the most useful points of departure for reviewing the role of authority in society has been advanced by the German sociologist Ralf Dahrendorf, who has persuasively argued the case that the basic conflict in society is a result not of the class structure but of authority structures. Dahrendorf's argument, in a nutshell, is that people may be divided into haves and have-nots with respect to power as well as property. The argument that conflict originates in authority structures is valid irrespective of the economic system—capitalist or communist. Conflict born of the authority structure can be seen in the nationalized coal mines in Britain, in the administration of Soviet science, or in plants such as General Motors' at Lordstown, Ohio.

A great deal of modern Russian literature has as its subject man struggling for his human identity against the power of modern bureaucracy. Essentially, we face the same problem in North America—but at least here we have the consolation of being able to retreat to the privacy of our homes in the suburbs to "cultivate our own gardens." But the basic challenge to authority is still with us, and growing.

CONCLUSION: COPING WITH THE CRISIS

How are managers going to cope with the crisis of authority? The answer is that they are. Managers intuitively recognize that the name of the game has changed. For example, previously managers spoke more in the terms of categorical inperatives, usually preceded by remarks such as, "Listen, this is what we are going to do." Now they are more likely to talk in terms such as, "Here is another input for you."

Put another way, the contemporary executive uses an information science grammar rather than a hierarchical one in talking to people. What this means is that many managers have lived right through the whole history of managerial philosophy in their own lifetimes. They inherited the classical theory of organization (Taylorism), helped to give birth to the human relations school, and switched to the systems approach of (Robert) McNamara's band in the late 1950s. Having survived such major changes, they are in the process of learning new styles of management appropriate to the postindustrial society.

It would be facile (and noncredible) to suggest that there is any one easy answer to be learned or available system to be put into practice. Lord Acton's "Power tends to corrupt" dictum is simple (and apparently highly memorable), but it is only one aspect or caution of the power complex.

In the 1950s, Robert Michels developed "the iron law of oligarchy," maintaining that corporate structure inevitably becomes oligarchic because the rank and file are not interested in democracy and because modern corporations are too large and sophisticated for participation to be practicable. We may say that the 1950s are a dead letter in view of intervening events; but that does not enable us to discard the empirical evidence that the rank and file frequently have shown a disinterest in democracy. Trade unions have moved from ideological zest to bureaucratic rigidity; in Britain neither nationalized industries nor profit-sharing have lived up to their promises of participation; the principle of co-determination has not worked out in Germany. We have mentioned elsewhere studies which show that some workers prefer noninvolvement and "hands off" attitudes.

On the other hand, there are studies such as the Glacier and Harwood projects which suggest other directions and preferences. There is little question that in North America democracy is clung to as a high value even when in practice it is being observed mostly in the breach. Our observation is that both education and experience frequently lag behind philosophies and principles; the U.S. Declaration of Independence enunciated that "all men are created equal" 100 years before slavery was abolished and at least 200 years before factual equality for Afro-Americans looked like a real possibility. But the principle is a magnet for the processes; in organizations, democracy as a goal may engender training for healthy nonconformity as well as the necessary conformity. Another observation is that it often takes a crisis to jolt the establishment into new patterns; self-government was not conferred upon the United States, or Canada, or India, by Great Britain but seized from below by dissenters who formulated their own power plays and had the confidence to exploit their opportunities. In that light, the crisis of authority may turn out to be a signal for innovation and new directions, in organizations and at every level of interaction.

So "the" new organizational philosophy (or the several new ones, if history is a guide) has not emerged. Adhocracy is one forerunner. One thing seems certain: new perspectives will be based on the science of information and will have to take cognizance of emerging existential values. With such ingredients, one hard and the other soft, the proportions and mixing are going to be crucial. A new kind of authority system will be hard to compute, but it already exists inchoately in many minds. The theorist, or perhaps poet, who can effect a love match between scientific realities and existential yearnings will take the crisis out of authority; but where will he put it?

REVIEW AND RESEARCH

1. Compare and contrast authority and power, using the following headings: source, behavioural relations (cognitive, affective, and action patterns) process, norms, share of the payoffs.

2. What caused the break-down in legitimacy between the student, the faculty, and the administration in universities?

3. Explain Max Weber's classification of traditional, charismatic, and legal authority.

4. What is risk syndication? How is it achieved in a management group?

5. Discuss the concept "zone of indifference." Subordinates have different levels of indifference. Why? How should a manager adjust his strategy to cope with these different levels?

6. At various times a manager can act (*a*) with authority, (*b*) in an authoritarian way, and (*c*) in an authoritative way. Compare and contrast these different styles according to (*i*) the task, (*ii*) position power, (*iii*) leader-member relations.

7. Describe a situation where either you had power over somebody or somebody had power over you. What was the source of power? How did it affect the relation, your perception of the other party, and the distribution of the payoffs?

8. In international politics, experts no longer discuss the "balance of power" but the "balance of prudence." What do you think might be the differences between these two approaches?

9. What is power equalization? How did students try to achieve it in the universities? Did they succeed? If not, why not?

10. Devise a revolutionary plan to take over the United States. What conditions are necessary to give your plan a 1:4 chance of success? In preparing your scenario, consider the following options (among others): a schizophrenic vice president, a repeat of the 1929 Wall Street collapse, the use of university ROTC units.

11. Why haven't work councils worked in the United States, although they have had a limited success in Europe?

12. How can you train executives to develop their skills in exercising power? Relate your answer to game theory, Fiedler's contingency theory, psychotherapy à la Berne, and physical exercise.

GLOSSARY OF TERMS

Authority. Legitimate or normative power, flowing from an "author" (person document, law), whose influence is accepted. Legitimacy—which implies a social contract based on consensus formation, risk syndication, and subordinate compliance—is the chief distinction between authority and other forms of power; authority cannot exist except in this moral climate.

Coercive power. Power which operates in a context of legality rather than legitimacy and functions chiefly through the use of rewards and sanctions, compelling behaviour rather than seeking consensus and compliance. Coercion is usually overt and more visible than other forms of power; it emerges when a system of legitimate authority breaks down.

Consensus formation. The process through which authority gains the compliance of subordinates or group members in general, though it is not necessarily unanimity or even majority rule; a powerful minority may agree on a course of action which the majority agrees not to oppose.

Crisis of authority. The break-down of legitimacy which gives rise to challenge, confrontation, and coercion.

Power. The source of the influence needed in organizations to direct, control, make decisions, and secure co-operation in achieving the organization's goals. Power has three major aspects (see definitions): authority, coercive power, and utilitarian power.

Risk syndication. The process of getting the parties who are involved to participate in making a decision and thus share in both the accountability for the decision and the distribution of the payoffs.

Utilitarian power. The pragmatic influence exerted on organization members by their desire to accomplish tasks and receive task rewards; a form of power implicit in organization structure and goal-orientation and thus more static (less dynamic) than authority or coercion.

Zone of indifference. The area of behaviour within which a subordinate is prepared to accept direction or influence; in general, he must see an instruction as within his jurisdiction and competence, and within the law and his value system, or he may be mobilized to oppose and reject it.

13

Stress, space, and
the executive

What makes man aggressive? Is he basically a "naked ape," monitored by the instinct of aggression which sets his endocrines off, pouring adrenalin and other hormones into his blood and forcing him back along the evolutionary trail to assume the role of the hunter or the hunted? Or is his aggression a function of the territory or space which society allows him? There is abundant evidence that aggression and social ecology are connected and, further, that executive man is increasingly experiencing stress as he moves further into the corporate jungle. Thus the triad of aggression, social ecology, and stress warrants more detailed consideration.

AGGRESSION CAN BE TRIGGERED OFF OR ON

A continuous, on-going debate among social scientists rotates around the subject of whether aggression is due to heredity or to environment. Freud once believed that aggression was one of two fundamental drives that motivated man, but later abandoned this view. Konrad Lorenz, the ethologist, who believes that aggression has survival value in that it helps to maintain social order in both human and animal communities, insists that aggression is inevitable because it was bred into man by natural selection in his early history.

But most behavioural scientists recognize that frustration triggers off aggressive behaviour. Frustration can arise from feelings of physical, social, or intellectual inferiority. Supporting the environmentalist optic is the fact that aggressive behaviour is learned. Many social scientists are convinced that violence on TV and in movies fosters violence in real life; others believe that media violence has a cathartic effect on the viewer.

In any case, no one doubts that the United States is a very violent society, with 16,000 criminal homicides in 1970. Such figures seems to underscore the validity of H. Rap Brown's dictum, "Violence is as American as cherry pie." Medical and behavioural scientists are experimenting with a wide variety of techniques to control aggression. It has even been suggested that pharmacologists should concentrate on a major effort to find drugs to control the levels of aggression of national leaders. Psychosurgical modifications of the brain to change or control some aspect of personality, are also undergoing a resurgence. The old-style lobotomies, which severed the connections with the frontal lobes of the brain (where it was once presumed the centre of personality was located), have now been abandoned because they resulted in improvements only half the time and turned many patients into "vegetables." Psychosurgery is only attempted after the more conventional approaches of shock treatment and drugs have failed.

It is safe to predict that over the next few years a frightening array of new techniques in psychotechnology will become available to control man's aggressive nature. Medical scientists regard the human brain as a very sophisticated computer which operates by virtue of trillions of minute chemical reactions and travelling electrical inputs, which can thus be influenced by the addition of certain chemicals or the insertion of carefully located electrodes. These two techniques for controlling the brain are known as chemical stimulation of the brain (CSB) and electrical stimulation of the brain (ESB), described in Chapter 6. The most famous demonstration of ESB was the experiment carried out by Jose M. R. Delgado, who by radio control stopped the charge of a "brave bull" in whose brain he had implanted an electrode. Both ESB and CSB have also been used to control aggressive behaviour in man.

But aggression is not only a function of heredity; it is also a function of environment; and how man interacts with his environment is what the subject of social ecology is all about.

SOCIAL ECOLOGY

The ecology of human behaviour—the nature of the mutual interaction between man and his environment—is a fascinating subject which is attracting a growing number of researchers who believe that if you get territorial matters right, everything else will be all right. E. T. Hall, an anthropologist, has come up with the name "proxemics" to describe the way in which man consciously or unconsciously structures his microspace. An increasing number of academics (from such disparate disciplines as architecture and psychiatry) have been engaged in the study of the ecological aspects of interpersonal conflict and stress.

Hall, in developing proxemics, neatly illustrates the ecological aspect of behaviour by his system, which defines four social distances in interpersonal relations. Starting with intimate distances of less than 18 inches and going to the other end of the scale with public distances of 12 feet or more, Hall has defined the cues and information exchange properties of each relationship in terms of kinaesthetic, body contact, thermal, olfactory, visual, and oral-aural factors.

Many studies have been made of subjects like social distance and eye contact. Other subjects of considerable interest include the limits of comfortable conversational distance and seating preferences in discussion groups.

Corporate executives and architects are turning to behavioural scientists for information on social ecology to help them plan physical layouts which are appropriate to the function of the structure to be designed. *Burolandschaft*, a word widely used by architects (literally translated as "office community," but widely used to mean "office landscaping"), aims to provide a stimulating (but not so stimulating that it is stressful) environment for work. An atmosphere which is aesthetically attractive results in higher morale and productivity. A good example of *burolandschaft* is the layout of the McDonald's Corporation office building in Oak Brook (near Chicago), discussed in Box 13.1. A major objective of *burolandschaft* is to reduce stress.

STRESS: A FOCUS FOR RESEARCH

The subject of stress has become a major focus of research for behavioural scientists who in increasing numbers have been leaping on this new research bandwagon. Conceptually, stress is interesting because of its location on the boundaries of so many social and biological sciences. On the practical side, answers are needed to ensure that people in key positions in such delicate areas as missile and aircraft control and international negotiations do not go to bits at the wrong time. And of course, in both business and politics, such knowledge would be helpful in making opponents go to bits at the right time.

Some behavioural scientists believe that fundamental research is the answer. But rude experience supplies most of the technology and concepts for inducing and reducing stress. Every American policeman or British intelligence officer worth his salt knows the value of the "hard man—soft man" routine for getting co-operation from prisoners. Likewise, tough-minded executives everywhere know more about how to cool off after a spell in the pressure cooker than their behavioural scientist cousins, armed only with their experience in the laboratory. Nevertheless, a behavioural scientist, Joseph E. McGrath, has come up with an interesting definition in *Social and Psychological Factors in Stress*:

> Stress is defined as the anticipation of inability to respond adequately (or at a reasonable cost) to perceived demand, accompanied by anticipation of negative consequences for inadequate response.

13.1: A rare hamburger headquarters

s probably the tallest office building in the world built on the profits from hamburgers.
t that is not all. When the executives of McDonald's Corp. abandoned their Chicago
op offices for a new eight-story building in suburban Oak Brook, they also left behind
eir traditional concepts of office layout. As a result, McDonald's Oak Brook head-
arters, opened last March, has a minimum of interior doors and walls, no offices in
e usual sense, and what may well be the only waterbed in the world of big business.
On each of the three top floors occupied by the company, there are large open
aces divided into "work stations" by tall green plants, file cabinets and movable
eces of mahogany furniture called TRMs (Task Response Modules). Each TRM con-
ns a closet, a chest of drawers, a bookcase and a built-in desk. In the larger work
as allotted to executives there are such traditional extras as upholstered chairs and
und or square oaken tables.
"At first it was horrible," admits Executive Vice President and Project Supervisor
hn Cooke. "We had people drifting in and out; whole families of curious sightseers
me to visit the building." There were also complaints about fellow workers who un-
owingly trespassed on the work space of others.
But most of McDonald's headquarters employees, 400 in all, adjusted quickly to the
de-open spaces. Now, says Market Research Coordinator Judy Stezowski, "You al-
ys know what's going on. You hear everything." The turnover rate among secretaries
d clerical help has dropped in some departments from 100% each year at the old
op offices to about 25% at the new Oak Brook base. Executives also feel that pro-
ctivity is up.
By far the most distinctive feature of the building is the "think tank," a sealed-off
ea on the seventh floor that is available to any employee, male or female, who reserves
nk time far enough in advance. President Fred Turner had the idea, after deciding that
me employees might want a taste of privacy now and then. The tank has two sections:
e a soundproofed workroom equipped with dimmable lights, a hassock, a beanbag
air, a desk that can be adjusted from sitting to standing height and walls, floor and
iling covered in beige pseudo suede.

Rich thoughts. A few steps away is the circular "meditation room," its walls covered
th suedelike material and concealing loudspeakers hooked to record-playing equip-
nt. The floor consists of a giant waterbed, 9 ft. in diameter, on which workers recline
think deep and presumably profit-making thoughts. So far, however, no big ideas have
erged, but several recliners have noted that lying on the bed is like lying on a giant
mburger.
That is as close to the real thing as McDonald's employees can get during working
urs. Because of local zoning laws, the nearest McDonald's hamburger stand is more
an a mile away.

me, February 28, 1972.

Figure 13–1 shows some stress factors from a stimulus-organism-
response view, according to input, transformation, and output. Stress may
arise, of course, from the perception of real danger in the environment.
Stress may also be generated by information overload or underload. The
personality may process information through a faulty perceptual filter
which transforms a neutral environment into a hostile one; or it may suffer from a physiological disturbance created by a faulty gene or an endocrine imbalance. The behaviour elicited may be inappropriate. Frustra-

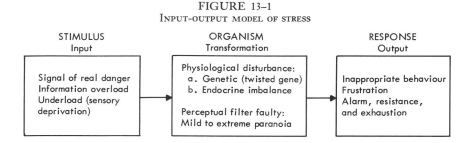

FIGURE 13–1
INPUT-OUTPUT MODEL OF STRESS

STIMULUS Input	ORGANISM Transformation	RESPONSE Output
Signal of real danger Information overload Underload (sensory deprivation)	Physiological disturbance: a. Genetic (twisted gene) b. Endocrine imbalance Perceptual filter faulty: Mild to extreme paranoia	Inappropriate behaviour Frustration Alarm, resistance, and exhaustion

tion is highly likely. When responses to stress are required too often, in increasing quantities, Hans Selye has pointed out that the probable result is alarm, resistance, and eventually exhaustion.

One of the curious things about stress is that in small quantities, stress improves performance. But as the stress increases, performance degradation in terms of psychomotor skills sets in. To measure the effect of stress on performance, speed, accuracy, number of errors, and error tolerance are measured. The subject of stress has been a major area of enquiry since the "shell-shocked" casualties of World War I startled the military into studying the problem. During World War II, with battle fatigue affecting 1 soldier in 10, the investments in stress research increased rapidly, especially in regard to the problems of combat pilots who faced a three-dimensional form of high-speed stress that the world had never seen before.

Sir Charles P. Symonds of the Royal Air Force Medical Service put forward his ideas on stress in "Use and Abuse of the Term Flying Stress":

> Flying stress might usefully be employed . . . to designate the special strains or stresses to which flying personnel are exposed. It might well in this sense be used in a quantitative way to denote the amount of strain to which a man has been put. Thus a man who had had a crash without injury to himself or others might be said to have been exposed to slight flying stress; a man who had had a similar crash with painful injury to himself or fatal injury to others, to moderate flying stress, and so on. Such estimates, especially as recorded by commanding officers would be of considerable value to the medical branch if the man subsequently became ill with psychological disorder. There will still be problems of flying stress for discussion by executives and medical officers: for example, how much flying stress can the average man stand without breaking down; what are the most important elements in flying stress for fighter, bomber, and reconnaissance personnel; what psychological types stand up to flying stress best or worst? But it should be understood once and for all that flying stress is that which happens to the man, not that which happens in him: it is a set of causes, not a set of symptoms.

During World War II, Allied flight surgeons developed rules of thumb which took into consideration information about personality, separation anxiety, and guilt processes, as well as such physical factors as weight loss, fatigue, and so on. Such personal factors were weighed against the importance of the mission and the chances of survival.

Stress is best thought of as a state of the total organism under difficult or extenuating circumstances. Capacity to withstand stress is a function of (1) the individual, (2) the situation, and (3) the social context.

STRUCTURE OF CHAPTER 13

Our first topic is aggression, and we examine the role of heredity and environment in determining aggression. Particular attention is paid to the work of ethologists such as Konrad Lorenz and anthropologists such as Margaret Mead. We briefly review the idea of the territorial imperative, which provides the bridge to our second topic, social ecology.

We begin Topic 2, the systematic study of social space, by looking at the subject of eye contact and then the geography of discussion groups. The issue is raised of how social space affects executive stress, which is our third topic.

Our treatment of stress begins by reviewing Hans Selye's work, which explains how organisms respond to stress by activating more and more defences until no additional ones are available and death ensues. Topic 3 then reviews the factors causing stress, including monotony, sensory deprivation, perceptual isolation, and information overload. Is a particular type of executive particularly prone to stress, and can he be identified? In discussing what stress can do, it is relevant to know that psychologists have identified a neurosis of success. There is a relationship between life events (including successful ones) and illness, so we look at the subject of executive health, with particular attention to the supposed predilection which executives have for coronaries.

To end the discussion on a broader sociological basis, Topic 4 takes up the theme of society, stress, and disease. Since stress is the basic theme of this chapter, we review the major topics as elements of our systems model —the dimensions and results of stress and the environment which produces it.

TOPIC 1
Aggression

Is aggression implicit in human nature, or does it constitute a response to the environment? Is it an instinct or a function of conditioning? This is far from just an academic question, for the answer to this fundamental question provides the best guide as to how a person views conflict.

Most discussions of aggression soon run into semantic difficulties. For example, in a narrow biological sense, "aggression" refers to patterns of behaviour associated with attacking another individual—an "attack posture"; but in a wider organizational context, the term includes competitiveness and self-assertiveness.

INSTINCT VERSUS CULTURE

Sigmund Freud, essentially in the 19th-century biological tradition, regarded aggression in its most extreme form as one of the two fundamental drives—as the death wish. Freud argued, and both common sense and language seem to take for granted, that sex and aggression are linked in some complex interlocking manner. How else can one explain the fact that most expletives have both sexual and aggressive connotations?

But the "aggression as an instinct" theory received a hefty blow from anthropologists, who produced evidence to show that not only did the pattern of aggression vary from society to society (in some societies, the woman is the aggressor) but also that in some communities aggression is virtually unknown. For example, Margaret Mead studied the Arapesh, a peace-loving tribe where aggressive leadership was hard to come by and where, as a result, festive occasions—which require an aggressive type to organize—were few.

For the ethologist, the received view is that aggression is innate, but serviceable in the sense that it helps to establish a stable pecking order which reduces the chances of internecine strife breaking out. Ethologists, including Robert Ardrey (*The Territorial Imperative*), Konrad Lorenz (*On Aggression*), and Desmond Morris (*The Naked Ape*) have collectively etched out the pseudoscientific pop-ethology cliché that man is a naked ape driven by a territorial imperative to satisfy a deep biological need for aggression. Anthropologists, particularly Margaret Mead, have in the main argued the other side of the human coin: that environmental considerations are the key determinants of whether aggression does emerge and, if it does, what form it will take.

Arguing against the pop-ethology view of aggression, Alexander Alland, Jr., an anthropologist, has entered the lists with a book entitled *The Human Imperative*, in which he argues that if man were innately aggressive, all societies would be characterized by violence. But anthropological research reveals the existence of societies that are nonviolent. Alland cites as an example of a nonviolent society the Semai of Malaya, among whom murder is unknown, children are never physically punished, and animals are adopted, named, talked to, and treated as if they were children. With such a pacific culture, the children growing up have no model of aggression to imitate. Apparently the Semai, when angry, restrict themselves to insults and the dissemination of malicious rumours. For the anthropologist, culture and genetic programming are the key factors determining the emeregence and characteristics of aggression.

Psychologists and psychiatrists recognize that the quality of living in early life can significantly determine the pattern of behaviour. In some primitive societies mothers, by deliberately frustrating their sons, make them very aggressive. (Anthropologists such as G. Gorer were able to explain the Russian personality as a reaction to the Russian habit of swaddling their young children.) This comes close to the celebrated frustration-aggression hypothesis of John Dollard, where aggression is seen as an exclusive and inevitable response to frustration. To-day this proposition still commands respect as specifying one source, but not the only source, of aggression. Aggressive behaviour may also be mimetic in origin; and, more importantly, aggression is regarded by contemporary social scientists as having survival value.

Witch hunts, modern and mediaeval

Frustration and anxiety in society generate aggression which must find an outlet. Witch hunts, modern and ancient, represent just one such outlet. While many innocent people were undoubtedly executed as witches, considerable historical evidence is available to show that witchcraft was a real movement. It has also been suggested by psychiatrists that witches' sabbat rites included delusions induced by taking drugs. The witches were controlled by the devils (in modern parlance, junkies and pushers). In contemporary society, stress causes not a few sensitive but socially inadequate people to get hooked; they in turn may act in a violent and aggressive way. The more apprehensive and less secure members of society displace their hostility onto the "acid-heads," and so the system is kept topped up with aggression.

Apes, au naturel and naked

On the question of whether aggression is instinctive or learned, the evidence of ethology (the science of animal behaviour) falls on both sides of the fence. S. Zuckermann's monkeys in London's Regent Park Zoo fought tooth and nail, but there the sex ratio was hopelessly wrong. Most important of all, they were confined to a zoo. Apes in captivity are aggressive; in their natural habitat, not so. Aggression, while it is innate, is also a function of population pressure. Apparently "fighting to the death" does not occur in most nonhuman mammals except in crowded conditions; a great deal of animal behaviour has been evolved as a means of overcoming overcrowding. This notion of linking "social space" and conflict could be validated by many human studies of delinquency in our cities, both British and American. Sociologists have argued that population pressures produce violence and crises in overcrowded school systems. Territorial imperatives are the hardest to resist for both animal and man.

The idea of man as a "naked ape" has come under considerable criticism for the following reasons: (1) the comparison is an insult to apes and (2) the theory is simplistic and male-oriented. David Pilbean, an associate professor of anthropology at Yale University and associate curator of anthropology at the Peabody Museum, has challenged the view of the animal behaviourists Konrad Lorenz, Robert Ardrey, and Desmond

Morris, who all claim they can explain man's "real" behaviour in ethological terms and describe its evolution from the behaviour of apes. Pilbean is disturbed by the fact that Ardrey's *African Genesis, The Territorial Imperative,* and *The Social Contract;* Morris's *The Naked Ape* and *The Human Zoo;* Lorenz's *On Aggression;* and Lionel Tiger's *Men in Groups* all argue that man's behaviour (particularly his aggressive and sexual behaviour) is status-oriented, related to a particular territory, and, most important of all, almost exclusively controlled by hereditary factors. Thus, according to this group of ethologists, man has no option but to accept his grotesque nature. Pilbean rejects this view and argues that (aside from our obsessive neophilia, which demands continuous titillation with new, original, and bizarre ideas) the "naked ape syndrome" serves only as a licence to the unpleasant to be offensive.

Other ethologists have argued that controlled aggression has survival value; that though dominance ultimately depends upon force, it leads to law and order. In *On Aggression,* Lorenz argues that aggression is a function of normal selection, that it produces an increased expectation of survival, and that it brings about a dispersal of individuals. Lorenz, whose experience of observing animals in their natural habitat is surpassed by few, believes that fighting may have the utility of generating a stable pecking order. This idea has an application to our own society, which is learning to allow dissent—but not unlimited dissent.

DISSENT AND CONSENSUS

Dissent and consensus are both integral to executive life. Aggression, apparently an essential characteristic of executives, makes many managers miserable with guilt. Adopting an "attack ethos" usually stands an executive in good stead; but his aggression is moderated by a need to maintain social acceptability.

The vital question is not whether aggression is a function of heredity or environment; it is a product of both. Certain environmental conditions are required to elicit aggressive responses, and these conditions must be defined by further research. New surgical techniques such as organ transplants and the use of kidney machines have forced doctors to consider that the patient's personality and attitudes may be significant factors in whether he will survive or not; the advantage apparently lies with the patient who has an aggressive lust for life. The plasticity of human aggression must be elaborated; aggression appears to be capable of very considerable modification in ways much like Freud's defence mechanisms—it is capable of displacement, sublimation, regression, and projection.

For the contemporary middle-aged executive, the real issue seems to be, "What will I do with my aggression (even if it is a diminishing quantity) which was once so valuable on the football field, in platoon warfare, and in aggressive selling?" The creative use of hostility requires further research, both to define what levels of aggression are acceptable and to ascertain the relation between aggression and such factors as social space, personality, group forces, and cultural matters. To examine one of these factors in detail, we now turn to the topic of social ecology.

TOPIC 2
Social ecology

A major focus of group dynamics research is the systematic study of spatial arrangements in groups. B. Steinzor first noted some unusual spatial effects while he was doing a study on other aspects of group interaction. Who takes the lead in discussions is to some extent a factor of location. So we can begin to understand social ecology by looking at clues to what is happening in individual and group encounters.

PERSONAL AND GROUP INTERACTIONS

How can you tell whether a person you have just met will be hostile or friendly? Behavioural scientists have come up with some pretty convincing evidence that the answers to such questions are contained not only in spoken words but also in the tone of voice, facial expressions, and body postures that emerge during the conversation. The nonverbal element is a message, according to Michael Argyle, a social psychologist from Oxford University, and it carries more weight than the actual words. Experiments at Exeter University in England have shown that a person has a way of signalling another person that he is about to claim the floor—which he usually does. Simply stated, humans can instantly assert their position in the pecking hierarchy by the exchange of single glance.

The ways in which people look at each other during a conversation reveal more than most people realize. The right amount of eye contact can be a vital factor in determining who is going to be dominant in a social encounter. Argyle has used dark glasses and cardboard shields in experiments to find out what happens in a conversation when you cannot see the other person's eyes or face. He discovered that seeing the other person's eyes is necessary to know when he intends to start or stop; with shielding, synchronization of the conversation becomes difficult. Shielding the other person's face creates further difficulties because his emotional reactions cannot be gauged. Exepriments in eye contact have shown that:

1. People who can see better dominate the conversation.
2. Women need and make more use of visual feedback.
3. People make more eye contact when listening.
4. People tend to look away when talking, especially if they are going over their "allotted time."

5. Eye contact promotes good relations only when associated with a friendly facial expression.
6. Different ethnic groups use eye expressions in different ways.
7. In discussion groups, members direct more comments to people opposite than people adjacent; but when a strong leader is present, members direct their comments to adjacent seats rather to those opposite.

Three factors that significantly affect the quality of relations are eye contact, posture, and distance. Researchers have identified what are called "correct conversational zones":

Conversational level	Distance	Classification
Soft whisper	3–6 inches	Top secret
Louder whisper.	8–12 inches	Highly confidential
Soft voice	12–20 inches	Confidential
Low volume	20–36 inches	Personal subject
Normal voice	5 feet	Nonpersonal information

Posture is also important, and a person can establish dominance by throwing his head back and speaking in a loud voice. If the person being addressed puts his hands behind his back he may well be seen as taking a subordinate role.

THE GEOGRAPHY OF DISCUSSION GROUPS

Recent research work has shown that certain combinations of places at a table are preferred to others. As shown in Figure 13–2, when two people want to converse, they will sit at right angles to each other across a corner of the table. If they wish to compete, they sit opposite each other.

This well-established principle of proxemics is frequently used by executives who shift from formal to informal seating arrangements depending on the intentions of the owner of the office. Besides the informal arrangement in Figure 13–3, the visitor may be placed at the side of the desk, away from the desk in an armchair setting, or (a current form of status

FIGURE 13–2

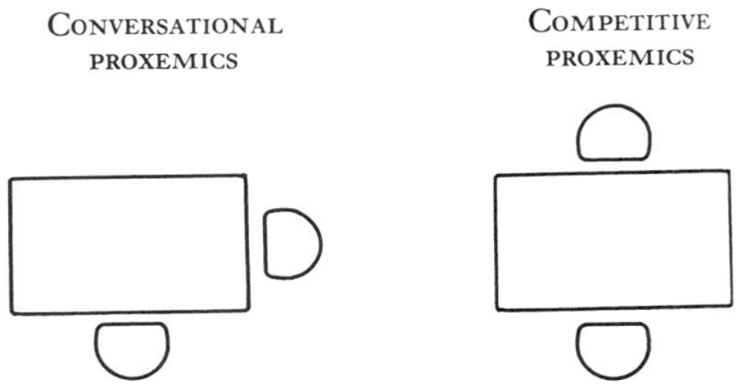

CONVERSATIONAL PROXEMICS

COMPETITIVE PROXEMICS

FIGURE 13-3

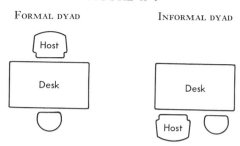

FORMAL DYAD   INFORMAL DYAD

symbol) the desk may have been concealed or banished from the office completely.

In discussion groups, it has been suggested that the more autocratic leader sits at the head of a table (Figure 13–4). This enables him to further structure the situation by putting hostile persons whom he wants to ignore close to him and putting his anchor men at or near the other end of the table where he can make easy eye contact with them. The more democratic leader tends to sit in the middle of the group, as in Figure 13–5.

It would be wrong to conclude that mere location is the critical factor determining the role which an individual will take up. It seems much more plausible to believe that dominant individuals select locations for reasons of tradition, or because this choice advertises the role they are going to take up.

Proxemics can be a subject of great importance in diplomacy, and matters of "who sits where" can create international incidents. For example, when the Vietnam peace talks were being arranged in Paris in 1968, the actual shape of the table to be used led to prolonged, acrimonious discussion which delayed the beginning of the negotiations for several weeks.

The design of a debating chamber can significantly affect the quality of debates. The British House of Commons is a relatively small room with quite insufficient seating for all members of Parliament; but its smallness

FIGURE 13–4
AUTOCRATIC GROUP LEADER

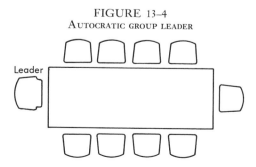

FIGURE 13-5
DEMOCRATIC GROUP LEADER

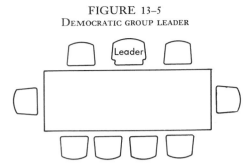

facilitates a debate which would be quite impossible in the more formal layout of the U.S. House of Representatives.

The actual "scene of the crime" can be of critical importance, as witness the fact that the Germans in 1940 insisted in bringing out the famous railroad car used at Compiègne for the 1918 armistice, to humiliate the French generals who were to sign the formal defeat of the French army.

SOCIAL SPACE AND STRESS

A major focus of ecological studies has been the interrelation of territorial behaviour, density, crowding, and personal space. Of particular interest is the effect of overcrowding on the behaviour of animals. For example a mass, unexplained die-off of a herd of Sika deer was believed to have been caused by endocrine imbalance (especially adrenal), brought on by social pressures generated by overcrowding. Apparently though the food supply was adequate, the deer could not cope with the increased population density with its attendant evils of loss of territorial sovereignty, increased competition for females, and loss of privacy. The same phenomenon was noted by J. B. Calhoun in his study of overcrowding among rats. Calhoun constructed a rat pen with food and water in a central location and in side areas. The king male rats established mafias with harems in the side areas, forcing most other male rats into a crowded behavioural sink in the centre. Social disintegration ensued. Some females died in pregnancy, others lost their litters, and many were less adept at nest building or taking care of their young. Males engaged in cannibalism, sexual deviations, and eating, drinking, and moving around when others were asleep.

Calhoun's rats behaved pretty much the same way human beings behave in similar circumstances. In the overcrowded slum areas of New York, London, or Montreal, the same social disintegration can be observed, with teachers' cars competing for space with children's need for elbow room in the playgrounds of our schools; dominant males running the gang; rampant diseases such as bronchitis, asthma, and "bad backs"; families fatherless; incompetent mothers being taught to budget by social workers;

and kids peddling drugs to calm the system down. And that precisely is what we are dealing with—a system: an integrated organization having interdependent parts with built-in feedback mechanisms, which is continuously adapting itself to the environment.

TOPIC 3
Executive stress

Stress research as a distinct field of enquiry has had an independent existence for only 20 years. The pioneer investigator into the implications of stress, Dr. Hans Selye of the University of Montreal, has defined stress as the nonspecific response of the body to any demand made upon it. Selye was the first to assemble a unified catalogue of the neuroendocrine consequences of physical and perceptual overload, reactions to demanding but anomalous stimuli.

One of Selye's most dramatic break-throughs was his discovery that he could take two similar groups of rats and dispose one group to heart disease by injecting an excess of sodium chloride and certain hormones. When both groups of rats were subjected to stress, none of the control group suffered but all of the predisposed group died. Selye drew the conclusion that the endocrine glands, particularly the adrenals, were the body's prime reactors to stress. What Selye found was that the adrenal glands were the only body organs not to shrink under stress.

Figure 13–6 illustrates some of Selye's theory from a systems view. Many external conditions, all defined as stressors, are seen as affecting the brain, which in turn signals the adrenal and pituitary glands. These glands

FIGURE 13–6
SCHEMATIC FLOW OF INFLUENCE AND FEEDBACK

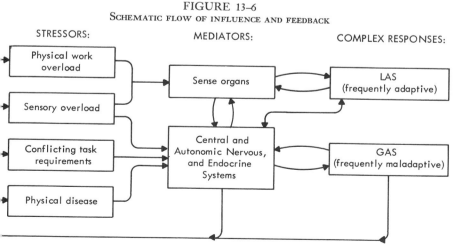

Reprinted by permission from Jan Berkhout, "Psychological Stress," in Kenyon B. DeGreene (ed.), *Systems Psychology* (New York: McGraw-Hill Book Co., 1970).

produce the hormones ACTH, cortisone, and cortisol, which stimulate protective bodily reactions. Selye defined the initial reactions to short-term stressors as the *alarm reaction* and the *local adaptation syndrome* (LAS), both of which have survival value and relevance in regard to immediate stressors. The LAS facilitates short-term homeostatic regulation of the body process; but in cases of extreme or prolonged stress, the body progressively brings in more subsystems of the body until the whole human system is mobilized. The end point of this tendency is the *general adaptation syndrome* (GAS), which may exacerbate or mask the symptoms of almost any medical problem. This stage is characterized by the features of chronic endocrine imbalance and deteriorated psychomotor performance. This condition of adrenal exhaustion indicates that the person, because his neuroendocrine system has been overmobilized for too long a time, is no longer capable of responding to new environmental conditions.

In summary, the initial reaction to stress is alarm, which is followed by a rallying of the body's defences. The sequence begins as mental stresses are transmitted from the cerebral cortex of the brain to the hypothalamus. The body seems to react to all threats, even purely semantic threats, as if it were dealing with a physical attack. Signals are sent through the sympathetic and parasympathetic nervous systems and adrenalin floods the blood stream. The whole endocrine orchestra comes into action, which causes tensing of the muscles, dilation of the pupils of the eyes, constriction of the skin vessels, paling, deeper breathing, pounding heart, and pressure on the bladder. If the stressor is countered, stability returns. But if the attack is prolonged, the defence system gradually wears down, and Selye's GAS ensues.

Walter McQuade, writing in *Fortune* (January, 1972) on "What Stress Can Do to You," has brilliantly summarized the impressive evidence that the chronic ailments afflicting middle-aged Americans are at least partly due to organizational stress and tension.

PSYCHOLOGICAL STRESS FACTORS

Genuine danger is, of course, the most obvious stress factor. In addition, there are many other factors, both physical and mental. Monotony is an obvious psychological stressor which has particular significance for automobile assembly plant operations. The management at General Motors is in the process of redesigning work assignments so that "larger" jobs can be found for shop floor workers.

Sensory deprivation and perceptual isolation also constitute stress factors. There is considerable disagreement among scientists studying sensory deprivation as to how long a person need be isolated to produce measurable stress responses. Nevertheless, military intelligence officers have been experimenting with such techniques as a means of breaking down a prisoner's defences.

Another factor increasing stress which is of great interest to executives is the disruption of circadian periodicity, the 24-hour cycle of night and day which is the most compelling organizing factor of human life. Disruption of this cycle—as everyone who has ever stepped on a transatlantic jet knows—constitutes a stress factor which can adversely affect not only psychomotor performance but also personal stability and executive judgement. Among airline staffs, this disturbance of the circadian cycle is recognized as a distinct stress factor. Reported shifts in eating and sleeping habits and changes in the endocrine balance are obviously interconnected.

Sleep deprivation, which is now a major field of psychological enquiry, causes a steady deterioration in performance of psychomotor tasks. Sleep is a complex, many-faceted process with many stages, each apparently serving distinct physiological and psychological functions. Research psychologists are paying a great deal of attention to rapid eye movement (REM) sleep, which is clearly associated with dreaming and whose suppression is conducive to bizarre behaviour patterns. Obviously, denial of REM sleep offers considerable potential for brainwashing and getting confessions from prisoners who, because of the stress induced, may quite well be willing to go along with their captors.

HOW EXECUTIVES REACT TO STRESS

Many behavioural scientists, as well as physicians, believe that cardiac disabilities may be as much a function of stress as of cholesterol level, blood pressure, smoking, glucose level, and the like. This is not a contradiction of the importance of these physical symptoms (which we will take up a little later). What appears to happen is that stress aggravates the level of cholesterol or blood pressure, and promotes such unhealthy activities as smoking and overeating. McQuade's *Fortune* article on "What Stress Can Do to You" reports:

> Management jobs carry higher risks than most. In a detailed study done for NASA at the Goddard Space Flight Center, the investigators from Ann Arbor found that administrators were much more subject to stress than engineers or scientists. Responsibility for people, French explains, always causes more stress than responsibilities for things—equipment, budgets, etc. The rise in serum cholesterol, blood sugar, and blood pressure among ground managers is much greater during manned space flights than during flights of unmanned satellites. Whatever their assignment, the administrators at Goddard, as a group, had higher pulse rates and blood pressure, and smoked more, than the engineers or scientists. Medical records revealed that administrators also had suffered almost three times as many heart attacks as either the scientists or the engineers.

Box 13.2 illustrates, from the same article, some of the ways in which different personalities respond to stress.

Box 13.2: Which executive type are you?

Walter McQuade's *Fortune* article reports some interesting research on executive types. Cardiologists Meyer Friedman and Ray H. Rosenman of the Harold Brunn Institute of Mount Zion Hospital in San Francisco maintain that behavior patterns and stress are principal culprits in the high incidence of coronary heart disease among middle-aged Americans—and that personality differences are of vital importance.

In studying reactions to stress, Friedman and Rosenman have gradually come to the conviction that people can be divided into two major types, which they designate A and B. Type A, the coronary-prone type, is characterized by:

Intense drive
Aggressiveness
Ambition
Competitiveness
Pressure to getting things done
Habitually pitting himself against the clock
Visible restlessness
An "existential" miasma of hostility which makes others nervous

Type B characteristics are:

A more easygoing manner
Seldom becomes impatient
Takes more time to enjoy leisure
Does not feel driven by the clock
Not preoccupied with social achievement
Less competitive
Speaks in a more modulated style

The extreme Type A is a tremendously hard worker, a perfectionist, filled with brisk self-confidence, decisiveness, resolution. He never evades. He is the man who, while waiting in the office of his cardiologist or dentist, is on the telephone making business calls.

He speaks in a staccato manner, and has a tendency to end his sentences in a rush. He frequently sighs faintly between words, but never in anxiety, because that state is strange to him. He is seldom out sick. He rarely goes to doctors, almost never to psychiatrists. He is unlikely to get an ulcer. He is rarely interested in money except as a token of the game; but the higher he climbs, the more he considers himself underpaid.

On the debit side, he is often a little hard to get along with. His chuckle is rather grim. He does not drive people who work under him as hard as he drives himself, but he has little time to waste with them. He wants their respect, not their affection. Yet in some ways he is more sensitive than the milder Type B. He hates to fire anyone and will go to great lengths to avoid it.

Walter McQuade, "What Stress Can Do to You," *Fortune,* January, 1972.

Many organizational problems seem to generate executive stress by creating role ambiguity, work overload, job insecurity, lack of a feeling of participation, and worry over difficult bosses or subordinates.

For example, air traffic controllers, who, of course, have a critical role to play in directing the increasing numbers of planes stacked up over congested airports, are exposed to considerable stress over long periods. Such

Type A, surprisingly, probably goes to bed earlier most nights than Type B, who will get interested in something irrelevant to his career and sit up late, or simply socialize. Type A is precisely on time for appointments and expects the same from other people. He smokes cigarettes, never a pipe. Headwaiters learn not to keep him waiting for a table reservation; if they do, they lose him. They like him because he doesn't linger over his meals and doesn't complain about quality. He will usually salt the meal before he tastes it. He's never sent a bottle of wine back in his life. Driving a car, Type A is not reckless, but does reveal anger when a slower driver ahead delays him.

Type A's are not much for exercise; they claim they have too little time for it. When they do play golf, it is fast-paced. They never return late from vacation. Their desk tops are clean when they leave the office at the end of each day.

But in the competition for the top jobs in their companies, A's often lose out to B's. They lose because they are too competitive. They are so obsessed with the office that they have attention for nothing else, including their families. They make decisions too fast—in minutes, rather than days—and so may make serious business mistakes.

Type B's differ little in background or ability from A's; they may be quietly urgent, but they are more reasonable men. Unlike Type A, Type B is hard to needle into anger. Friedman says, "A's have no respect for B's, but the smart B uses an A. The great salesmen are A's. The corporation presidents are usually B's."

What is most tragic of all in this picture of hopeful, driving, distorting energy is that the Type A's are from two to three times more likely than the Type B's to get coronary heart disease in middle age.

The test program that Friedman and Rosenman offer as their strongest body of evidence was undertaken in 1960 with substantial backing from the National Institute of Health. A total of 3,500 male subjects aged 39 to 59, with no known history of heart disease, were interviewed and classified as Type A or Type B. Then came complete physical examinations, which are still being performed on a regular basis as the program continues to accumulate data. So far, 257 of the test group—who are roughly half A's and half B's—have developed coronary heart disease. Seventy percent of the victims have been Type A's.

One pointed criticism that opponents make of the Friedman-Rosenman studies is that their method of classifying individuals into Type A or Type B is subjective, relying heavily on signs of tension as observed by the interviewer. The two cardiologists do not deny this, but point out that a good deal of all medical analysis is subjective. Says Rosenman, "A migraine is subjective, too."

Now that even cardiologists are beginning to believe that heart disease can be traced to unrelenting competitiveness, will a wave of concern over stress sweep over this country? Quite likely. There is nothing more fascinating to the layman than folklore finally validated by reputable scientists.

high information levels and the attendant decisions—any one of which may lead to a calamity—induce a level of stress which is unremitting and which has serious consequences for their digestive tracts. A study of the Academy of Air Traffic Control Medicine in St. Charles, Illinois, showed that the incidence of ulcers among control-tower personnel is alarmingly high. One group of air controllers was examined by Dr. R. Grayson who found that three quarters of the members required further tests. These tests revealed that almost a third had ulcers. The incidence of ulcers for American physicians is between 2.5 and 4 per cent; even for alcoholics the rate is only 9 per cent. Perhaps the cause of this level of ulcers among air traffic controllers is unremitting stress, generated partly by information and decision overload.

THE NEUROSIS OF SUCCESS

One of the most interesting lines of stress research has been the study of the relationships between life's events and illness. A life event is any change in a person's circumstances to which he must adapt. This research work was initiated by Harold Wolff and Lawrence Hinkle, who investigated the health records of American employees of the Bell Telephone Company and were surprised to discover that episodes of illness were not distributed at random, but that each employee tended to have a set annual amount of illness. Instead of illness being randomly distributed, a quarter of the employees suffered one half of the total illness, with 1 in 20 experiencing very little. Further, those employees with the most episodes of illness not only had a greater variety of illnesses but also had more serious physical and psychiatric illnesses. Wolff and Hinkle went on to show a clear link relating clusters of illness to periods during which the individual considered his life situation threatening or unsatisfying.

In this "human ecology" approach to medicine, Hinkle has argued that disease may not be the result of any single specific virus but a consequence of many factors, including the effect of change itself. A colleague of Wolff's, T. H. Holmes of the University of Washington School of Medicine, has developed a "life-change units scale" to measure how much change an individual has experienced in a given span of time. Holmes's brilliant insight was that the significance of the change lay not in its threatening or difficult characteristics but in the actual need to adapt to change, whether it was pleasant or unpleasant. Pleasurable and satisfying change takes its toll as well—a kind of neurosis of success. According to Holmes, the amount of stress (whatever its emotional concomitants) and the ability to adjust to it are the two elements in the equation of change whose lack of balance determines illness.

Arguing that different kinds of life changes strike us with different force, Holmes set out to list as many changes as he could and then try to assess the stress value of each. Holmes and his colleagues asked 394 adults to rate 42 common life events (a divorce, a marriage, a move to a new home, etc.) according to their subjective estimate of the degree of life change and the readjustment each would need. Which changes required a great deal of coping? Which a minor degree? To establish a standard, the event "marriage" was given an arbitrary value and the subjects invited to answer, "Does this event involve more or less adjustment than marriage? Would the readjustment take a longer or shorter period?" To Holmes's surprise, it turned out that there was a consensus among people questioned —irrespective of age, race, sex, education, marital status, social class, ethnic origin, and religion—as to which changes in their lives would require major adaptations and which minor adaptations.

When the mean scores for each item were calculated, the results were set out in a "schedule of recent experiences." In an experiment to predict the sickness patterns in a group of 3,000 U.S. Navy men, 90 per cent of the crews of three cruisers completed the schedule before the ships were about to depart for a six months' cruise. On the basis of their life-change unit scores, the men were put into high-risk and low-risk groups. At the end of the six months, a survey of the ships' medical records revealed a correlation between high scores and the amount of illness. Thus the schedule may be used to predict illness in otherwise healthy people.

A series of British research studies have studied the effect of bereavement on surviving relatives and have shown that nearly 5 per cent of close relatives actually died within one year of the bereavement (compared with seven tenths of 1 per cent in a control group). The risk was greatest for males and particularly high for widowed people.

Thus it seems reasonable to argue that stress affects health. Like money in the bank, stress, once it has been deposited, appears to bear interest in malice for the subject. The most striking confirmation of this "sleeper," interest-bearing aspect of stress has been rendered from studies of military life, where it is reckoned that one year of campaigning ages a man as much as three years in barracks. Writing on stresss of great severity—the experiences of POW's—Harold Wolff asks in *Stress and Disease:*

Is there any reason to infer that men who experience catastrophes of any kind, but who actually suffer no burns, direct effects of irradiation or physical injury, have shorter life spans than others? Do such persons grow 20 years older than their actual age?

Of the 94,000 United States prisoners of war captured in Europe in the Second World War and imprisoned for about ten months, less than one percent died before liberation. In the Pacific theatre, about 25,000 American were captured, remaining in prison four times as long as those captured in Europe and suffering more threats, abuse and humiliation. Their demoralisation was often extreme. More than one third of them died while in prison.

Six years after liberation, the fate of those who survived was investigated. The total number of deaths in the group during these six years was more than twice the expected incidence for a similar group of persons not so exposed, and three times as great as in the group of United States prisoners in Europe. The causes of death included many diseases not directly related to confinement or starvation. Twice the expected number died of heart disease, more than twice the expected number of cancer, more than four times the expected number of diseases of the gastro-intestinal tract, nine times the expected number of pulmonary tuberculosis. Twice the expected number committed suicide—and, most

Box 13.3: The managerial coronary: A myth?

Lawrence E. Hinkle, Jr., and his colleagues at Cornell University Medical College have investigated the long-held belief that rapid advancement in industry and high levels of responsibility are associated with an increased risk of heart attacks.

Their study was based on a five-year survey of all the episodes of coronary heart disease that occurred among 270,000 men in the Bell System throughout the United States.

Hinkle points out that the male population of the Bell System is made up of 22,000 men who have college degrees and 248,000 without college degrees. Both college and noncollege men typically enter the system in their twenties at the nonmanagement level and pursue their careers thereafter. Although a much larger proportion of the college men attain the highest levels of management, a significant number of the noncollege men also attain these levels. During the course of their advancement these men may experience many changes in job assignment, transfers from one department to another and transfers from one company in the Bell System to another.

The rates for coronary heart disease are highest among men not in management and decline at each step up to a higher level of the organization. The lower rates among upper level managers are primarily caused by the higher proportion of college men at these levels. Hinkle found that in all parts of the nation, in all age groups, at all levels of the industry, and in all departments, the rates for coronary heart disease are 30 per cent lower among college men than among noncollege men.

When the experiences of the college and noncollege men are considered separately the difference between the coronary heart disease rates among men at various levels is

This box was especially prepared for this volume from data furnished by L. E. Hinkle, Jr.

striking of all, three times the expected number died as a result of accident . . .

Those that were in "very poor health" had many different diseases, among them many that did not appear to be immediately related to incarceration—hernia, deafness, and diseases of bones, muscles and heart. There were ten times as many "impairments" as among the European prisoners of war.

Many executives are not puzzled by such findings, for they seem to fit their own experiences and their observations of other executives and go some way to explain the phenomenon of the executive who drops dead the day after he has been given a clean bill of health after a detailed medical examination. The examining physician might have improved his diagnosis if he had gotten his executive patient to complete Holmes's "schedule of recent experiences"; it might have been more revealing than his cholesterol level.

MONITORING EXECUTIVE HEALTH

Research psychologists believe there is a need for constant monitoring of body responses of key individuals in important man-machine systems such as spacecraft flying or airline piloting. Such new techniques are

not so great, but there is still no evidence that organizational mobility has an adverse effect. Men without college degrees who have risen most rapidly to the highest levels of management have rates that are no higher than those of nonmanagement men of the same age and background. Hinkle also found that men transferred between departments and managers promoted within the last year had rates no higher than those who had not been promoted for 10 years.

The slightly lower rates among upper level managers appear to be an unintended result of the process of advancement. This tends to select better educated men with good records of health and performance and leaves behind a larger proportion of those who have chronic conditions which enhance the risk of heart disease. There is also incomplete evidence which suggests that the college men as a group are taller, slimmer, healthier, and smoke less than the noncollege men.

Hinkle points out that his findings are supported by similar findings among employees of Standard Oil of New Jersey and of Du Pont, and by unreported data from other large corporations. All of these indicate that the idea that coronary heart disease is a special hazard for men at the higher levels of American corporations at the present time is a myth. However, he cautions that these findings for American industry should not be extrapolated literally to other societies, and especially not to those developing countries where workmen may not be as well nourished as managers; and he also cautions that these findings may not apply to other sectors of our own society, such as the agricultural sector, in which labourers may be of a different ethnic background than managers or proprietors and have a much higher level of physical activity.

known as integrated psychophysiological information-processing systems (IPIP). IPIP systems have been developed for the study of astronauts and have also been used tentatively at Moscow airport to monitor the stress reactions of air traffic controllers. There is a growing body of experimentation with the application of such techniques to monitor the performance of more ordinary people, including executives. It seems reasonable to expect that such integrated monitoring facilities will be built into decision systems in the near future.

Reading the early literature on executive health gives the clear impression that psychosomatic illness is a very common response to managerial stress. Despite a small but growing body of evidence to the contrary, a widely held myth is that demands made on executives are more stressful than those made on nonexecutives. While we have seen that stress factors do link up with hazards like coronary disease and ulcers, the question is whether executives in general are as subject to stress, as, say, air traffic controllers.

According to Lawrence Hinkle, the executive's liability to coronary attacks is not as bad as some of the earlier writers in this field would have had us believe (see Box 13.3). Understandably, a topic of vital interest to both American and British executives is the incidence of coronary thrombosis in the management group. The major finding of modern research in the field of executive health is that executives enjoy pretty much the same standard of health as other members of the socioeconomic class of which they are members. Not only is their objective health record good but, compared with less well-off social groups, a higher proportion of the executives report that they enjoy good health; and apparently factors such as stress play a relatively insignificant part. As is now generally accepted, the incidence of coronary disease is closely related to obesity, lack of exercise, and cigarette smoking.

Occupational health is now a significant focus of research. For example, Professor D. Morris and his group at the Social Medicine Research Unit in London have shown that the less active bus driver has a much higher rate of myocardial infarction and deaths from this condition than the more active conductor, whose survival is attributed to the repeated climbing of steps in double-decker buses.

A similar discovery was also made in regard to postmen, who had a better health record than their more sedentary colleagues such as the letter sorter and telephonist. Aside from cigarette smoking, the two factors of greatest interest are related to the need to avoid obesity and the matter of taking more physical exercise.

It is now generally accepted by insurance companies that obesity is associated with an increased liability to death from degenerative diseases. Executives, perhaps in response to C. P. Snow's denunciation of the expense-account lunch, are well placed to take advantage of the necessary dietary requirements of the new regime. Diet, especially protein intake, appears to be a function of socioeconomic class. But obesity can only arise when energy from food exceeds energy utilization. Some medical authorities have argued that the obese eat no more (in some cases less) than the slim, but exercise less.

It is as well to remember that the relations between weight, diet, and exercise have not been settled in a final and conclusive way by scientific standards. But most doctors who have seriously considered the matter have agreed that a regular programme of exercise is not only good but necessary for executive well-being. Apparently the best exercise is walking, then jogging, then running.

Many organizations, realizing the importance of their investment in their executive group, have instituted medical examinations as a regular feature for their top-management group. Like their brothers who are pilots in the airline business, the matter of periodic medical review for executives evokes an ambivalent response. Many company physicians take the opportunity presented by these examinations to counsel top management on health considerations. Apparently quite a few executives report stress symptoms—including hysterical heart conditions—some of which, at least, must be iatrogenic (induced by the physician) in origin.

Such hysterical cardiac symptoms are not easy to allay even after an E.C.G. has been prepared. The afflicted executive studies his skin pallor carefully, keeps a close check on his weight, watches his diet, nags his wife for being indifferent to his fate, keeps feeling his heart and pulse, is an avid reader of any medical literature on cholesterol levels and arteriosclerotic disorders, and has such "an advanced knowledge of biochemistry and physiology" that many overworked doctors express the wish that the *Reader's Digest* would abandon the field of medical education. The best advice for the hysterical cardiac seems to be "live dangerously" (i.e., take exercise) under medical direction; and, if he survives, to make a virtue of "hysteria is better than nothing."

TOPIC 4
Society, stress, and disease

Even a brief glance at the evidence in behavioural science, ethology, and medicine should be sufficient to convince most reasonable men that there are links between aggression, social ecology, and stress. Figure 13–7, modeling stress as a system, indicates the probable role of aggression as being among the physiological and psychological stress factors. The "processes" for dealing with stress—the adaptation syndromes—are difficult to detail; it is obvious that society in general (and North American society in particular) has not developed enough ways either to prevent or to deal with the causes and results of stress.

FIGURE 13–7
Stress as a system

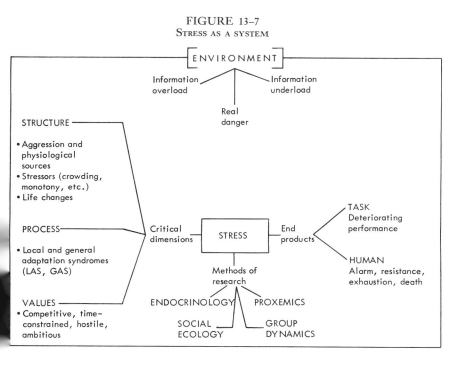

In the long run, aggression may be controlled by ESB or CSB. As Kenneth B. Clark argued in his presidential address to the 1972 American Psychological Association, in which he stressed the need to develop a "peace pill" that "all power-controlling leaders" would be required to take:

> This form of psychotechnological medication would be a type of internally imposed disarmament. It would provide the masses of human beings with the security that their leaders would not or could not sacrifice them on the altars of their personal ego, pathos, vulnerability, and instability.

In time, as scientists get a better understanding of how the brain functions, there may well be such things as enzyme-assisted instruction, protein memory consolidators, and electrical stimulation of the brain to control aggression; but the problem must be dealt with in the interim. And presumably, as behavioural scientists get a better insight into social ecology and proxemics, we can expect improvements in the design of the spaceship Earth and its life support systems. New technologies like *burolandschaft* will have to be created and developed to help re-create this environment. But this is only scraping the surface of the problem.

There is something seriously wrong with the postindustrial society, which is revealed in such facts as the statistics showing that Americans do not live as long as the people of many other countries. Though the United States is ahead of the rest of the world in most measures of material success, in life expectancy it ranks 24th for men and 9th for women. Men live longer in most Western European countries, as well as Japan, Israel, and Greece. One of the reasons why the United States ranks so low is that so many nonwhites do not receive the benefits of sound nutrition and medical care. But perhaps more important is the fact that the American, especially the American male, consumes too much in terms of calories and cholesterol, nicotine and alcohol, while striving tirelessly for success for himself and his famliy. The persistent endeavour of the meritocracy takes its toll, with the death rate from cardiovascular disease 50 per cent higher in the United States than in Western Europe and 25 per cent higher than in Canada.

There is also abundant evidence that sudden changes in the structure of a society can have marked effects on the prevalence of particular diseases. When Britain went to war in 1939, the death rate from suicide and alcoholism dropped to almost zero. After the Netherlands were occupied in 1940, there was a sharp increase in the incidence of peptic ulcers; whereas peptic ulcers were extremely rare among prisoners in German concentration camps, presumably because life for the prisoners, in spite of the terribly cruel conditions, had a dramatic simplicity in moral terms.

The conclusion is inescapable that there is something seriously wrong with the affluent life style of North Americans which is having dramatic consequences for them in terms of life expectation; and the curious thing is that the rest of the world is struggling to increase its affluence. One interesting fact to emerge from the World Health Organization's report "Society, Stress and Disease" is that an Italian-settled community—Roseto, in Pennsylvania, with a population of 1,700—has a death rate from heart disease which is less than half the rate for the United States as a whole. Roseto has a cohesive social structure, with the men as the unchallenged heads of families, and where the elderly are revered and their advice sought. The net result is a community of mutual support and understanding, where (in spite of the existence of the usual risk factors of overeating, oversmoking, and overconsuming) people live longer.

Perhaps the explanation for the American male's poor life expectancy is to be found in the emancipation of wives and children—or, looking at the other side of that coin, in his reactions to the changing role signals and expectations caused by such liberation. Perhaps society's callous attitudes towards older people shadow his outlook even in the prime of life. Many people are fascinated by studying such "Shangri La" communities as Roseto, the Arapesh and Semai tribes, and other remote spots where people seem to live longer and happier lives; the evidence from such studies does not pinpoint any single answer, but does indicate many possible factors. In any case, it is clear that social customs have a profound effect on the incidence of disease, and that further research is needed to clarify the relationships and see what factors are pertinent to modern societies.

Sufficient evidence is available to make it clear that the way organizational life is arranged and the kind of occupation which a person chooses can give rise to stresses which, in turn, can cause disease. For example clergymen, scientists, and teachers live longer than the average; Supreme Court justices often live beyond 80; and such life expectations seem to be a function of regular hours and a minimum of pressure and tension. The poor corporate executive is left in a hair shirt of competition, responsibility, and decision making. Society has built up his needs to achieve and to win power, all through the exercise of bureaucratic *real-politik*, leaving him with an existential miasma of hostility which makes him a "cert" for a coronary—or so some medical and behavioural scientists would imagine the executive life.

Organizational life works out a little differently from this macabre vision of the corporate coronary case, hassled and harassed all day long. Corporate executives live longer than their subordinates, as any good book of actuarial actualities would tell you. They have transformed many organizations into monastic institutions where they begin the day with the matins of reading from the great teachers of our times in the *New York Times* or *The (London) Times*, follow with prayer meetings to sing the praises of their corporate betters, and, after returning the telephone calls of the favoured few, repair to the club for a frugal lunch of filet of sole and white wine. Afterwards, they return to the postprandial relaxation of a boring meeting. And so the day wears on, as they turn the hustle and bustle of corporate life into a behavioural pabulum (à la R. M. Cyert and J. G. March). Even such a dangerous subject as conflict can be knocked into shape; so that if it cannot always be presented in the form of an algorithm, at least there are some heuristics at hand to guide the executive. Aggression and stress are for the lower orders. Thus our next subject is conflict—its models and management.

REVIEW AND RESEARCH

1. What is aggression in (*a*) hereditary, (*b*) biological, and (*c*) environmental terms?
2. Why do executives have a territorial imperative?
3. Why are dissent and consensus integral to executive life?
4. Devise and execute an experiment to study how people group themselves in a leisure area such as the cafeteria. Make a comparative study of people grouping in the library.
5. Design two layouts for discussion groups: (*a*) for a democratic and (*b*) for an autocratic group. Discuss the role of eye contact in discussion groups.
6. What generates executive stress?
7. Compare and contrast Friedman and Rosenman's view of the executive cardiac type (see Box 13.2) and Hinkle's view (see Box 13.3).
8. What is "the neurosis of success"?
9. How would you set about changing your life style? How would you measure achievement?
10. "There must be something good to life if it ends with death" and "Death must have something going for it, if they save it for the end" represent two typical death-wish statements. Construct an existential thanatology for M.B.A. students that will keep them slim, trim, noncigarette-smoking full of pep, zip, and panache, and yet ready to go at a moment's notice.

GLOSSARY OF TERMS

Adaptation to stress. Ways of coping with stressors. According to Selye stressors affect the brain, which signals the adrenal and pituitary glands. Re actions to short-term stressors are (1) alarm, and (2) the local adaptation syndrome (LAS), which facilitates short-term homeostatic regulation o body processes. Under long-run stress, more subsystems are activated until the entire body is mobilized; the end point of this process is the general adaptation syndrome (GAS), characterized by chronic endocrine imbalance deteriorating psychomotor performance, and adrenal exhaustion; finally the person is unable to respond to environmental conditions.

Aggression. In a narrow biological sense, patterns of behaviour associated with attacking another individual, or an "attack posture"; in a wider organiza tional context, includes competitiveness and self-assertiveness.

Proxemics. The ways in which man consciously or unconsciously structures his micro-space.

Social ecology. The ecology of human behaviour, or the nature of the mutual interaction between man and his evironment, including factors such as spatial layouts, territoriality, and body language.

Stress. The anticipation of inability to respond adequately (or at a reasonable cost) to perceived demand, accompanied by anticipation of negative consequences for inadequate response.

Territorial imperative. The belief that a definite area is needed to survive, so widely observed by ethologists in their study of animal communities that many social scientists are coming around to the view that territoriality is a kind of instinct.

14

Conflict

In our turbulent environment, where conflict is the order of the day, it is small wonder that many corporate executives are bewildered by the forces of organizational change. Old concepts of human relations, including the notion that conflict per se is harmful and should be avoided at all cost, do not square with the facts any longer. Indeed, the new approach is that conflict, if properly handled, can lead to more effective and appropriate arrangements.

Contrary to conventional wisdom, the most important single thing about conflict is that it is good for you. While this is not a scientific statement of fact, it reflects a basic and unprecedented shift of emphasis—a move away from the old human relations point of view where all conflict was seen as bad.

The modern organizational revolution has been characterized by an acceleration of healthy subversive tendencies which gathered force and speed in the 1960s in protest against the brittle iron law of corporate oligarchy; a protest against the presumption that, in organizations, policies and instructions flow down the hierarchy and reports flow up.

It is a protest against the cozy paternalistic world of classical management theory where top management carries total responsibility. It is a protest exemplified by the success of Lawrence Peter and Raymond Hull's *The Peter Principle*, which was on the best seller lists for many months. It is increasingly a middle-class protest by executives and professionals and decreasingly a protest from a diminishing shop floor. It is a protest with its own particular diabolism; some of the games played in executive suites make Edward Albee's "Get the Guests" and "Bring up the Baby," as portrayed in "Who's Afraid of Virginia Woolf?" seem like nursery pastimes.

In brief, in our new frontier environment, conflict is the order of the day. The new look is so radical that many top managers wonder just how this change came about. Not that most knowing managers have not adopted a different posture towards conflict management; most have mastered the new argot that includes such choice phrases as "structure me a meeting," "let's go for confrontation," "they're definitely going to escalate this one," "minimize our maximum losses," "let's introduce a little uncertainty into the situation," and so on. Most experienced executives recognize the script and know they have learned new parts, but are curious to discover how it all came about. This is not only intellectual curiosity as to what happened in the past; it also conceals a deep and pervasive need to try to guess the practical implications of "conflict nouveau." The old concept, or human relations view, of conflict fails to acknowledge its importance as a creative force in today's society. The executive needs a new view of conflict that will make conflict work for him.

REALISTIC REASSESSMENT

The emerging view of conflict, as shown in Table 14–1, reverses many of the cozy nostrums of human relations management which had its intellectual origins in the famous Hawthorne studies of the 1920s. These studies "proved" the then startling proposition that interpersonal relations counted more for productivity than the quality of the physical environment, such as the level of illumination. An entire school of management

TABLE 14–1
HUMAN RELATIONS AND REALISTIC MODELS OF CONFLICT

Old view	New look
Conflict is by definition avoidable.	Conflict is inevitable.
Conflict is caused by troublemakers, boat rockers, and prima donnas.	Conflict is determined by structural factors such as the physical shape of a building, the design of a career structure, or the nature of a class system.
Legalistic forms of authority such as "going through channels" or "sticking to the book" are emphasized.	Conflict is integral to the nature of change.
Scapegoats are accepted as inevitable.	A minimal level of conflict is optimal.

grew up around the notion that if people were well treated, they would produce. Conflict, by definition, was harmful and should be avoided. Those who generated conflict were troublemakers and were bad for the organization.

The new view is that perfect organizational health is not freedom from conflict. On the contrary, if properly handled, conflict can lead to more effective and appropriate adjustments.

There is a curious link between conflict management and anxiety. At one time, psychologists believed rather naively that anxiety, in any form or level, must by its nature be bad. But research studies strongly suggest that a moderate level of anxiety may be adaptive and facilitate survival. Other researchers reinforce this point by arguing that an environment devoid of novelty can be unbearable to human subjects. In other words, there seems to be an optimal level of uncertainty for effective functioning.

Conflict management recognizes that executives have aggressions to expend, can withstand a fair amount of anxiety, and welcome uncertainty as an opportunity to restructure their environment. Hence the way conflict is *managed*—rather than suppressed, ignored, or avoided—contributes significantly to a company's effectiveness.

TURNING POINTS

What are the intellectual origins of this new approach to conflict management? Some executives, perhaps jaundiced by the distressing skill that social psychologists have shown in managing and eventually dissipating conflict in laboratory situations, have blamed the behavioural scientists. The more mathematically oriented executive might be tempted to think it all began with game theory—a mathematical technique which finds an optimal strategy for a player, taking into consideration all options open to an opponent. Reflection suggests, however, that the assumptions of game theory are too abstruse, abstract, and mathematical to have much relevance, though a few managers like the argot—"zero sum games" and "minimax strategy," for example. Other executives blame the cold war and quote Thomas C. Schelling, who pointed out in *Strategy of Conflict:*

> The precarious strategy of cold war and nuclear stalemate has often been expressed in game-type analogies: two enemies within reach of each other's poison arrows on opposite sides of a canyon, the poison so slow that either could shoot the other before he died; a shepherd who has chased a wolf into a corner where it has no choice but to fight, the shepherd unwilling to turn his back on the beast; a pursuer armed only with a hand grenade who inadvertently gets too close to his victim and dares not use his weapon; two neighbors, each controlling dynamite in the other's basement, trying to find mutual security through some arrangement of electric switches and detonators.

A more fundamental reason has been the demise of human relations as a management philosophy and the emergence of the task approach to conflict management, where the emphasis has been on developing the optimal organization by considering both the task to be done and the resources available. In the task approach, the exploitation of crisis becomes a major avenue of development.

For example, in the Apollo project, the capsule fire which took the lives of three astronauts was seized as an opportunity to change relations between NASA officials and executives of contracting companies. Whereas before the fire two parties had met in a negotiating context, after the fire they got together to solve problems. The result was not only increased effectiveness but the beginning of a change in the role of the liaison executives; their companies began to question to whom they owed their allegiance—NASA or the contractors.

CRISIS: USE AND MISUSE

In the creative use of crisis, the effective executive welcomes uncertainty and plans for its exploitation, if not its creation. An example of this is provided by the experience of a British manufacturing company which reacted to the government's introduction of a payroll tax by grasping the chance to reorganize and rationalize its product lines, so that each factory was charged with the making of one component instead of two. What is significant about this case is not only that the company subsequently had the tax and a bit more refunded to it, but also that the chief executive exploited the chance to make dramatic organizational changes which he had been mulling over for some time. In other, more tranquil circumstances, such changes would have been subject to considerable and sustained negotiations, both in the front office and in the work councils.

In the turbulent environment of contemporary business, suffused with ambiguity, the hard-headed executive with strong nerves and a feel for the moment of drama that a crisis affords has the chance to restructure the organizational scene in a way which may well meet his needs for self-fulfilment as well as the interests of the institution.

Moreover, the social science "angels" would be on the side of this hard-headed but imaginative executive. Research evidence suggests that tension needs to be reappraised and that the exploitation of healthy tension can stimulate learning, serve to "internalize" the problems of other managers, increase critical vigilance and self-appraisal, and induce decision makers to examine conflicting values (including their own) more discerningly when making decisions.

There is also considerable and growing research evidence from the study of creative tension and scientific performance that research scientists, if they are going to function effectively and achieve excellence, require an intellectual and social environment made up of two sets of apparently inconsistent factors, one set related to stability, confidence, or security, and the other to an optimal level of disruption, intellectual conflict, or challenge. The most effective researchers are those who control their product mix of personal interaction in such a way that they get sufficient critical feedback from competitive colleagues; they also have a steady supply of generally supportive human back-up which they can use as a form of psychic heavy water to keep the fissions and fusions of intellectual ferment from becoming critical and detonating.

In brief, what social scientists are saying is that an optimal level of anxiety, arousal, and conflict is needed for man to function effectively. Fortunately, this intelligence is coming to business leaders at an appropriate moment because, both at home and abroad, conflict is manifesting itself in ways which challenge conventional wisdom in management theory.

To make this point of theory meaningful, it is necessary to distinguish between structure and process. The structure, in terms of organization shapes, definitions, and roles, we seem to know a lot about; but about the process, in terms of what actually happens within or without the structure, we seem to know very little. The student revolution, with its emphasis on confrontation, conflict, and crisis, is but one vivid example of the organizational process bursting the conventional structure of bureaucracy.

THE PERSONAL FACTOR IN CONFLICT

While it is clear that conflict is ultimately structural in origin—i.e., it is a function of the shape of the class system, of the way technology structures interaction, or of the geographical layout of a community or a building—there is nevertheless a personal factor involved. Nowhere has this personal factor been better demonstrated than in the study of the personal characteristics of skyjackers and political terrorists. Dr. David G. Hubbard, a Dallas psychiatrist who has made a special study of air piracy, has concluded that skyjackers and political terrorists are almost always paranoid schizophrenics with overt suicidal tendencies. Thus airline administrators and government officials who have to deal with this deadly species have to recognize that one of the options open and attractive to their opponents is suicide. But this also makes it possible to make some predictions as how such terrorists operate; and provided the air crew and hostages work within these rules in a mood of "We're in this together," events can be programmed to some extent.

What is relevant about this for the student of organizational life is that a great deal of the industrial relations scene in both business and the university is characterized by the presence of political personalities to whom the suicidal option is an attractive proposition. For example, many university confrontations begin with fairly small academic or administrative issues and are only blown up when the review process which was set up to get the facts, weigh and decide, and make recommendations is challenged. Now follow the "nonnegotiable" demands, and the agonizing begins. Invariably the administration is locked into a very narrow range of options which have been predetermined for it by virtue of the contracts which exist between the administration and faculty, between the administration and the government, and, for that matter, between the administration and students who are involved in the confrontation. But the confronting students have a different constituency, which may also include political organizations remote from the scene of the action. Thus an option open to the students challenging the system is to engage in illegal activities, such as occupying buildings, destroying particular professors' classes, or destroying computers, which may lead to their arrest, trial, and possible imprisonment. This last consequence may not be so unacceptable to them as one might think. The attendant publicity functions as a platform for the expression of their personalities and philosophies.

Taking one step nearer to apparently "normal" organizational activities, it seems reasonable to argue that many effective executives appear to be affected by the suicidal option, and that they seem to be capable of steering their lives and careers very close to the disaster line while (usually) staying on the safe side of it. A great deal more can be said of legendary film stars in regard to this ability to live dangerously and well. In the executive scene, apparently suicidal career options include threatening to resign, open confrontations with bosses, staging spectacular outrages intolerable to the organization, going over everybody's head to the president, publishing and perishing, and so on.

How can organizations cope with the modern urban guerrilla who is armed with behavioural science techniques and knowledgeable about group dynamics and the principles of subversion? Why do the more intractable organizational conflicts attract a particular fanatic to whom the game, the ritual of confrontation, escalation, crisis, and further escalation, is an extremely attractive option? Until social scientists come up with a better researched description of conflict's profiles and preferred processes, management will go on fumbling through such confrontations—and shaking their heads afterwards, more in sorrow than in anger, wondering what in fact happened. Perhaps the picture would be clearer if they accepted that conflict is structural in origin; follows a particular, definable process; and is characterized by a specific value system—and that this social lattice attracts a particular personality type.

STRUCTURE OF CHAPTER 14

Topic 1 reviews conflict at the individual, group, and organization levels. Beginning with the frustration-aggression hypothesis, we go forward to look at the effect of aggression on perception, which can generate intolerance of ambiguity. Under the heading of group conflict, we consider both conflict within groups (intragroup) and among groups (inter-group). Intragroup conflict can arise from differences in interpretation of values, norms, rules, roles, and relations. Intergroup conflict typically arises between groups who are competing for a limited resource, especially where the groups have different aims. Organizational conflict can also be divided into intra- and interorganizational forms.

Topic 2 deals with organizational conflict in depth. Having quickly reviewed game theory and tacit bargaining, we turn to the subject of organizational attrition. Three short cases illustrate different aspects of the management of conflict. We are then in a position to formulate a set of ground rules for the various parties to a conflict: the initiator, the defendant, and the conciliator; and to review the techniques for alleviation of conflict: negotiation, mediation, and arbitration.

Topic 3 models conflict as a system, and suggests some answers to the ancient question, What's in it (conflict) for me?

TOPIC 1
Conflict at the individual, group, and organization levels

CONFLICT AT THE INDIVIDUAL LEVEL

Conflict occurs at many different levels, not the least important of which is the level of the individual. In this particular discussion we are not concerned with intrapsychic conflict except in so far as this might provide a useful model to explain organizational conflict. The most useful starting point is to take up the discussion of aggression we began in Chapter 13. Much of the early psychological work on aggression was based on research conducted by S. Zuckermann, who studied a community of baboons living on Monkey Hill in the London Zoo and concluded that the most common cause of aggression was fighting over possession of objects, usually females or food. Many of the findings of this early research on aggression have been countermanded by more recent studies of baboons in their natural habitat which support the notion that adult male baboon populations establish a well-integrated social system based on dominance and seldom come into conflict. A great deal of innocent amusement can be had from finding parallels between Zuckermann's study of baboons on Monkey Hill and the behaviour of English mutineers from *The Bounty* on Pitcairn Island. Apparently a group made up of 9 English seamen, 6 native men and 11 native women landed on Pitcairn after fleeing from Tahiti with the Royal Navy in hot pursuit. Internecine strife broke out over the possession of the females and after 10 years on the island, 12 of the 15 men had been murdered and peace only broke out when the island population had been reduced to 9 native women, 25 children, and 1 lone Englishman.

THE FRUSTRATION-AGGRESSION HYPOTHESIS

The modern approach to human aggression is founded on John Dollard's frustration-aggression hypothesis: that some link always exists between aggressive behaviour and frustration. It may be useful to define frustration as the motivational and emotional state accruing from the persistent blockage of goal-directed behaviour; it is possible to define aggression as the attack upon an obstacle or barrier blocking satisfaction or displacement of the attack to an object or person (see Box 14.1).

Dollard has stated the now classical frustration-aggression hypothesis in the following terms: "The proposition is that the occurrence of aggressive behaviour always presupposes the existence of frustration and, contrariwise, that the existence of frustration always leads to some form of aggression." Personal frustration is tightly woven into the fabric of social life and makes aggressive response an inevitable human reaction though it is perhaps as well to point out that, while there is frequently an apparent link between aggression and frustration, it may not be the invariable case.

Under conditions of frustration, the behaviour of the individual may revert to an earlier, less objective phase; or frustration may produce extremely rigid behaviour. Sometimes aggression may produce flight rather than fight. In conflict, the individual may find himself in a situation in which there are two mutually exclusive motives or goals available to him. To simplify analysis, this kind of conflict can be subsumed under three headings:

1. "Approach-approach" conflict, where a choice must be made between two mutually exclusive positive goals; e.g., the choice may be between apple pie and rice pudding for dessert.
2. "Approach-avoidance" conflict, where the subject is placed in an ambivalent position with respect to a goal which has both positive and negative aspects; e.g., the choice may be between a trip to a café or doing one's homework.
3. "Avoidance-avoidance" conflict, where the subject faces barriers involving two or more threats; e.g., the choice may be between smoking or overeating.

AGGRESSION AND PERCEPTION

Inevitably, perception and aggression interact. In the simplest terms, perception is the process whereby a person becomes aware of his environment. This oversimplified definition of perception does scant justice to the complex mental processes that lie between impression and expression. Nevertheless there seems to be abundant evidence to support the notion that individual aggressive posturing structures perceptions. Social psychologists and sociologists have been drawing up mirror images of the American view of the Union of Soviet Socialist Republics and the Soviet view of the United States. In other words, different individuals with dif-

Box 14.1: Aggression and leadership

Robert C. Day, a sociologist at Washington State University, and Robert L. Hamblin, a sociologist at Washington University in Missouri, carried out an experiment on four-person work groups, under controlled conditions, to test the effects of two supervisory styles on aggressive responses of subordinate workers. A confederate was trained to emit varied rates of instructions along with hovering and watching behaviour in the *close* style and to interject specified negative, sarcastic remarks at varied rates in acting out the *punitive* style. The experimenters were interested in finding out whether close leadership engendered as many aggressive feelings and verbal remarks against the leader and co-workers as punitive leader behaviour; what effects these leadership styles would have on productivity; and whether these effects would be influenced by a personality variable, self-esteem.

The experimental design

A two-by-two factorial design employing low-high variations of the two leader styles was used. Twenty-four groups, each consisting of four undergraduate, middle-class women, were run all together. The experimental situation was designed to simulate an industrial work station. Subjects were given a manual task, assembling molecular models, using "blueprint" drawings of complex molecules. The total task was broken up into subcomponents and arranged along an assembly line sequence around a curved table, allowing face-to-face interaction. The resulting task interdependency and visual contact elicited interaction and discussion between subjects when the "supervisor" left the room periodically during the experiment. The low-high variations of the close style were operationalized with 8 and 40 instructions, respectively, during the 40-minute work period. Zero and 40 standardized sarcastic remarks, respectively, were used in the low-

R. C. Day and R. L. Hamblin, "Some Effects of Close and Punitive Supervision," *American Jour of Sociology*, Vol. 69 (1964), pp. 499–510.

ferent foci to their aggressive attitudes develop a different picture of reality. This ability to select appropriate perceptual clues, linked with the principle of selective recall, leads to a situation where individuals develop stereotypes which have immensely strong resistance to modification. The approach of early psychologists (such as William McDougall with his emphasis on the instinct of pugnacity, and the bizarre and esoteric aspects of the psychology of Sigmund Freud with his death instinct) has now given way to a more modern view which recognizes that while aggression has a biological base, it must be thought of as a secondary phenomenon arising from environmental factors. For example, in the frustration-aggression situation there may be a significant mobilization of energy when a barrier is encountered. This mobilization may be adequate and sufficient to remove the barrier. In other circumstances it may not, and the energy mobilized may overflow into the generalized destructive behaviour which R. F. Maier categorized as "behaviour without a goal."

Intolerance of ambiguity

Aggression at the level of destructive behaviour may well represent a serious social danger. A person finding himself in an aggressive state may

high variations of punitive leadership. A self-esteem scale was administered before the experiment. Measures of productivity, aggressive verbal behaviour, and aggressive feelings were taken during and after the experiment.

Close supervision, aggression, and self-esteem

Close supervision produced significant increases in aggressive feelings towards the supervisor and in indirect aggression towards the supervisor through lowered productivity; an insignificant increase in verbal aggression towards the supervisor; and an increase of borderline significance in aggressive feelings towards co-workers. Punitive supervision produced significant increases in indirect aggression through lowered productivity and in verbal aggression, but no significant increases in aggression towards co-workers. The relationship between close supervision and aggressive feelings appears to be mediated by the self-esteem of the subordinate; an increase in aggressive feelings occurred only in subjects having low self-esteem.

The results indicate that close supervision is frustrating to subordinates, especially those with low self-esteem; and under some conditions, which have yet to be fully specified, it seems to lead to significant drops in output and to increased tendencies to displace aggression against co-workers. Punitive supervision, on the other hand, apparently is recognized as overt aggression and elicits direct verbal counteraggression from subordinates rather than displacement against substitute targets such as co-workers. Generally, the study suggests the need to further test the effects of leader behaviours, including various reinforcing as well as punishing behaviours, under varied organizational contingencies (i.e., varied wage and promotion systems) and to *simultaneously* explore the influence of the personality of the subject on the results.

experience certain perceptual changes. For example, an individual suffering from aggression may develop tunnel vision; that is, he focuses upon an enemy or the object of danger to the extent of excluding other perceptual cues. Polarization may develop to such an extent that he is unable or unwilling to recognize delicate shades of grey and sees every problem in straight blacks and straight whites.

Else Frenkel-Brunswik has argued that such phenomena as tunnel vision and perceptual polarization represent specific examples of a more generic phenomenon called intolerance of ambiguity—the very fundamental need that individuals have to impose meaning and structure on unstructured, inchoate, ill-defined situations. This ability to structure one's perception almost certainly has survival value for the individual in the sense that it enables him to test whether the environment is threatening or not. There is apparently a variance between those who can tolerate a high level of ambiguity and conflict and those who can tolerate only a low level.

Conflict situations inevitably are made up of at least two individuals who hold polarized points of view, who are somewhat intolerant of ambiguities, who ignore delicate shades of grey, and who are quick to jump to conclusions. Given a frozen situation like this, it is extremely difficult to deal with conflict. The important cognitive problem is to introduce

Box 14.2: A conflict model

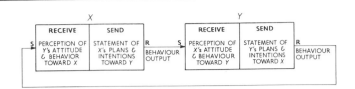

An extremely valuable and widely used model for understanding conflict is shown above
This particular model has the following advantages:

1. It has very wide generality. It can be used to analyse conflict between countrie
   organizations, groups, or individuals. For example, if *X* = America and *Y* = Russi
   a very useful model becomes available for discussing international conflict.
2. It exploits the systems approach and underscores the fact that conflict is frequent
   cyclical and self-locking (a vicious circle).
3. The model combines two basic behavioural science paradigms, viz:
   a. Stimulus + Attitudes = Perception
   b. Stimulus ⟶ Response

In this model, *X*'s perception of *Y*'s behaviour leads to *X*'s response, which is the
interpreted by *Y* according to his attitudes toward *X*; this structures *Y*'s response. S
the vicious circle is maintained.

This model can be used very successfully to collect data about *X*'s perception of
and vice versa. The next stage in the exercise is "the confrontation of stereotypes." Th
procedure has been used to research stereotypes in both management-labour contex
and American-Russian confrontations. It has the practical advantage of providing th
action-oriented researcher with a source of hard data about stereotypes which, wh
presented to the parties to a dispute, frequently induces a sense of cognitive dissonan
which may in turn lead to the breaking up of well-established and "frozen" prejudic
In other words, this model emphasizes the important fact that perceptions play an i
portant part in shaping and maintaining conflict positions; and further, that factua
defining perceptions allows the conflict system to be explicated and may facilita
attitude changes. "Stereotype confrontation" may change stereotypes.

Specially prepared by J. Kelly for this volume.

dissonance into the system. Basically this is achieved by providing intelligence that the opposition has characteristics or displays behaviour similar
to one's own. Such intelligence helps to break up both hostility and hard-
ened images and offers the possibility of restructuring at a more favourable
level (see Box 14.2).

CONFLICT AT THE GROUP LEVEL

There has been relatively little systematic study of conflict either within
groups (intragroup conflict) or between groups (intergroup conflict)

Looking first at intragroup conflict, it is perhaps useful to remember that a group may be thought of as consisting of a number of people whose interactions at a given time have generated the following characteristics: a system of values, norms, and sanctions has emerged appropriate to the nature of the task on which they are working, which has created a set of fairly well-defined role and status relations which are interdependent.

Intragroup conflict may arise in at least three ways: (1) when the group faces a novel problem or task, (2) when new values are imported from the social environment into the group, or (3) when a person's extra-group role comes into conflict with his intragroup role.

A good example of the change of task generating conflict can be cited from the case of a factory primary working group required to perform a new function with semiautomated equipment. In a component-manufacturing plant which the author studied, one particular line of manually operated machines was replaced by a semiautomated line, where automatic machines were linked with transfer equipment. With this change-over, the role of the supervisor became less important and there was a deeply felt need for two new roles: a super-machine operative who could set a large number of the machines, and a "slip-man" who could relieve the operatives so that they could get a break without stopping the machines. Working at a new task like this threatened to produce tremendous and far-reaching changes in the structure and function of the primary working group. It was obviously in management's interests to get the workers to stagger their tea breaks, which would inevitably have produced immense changes in the informal group.

An example of how conflict can be engendered by the importation of values from the environment is provided by examination of the effect of the Closed Brethren Religion on the manning of fishing boats in the East of Scotland. One of this sect's tenets is that members must not associate with nonmembers either at work or leisure. As well as leading to tremendous domestic difficulties, observance of this rule created a preference for smaller fishing boats which, in turn, require smaller crews, thus reducing the difficulty of guaranteeing that all members of a crew share the same religious point of view. A similar sort of finding was made by Melville Dalton, who found that many rate-busters came from quite different socioeconomic backgrounds and had political and religious views quite different from the majority of their fellows on the shop floor.

Another source of intragroup conflict has its origins in role conflict. This may arise where there is some kind of conflict between a person's role within the group and his role without. There has recently been some study of this type of role conflict, mainly in researches into disasters. For example, the father of a family who is a policeman or fireman may have to decide whether to stay and try to save his own family or to report for duty to work for the survival of the community. This type of situation inevitably and not unnaturally induces severe role conflict.

Margaret Mead and Rhoda Metraux in "The Anthropology of Human Conflict" describe an interesting method for dealing with intragroup conflict:

> For example, examination of the handling of submarine crews during World War II showed that all the European participants hit on a common solution to the dangers of intragroup conflict within the confined space of the submarine—continuous access to food. The types of food differed by nationality, but the solution was the same.

INTERGROUP CONFLICT: HAWKS VERSUS DOVES

When intragroup conflict becomes sufficiently strong it may lead to a situation where two new groups are formed which are in conflict with one another and thus give rise in fact to intergroup conflict. A good model of intergroup conflict is provided by the "hawks versus doves" paradigm which has been frequently cited to explain how conflict in the upper echelons of the American government is regulated in response to crises such as the Cuban missile situation. This phenomenon has manifested itself a number of times at the Cabinet level in American crises, and it would seem not unreasonable to suspect and to hope that this process has now become institutionalized. The technique of naming a process helps to legitimize it and thus facilitates its institutionalization.

Groups commonly come into conflict when they have different aims such that one group can only achieve its objective at the expense of the other. In such circumstances research and common sense join in telling us that the members of one group will become hostile to the members of the other. This hostility may well manifest itself in the use of derogatory terms by the "good guys" to describe the status, physical appearance, ethnic origin, achievement, and aspirations of the "bad guys"; but a major effect of intergroup conflict is to heighten morale within each group.

Social psychologists, who have shown a frightening skill at making and breaking conflict in experiments, have devoted considerable effort and ingenuity to devising ways and means of replacing intergroup conflict with co-operative interaction by such techniques as the introduction (even invention) of a common enemy, dissemination of favourable information about the other group, and exchange of persons between groups (see Box 14.3). All these techniques are widely used as a means of pulling diverse and disparate work groups together. The "common enemy technique," in the form of a threat of a takeover or of heightening economic competition, may be used as a means of welding different sections of the same organization together. A great deal of management education can no doubt be justified when it serves to provide favourable information about other sections of the enterprise. And job rotation undoubtedly serves to reduce competition by giving "the new boy" a better chance to find out what the other fellow is doing.

CONFLICT AT THE ORGANIZATION LEVEL

In an organizational setting, conflict may manifest itself in a number of different modes. It is useful to distinguish between interorganizational and intraorganizational conflict. Interorganizational conflict includes:

1. Conflict between organizations, e.g., Ford versus General Motors.
2. Conflict between the headquarters organization and an operating organization, e.g., the head office versus a manufacturing plant.
3. Conflict between a government agency and a business organization, e.g., the Defense Department and an aircraft company.

Intraorganizational conflict includes:

1. Hierarchical conflict, e.g., management versus foremen.
2. Functional conflict, e.g., work study versus personnel.
3. Professional versus functional conflict, e.g., accountants versus production control.
4. Management versus shop floor conflict, e.g., managers versus shop stewards.
5. Union versus union conflict, e.g., a craft union versus a general workers' union.

THE UNIVERSAL CHARACTER OF CONFLICT

One of the propositions that many executives find difficult to accept about conflict is its universal character. Conflict appears to be endemic to the organization irrespective of its nature. The rationale for this catholicity of conflict appears to be that an organization represents systems of roles where authority is distributed asymmetrically. This inevitably produces conflicts between the organizers and the organized, between the powerful and the weak, between the governor and the governed.

Even in such organizations as prisons and military units, where the officials have apparently total power, we still find conflict. Gresham M. Sykes, in his study of corruption of authority in a maximum security prison, provides a brilliant illustration of the limits of totalitarian power. Sykes makes some very intriguing observations regarding the nature of the process which removes the power from the guards and puts it into the hands of the prisoners. In essence this shift of power arises because the guards, in order to survive, are forced to acknowledge the prisoners' informal system. This corruption arises partly from the fact that the guard is exposed to a kind of moral blackmail and partly because he is dependent on the prisoners for the satisfactory performance of his duties. Thus the view of a bureaucracy as a system where orders flow down the line and are translated into actions by the people at the bottom to achieve the objectives of the top bureaucrat must be moderated by the fact that even in

Box 14.3: From conflict to co-operation

A brilliant psychologist, Muzafer Sherif, carried out a series of experiments on conflic in the late 1940s and early 1950's. Sherif's experimental studies combined field and laboratory methods in studying group formation and intergroup relations under con trolled yet lifelike conditions. Sherif was convinced that measures to mitigate inter group tensions can be achieved only by defining the conditions generating conflict and co-operation.

THE EXPERIMENTAL SETTING

Boys' camps were chosen as sites for the research due to the fact that (a) conditions could be controlled and reproduced in the future, and (b) groups formed at summe camps would be informal and made up of boys who were unacquainted prior to the experiment. The subjects selected were similar in background, "healthy, well-adjusted boys, somewhat above average in intelligence and from stable, white, Protestant, middle class homes." The experimental situations were kept lifelike by choosing activities characteristic of such camps, including canoeing, but usually requiring obstacles to be overcome first.

Data collection methods were disguised or made a natural aspect of the setting Several methods were used at each step for purposes of cross-validation. The experi ments were designed in successive stages, each lasting about a week. Stage 1 was devoted to the formation of the two groups, Stage 2 to the development of conflic between the groups, and Stage 3 to the reduction of conflict.

Stage 1: Formation of groups

Stage 1 was characterized by the formation of status and role relations and norm within the separate groups. Tasks were provided and soon leaders and lieutenant emerged. Observer ratings and informal opinions from the boys indicated when the group had established a structure. Sociograms were constructed on the basis of these observations. As the groups established themselves, rituals, nicknames, secret symbols and group names were also adopted.

Stage 2: Intergroup conflict

Stage 2 introduced intergroup conflict. Activities in which only one group could achieve its goal at the expense of the others (e.g., tugs-of-war, baseball games) wer

M. Sherif, "Experiments on Group Conflict and Co-operation," *Scientific American,* Vol. (November, 1956), pp. 54–58.

circumstances where bureaucracy appears to concentrate total power in the hands of the officials, there is inevitably a backlash by the organized against the organizer.

To many minds the ideal of the organization as a machine was the World War II German war machine, in particular the German general staff. But even this august institution had built-in mechanisms to allow conflict, as described by D. J. Goodspeed in *Ludendorff:*

In theory, and to a large extent in practice, the officers of the General Staff lived sequestered from the main currents of German life, aloof from politics and untouched by the ferment of industrial expansion and pros-

used. This led inevitably to animosity between groups, often to the extent that a boy who once gave a boy in the other group a "best friend" rating now gave him a negative rating. But the effect of intergroup conflict was to increase solidarity, co-operativeness, and morale within each group.

Stage 3: Reduction of conflict

Stage 3 was devoted to reducing the conflict established in Stage 2. At first, events were introduced involving extremely pleasant contact between the groups but not requiring interdependence; instead of reducing conflict, these situations provided avenues for further hostile incidents.

Activities requiring mutual assistance were then introduced. The "superordinate goals" were appealing to both groups but necessitated the co-operation of both groups if they were to be achieved. An example of this type of activity was as follows: a lorry was to go for food, but "broke down" when everyone was hungry. The boys got a rope and, working together, managed to start the truck.

Eventually the groups became more friendly and positive ratings began developing across group lines. Best friends appeared quite often in the other group.

CONCLUSIONS

. Conflict is not primarily a result of individual neurotic traits but arises under given conditions even when the people involved are well adjusted.
. Intragroup co-operative and democratic procedures are not directly transferable to intergroup relations. On the contrary, intragroup solidarity was greatest when intergroup conflict was most pronounced.
. Interaction between warring groups as equals in pleasant circumstances does not necessarily mitigate conflict.
. Interaction between groups requiring co-operation and working toward superordinate goals helps to establish good relations between groups, but single episodes are not sufficient.
. A number of co-operative situations involving working toward superordinate goals has a cumulative effect in mitigating intergroup hostility.

perity in the Reich. In many ways they were as withdrawn and dedicated as members of a religious order. Like a religious order, too, they managed to combine the opposing principles of autocracy and democracy, exacting the best from both systems. They regarded rank less highly than intelligence; they debated military problems freely and often heatedly until the moment of decision; and although a junior was expected to carry out any positive order scrupulously, he was expected as well to advise honestly and without subservience.

In short, the logic of conflict seems to be: it is inevitable, endemic to the organizational milieu, a necessary consequence of change; therefore, let us plan for this catholicity of conflict so that its regulation and control will optimize the outcome for the organization.

TOPIC 2
Organizational conflict in depth

If it is accepted that conflict is endemic, inevitable, and necessary to organizational life, then its specification becomes a central problem for organizational analysts. L. A. Coser in "The Function of Social Conflict" has defined conflict as "struggle over values and claims to scarce status, power, and resources in which the aims of the opponents are to neutralize, injure, or eliminate their rivals."

In an organizational setting, conflict must be seen as one of the core problems of communication. The contemporary organizational analyst regards conflict as a means of achieving some kind of unity out of divergent interests. Inherent in this view is the belief that conflict constitutes a device which facilitates social cohesion, principally because its development calls into being forces which emphasize common interests and values.

The modern approach to conflict analysis is based on game theory, which is rapidly becoming *de rigueur* for all behavioural scientists. Game theory is a set of mathematical operations developed to provide a solution to the problem of selecting the optimal strategy for a player, taking into consideration all possible actions open to an opponent. In essence, in game theory an attempt is made to develop models which will define outcomes in terms of utilities and probabilities. Game theory may be thought of as a model of conflict among several people where the principal modes of resolution are collusiin and conciliation. Many executives have found its hard-headed, scientific language particularly useful. Terms such as rules, players, moves, strategies, and payoffs fit easily into executive argot.

Nevertheless, there is considerable and continuing controversy regarding the relevance of game theory to the study of corporate conflict and strategy. Many executives believe its mathematical assumptions are too abstract for it to have much organizational relevance. But the significant and decisive advantage of game theory is the fact that it compels an individual in a conflict situation to consider his own reactions to an opponent's response to his potential moves, with a view to evolving strategies and tactics designed to make his opponent involuntarily select a strategy favourable to him. For this reason game theory is a "must" for the executive.

TACIT BARGAINING IN GAMES

Much of the early discussion in game theory was concerned with zero sum games, where what one player wins the other loses, so that the pluses and minuses always total zero. What is more interesting to the organizational analyst is the nonzero sum game, which involves some degree of mutual dependence. T. C. Schelling has studied conflict situations in which there is a common interest as well as conflict between opponents. He has focused analysis on bargaining or mixed motive games which contain elements of both conflict and co-operation. For example, in tacit bargaining, where communication between the parties is incomplete or impossible it may be possible to set limits to conflict without overt negotiation. There is an improved probability of finding tacit agreement if we understand better where to look for the terms of the agreement. Schelling argues in *Strategy of Conflict* that:

> (1) tacit agreements or agreements arrived at through partial or haphazard negotiation require terms that are qualitatively distinguishable from the alternatives and cannot simply be a matter of degree; (2) when agreement must be reached with incomplete communication, the participants must be ready to allow the situation itself to exercise substantial constraint over the outcome; specifically, a solution that discriminates against one party or the other or even involves "unnecessary" nuisance to both of them may be the only one on which their expectations can be coordinated.

In other words, conflict involves bargaining between A and B, and the ability of A to achieve his objective is dependent to a significant degree on the moves that B will make.

The nuclear stalemate which has caused peace to break out between the Union of Soviet Socialist Republics and the United States represents a slap in the face to the argument of Christian charity or meekness as a means of abolishing large-scale wars. Both sides opt for peace not only because of their ability to overkill each other but also because the power of both nations can be fully explicated and made visible to the other party.

Much the same is true at an organizational level. What is necessary is for the organization, in the first instance, to make explicit the objectives, value systems, powers, and resources of its various members. Secondly, the environment must be examined to ascertain and define the external value systems, with a view to testing for legitimacy any moves that are proposed.

ORGANIZATIONAL ATTRITION

Conflict always involves some testing of the power situation. A typical example of organizational conflict is revealed in the following case, based on an actual but disguised corporate situation.

Bill Jones, a department manager, was sent to a management course and on his return found that his auxiliary but highly valued position of assistant general manager was apparently up for grabs. Before his departure, his name had appeared on the organization chart set aside for assistant general manager, as shown at the top of Figure 14–1. On his return, he found that

FIGURE 14–1
TYPICAL EXAMPLE OF ORGANIZATIONAL ATTRITION

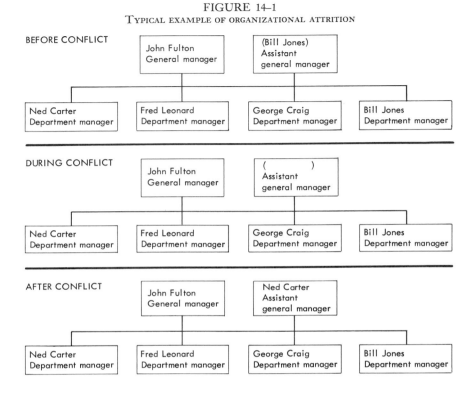

a new organization chart had been issued, but that this particular box had been left empty.

Jones was thus faced with a dilemma: Had it been done deliberately? The decision which he had to make at this stage was whether he ought to keep silent and bide his time or raise this matter with the general manager, John Fulton, to try to have his name put back in this box. As it was, he decided to follow a policy of "wait and see." But when he returned from his annual vacation, he discovered that the name of a rival department manager, Ned Carter, was in the assistant general manager's box.

Taken with other signs, Jones realized he was getting the treatment. His boss was using the technique of "nonlosing hazard," a strategy that can produce a win but not a loss for the general manager, and one which put Jones at a considerable disadvantage. In other words, if Jones had reacted to the first move of leaving the box empty, the general manager might have acquiesced but accused him of being paranoiac and generally oversensitive. In fact, Fulton continued the squeezing process, circumscribing Jones's role by establishing very close standards of performance for his department and leaving him without much organizational slack. Fulton, in his inspection tours, freely criticized the department's performance. Jones experienced a good deal of stress and anxiety, and he had to exercise considerable restraint to ensure that he did not transmit his anxiety to his subordinates, who were already under enough pressure from the more exacting performance standards required by the general manager. In view of this level of conflict, Jones understandably began the search for a more secure niche elsewhere in the corporation.

DILEMMA AND DEFENSE

The type of organizational conflict we have just seen starts in a very low key. The first move, omitting the name, faces the department manager with alternate choices, neither of which is particularly attractive—to accept or protest. With the latter strategy, it might be possible to go over the general manager's head to the divisional vice president. Most department managers would likely regard this move as a strategy of last resort. If Jones had protested to the general manager, Fulton might well, with bad grace, have acquiesced and allowed the name to be reinserted; or, alternatively, "suggested" a postponement of decision, say, for three months, when a new organization chart would be issued in any case.

Once this first strike had been successfully launched, the way was open for the general manager gradually to escalate the conflict. The ensuing anxiety and the vagaries of organizational life make it difficult for the target victim to function effectively. In such circumstances, various defensive postures are usually invoked—from depersonalization ("try to imagine it's happening to somebody else"), adaptive segregation ("keep out of direct contact"), or rationalization ("man is made to suffer"), to the formation of new coalitions, placatory behaviour, and so forth.

One of the most depressing features of this type of organizational conflict is the fact that it may well be incomprehensible to nonmembers of the organization, such as the wife of the victim, who may well wonder about his anxiety when matters of pay are not involved.

But let us look at the problem from the viewpoint of the general manager. The sophisticated manager has a great interest both in breaking traditional modes which are no longer appropriate—and which bind the business to conditions no longer existent—and in establishing a new consensus defined by the emerging legitimacy.

COMMITTEE CONSENSUS

Perhaps the most misunderstood word in executive parlance is "consensus." In order to understand how consensus is achieved in executive meetings, we need to review the brilliant research of Harvard professor R. F. Bales on group dynamics. Bales described the process of groups in terms of clarification, evaluation, and decision; and the structure in terms of roles, with the task specialist and the human relations specialist as the most critical roles. These principles apply to executive meetings as well as to other group situations.

But executive meetings have not stood still. A dramatic change in tone and content has become more obvious in the last five years. The significant difference is the emergence of naked conflict in managerial meetings, conflict which is so common and visible that executives have been compelled to find both a rationale and a ritual for it.

One such ritual is the "hawks versus doves syndrome," which gained considerable currency after its creation during the 1962 Cuban missile crisis. One of the most curious conclusions suggested by a careful reading of Robert F. Kennedy's account of this confrontation is that the dialectic of the situation had to be polarized in this way. Thus, if the hawks had *not* existed, they would have had to be invented (*a*) to give the Kennedy-McNamara axis an opposition and perspective to test and present their ideas against, and (*b*) to give President John F. Kennedy an alternative which he might need. Such are the complexities and complications of the new-style executive meetings.

Within the foregoing context, it is possible to define consensus. No longer are chief executives prepared to be guided by simple majorities; nor for that matter are they prepared to wait for unanimity. They shoot for the consensus, which implies two conditions—one positive and the other negative. On the positive side, the presumption is that the significant authorities endorse, or at least tolerate, the proposed solution. On the negative side, sufficient feedback is available to indicate that a vociferous minority will not emerge which will make the solution inoperable.

Such is the nature of the modern management process; risks are high, stakes are high, and the risks must be syndicated among the executives.

The principle invoked is one of deadly simplicity, capable of wide application, but difficult to understand and even more difficult to apply. It is the proposition that in an organization, executive action must take cognizance of the interdependence of roles.

If this statement seems simplistic, invite someone in your peer group to define his role. The answer usually involves a list of functions and decisions emphasizing responsibility to the person's superior. Such a "worm's eye" response reveals an underlying organizational philosophy where the emphasis is on the exclusively vertical dimension of bureaucracy and where a person can be held totally responsible for something. A more intelligent answer, emphasizing the concept of interdependence, would be, "You define your role and then I'll try to define mine." More briefly, a role can only be delineated by defining a set of roles. Consider the following illustrative scene.

The time is late Friday afternoon and the locus is the general manager's office of a medium-sized engineering firm which makes components for the aerospace industry. The general manager; G. B. Macdonald, is in the process of firing his personnel manager, Bill Murray.

MACDONALD: You're all washed up, Murray. You're through.

MURRAY: I'm sorry, but I didn't quite catch that.

MACDONALD: Look, I'm telling you that you've done your last job around here. The way you really botched up that negotiation with the shop stewards on the new contract is unforgivable. Besides, I'm sick of the way you keep coming back to me for policy decisions. If I heard you say, "Could I have your policy input?" once more, I'd go right out of my skull.

The one-sided tirade continues for some minutes with Murray, his back to the wall, silently waiting for his chance. Abruptly and unexpectedly, the general manager begins to fumble for feedback.

MACDONALD: Well, Murray, isn't it valid? You keep coming back to me, then botching it?

MURRAY: Sir, could I ask you to cast your mind back to when you *invited* me to become your personnel manager. Your very words were, "As general manager, I shall retain the executive function, whether it is programming, technical, or personnel. You are merely the personnel extension of my role." I accepted the job on those terms. With all due respect, in firing me, you are really firing yourself.

MACDONALD: What are you driving at?

MURRAY: I'm merely saying that as the "personnel executive," you are unjustifiably blaming me for living up to your own prescribed terms.

MACDONALD: Wait a minute, Bill. I'll get the sherry bottle from my liquor cabinet. . . .

What is significant about this incident is the exploitation by Murray (and perhaps more important, the general manager's acceptance) of a line of argument that 10 years ago would have been unthinkable.

In more general terms, conflict is always moral conflict. Where there is a dispute, values, norms, roles, and statuses will be involved. What this means for the hard-pressed executive is that he must dig beneath such clichés as, "It's a problem in communication." Searching behind such gadget words for their value orientation makes the latter-day executive a thoughtful man who understands semantics.

NEW PERSPECTIVE

An excellent test of a graduate business administration student's understanding of the new behavioural approach to management would be to ask that he reconcile the psychologically distant, task-oriented executive of the 1970s with the human relations–directed, democratic manager of the 1940s. It would be impossible for him to respond properly without getting involved in a discussion of the new morality.

Traditional morality is dead. It is a victim of the new technology exemplified by organ transplants, instant communication, and zero privacy (generated by electronic bugging devices). Its demise was aided and abetted by a new organizational logic which somehow resolves the dilemma of trying to integrate self-fulfilment and loyalty to the traditional institution—whether it be the corporation, the church, or the crack combat unit. The mobicentric (mobile) manager has considered the permissiveness of Freud, worried with Sartre about the futility of choosing to act unfree, knows something about game theory, and feels a diminishing loyalty to traditional forms of organization. In his view, "Everything is up for grabs; the next move is yours."

A CASE EXAMPLE

Let us turn to a case illustration of how conflict technology can be used as a means of improving corporate effectiveness. This will serve to set up the ground rules for the several roles the executive may have to play in a conflict situation.

In the past, an independent social science research institution had achieved considerable success and growth by creating a democratic work atmosphere in which some of the best social scientists in North America had done research, mainly for the government but also for large corporations. All major decisions were agreed on by the heads of the various departments, and this executive consensus was then pumped through a corporate research council which met every month.

The director—who was younger than any of his department heads, and who had managed the institution to its present dynamic position by a combination of aggressiveness, political acumen, and administrative know-how rather than research excellence—was dissatisfied with the institution's present performance. He had made up his mind to do something about it, and he planned his moves most carefully.

In the evolution of this research institution, three large departments had evolved, each of which was run by a department head who was distinguished in his own field. One of the many anomalies in the institutional structure was that the "behavioural science group" handled marketing projects. The rationale for this was never fully explicated. One view was that when the company got into marketing, much of the work had been concerned with exploring consumer attitudes to new products; thus a psychologist had been nominated for this function and located in the behavioural science group.

Starting at a lower level, the director decided he was going to transfer the marketing function to the "computer science group." He began his strategic ploy at a private meeting in his office with the department head of the behavioural science group. After some general discussion of the group's performance, the director began his attack on the specific situation.

DIRECTOR: I am going to initiate a major change of policy; in fact, a large reorganization of our existing structure. I am going to move marketing from your behavioural science group. I want this out in the open. I am not going behind your back in this. I want the discussion to be all above board.

DEPARTMENT HEAD: I have no strong views on this either way, but I would like to consult with my group.

DIRECTOR: Marketing is not functioning well at the moment because we can't get the people we need who can do forecasting using mathematical models; that type of person would be more at home in the computer science group.

Ten days after this meeting, at which no decision had been made, the director launched his second strike at the situation at the weekly meeting of the department heads; he invited the head of the behavioural science group to raise the question of the location of marketing in his department. This the department head did. Opinions among his subordinates had varied, he reported, but the majority had agreed that for political purposes they wished to hang on to marketing.

The director made his move. He first asked for the documentation of the decision and then asked for and received permission to attend the next meeting of the department. At that subsequent meeting, the director presented his plans for how the marketing function would have to be developed and challenged the department to reveal its plans (if any) for marketing. Considerable uncertainty had been aroused that had focused on how the company got research contracts in the first place and, second, on how they were processed. But still no agreement was reached to release marketing.

The director then decided to change direction. At the next meeting of the department heads he put forward the proposal that an organizational analyst spend sufficient time with the company to thoroughly assess the entire situation. This was agreed on, and some six weeks later, the analyst came up with this proposition:

> The company is a "gourmet" organization which specializes in finding interesting problems and then solving them. In such a context, the conventional form of organization is quite inappropriate and an organic rather than mechanistic model is needed.
>
> In a task-oriented business, R&D can be defined and therefore managed; objectives are specified; programs are produced and policed. Research standards are of necessity less detailed, but both modern behavioural science investigation and executive experience confirm that social scientists are able and willing to work within such constraints.
>
> The conventional departments should be abolished and the task-force concept used—with interdisciplinary task groups set up to handle the specific problems which arise; further, these groups should be headed by the person most expert in that problem.

A special weekend meeting of the corporate research council was called, and over a period of three days the researchers debated their future and presented position papers. The proposal to dissolve the departments and replace them with task forces was regarded as too radical; but it was acceptable that task forces would be created from department members who would still be part of their respective departments for "pay and rations."

What does examination of this case tell us about conflict management? The most significant point to emerge is that it is not always necessary to have a clearly stated set of operational objectives in mind before you initiate change. It is necessary, of course, to have a set of criteria to judge the efficiency of the change (e.g., return on investment, share of the market, and so on).

The director started from a vague but strong hunch that performance could be improved. Instead of issuing an order to move marketing from the behavioural group to the computing group (which he legitimately could have done), he opted for a more general revision which led to a major change in policy—that is, the use of the concept of task forces. This was a concept not imposed by fiat, but one that the whole organization had a chance to look at and debate.

In brief, what the director did was to work systematically through a well-conceived plan for achieving change by initiating conflict. Because he understood the inevitable process of conflict, he was able to maintain balances between creating uncertainty and maintaining a data base, and between getting people to participate and keeping direction.

GROUND RULES

To this point in the discussion, we have been looking at theories of conflict. Next, let us turn our attention to specific guide-lines which may help the hard-pressed executive to apply these theories in such a way that conflict can be meaningfully exploited. The important thing is that the objective must be to achieve, at all times, a creative, acceptable, and realistic resolution of conflict.

One of the most effective means of formulating ground rules for executive conflict is to consider the three roles which an executive might play in a conflict situation. He can be: (*a*) the initiator, (*b*) the defendant, or (*c*) the conciliator. At one time or another, most executives are called on to play each of these roles.

When the executive is the initiator of conflict, he should:

1. Start at a low level and advance on a narrow front on one or two related issues, following a well-documented route.
2. Maintain second-strike capability.
3. Pick the terrain with care; where and when the case is heard is vital.
4. Be prepared to escalate, either to a higher level in the organization or to a meeting of peers.
5. Make it objective, private, and routine; above all, keep it formal.
6. Search for reaction and remember that he may have to settle for token conformity in the first instance.
7. Reinforce success and abandon failure.

When his role is that of defendant, the executive should:

1. Not overreact; keep his cool; let the initiator state his case; listen carefully and neutrally.
2. Ascertain the scale of the strike; try to build a decision tree with "go, no go" decision rules.
3. Ask for the name of the game. Is it the game of "courtroom"? If so, he should ask for the counsel for the defence.
4. Ask not only for an exact definition of the "charge," but also for the evidence with, if possible, identification of the sources.
5. If it is a "minor crime," be prepared to plead guilty.
6. Ascertain the various lines of appeal.
7. Consider the option of keeping a waiting brief and be prepared to reserve his defence; take notes; above all, let the initiator score somewhere—and then try for informality.

When the executive is the conciliator, he should:

1. Get the parties to the dispute to realize that conflict is not only universal but a necessary requisite of change.
2. Break down the attitudinal consistency of each disputant (the belief that his attitudes do not contain contradictory elements).
3. After breaking down frozen but antithetical attitudes of the disputants, minimize the individual loss of face.
4. Break the conflict into fractional workable components.
5. Consider common-enemy, high-interaction, shared subordinate goal strategies.
6. Remember that nobody loves a go-between.

CONCILIATION AND CONFLICT

Conflict is the central problem of organizational life. The modern techniques of operations research enable organizations to quantify measures of end products and to police performances to such an extent that organizations inevitably come under a considerable degree of control, which is usually achieved by the removal of organizational slack. Such structuring of behaviour very often serves to increase the amount of conflict and tension within the organization.

The general techniques for the alleviation of conflict may be described under the generic heading of conciliation. The major techniques of conciliation are negotiation, mediation, and arbitration.

Negotiation

Many organizational conflicts get balked at the level of negotiation. Negotiation is the process whereby the parties to a dispute come together with a view to determining the terms of a contractual exchange which will be acceptable to both parties. Intellectually, negotiation consists of defining the *quid pro quo* which is acceptable to either party; emotionally, negotiation consists of defining and testing the power situation between the parties; behaviourally, negotiation is usually the process of bringing the parties together in a face-to-face situation where the terms of the bargain can be worked over.

Mediation

In the process of mediation, a third party is invited to try to resolve the difficulties facing disputing parties. Mediation is especially important because frequently the power displayed at the phase of negotiation produces such a sharp polarization of behaviour and sentiment that the parties become isolated from one another. In such circumstances the mediator frequently is able to maintain some degree of contact and communication between the parties, who now may well be located in different places far away from the conference room.

Arbitration

If mediation fails, disputes sometimes go to arbitration, the process whereby the dispute is referred to a third party who is given the power to formulate a settlement binding on both parties. It is usual to distinguish between compulsory and voluntary arbitration. Compulsory arbitration occurs when the parties are compelled (e.g., by law) to accept arbitration; voluntary arbitration is that agreed to by the parties without such compulsion.

THE DYNAMICS OF CONCILIATION

The first step in the process of conciliation is the recognition by the parties in dispute that conflict is not only universal but a necessary prerequisite of organization change. Basic to this approach is the belief that conflict contributes to functional effectiveness. The function of conflict is to save the system from ossification.

A second major difficulty in trying to establish conciliation arises from man's need for attitudinal consistency. Attitudinal consistency, or cognitive consonance as it sometimes is called, refers to the need that man has to ensure that his beliefs do not contain elements which are mutually contradictory. This "it is a question of principle" attitude appears as a major stumbling block to effective conciliation. A significant difficulty of the conciliator in a dispute is to break down the frozen but antithetical attitudes of the disputants; the problem here is the need to introduce inconsistency to the minds of both parties, which frequently have viciously snapped closed. Once both parties have admitted the possibility of inconsistency in their beliefs, even in a limited context, the way has been opened for further development.

A significant advantage of employing a professional or expert conciliator is the hope that he can find a formula that will minimize loss of face for both parties. As well as finding face-saving formulae, conciliators often succeed by breaking down the dispute into workable components. The ability to fractionate a problem into its component parts is a major part of the process of conciliation.

Tolerance—at least on the surface—is a very useful virtue for conciliation; but as E. M. Forster pointed out in *Two Cheers for Democracy*,

> Tolerance is a very dull virtue. It is boring. Unlike love, it has always had a bad press. No one has ever written an ode to tolerance, or raised a statue to her. Yet this is the quality which will be most needed. . . . This is the sound state of mind which we are looking for. This is the only force which will enable different races and classes and interests to settle down together.

As was pointed out earlier, understanding conflict has been greatly facilitated by the development of the theory of games. Anatol Rapoport, a mathematician, has made a significant contribution to the use of games for understanding conflict. Rapoport makes a distinction among fights, games, and debates. In fights the aim is to injure, destroy, subdue, or drive away the enemy. In games the enemy is accepted as being integral to the situation rather than an irritant, and he is regarded as a mirror image who has rather similar but irreconcilable needs. In debates the aim of the parties is to convince rather than to injure or score off the other.

TOPIC 3
Making conflict work for you

For the contemporary manager, one of the most exciting organizational developments may well be the efforts of behavioural scientists to approach conflict as a subject whose structure and process can be properly exploited as a means of promoting effective change. Understanding conflict from this systems point of view is the most important factor in learning how to manage conflict.

Figure 14–2 is a systems model which incorporates the more important concepts presented in this chapter. Guided by realistic models of this sort, scientists are now searching for hypotheses about conflict to test both in the laboratory and in the executive suite. Their methods of research include game theory, group dynamics, and ethology. The works of Konrad Lorenz, Desmond Morris, and Robert Ardrey have triggered the interest of both scientists and managers who recognize the truth of linking human conflict factors to those observed in studies of other animals. Men, like other animals, have some kind of pool of aggression that, when properly mobilized, facilitates the emergence of stable social structures.

The systems concept always supposes an interlocking network in which, if one element is changed, some or all of the other elements will be affected. Thus part of the structure of conflict relates to the personal factor of aggression and frustration. Zoos drive apes psycho; the corporate zoo drives men anomic. Another structural factor is the structure of the organization; the systems concept of interacting change elements is one of the things that produces conflict.

FIGURE 14–2
Conflict as a system

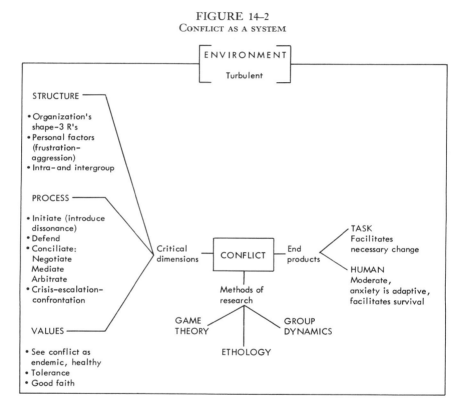

A realistic model of conflict includes the knowledge that the environment of the modern organization is turbulent. In this state of social turbulence, the rate of change in the environment inevitably outstrips the rate of change in the organization, leaving it in a maladapted state. Less powerful members of the organization have a vested interest in recognizing this phase lag, more powerful members in denying it; hence the more powerful must be more alert if they are not to lose control of the situation.

While conflict may sometimes be the unintended result of poor coordination, we have mentioned several reasons why an important process is the deliberate initiation of conflict. It can compel the organization to define goals, change processes, and reallocate resources. But conflict is only likely to produce constructive change when there is a rough balance of power between the parties to the dispute.

THE MODEL IS PREDICTABLE

Conflict usually follows a particular pattern and is frequently quite predictable. For example, the pattern of wage negotiations is well established, although a change in economic conditions, such as the government's fiscal policy defining its reaction to inflation, can affect the ritual.

Most organizations have evolved procedures that deal with such contingencies, but not all. University administrators in the late 1960s discovered to their horror that they had no procedures for dealing with conflict, and no properly constituted lines of appeal. In fact, even a cursory examination of the student revolution emphasizes that the pattern is predictable: (1) *crisis* (the establishment commits a "crime"), (2) *escalation* (occupation of administrative offices), (3) *confrontation* (show-down with officials), and (4) *further crisis* (challenging the legitimacy of the committee appointed to investigate the original charge). And when the immediate fight is over, the organization is left to build not only a new hierarchy and an appeals system, but also a new code of ethics.

None of the processes will work, however, unless executives fully understand the concept of good faith. Good faith demands that in communication one party does not deliberately control the flow of information in such a way as to manipulate the interests of the other party. In the new approach to organizational behaviour, which is based on information science concepts, legitimate authority is defined in terms of three factors: location, function, and reference. Location refers to a particular node in the matrix of information processes; function describes the requirement the manager has to search out, collect, process, and disseminate particular kinds of information; and reference defines the constituency which he represents.

To the information scientist, a measure of the amount of information that a message contains is the degree of surprise it induces, but the breach of good faith also produces a surprise. The offended party invariably feels that he was not given the necessary information to participate in the exchange. Even the way the information is sequenced may well induce this feeling of bad faith. A great number of managers have experienced this sensation, which they usually describe as a manipulation. Knowledge of the management of conflict may give one party in a dispute a significant advantage over his opponent, and his use of such knowledge may in itself be seen as an act of bad faith by those who have little knowledge or skill in this area.

Thus the need for more managers to familiarize themselves with the structures and processes of conflict becomes more pressing. How to make conflict work for you is going to be an increasingly crucial management issue in our rapidly changing industrial society.

REVIEW AND RESEARCH

1. Why is conflict good for you? Under what conditions? Why has there been a radical change in viewing organizational conflict?
2. What have university students taught administrators about the conflict process?
3. Critically evaluate the two models of conflict.
4. How can conflict within the group be controlled? Illustrate your answers by considering a group such as a football team, a platoon, a work group, or a fraternity committee.
5. How can conflict be mitigated between a production work group and a marketing group in a particular industry? Select an industry with which you are familiar.
6. Develop a plan of action to regulate the conflict between an automobile manufacturer and its franchised dealers.
7. Develop a model using the "prisoner's dilemma" game as a means of gaming a situation where two companies are in collusion and are the only bidders for a building with a city administration.
8. Develop a theory of conflict to cover the matrix:

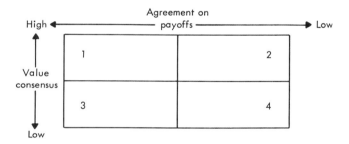

What circumstances would generate cells 1, 2, 3 and 4? What should be the best strategies for handling each contingency?
9. Define the roles of the initiator, the defendant, and the conciliator. Select an example from your own experience and describe the attitudes, behaviours, and strategies of each party in the conflict.
10. How can you make conflict work for you?
11. Compare and contrast the relative merits and disadvantages of using confrontation versus mediation in a conflict situation.

GLOSSARY OF TERMS

Arbitration. The process whereby a dispute is referred to a third party acceptable to both disputing parties, who ask the third party to formulate a settlement which will be binding. Arbitration may be voluntary (entered into freely by the two parties) or compulsory (forced upon the disputants by some outside power, such as government).

Cognitive consonance. Attitudinal consistency; the need that man has to ensure that his beliefs do not contain contradictory elements.

Conciliation. The process of bringing into harmony, or effecting a settlement between conflicting parties. The major techniques of conciliation are (see definitions) negotiation, mediation, and arbitration.

Conflict. Opposition or dispute between persons, groups, or ideas, which may be discussed according to two models:

Human relations model. The more classical view that conflict is unhealthy and should be avoided; this "old look" assumes that every society is a well-integrated, relatively persisting configuration of elements which contribute to its functioning through a fundamental consensus, and that conflict is caused by malfunction or by troublemakers.

Realistic model. The "new look" at conflict sees it as endemic, inevitable, and healthy, and looks at the management of conflict as the central problem for organizational analysts. This model assumes that change and conflict are ubiquitous, and that society rests on constraint of some of its members by others. The value of conflict lies in its facilitation of needed change and, because its proper management emphasizes the need for common interests and values, of eventual social cohesion.

Frustration-aggression hypothesis. The theory that frustration (persistent blockage of goal-directed behaviour) leads to aggression (attack on the perceived blockage), and that aggressive behaviour presupposes frustration.

Game theory. The set of mathematical operations through which game players learn to evaluate and predict reactions and potential moves (their own and other players'), bargain, and evolve tactics and an optimal strategy; the development of models which define outcomes in terms of utilities and probabilities; a model of conflict among several people in which the principal modes of resolution are collusion and conciliation.

Intolerance of ambiguity. The fundamental need of man to impose meaning and structure on inchoate, ill-defined situations. This ability to structure a perceptual environment has survival value for the individual; however, when change and conflict are seen as necessary, the individual must also learn some degree of tolerance for ambiguity to survive.

Mediation. The process whereby a third party is invited to try to resolve the difficulties facing the parties to a dispute, often by acting as a go-between.

Negotiation. The process whereby the parties to a dispute come together to bargain over terms which will be acceptable to both parties.

Tacit bargaining. Element of game theory which assumes a degree of interdependence between disputing parties, so that, even without complete communication, both parties accept that co-operation and mutual constraint will be necessary to resolve their conflict.

Zero sum game. A game in which whatever one player loses, the other wins; the plus and minus balance is always zero. Nonzero sum games are those in which conflicting parties can achieve pluses in excess of their minuses (or the reverse).

15

Communications

Communication may be thought of as the sharing of information between at least two people. The term information is used in this context on the assumption that it is possible to communicate not only facts but also sentiments and attitudes. It is important to realize that most communicators have a particular audience in mind, and that communication is seldom random; as is well known, organizations are heavily dependent for their survival and growth upon having an effective communications system. A business organization cannot function properly without decision making; decision making is impossible without communication and, of course, further communication is required to implement the decisions reached.

According to R. S. Weiss, all problems facing an organization can be subsumed under three headings—allocation, adaptation, and co-ordination. *Allocation* refers to the "responsibility for apportioning functional activities"; *adaptation* means the "acceptance of responsibility by members of the organization"; *co-ordination* is the "harmonious integration of the functional activities of members." All of these functions require or presuppose some measure of communication.

DEFINITION OF COMMUNICATION

The term "communication" has been so overworked that it has emerged as a gadget word which has come to mean different things to different people. For those who speak in panoramic phrases, it is the nervous system of an organization which provides the information and understanding necessary to achieve both high productivity and high morale. Nevertheless, management is giving increasing recognition to the importance of communication as a subject of inquiry and research; and effective managers are beginning to realize that good communications are vital to good relationships.

In formal terms, communication may be defined as the field of inquiry concerned with the systematic use of symbols to achieve common or shared information about an object or event. Three important aspects are stressed in this definition. First, it emphasizes the systematic aspect, the way in which the elements of communication are related to one another in a purposeful way. Second, it draws attention to the fact that communication is a symbolic process in the sense that it refers to something which is external and real. Third, it underscores the fact that communications are need-related, that is to say, they are used for the purpose of achieving something or getting somewhere. This "something" may be the achievement of a task, such as producing so many cars per day or inventing a new product; or an increase in human satisfaction, such as improving the motivation and morale of employees.

These aspects of communication provide a useful framework for the study of three important subjects: the syntax, semantics, and pragmatics of communication.

Syntax is the systematic analysis of the grammar of the process and includes the relations internal to the system of symbols. The subjects of mathematics, logic, and grammar fall into this category.

Semantics is the relation between the symbols and the reality to which they refer. The validity of a scientific theory and the phenomenon it covers would be considered under this heading. Semantics is sometimes cynically described as being preoccupied with the meaning of "meaning."

Pragmatics is concerned with assessment of the effectiveness of the process and judges the efficiency of the communication in relation to the extent to which it achieves its purpose.

Studies of executive behaviour reveal that executives spend a large proportion of their time in transmitting and receiving not only information but also ideas and feelings, as well as issuing and receiving instructions. It is obvious that organizations are heavily dependent on the proper use of communication for their survival and the maintenance of effectiveness. Only naive managers can believe that the communication process can be summarized by saying that instructions and directives flow down the organization and reports flow up. For such managers it is, therefore, all-important for the efficiency of the organization that the information to be transmitted is precise and relevant and that instructions are firm, clear, and unambiguous. Modern research findings do not support this unsophisticated view.

STRUCTURE OF CHAPTER 15

Topic 1 deals with perception, personality and language. Since communication is concerned with the transmission of meaning, and perception in the cognitive process is concerned with the interpretation of meaning, we begin by looking at the "laws" governing perception, and then turn to the related subjects of cognitive dissonance and balance theory. We then attempt to link personality and language by looking at the subject of psycholinguistics.

Our second topic is dyadic communication—how A communicates with B, and B with A. Particular attention is paid to the subject of feedback.

Within Topic 3, communication in a group setting, four items are considered: the committee meeting, the command meeting, brainstorming, and Eric Berne's theory of games.

The fourth topic deals with communication and organization structure. The basic issue here is whether structuring communications is a good thing. The answer appears to be a function of what you are trying to achieve. The interrelation between vertical and lateral lines of communication is examined for the light it throws on operating effectiveness.

Topic 5 is managing the organizational interface. It deals particularly with the strategy and tactics of lateral interactions. The chapter is concluded by trying to specify what advice the behavioural scientist can give the executive on the thorny subject of the practical art of communicating.

TOPIC 1
Perception, personality, and language

COMMUNICATION AND PERCEPTION

Perception significantly affects communication. Communication is concerned with the transmission of meaning, while perception involves the interpretation of sense data, which is intimately bound up with questions of meaning. Perception is influenced by both external stimuli and personal factors. In other words, perception requires the selection of the relevant sense data, which are then arranged in a meaningful way.

Gestalt psychologists attach great importance to the role of insight in the interpretation of communication and in learning. The more intelligent a person is, the more capable he will be of insight, but this faculty is also increased by experience.

In the course of communication, people normally try to elicit reaction from the person they are addressing which tells them that the recipients have insight into the meaning which the communicator is trying to convey. Phrases such as "D'you get me?" and "Do I have to spell it out for you?" characterize this attempt. If the person being addressed cannot grasp the meaning immediately, he may console himself by thinking that "the penny will drop" later. Thus he may go on trying to make sense of the message even after the communication has ended.

Personal factors are very important in communication, for an individual's past experience determines how he interprets a communication. He is likely to analyse the situation in terms of the stereotypes he has built up in the past.

THE DANGERS OF A SIMPLISTIC MODEL

Many managers take a somewhat unscientific and uninformed approach to the problems of communication. Implicit in the minds of such managers is the belief that fairly simple statements can be made regarding the communication process which will cover all contingencies. Some managers go further and codify their views, giving them unscientific titles such as "The Ten Commandments of Good Communication." Typical examples of these commandments are: "all communications should be brief, terse, relevant and accurate" and "all communications should be two-way." The idea is firmly fixed in many people's minds that two-way communication is somehow democratic and therefore good.

Research by behavioural scientists suggests that there are few simple statements which can be made regarding communication in general. In tackling a problem in communications, it is best to start by defining the purposes of the communication process. Broadly speaking, these purposes can be divided into two categories: task and human satisfaction. Certain questions spring to mind when one looks at the task category in more detail: Is the task simple or complex? If it is reasonably simple and likely to be clearly understood by both the initiator and the recipient, then it is possible that a one-way communication system will be more appropriate; it will at least be faster and more effective. If the task is more complex, involving a nonroutine situation, two-way communication may be better, especially if accuracy is being emphasized.

On the other hand, if a two-way system is used, the initiator may come under criticism from the recipient, which will undermine his confidence. It is important to realize that two-way communication does not necessarily improve mutual confidence. This is because emotions are communicated as well as facts. Emotions may generate noise in the system.

It is too often forgotten that communication is not only by the spoken or the written word; it is dependent upon the inferences drawn by one person from the behaviour of another of what the communicator is trying to convey. When two people are communicating, they do not respond only to the words spoken, they also try to "read between the lines." All communication involves an effort towards meaning. This point is well illustrated by the number of times phrases such as: "you know what I mean" and "we know each other" occur. When the other person fails to get the meaning, it is not uncommon to hear questions like: "Are you with me?" and "Am I making myself clear?"

Questions of meaning are always of paramount importance in communication. They may be relatively simple or of considerable complexity, depending on circumstances. It is important to distinguish between denotative and connotative meanings (see the section on "Semantics" below). In ordinary speech in our society, most words have connotative meanings, the wider penumbra of ideas, emotions, and actions which are associated with the word: For example, "democracy" is a word with many connotations.

COMMUNICATION AND PERSONALITY

It is widely believed that the individual's linguistic style reveals his underlying personality. A number of investigations, conducted mainly in the United States and Germany, have included very detailed analyses of speech styles. It has been argued that the style of speech a person uses reflects his basic personality.

A communication may not produce insight immediately; there may be a delay of several hours or days, or for that matter years, before its meaning becomes clear. In some respects the process is like that of inspirational thinking, which has been analysed into four stages: preparation, incubation, illumination, and verification. Most of the hard work of assembling facts is done in the first stage. Incubation is largely an unconscious process which allows this information to interact to form new intellectual constructs. Illumination occurs when insight is gained, associated almost invariably with the sudden emergence of a solution. Verification requires application of cold logic to test if the idea is workable.

The perceptions of members of a communicating group are selectively organized and developed into a pattern whose configuration is determined partly in accordance with the principles of stimulus organization and partly by personal factors. The properties of a perceptual system are influenced by those of the system to which it belongs. A change may be introduced in a cognitive field by changing the individual's information and wants. To some extent, a person's perceptions are influenced both by his previous experience and personality factors. Early studies of perception regarded the perceiving organism as empty, but contemporary research in the field of perception is predicated on the principle that the organism is "filled" with needs and attitudes which may structure the perception.

THE IMPORTANCE OF STEREOTYPES

Stereotypes influence perception and therefore communication to a very considerable extent. For purposes of analysis, social situations may be thought of as giving rise to sense data which are interpreted by the individual. In order to organize these data more easily the individual makes use of "simplified pictures of people," or stereotypes. Stereotypes are relatively simple cognitions which are widely held by the members of a particular group. Inevitably one's perceptions of a member of a particular group are influenced by his stereotype of that group. It is important to realize that stereotypes should not be equated with prejudices; they are essentially rationalizations which organize these prejudices. Our behaviour in relation to categories is rationalized by the exaggerated beliefs or stereotypes which we associate with these categories. Stereotypes ought to be regarded as only symptoms reinforcing hostile attitudes.

COGNITIVE DISSONANCE AND BALANCE THEORY

Cognitive dissonance exists when a person holds irreconcilable beliefs. It is usual to do something to balance the situation, perhaps by rejecting the communication or the communicator who introduced the dissonant element. For example a person who (a) accepts that there is a link between lung cancer and cigarette smoking and (b) continues to smoke is inevitably in a state of cognitive dissonance. He may at first seek to balance his cognitive system by denying that there is good evidence of a causal link between cigarette smoking and lung cancer. When the appearance of more evidence supporting the existence of a link makes this position untenable, he may resort to rationalization to bridge the gap in his cognitive structure and argue that if he stopped smoking he would be liable to put on weight, increasing the risk of coronary thrombosis. Deprived of this prop by the evidence that there is a link between smoking and heart disease, the harassed smoker may try to convince himself that his habit is of psychotherapeutic value and that if he stopped it he would probably get ulcers or some other psychosomatic disorder. This person has an unconscious need to stop smoking which he cannot satisfy because he cannot break the habit; at this stage he may need help to stop him trying to stop smoking. This imaginary case illustrates the lengths to which people will go to establish a consonant cognitive system with harmonious components.

Balance theory is closely allied to this analysis of cognitive dissonance. A cognitive system is said to be balanced if the units which form it are not contradictory. Consider this example of cognitive dissonance: Proposition 1, "I am in favour of free speech for everyone"; Proposition 2, "this man is preaching against personal freedom"; Proposition 3, "I am in favour of withdrawing his freedom of speech." Balance theory is predicated on the principle that unbalanced systems move towards equilibrium. F. Heider, whose research work is associated with balance theory, used this concept of balance in the analysis of interpersonal relationships. In Heider's analysis there are three elements in the system analysed in Figure 15–1: two people, A and B, and an object X, the Republican party. A triadic system

FIGURE 15–1
BALANCE IN TRIADS

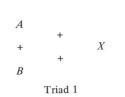

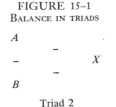

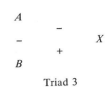

Triad 1

Triad 2

Triad 3

A and *B* both support the Republican party and like each other. Three plus signs, the system balances.

A and *B* both oppose the Republican party and dislike each other. Three negative signs, a state of imbalance.

A opposes the Republican party and dislikes *B* whom he sees as supporting it. Two negative signs and one plus sign, the system balances.

is unbalanced when there is only one or an odd number of negative signs in it; the system is balanced if there are no negative signs or if there is an even number of negatives.

Some people have a lower tolerance of cognitive ambiguity than others; they tend to dichotomize the world into blacks and whites. It might be argued that their minds are closed to new information. Milton Rokeach considers that closed-mindedness is a general personality trait and has devised a scale to measure it.

SERIAL REPRODUCTION

Serial reproduction is the transmission of information from one person to another who, in turn, passes this message to a third person and so on. The process is often demonstrated by the following experiment: subject A is told a short story by the experimenter, then allowed to write it down from memory; he tells his version to subject B, who writes down what he can remember and then tells subject C, and so on. The "story" emerging at the end is seldom completely accurate, although the outline usually persists, frequently built round a number of clichés; it is as if clichés were hooks on which the rest of the story could be hung. The style of the story may change in the telling. Although the overall length is likely to be cut, details are characteristically elaborated, sometimes until the original emphasis has been lost. Not unexpectedly, dramatization takes place.

Such experiments in serial reproduction throw some light on the way rumours grow as they spread. Rumours are related to the needs of the people spreading them and reach their most spectacular heights in times of general anxiety, for example, during a war. During World War I, a generally held anxiety over the shortage of manpower (no doubt caused by the attrition of the Western front) was reflected in a persistent rumour of Russian troops, "the snow still on their boots," marching through England. In the same war, sketchy accounts of German atrocities in Belgium were elaborated into detailed stories. In 1940 the linking of British experiments on the effect of setting fire to floating oil and the discovery along the south coast of the burned bodies of German soldiers (who were killed on the other side of the channel) gave birth to a rumour that a Nazi invasion had been repelled by setting the sea alight. This story gave people the reassurance of Britain's strength which they so desperately needed.

The perception of two-sided messages

David F. Wrench in "The Perception of Two-Sided Messages" has argued that some people, especially politicians, try to be all things to all people. On the basis of this research, Wrench concluded that,

> . . . it would appear that most people will tolerate a great deal of internal contradiction in a message before becoming incredulous. In one sense, then, it appears practical to present two-sided communications. They will not necessarily be rejected as self-contradictory and illogical. Further research is needed to see whether incredulity would be more of a factor in areas where the subjects had more structured opinions than undergraduates have about international relations.

It is possible to explain Wrench's conclusion by relating his findings to the principle of perception established by psychologists in psychophysical studies and studies of the perception of simple opinion statements. These studies show that stimuli (i.e., in this case, statements) falling close to major anchor points tend to be assimilated and that the subject's own attitudes act as significant anchor points.

Perhaps more important still is the fact that statements similar to those held by the subject may well be perceived as being even more similar to his own picture of the situation than they are in fact. Wrench argues from his study that:

> These results suggest that more research is necessary to assess the effectiveness of trying to be all things to all people. The experimental situation differs from a real-life one, for in a real-life situation the members of any given communication chain are likely to have more than chance agreement about the topic which they are discussing. This being the case, it is quite possible that the ambiguous two-sided message might be assimilated to the norms of varying subgroups of society to a greater extent than a less ambiguous one-sided communication. If this occurred, the communicator would indeed succeed in having differing groups of people each believe that he agreed with them.

COMMUNICATION AND LANGUAGE

The complexity and growth capability of his language distinguishes man from the great apes by enabling him to communicate meaning and to share experiences with his fellows; and, of course, it is largely through language that society is able to create and transmit a culture.

Communication theorists, who are fond of thinking of things as tools, have defined language as a tool for communicating. An outstanding characteristic of language is its social nature. J. Piaget has distinguished two speech forms in children: egocentric and social. In egocentric speech, apparently an audience is unnecessary; the child is literally talking to himself. Social speech, on the other hand, is directed towards someone. This distinction of Piaget's has been challenged by other psychologists who consider that all communications must inevitably be directed at some kind of audience, real or imaginary. Executives are inevitably limited by the sophistication of the language which they use. A language is a particular way of structuring or organizing reality, and the executive's view of business life is limited by the verbal structures which he employs to make his experience explicit.

Linguistics is the field of inquiry which is concerned with describing the different languages that people use, and it is useful to realize that men make use of a number of languages, which one depending upon the actual occasion. For example in the language of advertising, negatives are forbidden, the past tense and the passive voice rarely used; the use of verbs is minimized except in the imperative form (go, get, buy, win). Analysis of the language of advertising suggests that it is only on the surface that advertisements appeal to our rational and observational faculties; at a deeper level they seek to keep these functions dormant and operate, in fact, on our emotions.

Words can be used in three different ways: as symbols, attributes of objects, or objects. A word may be thought of as a symbol in so far as it stands for something other than itself. The ability to use words as symbols or objects is usually a mark of cultural sophistication. The mistaken assumption that there must always be a connection between a word and the object which it represents can cause trouble.

ORGANIZATIONAL LANGUAGES

All organizations develop particular languages that are peculiarly their own. All corporate entities apparently develop a cryptic argot whose use facilitates communication. For example, marketing managers, more particularly advertising specialists, seem to have a vested interest in evolving a special language. Examples of the advertising argot include:

Talking off the top of my head (decerebrated dog image).
This is only an Aunt Sally, to be shot down (hunting, shooting, fishing theme).
See if this idea goes into orbit (space speak).
Run this one up the flag pole and see who salutes (military mumbo jumbo).
How does this idea hit you? (the intellectual cafeteria syndrome).
Put that idea in a stacking orbit (jet-set theme).
Running into organizational static (physics model).

The 1973 Watergate scandals supplied us with a whole new vocabulary, with a wide choice of bromides including "at that point in time," and "in that time frame." Executives everywhere seem to have the knack of enveloping a subject in a cocoon of marshmallow, by using such rules as "Never use a word when a sentence will do," "Quote several conflicting sources," and "Obscure, don't clarify."

In developing these new organizational argots, executives make extensive use of the language of computers, the military, and football. "Zero-defect system" is used for perfection. "Here's another input for the hopper" precedes the giving of an opinion. "Preemptive strikes" (hit the other guy first) are backed up by "second-strike capability" (reserve position). And from former Attorney General (and football coach) John Mitchell we learned at Watergate, "When the going gets tough, the tough get going."

Watergate produced a whole new lexicon straight out of *Alice in Wonderland.* "Breaking and entering" was disguised as "intelligence-gathering operations." Papers were not deliberately lost; they were "deep-sixed." "White House horrors" became a euphemism to make palatable "government-sponsored crimes." Basically, the White House aides were on the side of Humpty Dumpty when he said to Alice, "When *I* use a word . . . it means just what I choose it to mean." Nowadays there is a good deal of *Alice* around, and not only in the White House. George Orwell could have had organizations in mind when he pointed out not only does thought corrupt language, but language can also corrupt thought.

In discussing language, executives should keep in mind that they have a particularly poor reputation for expressing themselves. Business today is regarded by many sophisticated people in the professions as being a major source of "gobbledygook," a term widely used by President Franklin Roosevelt to describe polysyllabic, ugly-sounding words held together by tortuous syntax. Examples of gobbledygook include "overkill," "cost-effective," and "explicate" (instead of explain). Executives appear to have a penchant for vogue words, such as system capability, relevance, charismatic, dialogue, parameters, which they then proceed to work to death. Of course, big words in the right mouth, put together properly, can be devastating—for example, the way Prime Minister Disraeli lambasted Gladstone in that beautiful piece of invective:

> A sophisticated rhetorician, inebriated with the exuberance of his own verbosity, and gifted with an egotistical imagination that can at all times command an interminable and inconsistent series of arguments to malign an opponent and to glorify himself.

Not all executives can manage this level of prose style; but by selecting their language carefully, they can go a long way to reduce the hideous corpus of jargon and incomprehensibility that envelops much discussion on business topics.

SEMANTICS

Semantics is the field of inquiry concerned with exploring the correspondence between the symobls used and the reality being communicated about. A semantic definition of communication is the interchange of meanings between persons. Many contemporary psychologists are deeply concerned with questions of meaning, which may be defined as the total disposition to exploit or react to a linguistic form. There are two kinds of meaning, denotative and connotative. The denotative meaning of a word refers to that to which the word points and argues an explicit definition of the referent. The language of mathematics and logic is denotative, or if you like, a "thing language" where a word means only one thing. Connotations are the constellation or complex of ideas, sentiments, and action tendencies which are associated with a particular word and the implicit and attitudinal dimensions of meaning. "Democracy," "profitability," "them," "us," and "insane" are all words of wide connotation. It is easy to befog an argument by using terms with a wide range of connotative meanings, and (although this is frowned upon in academic circles) it may also be thought of as a technique which can be used to influence others. Politicians are expert at using terms of wide connotation which have appeal both for the duke and the dustman.

THE MEASUREMENT OF MEANING

C. E. Osgood devised a technique for measuring semantic differentiation. The belief underlying Osgood's technique, known as the semantic differential, is that some of the significant components of the meaning of a concept can be measured by inviting subjects to rate the concept on a number of bipolar adjectival scales. This is an extremely useful research technique for both psychologists and writers of advertising copy. For the latter, of course, it is particularly valuable to know the connotations of different terms.

Osgood's technique conceives of meaning as multidimensional. Using factor analysis, Osgood has been able to define three dimensions of meaning: (1) evaluative—Has the word good or bad, pleasant or unpleasant connotations? (2) potency—Is it weak or strong, big or small, heavy or light? (3) activity—Is it active or passive, fast or slow? Using this research technique, it is possible to build up a profile of a word on these various scales.

STEREOTYPES OF "FOREIGNERS"

A major source of difficulty in intergroup communication is the difference in the meaning attached to the same word by different groups. As is widely known, people often have stereotyped pictures of foreign national groups. For example, after the Cuban crisis, many Americans seemed to expect Russia to do something to compensate for its loss of face; what was happening here was that the American stereotype of a nation obsessed with status had been transferred from China to Russia.

Margaret Mead and Rhoda Metraux, writing about the application of theorizing about culture to international affairs in an article entitled "The Anthropology of Human Conflict," have argued:

> An understanding of the Russian preoccupation with full use of strength, their insistence on testing the limits, and their willingness to abide by them provides a framework within which Soviet behavior becomes more intelligible and therefore more predictable. The characteristic Russian response to opposing strength greater than their own is strategic withdrawal accompanied by the sense that this will enable them later to return to the conflict in greater strength because of the maximum effort made previously. But if this strategic withdrawal is interpreted by Americans as a sign of weakness and defeat, two undesirable results obtain. Americans begin to act in ways which are appropriate (in American culture) for us with those whom we believe can be bluffed by a show of strength—as in the Dulles type of brinkmanship; and Russians, in response, must keep their stance of intransigency. In contrast, when Russian negotiators recognize that the opposition respects their strength, their pride in this recognition is a facilitating factor. Spelling out these conditions for the interpretation of a set of United States–Soviet Union negotiations means taking into account the culturally crucial question for Russians: "Did I put forth my full strength?" and the culturally crucial question for Americans: "Did I win or lose?" Where English values must also be included, a third culturally crucial question must be taken into account: "Was this the best possible compromise?"
>
> The kind of pressure exerted by the United States on the Soviet Union in the 1950's and the interpretation to Americans of both our own and Soviet behaviour in this situation was a poor preparation for an American understanding of the sequence of events in the Cuban crisis. One result was that we erroneously worried about Russian "face-saving"—a misapplication to the Russians of our misunderstood ideas of Chinese (or even "Oriental") standards of behavior.

These are presumably stereotypes held by anthropologists. The influence of stereotypes is particularly important on communications between national groups. Fundamental to this problem of stereotyping is the question, Is it possible to get value-free facts? Probably not, as all communications are more or less "contaminated" with values. As a result, the process of communication is bedevilled by the possibility that the person with whom you are communicating may not share your value system. In the physical science facts can be expressed in terms of spatial co-ordinates, mass, and time; and simple physiological facts, such as pulse rate, can also be defined in this way. Complicated physiological facts such as life or death depend to some extent, however, on subjective judgements, as do many behavioural facts.

Questions of value judgements arise in all interclass communication, for our source of current moral attitudes is pluralistic. Each different social class in our society makes different assumptions in regard to value which may be extremely significant in communication. Although grossly simplified, Table 15–1 may be of interest as a broad example of such differences.

TABLE 15–1
CLASS, MORAL VALUES, AND IDEOLOGY

Class	Occupation	Moral Values	Ideology
Upper	Owners	All effort is "bad form." Leisure and conspicuous idleness are to be preferred.	Ancient values such as chivalry and honour.
Middle	Managers	The business ethic—thrift, self-help and initiative.	Aspire to overachieve.
Working	Workers	Group loyalty—don't rate-bust, don't be a squealer, don't be a chiseler, don't be officious.	Pessimistic about chances of advancement—"stand by your mates."

What executives must realize is that in our industrial society too many managers speak in terms which imply a shared moral vocabulary between social classes. The extent to which values and attitudes are shared between classes is uncertain. Of the three occupational groups, managers find themselves under the greatest pressure, in the sense that they are required to get the workers to do the work (which the workers have a vested interest and moral belief in restricting) for the owners (who do not wish to work themselves and, worse still, believe that all effort is in bad taste). These questions of the moral values of different social classes, though largely unexplored, require to be defined by careful research by moral philosophers working with social psychologists. In modern terms, such differences are perhaps less a function of class and more a function of life styles, value systems (which cut across class lines), age, and other such factors.

TOPIC 2
Dyadic communication—A interacts with B

To be minimally human is to use symbols, both verbal and nonverbal, when engaged in face-to-face interaction. "No man is an island" means that to be fully human a person must have regular personal involvement with others. But what happens when two people interact, when A interacts with B? At the simplest level, there is stimulus and response:

$$A \underset{\text{Response}}{\overset{\text{Stimulus}}{\rightleftarrows}} B$$

When A communicates with B, B communicates with A. Typically B's response to A elicits some surprise in A, and A may well wonder whether he has got the message through to B. A may guess that he is not transmitting on B's frequency; if he is of an analytical turn of mind, he might ask B to elaborate on his reaction. If both A and B use a VANE model, some progress may be made:

$$A \begin{vmatrix} V \\ A \\ N \\ E \end{vmatrix} \begin{array}{c} \longrightarrow \\ \longleftarrow \end{array} \begin{vmatrix} V \\ A \\ N \\ E \end{vmatrix} B$$

If A and B are to communicate effectively they will both need to know something of each other's values, attitudes, needs, and expectations. What is implied is that the person's perceptions are influenced by the frame of reference which he uses to evaluate incoming information, which in turn is largely determined by his VANE.

As A interacts with B, the hope is that both will develop the ability to see things from the other man's point of view. This taking the role of the other is an essentially human characteristic. The capacity for empathy—to get into the psychological processes of the other, to anticipate his possible actions and responses vis-à-vis one's own action and responses—is integral to the whole subject of human relations. Communication thus involves emotion and cognition, as well as perception through the VANE:

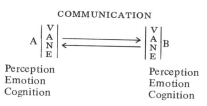

COMMUNICATION

Perception Perception
Emotion   Emotion
Cognition   Cognition

One interesting conclusion which emerges from this model, which has been confirmed by research, is that the prospect of increased interaction makes A and B like each other more. If A and B are to communicate, then there must be some degree of value consonance. If they wish to communicate, they must tune their value systems (like the variable condensers in radios) in to each other to reduce any value dissonance.

A good illustration of this principle of value tuning is the prisoner who learns to like his interrogator. What happens in interactions is that A rewards B for adjustive value tuning and B rewards A for his attempt to tune in. Many of the Dale Carnegie subroutines are based on part of this principle, that you imply with smiles and a show of goodwill that you appreciate the other man. But what is really needed is a meeting of minds. This is precisely what is implied in the concept of good faith—that you do not prejudge issues and other peoples' values. The black-white dialogue in the United States has evolved many subroutines to make white administrators realize this principle. For example when the administrator says, "I know exactly how you feel . . . ," he is cut off in midstream and treated to, "How could you possibly know how I feel? You're white." The liberated female-male chauvinist dialogue uses a similar routine. If good faith is present, such routines may lead to a true communication process where the dissonance is lowered. Unfortunately, too often what is actually going on is a double monologue (with no one listening) instead of a real dialogue.

An effective interviewer has to be capable of value tuning to communicate with a large number of different people. Individuals with very strong, highly structured value systems find it difficult to tune in to people who don't share their value systems.

FEEDING BACK FEEDBACK

A good description of the feedback process is furnished by A. G. Smith in *Communications and Culture, Readings in the Codes of Human Interaction*:

> In a communication network a signal goes from point A to point B with more or less fidelity. It also goes from point B back to A with more or less fidelity. The signals sent out are often sent back in order to control what is sent out. In human communication particularly, the signal A sends to B is largely determined by the signal B sends back to A. A can even react to his own output himself. This is feedback. Feedback serves to control and correct the signals fed forward. It serves to realign all the signals within the networks to one another. It makes A and B truly interacting members of a communication system.

In our contemporary existential society, there is a general presumption that any system with feedback is superior to one without. The logic behind this proposition is based on the notion that anything democratic (allowing or encouraging participation) is good, and the converse, anything not democratic is bad.

Let's start by examining some of the factual evidence favouring feedback and postpone for a moment the case against. When the task is relatively simple and capable of objective verification, feedback improves performance. For example, riflemen on a range get higher scores if the marker in the butts signals back right away where the shot has landed. Three points are worth understanding:

1. Information is objective.
2. Feedback follows performance almost immediately.
3. Improved performance follows, i.e., reinforcement takes place.

In a similar vein, but with less objective information, management trainees also improve when given feedback about their performance.

Encouraged by such experimental results, managers today spend a fair amount of their time giving and receiving feedback. Previously a good deal of such feedback was given in the annual review of performances. The trend is now away from such dyadic exercises; increasing use is being made of group experiences. The disadvantages of the dyadic approach were mainly:

1. The traffic of information was largely one-way, superior to subordinate.
2. Peer and subordinate sources were neglected.
3. For rewards such as salary increases, it was difficult to separate counselling from appraisal.
4. Validation of data was made difficult by having apparently only a single source of feedback (and the superior was often presumed to have perceptual astigmatism).
5. A limited number of rituals or routines were available for the actual process.

The modern alternative for supplying feedback has emerged from the T group. Most organizations get involved with T groups by sending selected individuals to sample the stranger group (one where nobody knows anyone beforehand). If they like it, cousin groups (peers from different departments) are set up; if this is a success, vertical groups are the next experiment; and so on, with departmental groups as the final development.

The advantages of the stranger T group include:

1. You are judged on your "here and now" performance.
2. The other members' perceptions cannot be based on your previous performance, so there is minimal prejudice based on your past efforts.
3. The fact that it is improbable that you will meet other participants again usually facilitates candour.
4. Perceptions can be validated against other members' judgements.
5. The exercises are carried out only when trust, interdependence, reciprocity, and calculated risk taking have been achieved.
6. The procedures are highly routinized, facilitating the development of rules, roles, and relations. A great many interesting and valuable games can be played.
7. The T group leader holds the reins, keeps the exercises meaningful and relevant, and intervenes before the exercises become completely destructive.

PRINCIPLES OF FEEDBACK

Accepting the overriding principle that feedback—though it is still dyadic in the particular instance—should be given in a group setting, the three following principles can be added as broad guide-lines. As in most management processes, the cookbook approach must be avoided.

I. ACCEPT PEOPLE AS THEY ARE

The presumption is—and this won't always hold—that there are no pathological types (psychotics) in your group. If you presume that the other guy is moderately well adjusted, it is safe to bet his personality is reasonably well structured. If this is the case, your chance of changing his personality in a large way is minimal. What's the point of feedback, if such is the case? Within this frame of reference, there are several initial advantages.

If the feedback is accurate and the recipient is perceptive, it will allow him to define more accurately the effect he is having on other people. The successful executive will only attempt to make marginal adjustments in his behaviour. For example if he is told he talks too much, that he hogs the conversation, should he immediately make a firm resolution to bite his tongue every time he feels like talking? Such a strategy, a self-denying ordinance, is a self-defeating ploy. More useful leads with an overtalkative executive could include:

1. Get him to use nonverbal modes of communication.
2. Help him practise standard psychiatric responses such as "Aha," "Hm," "That's interesting," "What happened next?" and so on.
3. Advise him to study group dynamics at meetings.
4. Insist on his using the one-sentence comment.
5. Suggest that when he feels tempted to make longer statements he punctuate his observations with phrases such as, "Do you want me to develop this point at this stage?" This will compel him to organize his thoughts and encourage him to begin with an encapsulated version which, with a bit of luck, will have some consumer choice built in.
6. Put it to him that he ought occasionally to say, "I talk too much," and watch for reactions.
7. Try to persuade him to look at the research findings on eye movements as punctuations of conversations.
8. What the group ought to examine is whether he has the kind of occupational organizational role that exploits his neurosis, or quirk, or advantage.

What the group ought not to do is to tell the person concerned not to say anything until the group invites him to participate. The list above gives enough detail to emphasize that most groups basically don't have at their fingertips a wide enough range of options to select from in giving advice to particular members.

Most cases are taken on an individual basis, without proper allowance for the fact that top management is concerned with developing effective executive teams rather than effective individual managers. Intuitively, top management has been acting on the law of requisite variety: that it takes complexity to control complexity. Such control complexity is unlikely to reside in any one person but is more likely to be found in a team of executives who have diverse talents, postures, and perspectives.

II. Develop a model for handling feedback

A useful model for dealing with feedback is the VANE model given earlier. Since the model takes into account the values, attitudes, needs, and expectations of both, the rating tells you something about the rater as well as the ratee.

Frequently it appears that the one giving the feedback is acting on the assumption that the ratee is simple and uncomplex, whereas he himself is complex and interesting. A model which avoids this trap is shown in Figure 15–2; it takes a systems approach, recognizing several interacting factors. This model was suggested by the work done by John Anderson at the Procter & Gamble Company.

FIGURE 15–2
Model for giving and receiving feedback

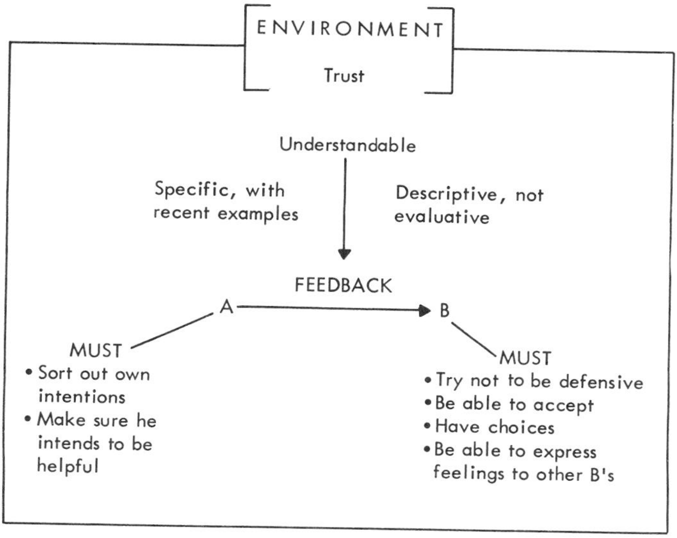

III. NOT ALL FEEDBACK NEED BE ACCEPTED AT FACE VALUE

The rater may well try to transfer to the ratee his own anxieties. Projection of this type is difficult to deal with unless the ratee keeps his cool and pursues the following strategy:

1. Ask for evidence.
2. Suggest that the rater check his perceptions with other members of the group.
3. Admit the existence of the behaviour, but offer, if appropriate, an alternative explanation.

TOPIC 3
Communications in a group setting

Before considering three different types of meetings that are common in businesses, it is well to remind ourselves that in order to guarantee their survival and optimize their efficiency, organizations must establish and exploit effective communications systems. In the light of recent research findings, the traditional picture of communication flow in a business setting—of instructions and orders flowing down the organization while information, reports, and criticisms travel up—is too naive. A realistic picture of the communications process will include gate-keepers who censor information moving upward in the organization so as to give a favourable picture of subordinates. Since the 1940s, social scientists have been most concerned with developing and defining the most efficient system of communications. But efficient for what? The efficiency of a system of communications may be measured in terms of accuracy, speed, freedom from error, lack of ambiguity, and sometimes ability to create or innovate. Before a system is established it is essential to define what is required of the system; research suggests that no system can be good on all counts. An air defence system must give priority to speed and accuracy of communication, but a manufacturing concern may decide that accuracy is less important to it than speed. Sometimes feelings, not information, are to be communicated and the system must be designed accordingly. A still different communication set is required if the object of the exercise is to develop a climate in which innovation is likely.

COMMITTEE MEETINGS

Under this heading are included all encounters of groups of people who come together to take part in a semantic exchange.

Examination of the more recent literature of management reveals a reaction against committees; they are often identified with a sloppy, irresponsible, uncertain, and unrealistic way of tackling organizational problems. Although many management theorists consider committees inappropriate to the present task-oriented state of business, most workers feel that committees are somehow good because they are democratic. A major criticism of the use of committees is that they are often entrusted with work that would be better handled by a staff officer. Not untypical of the view of such critics is the assertion that "the best committee is a three-man committee with two members absent."

If a group is not in agreement it is as well to start with the facts and argue forward from them. Once a factual perspective has been achieved, it is advisable to explore attitudes and sentiments before trying to reach a decision. The first stage of a meeting is primarily intellectual; emotional considerations enter into the second stage; and in the final part, both elements (the logical and the psychological) are combined.

The role of the chairman of a discussion group is to hold the reins. To discharge his role properly, he must understand the dynamics of decision making. Following R. F. Bales's analysis, he should begin by clarifying the problem to facilitate discussing it intelligently. It is vital to make the objectives of the meeting clear to the members. Unfortunately, it is usually so difficult to focus on objectives that attention is speedily displaced to means. The essence of the greatness of Winston Churchill as a committee-man lay in his outstanding ability to bear down on objectives. The chairman must go on repeating the objectives until they are clear to the meetings. "All arguments are ultimately repetitious," observed Kant; dialectical efficiency depends on skill in repetition—on the ability to restate the aim in terms which are meaningful to the members of the group.

The culture of our society is such that a group of people placed around a table will sooner or later spontaneously start discussing something. A chairman should not try to speed things up by buttonholing particular members; before long someone will take off and start on the problem. Once the discussion is under way, the chairman should keep it task-oriented and make occasional objective summaries of arguments.

COMMAND MEETINGS

The term command meeting is used to describe a meeting between a manager and his subordinates. This concept was developed by Wilfred Brown, the former chairman of the Glacier Metal Company. Command meetings are presumed to lack that element of corporate responsibility which characterizes committee meetings; according to Brown, the manager of the command meeting alone is responsible for decisions made in this context. This being so, his subordinates are obliged to give him the benefit of their opinion on the matter at hand. Much time can be wasted by failure to distinguish between committee and command meetings. Brown further argues that the term "industrial democracy" should be dropped because of its wide connotations. Here, the difficulty is that subordinates in a group setting with their boss feel compelled to behave like M.P.'s and express opinions on everything; worse still, they often act as "the opposition."

A command meeting is designed to permit an interchange of information with subordinates; the manager can clear up misunderstandings, state policy, and spell out instructions. It is up to the manager to decide where and when such a meeting should take place and what procedure should be adopted.

Although in many situations responsibility does indeed rest solely with the manager, many people go to a meeting with an expectation of expressing their feelings and ideas. Having voiced these they feel morally as well as structurally committed to any decision made at the meeting. There is no moral obligation on the part of the members to implement the decisions of a command meeting.

BRAINSTORMING SESSIONS

The technique of brainstorming was developed in 1939 in an American advertising agency; since then it has been widely used by business, government, and military institutions. The principles of brainstorming are: (1) no ideas are criticized, (2) freewheeling is encouraged—the more outlandish an idea the better, (3) the emphasis is on quantity of ideas, and (4) synergy—the creative putting together of diverse ideas—is encouraged.

Before a session begins everyone must clearly understand the objectives of the meeting. A time limit, usually under an hour, should be set. During the session absolutely no negative statements are allowed and criticism must be kept to a minimum.

Donald W. Taylor, Paul C. Berry, and Clifford H. Block, in "Does Group Participation When Using Brainstorming Facilitate or Inhibit Creative Thinking?" point out:

> In an experiment designed to answer the title question, twelve groups of four men each and forty-eight individuals followed the four basic rules of brainstorming in attacking the same three problems in the same order. Upon completion of the experiment, a table of random numbers was used to divide the forty-eight individual subjects into twelve nominal groups of four men each. The performance of each nominal group was then scored as though its members had actually worked together. The achievement of these nominal groups thus provided a measure of the performance to be expected if group participation neither facilities nor inhibits creative thinking. When compared with that of the twelve nominal groups, the performance of the twelve real groups was found to be markedly inferior with respect to: (*a*) mean total number of ideas produced; (*b*) mean number of unique ideas produced; (*c*) three different measures which weighted the ideas produced differentially with respect to quality. To the extent that the results of the present experiment can

be generalized, it must be concluded that group participation when using brainstorming inhibits creative thinking.

Brainstorming is regarded by many people as a very good way of exchanging ideas and of sparking off new lines of development, but scientific research has cast doubt on the validity of the technique, suggesting that it may not be as creative as was first thought. "We think" may not be as creative as "I think."

COMMUNICATION THROUGH GAMES

People tend to spin out their lives by engaging in certain "games." In a brilliantly witty book, Eric Berne, a psychiatrist from San Francisco, has explained why people play games: to avoid facing reality, to hide their real motives, to rationalize their behaviour, or even to avoid actual participation. In his widely read and even more widely acclaimed *Games People Play*, which has the subtitle "The Psychology of Human Relationships," Berne strips the surface innocence of conventional relations and reveals what is simmering just below the surface in most human encounters.

Berne's penetrating and stimulating analysis takes as its starting point the idea of stimulus hunger—which he summarizes by noting, "If you are not stroked, your spinal cord will shrivel up." Berne, who specializes in the technique of transactional analysis, uses this term "stroke" to describe a social stimulus such as "Hallo," and he defines a transaction as an exchange of strokes. According to Berne:

> The advantages of social contact revolve around somatic and psychic equilibrium. They are related to the following factors: (1) the relief of tension, (2) the avoidance of noxious situations, (3) the procurement of stroking, and (4) the maintenance of an established equilibrium. All these items have been investigated and discussed in great detail by physiologists, psychologists, and psychoanalysts. Translated into terms of social psychiatry, they may be stated as (1) the primary internal advantages, (2) the primary external advantages, (3) the secondary advantages, and (4) the existential advantages.

Berne defines five different activities in which people can engage which require social interaction; procedures, rituals, pastimes, games, and intimacy. A procedure is a simple direct operation such as building a boat; a ritual is a conventional pattern which is carried out to pass the time but does not require any original activity on the part of the participants. As Berne points out,

> From the present viewpoint, a ritual is a stereotyped series of simple complementary transactions programmed by external social forces. An informal ritual, such as social leave-taking, may be subject to considerable local variations in details, although the basic form remains the same. A formal ritual, such as a Roman Catholic Mass, offers much less option.

A pastime is an activity, usually a conversation (very often described as chit-chat), where the participants go through the motions of making the appropriate noises to pass the time. Much car talk fits this category. Berne defines a game as:

> . . . an ongoing series of complementary ulterior transactions progressing to a well-defined, predictable outcome. Descriptively it is a recurring set of transactions, often repetitious, superficially plausible, with a concealed motivation; or, more colloquially, a series of moves with a snare, or "gimmick." Games are clearly differentiated from procedures, rituals, and pastimes by two chief characteristics: (1) their ulterior quality and (2) the payoff. Procedures may be successful, rituals effective, and pastimes profitable, but all of them are by definition candid; they may involve contest, but not conflict, and the ending may be sensational, but it is not dramatic. Every game, on the other hand, is basically dishonest, and the outcome has a dramatic, as distinct from merely exciting, quality.

THE REPERTOIRE OF EGO STATES: THE PARENT, THE ADULT, THE CHILD

To explain games, Berne makes use of the idea that each individual has a limited repertoire of ego states (see Figure 15–3):

FIGURE 15–3
BERNE'S
REPERTOIRE
OF EGO STATES

a. Ego states similar to those of the parental figure.
b. Ego states which are concerned with the objective appraisal of reality.
c. Ego states which are fixated in early childhood.

In talking about the Child ego state, Berne is careful to avoid the words "childish" and "immature." In "the Child" are to be found intuition, creativity, and spontaneous drive and enjoyment. "The Adult" is essential for survival because of its reality-testing function, which enables it to process and analyse data and compute probabilities. "The Parent" has two functions: it enables an individual to assume the role of parent and it automates many decisions. According to Berne, these three aspects of personality are necessary for survival.

Salesmen are professional game players, as the following example provided by Berne illustrates:

SALESMAN: This one is better, but you can't afford it.
HOUSEWIFE: That's the one I'll take.

An analysis of this transaction is shown in Figure 15–4. At the conscious, ostensible, social level, the salesman (Adult ego) is stating two objective facts: "This one is better" and "You can't afford it." At the Adult level, the housewife should reply, "Right, both times"; however, an ulterior or psychological vector was aimed at the housewife's Child. The validity of

FIGURE 15–4
Transaction between salesman and housewife

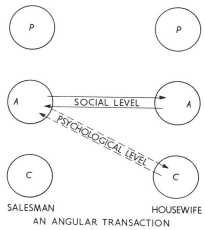

SALESMAN   HOUSEWIFE
AN ANGULAR TRANSACTION

the salesman's judgement is vindicated by the Child's response, which in effect is "Irrespective of cost, I'll show you that I'm as good as anybody."

Another good example of game theory is provided by consideration of the game of "courtroom." "Courtroom" is usually played by three people, though any number can play. The principal parts are the husband (the plaintiff), the wife (the defendant), and a guest (the judge). The game usually begins with the husband saying, "Did I tell you what my wife did last night. . . ." The wife replies, "Let me tell you what really happened. . . ." The guest may now comment in terms such as, "I don't want to stick my nose into other people's business, but might I suggest. . . ." Other guests can be cast in the role of jury.

Berne's theory of games has considerable relevance for the student of organizational behaviour. For a start, Berne's idea of stroking certainly has relevance to the way in which salutations are exchanged by executives. Most managers are at least intuitively aware of the significance of the way in which they are greeted *or not* by their colleagues when they arrive at the office in the morning. To be greeted by, "Hallo, Bill. How is it going?" is regarded as quite satisfactory. "Good morning" may well only signify the formal discharge of the need to acknowledge your arrival. The total absence of any signal of recognition nearly always is registered in some way. By itself, it may not be sufficient evidence on which to base an evaluation of the relation; but if it happens on several occasions, it may produce a diffuse feeling of anxiety that something is wrong, although precisely what is impossible to say. It is just this uncertainty, coupled with the difficulty of diagnosing its source, which gives the free-floating anxiety of the executive the opportunity to find a focus. Testing for fit of focus of anxiety is the first step in the agonizing reappraisal which seems to be an integral part of executive life. To minimize anxiety, most managers apparently spend a significant part of their work day testing social circuits and making appropriate adjustments. Unfortunately, this circuit-testing process may achieve functional autonomy and continue even when it has no real operational significance.

The experienced executive quickly develops techniques to deal with the problem of reduced stroking. For example, he may decide to establish contact with the person concerned by rearranging his schedule or inventing a problem. Operating on this basis, he may be able to reestablish contact and identify the difficulty. In any case, modern research findings in group psychology suggest that increased contact, on balance, reduces hostility.

Again, the experienced executive may accept the confrontation and set out to test the strength of his opponent. In the early stages of this exercise, our executive may decide to "deadpan it"—to present an expression that is neither for nor against the other fellow and await reaction. On balance, the advantage would seem to lie with the person who decides on his "relations policy." The ability to maintain a neutral expression seems to be well developed among military personnel, prisoners, and executives.

Although Berne's theory lacks theoretical consistency and has no considerable body of empirical data to lend it validity, it has considerable pragmatic relevance. Reverting to the vexed problem of psychotherapy, a psychiatrist who refers a troubled patient to the works of Freud, Jung, or Adler runs the risk of adding mental confusion to the patient's other problems; but a copy of *Games People Play* may give him a valuable insight into his own personality dynamics. As a tool for analysing organizational behaviour, it has considerable potential, to say nothing of the fun its use may give.

I'M OK—YOU'RE OK

Dr. Thomas A. Harris, a psychiatrist, has developed the ideas of Eric Berne into a teaching and learning device which is of great interest to executives because of its simplicity, ease of understanding, and the extent of its application to organizational problems. According to Harris, the central thesis of transactional analysis is that most people suffer from a vague sense of inferiority (they feel that they're "not OK").

Transactional analysis looks on every human interaction as a transaction, and much depends on whether the Adult (the mature ego state) keeps in the proper balance his Child aspects (immature, emotional) and his Parent promptings (authoritative dicta inculcated by parents and society). Differing balances among these ego states result in four basic life positions:

1. I'm not OK—you're OK (the anxious, dependent position).
2. I'm not OK—you're not OK (the "give-up" position).

3. I'm OK—you're not OK (the thug position).
4. I'm OK—you're OK (the balanced, Adult position).

Since, according to Harris, everyone starts life in the Child's "I'm not OK —you're OK position," the trick is to work one's way out of that, avoid the other two unbalanced positions, and achieve an existential Adult response in most transactions.

A useful tool in analysing transactions is the diagram in Figure 15–4. Each individual has each of the P-A-C elements; a transaction may involve, say, the boss's Parent and the worker's Child. If each is content with his role, the transaction is complementary; but suppose the worker instead tries to respond as Adult to Adult, or tries to impose his Parent on the boss's Child? Harris has evolved rules in such situations:

> *Rule 1.* When stimulus and response on the P-A-C diagram make parallel lines, the transaction is complementary and can go on indefinitely.
> *Rule 2.* When stimulus and response cross on the P-A-C diagram, communication stops.

An example of a crossed transaction is:

PATIENT (ADULT): I would like to work in a hospital like this.
NURSE (PARENT): You can't even cope with your own problems.

In crossed transactions, further communication is impossible unless "something gives"; Harris's advice is to try to "hook" (appeal to or invoke) the other person's Adult by an Adult response. If the worker can succeed in hooking the boss's Adult, or the patient can do so with the nurse, they can begin a real process of communication with each other. Complementary transactions are not necessarily true communication; only Adult to Adult exchanges are in fact desirable.

The beauty of the Berne-Harris approach lies on its comprehensibility and utility, not in its originality. Nevertheless, T.A., because of its accessibility and the colloquial language in which it has been presented, has captured the interest of many academics and executives who find R. D. Laing's concept of "mapping" too complex. In spite of the carping criticism of the psychiatric establishment, it is worthwhile looking at T.A. in more detail, for the system has offered therapy to many thousands and has been considered as a potential source of advice and counsel for millions more. Like many other neat and tidy explanations of personality, T.A. fails ultimately because it is hermetically sealed to outside influences (i.e., it is a relatively closed system); but it has value as an arithmetical stepping stone to the more complex calculuses of Freud and R. D. Laing, which offer real opportunities for learning and growth experiences.

Transactional analysis can be taught to executives and other employees —and in spite of its simplifications, it is useful. For example, in the American Airlines training school for stewards and stewardesses, trainees spend a fair amount of time learning about ego states. Having figured out the

Berne gospel that the world is divided into three types—the Parent domineering and scolding, the Adult reasoning and reasonable-with, and the Child creative and innovative but also likely to throw a tantrum or sulk—the trainees are encouraged to covertly categorize their passengers and react accordingly. Having been introduced to the mysteries of Berne and Harris, they move on to learn T.A.C.T.—Transactional Analysis and Customer Treatment.

TOPIC 4
Communication and organizational structure

It is obvious that collecting information is a necessary prerequisite to decision making and, further, that the information required for making a decision is likely to be located at a number of diverse points within the organization. The routes along which this information flows are referred to as the channels of information. In business organizations, communications are usually highly structured. In formal organizations it is usually necessary to spell out who can communicate with whom, who can initiate contacts, who can sanction what, what information is to be limited in circulation and so on.

But the question may be raised as to why it is necessary to "stick to channels." There are three reasons for sticking to channels: (1) if information is not transmitted through channels, it may cause chaos in the organization; (2) it is usual to assume that the organization has a better chance of being successful if certain messages are kept secret; and (3) research findings in group dynamics support the view that structured communication is usually more effective than unstructured.

THE VERTICAL DIMENSION

Conventional wisdom in regard to hierarchical communications emphasizes that information and reports flow up the hierarchy and orders, instructions, and policies flow down. The implication is that a one-way, exclusively vertical communication channel exists between top management and the lower echelons. Many organizations seem to have a vested interest in maintaining the myth that all communications are exclusively vertical by producing job descriptions that talk only of vertical relationships. Arguing against this picture of vertical simplicity, modern research findings show that horizontal (lateral) communications can be important too. With the uncertainty and complexity of the modern technological organization, there is likely to be a lot of communication among peers to fill in gaps in the information travelling vertically up and down the organization. As yet management theory largely fails to take proper cognizance of communication among peers.

The modern approach to communications recognizes the "instrumentality" of upward communication. Subordinates tend to regard those with greater power as instrumental to their needs satisfaction. Thus "lows" behave towards "highs" in a way which is calculated, perhaps unconsciously, to maximize good relations and minimize anxiety in interacting with those who are in positions of power in the organization. In this way, hierarchies automatically develop restraints against free communications, especially hostile criticism by subordinates against superiors. In a study entitled "Upward Communication in Industrial Hierarchies," W. H. Read concluded:

> The results have generally supported the major prediction that, in industrial hierarchies, mobility aspiration among subordinate executives is negatively related to accuracy of upward communication. The findings have paralleled those of small-group studies which have rather consistently shown that individuals in power hierarchies tend to screen information passed upward, and to withhold or refrain from communicating information that is potentially threatening to the status of the communicator. The present study confirms that this tendency prevails in formal, large-scale organizations, is stronger among upwardly mobile members, and is strongly modified by the communicator's attitudes towards those above him in the hierarchy.

FIGURE 15–5
POLICY, PROGRAMME.
INSTRUCTIONS

The conventional picture is of the board of directors devising policy, which is developed into a programme by the departmental managers and then broken down into departmental assignments by foremen. If a job is highly mechanized (for example, the assembly of cars), technology becomes the major determinant structuring communication flow. What the assembly worker does next and the pace at which he works is fixed by the assembly track. In a car factory, where work flow is vital, there is likely to be a lot of horizontal communication; but where there is less mechanization (for example, in the case of a gang digging a road), vertical communication will be more in evidence.

In their book *Formal Organizations*, P. M. Blau and W. R. Scott analyse in considerable detail this question of hierarchical communications. They deal firstly with the dysfunctions of hierarchical communications. Secondly, they argue that groups are superior to individuals because they permit suggestions to be sifted, thus reducing error; give valuable social support; and mobilize energies of the members of the group by creating a spirit of competition. Blau and Scott at first suggest that hierarchical organization appears to curtail this process. Studies of bureaucracies show that social interaction follows status lines and is inhibited by status boundaries. Thus theoretically the existence of a hierarchy can be expected to reduce the effectiveness of communications; but in fact, research in group psychology has shown that groups with leaders usually perform better than leaderless ones. There is a significant body of evidence to support the idea that having a leader facilitates problem solving in groups. R. F. Bales has produced a wealth of research data showing that leaderless groups attempting to solve human relations problems did better if they developed a status gradient. The burden of modern communication research suggests that, subject to certain reservations (such as the need to innovate), structuring communication flow improves performance of work groups.

THE LATERAL DIMENSION

Blau and Scott made a rather revealing study of communication among peers in a U.S. law enforcement agency. The main job of the agents was to investigate business organizations to find out if they were in fact complying with two particular federal laws. According to Blau and Scott, the agents derived great satisfaction from their work, which required, in addition to a knowledge of the law and administrative precedents, considerable discretion. Although the agents were allowed to exercise their discretion in making investigations, no check was made on how they spent their time. But rigid conformity to the law and established operating procedures was expected of them in terms of their decisions. Their superiors, as Blau and Scott pointed out, judged them on their results.

The results of this policy suggested that evaluation on the basis of results achieved rather than methods employed fostered disciplined responsibility among agents. "Not the road taken but the destination reached was the test of performance."

The formal procedure required that an agent faced with difficulties go to his boss, who might send him to a staff attorney; officially agents were forbidden to ask each other for advice. However, as their work was reviewed by their superiors, the agents were reluctant to turn to them for advice, and instead consulted their peers. This practice improved decision making and helped both the agent asking for advice and the one giving it. The agent whose advice was sought gained experience in analysing problems and, being free from anxieties about the situation, was better able to analyse situations and thus improved his skill. As a result his self-confidence rose.

LATERAL COMMUNICATION—WHO CONSULTS WHOM?

The most competent agents were most often consulted; but people tended to form dyads for consultation, since going frequently for advice to a person who never consults you gives superior status to the person consulted. Besides, if too many people consult "the expert," he will be prevented from doing his work; and so in self-defence he must adopt an approach which discourages or at least minimizes consultations. Members of dyads in the law enforcement agency would consult each other.

Similar behaviour can be observed in universities. Partnerships are formed to pool information about useful topics to investigate, methods of research to be employed, channels for publication, and so on. Likewise, students prefer to seek advice from a classmate of approximately equal ability rather than from the brightest student. Blau and Scott concluded from their study that:

> The formal status hierarchy in an organization creates obstacles to the free flow of communication. Specifically, dependence on superiors for formal rewards restricts consultation across hierarchical boundaries. Under special conditions, it may also discourage consultation among colleagues, but probably the more typical situation is that hierarchical obstacles to communication foster consultation among peers. The processes of consultation among peers give rise to an informal differential of status, because some members of the colleague group earn more respect as consultants than others. Such emerging distinctions of informal status also create obstacles to the free discussion of problems, just as formal status differences do. These obstacles may further redirect the flow of consultation, so that the highest frequency occurs between persons of equal informed status. But even consultations among persons of equal competence probably improve the quality of performance, for anxiety interferes less with making decisions on a colleague's cases than with making decisions on one's own.

In a study conducted in an engineering plant by the author, it was found that foremen in charge of batch production had to consult with each other before they could begin on a batch. Foreman B might have to approach foreman A about the materials he needed, then ask C if he might fit the new job into the schedule. Arrangements for the day were usually made at the morning tea break, which was extended, without managerial protest, from the set 10 minutes to about 45 minutes to allow time for discussion. Where long production runs were the norm, there was much less peer interaction, which suggests that technology can have a major influence on communication patterns (See Box 15.1).

In some vertical communication with superiors, disagreement is minimized to present the subordinate in the most favourable light. There are many homely expressions for this kind of behaviour. Instead of travelling up the chain of command without restriction, reports are often censored. Often the person making a report will try to present it not to his immediate superior but to the superior's boss, and in this way levels of management are skipped.

Box 15.1: Vertical versus horizontal communication

Professor Richard L. Simpson, a sociologist at the University of North Carolina, cor
ducted a survey of eight supervisors in the spinning department of a synthetic texti
mill in order to test the hypothesis that "work related communications between official
are more often vertical than horizontal."

The method employed by the researcher was a structured but open-ended intervie
procedure. The question put to the supervisors was: "About how often do you talk wit
——————— on business? Don't include times when you just say hello or pass the tim
of day; just the contacts needed to get your work done. . . . What kinds of things d
you talk about with him?" Some of the findings and interpretations were:

> The contacts of the three men at the higher levels—A, B–1, and B–2 (see
> organization Chart)—were overwhelmingly vertical; but they could hardly have
> been otherwise. A, being the only man at his level could not possibly have any
> horizontal contacts. B–1 and B–2 could communicate horizontally only with each
> other, but they could communicate downward with several foremen and upward
> with A. They seldom had to communicate with each other, since the work rela-
> tions between their sections were coordinated mainly through horizontal contact
> between their subordinates. . . .
>
> On the C-foreman level most contacts were horizontal except those of C–3. . . .
> Three of these five foremen—C–1, C–2, and C–5— had markedly fewer vertical
> and more horizontal contacts than would have occurred on the chance expecta-
> tion that every man communicates equally with every other man. The contacts of
> C–4 were mainly horizontal, in about the same proportion as would be expecte
> on the basis of chance. . . .
>
> The preponderance of horizontal communications reported by four of the five
> first-line foremen (level C) is understandable if we examine the content of the

R. L. Simpson, "Vertical and Horizontal Communication in Formal Organizations," *Administr*.
Science Quarterly, Vol. 4 (September, 1959), pp. 188–96.

THE DILEMMA OF STRUCTURING COMMUNICATION

Research in group dynamics shows that decisions worked out by the
group are more acceptable than ones imposed by authority. In our society
it is usually felt that if a person was present when a decision was reached
and made no objection, he ought to go along with the decision. A study
conducted by L. Coch and J. R. P. French in a pyjama factory in the
southern United States indicates that total participation in decision making facilitates the greatest change in behaviour. Attitudes can, however, be
influenced in many subtle ways; for example, a person may be more likely
to change his attitudes as a result of overhearing a communication than
after having one specifically directed to him.

Blau and Scott, in *Formal Organization*, concluded that a hierarchical
organization, because it restricts the free flow of communications, improves co-ordination. On the other hand, this hierarchical differentiation,
while it is extremely important for co-ordination, tends to block or at least
inhibit the communications that are so necessary for stimulating innovative
activities and facilitating decision making. In a manufacturing industry

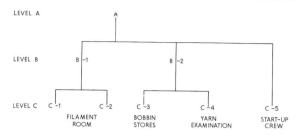

ORGANIZATION CHART OF SPINNING DEPARTMENT SUPERVISORS

communications they reported. Very few communications involved the issuing of commands or the reporting of results—the standard types of vertical communications. Most contacts of men at level C involved either (1) joint problem-solving or (2) coordination of work flow between sections. These were mainly horizontal communications. . . .

It is noteworthy that they [the level-C men] worked out these problems without consulting or informing their superior.

The findings neither confirmed nor rejected the hypothesis but led to a modified hypothesis:

Mechanization reduces the need for close supervision (vertical communication), since instead of the foreman the machines set the work pace; but automation (i.e., extreme mechanization) increases the need for vertical communication, to deal with the frequent and serious machine breakdowns.

such as the assembly of motor cars, a highly structured communications system is required to ensure the necessary level of co-ordination. On the other hand, in a research organization such as a chemical research laboratory, the absence of hierarchy facilitates inventiveness and discovery. In research laboratories, technological gate-keepers play a critical role in structuring the information flow.

The importance of structure raises questions such as, Is disagreement good or bad? E. P. Torrance has made a number of studies on the effect of disagreement in small group processes. He found in a study of air crews in combat in Korea that the more effective crews were more tolerant of disagreement. In his study of USAF jet aces in Korea, Torrance found that, compared with their less effective colleagues, the aces were less likely to take no for an answer; they went to the limits in opposition to accepted procedure in order to test the situation and tried to get the maximum from themselves and their aircraft.

In his studies, Torrance found that structure was not always the main requirement of the communication process. His research at survival-training schools made it clear that the type of communication pattern or structure required after a plane has crashed is quite different from the pattern required to fly the plane efficiently. Torrance argued that most managers have been taught to believe that disagreement about the task is always bad; in his view it is necessary to foster a willingness to disagree.

More research is required to define the factors that impede the expression of disagreement. Psychologists have focused attention on the problems that arise where there is lack of consonance in the beliefs held by a person. Cognitive dissonance arises when a person is exposed to a communication which differs from his own opinion. In these circumstances the person may change to a position closer to the communication or denigrate both the communication and communicator.

To try to throw some light on the dilemma of structuring communications, behavioural scientists have developed a new experimental design called the communication net.

COMMUNICATION NETS AND STRUCTURING INFORMATION FLOWS

Communication net is a term used to describe the arrangement of information channels. In a business, organization charts may be thought of as devices or visual aids used to spell out or make explicit the structure of the management team and to show how information should flow through the firm. It follows from this that the organizational structure may be thought of as synonymous with the communication net. There have been many studies of organization structure, mostly in a business setting.

In 1950, Alex Bavelas conducted the first laboratory experiments in communications and developed a very interesting and useful procedure to

FIGURE 15–6
EXAMPLES OF COMMUNICATION NETS

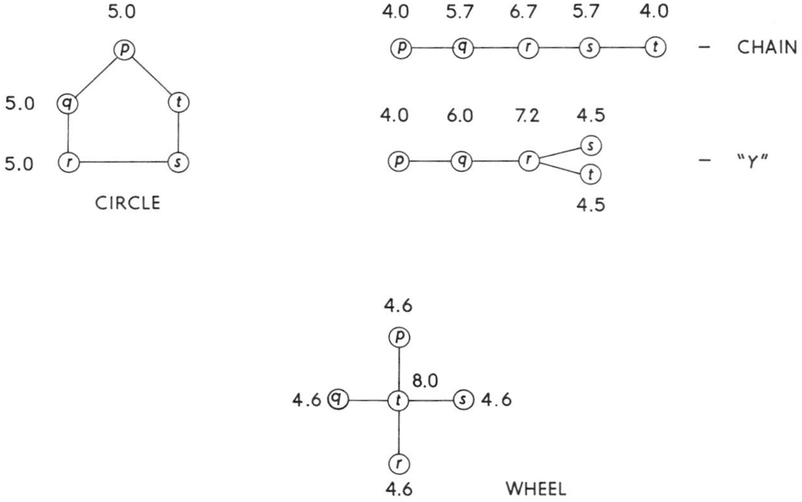

determine which of several logically adequate communications networks gives better performance. The subjects in these experiments were isolated and put to work on a laboratory task while the experimenter controlled the channels of communication to form any desired pattern or net. The usual procedure was to seat five people at a table and separate one from another by vertical screens. The only form of communication allowed was by means of notes passed through slits in the screens.

Basic to this research design is the assumption that the distance between any two people in the network is one. Figure 15–6 shows examples of patterns, such as the wheel, the circle, the chain, and the "Y." Communications among the five people in each net can take place only through the channels indicated. The index of relative centrality is calculated by dividing the sum of all internal distances in a pattern by the sum of distances from any one position in the pattern. This can be calculated on the assumption that distance between two adjacent people is one. For example, for the wheel the distances are:

p to $q = 2$	q to $p = 2$	r to $p = 2$	s to $p = 2$	t to $p = 1$
p to $r = 2$	q to $r = 2$	r to $q = 2$	s to $q = 2$	t to $q = 1$
p to $s = 2$	q to $s = 2$	r to $s = 2$	s to $r = 2$	t to $r = 1$
p to $t = \dfrac{1}{7}$	q to $t = \dfrac{1}{7}$	r to $t = \dfrac{1}{7}$	s to $t = \dfrac{1}{7}$	t to $s = \dfrac{1}{4}$

The sum of all internal distances is $7 + 7 + 7 + 7 + 4 = 32$. The centrality index for person p is $32/7$, for q it is $32/7$, etc. It should be obvious that the greater this index is, the greater is the degree of centrality. Figure 15–6 gives the index for each participant in each net.

In the circle notes can be passed to left or right. In the wheel only t can communicate with all four others. In the circle, all positions are equally central; in the wheel only t is central.

In one experiment, each subject was given five of a possible six symbols. The task of the group was to discover which symbol was held in common by all. In this simple problem, the wheel was most effective. Using such experiments, a number of conclusions were reached about relative effectiveness of the various nets.

The network with the least centralized structure was found to have on the average more errors than that which was most centralized. The more centralized nets had greater agreement on who the leader was. Wheel groups required less time to solve simple problems, but circle groups solved more complex problems faster. The availability of information is the key to the solution of simple problems, provided the problem can be solved by anyone in the net; and. so the wheel pattern is superior for tackling such problems. With complex problems it is desirable that everyone in the net have a chance to contribute so that the full range of intellectual resources may be exploited, and in these cases the circle is better than the wheel. With a complex problem the hub-man may become saturated with information and be unable to function properly. To avoid this difficulty, military and other organizations are often designed with several headquarters groups which can be used to carry out, with the same basic military formation, a number of consecutive operations.

In general terms it is safe to say that the all-channel net, where everyone can communicate with everyone else, is most advantageous. Its superiority has been attributed to its flexibility: if the task is simple the net can appoint a leader to maximize task performance; if it is complex, everyone can contribute to the development of the solution. Nevertheless, in 1955, H. Guetzkow and H. A. Simon, who had replicated and extended the work of Bavelas and his colleagues, concluded in "The Impact of Certain Communication Nets upon Organization and Performance in Task-Oriented Groups":

> The current management literature on the topic of communication leaves one with the expectation that certainly a reduction in communication restrictions should lead to a more adequately functioning organization. Yet, our findings in this experiment indicate that assertion of a one-to-one relationship between effective functioning and freedom in communication is unwarranted. Had our analysis not separated the organizational problems from the operating problem, it would have seemed paradoxical that complete freedom of communication is at times more limiting than restricted communication. The findings warn the practical communications expert working in industry or government that a change in communications structure may have quite different consequences for the efficiency of immediate day-to-day operations, and for the ability of the organization to handle changes in its own structure.

It is possible to summarize some of the findings of this research on communication nets by noting:

1. The greater the degree of connectiveness, the higher the level of satisfaction.
2. The probability of emerging as a leader increases with the centrality of one's position.
3. Members' morale is related to their centrality.

EXPERIMENTS IN COMMUNICATION

A number of experiments have been conducted to compare the efficiency of individuals and groups in problem solving. The conclusion of most of this research is that groups are superior to individuals. It has been argued that the superiority of groups over individuals is derived from the fact that social interaction in the group setting produces a correcting mechanism for sifting ideas and also provides a supportive environment for individual members, who therefore try harder. As is widely known, problem solving frequently engenders anxiety. When a person takes the first step and stops to consider whether it is correct or not, there is always the possibility that a mental blockage may develop and the whole process may be brought to a halt. In a group situation, on the other hand, useful suggestions are likely to receive some form of verbal approval. This process in turn encourages individual members to produce suggestions likely to help the group to resolve its problems. The superiority of the group over the individual may be attributed to (1) the sifting of suggestions by social interaction, which may be thought of as an error-correcting device; (2) the extension of social support; and (3) the effect of competition among individual members, thus mobilizing their energies for problem solving.

THE NEED FOR FLEXIBILITY

Managers know only too well that information is expensive, but also that the lack of information may be even more expensive. The development of computers has added greatly to the amount of data available to provide an informational background for organizational decision making. To operate effectively, the organization must make best use of these data. It is obvious that communications systems have been greatly complicated by the need to find ways of processing large volumes of information quickly. Inefficient communication leads to dysfunctional consequences which are partly due to organizational complexity but more often than not are reinforced by personal failure. Some business organizations are overcomplex, perhaps in that they may have too many levels or are too large, or perhaps because they fail to resolve the problems of communication between line and staff. Organizations, to-day, must be flexible, and thus a frozen communication system is inappropriate. The organization must be adaptive; new structures must be devised to deal with fresh tasks.

TOPIC 5
Managing the organizational interface

MANAGING THE VERTICAL DIMENSION

A decisive reason why most American prisoners held in North Vietnam were able to stand up to both physical and psychological torture was the fact that a fixed command structure was set up to control the flow of information among the captives. The senior officer according to rank assumed command and everybody else fell into place. Thus tying information channels to hierarchy converted what normally would have been an informal apparatus into a powerful formal instrument which wielded tremendous power and saved the prisoners from the personal degradation which was the fate of so many U.S. prisoners during the Korean war.

The same argument for structuring communication applies to business organizations. The issue is not whether structuring is good or bad, but rather how much, where, and when.

We know from our work on path-goal motivation that structuring reduces ambiguity and facilitates effort, but only in certain circumstances. Further, we know that supervisors who initiate structure are more productive not only of task output but also of grievances. So structure can generate noise and dysfunctions in terms of grievances. But as you ascend the hierarchy, research seems to support the view that initiating structure is sufficient to generate both productivity and satisfaction.

An intriguing and revealing insight into the relation between structure and language has been provided by Lena L. Lucietto of the University of Chicago in a research report entitled "Speech Patterns of Administrators." She found that, first, school principals high in initiating structure use fewer "self" words. But when they do use words like "I" or "me," they employ them in direct, specific, and forceful contexts:

> *I* want to know why you would reject it.
> Now this is *my* responsibility.
> Let's get your reaction to some of the statements *I've* made.
> Remember what *I* said to you, though.

On the other hand, principals perceived by the teachers under them as low in initiating structure use more "self" words and use them in contexts of co-operation and agreement:

> *I* kind of thought you were.
> It's all right with *me*, in a way.
> *I* agree with you that the other would be top priority.
> *I'm* not trying to be—I don't want to be dictatorial here.
> And *I* do too, you know.
> No, *I'd* agree with you.

Principals high in initiating structure were distinguished from those perceived as low by their use of "attempt" words, like "try," "pursue," and "effort." Principals perceived as low in initiating structure use similar words, but in a less direct way. The sense of strength which might have been conveyed by the attempt word is attenuated by the word "think" proceeding it:

> I *think* that if you *try* something like that, I think along those lines, you may have some success with John.

MANAGING THE HORIZONTAL DIMENSION

Lateral transactions are seldom shown on the classical organization chart, but horizontal interactions are often as important as vertical ones. When an organization faces a uniform task, communications can be more bureaucratic and vertically structured. Wilfred Brown of the Glacier Metal Company invented the command meeting to achieve more vertical integration. The command meeting worked in some departments but not in others; to some extent its success was a function of technology (automatic versus individual machine lines) and the length of the production run (batch versus long run). Glacier, like most contemporary large-scale organizations has to deal with both uniform and nonuniform tasks. When the command meeting was insufficient to meet the needs of a situation, the Glacier managers invented additional lateral communication tissue (meetings in the cafeteria, informal telephoning, and car pools) to solve the problems involved.

Paul Lawrence and J. W. Lorsch have shown from their studies of six plastics organizations that the departmental structure (tightness of rules, narrowness of the span of supervisory control, frequency and specificity of performance services) is a function of the orientation towards the environment (technological, economic, and marketing). In other words, there is an optimal level of structure which is largely a response to the uncertainty of the environment. Thus, the environment, technology, and the length of the production run also contribute to determining the mix of vertical and lateral communications.

THE TACTICS OF LATERAL INTERACTIONS

There is a rapidly growing literature on the tactics of lateral communication. M. Dalton has described how staff units were encouraged by top management to keep an eye on line units, who retaliated by blocking the creation of staff units and their promotion. Dalton's study focused on the formation in the line departments of coalitions of cabals and cliques which "fixed" the information top management was to receive. George Strauss has reported on how purchasing officers attempted to get leverage over engineering and production by inventing restrictive rules and then, relying on personal contacts and persuasion, proceeded to break their own rules and thus subvert and alter the organizational structure.

What tactics are employed is essentially a function of power, which in turn is a function of such factors as the unit's ability to cope with uncertainty, how easily the unit's work can be replaced, and how central the unit is in the work flow. All this follows D. J. Hickson's view of power as a systems variable. Different departments hold the decision power in different circumstances; different contingencies produce different tactics. In Lawrence and Lorsch's 1967 studies, the research department was most influential in two food-processing firms, co-ordinating and integrating units were most influential in the six plastics firms, and sales most influential in the two container-manufacturing organizations. Both research and common sense argue that maintenance can often be the decisive subunit, even with programmed maintenance (apparent low uncertainty).

Richard E. Walton and John M. Dutton have suggested that there are two basic ways of handling the external relation, the integrative (problem solving, information exchange, conscientious accuracy in transmitting information, flexibility, and trust) and the distributive (bargaining, careful rationing, information distortions, rigidity, and hostility).

MANAGING THE LATERAL INTERFACE

Modern research findings argue for the management of the lateral interface. But how? The greater the degree of differentiation between depart-

FIGURE 15–7
TACTICS OF LATERAL INTERACTION

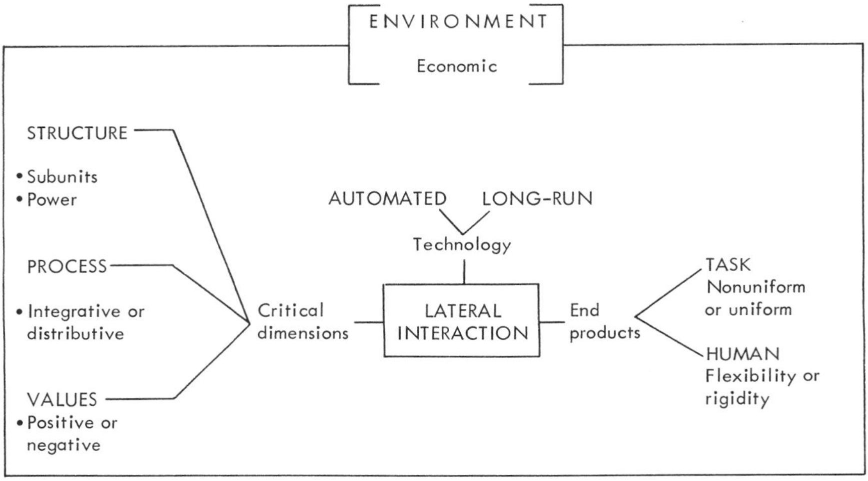

ments, the more complex must be the interface management techniques. Lawrence and Lorsch reported that the most differentiated firm in their study even had a separate integrative department. According to Lawrence and Lorsch, such integrating units must have respected staff members who are organized according to a structure intermediate to the units to be coordinated and who can help managers to confront rather than smooth over conflict.

The whole operation of structuring lateral interactions is far trickier than structuring vertical communications. In any case, subunits which fail to sort themselves out are frequently reorganized. Close examination of organizational design for lateral communication suggests how particular pitfalls can be overcome. For example, Figure 15–7 models lateral interaction as a system; such models can help to develop sophisticated designs which can respond to different contingencies.

SUMMARY; COMMUNICATION AS A SYSTEM

The term "communications" covers a wide spectrum of human activity which has become a major focus of research and interest for social scientists, many of whom consider a knowledge of this subject essential to an understanding of organizational behaviour. For example, at one end of the scale there is research which is concerned with the biochemistry of the neuron; and at the other end of the scale there is the social scientist who may be preoccupied with the study of methods of mass communication such as television. The lumping together of these different approaches had led to a somewhat confusing transference of terms. Today the subject of communications has become an amalgam of information theory, semantics, cybernetics, computer technology, and group dynamics.

A major focus of interest which research workers have ignored is the ways in which communication may be inhibited; on many occasions it is undesirable to keep everyone informed of all developments. The restrictive practices of communication are surely deserving of attention and ought to be more fully investigated. Some executives who are psychologically distant from their subordinates show great skill in blocking communications, and a situation may develop in which failure to communicate becomes a significant stimulus of further organizational behaviour.

This lacuna in the experimental work illustrates the point that it is difficult to generalize about communication in a way which is valid in all situations. Figure 15–8, modeling communication as a system, takes the systems approach of identifying the many interacting elements which need to be considered, studied, and integrated in organizational designs.

Organizational scientists and managers should appreciate that lists such as "The Ten Commandments of Good Communication" must be treated with some caution, as no single form of communication can be guaranteed to be effective in all circumstances. Before commenting on the validity of the communication it is necessary to start off by deciding what constitutes effectiveness in communication; what is vital, here, is to decide whether it is speed, accuracy, freedom from error, clarity, success in improving human relationships (perhaps by changing perceptions, needs, and beliefs), or innovation. The objectives of the communication must be clearly defined before the criteria for its effectiveness can be identified. Too many executives remain frozen in one particular communications posture which, in their ignorance, they believe is valid for all circumstances and for all purposes.

The "cookbook" approach to effective communications assumes that it is possible to spell out simple laws whose observance will make for good communications in all circumstances. The "how to do it" book is usually platitudinous in the extreme and frequently starts by observing that "all communications are of two types—the written word and the spoken

FIGURE 15-8
COMMUNICATION AS A SYSTEM

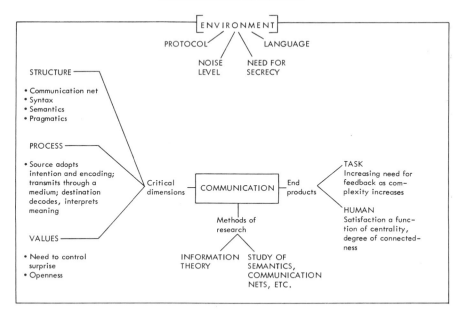

word"; and its best "advice" is to get two-way communication, to keep everyone informed, to use a wide range of media—television, posters, talks, and so on—and above all, to ensure that all communications are short, terse, unambiguous, and relevant. The burden of research findings of contemporary work on communications would be to reject this kind of universal platitude. It is more realistic to define the object of communication as the reduction of uncertainty. Having received a communication, the respondent should be in a position to analyse his social environment so as to achieve the goals of the sender. Most laboratory experiments on communication are too simple to have much relevance for everyday life. For example, too little empirical work has been done on communication in crises; a reading of William Manchester's *Death of a President* suggests that some useful research could be carried out in this area.

GUIDE-LINES

Some guide-lines for effective communication can be given, to flesh out the "Process" section of Figure 15–8:

1. Before communicating, a person should analyse his problem in as great detail as possible in order to determine exactly what he wishes to communicate. As is often the case in business, he may not be able to clarify the issue completely, unless his problem is very simple. But any effort in this direction will bear handsome dividends.

2. The purpose of the communication should be defined. Specify your intention, then define your aim.

3. The physical and human environment should be considered, i.e., timing, location, social setting, and previous experience. It is worth repeating that communication is not exclusively verbal.

4. Consult with others if this is thought to be necessary. Often authority to communicate must be sought before a message is sent, or someone must be put in the picture in regard to the action that is to be taken. It is useful to remember the headings "For Action" and "For Information," when communications are being planned.

5. Objectivity is not always necessarily a criterion of good communication in every circumstance; sometimes two-sided messages are useful. As well as the message itself, communications frequently contain peripheral elements; and nuances of meaning conveyed by the timbre of the voice or the choice of language may turn out to be the significant stimulus. The cookbook approach to communication recommends use of words with a limited range of connotations; but often words with wide connotations are best for producing attitude changes in members of work groups.

6. Try to influence the person with whom you are communicating; try to see things from his point of view. Remember different people have different perceptual slants.

7. Assess the effectiveness of the communication if this is possible. This is usually done by encouraging feedback.

8. Choose carefully the type of communication process best suited to your purpose. For example, in military parlance it is useful to give a warning order, then an executive order. Sometimes this approach may be relevant in a civilian context. Politicians sometimes communicate their plans to the public by the calculated leak; reaction to the leak helps them to decide whether to introduce the intended change or not. Excessive use of calculated leaks may produce a credibility gap between what politicians say and the public believe.

9. Many executives seem to believe that it is possible to manage by exclusively vertical forms of communications, but research reveals that a great deal of communication is lateral. If the situation is inchoate or ill-defined, superiors cannot give precise positive instructions that cover all contingencies, and so subordinates must get together to decide what is possible and in the best interests of the organization. Though lacking in hierarchical logic, such horizontal communication has its own organizational logic.

In view of the obvious need for more research into communication theory and practice, it is unfortunate that there is such a gap on this vital subject between the approaches of behavioural scientists and those of practising managers. Social scientists, to the mind of many a practising manager, seem excessively preoccupied with experimental situations that

Box 15.2: How primacy of presentation persuades

C. I. Hovland and his colleagues at Yale University have conducted an extensive series of communication experiments "designed to test a variety of theoretical formulations concerning the order in which persuasive material is presented to the audience." Their main findings are the following:

1. When two sides of an issue are presented successively by different communicators, the side presented first does not necessarily have the advantage.

2. If, after hearing only one side of a controversial issue, a response is made which publicly indicates one's position on the issue, the effectiveness of a subsequent presentation of the second side of the issue is reduced, thus entailing a primacy effect.

3. The mere act of stating one's opinion anonymously on a questionnaire after hearing only one side of an issue does not significantly reduce the effectiveness of the second side.

4. When contradictory information is presented in a single communication, by a single communicator, there is a pronounced tendency for those items presented first to dominate the impression received.

5. The primacy effect found in presenting contradictory information in the same communication was reduced by interpolating other activities between the two blocks of information and by warning the subjects against the fallibility of first impressions.

6. Presentation of information relevant to the satisfaction of needs after these needs have been aroused brings about greater aceptance than an order which presents the information first and the need-arousal second.

7. Order of presentation is a more significant factor in influencing opinion for subjects with relatively weak desire for understanding than for those with "high cognitive need."

8. Placing communications highly desirable to the recipient first, followed by those less desirable, produces more opinion change than the reverse order.

9. When an authoritative communicator plans to mention pro arguments and also nonsalient con arguments, the pro-first order is superior to the con-first order.

C. I. Hovland *et al., The Order of Presentation in Persuasion* (New Haven, Conn.: Yale Universi Press, 1957).

can be treated with great accuracy but seem of little relevance to the busy executive who is heavily committed to sorting out his immediate organizational difficulties.

A CHECKLIST FOR COMMUNICATIONS

For the purposes of analysis, it is useful to look at:

The message. What is this supposed to be? What language is it to be put in? What information does it contain? How should it be sequenced (see Box 15.2)?

Communicators. Who are they? What are their roles? Where do they stand on the status scale? Is there a status gradient? Does either or do both have a vested interest in communicating the message? Are their personalities likely to interfere with the communication process?

Media. What form should be used? What are the mechanics of the information handling? What is the density of the communication system? What is the time pattern?

Environment. What are the circumstances of the communication? Who must know and who must not? Is there a protocol which is appropriate on this occasion? What about situational factors, especially social setting?

Effects. How effective is the system? How capable is it of adaptation? What are its aims? Are they being achieved?

The study of communications, which is closely related to that of leadership and decision making, is already a major focus of research, and there is likely to be further extensive research. If this field continues to develop at its present rate, it seems probable that a more general analysis of the communication process cannot be far off; and as better and more detailed research findings become available, there seems a much greater probability that more effective communication systems can be designed for business organizations.

REVIEW OF PART THREE

Part Three was essentially concerned with the influence process: how organizations, by allocating authority and power, attempt to direct and control the behaviour and attitudes of their members. In the hurly-burly of organizational life, territories, tasks, and technologies are fought over and stresses, strains, and tensions are induced. All this conflict, which is structural and endemic to organizations, must be modulated and monitored. Structures, processes, and value systems must be invented to exploit the energy of conflict. Conflict must be communicated. But in what form?

Our review of communication has focused on the part played by perception and language in getting (and stopping) information flowing from A to B, where A and B can be persons, subunits, or organizations. Our brief look at A communicating with B points up the need to adopt sophisticated interpersonal (or interorganizational) strategies, depending on the contingencies. The major problem is that neither people nor organizations will stand still; and thus, to try to get a better handle on this problem of behavioural change, we turn in Part Four of the text to organizational growth and change, both now and in the future.

REVIEW AND RESEARCH

1. Why is the term "communication" so widely used in executive discussions? Why is it wrong to think that most organization problems are problems in communication? Why do so many managers attribute their problems to communication difficulties?

2. How are perception and communication linked?
3. Develop a semantic differential scale for measuring people's perceptions of black and white managers. Invite 10 of your associates to complete the scale. Collate the data on one scale. What conclusions can you draw from this pilot investigation?
4. Why are top managers cut off from knowing what is happening in the lower levels of their organizations? How do effective managers overcome this difficulty?
5. Why is oral usually preferable to written communication? In which circumstances is written communication superior? Why?
6. Why have committee meetings come under so much fire recently? How can the conduct of such meetings be improved?
7. What is a command meeting? What problems should be tackled through a command meeting?
8. Develop a set of rules for brainstorming. Use brainstorming with a group of your colleagues to develop a list of problems suitable for brainstorming.
9. Define a game à la Berne. What are the critical elements in a game? From your work experience, develop an example of the "games executives play."
10. Why is the structuring of communications essential in business?
11. What were the consequences of putting obstacles in the way of upward communication for the agents in Blau and Scott's study of a federal law enforcement agency?
12. When are two-sided messages appropriate?
13. Discuss the relationship between serial communication and the spread of a rumour.

GLOSSARY OF TERMS

Adaptation. The process or action of becoming more effectively adjusted to the environmental conditions pertaining to work or learning.

Brainstorming. A technique for generating ideas by means of highly intensive group interaction in which no ideas are criticized, freewheeling is encouraged, and the emphasis is on quantity of diverse ideas.

Cognitive dissonance. The mental state of holding irreconcilable beliefs. Cognitive dissonance arises when a person is exposed to a communication which differs from his own opinion; he may change to a position closer to the communication or derogate both the communication and the communicator.

Command meeting. A meeting between a manager and his subordinates in order to facilitate an interchange of information; the manager dominates the meeting (it is not democratic).

Communication. The field of inquiry concerned with the systematic use of symbols to achieve common or shared information about an object or event. The communication process can be thought of as a chain with at least three links; the sender, the medium, and the receiver. The sender encodes his message and transmits it through the chosen medium, and it is then decoded by the receiver.

Communication net. The arrangement of information channels. It is possible to summarize some of the findings of this research on communications nets by noting: (*a*) the greater the degree of connectiveness, the higher the level of satisfaction; (*b*) the probability of emerging as a leader increases with the centrality of one's position; and (*c*) members' morale is related to their centrality.

Entropy. The degree of randomness, ignorance, or chaos in a system; in a communication system, the noise which arises from errors and distortions.

Feedback. The response to a communication, in which B not only gives a reaction to A's message but also may control and correct further signals, thus making A and B truly interacting members of a communication system.

Game. As used by Eric Berne, an ongoing series of complementary ulterior transactions progressing to a well-defined, predictable outcome; a series of moves with a snare, or "gimmick." Games are clearly differentiated from procedures, rituals, and pastimes by two chief characteristics: (1) their ulterior quality and (2) the payoff; games are basically dishonest, and the outcome has a dramatic, as distinct from merely exciting, quality.

Noise. The elements of communications which are irrelevant or interfere with the transmission of the message.

Pragmatics. The area of communication theory that is concerned with assessment of the effectiveness of the communication process with respect to its purpose.

Semantic differential. C. E. Osgood's concept of the semantic differential is that some of the significant components of the multidimensional meaning of a concept can be measured by inviting subjects to rate the concept on a number of bipolar adjectival scales. Using factor analysis, Osgood has defined three dimensions of meaning—evaluation, potency, and activity.

Semantics. The relations between the symbols and the "reality" to which they refer.

Serial reproduction. Transmission of information from one person to another who, in turn, passes this message to a third person, and so on.

Syntax. The systematic analysis of the grammar of the process of communication.

Part four

Maintaining the organization's viability

Organizations as goal-seeking organisms have to adapt and learn in order to survive and prosper. This last section of our text begins with a discussion of organizational change and development and examines the special role that crisis plays in change. No organization can maintain its viability without looking to the future; so we end with an attempt to look at the beginning of tomorrow.

CHAPTER 16

Chapter 16 links change strategies to each of the major organization theories: the classical to structural changes; the human relations school to process changes; and the systems approach to integrated structure, process, and value changes through organizational development (O.D.). T group technology is the modus operandi of O.D. change. The most successful practitioners of O.D. using laboratory techniques are still R. R. Blake and J. S. Mouton, whose managerial grid fused behavioural science and corporate excellence; but much is expected of more recent developments such as Chris Argyris's intervention strategy and Edgar Schein's process consultation. Chapter topics are:

1. Change strategies.
2. From T group technology to organizational development.
3. Organizational development.
4. Process consultation and intervention strategy.
5. Organizational development in the future.

CHAPTER 17

Futurology is a major growth industry. Some research methods of looking at the future are the Delphi method, the scenario, computer simulation, and technological forecasting. A computer simulation predicting world catastrophe is examined in some detail. Other leads to the future corporate environment are provided by Herman Kahn, Anthony Wiener, John Kenneth Galbraith, and Harold Leavitt. We examine the impact of new information technologies on executive life, as well as on the organization; and take a look at the adhocracy as an organization style. Life style is also significant in the emergence of the counterculture; and we are led, finally, to consider the confrontation between systems man and existential man. Chapter 17 topics are:

1. Population, production, and pay.
2. The corporate environment, 1975–85.
3. The adhocracy.
4. The counterculture.
5. The futility of futurism.

16

Organizational change
and development

Like human beings, organizations are born, grow, mature, achieve
uniqueness, decline, and die. To be effective, executives must be sensitive
to the growth characteristics of their businesses; they must know what
stages of development their organizations have reached if they are going
to be able to predict the consequences of their policies. And if their predictions are going to have any validity whatsoever, they must be concerned with the organization's relation to its environment.

But—are organizations human? Are they another class of living things,
beings who have captured organization men, computers, data, energy,
matter, and markets—and made off with men's souls in the process? Possibly, if not probably. It is certainly worth pursuing the question further to
see how far the principle can be stretched.

Like man or any living system, an organization has an anatomy (structure), a physiology (processes), and a nervous system (a communication
network of people, computers, and linked data transmission equipment).
Organizations trade with their environment; they import such things as
matter, energy, and information, and export a product.

Health for an organization is measured by its ability to mobilize, develop, and operationalize the appropriate structures, processes, and values
to generate enough productivity and satisfaction. But production of what
and satisfaction for whom? The answers vary from year to year, day to
day, even from minute to minute. Effectiveness means innovation and
adaptation.

To get innovation means responding to the imperatives of technology and the pressures of the marketplace. Innovation means living dangerously, which means incentive payments to organizations in the form of profits. Guaranteeing profits means fixing the "fix": control of suppliers and manipulation of the market. To stay healthy the corporate organism must grow. And it does. In 1968, the 200 largest American corporations owned 60 per cent of manufacturing assets, up from 45 per cent in 1945.

To get growth the corporate amoeba, faced with overall uncertainty but governed by the need for rationality, engages in the generation of a complexity of subsystems, each of which operates under conditions of certainty or near certainty. A good example of this growth paradox of certainty-uncertainty has been provided by International Telephone and Telegraph, which was once the low-profile manager of telephone exchanges in South America and is now in hotels (Sheraton), car rentals (Avis), insurance (Continental), and home building (Levitt), as well as electronics, domestic and defence. Harold Geneen, president of ITT, a chartered accountant and a master of financial control, insisted on such elaborate and esoteric control procedures for subsidiaries and divisions that he was able to maintain the "fact-fiction" of increasing the return on investment for more than 20 quarters in a row. But the management of the certainty-uncertainty nexus took ITT into the political back yards of governments, including both the United States and Chile.

Organizations, like human beings, get sick, suffer from growing pains, and sometimes grow obese. They get flabby and have to be trimmed down by organization doctors. Darwin would have been delighted by how the law of natural selection works so swiftly to kill off new organizational strains; yet some, like the Catholic Church, have immense staying power. They have slick names that look impressive and mean business. Some even have a sex. Many carry on illicit relations that would make a polymorphous sexual pervert look normal. They combine with their competitors secretly, tie up with brothers and sisters, and deny the original ideology that gave them birth. In fact, one might say they would do anything for a buck.

The organization—the machine, the apparatus, the system, call it what you will—has all sorts of interesting human characteristics. At first sight, it looks amoral, but it isn't—it has morals somewhere; like human values, they are not always obvious or logical but they're there. Morals, mores, cultural values are the endocrines which keep the organization going while it figures out exactly what it should do.

Organizations have stereotypes about other organizations, although of course, they all work the same way. The Mafia, the Marines, IBM, General Motors, ITT, the Roman Catholic church, the Communist party, the Kennedys. They all work the same way—or do they?

In the corporate jungle, organizations are organivorous and live off the carrion of other organizations they have eliminated. Like Penn Central or Rolls-Royce, they can attempt suicide. But everybody loves and hates them, and they are usually resurrected, even if they have to have surgery afterwards, followed by marriage to a stronger cousin. Of course, they are completely agnostic and apolitical, neither for or against the establishment. They are proper social harlots. You just have to own them, rent them, invent them, or grow them. They'll work for anyone.

But are they human?

THE ORGANIZATIONAL CRISIS

The most striking point about organizational growth is that as an organization moves from stage to stage it experiences a sharp crisis. Organizations, like human beings, have a life cycle: they are born, find a name, stake out a territory and a function; they grow up a bit, go through the crisis of puberty as they fight to establish their stability and win a reputation for themselves; next they struggle for uniqueness and adaptability; only to be cast into the menopause, from which they emerge with the serenity of resignation to try to figure out their debt to society and what sort of contribution they can make.

Gordon L. Lippitt and Warren H. Schmidt, in "Crisis in a developing Organization," set out to study the crises which organizations go through. If their scheme of organizational growth (shown in Figure 16–1) is accepted, the critical issue in changing organizations becomes the management of crisis.

FIGURE 16–1
STAGES OF ORGANIZATIONAL DEVELOPMENT

Developmental stage	Critical concern	Key issues	Consequences if concern is not met
Birth	1. To create a new organization	What to risk	Frustration and inaction.
	2. To survive as a viable system	What to sacrifice	Death of organization. Further subsidy by "faith" capital.
Youth	3. To gain stability	How to organize	Reactive, crisis-dominated organization. Opportunistic rather than self-directing attitudes and policies.
	4. To gain reputation and develop pride	How to review and evaluate	Difficulty in attracting good personnel and clients. Inappropriate, overly aggressive, and distorted image building.
Maturity	5. To achieve uniqueness and adaptability	Whether and how to change	Unnecessarily defensive or competitive attitudes; diffusion of energy. Loss of most creative personnel.
	6. To contribute to society	Whether and how to share	Possible lack of public respect and appreciation. Bankruptcy or profit loss.

Change and luan

All systems, both physical and social, appear at different stages of development to be at different levels of equilibrium. Apparently, to move the system from one level to another demands a considerable quantum of energy. In physics, high-energy machines are used to smash the atomic nucleus. With social systems, powerful energy inputs are also needed to move from one level of equilibrium to another. For example electroshock therapy, which has been likened to simulated death, is still used (though somewhat infrequently in today's world of psychotherapeutic drugs) to shift the schizophrenic, who is locked in his own world of delusions, into a different and hopefully more realistic world.

This unfreezing aspect of the change process has attracted a growing number of clinical psychologists and psychiatrists in recent times. One such psychiatric theory is the theory of positive disintegration, which maintains that neuroses are not mental illnesses at all but may be better thought of as accelerated human developments. While few established psychiatrists would accept such a theory, many recognize that personality growth may be associated with the break-down of a particular self-concept. And presumably a change in personality is associated with or preceded by a state of self-alienation. Eric Erikson, we may recall, suggests that a moratorium or an in-between rest period of tranquility is required between each change.

The idea of unfreezing or breaking up structures is integral to the modern approach to organizational development, which essentially utilizes a process analysis. As we have noted, Edgar H. Schein developed this unfreezing-changing-refreezing model as a result of his experiences of studying both brainwashing techniques and the T group process, which puts its members in an unstructured social vacuum. The danger of this approach is, of course, that the unfreezing may be so traumatic that the individuals unscrambled may not be able to get themselves together again; or if they do, the actual integration achieved may be at a lower level of sophistication, relevance, and effectiveness. Undoubtedly this negative disintegration does happen from time to time in T groups, and even the most skilled trainer cannot completely avoid dysfunctional outcomes of this kind.

The curious thing about this unfreezing aspect of the change process is that not only can it be applied to individuals and groups but it also can be applied to societies. The most striking illustration of this unfreezing element in the change process has been provided by the study of the cultural revolution in China engineered by Mao Tse-tung, who has engineered a social happening without parallel in modern social history. This was a revolution by anarchy in which Chinese society was deliberately subjected to a trial by chaos. This chaos was begun by the Red Guards of Tsinghua

University, who set out to "turn the old world upside down, smash things into chaos, smash things *luan-luan-ti*, the more *luan* the better." Mao expressed the view that "a few months of *luan* will be mostly for the good and little harm will result from this confusion."

Luan is the Chinese word for chaos, and chaos spread all over China. It took a massive effort on the part of 30,000 Peking workers, unarmed and chanting, "Use reason, not violence; use reason, not violence," to bring the hysterical students of Tsinghua out from behind the barricades. Yet today many Chinese apparently regard the cultural revolution as the most profoundly moving experience of their lives.

Luan is nearly always present in organizational change, at least in the early changes. Experienced senior corporate executives seem to understand the need for occasional bouts of chaos. These executives also recognize and exploit external management consultants as political agents to facilitate and create *luan;* not infrequently, new, fresh, M.B.A.'s are employed as "Red Guards" to act as catalysts in the fermentation process. Inevitably, the M.B.A.'s (like their Chinese counterparts) come to a bloody end once they have served their purpose; and of course, consultants have a limited contract or life span. Therefore the freedom of operation and independence of action afforded most consultants may well be motivated, not necessarily by a spirit of scientific enquiry on the part of corporate officials, but rather by a spirit of benign neglect springing from intuitive knowledge of the need for a *luan*-generating role. For such corporate officials, a critical question is, will growth evolve into revolution?

PHASES OF GROWTH

In the midst of the current preoccupation with interpersonal relationships, personal growth, and self-actualization, it is important to remember that the overall organization structure may still be the most significant factor in determining the success of the enterprise. A. D. Chandler was the first to outline the importance of correlating organization structure with the business strategy of the firm; now Larry Greiner, building on the base established by Chandler, has advanced the intriguing view that organizational change is necessitated by an inevitable reaction to the historical structure of the firm. Unlike Chandler, Greiner does not feel that change is necessarily a planned concomitant of variations in business strategy which result from alterations in the economic and social environment of the firm. Rather it comes as a result of the stresses that business growth places on every kind of management structure.

Greiner describes five phases in the history of an organization's management practices—each one an outgrowth of problems which developed in the previous phase. The periods of turmoil when these problems come to a peak are described as revolution, while the intervening periods of relatively lengthy and peaceful growth are called evolution. The frequency of revolutionary change is felt to increase with the size of the organization and the growth rate of the industry in which it operates. Older organizations may have institutionalized practices which inhibit change, and high profits may defer the need for new structures. However, continued growth of the firm appears to lead inexorably to a need for changes in management practice. If these are not effected, decline and bankruptcy are predicted. Greiner's five phases are listed below.

Phase I: Creativity. A new firm is primarily concerned with producing its product and finding a market for it. Leadership is entrepreneurial and individualistic, communication is informal, and achievement is measured by market results and rewarded by ownership in the business. Successful growth leads, however, to a crisis of control as the leader is no longer able to fulfill the multiple demands on his time. This leads to Phase II.

Phase II: Direction. A formal, directive leadership is established to make operations efficient. Standards and cost centres are set up to control the organization, and rewards are given in the form of salary increases. Functional specialists are developed, but the centralized structure does not allow them to utilize their knowledge in the decision-making process. This leads to frustration and, if widespread dissatisfaction and turnover are to be avoided, the organization must move toward Phase III.

Phase III: Delegation. Operations are decentralized into geographic or product-oriented profit centres. Management is by exception, and rewards by individual bonus. Management often concentrates on new acquisition. The general reduction of communication leads to parochial attitudes and loss of control. Since the scope of the organization is too great for a return to centralized management, the next phase is co-ordination.

Phase IV: Co-ordination. Units are merged into product groups, and formal planning and co-ordinating systems are established by corporate staff groups. Review of capital expenditures and investment returns is used to control operations. Corporate incentives such as stock options are used as rewards. Conflict arises between line and staff and the organization becomes bound by red tape. To remain flexible enough to meet business needs, a new phase is entered.

Phase V: Collaboration. Formal control systems are replaced by emphasis on social control and self-discipline. Interpersonal behaviour skills are fostered to reduce the need for rigid communication channels. Cross-function teams are set up to handle project assignments, and the organization frequently develops a matrix type of structure. Rewards are geared to team achievement.

This type of structure may be considered to-day's ideal, but Greiner predicts that the psychological strain caused by the pressure for teamwork and innovation will force further revolutionary changes. His tentative solutions include job rotation, job interchangeability, sabbatical leaves, and the creation of a dual structure which would permit members to interchange reflective and executive tasks.

Greiner's thesis has considerable explanatory and practical usefulness. In focusing attention on the negative aspects of various management styles, he explains the disenchantment that seems to eventually follow even the most highly regarded new systems.

The concept of different phases of development explains why solutions which succeed in one organization often fail in another. By examining the historical pattern of the firm, management can better understand current problems and predict and plan for the actions that will be required in the future. Most important, by understanding the organizational consequences of a particular strategy, management can evaluate the strategy more accurately. The entrepreneur may elect to forgo growth in order to remain in control of the organization as he created it. Or, as L. E. Fouraker and J. M. Stopford point out, a firm may elect to remain in Phase II and concentrate on becoming more cohesive, integrated, and capital-intensive rather than taking on the problems of diversified growth. A realistic appraisal of organizational capabilities as well as environmental opportunities is required to maintain successful operation. By providing a theoretical framework for the practice of organizational change, Greiner has increased the probability of success in the organizational development effort.

An understanding of these stages of development will help managers to cope more effectively. But to cope with change, management has to focus on the rapidly changing quality of the environment. Change arising from computer technology and electronic technology (e.g., evaluating the opportunities and hazards of the hybrid domestic computer–copying machine–videotape recorder expected in the 1980s), the proliferation of rapid transit systems, the development of new managerial technologies, the growth of international trade, and the demand for ethnic and sexual equality are turning organizations upside down, shaking them all about, and making them do the twist. The more sophisticated managements are not prepared to wait it out and let such changes dominate them, but are entering into the spirit of the times and trying to exploit these change options.

In "Patterns of Organizational Change," Greiner has reviewed the common approaches to change along a "power distribution" continuum ranging from unilateral action (by decree, by replacement, by structure) to power sharing (group decision making and problem solving) to delegated authority (by case discussion, by T group sessions). Greiner sets out the success pattern for organizational change, which essentially assumes that (1) top management comes under considerable and growing pressure as performance falls off; (2) a new top man or a consultant is brought in and the agonizing reappraisal begins; (3) top management backs him as he gets everybody involved in fact-finding problem solving; and (4) slowly the whole change ethos spreads throughout the system. To facilitate such changes, behavioural scientists have invented powerful change strategies, known collectively as organizational development (O.D.), which utilize T group technology to facilitate change.

ORGANIZATIONAL GROWTH AND PLANNED CHANGE

Organizational growth is not spontaneous but is the result of careful planning and decision in an attempt to achieve an optimal state. Growth is achieved as customers demand a complete range of services or as new technologies are exploited, and also because companies which do not expand contract—they cannot stand still.

Some cynics regard the organizational growth concept as a cancer model and believe that unlimited and unsupervised prolific growth is bad for society. To their minds, if executives like to gamble on new activities which will enhance their prestige, power, and job security, they should start playing Monopoly. Critics of corporate growth are sustained by Parkinson's "easily expanded executive empire" thesis and by Peter's aphorism that "an executive is promoted to his own level of incompetence." Organizations, in this cynical view, represent a coalition of managers, workers, stockholders, suppliers, and customers; and when the firm's survival is not the crucial issue, the managers, who are the dominant force, operate the organization to optimize their own utility function, which emphasizes salaries and staff while satisfying the stockholders and the workers. Further organizational growth facilitates stability, as large organizations face a more stable environment than small ones.

Adaptation and growth

The organization cannot grow unless it goes through what Schein has called the "adaptive-coping cycle." When the enterprise is faced with changes in the environment, either external or internal, which upset its equilibrium, the organization has to respond to this change. Adaptation is a clear prerequisite for survival, and survival a clear prerequisite for growth.

Growth depends on the organization's ability to exploit opportunities created by environmental change. Planned organizational growth is the process of initiating, creating, and confronting such environmental changes so that the organization becomes more viable.

Planned change

But if an executive is going to play his full role and not be an innocent bystander watching change take place, he will want to know what behavioural scientists have to say about directing and implementing change. Such a theory must recognize the following factors:

1. Organizations go through different stages of development in their growth; these stages can be identified and managed.
2. The shift from one stage to another is associated with a crisis. These crises can be exploited and controlled.
3. Energy inputs are needed to facilitate change.
4. It is necessary to identify where the energy in the system is located and what levers control the flow of energy. Change is a function of power, and the powerful have influence.
5. Particular organizational structures favour assimilation of new technical ideas.
6. Change is not always resisted. There is an optimal level of change which people and organizations can handle.
7. Change has been facilitated by the emergence of a new profession known as organizational development; O.D. consultants specialize in the art of facilitating change by using behavioural science concepts, methods, and technology.

STRUCTURE OF CHAPTER 16

Five topics are considered in this chapter. Our first topic reviews change strategies from three different theoretical optics. The first optic, classical theory, represents an essentially structural approach where change is achieved, for example, by revising organization charts, role descriptions, and policy statements. The second optic, the human relations approach, represents an attempt to introduce participative management and is essentially concerned with process. The systems optic utilizes the model of unfreezing, changing, and refreezing and involves the use of power equalization and T group technology.

Topic 2 takes us from T group technology to organizational development. The aim here is to explain how T groups began and to get some insight into their effectiveness and dysfunctions. In this topic, the subject of videotape recording (VTR) is also considered.

Our third topic is organizational development or O.D. We begin the subject by setting out its assumptions, which include the fact that O.D. represents training the system by changing corporate posture, perspective, and process, all through the use of T group technology. One particular O.D. strategy, the managerial grid, is discussed in considerable detail.

Topic 4 deals with process consultation and intervention strategy, which have been developed primarily by E. H. Schein and C. Argyris, respectively. These new strategies—which make use of confrontation, but only after carefully defining the psychological contract and collecting actual data—are compared to the revolutionary tactics of dissident students.

Topic 5 looks forward to the role of O.D. in the future, and an attempt is made to explain O.D. in the metaphor of the theatre.

TOPIC 1
Change strategies

Modern change strategies owe much to the young Karl Marx, who asserted that the point is to change the world and not merely to interpret it. Change advocates intuitively accept and act on a dialectical or critical conception of knowledge and truth. A description of the status quo is only a necessary preliminary to changing it.

Corporate change agents need a dialectical imagination which can comprehend the organizational world, not only as it is but as it could be. "Is" and "ought" are dialectically interlocked in an imperative for change. Research is defined as a form of action. To get into action means that the change agent gets involved in the actual change; action and knowledge are inextricably one. In this transactional paradigm, participation becomes both a prerequisite and a prerogative, and people discover both their potential and power: their potential for growth and self-actualization and their power to break boundaries, laws, and promises without perishing in the process. Participation, potential, and power make a shambles of the traditional means-ends schema.

This is a value-loaded science of change which pays but scant heed to the value-free world of traditional behavioural science—the ever-decreasing microcosm of "all I want is the facts." In organizations there are no "facts" that are sterile, clean, pure, untouched by the human hand. Everything is contaminated by human values. Rather than resenting this human contamination, the effective change agent develops his dialectical imagination by seeking to combine action and thought in trying to change organizations in a systematic way.

STAGES OF CHANGE

The principal stages of change are organizational diagnosis, implementation, and evaluation. As shown in Figure 16–2, each stage has critical steps. Diagnosis involves, first, searching for and *identifying* significant organizational problems. From his general analysis, a change agent should be able to isolate specific problems, assess the magnitude and direction of each problem identified, and attach to each problem a measure of relative importance. Second, he must *diagnose* the nature of the problem and its significant dimensions through a sound and methodical approach, and bring to bear the important aspects of relevant disciplines. Third, the change agent *formulates alternatives*, devising a reasonably comprehensive set of viable solutions.

The stage of implementation involves *developing decision rules* to judge the relevance and appropriateness of a particular solution. The change

FIGURE 16–2
STAGES OF CHANGE

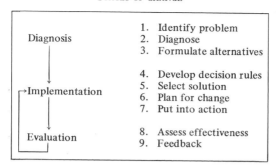

	1. Identify problem
Diagnosis	2. Diagnose
	3. Formulate alternatives
	4. Develop decision rules
Implementation	5. Select solution
	6. Plan for change
	7. Put into action
Evaluation	8. Assess effectiveness
	9. Feedback

agent must be competent to choose and justify the set of criteria used. He then *selects* an optimum solution consistent with the criteria. Working out the implications of his decision, he *plans* the change and then *puts it into action.*

The final stage is evaluation of the change. This involves *assessing* the effectiveness of the programme in achieving objectives. *Feedback* is essential to evaluation, and is used to make necessary adaptations in the further implementation of the change process.

These stages need fleshing out with consideration of techniques, processes, and possible pitfalls, as outlined in the following sections.

DIAGNOSIS

Organizational diagnosis is essentially concerned with the identification, delineation, and definition of the specific problems (issues, challenges, opportunities), their causes, consequences, and likely effect on the organization's viability. Most executives are so closely integrated with the corporate tissue that they find it difficult, if not impossible, to come up with answers that group symptoms into meaningful patterns. In fact executives given to making diagnoses are seen by their colleagues as engaging in special pleading and are usually thrown into states of guilt and anxiety.

A fantastic variety of diagnostic techniques is currently in use, including observation (e.g., attending management meetings), interviewing (e.g., ask two representatives of each department, "How do you feel about the present crisis in your department?"), and examination of documents (e.g., newspaper reports, annual reports, policy papers, minutes of meetings). While O.D. specialists use all of these methods, most have a penchant for particular techniques such as questionnaires, surveys, confrontation meetings, or T groups. The questionnaire survey—using scales like those used by Rensis Likert, which scale organizations on several dimensions like authority, communication, and leadership—is widely used to pigeon-hole the organization as to whether it corresponds to Likert's System 1, 2, 3 or 4.

Diagnosis is essentially concerned with establishing a bank of reliable and reasonably valid data about the state of the organization which reflects a variety of sources, levels, and optics.

IMPLEMENTATION

Increasingly, corporate executives are making a conscious, deliberate, and collaborative effort to introduce change. Basically such executives are trying to link organization theory into strategic planning, operational handling, and tactical activities. In terms of strategy, goals or objectives have to be defined; operationally, a well-defined line of approach must be worked out; and tactically, a sequence of detailed steps will have to be invented to facilitate progress along operational vectors.

This plan for change must fit the organizational diagnosis. For instance, if the basic problem appears to be one of destructive conflict among students, faculty, and administrators arising out of three separate socio-occupational systems that are out of contact, it is hardly sufficient to set a general goal of "increased communication." Likewise "sending people on courses" is unlikely to be successful. What are needed are new structures of government; different processes of consultation, decision, and appeal; and new, overlapping value sets. It is unlikely that the changes in structure, process, and values can be kept in balance, so inevitably resistance will be encountered. Only careful tactical planning will overcome such resistance.

The most important thing to know about the planning of change is that it is not so much a programme as a process. Change is a process where diagnosis, formulation of alternatives, implementation, and evaluation succeed and interact with each other without reaching a full stop. The process is both iterative and participative.

Planning, to be participative, must allow "the people being planned" to input their ideas into the body of planning. This kind of *planification*, as the French term it, calls for continuous dialogue, *animation sociale*, negotiation, and bargaining among interest groups. Planning is both a technical and a political process. As a political process, change advocates have to know what it takes to make a planning decision legitimate, who can vote, how polling is to take place, what counts as a mandate for (or veto against) action, who has to be paid off or allowed to mislead himself. Rarely, of course, does planning for change involve actual voting—but many are polled in some form of consultation. Planning for change is a collaborative, democratic, and iterative process; it establishes a basis of legitimacy for modes of action that facilitate the mobilization of the power centres of an organization to maintain its viability and adaptability to changes in the environment.

Plans must be implemented to be meaningful. The plan must clearly state who, what, where, when, how, and how much. Getting into action with a plan for change can be a real hassle, especially if the top brass have not been properly sold on the problem, perspective, and prospects. Top management is unlikely to introduce large-scale changes unless they feel themselves under intense pressure. Given this level of tension, the change advocate will have to show real human relations skill in helping his senior colleagues to handle their tensions and anxieties.

EVALUATION

When change agents are allocating resources to the three major stages of change, they should budget a little extra for the follow-up. Once the change is underway, there is a real danger of slacking off in terms of effort. Did the plan work out? To what extent were the objectives reached? What dysfunctions were generated? Assessment may require the employment of fairly sophisticated statistical experimental designs with control groups to ascertain if a real change took place. At least the opinions of participants should be polled.

Changing is a way of life in organizations, and trying to answer a question usually generates more questions than answers. All questions concerned with evaluation turn around the basic issue, "What are managers trying to achieve by planned change?"

OBJECTIVES OF CHANGE

As Kurt Lewin once observed: if you want to understand some social system, try to change it. Thus it frequently happens that management's feel for new organizational structure, process, or values only emerges after the start of an intensive change strategy.

But what are managers trying to achieve by change? What are their objectives? Twenty years ago, the answer would have been relatively simple. The aim of change could have been stated in terms of increased profitability and productivity, which typically could be achieved by the installation of new management techniques such as work study, production planning and control, budgetary control, or perhaps by redesigning the organizational structure and rewriting role descriptions. This approach to change essentially presumes the use of the classical model.

In the human relations phase, the aim of change was to change attitudes, improve motivation, and raise morale, but again in the hope that such psychological changes would enhance task effectiveness.

In the systems approach, the aim is changes in the organization's level of adaptation to its environment through changes in the internal behavioural system. Thus because of the turbulence of the environment and its built-in uncertainties, management is continuously involved in the process of making internal organizational changes which represent a reaction to such factors as rising competition, rapid technological change, changing social values, and new government legislation. The internal change in the system approach is largely related to information-processing and decision-making behaviour and is concerned with changing ideology. Instead of shooting directly for behaviour change, the aim is to achieve a change in ideology (values and norms) which in turn will change executive life styles, which will, of necessity, require changes in behaviour.

FIGURE 16-3
MODEL FOR STUDYING ORGANIZATIONAL CHANGE

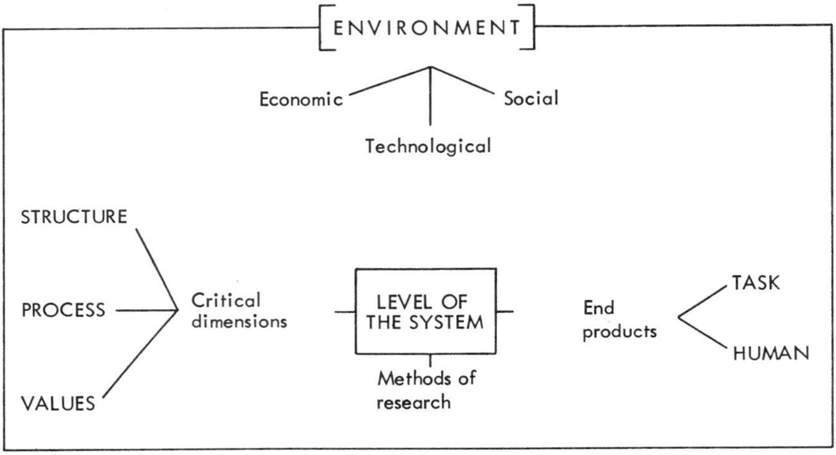

ANALYSING ORGANIZATIONAL CHANGE

Organizational change can be approached from a large number of optics. A quick glance at Figure 16–3 will suggest a variety of perspectives for processes of change based on our system model. The following sections emphasize in particular the influence of structure, process, values, and the environment.

STRUCTURAL OPTIC

Structural changes are introduced by modifying the organization chart and rewriting job descriptions; spelling out new formal guide-lines and procedures; clarifying such matters as delegation, staff work, and line-functional relations; and development of more extensive, pervasive, and penetrating control techniques such as production planning and control, budgetary control, and so on. Essentially what is being changed is the structure, that is, the communications and authority network. Also included under structural changes are such issues as centralization versus decentralization.

The structural optic has been the major mechanism of the classical theory management consultant of the 1940s and 1950s, who earned his fees (and our anguish) by coming up, after careful study, with a new organization chart optimizing such matters as the number of hierarchical levels (five in medium-sized and seven in medium-sized-plus firms), the span of control (3 at the top, 15 at the bottom), committee structures, flow process charts, and incentive plans. At the shop floor level, sophisticated forms of work study such as methods time measurement (MTM) were developed. The curious thing about these early structural strategies were that they worked in spite of their formal, legalistic, military-based, abstract, theological, and inadequately empirical character. Why? Ultimately, presumably because such structural changes were consonant with what the people of the industrial societies of the 1940s and 1950s believed.

In retrospect, the values which emphasized achievement, affluence, aggression, independence, and postponement of consumption seem archaic. They are essentially class-loaded, male chauvinistic, tied to an economy of scarcity, imperialistic, and self-destructive. But these same values created the new technological postindustrial society, where the existential ethic is now appropriate.

Integral to the structural approach is the presumption that the initiative for change lies with the most powerful at the top of the hierarchy. As Larry Greiner of the Harvard Business School has pointed out, such structural changes involve unilateral action, where the change is achieved by decree or fiat and the option of replacement (firing and hiring) is always there. But the modern approach to structural change is quite different. Armed with the new contingency theory of organization, behavioural scientists are taking a leaf out of J. W. Lorsch and Paul R. Lawrence's *Studies in Organizational Design* and proposing sets of rules which will help executives to choose the one ideal organizational design. The presumption in the contingency approach is that if certain environmental, technological, and preferred outcomes (both task and human) can be identified, then the best form of organizational structure can be determined. Much of this ground was covered in Chapter 2 when we reviewed the work of Thomas Burns and G. M. Stalker and of J. Woodward. Lorsch and Lawrence have refined the analysis by arguing that corporate success requires an optimal mix of differentiation and integration consistent with the demands of the environment—information uncertainty, length of feedback time, technological complexity, market factors. But such exercises are largely descriptive of actualities. What happens when a behavioural scientist tries to act prescriptively in setting up new organizational designs?

The first point to note is that few behavioural scientists are involved in organizational design. Contemporary organizations are not job-enriched, Theory Y, participative, System 4, decentralized organic structures constantly locked in suboptimization exercises deciding between corporate excellence and existential hell. Corporate behavioural scientists are involved largely in putting on theatrical, training, and therapeutic happenings which can be useful, entertaining, and even enlightening nonevents. These non-events include management by objectives, attitude surveys, T groups, early parts of the grid, and motivation-hygiene. They can be magnificent, but they are not corporate war; that is reserved for a different kind of person, the tough, pragmatic, experienced, and trusted executive. Now behavioural scientists are working with executives to formulate new design answers. With a contingency approach, they can be useful.

It is useful at this juncture to summarize why the structural optic was successful and why it has now largely fallen into disuse. The successes of the structural change arose because:

1. It clarified organization structure, specifying information flows, and identified decision nodes, spelling out who should do what and who should be held accountable for what.
2. It focused on performance and quantitative measures of achievement by continually evolving control techniques.
3. It developed a common language which facilitated communication. This language both assumed and reinforced the classical value system.
4. It harnessed the scientific method to problem solving, which facilitated the development of operations research.
5. It spelled out the values for managerial talent, who could make progress once they knew the "score."

The structural approach fell into disuse because:

1. It represented an essentially one-shot treatment.
2. The underlying behavioural science model of man was too simplistic.
3. The actual process of change was not understood. Many of the changes were caused by the intervention, not by the specific structural recommendations.
4. The method was out of kilter with the values of the postindustrial society.
5. Human engineering ensured that Taylorism was designed into the machines. For example, the design of the controls of modern cars, aircraft, and engineering machines increasingly compels the operator to employ the safest and most efficient procedures.
6. Ultimately and fundamentally, the model of organization employed was irrelevant when compared to the systems approach, which presumes an existential information-processing optic.

In brief, the structural approach was right for its time, but probably its effectiveness arose mostly from defining standards of performance, reinforcement of the prevailing culture, the actual intervention process, and pointing out the road to the top managerial talent. Basically, successful structural strategies emerged not primarily from freezing organizational structures but rather from the method of introducing change. It was not what you did, but how you did it—and, more important, who did what with whom—that counted. Thus a critical factor in introducing change is the actual change process.

PROCESS OPTIC

The process is the actual sequence of organizational events. In the process approach to change, the seminal conception has emerged from the three-step model proposed by Kurt Lewin: unfreezing, changing, refreezing. Integral to this model is the notion that behavioural and attitudinal change follow a basic sequence.

FIGURE 16–4
THE CHANGE PROCESS

	UNFREEZING	CHANGING	REFREEZING
Goal	Inappropriate	Generalized	Specific
Social relations	Break-up	New and tenuous	New, reinforced
Self-esteem	Anxiety, tension	Growth	New integration
Motive for change	External	External/internal	Internal

Figure 16–4 models this basic sequence. Unfreezing must be understood as a process of mobilizing frustration, increasing tension, and fostering disintegration and dependency. Change is thus made possible by the disintegration of old and inappropriate group relations, behaviour patterns, and life styles. The crux of the changing phase is facilitating the group formulation of new goals, strategies, and processes relevant to its needs and aspirations. These processes maximize participation, enhance authenticity, and improve communication flow. The refreezing phase is essentially concerned with the reintegration of system forces through the formulation of a new set of rules, roles, and relations. In the refreezing phase, a new set of values, norms, reinforcements, and sanctions is confirmed and internalized.

Before this paradigm of change can be invoked and operationalized it is necessary for a considerable level of tension to exist in the system. Thus change may well require as an antecedent condition a fair amount of extant organizational tension. Typically, substantial levels of tensions have been generated by some technological failure, economic change, or a merger, and this energy mobilization is what the consultant or the change agent seeks to exploit. Much evidence has already been produced in regard to the importance of tension, anxiety, and guilt as facilitants of change from studies of subjects in psychotherapy, managers in T groups, and prisoners of war.

A second requirement for successfully induced change is that the change agent who initiates the process must be seen as a respected, trusted, competent executive or professional who has the necessary experience and power-manipulation skills to facilitate the change. Thus typically when change programmes are being introduced, it is optimal to begin at the top and then (counting on top management's support) set about changing middle and lower management. For example, in the Harlow studies, the behavioural scientists had the support and active backing of the president; and in the Glacier studies in England, Elliott Jaques of the Tavistock Institute had Wilfred Brown, the managing director of the Glacier company, behind him.

FIGURE 16–5
SUCCESS PATTERN OF CHANGER-CHANGEE RELATION

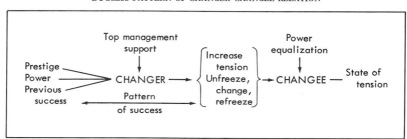

In brief, there is considerable evidence to support the proposition that there is a link between prestige and influence. Research work in clinical psychology suggests that even brief contacts with a prestigious psychiatrist can have therapeutic effects for patients. Presumably this "hail and farewell" effect has a correlate in process consultancy, where important organizational clients are prepared to pay large fees to have a distinguished consultant pay infrequent and brief visits to their organizations. Figure 16–5 indicates how a consultant or change agent establishes a successful pattern.

The mention of "power equalization" in Figure 16–5 is a reminder that the process optic has gone through distinct historical phases in its approach to people. The earlier phase, associated with the human relations movement, was essentially manipulative in character and dealt with such matter as, "How can we get people to do, feel, and act as we want them to?" and "How can we get them to do our thing without even being aware of it?" The Dale Carnegie *How to Win Friends and Influence People* approach typifies this phase. Salesmen given this kind of training boasted that they could "sell refrigerators to Eskimos." The second phase was closer to the legitimate social science approach of process consultation; but even in this phase, some behavioural scientists regard techniques for "overcoming resistance to change" as essentially manipulative in character.

But more recent efforts in process consultancy utilize a power equalization (P.E.) model, where it is recognized that the changee will achieve a more stable, appropriate, and adaptive change if he has an equal share of power with the changer. The aim is not to solve a problem (i.e., achieve a specific structural solution) but to assist the system to grow in a responsive and responsible way to the environment.

An excellent illustration of a ´technique which facilitates P.E. is the T group, where the trainer becomes a "resource person" who is an expert on group process but is not committed to a particular substantive change. The basic core of group development through T groups is the renunciation of traditional authority and dependency and all its works and pomps. The T group, by virtue of its very lack of structure, facilitates a rapid movement through the phases of unfreezing, changing, and refreezing; it demands a degree of subversiveness, which may well include the rejection of the leader, as the group finds its reality in the testing of new rules, roles, and relations. Thus P.E. has become a crucial ingredient in any collaborative process for achieving planned change.

Summing up, the advantages of the process optic include the following:

1. The use of a specific model, unfreezing-changing-refreezing.
2. An experimental, probing attitude which does not lock the system to a specific solution.
3. The use of a prestigious, successful, charismatic change agent.
4. The use of power equalization, which maximizes participation.
5. The use of T group technology to establish group dynamics principles.
6. The exploitation of tension, frustration, and anxiety.

The disadvantages include:

1. Uncertainty in regard to desired end states.
2. A possibility of exploitation and manipulation of people.
3. A failure to integrate the information science approach.
4. Insufficient attention to structured solutions to problems such as those suggested by modern decision theory and path-goal strategies.

The real trick is to use process tactics to achieve structural solutions to organizational problems. Structural solutions are likely to emerge from the on-going research which utilizes the path-goal paradigm.

Value optic

The value optic approach to change presupposes that new values are imported into the system which in turn have a significant effect on changing structure and process. Many organizations typically achieve value changes by introducing personnel who have been exposed to a different culture. For example, value changes in organizations are frequently achieved by introducing M.B.A.'s from different schools according to the predilection of top management.

This type of value assimilation represents an interesting example of the prefigurative culture, where the older members of a system learn and acquire life styles from the younger members of the system. Presumably the new existential systems approach to organizations will percolate into institutions through the new generation of M.B.A.'s.

ENVIRONMENTAL OPTIC

It seems wholly convincing to believe that the major source of change will come from environmental changes. The picture of turbulence in the environment developed by F. E. Emery and E. L. Trist seems eminently appropriate to contemporary society. For example, the major change in organizational theory and thinking that has emerged in the last 20 years is the reaction to and exploitation of the possibilities of high-speed, large-scale data processing made possible by the computer. Such technological changes are accelerating.

But not only do organizations have to cope with technological change, they have to be responsive to economic changes as well. Economic changes such as balance of payment problems, levels of unemployment and inflation, and variations in international trade—to say nothing of anti-trust legislation and energy shortages—often have a decisive effect on organizational change.

The other great environmental factor is the social fabric of which the organization is a part. We are currently witnessing a drastic change in social values in regard to the rights of minority groups (including the "majority minority," women) which will have far-flung consequences for organizations.

For our purposes, the existence of such powerful and pervasive change elements in the environment points up the need for organizations to make a fetish of the change ethic. A major tool in the change ethic is the T group, the subject of Topic 2.

TOPIC 2
From T group technology to organizational development

The use of T group technology marked a decisive turning point in the search for change strategies which management could exploit to make things happen the way they wanted in business. In the T group, people gather in seclusion under the guidance of a resource person, usually a psychologist, who refuses to give direction or leadership in the expected sense. There are no rules, no agenda, and the people in this planned vacuum develop from a bunch of strangers into a real group. In the process they "rediscover the wheel" of group dynamics. The three R's of group life—rules, roles, and relations—become obvious by direct experience, and different life styles become clearer.

These "laboratory groups" who meet in a "social island"—a residential setting away from the hurly-burly of business—dissect their own behaviour and critically explore their own perceptions, attitudes, and roles in an effort to find out what is happening in the "here and now" situation. There are no rules of procedure. The optimistic hope is that the participant will reveal his life style. Using this mode of training, the perceptive executive should improve in a dramatic way through understanding and insight into his own behaviour and becoming aware of its effects on others. The rationale is that in a structured social vacuum the autocratic type will sound bossy, the submissive type will be seen to give way to argument, and the hostile type will be exposed for what he is.

T group training has been described as "a learning experience for normals," the presumption being that the really neurotic or psychotic person is too engrossed in his own hang-ups to understand the other person's problem. Ever since the film "Bob and Carol and Ted and Alice," the title human potential movement, to use a more generic name, has been gaining increasing recognition at the expense of the more sensational terms— encounter group, "the bod biz," the acidless trip. The *cri de coeur* of the movement is "no man is an island," and the supposition is that nobody can define himself without an examination of the web of relations and exchanges between one man and all the others in his life.

HOW TO SURVIVE IN A T GROUP

The promise of the T group is that people can learn to be more loving, honest, creative, zestful, joyous, responsive, trusting, responsible, open, compassionate, integrated, complete, and alive! The basic underlying assumption is that most people have untapped, often unsuspected, potential for richer, fuller lives; and on the negative side, that life in the seventh decade of the 20th century is strangling the human being inside all of us.

The T group is part of the human potential movement, which has emerged to provide man with a new type of behavioural science–religious experience to counter the terrible and pervasive loneliness of our new, mobile, nonhostile urban society. We may, with 20th-century communications technology, live in the global village, with almost instant replay of man's first step on the moon and the assassination of a President; but we find ourselves isolated from the man next door or the fellow in the office across the hall.

Many executives and professionals, brought up on the proposition, "If you can't beat 'em, join 'em," are disappointed at being the vehicles of old-fashioned Calvinist values with their emphasis on achievement and acquisition, and are vaguely seeking a higher level of awareness and authenticity. Many middle-class people are vaguely troubled about the lack of a moral consensus; unable to pinpoint the source of their malaise, they still experience a sense of being up-tight and bewildered.

What the T group does not set out to do is to make participants better adjusted—which frequently, in our increasingly faceless society, is just another name for some form of conformity—but it does set out to confront a person with his own existence. The aim of the T group is simply to get people to turn on; to turn on to other people, but most important of all to turn on to themselves. By "getting in touch" they hope to achieve intimacy, trust, and awareness, all through candour.

A T group is a gathering, sometimes for a few hours, sometimes for up to 14 days, of between a dozen and a score of normal, responsible people who have come together to discover "where it's at." Mostly they have never met before; but soon, at least in the successful groups, they are turned on physically, emotionally, and sometimes sexually.

T groups, or encounter groups, differ from therapy groups. To encounter-group man, therapy is concerned with the historical roots of behaviour—with personal archaeology and museum pieces—whereas the encounter group deals with the immediate here and now and, what's more, spells out what to do about it. Therapy groups rebuild; encounter groups educate.

THE OBJECTIVES OF THE T GROUP

The objectives of the T group include:

1. To give members an insight into their own personality dynamics—not only their anxieties, obsessions, and defences, but also their creative strengths, such as the value of a strong ego in a well-integrated person.

2. To facilitate insight into the interpersonal process (for example, how others react to them); to develop listening skills; and to identify, extend, and utilize stereotypes.

3. To make members aware of the group process, particularly how groups grow and develop and how roles emerge, and generally to get a better understanding of the three R's of the group—rules, roles, and relations.

4. To help members to accept a more realistic understanding of conflict, especially how conflict can be managed; to get a better understanding of the fact that not everybody in the group shares the same objectives, commands the same resources, or believes in the same values, and that they are not equally vulnerable or powerful. Above all, the hope is to bring the member face to face with his own stereotype.

5. To enable members to step out of their own frozen role positions and look existentially at the choices that face them.

6. To accept oneself and others as they basically are and to try not to manipulate them, but rather to adopt a supportive attitude in helping others to look at themselves and make their own decisions.

WHAT HAPPENS IN THE T GROUP

But this discussion of the purposes of the T group seems very remote to the neophyte as he steps into his group. For a start, what is the trainer up to? He seems to have surrendered his responsibilities in refusing to give the group the direction it so earnestly craves. At the outset, the group is faced with unusual freedom, and as a result considerable anxiety is generated. Members are scared and apprehensive. Complaints are made. But participants have to face the fact that there is no structure except that which they generate themselves.

In any case, group members begin to do and say things. The salient tactic of this type of training is for the participant to analyse and understand this behaviour, but it is behaviour of the *here and now*. It is not the behaviour of the *there and then*, so beloved of the psychoanalyst, which the group deals with, but what is happening right now.

The strange thing is that in spite of the anxieties and ambivalence of the situation, participants begin to express themselves about how they feel about things in general and, as they gain more experience, about each other. At this stage of the group's development, it can be readily understood that much of what is said may be negative, either about other members or the leader.

GROUND RULES

At the beginning of the T group, what the trainer is trying to get the group to agree to is that helping the group to formulate a programme works best if participants are:

Open. Members should express themselves freely about their own feelings and behaviour as well as those of others. If you are open, it will surprise other members and may well lead them to . . .
Reciprocate. Honest expression of opinion on personal matters usually invokes some kind of reaction. This will work best if you . . .
Level with one another. If you don't say what you feel, other people will be aware of it in some way. This will work better if there exists . . .
Trust. At the beginning you will have to take it on faith that this is an effective learning process. In any case you are encouraged to . . .
Bet. Pitch what you want to say at the right level. Control your level of candour. Get your risk strategy in perspective.

When the ground rules have been discussed, members of the group are given the task of identifying their needs so that the programme can be custom-built around them.

HANG-UPS

A word about anxiety. Everybody experiences anxiety. Nobody should be ashamed of this. Without anxiety no one could survive. Real anxiety is what alerts us to the physical and social dangers in our society. A man without fear is a fool. Neurotic anxiety is related to irrational fears. Try thinking about the following statement: "A few people are psychotic nearly all of the time, a larger number are neurotic most of the time, and everybody is neurotic some of the time." Anyway—who would want to be well-adjusted to the kind of environment we have produced?

We are living in a postindustrial society where people have no mythology to handle the guilt generated by the crises of our times. We are in the process of inventing a new mythology and a new language which will allow us to relate ourselves to the meaningful crises of our lives. Ours is an age of angst because we are caught between two systems: one that is going and one that hasn't yet arrived. The one that is going is based on respectability, hard work, keep to yourself, a buck is your best friend—all in an environment "where men worked and women wept" to keep the wolf from the door. If things were bad in this world, they would be better in the next; and at least there was the comaraderie of fighting for jam tomorrow, if not jam to-day. And now, when the jam has arrived, where are we? We are all like the hero of the movie "Joe," looking agog at the younger generation who are coming on strong, who never did a hard day's work in their lives, who never wonder where the next meal is coming from, but who are turned on, tuned in, and having a ball, untrammelled by conflict. They are switched on but freaked out of the value system we inherited, once accepted, and now cannot justify. They may or may not be worth following, but they are front runners of something which hasn't arrived. Meanwhile, at the T group we are the guys caught in between. As Rollo May put it, "We are at a point of historical change where one age is dying and the other has not yet been born."

In the T group you are going to talk about your anxieties. So you might as well get ready. What kind of anxieties have you got going for you? Are you hung up with having too much aggression? You may think, "Hell, that's nothing! Aggression is really useful in our society." But does it worry you that your aggression might get out of hand and you might destroy yourself? What's it for, anyway? What are you scared of?

Maybe aggression is not your bag. What is it? Is it that you give way too easily when the other guy starts to apply pressure? That's not too bad—some people have to comply to allow our system to work. But is what scares you what you might do one day in this situation? Yes, you might. . . .

If you haven't got a hang-up, you had better invent one, because the group will give you one anyway. Before you invent or discover your own hang-up, it might be useful to remind yourself of the objectives of the T group.

Handling Criticism

As the group first comes together, the statement of objectives may look like a pretty formidable list. If members are honest and level with one another, a good deal of criticism is going to be flying around. A question you should put to yourself is, "How should I respond to being criticized?" You have probably evolved your own strategy and tactics for responding to criticism, but let's try a different tack.

For starters, how do you react to being criticized in the back-home situation, at work? Do you fly off the handle because it seems unjust? What do your colleagues say about you? Do you know? Is there some pattern or thread running through their comments? Maybe you don't get any criticism. What does this tell you about your level of work, your risk taking, or the power relationship?

In any case, for the record, most people react badly to criticism (I do, myself). They overreact or they withdraw. Overreaction in an organizational context is frequently quite a good strategy—at least it gives the other guy some feedback, makes him realize you are not going to take it lying down, and usually concentrates his mind wonderfully. Anyway it may be expected of you and its absence may make your detractor feel guilty. You can hope that an honest reaction will allow a statement of different positions to be worked out. Probably, in the work situation, the best advice is to hang in and see what happens. And if you don't get a complete mental blockage when you get hit, you can usually figure out the ground rules: join the game and have a bit of fun.

But in the T group, which is a new point of departure, a number of different strategies are open to you. Say one member of your group comes after you for always intellectualizing; how should you react? Nobody can really advise you as to the best answer.

It is probably best to try to keep your cool, act like a masochist, and listen carefully to what your critic is saying. Try to figure it out. Is he trying to get at you or, more hopefully, is he really puzzled by what you have said? If you feel his judgement is not valid, ask the other members for their perceptions. Usually by then they have something to go on and can give you an opinion. Try to evaluate the situation again; and above all, try to get the group to help you.

Of course it doesn't always work out. Sometimes you feel you are taking a pounding to no good effect. In this case, you'll have to try some other strategy. A useful point to keep in mind is that "the rating tells you as much about the rater as the ratee." For example, if someone tells you that you are too clinical, that you have been playing Perry Mason, it would seem reasonable to suppose that he or somebody else feels that they have been probed in an unsympathetic way. It is probably best to accept this criticism at face value—if you think it has some validity. Responding with, "Yes, you are right. How does it affect you?" may help you to gain useful insights.

But nobody will be able to handle criticism in a completely rational fashion. Adrenalin levels are going to go flying up. You will see all sorts of odd adjustments and you will make some of them yourself. Some members are going to withdraw within themselves, others are going to pound the table, a few are going to burst into tears. That's one of the major reasons for having a professional trainer: to insure that nobody gets hurt more than they can take and to make sure the whole thing keeps going as a learning experience.

After all, you will probably go wrong if you allow yourself to get hung up on this criticism thing; it is the big picture that counts—what's happening in the group overall.

GROWTH OF YOUR GROUP

Meanwhile, back at the farm, your group is emerging. The members have been battling with a task as if they were suffering from amnesia—trying to figure out who they are. As they begin to get glimpses, people take up their roles. Old Papa Freud is there, playing out the therapist: "Yes, yes. That's very interesting. Do people often affect you like that? Has it been going on for long?" And Papa Hemingway is there too, shooting the breeze, being upright and handsome, free from all taint, following the good extraverted life: "Nobody in here needs your psychotherapy." Often some woman with more than just a whiff of nymphomania is nonverbally promising to make it with all the guys rather than trying to solve her problems. Father figures, mother figures, guys who make like Bogart, old hippies, hard-nosed WASP's—all are there. But somewhere out there, there are human beings. As the time goes on, the many skins of the persona are peeled aside, and people come to accept themselves as they really are.

But what a crisis it is to get there (see Box 16.1). When the group is really going, it has escaped from its original floundering around, settled, established ground rules, psyched out the trainer, and got to work on itself. Once the group gets to this stage, it becomes a real ego trip; members can't believe how much they really like, almost love, each other.

THE DEEP-FREEZE PRESSURE COOKER

Is there an overall scenario for the T group?

The trainers often picture the process as unfreezing—changing—refreezing. This is probably an optimistic oversimplification. Certainly, at the beginning of the exercise people are apprehensive but expectant; but expectant of what, they just don't know. T groups have been enveloped in myth and mystery, and nobody seems to be able to transmit their essence in any rational way. (Maybe you have guessed this already.) If at the beginning of the group you ask members what they expect, the most common and honest answer is, "You tell us what we are getting." So much for that start.

The group is apprehensive and the trainer will not give them the direction they want. In the first part of the T group, the trainer will "introduce his personality" to the group. This still puzzles the group. Usually trainers are seen as being open, accessible, very extraverted, flip, and above all, cool. A few members will despair, thinking that with such a type they will get nowhere.

What happens next is that trainers "test the mikes" by encouraging members to talk about their expectations. Nothing much in a logical sense is happening at this stage, but the group is loosening up.

The next step is escalation. The group must make a go, no-go decision—whether to proceed or not. Usually a few members have had experience with group work. One for and one against should be invited to debate the pros and cons of the T group with the trainer, with the balance of the group studying the behaviour of this triad. After this discussion of the discussion, members are invited to voice questions and comments. Then the trainer insists on the group deciding to go or not to go. This is the first crisis, and they are off. The trainer must get some commitment and the group must get some information. The trainer must frustrate the group by refusing to accept token compliance in order to get commitment. Following this first decision (if it is go), the members work out the ground rules.

So the group wanders off into the mysteries of sensitivity training. Somewhere along the road lies *the* crisis. It is all rather like the student revolution on a miniature scale and usually has the sequence:

Incident
Investigation
Escalation
Crisis
Confrontation
Further escalation
Replay

The incident can take a great number of forms, including rejection of the training or the trainer, someone breaking down and crying, or a member producing a confession which shocks the group. But the tension and the mystique practically guarantee a crisis.

In one particular group, it started when one member asked the trainer, "What would you do if I walked out?" When he was told "nothing,"

Box 16.1: How groups develop

To construct a broadly useful theory of group development, it is necessary to identify major areas of internal uncertainty, or obstacles to valid *communication* within the group. The two major areas of internal uncertainty are: (1) dependence (authority relations or members' orientations towards the handling and distribution of power in the group) and (2) interdependence (personal relations or members' orientations towards one another). These two areas are not independent of each other and yet they are two distinct concepts.

The core of Warren Bennis and Herbert Shepard's theory of group development is that the principal obstacles to the development of valid communication are to be found in the orientations towards authority and intimacy that members bring to the group.

The orientations towards authority are regarded as being prior to, or partially determinant of, attitudes towards other members. In its development, the group moves from preoccupation with authority relations to concern for personal relations. This movement defines the two major phases of group development. Within each phase are three subphases, determined by the ambivalence of orientations in each area.

PHASE I: DEPENDENCE

Subphase 1: Dependence-flight. The first days of group life are filled with behaviour whose aim is to ward off anxiety. The search for a common goal is aimed at reducing the cause of anxiety, and should best be understood as a dependence plea. The trainer is seen as the cause of insecurity, since he is presumed to know what the goals are or ought to be.

This period is characterized by behaviour that has gained approval from authorities in the past. Thus the trainer's reaction to each comment is surreptitiously watched.

Subphase 2. This subphase is marked by a paradoxical development of the trainer's role into one of omnipotence and powerlessness, and by division of the group into two warring subgroups. Power is much more overtly the concern of group members in this subphase. The undertones of the discussion are no longer dependence pleas; the trainer's abdication has created a power gap, but no one is allowed to fill it.

Subphase 3: Resolution-catharsis. Resolution of the group's difficulties at this point depends upon the presence in the group of other forces. The independents, who have until now been passive or ineffectual, become the only hope for survival, since they have thus far avoided polarization and stereotyped behaviour.

A group member may suggest that the trainer leave the group "to see how things go without him." There is a sudden increase in alertness and tension as the trainer is thus directly challenged. The principal function of the symbolic removal of the trainer is freeing the group to bring into awareness the hitherto carefully ignored feelings towards him as an authority figure, and towards the group activity as an off-target dramatization of the ambivalence towards authority. The event of subphase 3 is always marked in group history as a turning point: "the time when we became a group," "when I first got involved," etc.

Warren G. Bennis and Herbert A. Shepard, "A Theory of Group Development," *Human Relatic* Vol. 9 (1965), pp. 415–57.

the group was off, started on its training. In another group, a member said to the trainer, "Can we fire you?" Again the real training began at this point. Working through these crises is the essence of training. If this crucial point is carried through properly, the group begins to gel and solve some of its real problems.

PHASE II: INTERDEPENDENCE

The resolution of dependence problems marks the transfer of group attention to the problems of shared responsibility. The distribution of affection occupies the group during Phase II.

Subphase 4: Enchantment-flight. Now begins a happy sense of group belonging. Individual identity is eclipsed by a "the group is bigger than all of us" sentiment: "We've had our fighting and are now a group." But this integration is short-lived; it soon becomes perceived as a fake attempt to resolve interpersonal problems by denying their reality. The solidarity and harmony become more and more illusory. There is a feeling that, "We should work together but cannot." In the later stages of this subphase, enchantment with the total group is replaced by enchantment with one's subgroup; and out of this break-down of the group emerges a new organization.

Subphase 5: Disenchantment-fight. This period is marked by a division into two subgroups based upon orientations towards the degree of intimacy required by group membership. The counterpersonal members band together to resist further involvement. The overpersonal members band together in a demand for love. A common theme underlies both moves: the subgroups share in common the fear that intimacy breeds contempt.

Subphase 5 belongs to the counterpersonals as subphase 4 belonged to the overpersonals. It seems probable that both of these modalities serve to ward off anxieties associated with intimate interpersonal relations. There is a generalized denial of the group and its meaning for individuals. In sum, the past two subphases were marked by a conviction that further group involvement would be injurious to members' self-esteem.

Subphase 6: Consensual validation. Two forces which combine to press the group toward a resolution of the interdependency problem are the approaching end of the training session and the need to establish a method of evaluation (including course grades).

Turning the task of evaluation and grading over to the trainer is a regression to dependence; and refusal to discriminate and reward is a failure to resolve the problems of interdependence. If the group has developed, the reality of termination and evaluation cannot be denied. But evaluation is a risky activity. The counterpersonals resist evaluation as an invasion of privacy. The overpersonals fear discrimination among the group members.

The activity that follows group commitment to the evaluation task has its chief characteristic in the willingness and ability of members to validate their self-concepts with each other. The fear of rejection and the tension which developed as a result soon disappear. Instead, what ensues is a serious attempt by each group member to verbalize his private conceptual scheme for understanding human behaviour. This activity demands a high level of work and of communicative skill.

Finally, the evolution from phase I to phase II represents not only a change in emphasis from power to affection, but also from role to personality.

Make no mistake about it, this type of training is very demanding, very tiring, and, it is hoped, very rewarding. But not everybody can hack it.

T GROUPS ARE NOT FOR EVERYBODY

Not everyone can take this type of training. T groups are for neurotic normals, not for those who are truly neurotic. A reasonable estimate, in my experience, is that two thirds to three quarters of members of the group will get something out of it. The balance—no. So this training must be voluntary.

Research is currently going on to identify the personality types who can and cannot profit from this training. Those who benefit most, in my experience, seem to be more open-minded and not too up-tight, can laugh at themselves a little, can reorganize their own neurotic traits, and are not so neurotic that it stops them from learning.

There seems to be quite a variety of people who can't make it in the T group. In my experience, women outnumber the men in this category. Most typically, they just drop out of the group. On the other hand, women who stay are frequently more effective than their male counterparts, mainly because they are more willing to express themselves emotionally.

THE REENTRY PROBLEM

When it is all over, the members of the group have to make it back to the real world and this can be a significant problem. Most people experience difficulty making this transition. Transferring the learning of the T group is a tricky problem. One member of a group, after completing his T group, walked into his house and said to his wife, "Don't speak to me, I'll tell you when I'm ready to talk."

Sometimes executives return to their companies and display the new attitudes and insights that they have picked up at the T group and are promptly dubbed "human relations fanatics." Not too surprisingly, such executives sometimes form pockets of resistance, a sort of human relations underground.

What is the answer to this reentry problem? One answer is to give colleagues and spouses time to adjust to the "new you" before switching over completely. A more long-term answer, but one which is open only to senior executives and training directors, is to arrange for sections of organizations (such as department groups) to train together in the new organizational development context.

T groups are the new religious-scientific experience of the post-industrial society; and it is going to take quite a bit of time to work out the rules, rituals, and processes for both members and trainers. As with most religions, there are going to be a fair number of schisms before a sufficient variety of religious experiences à la T group are available to meet the endless kinds of human needs that have to be served. Roll on the encounter groups.

THE ROLE OF THE TRAINER

The trainer's role is to observe, record, interpret, sometimes to lead, and always to learn. In my view, the trainer learns most in the T group; if this is true, it runs counter to the basic premise of T group training—that you can only really learn about groups by experience in the group.

In regard to the observation function of the trainer, it is usual to videotape-record the discussion. It is also useful to do a Bales Process Interaction Analysis of the actual discussion. R. F. Bales's system classifies behaviour into two major categories, task and human relations, each of which is further divided into positive and negative categories. Using Bales's categories it is possible to ascertain who are the task specialists and who are the human relations specialists in the group. If this analysis is carried through in the objective manner dictated by the Bales system, it is seen as such by the trainees and more readily accepted. It is also valuable to do a distribution of speaking time which tells members how long each person spoke. This kind of information can often have a salutary effect on the length of subsequent contributions. These duties can be carried out by assistants.

The trainer's principal function is to observe what happens in the group. In my experience, to observe the group effectively, it is necessary to have three large cards available for recording (*a*) psychological phenomena, (*b*) subjects discussed, and (*c*) actual quotes or behaviour observed.

As he gains more experience in running this type of training, the trainer inevitably gets a feeling of *déjà vu*—a feeling of having seen it all before. This, to my mind, constitutes vivid evidence of the validity of the science of group dynamics—i.e., it is possible to predict the behaviour of the members of the group—and reinforces the view that the trainer learns from the group.

From the trainer's point of view, the T group represents an ideal training technique in the sense that the method can be applied in an industry without the trainer's having any prior technical knowledge. Indeed, the method can be used, inter alia, as a means of collecting ideas and feelings about particular problems.

The T group has sometimes cynically been described as, "The participants shoot each other and then the trainer gets the participant observers to help him to bury the dead." In any case, the training has the effect of generating considerable anxiety which, in turn, enables the mobilization of sufficient energy to solve the problem. Understandably the training frequently assumes the form of a crisis, and as members work through the problem, they are able to clarify their roles.

For the trainer, the situation can take the form of a personal emotional crisis—especially if the group is composed of executives from the same organization who band together to reject the training. Thus ideally the trainer must combine a powerful and resilient ego with a sensitive, penetrating mind capable of recognizing roles, motives, and defence mechanisms. Few, if any, trainers meet this demanding specification; most try to survive by learning quickly, which usually involves a considerable amount of personal buffeting. Experienced trainers, who seem to operate like good film or stage directors, are quick to recognize when a change of scene is in order or a close-up is required; they also have the ability to use the flash-back technique to explain immediately behaviour in terms of previous group incidents. Another technique they use is the immediate replay of a particularly significant event using videotape recording.

Videotape recording, or VTR, is well on its way to revolutionizing human relations training and as such is widely used in T group training. A major factor facilitating this VTR development has been the sharp reduction in the price of the hardware (TV camera, videotape recorder, and monitor), which over a period of 10 years dropped from over $70,000 to about $1,500 for a portable TV camera and videotape recorder. Thanks to the development of transistors and printed circuits, small, reliable, and relatively inexpensive portable cameras are now available.

But a curious thing about the VTR business is that many businesses and public authorities have bought the hardware, but most are unable to use it. Just as in many underdeveloped countries the tractors sent by the United Nations are lying at the docks, their batteries rotting away, so in many training departments expensive VTR equipment lies unused. Training specialists have been thrown into a state of future shock, unable to cope with supermodern technology.

What is the hang-up? Is it technological? The main problem is not technological, for modern technology has produced cameras which can be used in normal classrooms without special lighting and equipment which can record sound without the soundproofing of a TV studio. And the equipment is relatively easy to operate. What is the problem?

The trainer as movie director

The real problem in using VTR lies not with the hardware or its operation but rather with the software—the planning, scheduling, programming, and subroutine aspects. There are two major problems: what to do with VTR and how to do it. To get into the act, the trainer has to be prepared to assume the canvas chair of the movie director and get into the atmosphere of the theatre, where the participants can become the performers, then the audience, then the "film" critics (one vital point of VTR protocol—never talk about "film," always talk about "tape").

There are certain basic ground rules which may help the budding TV director–training specialist:

1. Identify events or incidents which are suitable for VTR treatment. Possible events include:
    a. Five-minute lecturettes.
    b. A 15-minute employment interview.
    c. A counselling interview.

d. Brief role-playing exercises.
e. Group dynamics exercises such as the leaderless group.
f. Behaviour sampling such as recording the expressions of customers as they pay at the check-out point of a supermarket.
g. A salesman talking to a customer.
h. A skill-training incident such as the operation of a film projector.
i. Psychological experiments such as serial communication.

Two points are worth stressing. The material must be interesting and reveal a variety of behaviours, and the incident should preferably take 5 minutes to record (anything over 15 minutes is difficult to exploit).

2. The actual process should include:

a. The event.
b. Discuss the event to see what ideas can be extracted before play-back.
c. Play back the tape, with interruptions to illustrate particular points.
d. Discuss the complete incident further.
e. Play back the complete tape without interruption.
f. Make the tape available for participants so that they can view it at their leisure if they wish.

What should the camera look at?

Most inexperienced TV camera operators get fixated by the equipment, point the camera at a particular person, and concentrate on getting a good picture in terms of quality, focus, definition, and depth. Like the operation of a light machine-gun, a two-man team is needed for better operation. Number one should operate the camera and number two should identify worth-while targets and signal them to number one. In recording a group, good, indicative shots might include:

1. Foot movements.
2. Hand movements. Chopping movements indicate how participants break a subject into component parts; finger tapping often indicates mounting tension and frustration; stroking (perhaps the arm of a chair) and touching movements indicate pseudo-courting or attention-getting attempts; and so on.
3. A noncontributing participant's lips moving as he prepares to make a point.
4. Selective head nodding or shaking, as feedback.
5. Participants' moving forward to get into the group.
6. Participants' moving back to withdraw from the group.
7. The body rigidity of isolates.
8. Panning shots of the whole group, to ensure that everyone appears in the playback.

The vital point to keep in mind in terms of camera work is to make sure that illustrative behavioural data is recorded even though picture definition and focus may not be of first quality. What should be emphasized is that VTR is an audiovisual aid or an adjunct—it is not an end in itself.

"The medium is the message" is a real danger in this situation. This aphorism suggests that the smoother and more perfect the TV programme is, the less the receiver is aware of the message and the more he is aware of the medium. Thus the VTR training specialist has a vested interest in making his VTR incident a less than perfect programme. If he is too successful in recording an incident, he must be doubly careful to make sure that he introduces discontinuities (without which learning is not possible) in the playback.

VTR is a dramatic new learning process which exploits human narcissism and has a *cinéma vérité* quality which few people can resist. It represents the new wave in human relations training, and it is going to be subject to our usual exponential growth pattern. It can only work while people believe the lie that "the camera can't lie."

BEYOND THE T GROUP

Two points are worth making about the T group experience from the individual point of view. Firstly, the experience can be extremely painful. When it is successful, a kind of agape develops; but when it fails, it really fails, and nervous break-downs can result. Secondly, the principal beneficiary of the T group is the trainer, who by virtue of seeing and acting in the same play week-end after week-end gets extremely perceptive insights not only into the structure, processes, and values of groups but also into the change process.

The dangers mentioned under the first point, as we have already noted, led to a waning in popularity for the T group during the 1960s; the initial enchantment was over. But the technology of group dynamics lingered on. R. F. Bales had "discovered" the two functions of groups, task effectiveness (productivity) and human satisfaction (the people factor), and unscrambled these functions in terms of roles, relations, and processes. In the 1960s, this kind of technology was transferred to organizational settings to solve real operational problems.

Bales's work formed the theoretical base for the managerial grid developed by Robert Blake and J. S. Mouton. Blake was among the first to realize that laboratory training could be harnessed to the problem of organizational development. The grid, which allowed managers to think about productivity and people simultaneously, was a dramatic breakthrough and has been used extensively. It will be described and discussed in Topic 3; the point here is to realize that Blake saw the need to get beyond the group into the organization and developed a plan of action which was like a social science blitzkrieg compared to conventional change strategies.

The overall strategic scenario of the managerial grid operation is reminiscent of a military plan: break in, clear the mine fields, consolidate, regroup, and attack on a larger scale, bringing in larger units at each stage. Blake's strategy begins with explaining the grid to key members of top management, who then select "diagonal slices" of their personnel for training in the grid. Further stages involve team exercises in problem solving, working on intergroup (e.g., production versus sales) relations, and so on, until the whole organization as an open system has become the unit of change. There are intellectual limitations to the grid, and to its base in group dynamics, and the movement has now passed its high point; but it did recognize the need to get beyond the small group.

What was needed was an understanding of how organizations operate and change. This is what organizational development is all about, and it is what research workers have been trying to discover in the past decade— what makes organizations tick, grow, develop, and ultimately decay. It has turned out to be much more difficult than figuring out what happens in groups. For starters, it is usually possible to get a group into one room and study its workings. An organization, besides being too large for one room, nearly always has a complex technology which affects behaviour in peculiar, little-understood ways.

The new strategies of O.D. involve an understanding of conflict technology and require confrontation techniques. The organizational development approach requires viewing organizations as sociotechnical systems reacting to the turbulent environment. The definition, understanding, and control of these reactions requires not only a lot of field research but also a new conceptual frame of reference. Systems theory offered the only frame which could handle the complexities involved, and even this approach—which is more philosophical than scientific—was something of a shot in the dark.

TOPIC 3
Organizational development

Organizational development (O.D.), which is a major growth activity in the 1970s, is an attempt to achieve corporate excellence by integrating executives' need for growth with organizational goals. It is concerned with changing posture, perspective, and process; but it is a value change in a system context which is appropriate to our contemporary turbulent environment with all its built-in uncertainties.

To get to the heart of what is involved in this kind of change, it is necessary to think of an organization as a giant protein-like molecule with lots of small radicals stuck on and with roles for atoms. Traditionally, these giant molecules have achieved their success by virtue of specifying authority, defining lines of communication, setting out areas of delegation, and generally operating in a relatively placid, fairly well-defined environment with a fair measure of control. This earlier approach to organizations is substantially structural in character. What is neglected in this structural optic is the notion of organizational culture.

Organizational culture includes the rules, policies, rituals, folkways, rubrics, and all the various subroutines which form the corporate subconscious. The O.D. consultant, to act properly as a change agent, must be a sort of corporate Freud who helps his group in the systematic exploration and management of this culture. He assists the group in identifying its corporate philosophy, business strategy, and operating tactics by examining these cultural beliefs, many of which are buried in the minds and behaviours of the executives in his group. A complete cultural renaissance is needed if the corporation is to escape from the cataleptic conventions of red tape and moribund procedures that inhibit effective decision making.

Going back to the model of the organization as a giant molecule with roles for atoms, it is possible to think of the structural forces as the bonds which link the various roles in the system, specifying who can speak to whom, who can initiate contacts, and who can spend what. It is possible to think of the culture as the electrostatic field—silent, pervasive, lying below the surface—which holds all these various roles in position and which helps to define and reinforce the forces flowing along the bonds. Therefore, in terms of O.D., if it is possible to change the cultural frame of reference (that is, the value system), then all the various structural relations will be correspondingly affected. Training the system to facilitate this cultural reformation is the essence of O.D.

ASSUMPTIONS OF O.D.

The new approach to organizational development is founded on certain assumptions which are described in the following paragraphs.

1. Structural innovations by themselves are insufficient. They must be reinforced by cultural changes. The effective ethos must be explored, defined, and developed. Structural changes such as redesigning organizational charts and rewriting role descriptions are still used, but the significant extra is the attempt to change cultural frames of reference. This does not mean that executives are expected to become more democratic; they are likely to be more selectively democratic (avoiding the democracy of overdependency) but more confident and effective as they come to understand and become more conversant with the new behavioural science insights and techniques. The objective in cultural terms is to get managers to reorganize their needs for dependency and shift them into a posture of interdependence (independency and dependency). They must also

recognize both their own and others' existential integrity; that they have choices and must choose; and that choices involve values and values are not completely arbitrarily determined.

2. The organization, suborganization, department, or section is the basic unit to be trained. O.D. involves a total system—ideally it should, in stages, encompass an entire corporation.

3. The substance of the training is the real-time on-line problem that currently faces the unit. Traditional cases play no part.

4. The focus is on activities, processes, and planned changes rather than on end states. Theological statements of the purpose of the organization are rarely relevant in such a context. O.D. is a method, a way of operating, not an end in itself.

5. Powerful new techniques in behavioural sciences are mobilized to facilitate changes. Specifically, T group technology becomes the medium for transforming organizational actualities. More specifically:

a. T group technology is used, not to explore psychopathology in terms of anxiety, phobias, or Oedipal fixations, but rather to define managerial styles, roles, role sets, and dissonance, and to facilitate feedback (see Box 16.2).

b. Power equalization is achieved and maintained to facilitate exploitation of the creative forces of conflict.

c. The content of the training is not the traditional case but real problems that actually exist in the organizational here and now. The T group is not a stranger group, nor a horizontal slice (nor even a diagonal slice) of the organization, but consists of a department or section or nuclear command group. In this way the problem of transfer of learning is avoided. The reentry problem (transferring ideas and insights that one has picked up in an executive development programme and installing them in the back-home situation) is avoided because the members of the group have never, in fact, left home.

6. The demarcation between training and operating is removed. When O.D. has been effective, preferred styles and techniques are incorporated into everyday operations. What this means is that planning a production schedule, setting up a new appointment, or incorporating a computer system becomes in itself an educational process within which people feel that they can be creative and learn. As the training becomes institutionalized, managers begin to incorporate the new styles into their everyday operations.

7. Training proceeds in steps, starting at the top of the organization and working down.

8. The O.D. approach aims to facilitate cultural changes which will create a more open problem solving climate; to change the authority base from the structural (position) to the sapiential (knowledge and competence); to have all corporate goals "owned" by all corporate members;

Box 16.2: Successful organizational change

According to Larry Greiner's study of organizational change, three major methods are used to introduce change:

1. Unilateral authority.
2. Shared approaches.
3. Delegated approaches.

The unilateral authority method is based on the authority of a man's hierarchical position in the company. He has three ways to do the job: (1) by decree, in the form of policy statement or memorandum; (2) by replacement, with the basic assumption that organizational problems tend to reside in a few strategically located individuals and that their replacements will bring about sweeping and basic changes; and (3) by structure, where the assumption lies in the statement that people behave in agreement with the structure and technology governing them.

More toward the middle of the power distribution continuum are the shared approaches, which are utilized in two forms: (1) group decision making and (2) group problem solving. The main assumption in group decision making is that individuals develop more commitment to action when they have a voice in the decisions that affect them. The assumption in group problem solving is that not only do people gain greater commitment from being exposed to a wider decision-making role but they also have significant knowledge to contribute to the definition of the problem.

The delegated approaches appear in two forms: (1) case discussion and (2) T group sessions. The first form assumes implicitly that individuals, through the medium of discussion about concrete situations, will develop general problem-solving skills to aid them in carrying out subsequent individual and organizational changes. The basic assumption in the second form is that exposure to a structureless situation will release unconscious emotional energies within individuals, which in turn will lead to self-analysis, insight, and behavioural change.

In his survey of 18 studies of organizational change, Greiner was able to identify five major success patterns:

1. Top management must be under considerable pressure for improvement long before an explicit organizational change is contemplated.
2. A new man, known for his ability to introduce a change, must enter the scene.
3. Top management must assume a direct and highly involved role in reexamination of past practices and current problems within the organization.
4. The new man must engage several levels of the organization in collaborative, fact-finding, problem-solving discussions.
5. As solutions and decisions develop, the success experiences must gradually spread and become absorbed permanently into the organization.

Larry E. Greiner, "Patterns of Organizational Change," *Harvard Business Review*, May-June,

and to replace traditional values of overachievement, aggression, and acquisition (with their correlates of anomie, alienation, apathy) with existential values where the emphasis is on authenticity, awareness, and interdependence. In the emergent value system, competition can be made more relevant to corporate goals and collaboration becomes more feasible.

9. Decision making is located as close to informational nodes and accountability centres as possible.

Viewing the change process as a whole, the overall success of change hinges on one key notion—that there must be a redistribution of power within the structure of an organization. The power redistribution should occur through a development process of change, which is best explained by dividing it into six phases which are illustrated in the figure below.

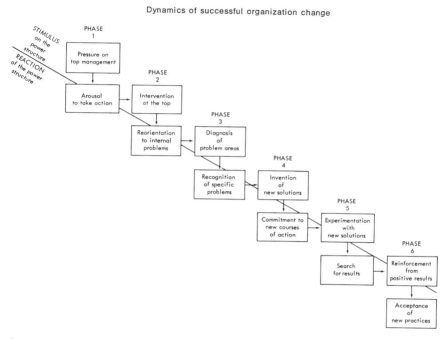

Dynamics of successful organization change

1. Pressure and arousal

Strong pressures in areas of top management responsibility that are most likely to provoke the greatest concern for organizational change should come from two broad sources: *(a)* serious environmental factors, e.g., lower sales or stockholder discontent; and *(b)* internal events, e.g., low productivity or interdepartmental conflict.

10. The ultimate goal is to make O.D. a self-perpetuating process for continuing organizational renewal.

THE INEFFECTIVENESS SYNDROME

How does O.D. get started? A great number of O.D. exercises begin when a chief executive, senior manager, or corporate personnel officer becomes concerned about the performance of his work group and is perplexed by his inability to identify the causes of this ineffectiveness.

2. Intervention and reorientation

Intervention by an outsider at the top of the organization is facilitated by the fact that he is respected for his skills at improving organization practices. This respect allows him easy access to those people who make decisions affecting the entire organization while his reputation is likely to give added weight to his initial comments about the organization. Thus, the newcomer is in an ideal position to reorient the power structure of the organization.

3. Diagnosis and recognition

As attempts are made to seek out the location and causes of problems by various levels of organization personnel, a shared approach to both power and change makes itself evident during this stage.

The significance of this stage is the fact that in front of every subordinate there evidence that (a) top management is willing to change, (b) important problems are being acknowledged and faced up to, and (c) ideas from lower levels are being valued by upper levels.

4. Invention and commitment

Once problems are recognized, effective solutions must be developed and a full commitment obtained for implementing them. The potency of obtaining quality decision and high commitment to action is essentially dependent upon participation by all members, who are required to collaborate and invent solutions that are of their own making and endorsement; for the temptation is always there for the old power structure to apply old solutions to new problems.

5. Experimentation and search

This stage is the stage of "reality-testing" before large-scale changes are introduced. All decisions made in the fourth phase come under careful scrutiny. Instead of making only big decisions at the top, a number of small decisions are implemented at all levels of the organization. Further, these decisions tend to be regarded more as experiments than as final, irreversible decisions.

6. Reinforcement and acceptance

Each of the studies of successful change reports improvements in organization performance. Obviously positive results have a strong reinforcing effect; that is, people are rewarded and encouraged to continue and even to expand the changes they are making. The most significant effect of this phase is probably a greater and more permanent acceptance at all levels of the underlying methods used to bring about the change. The use of shared power is more of an institutionalized and continuing practice than just a "one-shot" method used to introduce change.

Most executives are only too familiar with the "ineffectiveness syndrome"—cost overruns, failure to meet deadlines, low-level innovation in group problem solving, interpersonal conflict that is not dealt with directly, distrust leading to filtering and suppression of information, disowning of personal responsibility and accountability. A sensitive and aware chief executive somehow realizes that the traditional way of overcoming the ineffectiveness syndrome is no longer an appropriate way of accomplishing his organization's goals.

Not untypically, such a chief executive has attended a T group on the managerial grid for presidents or top managers, where he will have discovered for himself some of the advantages of trust, openness, levelling, giving and receiving helpful feedback, risk taking, and confronting conflict. Such a chief executive may decide to begin his O.D. effort by sending some of the key people in his group for laboratory training, which is an integral part of the managerial grid.

THE MANAGERIAL GRID

In "Breakthrough in Organization Development," Robert R. Blake argued:

> There have been many earnest attempts to make the behavioral sciences useful to business, government, and service institutions. But, because of the complexities, success has been elusive. . . . Most typically, in-company human relations training programs are established for foremen or other lower level managers. The almost universal response of participants in these programs is, "I wish my boss could learn what I've been learning." Then, as in the famous study of the International Harvester training program, most trainees go back to the job and apparently conform to their bosses' expectations, often at the expense of human relations concepts set forth in the program.
>
> In short, the overall results of human relations and behavioral science training are questionable, at best, for on-the-job practitioners. Individual benefits are thought to be great, and personal testimonials are abundantly favorable. However, the question of mobilizing these insights into collective organizational efforts has remained a serious issue.

To overcome the difficulties, Blake and J. S. Mouton developed the managerial grid concept, which assumes that all executive styles can be plotted on a grid with two dimensions, concern for production and concern for people. As shown in Figure 16–6, a manager's style is plotted by rating him from 1 to 9 on each of the dimensions. Blake and Mouton recognize five principal styles, which have been plotted in Figure 16–6:

A rating of 1,1 indicates *impoverished management:* exertion of the minimum effort to get the required work done to maintain organization membership. Task effectiveness is unobtainable because people are indolent, passive, and apathetic. Satisfactory human relations are difficult to achieve; but then, human nature being what it is, conflict is to be expected.

A rating of 9,1 indicates *task management:* the manager is high in task efficiency but low in concern for human satisfaction. Men are regarded as just another commodity—another instrument of production. Productive efficiency is achieved by arranging the conditions of work so that "human interference" is minimized. The manager's job is to plan, direct, and control his subordinates' work.

FIGURE 16-6
THE MANAGERIAL GRID

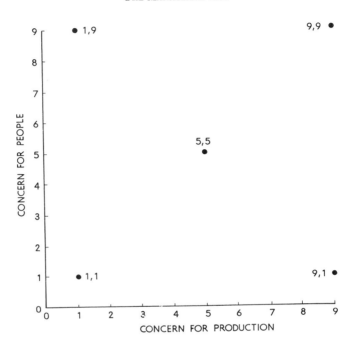

A rating of 1,9 indicates *country club management:* high human satisfaction but low work tempo. Production is incidental to the elimination of conflict and the establishment of good fellowship. Being nice and considerate leads to a comfortable, friendly, home away from home atmosphere which allows and requires an easy-going work tempo.

A rating of 5,5 indicates *middle of the road management:* adequate task performance while maintaining morale at a satisfactory level. A certain amount of production push—but don't go flat out. Be fair; be firm.

A rating of 9,9 indicates *team management:* high task achievement from committed people who have a common stake in the firm's purposes, with good relationships of trust and respect. Production is achieved by the integration of task and human requirements into a unified system.

THE BLAKE SIX-STEP PLAN OF IMPLEMENTATION

The Blake system of managerial grid can be applied in six phases to the training of management. Phases 1 and 2 include management development. The last four phases build on this development.

1. Laboratory-seminar training. This involves a one-week conference designed to introduce the manager to the grid system. From 12 to 48 individuals are brought together as members of problem-solving teams. An interesting feature of this type of training is that these sessions are conducted by line managers who already have been through the Blake lab.

The seminar starts with the analysis and assessment of one's own managerial grid style of behaviour. This part of the programme lasts for 50 hours and deals with problem solving; it also includes evaluation of individual and team performances. The problems selected are those which will illustrate how interpersonal relations affect task effectiveness. It is assumed that a team which performs poorly at first will get feedback and be able to improve its subsequent performances.

Phase 1, according to Blake, is not meant to produce immediate organization improvement, but is intended more as "a trigger which creates a readiness to really work on human problems of production." Participation in a grid seminar is set up to include a "diagonal slice" of the organization chart. No man is in the same group as his boss or immediate work colleagues. At the same time, this diagonal slice arrangement permits many organizational levels and departments to be represented in each session.

2. Team development. This represents an in-plant application of the first phase. Each department works out its own 9,9 ground rules. According to Blake, phases 1 and 2 provide conditions designed to:

> ... enable managers to learn Managerial Grid concepts as an organizing framework for thinking about management practices;
> ... increase the self-examination of personal performance characteristics;
> ... increase a manager's willingness to listen, to face and appreciate work-related conflict, to reduce and work out interpersonal frictions, and to reject compromise as a basis for organizational decision making;
> ... build improved relationships between groups, among colleagues at the same level, and between superiors and subordinates.

3. Intergroup development. This involves group-to-group working relationships and focuses on building 9,9 ground rules and norms beyond the single work group. Situations are established whereby operating tensions that happen to exist between groups are identified and explored by group members or their representatives.

4. Organizational goal setting. This involves issues of major importance to all managers. Organization development moves beyond team areas into problems that require commitment at all levels. Such broad problems include: cost control, union-management relations, safety, promotion policies, and overall profit improvement. These problems are identified by special task groups, which may again come from a diagonal slice of the organization chart.

5. Goal attainment. This uses some of the same educational procedures used in phase 1, but here the issues are major organizational concerns and the stakes are real.

6. Stabilization. This final phase is designed to support the changes brought about in the earlier phases. These changes are assessed and reinforced to withstand pressures which could cause regression. This phase also gives management an opportunity to evaluate its gains and mistakes under the organizational development programme.

A COMMENT ON THE GRID SYSTEM

Managers have made good use of the managerial grid, and learned from the experience. It is useful to recall that the grid was preceded, in the 1950s, by research such as that of Daniel Katz and R. L. Kahn, which seemed to imply to many managers that the effective executive should be an employee-centered, democratic, human relations specialist. This can be contrasted with the work of F. E. Fiedler, who showed that the more effective executive was psychologically distant with subordinates and could be described as a task specialist. The dilemma had been posed: How can you reconcile the human relations specialist of the 1950s with the psychologically distant task specialist of the 1960s? The managerial grid provided an excellent framework for discussing this dilemma.

Managers in group relations training are keen to specify their managerial styles. It is not uncommon to hear managers, when the grid is first introduced, express the view that the scheme is too black and white and does not allow for delicate shades of grey. But, when the managers gain more experience and get more confidence in using the system, they are not slow to recognize that:

1. Managerial styles represent responses to the situation and change accordingly.
2. Managers frequently use a number of different styles.
3. The style your boss uses affects your own adaptation. For example, if your boss is a task specialist, you have to do more human relations work.
4. The grid provides a very useful framework for discussing the performance of subordinates.

The principal advantages of the Blake lab training are that it emphasizes task effectiveness as well as concern for human satisfaction; that this training is given by line managers and not the diabolical psychologists; that the training is given through "concrete" case studies in the first instance; that a relatively simple theory of management (the grid concept) is used rather than some esoteric mathematical-behavioural science model; that all the managers are trained, not just the junior executives and foremen; and finally, that the method is carried over into the back-home situation. The Blake lab has many advantages over the earlier type of sensitivity training. In spite of its theoretical oversimplifications (many managers believe that absolutely maximum effort can only be achieved by a certain loss of human satisfaction; therefore, for them top performance would be 10,8), it continues to be the subject of many experiments by firms and universities.

However, there are new and promising thrusts in organizational development which are bidding to replace older techniques like the grid. Two of the most promising are process consultation and intervention strategy.

TOPIC 4
Process consultation and intervention strategy

Process consultation is the new modus operandi used by organizational psychologists who have graduated beyond T groups and who believe with Kurt Lewin that "If you want to understand something, try to change it." Process consultants such as Edgar Schein and Chris Argyis see themselves as sociotherapists who, through the concepts of "diagnosis" and "helpful intervention," work with healthy organizations. These "alive" organizations can achieve more growth through process consultation, both in economic and interpersonal terms. The organization being helped plays a key part in the process. As Schein points out in *Process Consultation:*

> The job of the process consultant is to help the organization to solve its own problems by making it *aware of organizational processes*, of the consequences of these processes, and of the mechanisms by which they can be changed. The process consultant helps the organization to learn from self-diagnosis and self-intervention. The ultimate concern of the process consultant is the organization's capacity to do for itself what he has done for it. Where the standard consultant is more concerned about passing on his knowledge, the process consultant is concerned about passing on his skills and values.

TYPES OF CONSULTANCY

It is possible to classify consultation into three categories according to the focus of the change: the structural model, the process model, and the value model. Table 16–1 indicates the objectives and methods of each

TABLE 16–1
THREE KINDS OF CONSULTATION

Type of consultancy	Objectives	Method
STRUCTURAL	To improve economic effectiveness	Careful analysis of structure and performance
PROCESS	To help the client to diagnose and process his problems	Study processes of executive groups in action
VALUE	To change the client from traditional to existential values	T groups

model. The most common form of consultation invokes the structural model, where the client purchases expert information or the services of an expert. It results in the formulation of specific structural changes. Structural recommendations usually include a fresh drafting of the organization chart, the writing of new role descriptions, prescriptions on the functions of delegation and staff work, and the specification of tighter control systems. There are still substantial advantages to this type of structural consultation, and many consultancy companies still devote a major part of their activities to this type of work. But there are also substantial disadvantages. Frequently the structural consultant installs in the client organization a system with which he is familiar and which has worked elsewhere but which may not be relevant to the needs and interests of his present client.

Process consultancy, right from the first moment, involves the client with the consultant in the process of joint diagnosis. The consultant enters the organization without a clear mission in terms of structure but with a set of process concepts which will help him to help the client to identify his real problems. Schein has defined process consultation as follows:

> *P-C is a set of activities on the part of the consultant which help the client to perceive, understand, and act upon process events which occur in the client's environment.*

The value and process types of consultancy use the T group approach. The presumption is that what the members learn about group dynamics can be taken back to the work situation and applied to improve both performance and satisfaction. The more sophisticated behavioural scientists regard T groups as a source of technology and personal training which can be very effectively used to facilitate organizational development, that is, to solve real organizational problems. A good number of executives, while unwilling or reluctant to get involved in T groups, welcome the confident approach of the process consultant who can use T group technology to help an executive group solve organizational problems. In *Process Consultation*, Schein has set out the assumptions underlying process consultation as follows:

1. Managers often do not know what is wrong and need special help in diagnosing what their problems actually are.
2. Managers often do not know what kinds of help consultants can give to them; they need to be helped to know what kind of help to seek.
3. Most managers have a constructive intent to improve things but need help in identifying what to improve and how to improve it.
4. Most organizations can be more effective if they learn to diagnose their own strengths and weaknesses. No organizational form is perfect; hence every form of organization will have some weaknesses for which compensatory mechanisms need to be found.
5. A consultant could probably not, without exhaustive and time-consuming study, learn enough about the culture of the organization to suggest reliable new courses of action. Therefore, he must work

jointly with members of the organization who *do* know the culture intimately from having lived within it.

6. The client must learn to see the problem for himself, to share in the diagnosis, and to be actively involved in generating a remedy. One of the process consultant's roles is to provide new and challenging alternatives for the client to consider. Decision-making about these alternatives must, however, remain in the hands of the client.

7. It is of prime importance that the process consultant be expert in how to *diagnose* and how to *establish effective helping relationships* with clients. Effective P-C involves the passing on of both these skills.

Schein has also defined the steps in process consultation as:

1. Initial contact with the client organization.
2. Defining the relationship, formal contract, and psychological contract.
3. Selecting a setting and a method of work.
4. Data gathering and diagnosis.
5. Intervention.
6. Reducing involvement.
7. Termination.

How process consulting operates

In process consulting, when the consultant is called in, he is unusually careful to ensure that his contract is properly understood; that he is with the organization, not to come up with pat ideas but rather to be maximally available for questioning and two-way communication. Typically the consultant, after having gone through the exploratory meeting which defines his terms of reference, will want to have the opportunity to observe his client group in action by being present at, for example, the weekly executive group meeting. The consultant will nearly always spend a fair amount of time interviewing different members of the executive group, and may on occasion arrange workshops which deal with organizational problems.

Figure 16–7 shows the P-C sequence: collecting data from the executive group through direct observation and individual and group interviews; using the data as feedback; and changing the structure, processes, and values of the group by this process. Thus the second kind of consultation, process, becomes the third type—value consultation is the end result.

The P-C man operates by collecting data, feeding it back to the group, and helping the individuals in the group to face up to the choices and challenges that confront them. Invariably the P-C man makes use of some form of intervention strategy.

INTERVENTION STRATEGY

The intervention strategy requires the behavioural scientist to go right into the organization and confront the executives with the actualities of

FIGURE 16–7
PROCESS CONSULTATION SEQUENCE

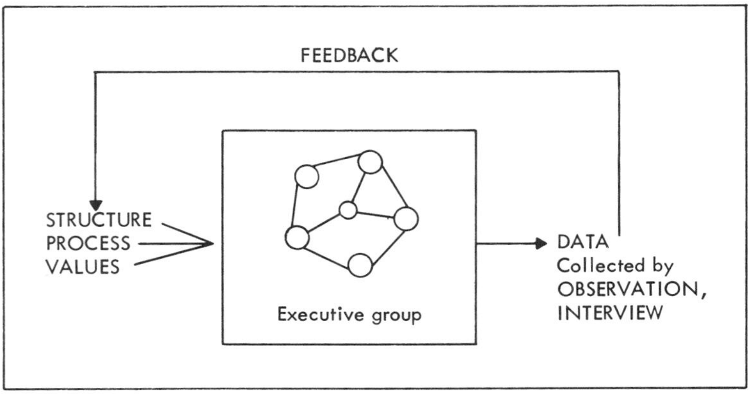

their business. The modus operandi requires the interventionist to be a kind of walking T group apparatus.

The basic assumption of intervention strategy is that there is something wrong with our organizations—that they are suffering from organizational dry rot. To the behavioural scientist who sees himself as an interventionist, this ineffectiveness in organizations is a function of the increasing rigidities generated by turning up the volume on the control system and refusing to face up to conflict and paternalistic personnel policies. The sequence seems to be: "Failure in performance requires tighter controls, which cause conflict, which we don't talk about around here; just be nice to everybody, and maybe the problem will go away."

To break this cycle, the interventionist steps in and makes the parties confront each other. He carries through the exercise with a mixture of charisma, organization theory, and T groups. How can behavioural scientists convince top management that they ought to try intervention-confrontation dynamics? Dead easy. The behavioural scientists are following in the footsteps of the radical youth of our society, who learned confrontation dynamics not in the psychology laboratory but in chasing university presidents and deans out of their offices; and what a ball they had in the process.

Interventionists work in a rather similar way to radical students. Once they get into an organization and create an incident, they insist on the incident being investigated fairly and objectively; a process is set up to investigate the incident. Quick as lightning, the process is challenged, and a process to investigate the process is needed. This is their bag—inventing a process to challenge the process which was meant to investigate the incident. Shades of the Chicago Seven trial—the whole technique is irresistible.

The assumptions of intervention strategy

In North America, the behavioural scientists who are at the frontier of their field have been exploring the use of confrontation techniques as a means of doing what students have been doing in universities—challenging the structure, process, and values of contemporary institutions. Both the behavioural scientists and the students are operating from the same assumptions:

1. Contemporary institutions are out of kilter and are not responding to social needs.
2. Technology has dated extant systems.
3. Complex sociotechnical systems are easy to sabotage (a study session of 10 computer programmers can stop a large car plant of 5,000). Thus, properly won commitment is necessary for operating normally.
4. Complexity produces the opportunity for power equalization.
5. Formal leaders are uneasy and uncomfortable about their own value systems, which they find difficult to justify.
6. Most formal leaders, while having only a vague, inchoate idea of what it is, believe in democracy. Hence problems must be discussed, and discussed in a rational way.
7. The process, *not* the problem, is the prime focus for activity and analysis.
8. Dilemma analysis is a valuable tool; it can be derived from a variety of intellectual sources, including the Marxist dialectic. This analysis typically includes thesis, antithesis, and synthesis (the negation of the negation).
9. Great emphasis is placed on the expression of feelings. For the 1960s student, the question might have been, "How do you feel about Vietnam?" If you answered intellectually, with the domino theory, the question was put again, with the intention of getting a statement on "feelings." The behavioural scientist's question may take the form of "How did you feel when A spoke to you?"
10. A high capacity for self-criticism, endurance, and articulation is required.

If it is any consolation, this process is going on all over the world. The Red Guards are everywhere; and of course, the technique can be learned.

Both the behavioural scientists and the radical students are out of the same intellectual and emotional nest. The students, nurtured by Dr. Spock, believe in a wide open, free-wheeling, swinging approach; business must be settled in good faith, which will allow people to be creative, "together" (integrated), and not up-tight. The behavioural scientists, spoon-fed on Freud, Jung, and Adler, prefer the openness of the T group; seek self-actualization (being "together"); and believe problems can be solved if they are identified and if people are given choices and commitment is thus established.

In the ranks of behavioural scientists, Chris Argyris has been in the forefront in using intervention strategy to get at organizational problems. In *Intervention Theory and Method*, Argyris set out three basic requirements for intervention activity:

1. Valid and Useful Information

First, it has been accepted as axiomatic that valid and useful information is the foundation for effective intervention. Valid information is that which describes the factors, plus their interrelationships, that create the problem for the client system. There are several tests for checking the validity of the information. In increasing degrees of power they are public verifiability, valid prediction, and control over the phenomena. The first is having several independent diagnoses suggest the same picture. Second is generating predictions from the diagnosis that are subsequently confirmed (they occurred under the conditions that were specified). Third is altering the factors systematically and predicting the effects upon the system as a whole.

2. Free Choice

In order to have free choice, the client has to have a cognitive map of what he wishes to do. The objectives of his action are known at the moment of decision. Free choice implies voluntary as opposed to automatic; proactive rather than reactive. The act of selection is rarely accomplished by maximizing or optimizing. Free and informed choice entails what Simon has called "satisficing," that is, selecting the alternative with the highest probability of succeeding, given some specified cost constraints. Free choice places the locus of decision making in the client system. Free choice makes it possible for the clients to remain responsible for their destiny. Through free choice the clients can maintain the autonomy of their system.

3. Internal Commitment

Internal commitment means the course of action or choice that has been internalized by each member so that he experiences a high degree of ownership and has a feeling of responsibility about the choice and its implications. Internal commitment means that the individual has reached the point where he is acting on the choice because it fulfills his own needs and sense of responsibility, as well as those of the system.

THE ORGANIZATION'S "REAL PROBLEM"

The interventionists believe that the real problem of an organization has nothing to do with the balance of payments crisis, the value of the dollar, foreign competition, racism, poverty, class conflict, the pill, pollution, or inflation. The real problems for organizations arise because organizations are hierarchical pyramids; because executives spend all their time thinking about how to get the job done instead of about people; because executives are being too rational (they don't show their feelings); and because executives maintain direction through control and coercion as well as rewards (carrot-and-stick style). For the student, "organizational imperialism" sums it up.

To get organizations to function better, the interventionist will help the executives to be more open and candid, to face up to their problems, and to commit themselves to a course of action. This sequence constitutes the primary intervention cycle, which is made up of three steps: (1) collecting valid information, (2) making an informed decision, and (3) developing commitment to that decision.

Getting at the real problems means operating at several levels consecutively. This jumping between levels of discussion can knock clients sideways.

EVALUATION OF PROCESS CONSULTATION AND INTERVENTION

One would not be surprised to discover that many client organizations are well pleased with the result of the interventionist's strategy. What is achieved? At a personal level, executives can be helped to become more honest, candid, and open. They can be taught the principal processes and techniques of conflict management. And so on for the whole book on organizational behaviour.

But something else happens. Some executives emerge from confrontation exercises believing that threat-free environments exist; that conflict is primarily caused by bad personal relations; that when people talk openly about problems, the problems will solve themselves. Executives who have gone through such exercises talk in a peculiar way which may well disturb other executives who are not familiar with intervention semantics.

The executive-turned-interventionist is given to such expressions as "I am conflicted" when faced with, say, a choice of talking with his boss or a colleague. When the boss absolves him with, "Go ahead, sort this out with your colleague," he is no longer "conflicted." Again, he is much given to offers to "help you." When you explain, "I'm not willing to play patient so that you can play therapist," a painful silence may ensue. If you challenge the executive-turned-interventionist, he may reply, "I don't understand what you're saying. I hear you, but it seems to me there are two agendas in what I hear." You are back as patient, and he is back as therapist.

The new-style interventionist displays new attitudes. Typically he cares little for formal procedures, such as working through the formal agenda at a meeting; instead he wants to know, "Where's the energy at in this meeting?" and you're off to the races. He has a vested interest in making something a "problem": if he creates a problem, he can solve it. He has a great interest in the hippie-existential culture, and frequently won't work with clients whose values are too far removed from his own. He never seems to be anywhere specific in terms of personal growth; you always seem to find him in the "in betweens," the kind of moratorium described by Eric Erikson. His boss is more than likely to be disconcerted when he comes up with, "In what ways is my behaviour or style holding you back from fulfilling your role?"

Such executive responses and attitudes give process consultation and intervention strategy a bad press. They make the more hard-headed manager who is unfamiliar with the techniques wonder whether behavioural science is slipping back into the marshmallow of the soft human relations approach. To emphasize that this is not the case, the basic question is: What is process consultation trying to achieve?

What P-C attempts is to change the values and interpersonal skills of its executive clients. In terms of values, effort is directed at bringing into better balance the process of suboptimizing between task effectiveness and human satisfaction, between structure and process, and between short-run and long-run effectiveness. In terms of interpersonal skills, the aim is to enhance the executive's ability to understand that other individuals have different perceptions of his behaviours and attitudes.

In essence, process consultation tries to develop the existential aspect of the executive's personality: to make him more aware, authentic, and self-actualizing. It remains to be seen how this new approach will develop; we can only try, in the next topic, to look ahead to the future of organizational development.

TOPIC 5
Organizational development in the future

There are still a number of problems associated with the future of organizational development. To start with, O.D. has a tremendous ambience of manipulation for those who've been on the inside track of its development. To the neophyte, it appears nonmanipulative, spontaneous, and creative. In many respects, it's easier to describe O.D. in terms of concepts derived from the theatre. It represents a kind of *coup de théâtre* in that, to the participants, it is unstructured and appears to grow along with the particular problems that are generated by the group; but for the O.D. analyst, it is a fairly structured type of training. Many of the training techniques are rather like thematic apperception tests, with a fairly wide range of responses which can nevertheless be structured into a number of different categories.

The O.D. consultant who has had a fair amount of experience often gets the feeling of *déjà vu*; he's seen it all before. This can be understood if it is accepted that the consultant controls the script, plot, roles, props, and games, and that he himself acts as the director. Many consultants would answer this charge by saying that professionalism is always a manipulation, but a manipulation with good intentions.

To pursue the analogy of the theatre further, O.D. is frequently the theatre of the absurd and occasionally the theatre of cruelty. "Theatre of the absurd" is not all that inappropriate, because management itself is so often absurd—a pulling of levers and switches, sometimes at random, to control a complex of black boxes, watching hopefully to see what will happen. But when things are working well, O.D. is good theatre, therapeutic (giving cartharsis), entertaining (providing comic relief), transporting the subject (providing an ego trip), and containing a message. The danger lies in the McLuhanesque madness of "the medium is the message"; the form of the T group may take over. But O.D., like good theatre, deals with real problems, although they may not always be epic ones.

The medium of O.D. is the process of the T group, and as such is partly cerebral, partly sensual, very experimental, and always existential. Mixing this behavioural martini involves not only a lot of judgement but a lot of luck. In the Age of Aquarius, in a world which is more physical and more gutsy, most executives (about two thirds to three quarters) react positively to this expressionist mode of problem-solving therapy.

Can anything intelligent be said about the T group? Like any religious experience, it causes an alteration in our brain waves and the adrenalin level of our blood. In both prayer and the T group, sparks are struck from some part of our cerebral cortex that knows no language. The sparks from prayer fly up; the sparks from the T group fly in all directions. For a minority of participants, some fly down to release butterflies in the stomach and set the heart pounding; for another (hopefully, larger) group the flying is a trip—an ego trip, a tremendous feeling of liberation. Perhaps the answer for most is that the T group, like prayer, is good for you in small quantities. But there is always a minority of religious maniacs whose whole life is one long T group. Most executives hope a sensible balance can be achieved.

Few serious and thoughtful managers can regret the passing of the executive development courses of the early 1960s with their slick gimmicks, superficiality, entertaining ploys, endless flip charts with final solutions, and remote cases of Company XYZ or Battleship M with no staff solutions. Organizational development represents a stage beyond management development. Management development, a training phenomenon of the 1950s and early 1960s which was conceived to teach the executive new skills and expand his conceptual frame of reference, was predicated on the notion that there was something wrong with the manager. And understandably met quite a lot of resistance. O.D., on the other hand, creates an open problem-solving climate throughout the corporation within which decisions are made on the basis of competence; and the presumption is that there is something wrong with the system.

O.D. involves a high-risk strategy, deals with real problems such as those arising from merger and acquisition activity, and tries to solve the problem on the job. It uses a policy of selective intervention and confrontation and assumes the new view of conflict. It is possible to summarize the position of O.D. among organizational methods as shown in Table 16–2.

TABLE 16–2

Skill	Subject to be trained	Method
Trade	Apprentice	Serve time
Operating	Operator	"Sitting next to Nelly"
Supervising	Foreman	TWI (training within industry)
Knowledge of management	Manager	Management training
Interpersonal skills	Executive	Executive development
Problem solving	System	Organizational development

The critical advantage of O.D. is that it deals with real organizational problems in a different power distribution context, and with the significant extra that the whole process can be illuminated by the flashbacks of observers.

Only with the recognition that O.D. is still in an evolutionary state can we attempt to model it as a system, as we do in Figure 16–8. Since change in organizations is what O.D. is all about, this model incorporates "methods of change" rather than "methods of research"—although they may amount to the same thing. Organizational literature has a dearth of written-up projects describing the kinds of problems that can be tackled using O.D. approaches, so the need for research is evident.

It seems unrealistic to believe that O.D. can solve all corporate problems. Corporate development people and O.D. consultants will have to be sensible about overselling this new training art form, especially in terms of the size and complexity of the problems it can solve. Only corporate managers can solve complex, long-term organizational problems, for only they are ultimately accountable; only they control the real power and resources. Corporate officials are the licensed pilots of our jumbo-jet-enterprises; they have their hands on the controls and are not about to relinquish them.

O.D. is a new flying-simulator technique which starts as a method for training the system, for revealing processes, and for changing perspectives and evolving new values—all through creative problem solving. It hopes

FIGURE 16–8
Organizational development as a system

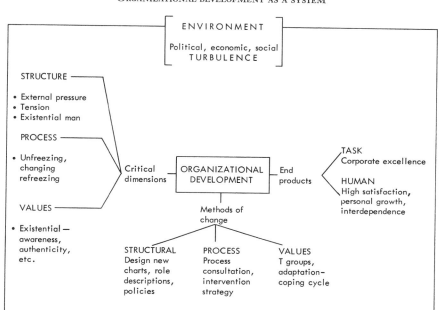

to become a way of life, a corporate zeitgeist which somehow permeates the mysteries of management, freeing up the executive to make effective decisions in a context where he can truly say, "Nothing human is alien to me."

REVIEW AND RESEARCH

1. Develop an outline plan of the changes that have taken place in the airline business since 1920. Make sure your answer includes references to the introduction of jets, jumbo jets, and SST's, cargo carrying, charters, feeder airlines, airport facilities, passenger attitudes, and the military-industrial complex. Include in your answer a scenario to explain the future decline of the airline business.

2. How can planned change be introduced in organizations? O.D. is not always a necessity in introducing change. In fact, it may be a positive disadvantage. List the kinds of change where O.D. would be inappropriate.

3. What are the stages through which a T group goes? If a member knows about these stages, the roles likely to emerge, and the process itself, does he leave himself open to the charge of manipulating his fellow group members if he "plays along" with his group? If the answer is yes, what does one say about the T group trainer? Can these difficulties be overcome?

5. Critically evaluate process consultation.

6. Discuss: "Life to-day is just one amusing (boring) T group."
7. What are the objectives of O.D.? Develop an O.D. plan for your business school.
8. Critically evaluate the managerial grid. Develop a new three-dimensional grid based on information processing, system sophistication, and tradi-tional-versus-existential value dimensions. How would you implement this grid?
9. Develop a new plan of training that goes beyond O.D. and takes cogni-zance of the effects of the environment. Entitle your paper "Eco-systems Training."
10. Develop a training programme to make executives more creative. Make sure that in your answer you consider the possibilities of using encounter groups, the women's liberation movement, and "the power of lateral thinking."

GLOSSARY OF TERMS

Intervention strategy. Strategy used by the behavioural scientist or con-sultant who intervenes directly in organizational life and confronts execu-tives with the actualities of their behaviour. The interventionist uses T group technology to bring process and value change.

Leaderless group. A type of T group in which no official leader is appointed or chosen, but members are asked to work on a problem; the intended result is that the group structures itself in a particular way, roles (including different kinds of leadership) emerge, and people take up these roles.

Managerial grid. A concept put forward by R. R. Blake and J. S. Mouton in which managerial styles are identified by plotting a manager's concern for production and his concern for people on a grid which rates each dimen-sion on a scale of 1 to 9. Blake and Mouton identified five principal *manage-ment styles* according to their position on the grid: 1,1, impoverished; 9,1, task; 1,9, country club; 5,5, middle of the road; and 9,9, team management.

Organizational development. An attempt to achieve corporate excellence by integrating executives' need for growth with organizational goals. O.D. is concerned with changing postures, perspectives, and processes, primarily through value changes in a systems context which is appropriate to the contemporary turbulent environment, with its inherent uncertainties.

Power equalization. A model which recognizes that the changee will achieve a more stable, appropriate, and adaptive change if he has an equal share of power with the changer.

Process change. The principal mode of process change is Kurt Lewin's un-freezing-changing-refreezing model. Unfreezing involves mobilizing ten-sion and frustration in the system to disintegrate inappropriate behaviours; changing means facilitating the formulation of new goals, strategies, and processes; refreezing is concerned with reinforcing and confirming new values and norms until they become internalized.

Process consultant. An organizational development scientist who helps the organization to solve its problems by making it aware of its processes, the consequences of these processes, and the mechanisms by which they can be changed. The process consultant stresses self-diagnosis and self-intervention, and his ultimate concern is to pass on his skills and values so the organization can continue to do for itself what he has done for it—in contrast to the structural consultant, who is concerned with passing along his knowledge.

Process consultation. A set of activities through which a consultant helps a healthy organization to perceive, understand, and act upon process events which occur in its environment, with a view to changing and improving its processes. Process consultation incorporates value consultation, since value changes are implicit in process changes; and it uses intervention strategy on the part of the consultant. E. H. Schein describes seven steps in process consultancy: (1) initial contact; (2) defining the formal and psychological contracts between client and consultant; (3) selecting a setting and a method of work; (4) data gathering and diagnosis; (5) intervention; (6) reducing involvement; and (7) termination.

Reentry problem. The difficulty of putting into effect in the company setting what one has learned in the T group.

Sensitivity training. A method of training which attempts to make the individual more aware of his personality dynamics, for example his motives, defence mechanisms, anxieties, effect on others, adaptation to a group role. Research indicates that sensitive people are above average in intelligence, tolerance, independence, responsibility, and considerateness; less consistent results indicate that the sensitive are more imaginative, more domineering, and less gregarious than average.

Structural consultation. The traditional approach to helping organizations (usually organizations in more or less trouble) through structural changes— changing organizational charts, guide-lines, and procedures; clarifying roles, delegation of responsibility, and line-staff relations; and developing more pervasive control techniques such as production planning and budgetary controls.

T group. Initially an unstructured, leaderless group in which individuals participate in order to learn about themselves (see *Sensitivity training*) and about group dynamics. The desired benefits for participants are: (1) insight into one's own personality dynamics, behaviour, and attitudes, and into those of others; (2) increased openness, receptivity, and tolerance of differences; and (3) improved operational skill in interpersonal relations, associated with greater willingness to take risks and try out new relationships.

Value consultation. Consultation which strives to import new values into the system. This is, in actuality, part of process consultation, rather than a separate technique, since the data gathering and feedback used in process consultation are intended to have an impact on the organization's value system (and, incidentally, on its structure if necessary). Many organizations achieve value changes by introducing personnel who have been exposed to many different cultures.

17

Organizational futuristics

Forecasting the future is not reserved exclusively for charlatans and fortune tellers but is also a major activity of social scientists. Social science fiction, in spite of its many failures, is a growth industry. In the United States, some of the forecasts of the past two or three decades have been quite wild. But many decisions made today commit future generations. Therefore there is a powerful need for these long-range forecasts to be made more rational. By making proper forecasts, it is possible to explicate what decisions are required and to identify what mistakes can be avoided. From bitter experience, many executives are only too well aware of the complications and errors of forecasting. Some problems associated with forecasting include:

1. How can forecasting, which requires sophisticated mathematical and social science techniques, be made credible to the lower level executives and politicians who are frequently called upon to make decisions with long time spans?
2. How much should be invested in forecasting?
3. Forecasting seems to work best when intuition is used to combine imperfect data and partial predictions from other forecasters.

To make forecasts about organizational behaviour requires strong nerves and the ability to walk on thin ice. For the forecasts to have any relevance whatsoever requires that they be based on findings from a number of disciplines, some of which must lie outside the competence of the forecaster.

To give forecasters the courage they need to stick their necks out, it is useful to make a trip to the graveyard of revolutionary predictions—the last chapters of books on organizational behaviour. After looking over the passing parade of George Orwell's *Animal Farm*, Aldous Huxley's *Brave New World*, H. J. Leavitt's "Unhuman Organization," and C. P. Snow's "Intellectual Luddites" and "Robot Executives," our forecaster (if he is not too bewildered) might take a look at the prophecies of John Kenneth Galbraith, who minted the phrase "the affluent society," and who, in *The New Industrial State*, predicted the "rise of the technostructure."

STRUCTURE OF CHAPTER 17

Our first topic is population, production, and pay. Beginning with the economic boom which was expected to characterize the 1970s, we look at the GNP tables which show Japan and France as the hot favourites. We then turn to the new Malthusians, Dennis Meadows and Jay W. Forrester, who, using their computer simulation of the world, forecast disaster in every direction.

While the "limits to growth" thesis has been sharply criticized, it has set the scene for a serious discussion of ecological problems. One answer to the problem is zero population growth, which is considered in this topic. We then briefly review some research methods for forecasting the future, including the Delphi method, the scenario, computer simulation, and technological forecasting.

Our second topic is the corporate environment, 1975–85. Here several predictions are examined, especially forecasts of Herman Kahn and Anthony Wiener of the Hudson Institute. One particularly worrying problem is the issue of structural employment, which is rapidly becoming a fact of life. We then examine, in terms of the future, the industrial system à la Galbraith, the firm of the future, and the development of the multinational company.

Topic 3 is the adhocracy, the contemporary organization which is designed specifically to cope with transience and change.

Our fourth topic is the counterculture, the new hippie-existenial life style which has developed a set of values which are decidedly anti-establishment. The future will have to take account of fluid, chasging value systems.

Topic 5, the futility of futurism, acknowledges the difficulty of predicting even a few months, to say nothing of a few years, into the turbulent future. Yet we venture to suggest that the underlying sruggle in future organizational systems will be between mechanism and mysticism.

TOPIC 1
Population, production, and pay

Most blueprints of the future have concentrated on three basic factors: population, production, and income and expenditure. Population estimates (based on extrapolation from past trends) have to be revised frequently. Both in the United States and Britain, the overall population is expected to increase. The structure of the population in both societies is moving away from the pyramid to the coffin-shaped structure which contains a diminishing proportion of blue-collar workers and an increasing proportion of white-collar workers, with the proportion of technocrats increasing most swiftly.

Not only production but also productivity will continue to rise. Even in Britain, plans are being prepared on the pessimistic assumption that productivity per worker will rise at the rate of 2½ per cent per year. The *rate of increase* in productivity in the United States is nearer the British than the faster Common Market countries. But present productivity in many industries in the United States, as measured by the added value concept, is three times that of the British.

When the factors of population and productivity are considered together, it is possible to estimate future levels of affluence. For example, in 1968 Mark Abrams predicted that in Britain the average gross personal real income per head could be about 50 per cent higher by 1983. Starting from a very much higher base, the rate of growth of real income in North America seemed almost certain to be higher.

In 1971 and 1972, the United States appeared to be in the midst of a new economic boom which would double its GNP within the 1970s to bring it to the $2,000 billion level. Many leading economic analysts believed that the United States would enjoy real gains of 6 per cent in GNP for 1973, and that such high levels might persist right through the decade. The thrust for this growth had come from consumer demand triggered by increased incomes, reduced joblessness, and the absence of strife on the industrial relations front. In this atmosphere of confidence, the presumption was that Americans would go on buying 11 million new cars, two million new homes, and large quantities of consumer durables each year. By early 1974, the crisis of confidence in government, the Mid-East strife and oil crisis, and the cut-backs caused by energy shortages cast doubt on such economic optimism.

In Europe, the forecast is that France will be the top economic power, with Britain in 9th or 10th place behind Spain, Austria, and Greece. According to a report prepared in 1972 by the Hudson Institute, France will become the third richest nation in the world, outranked only by the United States and Japan. France's economy, which has already outstripped Germany in output per head, is expected by 1990 to be the highest in

Europe, with a GNP per head twice that of Great Britain. With its superior educational system—and in spite of its poor policy on housing, poor health service, repressive police system, and extremes of wealth and poverty—France will go to the top of the European economic league, leaving Britain and Germany as the "have-not" nations of the 1980s and by its very success threatening the stability of the European Common Market.

THE NEO-MALTHUSIANS AND THE DOOMSDAY SYNDROME

By the beginning of the 21st century it is estimated (at present growth rates) that world population will have doubled, to 7 billion; that by 2050, it will have reached 20 billion; and that by the beginning of the 22d century it will have reached 50 billion. "Standing-room-only day" (one person for every square foot of earth) will arrive in about 700 years.

Uncontrolled population growth has been a favourite topic of discussion since Thomas Malthus put forward his famous theory that population increases at a geometric rate while food supplies grow at an arithmetic rate, and that the growth of population could only be limited by war, poverty, or famine.

To many academics and social reformers, the growth of technology, industry, and population has clearly outstripped the ability of our social and political institutions to control this growth. But in economics, growth has been regarded as an almost indispensable prerequisite of the good life. Now many social scientists and laymen have begun to view perpetual economic growth as a kind of social cancer which has got out of hand and is now destroying the body politic. The gnawing fear is that production increases will destroy civilization by stripping the earth of its natural resources and completely fouling with pollution our life support system, the biosphere. So strong is this reaction against economic growth that its proponents have been assailed with titles such as "growth maniacs" and "abominable growthmen."

The neo-Malthusians of modern times include a group from the Massachusetts Institute of Technology who developed a computer simulation of the growth of the world's capital, population, food resources, fuel supplies, and pollution. Jay W. Forrester built a mathematical model which attempted to document the relations between these five variables that govern the quantity and quality of life. With his model of the world, Dennis Meadows and his wife and other colleagues at M.I.T. fed into the computer masses of data on the five parameters and built in feedback loops to interlock variations in one parameter with variations in the others. Their results were published in the book *The Limits to Growth*.

The study was sponsored, approved, and publicized by the Club of Rome, an organization of distinguished industrialists and scientists from 25 countries. The organization stated its aims as:

> Our goal was to provide warnings of potential world crisis if these trends are allowed to continue, and thus offer an opportunity to make changes in our political, economic and social systems *to ensure that these crises do not take place.* . . . But we wish to underscore the *challenge* . . . rather than the difficulty of mapping out the road to a stable state and society.

Its general conclusion is that if current trends continue, man cannot avoid catastrophe. For Forrester and the Meadows team, there is no possibility of:

1. Sufficient technological and cultural progress to support this planet's projected population.
2. The majority of people in the developing countries even achieving the living standards of the developed world (North America and Europe).

The demon in the computer which turned it into a latter-day Malthus prophesying doom in the form of "a rather sudden and uncontrollable decline in both population and industrial capacity" sometime before the beginning of the 22d century is "exponential growth" at a regular annual percentage. In the Meadows computer, bad things are growing exponentially and good things are not. So, inevitably, "all growth projections end in collapse."

This apocalyptic vision of disaster emerges from a computer simulation of the world which, according to its critics, can be boiled down to about a dozen equations. Using these equations, Meadows set out to show that pollution and poverty cannot be attacked directly, but only by stopping economic growth. There is one way out: zero population growth must be established sometime in the next 20 years; but this prescription for global dynamic equilibrium has little prospect of being implemented.

The new Malthusians have been severely criticized for the assumptions which they made in their model. Peter Passell, Marc Roberts, and Leonard Ross, reviewing *The Limits to Growth* in the *New York Times* on April 2, 1972, argued that:

> "The Limits to Growth," in our view, is an empty and misleading work. Its imposing apparatus of computer technology and systems jargon conceals a kind of intellectual Rube Goldberg device—one which takes arbitrary assumptions, shakes them up and comes out with arbitrary conclusions that have the ring of science. "Limits" pretends to a degree of certainty so exaggerated as to obscure the few modest (and unoriginal) insights that it genuinely contains. Less than pseudoscience and little more than polemical fiction, "The Limits to Growth" is best summarized not as a rediscovery of the laws of nature but as a rediscovery of the oldest maxim of computer science: Garbage In, Garbage Out.
>
> It is no coincidence that all the simulations based on the Meadows world model invariably end in collapse. As in any simulation, the results depend on the information initially fed to the computer. And the "Limits" team fixes the wheel; no matter how many times you play there is only one possible outcome. Critical to their model is the notion

that growth produces stresses (pollution, resource demands, food requirements) which multiply geometrically. Like compound interest on a savings account, these stresses accumulate at a pace that constantly accelerates: Every child born is not only another mouth to feed but another potential parent. Every new factory not only drains away exhaustible resources but increases our capacity to build more factories. Geometric (or as mathematicians prefer to call it, exponential) growth must eventually produce spectacular results. If the Indians who sold Manhattan 300 years ago for $24 could have left their money untouched in a bank paying 7 per cent (a number chosen no more arbitrarily than many in "Limits") they would have more than $25-billion today.

While the team's world model hypothesizes exponential growth for industrial and agricultural needs, it places arbitrary, non-exponential, limits on the technical progress that might accommodate these needs. New methods of locating and mining ores, or recycling used materials, are assigned the ability to do no more than double reserve capacity; agricultural research can do no more than double land yields; pollution can cut emissions from each source by no more than three-fourths. Hence the end is inevitable. Economic demands must outstrip economic capacities simply because of the assumption of exponential growth in the former.

Meadows and his team have been accused of "rear-view mirror driving" because they have failed to grasp that all their exercise proves is that the past is a bad guide to the future. In essence, what has been challenged about *The Limits to Growth* is the basic set of assumptions on which the whole edifice of argument is built. But what is useful about the book is that it has triggered off a debate which attempts to explore the "complex of troubles affecting men of all nations" which threatens the survival of our species. For Meadows, these apparently divergent problems are in fact part of a single "world *problematique.*" It is also to the good that as a result of this debate, the current methods of measuring GNP have been challenged and attention focused on developing measures of the quality of life. Above all, the message of *Limits to Growth* for many is that man's existential life style, rather than his piles of consumer goods, must be allowed to grow exponentially. But isn't there a danger, in pursuing the quality of life, that the drive to "get things done" will become passé? For those who believe that zero growth is the answer to the evils of industrialization, the case of Britain, where growth rates typically run at a level between zero and 2 per cent, provides a disturbing example.

As recently as 1960, Britain produced more than any other country in Europe; but by 1970, in terms of GNP per capita, Germany and France produced 35 per cent more than Britain, leaving Britain 11th in Europe (below Finland and a little above Austria). Britain is still a most civilized and comfortable country to live in; but economically, the system is a disaster, with strikes steadily increasing. The essence of the problem seems to be that the population's expectations in terms of income, consumption, and social and medical security are continuously rising (perhaps driven up by American movies and TV) at a time when the British élite, the upper middle classes, is bored with business and growth and is no longer prepared to give itself over to the obsessive policy of total push that is required to make large organizations take off economically. The upper classes can rest on their laurels and annuities, while the working classes are still passionately anxious to move up. The moral of the British case of virtually zero growth may be that if the more powerful societies opt for slower GNP growth, the GNP's of underdeveloped countries may be frozen at a very low level.

"No growth" is not a viable policy for any society today. What is needed is an effort to rethink concepts of the basic purposes of growth and to develop a frame of reference for enriching lives and extending opportunities for all. Man need not accept the doomsday syndrome put out by Meadows; but as Maurice Strong of Canada, the Secretary General of the United Nations Conference on the Human Environment at Stockholm in 1972, put it (quoted in the *New York Times*, November 6, 1972):

> There is much difference of opinion in the scientific community over the severity of the environmental problem and whether doom is imminent or, indeed, inevitable. But one does not have to accept the inevitability of catastrophe. We need subscribe to no doomsday threat to be convinced that we cannot—we dare not—wait for all the evidence to be in. Time is no ally here unless we make it one.

We have become preoccupied with the question of continuous economic growth, which has been described as "the unwritten and unconfessed religion of our times." A moratorium is necessary, not a time of benign neglect. The insane demand for growth must stop, but innovation must not stop. As Dennis Gabor, winner of the 1971 Nobel Prize in Physics for the invention of the holograph (a three-dimensional "picture"), points out in *Innovations: Scientific, Technological and Social*:

> History must stop, the insane quantitative growth must stop—it must take an entirely new direction. Instead of working blindly toward things bigger and better, it must work toward improving the quality of life rather than increasing its quantity. Innovation must work toward a new harmony, a new equilibrium; otherwise it will only lead to an explosion.

Perhaps nowhere are the dangers of growth more evident than in the field of population growth.

ZPG: Zero population growth

Zero population growth has been one of the major goals of population experts, but odd things begin to happen once ZPG becomes a reality in a developed country.

According to the birth data for the first quarter of 1972, births in the United States have dropped sharply even from the declining 1971 rate and may have reached the threshold of ZPG. The total fertility rate is practically at the replacement level. Further, the U.S. National Fertility Study reports that in just five years American women have decidedly reduced their estimates of the number of children they intend to have in the future. But caution is needed because of the fluctuation in recent American rates of number of children per family: 2.23 in 1937, 3.27 in 1947, 3.77 in 1957, and 2.57 in 1967. The demographic number of ZPG is 2.11. The current U.S. rate may be under 2.14. If ZPG were reached and maintained for perhaps 70 years, the population would be stabilized.

Experience in developed countries which have experienced rates lower than ZPG is that advanced countries are not prepared to accept the situation of the population merely replacing itself or even declining slightly. For example, in 1969 a Japanese research study, after noting that the fertility rate had been below the replacement level for 9 out of 11 years, argued for a small increase in the birth rate. Apparently the media took up the cry with a vengeance, and the government began to consider family allowances. In 1966 in Rumania, where the birth rate had fallen below replacement for five years, the government clamped down on abortions, made divorce more difficult, and stopped the importing of contraceptives—all with dramatic effects on the birth rate.

If the population growth rate in the United States falls too far, such experiences suggest a clear possibility: overreaction. But fluctuations in the economy, the values espoused by the women's movement and the younger generations, and the drop-off in religious opposition to family planning will also be important factors.

RESEARCH METHODS OF FUTUROLOGY

THE DELPHI METHOD

A major technique which has been frequently used to make predictions about the future is the Delphi method, which was developed by O. Helmer at the RAND Corporation. The Delphi method represents an attempt to pool the judgements of experts by trying to establish a group consensus through feedback.

The Delphi method requires the successive polling of experts (who do not necessarily meet on a face-to-face basis), with controlled feedback of both the data of the previous poll and the reasons advanced for particular judgements. Each participant is usually supplied with the median and the first and third quartiles of the first poll in regard to each of the variables which is being estimated, and is then asked in the second poll to reconsider his own answer. If a participant's estimate lies outside the middle 50 per cent, he is invited to state briefly a reason for his opinion. In the third poll, participants are invited to criticize "reasons advanced" if they considered them unconvincing. In the fourth poll, the experts are asked to include a self-rating of expertise.

Not unexpectedly from a group dynamics point of view, the use of the Delphi technique produces conformity, with the spread of opinions tending to converge on the median. Nevertheless, one advantage of this technique is that it helps the less powerful, who might well be overawed if the experts were in fact brought together in one room.

THE SCENARIO

Another major technique which has been extensively used by the Hudson Institute is scenario writing. Scenario writing, which has its origins in war gaming and the movie-making business, requires the development of a hypothetical narrative of a sequence of events. A typical scenario might begin, "When Ford flooded the market in 1978 with electric cars with a range of 300 miles. . . ." The advantages of the scenario lie in the fact that developing the story raises certain issues:

1. What are the branch points in the narrative where choices emerge and other choices vanish?
2. What conditions favour the reaching of particular ends?
3. What could hold you back from achieving particular ends?

The actual scenario—which after all is a heuristic which does not prove anything but rather suggests the obvious intuitively—is only as good as the story teller. Nevertheless, scenario writing is a major method in the social sciences.

COMPUTER SIMULATION

An extremely useful technique for making predictions about the future is computer simulation. Simulations are interrelated abstractions or analogues of the real world.

Simulation has proved its worth for testing engineering designs at little cost and at no risk to life. Instead of building a test aircraft, the plane's characteristics are condensed into a set of mathematical equations. For example, the Apollo spacecraft made a large number of flights in an IBM 360 before it was built. Simulation can also be applied to the social sciences to facilitate conceptualization, research analysis, test, and evaluation, and also to predict how the system will perform at a later date.

Simulation can be defined along three dimensions:

1. Level of abstraction.
2. Fidelity.
3. Degree of mechanization or computerization.

The level of abstraction can be measured by the "distance" from the real world, as shown in Table 17–1. Fidelity relates to the level and precision with which the real world is reflected in the simulation. The degree of mechanization can vary from pencil and paper simulation right through to complex computer simulations such as a computer test of Apollo or the SAGE air defense system.

But computer simulations can get out of hand and run away with the inventor unless proper checks are built in. Such checks include reliability and validity of data and feedback of the simulation data for comparison with real-world data.

TABLE 17–1

LEVELS OF ABSTRACTION

FROM THE REAL WORLD

REAL WORLD
Observation and measurement
Field studies
Training, simulation, simulators
Laboratory experiments
Psychological tests
Game simulation
Monte Carlo methods
Analytic models
Mathematical models

Source: Modified from Haythorn, as presented in Kenyon B. DeGreene (ed.), *Systems Psychology* (New York: McGraw-Hill Book Co., 1970).

TECHNOLOGICAL FORECASTING

Technological forecasting (T.F.), which began in a systematic way around 1950, is a means through which organizations and governments can assess the effects of technological change on their being. T.F. can be used to assess the effects of SST's, VTOL aircraft, domestic computers, electric cars, genetic engineering, organ transplants, and the like, on society. Speaking more technically, T.F. can be defined as the probabilistic evaluation of future developments and applications of physical, behavioural, social, and life sciences.

Typically, T.F. is concerned with future scientific developments—their date and cost of invention, and their desirability. There are two basic methodological approaches, exploratory and normative. Exploratory forecasts, which are quantitative and rely on such techniques as curve fitting, correlation analysis, network theory, and decision tree analysis, begin with what we know now and project forward, trying to identify what we need to do to achieve a goal. While exploratory forecasting is thus opportunity-oriented, normative forecasting is mission-oriented. Curing cancer is an example of the normative orientation, and inventing DNA-type structures for genes an example of the exploratory. Normative forecasting begins with needs and goals, is highly subjective and then involves working back to what is currently known.

Congress has set up an Office of Technology Assessment which is expected to be able to make predictions about which new technologies are going to be important and their long-range effects. As well as assessing the impact and the side effects of new technologies, the new agency will also decide which technologies are to be discouraged.

Oddly enough, technological forecasting is not currently well developed in U.S. companies, though many large companies are involved in T.F. through the Hudson Institute, the RAND Corporation, and other think tanks. What most companies do is to contract broad assignments of T.F. to research institutes and worry in a short-term way about customers' needs and suppliers' possibilities. Of course, T.F. became big business as soon as the general public began to worry about the quality of the environment. The most difficult problem to-day is placing normative forecasting in the correct time frame.

T.F. is more of an art than a science. The future impact of a new technology is difficult to estimate. A frequently cited example is DDT, which was developed during World War II to protect Allied soldiers against diseases such as malaria. None of the researchers who developed DDT and few of those who found it a great boon to agriculture for 25 years, realized the dangers of the chemical insecticide or that it was an environmental hazard.

Technological forecasting remains difficult to apply because the situations to be predicted are complex; because the techniques have not been proved; because T.F. is difficult to integrate into organizational planning, and errors in T.F. can put giant companies into bankruptcy (e.g., Rolls-Royce); and because the environment is so uncertain. Finally, T.F. often leads to forecasts being labelled doomsday syndromes because they represent a threat to vested interests.

The importance of the need for T.F. is easily demonstrated by considering, for example, the failure of governments to size up the impact of air travel on North Atlantic ocean travel. In the 1950s and early 1960s, European countries and the United States heavily subsidized new luxury liners just at the time passengers were quitting ships for airplanes. Similar failures can be recorded for predictions on (1) the effect of automation on middle management and (2) the rate of growth of computers.

In selecting a forecasting technique, the following criteria should be kept in mind:

1. Are the necessary input data available?
2. Will the technique answer the question? With what accuracy?
3. What will the forecast cost?
4. What is the objective of the forecast—to provide definite answers or to get people thinking?

5. Who will be the prime beneficiary: the government, a defence contractor, a research agency, a manufacturer of ecological equipment, the people?
6. Who will be threatened by the forecast?
7. How much time is available to make the forecast?
8. Are technological experts available?
9. Is a combined effort (of organizations) necessary?
10. How can the disadvantages of the technique selected be mitigated?

T.F. is a serious and important task which is the responsibility of management. Already quite a number of university business schools have shown a significant interest in futurology and T.F. Presumably it is necessary to train cadres of scholars who have fingers in several academic pies. A good example of this multidisciplinary activity was the training of the astronauts, some of whom managed to link their expertise in aerospace with studies in social and behavioural sciences.

Presumably T.F. will become very important when we learn to solve the problems in corporate planning. Perhaps that's what forecasting's prime function is—to test out corporate planning techniques in the glamorous, exciting, highly visible context of predicting the future. In fact, many future-oriented techniques such as the Delphi method, simulation, and gaming have already been used in the context of corporate planning, where the realism of what's happening next Monday puts what's happening five years from now into perspective.

Put more tersely, managers are intensely interested in the "here and now" problem; and since this is usually unthinkable enough, thinkers about the enormously unthinkable, like Herman Kahn, excite their imaginations. Future-tense thinking is easier than present-tense thinking; since you can't worry about everything, worrying about the future makes the present more attractive. Which means that futurology can become a kind of cosmic neurosis—a thought to which we will return in Topic 5.

TOPIC 2
The corporate environment, 1975–85

Anthony Wiener and Herman Kahn at the Hudson Institute have made a forecast of the corporate environment for 1975–85. They begin their forecast by stressing the need for further study of economic projections and technological developments. Particular importance is attached to the impact of technology on business, with production plants becoming more automated yet more subject to pollution control. According to this model, there will probably be significant developments in climate and weather control; transportation advances such as large SST and hovercraft developments; improved surveillance techniques along the lines of the movie

"The Anderson Tapes"; developments in PL and CAL learning systems; the development of automated universal credit, audit, and banking systems; and so on.

Such technological changes will be accompanied by the spread of the hippie counterculture life styles to the other social classes, particularly the middle classes. The effect of new value systems on corporate life styles will be considerable, and management will be compelled to invent, install, and maintain participation processes which will have little real relevance in actual decision making but will provide suitable democratic religious rituals.

The fourth great factor for Kahn and Wiener is the rapid proliferation on the multinational and international business firm. For example, consider Jean-Jacques Servan-Schreiber's thesis that the third great force in the world will be American business in Europe. Similarly the rising levels of international trade and the emergence of the Japanese economy (the biggest surprise in store for the Russians is the passing of the Soviet economy by the Japanese, without the need for a bloody revolution) are bound to be tremendous factors in shaping the corporate future.

STRUCTURAL UNEMPLOYMENT BECOMES A FACT OF LIFE

A dramatic change has taken place in the attitude towards the level of unemployment that is acceptable in modern industrial societies. In the early 1960s a 4 per cent level was regarded as dangerously high in the United States. The major reason for the new attitude which presumes that 4 and 5 per cent figures are not intolerable is the reexamination of the goals of full employment and price stability.

Until recently it was presumed, based on the work of Professor A. W. Phillips of the London School of Economics, that there was an inverse relation between wage changes and the percentage of the labour force unemployed. For the United States, a 1960 analysis by Paul Samuelson and Robert Solon suggested that an annual price increase of 4.5 per cent would accompany a 3 per cent level of unemployment. Later surveys have suggested that the price rise might be as high as 5.5 per cent to achieve a 3 per cent level of unemployment.

While there is a measure of disagreement among economists about the precise ratio, most agree that some trade-off exists. The 1971 unemployment rate of 5.9 per cent meant five millions without work, with the young and blacks being hardest hit of all. The curious point is that when the U.S. government has sponsored programmes such as JOBS (Job Opportunities in the Business Sector), in which private businesses were paid to train disadvantaged workers, and the Work Incentive Program, whose function was to move welfare mothers into paying jobs, it seems to have been knocking its head against a wall. For if unemployment is structurally determined by wage, productivity, and price levels, how can such programmes work? For example, economists have calculated that stable prices and a productivity and wage increase of 2.5 per cent would be accompanied by up to an 8.5 per cent level of unemployment. Given a nexus of structural economic forces that work in this way, society is compelled to change its values to act more realistically in deciding what trade-offs are acceptable to it.

THE FUTURE OF THE INDUSTRIAL SYSTEM

John Kenneth Galbraith, in *The New Industrial State*, has argued that the technostructure—the managerial and technical apparatus for group decisions in corporations—has taken over the powers of the entrepreneurs of yesteryear. Galbraith's administrative man (a species of the genus technostructure who has superseded economic man) is apparently able to predict what affluent man (second-generation economic man) will do, by the use of extensive and penetrating market research and persuasion techniques. For Galbraith, the entrepreneur, the professional manager, and the union boss are dead or dying; long live the technostructure!

As Galbraith points out, economic history records how power was taken from the landed gentry at the beginning of the 19th century by the great industrial magnates and men of capital. The present century has seen the further transfer of power from the entrepreneur to the professional manager. The revolution generated by sophisticated technology, automation, and computer science has caused a further shift of power to the technostructure. Power in corporations is diffuse and held by the technocrats, who have the necessary expertise to work the system and who, in cabals and cliques, decide what happens next and who gets what—including what the shareholders are going to get.

Galbraith reinforces Herbert A. Simon's point that corporations do not maximize profits by noting that the technocrats who have decisive control are so interested in maximizing their corporations' security, autonomy, and continued existence that they are content merely to optimize earnings, including their own, in subordination to that goal. The corporation avoids high-risk adventure, tries to develop freedom from the capital market, and opts for only a secure amount of growth and a rate of return that will keep investors reasonably satisfied.

On executive salaries, Galbraith makes the extremely interesting observation:

> Management does not go out ruthlessly to reward itself—a sound management is expected to exercise restraint. . . . There are few corporations in which it would be suggested that executive salaries are at a maximum. . . . Astronomical figures, though not exceptional, are usually confined to the very top. Stock holdings by management are small and often non-existent. Stock options, the right to buy stock at predetermined prices if it goes up in value, though common, are by no means universal

and are more widely valued as a tax dodge than as an incentive. So even the case for maximization of personal return by a top management is not strong.

But with the rise of the technostructure, the notion, however tenuous, that a few managers might maximize their own return by maximizing that of the stockholders, dissolves entirely. Power passes down into the organization. Even the small stock interest of the top officers is no longer the rule. Salaries, whether modest or generous, are according to scale; they do not vary with profits. And with the power of decision goes opportunity for making money which all good employees are expected to eschew.

Discussing the achievements of the industrial state, Galbraith eloquently observes:

> Three further changes are less intimately a part of the established litany of accomplishment. First, there has been a further massive growth in the apparatus of persuasion and exhortation that is associated with the sale of goods. Measurement of the exposure, and susceptibility, of human beings to this persuasion is itself a flourishing science.
>
> Second, there has been the beginning of the decline of the trade union. Union membership in the United States reached a peak in 1956. Since then employment has continued to grow; union membership in the main has gone down. Friends of the labor movement, and those who depend on it for a livelihood, picture this downturn as temporary or cyclical. Quite a few others have not noticed it. There is a strong presumption that it is deeply rooted in related and deeper change.
>
> Finally, there has been a large expansion in enrollment for higher education together with a somewhat more modest increase in the means for providing it. This has been attributed to a new and penetrating concern for popular enlightenment. As with the fall in union membership, it has deeper roots. Had the economic system need only for millions of unlettered proletarians, these, very plausibly, are what would be provided.

Some of Galbraith's conclusions are particularly worth summarizing for the educated executive:

1. The power of the technostructure will increase at the expense of that of the entrepreneur and professional manager.
2. Governments will have to accept more responsibility for managing the market.
3. Corporations, through market manipulation, have considerable—if not decisive—ability to structure demand. The consumer is no longer sovereign.
4. The role of unions will decline.
5. Ideologies are becoming less important. Efficient industrial societies are judged by their ability to provide appropriate affluence.
6. There will be a blurring of "work" and "nonwork." Earnings are to be preferred to leisure, because work is interesting anyway.

7. All economies are mixed; public-private dichotomies are "old hat." The Russian economic system is becoming more capitalist and market-oriented; and the American free enterprise system is more of a mixed economy, public and private, than many Americans would care to admit.
8. All industrial systems will converge on the same pattern.
9. Corporations, to be effective, require a considerable measure of autonomy.
10. The power of the military-industrial complex is immense.

THE FIRM OF THE FUTURE

A number of distinguished academies have had a go at identifying the significant factors that are likely to influence in a serious way the firm of the future. Some of the major ones are discussed below.

INFORMATION TECHNOLOGY

The rapidly expanding information technology derives its strengths from the concept of computers not simply as large, fast counting machines, but as devices which not only utilize advanced mathematical techniques to solve problems in the field of operations research but also have the capability of simulating human thought.

The most striking feature of computer technology is the rate at which it is growing. One curious aspect of this growth is that the software of computers (the methods relating to the input and output of data) is still relatively primitive. Using the computer, sophisticated management information systems have been developed, but most firms have encountered considerable difficulties making "integration and rationalization" a living reality. Management scientists have been slow to resolve the problem of real-time control of industrial processes and traffic flows, irrespective of whether the traffic be of parcels, vehicles, or information.

The major influence of sophisticated and comprehensive information technology will be in strengthening the power of top management, who will band themselves together in a tight group of oligarchs because they will be able to programme middle management more efficiently. Harold J. Leavitt and Thomas L. Whisler say, in "Management in the 1980's":

> *a*) Information technology should move the boundary between planning and performance upward. Just as planning was taken from the hourly worker and given to the industrial engineer, we now expect it to be taken from a number of middle managers and given to as yet largely nonexistent specialists: "operations researchers," perhaps, or "organizational analysts." Jobs at today's middle-management level will become highly structured. Much more of the work will be programmed, i.e.,

covered by sets of operating rules governing the day-to-day decisions that are made.

b) Correlatively, we predict that large industrial organizations will recentralize, that top managers will take on an even larger proportion of the innovating, planning, and other "creative" functions than they have now.

c) A radical reorganization of middle-management levels should occur with *certain classes* of middle-management jobs moving downward in status and compensation (because they will require less autonomy and skill), while other classes move upward into the top-management group.

d) We suggest, too, that the line separating the top from the middle of the organization will be drawn more clearly and impenetrably than ever, much like the line drawn in the last few decades between hourly workers and first-line supervisors.

DYNAMICS

In terms of *product* dynamics, the life cycle of products will become shorter. *Market* dynamics indicate that organizations will be forced into postures which favour finding new markets. In the field of the relation of the *firm and society*, the interaction among business, government, and the public will become more important.

The major influence of these factors will be to reinforce the need to accept change and to keep organizational structure and authority minimal to facilitate innovation.

NEED TO DIVERSIFY

The need to diversify to meet market and technological change will develop very strongly, creating an organizational situation where the ability to manage will be more important than actual technical expertise. According to Igor Ansoff in "The Firm of the Future":

> The firm of the future will see an increasing emphasis on a new type of staff activity which is already in evidence in many firms. This is the activity of technical and managerial decision analysis by planners, management scientists, and computer specialists. The traditional staff activity of data acquisition, compilation, and presentation will have been taken over by the computer.
>
> The representaive manager who will fill these new roles will be different from the typical manager of today. He will be much broader-gauged than his present counterpart. On the one hand, he will be representative of today's trend toward selecting managers who have a thorough understanding of the firm's technology. On the other hand, he will be representative of another trend toward statesmen-managers who are capable of dealing with problems on a combined economic-political-cultural level.

Paradoxically enough, the age of change and automation will call for increased management skills in human relations. In a climate of change, increasing importance will be placed on the manager's ability to communicate rapidly and intelligibly, gain acceptance for change and innovation, and motivate and lead people in new and varying directions.

Diversification, coupled with the dynamic forces mentioned in the preceding section, has led to the emergence of the international conglomerate which sprawls across continents, leaping tariff walls and disarming nationalism.

MID-ATLANTIC THESIS

The "brain drain," affluence, and bigger and better jets, coupled with universal higher education will further the mid-Atlantic thesis. That "executives will live in Europe, work in North America, and holiday in Peru" is not as farfetched as it sounds. There is bound to be considerable and increasing interaction between North America and Europe, not only in capital and technology but also in managerial personnel. New-style maps, drawn to a scale where distance is measured in hours taken to travel from A to B by the most efficient and appropriate means, will show that the "distance" between London and New York or London and Newcastle is narrowing very quickly. Already increasing numbers of top consultants, scientists, and academics are commuting on a weekly basis across the Atlantic.

In the aircraft industry, not only are components being built in Europe and assembled in the United States, but there have been examples of major design work being carried out in Europe for aircraft being built on the other side of the Atlantic. With satellite communication and new photocopying and transmission techniques, this type of business activity is likely to increase.

EMERGENCE OF THE MULTINATIONAL FIRM

Mergers and acquisitions will increase the speed at which international conglomerates will emerge. The dominance of firms such as IBM, General Motors, General Dynamics, and Du Pont will increase, and large British firms will be increasingly sucked into larger, mostly American companies to survive. This is already the case to a significant extent with the British car industry. To meet competition from IBM, the British computer industry is virtually completely concentrated in one firm. British airframe manufacturers are desperately involved in "temporary liaisons" with continental European companies in joint projects. In Britain, major electrical engineering companies have recently merged. The number of British shipyards has been drastically reduced by government-sponsored integrations.

Important factors affecting this merger and acquisition activity include:

1. *Facilitation of diversification* may make unsuspecting firms strange bedfellows. Overall financial viability may outweigh the need for technical or market compatibility in merging firms (e.g., the union of an electronics firm and a car-hire business).

2. *Technological and organizational transfusions* will be made between advanced technical firms who have exploited mass production techniques to produce sophisticated sociotechnical systems such as modern supersonic fighters or aerospace devices. An early example of this transfusion is the entry of aircraft firms into the shipbuilding business in the United States.

3. *The military-industrial complex* will facilitate such mergers to improve efficiency. It has been argued that the most important single consideration affecting American society since 1945 is the fact that the U.S. Air Force, when it achieved its independence, had no internal research and development element to specify aircraft designs. The result was that research and design were both subcontracted. Hence not only the emergence of "think tanks" such as the RAND Corporation but also the fantastic growth in university research resources and facilities. From such activities has emerged the proposition called "concept formulation–contract definition" (C.F.–C.D.). The more advanced American and British companies are using the C.F.–C.D. philosophy as a means of deciding which business they are in and then "convincing the client" and "delivering."

4. *Common Market* phenomena will increase the need for the international conglomerate as a means of getting under tariff walls.

The development of the multinational company

The multinational firm is already a major ITT in the world and includes such companies as Xerox, IBM, ITT, Volkswagen, Fiat, Shell, 3M, and General Motors, who by virtue of their size, economic power, technological excellence, and international connections are seen by many as "states" in their own right.

What is a multinational firm? One definition is that it operates in at least six countries and its foreign subsidiaries account for 20 per cent of its total assets, sales, or labour force. No company with less than $100 million in annual sales is deemed a multinational. Other characteristics include above average growth and profits. Most of these firms are high in technology, research, and advertising, and most are American. The classic example is General Motors, whose annual sales in 1971 were $28 billion, which exceeded the GNP of all but 14 or 15 countries.

The multinational firms, whose spread has been encouraged by the progressive reduction of trade barriers and the upsurge of economic development of all world regions (both dating from the end of World War II), have had substantial effects on their host countries, including:

1. Infusing new technological concepts and devices.
2. Setting a standard of excellence in terms of corporate management style.
3. Acting as a spur to economic effort in other firms in the country, since frequently the local multinational has a higher level of performance in terms of profitability, exports, and investment.
4. Creating a cadre of local executives who have gained the experience of working in an American academy company such as IBM.

The multinationals have been severely criticized. Sometimes the multinational is seen as a means of penetrating and controlling the economics of other countries. They have been accused of exercising undue political influence in host countries. For example, ITT has been accused of trying to protect its interests in Chile by plotting to overthrow President Salvadore Allende, an established Marxist dedicated to policies of nationalization.

In any case, the multinationals exercise tremendous political influence in countries like Britain, Canada, France, Switzerland, and Holland. A threat by Ford to transfer the manufacture of a particular car model from England to Germany can send the British government into a tizzy. Government and business work so close, hand in glove, that the partnership is frequently characterized by terms like "Japan, Incorporated." For example, if the "United States, Incorporated" were to repeal the auto pact which guaranteed Canada sales of 500,000 cars a year in the United States, it could turn the Canadian economy upside down. The Canadian economy is a largely branch-plant operation, with small outfits which are high in marketing and low in technology and research. There is little corporate structure. The effect is very bad in terms of developing a band of corporate entrepreneur-managers who have the risk-taking skills and profiles which are vital for national prosperity in manufacturing, in government and in setting the style for the rest of society.

And Canada is no exception. In Britain, many believe that U.S. multinationals are turning Britain into a nation of industrial helots, with the research, corporate planning agencies, and highly technological devices manufactured in the United States and the low-technology, large-labour products manufactured in Britain. Computers are made in the United States, adding machines and typewriters in Britain.

Another major criticism of U.S. multinationals is that they attempt to apply industrial relations principles valid in the United States but not in the host country.

Probable developments in multinationals

Most multinationals will probably move from a posture of "economic imperialism" to one more characteristic of the truly international firm.

What this means, essentially, is a smaller share of the profits for the head office, an increasing number of local directors and senior corporate officials, a better share of research and high technology products for "overseas" plants, and a better adjustment to local social values.

Multinational firms will act in a more circumspect manner; but no matter how quietly they step, they are still going to be a tremendous political and economic force in the host countries. The rise of the multinational firm has had a tremendous effect on international politics. Firms uninhibited by national loyalties advance their corporate interests by lobbying among national legislatures, competing for favours. Weary of this need, Carl A. Gerstacker, chairman of Dow Chemical, said in 1972: "I have long dreamed of buying an island, owned by no nation, and of establishing World Headquarters of the Dow Company on the truly neutral ground of such an island, beholden to no nation or society." Multinationals tend to manufacture in countries where business taxes are lowest, labour laws most restrictive, unions weakest, toleration of pollution greatest. There is a growing demand for international legislation dealing with principles and guide-lines to police their activities. Leonard Woodcock, president of the United Auto Workers, sounded such a note in response to Gerstacker's dream:

> Study is necessary as the basis for sound action. But the phenomenal growth and spread of the I.C.'s [international companies] emphasizes the need for both studies and effective intergovernmental action to be expedited if irreparable damage is to be avoided.
>
> Mr. Gerstacker has put us on notice. The world cannot afford to permit fulfillment of his wish that I.C.'s be allowed to operate "beholden to no nation or society."

The big question has been put by Raymond Vernon, Professor of International Management at Harvard, in his book *Sovereignty at Bay*. Vernon asks whether the multinational enterprise is undermining the capacity of nations to work for their own welfare. Noting that "the multinational enterprise as a unit, though capable of wielding substantial economic power, is not accountable to any public authority that matches it in geographical reach and that represents the aggregate interests of all the countries the enterprise affects," Vernon has argued for the creation of a global justice department to regulate multinational firms.

THE EXECUTIVE OF THE FUTURE

Looking at the 1975–85 corporate environment from the executive's optic, it seems likely that he will be affected by some of the following developments:

1. Expansion of the top management group, which will be increasingly affluent, numerate, and literate.

2. Control of organizations by small oligarchies who will manage by the flexible exercise of power, sustained by information which is fresh and salient at the expense of being comprehensive. They will manage with an amalgam of authentic but realistic leadership married to a flair for backing technological winners—a marriage, however, based on a sound knowledge of finance.

3. Strengthening of the power of the technostructure in organizations based on the combination of technical and managerial expertise will be balanced by the power of significant shareholders who, through their ability to merge, acquire, and conglomerate companies, will retain a considerable, if not the decisive, share of authority. The managerial revolution has run into the counterrevolution of the significant shareholder with his fingers in many pies.

4. Management consulting will continue to increase in importance. Consultants, whose original interests were in techniques such as work study, time study, and production planning and control, are now more interested in systems theory and operations research. The élite among management consultants are receiving assignments requiring them to help formulate policies at the top managtment level for some of the largest companies. Such high-level consultancies will generate more realistic but topdrawer solutions which client companies sometimes may not implement but which will produce radical rethinking among company executives. As well as being a major source of productive improvements, consultants are being increasingly involved as brokers of executive talent.

5. University business schools, strengthened by the addition of distinguished academics like Herbert A. Simon, will become powerhouses of organization theory. The hard-headed organization theorists of the 1970s speak with a clarity and probity about matters that scarcely interested an earlier generation of management teachers. But many business executives and not a few academics are concerned about the change in values of a few business school academics whose high level of earnings, augmented by substantial consultancy fees, has effected a shift in belief towards the conspicuous consumption ethos at the expense of professional probity.

6. The main problem for executives will be in the area of values. Technology is a major factor determining the nature of value systems. With a rapidly changing technology, value systems tend to be left behind, as the hierarchy of the Catholic Church discovered with the impact of the birth control pill on conventional Catholic attitudes.

7. Rapid development of executive trade unions to handle the problems of middle management who have been displaced—either by merger and acquisition activity or by the information revolution—is to be expected. Already in Britain there are growing signs that the ranks of the technocratic white-collar unions are going to be swollen by displaced executives declared redundant by "the integration and rationalization of organizations."

TOPIC 3
The adhocracy

A new type of organization is emerging which is challenging the bureaucracy of organization man. Alvin Toffler, of *Future Shock* fame, has called this new form the "adhocracy." The single most salient characteristic of the adhocracy is its short life span. This built-in obsolescence is a direct result of the rapid and unexpected change which is characteristic of the turbulent environment of the 1970s.

These new emerging adhocracies demand a radically different perspective and posture. Instead of permanence, the demand is for transience; instead of the organization man, we find the "mobicentric" (mobile) manager who is in tune with the high mobility between organizations and the constant reorganization within.

What will be the characteristics of the new organizations of the post-industrial society? According to Warren Bennis, the key word will be "temporary." The organizations that will emerge will be adaptive, rapidly changing, ad hoc structures manned by members of the technostructure who owe allegiance not to the company but to the professional association that is the custodian of their expertise and the recognized licensing authority which allows them to practise and to flit from one assignment to another.

Adhocracy, either in the form of matrix management, project management, or the task force, is a relatively recent development with its antecedents in aerospace, computers, and the military. It is an organizational creature with a brief life span, built to cope with tight deadlines and highly exacting specifications which would turn conventional organizations, with their rigid line-staff relations, upside down. In selecting structures for problems, it is the old case of "horses for courses and courses for horses"—which is but to argue that classical bureaucracy is appropriate for a company which is producing standardized products in high volume; but where considerable innovation is required, the matrix or project forms of management are more appropriate (see Box 17.1).

Two major problems of adhocracies must be addressed, one primarily organizational and the other essentially a problem of the individual members. The organizational difficulty relates to such matters as how the adhocracy is meant to interact with the host organization, or how a project management team's goals and demands for scarce resources (highly qualified personnel, computer time, secretarial help, laboratory and testing facilities) are to be integrated with corresponding demands from established departments. Two general solutions, one formal and the other informal, have been set out to this problem of integration. The formal solution is more appropriate where the parent organization has a number of project groups going simultaneously; here it is usual to appoint a "project group of project leaders" to oversee the various project groups. The informal solution requires the ad hoc aristocrat who is leading a project to have access to top management, who can be briefed on achievements, challenges, probabilities, resources needed, and timespans, and then in turn give decisions and directives facilitating integration.

In general terms, survey research in the aerospace industry reveals that the major advantages of project management include: better control of projects, improved customer relations, shorter development time, lower programme costs, improved quality and reliability, better profit margins, and better control over programme security. In personal terms, the advantages include "higher visibility" and enhanced rates of executive growth.

But there are disadvantages. While control and customer relations improve, internal relations become more complex; considerable frustration and anxiety are generated, which frequently spill over into the personal lives of the adhocracy managers and are manifested in the form of increased divorces and rising alcoholism. Many of the project members face considerable anxiety about the possible loss of employment at the termination of a contract. Even worse, in some respects, is the fact that key personnel are put on "make-work" jobs during the phase-out period.

Yet curiously enough, matrix men seem indifferent to the authority ambiguities of the adhocracy. The whole phenomenon is most odd. To the ordinary manager or professional who has corporate tenure with a built-in salary annuity, it is difficult to understand why employees opt for project work with all its uncertainties—which affect not only the work situation, but also domestic relations and even career path plans, including such matters as personal educational programmes (which frequently have to be abandoned). It seems reasonable to speculate that highly ambitious, competent executives and professionals see the adhocracy as a dramatic means of achieving a high profile of executive excellence swiftly. Perhaps, also, such tyros win through the recognition barrier by persuading "lesser" people to risk their careers by working with them for substantial short-term salary gains—which may in the middle term have disastrous consequences for them as the political and economic environment changes.

To pursue this discussion of the symbiotic interaction between the highly competent stars who are the core of project teams and the less competent peripheral members who are usually regarded as dispensable requires a more detailed analysis of the engineering profession in North America. This field at present includes a good proportion of both talented and mediocre engineers who have been "let go" as aerospace and electronic contracts have diminished. Perhaps this is a major strength of North American project teams—that such groups have a core of tough, professional, tenured personnel and a periphery of floaters who have technical know-how; who like interesting, challenging work; and who, between

Box 17.1: How matrix organizations work

With the development of computer-based management information systems, there exists a need for new approaches to systems development organizations. The first approach, the functional groups organization, was soon replaced by the project organization, an adhocracy approach in which project teams were formed from individuals with the various skills necessary to implement the system. The third approach, the matrix organization, is the newest concept, one which is fast replacing the project organization approach, according to Gerald R. Demaagd.

The matrix organization, as shown below, consists in part of functional elements—such things as programming, systems analysis, computer operation, and user liaison. Temporary project assignments are superimposed on the functional elements to complete the matrix. The matrix organization differs from the project organization in that the team members join or leave the team as required, whereas in the project organization members are "permanently" attached.

Functional Elements

F_1 F_2 F_3 F_n

Project P_1

Elements P_2

P_3

P_n

Gerald R. Demaagd, "Matrix Management," *Datamation,* Vol. 16, No. 13 (1970), pp. 46–49. Figu reprinted with permission of *Datamation®*, copyright 1970 by Technical Publishing Co., Greenwic Connecticut 06830.

times (like actors "resting"), can occupy their time in a variety of occupations which range all the way from house painting to the invention of new gadgets.

Thus in deciding whether the adhocracy, and which of its forms— project management, matrix management, or task force management, should be selected, the nature of the problem is of critical importance.

TOPIC 4
The counterculture

A supposedly novel feature of our society is the emergence of the counterculture, a separate and distinct culture whose *raison d'être* is opposition to the culture of white male chauvinism, with its worship of science and adoration of affluence. The counterculture has its own values, norms, heroes, villains, life styles, folk lore, and rationales. Before going further, the most curious aspect of this "counter" is that so many squares have

The projects are organized along the lines of the matrix concept, "to take best advantage of the resource utilization efficiencies of the Company's functional organization and at the same time having the focused attention of project organization."

Advantages of the matrix organization over the other two types of organization are that it:

1. Makes job enrichment possible by creating larger work packages and introducing shared responsibility relationships.
2. Helps to make organization goals coincide with group goals by specifying end products to a task team consisting of members with all the required skills to produce the desired product.

The matrix organization of shared responsibility and mutual interdependence requires management attention in the following areas:

A. *Interaction:* The matrix form is designed to operate in an interactive environment. The team leader must create a climate for effective problem-solving activity and maintain this activity.
B. *Changing roles:* Various members of the team will assume leadership from time to time as questions arise in each person's area of specialization. "All members of the team are essentially on an equal level and status is determined by the relative importance of their individual contribution at any particular time."
C. *Ambiguity reaction of professionals:* Specialists in a particular field such as computer programming may react negatively to the vagueness of specific task responsibilities inherent in the matrix method. Too much ambiguity creates excessive tension and anxiety in the individual and impedes problem-solving effectiveness.

shopped at it, selectively picking up the parts of this life style which appealed to them or which they thought they could get away with. Thus sideburns have gotten longer in the office, while beads have been reserved for the week-end.

Though the counterculture is basically the antithesis or negative image of the established culture, the movement is essentially religious, and phrases like "the politics of eternity" and "the energies of transcendence" pepper the pages of the writings of Theodore Roszak, who coined the term in his 1969 book *The Making of a Counter Culture.* Roszak argues for a return to "sacramental consciousness" as a countervailing power to the "treachery of technology" and the "scientized temperament." Members of the counterculture treat the rationality of science as a kind of cosmic absurdity and view the "suave technocracies" of the modern world as spurious successes which are increasingly consuming what is left of the world's scarce resources.

The counterculture should not be regarded as a social aberration. As Rene Dubos has pointed out in *A God Within:*

> For thousands of years there have been attempts to provide alternatives for the existing social order in response to the perennial grounds for dissent: hierarchy and privilege, distrust of bureaucracy, disgust with

hedonism and consumerism. These are more than the dreamy schemes of dropouts, because they represent man's search for ways of life really suited to fundamental human needs.

The American public has been brainwashed during recent decades into the belief that progress means introducing into our lives everything we know how to produce—an endless variety of food additives, even more powerful automobiles, higher and higher buildings serviced by high-speed elevators, a senseless consumption of electricity to create a more artificial life. This kind of progress demands little imagination and its likely outcome is at best a return to the dark ages. Fortunately, the future will not be a magnified form of the present, for the simple reason that the absurdities of current trends are generating forces which will soon change the course of technological societies.

The paradox of modern life is that while technology has raised standards of living for large numbers of people, the quality of life has been reduced in so many places. While standards of living may be measured in objective economic terms, the quality of life is a much more subtle and subjective consideration which cannot be measured in terms of cars and washing machines per capita but is related to the extent to which life has meaning, purpose, and splendour.

The splendour of life derives its colour from art, music, and poetry, and ultimately from a form of naturalism which accepts that every man, woman, and child has some day to die. Naturalism is the philosophy most likely to make some cherish the grave beauty of living things and search for values to give zest and meaning to our lives, making them more authentic, alive, intimate, and unique.

The great achievement of the counterculture is that it has persuaded the Establishment to challenge the rationality of unlimited economic growth; to face the evil demon of Science, with its attendant devils of industrialization, urbanization, and technocracy; and to try to formulate new social policies which somehow combine the productivities of the systems approach with the intangible values of man's existential needs.

THE NEW VALUE SYSTEM

Running against the mainstream of the American middle-class value system of careerism through educational achievement, respectability, and conventional morality is the new, hippie, existential counterculture, which is presumed to be a direct reaction to the experience of living in an advanced industrial society. This new movement rejects the primacy of technology and impersonal relations and the unremitting demands of the rat race of upward mobility. It has developed a new *Weltanschauung* which has a distinct core value system of its own.

The primary characteristic of this new value system is the existential notion of freedom—freedom to do what one wants when one wants;

above all, an unwillingness to act unfree. Closely linked to the need for personal freedom is the need for expressiveness, which requires giving full symbolic and bodily reign to feelings. This essentially sensate, sensuous, hedonistic approach to life is opposed to the intellectual and cerebral analytical problem-solving style which has served our society so well in the past. A sense of immediacy, of making things happen in the "here and now" is a distinct feature of the new existential life style. The hippie argot includes a large number of words and phrases in the active present tense, underscoring a different time perspective. Terms like "where it's at," "turn on," "tune in," "drop out," "copout," "grooving," "mind-blowing," "switch on," "rap," "put on," and "send up" have been borrowed (with slight changes in meaning) from Negro, jazz, homosexual, and drug cultures.

Another element in the new counterculture is an emphasis on authenticity, a concern with coming to terms with one's own destiny, living it out, and avoiding the phoniness of conventional roles. Hippie preferences include feeling over intellectualism, the spontaneous over the structured, the primitive over the sophisticated, the mystical over the scientific, and the communal over the private.

In seeking an explanation for this value system, it is hard to resist the view that it is essentially antiestablishment and that it derives its rationale from reaction to the dominant middle-class value system. Yet, as we have said earlier, it has touched the lives of the square and the hip, the young and the old, the haves and the have-nots; and it has prompted rethinking of all kinds of processes and values. No worth-while value system (including this one) ever suffers from periodic challenge, examination, and reevaluation.

TOPIC 5
The futility of futurism

Futurism has come under severe and sustained fire from several sources. The most penetrating criticism is that social engineers like Herman Kahn cannot make valid predictions even over a period as short as five years. For example, Kahn's book *The Year 2,000*, written in 1967, made no reference to pollution. Yet pollution emerged as an environmental issue because the hippie, existential young people of our postindustrial societies —perhaps to avoid finding themselves rebels without a cause—turned on pollution.

Again, there is no mention in Kahn's book of the Club of Rome, which sponsored and endorsed the Meadows *Limits to Growth study*. Now it is being argued that the industrialists behind the Club of Rome are forecasting disaster to get the market ready for the antipollution technology and systems which they are going to invent, manufacture, and sell. Such criticism reveals the gap between the "haves" and the "had"—between those who have a system for hire and those who are had by it.

In essence, two great forces are running in opposite directions, on a collision course. One force has its origins in the "mindless, liberal, techno-cratic, managerial vision" held by system theorists and behavioural engi-neers like Meadows, Forrester, Kahn, and Skinner, who believe the answers lie in studying large Gestalts (for example, the world) whose configuration can be solved by running equations through data-loaded computers and by treating people as if they were subatomic particles in the atoms of primary groups, which are held together in the molecules of organization, which in turn are part of the complex protein molecule known as a society, which in turn is . . . and so on until the ultimate Gestalt is reached.

The other force, sustained by a social form of Werner Heisenberg's principle of uncertainty, is existential man, who believes ultimately that all is chaos and anarchy and that all social arrangements are temporary, power-based, and thus nonbinding in any real sense. All meaning is a temporary mnemonic somewhat arbitrarily put together to facilitate communication.

As William Irwin Thompson, a professor of humanities at York University, has put it in his provocative book *At the Edge of History,* culture has split into mechanism and mysticism. The new mechanists— the Meadows-Toffler-Skinner axis—are obsessed with the power of the new technology. They essentially see man as an information-processing system whose life style can be controlled by changing the software, in terms of either the data fed into him or the programme or paradigm he is led to install. The new mechanists see the high ground of the modern battlefield in terms of who has first access to the computer print-out.

There can be no quarrel about seeing the future organization as an information-processing system. In Figure 17–1 we gather some of the heuristics of this chapter into our systems model framework to portray it as such. No doubt the futility of futurism means that we have overlooked elements that will turn out to be of great importance; but, in the areas of values and end products, we have included elements which can already be seen as paradoxical. The information-processing system is task-efficient; but it is also inherently antidemocratic. Even though sophisticated and sensitive systems analysts would like the processes to be participative, with all information made available to those whom it affects, it is near-impossible to see how that can be achieved in practice; for the powerful control the information-processing function and decide the timing, and more impor-tantly the sequencing, of the releases. The actual sequencing and timing, in Skinnerian terms, become a contingent reinforcement strategy which beckons the uninitiated fly, the "lowerarch," into the web of information values of the spider, the "hierarch." The new systems of tiered techno-

FIGURE 17–1
THE ORGANIZATION OF THE FUTURE

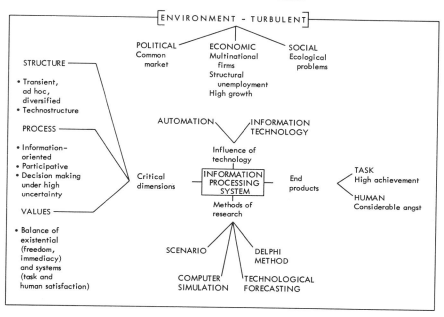

structures manned by mobicentric men are essentially layers of information strata; each successive layer as you move upwards is incapable of being digested by the lowerarch just below without it being predigested for him. Therefore, the new systems approach is essentially antidemocratic.

Existential man knows this and has turned to the counterculture in the form of Yoga, Zen, or the human potential movement in search of planetary mysticism—about which people like Meadows have nothing to say. It sounds incredible, but people want holiness back in their lives, to make life meaningful, so that personal needs like self-realization can be measured on a sanctified scale. And the more enlightened and sophisticated corporate philosopher-kings realize the necessity of humanizing technology by effecting a marriage of systems theory and existentialism. For if alienation, apathy, and anomie get out of hand, every Chevvy will have a better chance of having a milk bottle welded into its gas tank; every 747 will have a statistically higher chance of being skyjacked; every building put up (to replace the Pentagon when it is blown up) will have to have the resistance of Fort Knox—in short, every up-for-grabs thing will face the explosions of frustration euphemistically titled "ripping off."

The crucial issue is how these two forces, which are heading towards each other like space capsules in the same orbit but going in opposite directions, are to be docked. The first postindustrial society—heading for lower growth, zero population growth, and pollution control; peopled with existential men who are aware, authentic, and awakening—will have to negotiate with the second postindustrial society, in an atmosphere appropriate to nuclear disarmament talks. The answer is that the plan for the docking of systems theory and existentialism will not come from people who think in linear causal trains, but will emerge from the underground presses of those who prefer the cup of hemlock to the diet of sophistry that conventional wisdom offered.

Who's first for the hemlock?

REVIEW AND RESEARCH

1. Why is futurology such a rapidly expanding area of research?

2. List the principal methods of studying futurology. Classify each method under the following headings: suitable problems, kind of data collected, time span, choices high-lighted, and cautions.

3. Write a brief outlining a policy controlling multinational companies which the United Nations might adopt.

4. Compare managements in the United States, Europe, and Japan. How do they differ? How are they similar?

5. List the 10 most important changes in technology which have taken place in the last 10 years. How have they affected management?

6. Guesstimate the 10 most important changes in technology, biology, and behavioural technology that will take place in the next 10 years. How will these changes affect management?

7. How does a computer modify the structure of an organization? In the future, what effect will the computer have on the structure of an organization? How will it affect middle-rank executives? What plans should be drawn up now to help such executives?

8. What are the major difficulties in technological forecasting? What kinds of teams should be assembled to develop T.F.? Devise a set of principles to help in making T.F.'s.

9. What changes should be made in university business schools to take cognizance of developments in (*a*) technology, (*b*) behavioural technology, (*c*) ecology, (*d*) the counterculture? Devise a curriculum to meet the opportunities of the new society that these forces will create.

10. Effective participation in organizations depends on power equalization. How can this condition be achieved in business?

GLOSSARY OF TERMS

Adhocracy. The ad hoc style of organization, in the form of matrix management, project management, or the task force. Military, aerospace, and computer technologies brought about the emergence of the temporary organization manned by highly mobile members of the technostructure put together to perform a specific task and then disbanded.

Computer simulation. A research technique in which interrelated abstractions or analogies of the real world are modeled by feeding data into computers; used to forecast highly technical system operations.

Counterculture. A separate culture formed in reaction to the established value system; in our times, a value system stressing freedom, immediacy, authenticity, and awareness as opposed to control, manipulation, hypocrisy, etc.

Delphi method. A research technique which attempts to pool the judgements of experts by successive polling, with feedback of their previous answers and reasons for answers between polls.

Multinational firms. International conglomerates with above-average growth and profits, high in technology. Firms which operate in several countries, whose foreign subsidiaries account for at least 20 per cent of total assets, and whose annual sales are at least $100 million qualify in this class; most are American at present.

Scenario writing. A research technique which requires the formulation of a hypothetical narrative of a possible sequence of events.

Structural unemployment. The concept that the level of unemployment is a trade-off with such structural factors as wages, productivity, and prices.

Technostructure. J. K. Galbraith's term for the interlocking of large, mature, technologically sophisticated private corporations with government planning and economic policy (particularly in areas such as the military and space programs), necessitating the rethinking of past economic ideologies. An important concomitant of the technostructure is the co-operation of the educational system in producing the needed technocrats.

Technological forecasting. A research technique for the probabilistic evaluation of future developments and applications of physical, behavioural, social, and life sciences. T.F. is typically concerned with the desirability and cost of scientific developments; it may be exploratory or normative.

Bibliography

ABRAMS, MARK. "Britain: The Next 15 Years," *New Society*, November 7, 1968.

ACKOFF, RUSSELL L. "The Development of Operations Research as a Science," *Journal of Operations Research Society of America*, Vol. 4, No. 3 (June, 1956).

———. "Management Misinformation Systems," *Management Science*, Vol. 14 (December, 1967).

ADAMS, J. S. "Inequity in Social Exchanges," pp. 267–300 in L. BERKOWITZ (ed.), *Advances in Experimental Social Psychology*. Vol. 2. New York: Academic Press, 1965.

AIKEN, M., and HAGE, J. "Organizational Interdependence and Interorganizational Structure," *American Journal of Sociology*, Vol. 33, No. 6 (1968), pp. 912–31.

ALBERS, H. H. *Organized Executive Action*. New York: John Wiley & Sons, 1961.

ALDERFER, C. P. "An Organizational Syndrome," *Administrative Science Quarterly*, Vol. 12 (1967), pp. 440–60.

———. "Job Enlargement and the Organizational Context," *Personnel Psychology*, Vol 22 (1969).

ALLAND, ALEXANDER. *The Human Imperative*. New York: Columbia University Press, 1972.

ALLEN, THOMAS J. "Communications in the Research and Development Laboratory," *Technology Review*, Vol. 70 (October–November, 1967), pp. 1–8.

ALLPORT, G. W. *Personality: A Psychological Interpretation.* New York: Holt, Rinehart & Winston, 1937.

——. "The Open System in Personality Theory," *Journal of Abnormal and Social Psychology,* Vol. 61 (1960), pp. 301–11.

AMERICAN MANAGEMENT ASSOCIATION. *Manager Unions.* New York: A.M.A., June, 1972.

ANDERSON, JOHN. Proctor & Gamble Company document.

ANDERSON, R. C. "Individual Differences and Problem Solving," in R. M. GAGNE (ed.), *Learning and Individual Differences.* Indiana, Indianapolis: Bobbs-Merrill, 1967.

ANGELL, R. C. "Sociology of Human Conflict," in *The Nature of Conflict* (ed. E. B. McNEIL). Englewood Cliffs, N.J.: Prentice-Hall, 1965.

ANSOFF, H. I. "The Firm of the Future," *Harvard Business Review,* September–October, 1965.

ARDRESKI, S. *Social Sciences as Sorcery.* London: André Deutsch, 1972.

ARGYLE, M.; GARDNER, G.; and CIOFFI, F. "The Measurement of Supervisory Methods," *Human Relations,* Vol. 10, (1957).

ARGYRIS, CHRIS. *The Impact of Budgets on People.* New York: Controllership Institute, 1952.

——. *Personality and Organization.* New York: Harper & Bros., 1957.

——. "Individual Actualization in Complex Organizations," *Mental Hygiene,* Vol. 44 (April, 1960), pp. 226–337.

——. *Interpersonal Competence and Organizational Effectiveness.* Homewood, Ill.: Richard D. Irwin, 1962.

——. "Some Unintended Consequences of Rigorous Research," *Psychological Bulletin,* Vol. 70 (1968), pp. 185–97.

——. *Intervention Theory and Method.* Reading, Mass.: Addison-Wesley, 1970.

ARONSON, E., and MILLS, J. "Effect of Severity of Initiation on Liking for a Group," in D. CARTWRIGHT and A. ZANDER (eds.), *Group Dynamics.* New Yorker: Harper & Row, 1960.

ASCH, S. E. "Studies of Independence and Conformity. A Minority of One against a Unanimous Majority," *Psychological Monographs,* Vol. 70, No. 9 (1965).

ASHOUR, AHMED S. "The Contingency Model of Leadership Effectiveness: An Evaluation," *Organizational Behaviour and Performance,* Vol. 9, No. 3 (June, 1973).

ATKINSON, J. W. *An Introduction to Motivation.* Princeton, N.J.: D. Van Nostrand Co., 1964.

——, and FEATHERS, N. T. (eds.). *A Theory of Achievement Motivation.* New York: John Wiley & Sons, 1966.

BACKMAN, C. W., and SECORD, P. E. (eds). *Problems in Social Psychology.* New York: McGraw-Hill Book Co., 1966.

BAGEHOT, W. *The English Constitution.* London: Fontana, 1963.

BALES, R. F. "Some Uniformities of Behavior in Small Social Systems," in

S. E. Swanson, T. M. Newcomb, and E. L. Hartley (eds.), *Reading in Social Psychology*. New York: Henry Holt & Co., 1952.

————. "In Conference," *Harvard Business Review*, Vol. 32, No. 2 (April, 1954), pp. 44–50.

————, and Slater, P. "Role Differentiation in Small Decision-Making Groups," in T. Parsons, *et al.*, *Family Socialization and Interaction Process*. Glencoe, Ill.: Free Press, 1955.

Bandura, A. *Principles of Behavior Modification*. New York: Holt, Rinehart & Winston, 1969.

Banton, M. "Role," *New Society*, May 7, 1964.

Baritz, L. *The Servants of Power, A History of the Use of Social Science in American Industry*. New York: John Wiley & Sons, 1965.

Barnard, C. I. *The Function of the Executive*. Cambridge, Mass.: Harvard University Press, 1938.

Barrett, R. S. "Guide to Using Psychological Tests," *Harvard Business Review*, September–October, 1963, pp. 138–46.

Bavelas, Alex. "Communication Patterns in Task-Oriented Groups," in D. Cartwright and A. Zander (eds.), *Group Dynamics*. New York: Harper & Row, 1960.

————, and Strauss, G. "Group Dynamics and Intergroup Relations," in W. F. Whyte *et al.*, *Money and Motivation*. New York: Harper & Row, 1955.

Benne, K. D. "From Polarization to Paradox" and "History of the T-Group in the Laboratory Setting," L. P. Bradford, J. R. Gibb, and K. D. Benne (eds.), *T-Group Theory and Laboratory Method*. New York: John Wiley & Sons, 1964.

Bennis, Warren G. *Changing Organizations*. New York: McGraw-Hill Book Co., 1966.

————, and Shepard, Herbert A. "A Theory of Group Development," *Human Relations*, Vol. 9 (1965), pp. 415–57.

Berelson, B., and Steiner, G. A. *Human Behavior: An Inventory of Scientific Findings*. New York: Harcourt, Brace & World, 1964.

Berg, Ivar. *Education and Jobs: The Great Training Robbery*. New York: Frederick A. Praeger, 1972.

Berkowitz, N. H., and Bennis, W. G. "Interaction Patterns in Formal Service-Oriented Organizations," *Administrative Science Quarterly*, Vol. 6 (1961–62).

Berliner, J. "A Problem in Soviet Business Management," *Administrative Science Quarterly*, Vol. 1 (June, 1956).

Berne, Eric. *Games People Play*. New York: Grove Press, 1964.

Berry, D. F. *The Politics of Personnel Research*. Ann Arbor: University of Michigan Press, 1967.

Bion, W. R. *Experiences in Groups*. London: Tavistock Publications Ltd., 1961.

————. "Experiences in Groups," *Human Relations*, Vol. 3 (1950), p. 3.

Bird, C. *Social Psychology*. New York: Appleton-Century, 1940.

BLAIR, JOHN M. *Economic Concentration.* New York: Harcourt, Brace, & World, 1973.

BLAKE, ROBERT R. "Studying Group Action," in L. P. BRADFORD, J. R. GIBB, and K. D. BENNE (eds.), *T-Group Theory and Laboratory Method.* New York: John Wiley & Sons, 1964.

———, and MOUTON, J. S. *The Managerial Grid.* Houston: Gulf Publishing Co., 1964.

——— and ———. *Corporate Excellence through Grid Organization Develment.* Houston: Gulf Publishing Co., 1968.

——— *et al.* "Breakthrough in Organization Development," *Harvard Business Review,* November–December, 1964.

———; SHEPARD, H. A.; and MOUTON, J. S. *Managing Intergroup Conflict in Industry.* Houston: Gulf Publishing Co., 1964.

BLAU, PETER M. *Dynamics of Bureaucracy.* Chicago: University of Chicago Press, 1955.

———, and DUNCAN, O. D. *The American Occupational Structure.* New York: John Wiley & Sons, 1965.

———, and SCOTT, W. R. *Formal Organizations.* London: Routledge and Kegan Paul; San Francisco: Chandler Publishing Co., 1963.

BLAUNER, R. *Alienation and Freedom.* Chicago: University of Chicago Press, 1964.

BLOOD, MILTON R., and HULIN, CHARLES L. "Alienation, Environmental Characteristics and Worker Responses," *Journal of Applied Psychology,* Vol. 53, No. 3 (June, 1967), pp. 284–90.

BOTTOMORE, T. B., and RUBEL, M. *Karl Marx: Selected Writings.* London: Penguin, 1963.

BOULDING, KENNETH E. "General Systems Theory—The Skeleton of Science," *Management Science,* Vol. 2 (April, 1956), pp. 197–208.

BRADBURY, M. "The Institutional Joneses," *Punch,* February 10, 1960.

BRADFORD, L. P.; GIBB, J. R.; and BENNE, K. D. *T-Group Theory and Laboratory Method.* New York: John Wiley & Sons, 1964.

BRADLEY, C. "New Men at the Personnel Desk," *The (London) Times,* January 3, 1968.

BRADY, J. V. "Ulcers in 'Executive' Monkeys," *Scientific American,* Vol. 19, No. 4 (1958), pp. 95–100.

BRAY, D. W. "The Identification of Executive Ability," *Business Review,* May, 1967, pp. 140–47.

———, and CAMPBELL, R. J. "Selection of Salesmen by Means of an Assessment Center," *Journal of Applied Psychology,* Vol. 52, No. 1 (1968), p. 18.

BRAYFIELD, A. H., and CROCKETT, W. H. "Employee Attitudes and Employee Performance," *Psychological Bulletin,* Vol. 52, No. 5 (1955), pp. 396–424.

BRECH, E. F. L. *Organization—The Framework of Management.* London: Longmans, 1965.

BRITT, S. H. *Social Psychology of Modern Life.* New York: Farrar, Strauss & Giroux, 1941.

BROWN, R. *Social Psychology*. New York: Free Press, 1965.

BROWN, W. *Exploration in Management*. London: Heinemann Educational Books Ltd., 1960.

————, and JAQUES, E. *The Glacier Project Papers*. London: Heinemann Educational Books Ltd., 1965.

BRUNER, J. S. *The Relevance of Education*. New York: W. W. Norton & Co., 1971.

————, and GOODMAN, C. C. "Value and Need as Organizing Factors in Perception," *"Journal of Abnormal and Social Psychology*, Vol. 42 (1947), pp. 33–44.

BRUNSON, RICHARD W., SR. "Perceptual Skills in the Corporate Jungle," *Personnel Journal*, Vol. 51, No. 1 (January, 1972).

BUCHANAN, P. C. "Evaluating the Effectiveness of Laboratory T-Group Training in Industry," National Training Laboratories, Explorations in Human Relations Training and Research Series, No. 1, 1965.

BUCKLEY, WALTER. *Sociology and Modern Systems Theory*. Englewood Cliffs, N.J.: Prentice-Hall, 1967.

———— (ed.). *Modern Systems Research for the Behavioral Scientists*. Chicago: Aldine Publishing Co., 1968.

BUGENTAL, J. *The Search for Authenticity*. New York: Holt, Rinehart & Winston, 1965.

BURNS, TOM. "The Directions of Activity and Communications in a Departmental Executive Group," *Human Relations*, Vol. 7 (1954), pp. 73–97.

————, and STALKER, G. M. *The Management of Innovation*. London: Tavistock Publications Ltd., 1961.

BYHAM, W. C. "Assessment Center for Spotting Future Managers," *Harvard Business Review*, July–August, 1970.

CAMPBELL, J. P., and DUNNETTE, M. D. "Effectiveness of T-Group Experiences in Managerial Training and Development," *Psychological Bulletin*, Vol. 70 (1968), pp. 73–104.

————; ————; LAWLER, E. E.: and WEICK, K. E. *Managerial Behavior, Performance, and Effectiveness*. New York: McGraw-Hill Book Co., 1970.

CANNON, W. B. *The Wisdom of the Body*. New York: W. W. Norton & Co., 1932.

CAPLAN, R. "Organizational Stress and Individual Strain: A Social Psychological Study of Risk Factors in Coronary Heart Disease among Administrators, Engineers, and Scientists," unpublished Ph.D. thesis, University of Michigan, 1971.

————, and FRENCH, J. R. P., JR. "Final Report to NASA," unpublished, University of Michigan, 1968.

CAREY, A. "The Hawthorne Studies: A Radical Criticism," *American Sociological Review*, Vol. 32 (1967), pp. 403–17.

CARLSON, R. E. "Selection Interview Decisions: The Effect of Interviewer Experience, Relative Quota Situation, and Applicant Sample on Interviewing Decisions," *Personnel Psychology*, Vol. 20, No. 3 (1967).

CARLSON, S. *Executive Behaviour*. Stockholm: Strombergs, 1951.

CARNEGIE, D. *How to Win Friends and Influence People.* New York: Pocket Books, Inc. 1958.

CARTER, C. F., and WILLIAMS, B. R. *Science in Industry.* London: Oxford University Press, 1959.

CARTER, E. EUGENE. "The Behavioral Theory of the Firm and Top Level Corporate Decision," *Administrative Science Quarterly*, Vol. 16 (1971), pp. 413–28.

CARTWRIGHT, D. "Power: A Neglected Variable in Social Psychology," in W. G. BENNIS, K. D. BENNE, and R. CHIN (eds.), *The Planning Change.* New York: Holt, Rinehart & Winston, 1966.

———, and ZANDER, A. *Group Dynamics.* 2d ed. New York: Harper & Row, 1960.

CATTELL, R. B. *The Scientific Analysis of Personality.* Chicago: Aldine Publishing Co., 1965.

CHAMBERS, E. G. "Industrial Fatigue," *Occupational Psychology*, the quarterly journal of the National Institute of Industrial Psychology, London, Vol. 35, Nos. 1 & 2 (January and April, 1961).

CHAMBERS, S. P. "Statistics and Intellectual Integrity," inaugural address of the president of the Royal Statistical Society, November 25, 1964.

CHANCE, J. E., and MEADERS, W. "Needs and Interpersonal Perception," *Journal of Personality*, Vol. 28 (1960), pp. 200–210.

CHASE, STUART. *Men at Work.* New York: Harcourt, Brace & World, 1941.

CHANDLER, A. D., JR. *Strategy and Structure.* Cambridge, Mass.: M.I.T. Press, 1962.

CHINOY, ELY. "Manning the Machines—The Assembly Line Worker," in P. C. BERGER (ed.), *The Human Shape of Work.* New York: Macmillan Co., 1964.

CHRISTIE, R. "The Prevalence of Machiavellian Orientations," a symposium at the Annual Meeting of the American Psychological Association, Los Angeles, 1964.

CLARK, D. G., and MOSSON, T. M. "Industrial Managers in Belgium, France and the United Kingdom: A Comparison," *Management International Review*, 1967, pp. 2–3.

CLARK, D. H. *Administrative Therapy.* London: Tavistock Publications Ltd., 1964.

CLARK, RUSSELL D. III. "Group-Induced Shift toward Risk: A Critical Appraisal," *Psychological Bulletin*, Vol. 76, No. 4 (1971), pp. 251–70.

CLAY, M. J., and WALLEY, B. H. *Performance and Profitability.* New York: Humanities Press, 1965.

CLINE, V. B. "Ability to Judge Personality Assessed with a Stress Interview and Sound Film Technique," *Journal of Abnormal and Social Psychology*, Vol. 50 (1965).

COBBS, B. B. "A Report on the Health of Air Traffic Controllers Based on Aero-medical Examination Data," published report to the Federal Aviation Agency, University of Michigan, 1972.

COCH, L., and FRENCH, J. R. P. "Overcoming Resistance to Change," *Human Relations*, Vol. 1 (1948).

COLBY, B. N. "Behavioral Redundancy," *Behavioral Science*, Vol. 3 (1958), pp. 317–22.

COLBY, K. M. "Research in Psychoanalytic Information Theory," in I. G. SARASON (ed.), *Psychoanalysis and the Study of Behavior*. Princeton, N.J.: D. Van Nostrand Co., 1965.

COLEMAN, J. C. *Personality Dynamics and Effective Behavior*. Chicago: Scott, Foresman & Co., 1960.

COOLEY, C. H. *Social Organization*. New York: Charles Scribner's Sons, 1909.

COOPER, D. "The Anti-Hospital: An Experiment in Psychiatry," *New Society*, Vol. 11 (March, 1965).

COOPER, G. L. "The Influence of the Trainer on Participant Change in T-Groups," *Human Relations*, Vol. 22, No. 6 (1969), pp. 515–30.

COOPER, R., and PAYNE, R. "Extraversion and Some Aspects of Work Behavior" *Personnel Psychology*, Vol. 20, (1967), pp. 45–57.

COSER, L. A. *The Functions of Social Conflict*. New York: Free Press of Glencoe, 1955.

COUCH, PETER D., and STROTHER, GEORGE B. "A Critical Incident Evaluation of Supervisory Training," *Training and Development Journal*, Vol. 25, No. 9 (September, 1971).

CRICHTON, A. "Personnel Management in Working Groups," *Occasional Papers* No. 18, Institute of Personnel Management.

CRONBACH, L. J. "Processes Affecting Scores on Understanding of Others and Assumed Similarity," *Psychological Bulletin*, Vol. 52 (1955), pp. 177–93.

CROPLEY, A. J. "Creativity," in P. E. VERNON (ed.), *Creativity*. London: Penguin, 1970 and New York: Humanities Press, Inc.

CROZIER, M. *The Bureaucratic Phenomenon*. Chicago: University of Chicago Press, 1964.

CRUTCHFIELD, C. N. "A Study of Managerial Stereotypes," unpublished M.B.A. thesis, McGill University, April, 1968.

CUBBON, ALLAN. "The Hawthorne Talk in Context," *Occupational Psychology*, Vol. 43 (1969), pp. 111–28.

CUMMINGS, L. L. "Management Effectiveness II: Performance at the Graduate Student Level," *Academy of Management Journal*, Vol. 10, No. 2 (June, 1967), pp. 145–60.

CYERT, R. M., and MARCH, J. G. *A Behavioral Theory of the Firm*. Englewood Cliffs, N.J.: Prentice-Hall, 1963.

———; SIMON, H. A.; and TROW, D. B. "Observation of a Business Decision," *Journal of Business*, Vol. 29 (1956).

DAHRENDORF, R. "Towards a Theory of Social Conflict," *Journal of Conflict Resolution*, Vol. 2, No. 2 (June, 1958), pp. 170–83.

———. "Out of Utopia: Toward a Reorientation of Sociological Analysis," *American Journal of Sociology*, Vol. 64 (September, 1958), pp. 115–27.

DALE, ERNEST. *The Great Organizers*. New York: McGraw-Hill Book Co., 1960.

———, and URWICK, L. F. *Staff in Management*. New York: McGraw-Hill Book Co., 1960.

DALTON, M. "The Industrial 'Rate-Buster': A Characterization," *Applied Anthropology*, Vol. 7 (1948), pp. 5–18.

———. *Men Who Manage.* New York: John Wiley & Sons, 1959.

DANIEL, W. W. "How Close Should a Manager Be?" *New Society*, Vol. 7 (October, 1965).

DAVIS, A.; GARDNER, B. R.; and GARDNER, M. R. *Deep South.* Chicago: University of Chicago Press, 1941.

DAVIS, F. "The Cabdriver and His Fare," *American Journal of Sociology*, Vol. 65 (September, 1959) pp. 158–65.

DAVIS, K. *Human Relations in Business.* New York: McGraw-Hill Book Co., 1957.

DAY, R. C., and HAMBLIN, R. L. "Some Effects of Close and Punitive Supervision," *American Journal of Sociology*, Vol. 69 (1964), pp. 499–510.

DEAN, D. G. "Alienation: Its Meaning and Measurement," *American Sociological Review*, Vol. 26 (1961), pp. 753–58.

DECI, E. L., and VROOM, V. H. "The Stability of Post-Decision Dissonance: A Follow-Up Study of the Job Attitudes of Business School Graduates," *Organizational Behavior and Human Performance*, Vol. 6 (1971), pp. 36–49.

DEGREENE, KENYON B. (ed.) *Systems Psychology.* New York: McGraw-Hill Book Co., 1970.

DEIGHTON, LEN. *Bomber.* London: Pan Books Ltd., 1970.

DELGADO, J. M. R. *Physical Control of the Mind.* New York: Harper & Row, 1969.

DEMAAGD, GERALD R. "Matrix Management," *Datamation*, Vol. 16, No. 13 (1970), pp. 46–49.

DEVORE, I. "Primate Behaviour," *International Encylopedia of the Social Sciences*, Vol. 14 (1968), pp. 351–60.

DEWEY, JOHN. *Democracy and Education.* New York: Macmillan Co., 1916.

DICHTER, ERNST. "The World Customer," *Harvard Business Review*, July–August, 1962, pp. 113–22.

DIESING, P. "Noneconomic Decision-Making," *Ethics*, Vol. 66, No. 1, Part I (October, 1955), pp. 18–35.

DILL, WILLIAM R. "Environment as an Influence on Managerial Autonomy," *Administrative Science Quarterly*, Vol. 2 (March,1958), pp. 409–43.

DOLLARD, JOHN, *et al. Frustration and Aggression.* New Haven, Conn.: Yale University Press, 1939.

DRUCKER, P. F. "The Employee Society," *American Sociological Review*, Vol. 58 (1952), pp. 358–63.

DUBIN, R. "Power and Union Management Relations," *Administrative Science Quarterly*, Vol. 2 (June, 1957).

———. *The World of Work.* Englewood Cliffs, N.J.: Prentice-Hall, 1958.

———. "Business Behavior Behaviorally Viewed," in G. B. STROTHER (ed.), *Social Science Approaches to Business Behavior.* Homewood, Ill.: Richard D. Irwin, 1962.

———. *Theory Building.* New York: Free Press, 1969.

————, et al. *Leadership and Productivity.* San Francisco: Chandler Publishing Co., 1956.

DUBOS, RENE. *A God Within.* New York: Charles Scribner's Sons, 1972.

DUNCAN, R. B. "Characteristics of Organizational Environments and Perceived Environmental Uncertainty," *Administrative Science Quarterly*, Vol. 17 (1972), pp. 313–27.

DUNNETTE, M. D. *Personnel Selection and Placement.* Belmont, Calif.: Wadsworth Publishing Co., 1966.

————. "The Role of Financial Compensation in Managerial Motivation," *Organizational Behavior and Human Performance*, Vol. 2 (1967), pp. 175–216.

DUNPHY, D. C. "Phases, Roles, and Myths in Self-Analytic Groups," *Journal of Applied Behavioral Science*, Vol. 4, No. 2, (1968), pp. 195–226.

DYMENT, J. T. "The Soaring Future of Aviation," *The Montreal Star*, February 10, 1968, p. 9.

ECONOMIC COUNCIL OF CANADA. *The Canadian Economy from the 1960's to the 1970's*, Annual Review, No. 4. Ottawa: R. Duhamel, Queen's Printer, 1967.

ELKIND, DAVID. "Eric Erikson's Eight Ages of Man," *New York Times Magazine*, May 4, 1970.

ELLSWORTH, R. B. "A Behavioral Study of Staff Attitudes toward Mental Illness," *Journal of Abnormal Psychology*, Vol. 70, No. 3 (1965).

EMERY, F. E. *Characteristics of Socio-Technical Systems.* London: Tavistock Publications Ltd., 1959.

————. *Systems Thinking.* London: Penguin, 1969.

————, and MAREK, J. "Some Socio-Technical Aspects of Automation," *Human Relations*, Vol. 15, No. 1 (1962), pp. 17–25.

————, and TRIST, E. L. "The Causal Texture of Organizational Environments," *Human Relations*, Vol. 18, No. 1 (1965).

————, and ————. "Socio-Technical Systems," in C. W. CHURCHMAN and M. VERHUIST, (eds.) *Management Science Models and Techniques*, Vol. 2. New York: Pergamon Press, 1960.

EVAN, WILLIAM M. "Conflict and Performance in R.&D. Organizations," *Industrial Management Review*, Vol. 7 (1965), pp. 37–45.

————. "Indices of the Hierarchical Structure of Industrial Organizations," *Management Science*, Vol. 9 (1963), pp. 468–77.

EVANS, M. G., and McKEE, D. "Some Effects of Internal versus External Orientations upon the Relationships between Various Aspects of Job Satisfaction," *Journal of Business Administration*, Vol. 2 (1970), pp. 17–24.

EWING, D. W. "Tension Can Be an Asset," *Harvard Business Review*, September–October, 1964.

EYSENCK, H. J. *The Structure of Human Personality.* London: Methuen & Co., Ltd., 1953.

FAYOL, HENRY. *General and Industrial Management.* London: Sir Isaac Pitman, 1949.

FIEDLER, F. E. "The Leader's Psychological Distance and Group Effectiveness," in D. CARTWRIGHT and A. ZANDER (eds.), *Group Dynamics*. 2d ed. New York: Harper & Row, 1960.

———. "A Contingency Model of Leadership Effectiveness," in L. BERCOWITZ (ed.), *Advances in Experimental Social Psychology*. New York: Academic Press, 1964.

———. "The Effect of Leadership and Cultural Heterogeneity on Group Performance: A Test of the Contingency Model," *Journal of Experimental Social Psychology*, Vol. 2 (1966), pp. 237–64.

———. "The Contingency Model: A Theory of Leadership Effectiveness," in C. W. BACKMAN and P. F. SECORD (eds.), *Problems in Social Psychology*. New York: McGraw-Hill Book Co., 1966.

———. *A Theory of Leadership Effectiveness*. New York: McGraw-Hill Book Co., 1967.

———. "Validation and Extension of the Contingency Model of Leadership Effectiveness: A Review of Empirical Findings," *Psychological Bulletin*, Vol. 76, No. 2 (1971), pp. 128–48.

———; O'BRIEN, G. E.; and ILGEN, D. R. "The Effect of Leadership Style upon the Performance and Adjustment of Volunteer Teams Operating in a Stressful Foreign Environment," *Human Relations*, Vol. 22 (1969), pp. 503–14.

FILLEY, A. C., and HOUSE, ROBERT J. *Managerial Process and Organizational Behavior*. Glenview, Ill.: Scott, Foresman & Co., 1969.

FLANDERS, A. *Fawley Productivity Agreements*. London: Faber & Faber, Ltd. 1964.

———. *Collective Bargaining: Prescription for Change*. London: Faber & Faber, Ltd., 1967.

———. "The Case for the 'Package Deal,'" *The (London) Times*, July 9, 1968.

FLEISHMAN, E. A. "Leadership Climate, Human Relations Training, and Supervisory Behavior," *Personnel Psychology*, Vol. 6 (1953), pp. 205–22.

———, and HARRIS, E. F. "Patterns of Leadership Behavior Related to Employee Grievances and Turnovers," *Personnel Psychology*, Vol. 15, (1962), pp. 43–56.

———; ———; and BURTT, H. E. *Leadership and Supervision in Industry*. Columbus: Ohio State University Press, 1955.

———, and PETERS, D. A. "Interpersonal Values, Leadership Attitudes, and Managerial Success," *Personnel Psychology*, Vol. 15 (1962), pp. 127–43.

FOREHAND, G., and GILMER, B. "Environmental Variation in Studies of Organizational Behavior," *Psychological Bulletin*, Vol. 22 (1964), pp. 361–82.

FORRESTER, JAY W. *Industrial Dynamics*. Cambridge, Mass.: M.I.T. Press, 1961.

FORSTER, E. M. *Two Cheers for Democracy*. London: Harcourt, 1951.

FORSTER, J. "Status Race," *(London) Observer Colour Magazine*, December 5, 1965.

FOURAKER, L. E., and STOPFORD, J. M. "Organizational Structures and the

Multinational Strategy," *Administrative Science Quarterly*, Vol. 13, No. 1 (1968).

FRANKS, LORD. *British Business Schools*. London: British Institute of Management, November, 1963.

FRENCH, J. R. P., JR., and RAVEN, B. "The Bases of Social Power," in D. CARTWRIGHT (ed.), *Studies in Social Power*. Ann Arbor, Mich.: Institute for Social Research, 1959.

FRENKEL-BRUNSWIK, E. "Intolerance of Ambiguity as an Emotional and Perceptual Variable," *Journal of Personality*, Vol. 18 (1949), pp. 108–43.

FREUD, SIGMOND. *Introductory Lectures on Psychoanalysis*. London: Allen and Unwin, 1923.

FRICK, F. C., and SUMBY, W. H. "Control Tower Language," *Journal of the Acoustical Society of America*, Vol. 24, No. 6 (1952).

FRIEDLANDER, F. "The Impact of Organizational Training Laboratories upon the Effectiveness and Interaction of Ongoing Work Groups," *Personnel Psychology*, Vol. 20 (1967), pp. 289–308.

FROMM, E. *Escape from Freedom*. New York: Farrar & Rinehart, 1941.

———. *The Sane Society*. London: Routledge and Kegan Paul, 1956.

GABOR, DENNIS. *Innovations: Scientific, Technological, and Social*. Toronto: Oxford University Press, 1972.

GAGNE, R. M. (ed.). *Learning and Individual Differences*. Indiana, Indianapolis: Bobbs-Merrill, 1967.

GALBRAITH, JAY, and CUMMINGS, L. L. "An Empirical Investigation of the Motivational Determinants of Task Performance: Interactive Effects between Instrumentality-Valence and Motivation-Ability," *Organizational Behavior and Human Performance*, Vol. 2 (1967), pp. 237–57.

GALBRAITH, JOHN KENNETH. *The New Industrial State*. Boston: Houghton Mifflin Co., 1967.

———. *Economics and the Public Purpose*. Boston: Houghton Mifflin Co., 1973.

GAMSON, W. A. "A Theory of Coalition Formation," *American Sociological Review*, Vol. 26 (1961), pp. 565–73.

GEIS, L.; CHRISTIE, R.; and NELSON, C. "On Machiavellianism," a study carried out at Columbia University, New York, 1963.

GELLERMAN, S. W. *Motivation and Productivity*. New York: American Management Association, 1963.

GEORGE, C. S. *The History of Management Thought*. Englewood Cliffs, N.J.: Prentice-Hall, 1968.

GEORGOPOULUS, B. S.;. MAHONEY, G. M.; and JONES, N. W. "A Path-Goal Approach to Productivity," *Journal of Applied Psychology*, Vol. 41 (1957), pp. 345–53.

GERGEN, K. J. *The Concept of Self*. New York: Holt, Rinehart & Winston, 1970.

GERTH, H. H., and MILLS, C. WRIGHT. *From Max Weber*. New York: Oxford University Press, 1946.

GHISELLI, E. E., and HAIRE, M. "The Validation of Selection Tests in the Light of the Dynamic Character of Criteria," *Personnel Psychology*, Vol. 13, No. 3 (Autumn, 1960), pp. 225–31.

GIBB, C. A. "Leadership," pp. 877–920 in G. LINDZEY (ed.), *Handbook of Social Psychology*. Reading, Mass.: Addison-Wesley, 1954.

GOLDNER, F. H. "Demotion in Industrial Management," *American Sociological Review*, Vol. 30, No. 5 (October, 1965), pp. 714–25.

GOODMAN, P. S., and FRIEDMAN, A. "An Examination of Adam's Theory of Inequity," *Administrative Science Quarterly*, Vol. 16 (1971), pp. 271–86.

GOODSPEED, D. J. *Ludendorff*. Boston: Houghton Mifflin Co., 1966.

GORDON, T. J. *Ideas in Conflict*. New York: St. Martin's Press, 1966.

GORDON, WILLIAM J. J. *Synectics*. London: Collier-Macmillan Ltd., 1961.

GOULD, J., and KOLB, W. L. (eds.). *A Dictionary of the Social Sciences*. New York: Free Press, 1964.

GOULDNER, ALVIN W. *Studies in Leadership*. New York: Harper & Bros., 1950.

———. *Patterns of Industrial Bureaucracy*. Glencoe, Ill.: Free Press, 1954.

———. "Cosmopolitans and Locals: Toward an Analysis of Latent Social Roles—I," *Administrative Science Quarterly*, Vol. 2 (December, 1957), pp. 281–306.

———. "The Norm of Reciprocity: A Preliminary Statement," *American Sociological Review*, Vol. 25 (1960), pp. 161–79.

GOWIN, E. B. *The Executive and His Control of Men*. New York: Macmillan Co., 1915.

GRAEN, G.; ALVARES, V. M.; ORRIS, J. B.; and MARTELLA, J. D. "Contingency Model of Leadership Effectiveness: Antecedent and Evidential Results," *Psychological Bulletin*, Vol. 74 (1970), pp. 285–96.

———; ORRIS, J. B.; and ALVARES, V. M. "Contingency Model of Leadership Effectiveness: Some Experimental Results," *Journal of Applied Psychology*, Vol. 55 (1971), pp. 196–201.

GRANICK, D. *The Red Executive*. New York: Doubleday & Co., 1960.

GREAT BRITAIN. COMMITTEE ON HIGHER EDUCATION. *Higher Education; Report of the Committee Appointed by the Prime Minister, under the Chairmanship of Lord Robbins, 1961–63*. London: H. M. Stationery Office, 1963.

GREINER, LARRY E. "Patterns of Organizational Change," *Harvard Business Review*, May–June, 1967.

———. "Evolution and Revolution as Organizations Grow," *Harvard Business Review*, July–August, 1972, pp. 37–46.

GROSSMAN, B. A. "The Measurement and Determinants of Interpersonal Sensitivity," unpublished master's thesis, Michigan State University, 1963.

GUEST, R. H. "Of Time and Foremen," *Personnel*, May, 1956.

GUETZKOW, H., and SIMON, H. A. "The Impact of Certain Communication Nets upon Organization and Performance in Task-Oriented Groups," *Management Science*, Vol. 1, Nos. 3 & 4 (April–July, 1955).

GULICK, L. "Notes on the Theory of Organization," in L. GULICK and L. F.

URWICK (eds.), *Papers on the Science of Administration*. New York: Institute of Public Administration, 1937.

———, and URWICK, L. (eds.). *Papers on the Science of Administration*. New York: Institute of Public Administration, 1937.

GUTHRIE, TYRONE. *On Acting*. London: Studio Vista Publishers, 1971.

HABBE, S. *College Graduates Assess Their Company Training* (*Personnel Policy Study* No. 188). New York: National Industrial Conference Board, 1963.

HACON, R. *Management Training, Aims and Methods*. London: English Universities Press, Ltd., 1961.

HAGE, J., and AIKEN, M. *Social Change in Complex Organizations*. New York: Random House, 1970.

HAIRE, M. *Modern Organization Theory*. New York: John Wiley & Sons, 1959.

———. "The Concept of Power and the Concept of Man," in G. B. STROTHER (ed.), *Social Science Approaches to Business Behavior*. Homewood, Ill.: Richard D. Irwin, 1962.

———. *Psychology in Management*. New York: McGraw-Hill Book Co., 1964.

HALL, A. D., and FAGEN, R. E. "Definition of System," in WALTER BUCKLEY (ed.), *Modern Systems Research for the Behavioral Scientist*. Chicago: Aldine Publishing Co., 1968.

HALL, CALVIN S., and LINDZEY, GARDNER. *Theories of Personality*. 2d ed. New York: John Wiley & Sons, 1970.

HALL, E. T. *The Hidden Dimension*. New York: Doubleday & Co., 1966.

HALL, J., and WILLIAMS, M. S. "Group Dynamics Training and Improved Decision Making," *Journal of Applied Behavioral Science*, Vol. 6 (1970), pp. 39–68.

HALPIN, A. W. "The Leadership Behavior and Combat Performance of Airplane Commanders," *Journal of Abnormal and Social Psychology*, Vol 49 (1954), pp. 14–22.

———, and WINER, B. J. "A Factorial Study of the Leader Behavior Descriptions," in R. M. STOGDILL and A. E. COONS (eds.), *Leader Behavior: Its Description and Measurement*. Bureau of Business Research Monograph 88. Columbus: Ohio State University Press, 1957.

HAMACHEK, D. *Encounters with the Self*. New York: Holt, Rinehart & Winston, 1970.

HANSON, B. *Work Sampling for Modern Management*. Englewood Cliffs, N.J.: Prentice-Hall, 1962.

HARE, A. P. *Handbook of Small Group Research*. New York: Free Press, 1962.

———; BORGATTA, E. F.; and BALES, R. F. *Small Groups*. New York: Alfred A. Knopf, 1966.

HARTOG, P., and RHODES, E. C. *An Examination of Examinations*. London: Macmillan Co., Ltd., 1935.

HARRIS, THOMAS. *I'm OK—You're OK*. New York: Harper & Bros., 1967.

HAY, E. N. "The Validation of Tests," *Personnel*, Vol. 29 (1953), pp. 500–507.

HEIDER, F. *The Psychology of Interpersonal Relations*. New York: John Wiley & Sons, 1958.

HELLER, J. *Catch-22*. New York: Simon & Schuster, 1961.

HENRY, W. E. "The Business Executive: The Psychodynamics of a Social Role," *American Journal of Sociology*, 1949, p. 54.

HERZBERG, F. *Work and the Nature of Man*. Cleveland, Ohio: World Publishing Co., 1966.

———; MAUSNER, B.; and SNYDERMAN, B. *The Motivation to Work*. New York: John Wiley & Sons, 1959.

HESLIN, R., and DUNPHY, D. "Three Dimensions of Member Satisfaction in Small Groups," in B. W. BACKMAN and P. F. SECORD (eds.), *Problems in Social Psychology*. New York: McGraw-Hill Book Co., 1966.

HICKSON, D. J. "Motives of Work People Who Restrict Their Output," *Occupational Psychology*, Vol. 35 (1961), pp. 110–21.

———, *et al.* "A Strategic Contingencies Theory of Intra-organizational Power," *Administrative Science Quarterly*, Vol. 16 (1971), pp. 216–29.

———; PUGH, D. S.; and PHEYSEY, D. C. "Operations Technology and Organization Structure: A Reappraisal," *Administrative Science Quarterly*, Vol. 14 (1969), pp. 378–97.

HILL, W. "The Validation and Extension of Fiedler's Theory of Leadership Effectiveness," *Academy of Management Journal*, March, 1969, pp. 33–47.

HODGES, HAROLD M., JR. "Peninsular People: Social Stratification in a Metropolitan Complex," pp. 5–36 in CLAYTON LANE (ed.), *Permanence and Change*. Cambridge, Mass.: Schenkman, 1969.

HOLLANDER, E. P. "Conformity, Status and Idiosyncrasy Credit," *Psychological Review*, Vol. 65 (1958), pp. 117–27.

———, and HUNT, R. G. (eds.). *Current Perspectives in Social Psychology*. 2d ed. New York: Oxford University Press, 1967.

———, and JULIAN, J. W. "Contemporary Trends in the Analysis of Leadership Processes," *Psychological Bulletin*, Vol. 71 (1969), pp. 387–97.

———, and WILLIS, RICHARD H. "Some Current Issues in the Psychology of Conformity and Nonconformity," *Psychological Bulletin*, Vol. 68 (1967), pp. 62–76.

HOLLINGWORTH, H. L. *Vocational Psychology and Character Analysis*. New York: Appleton-Century, 1929.

HOLMES, T. H., and RAHE, R. H. "The Social Readjustment Rating Scale," *Journal of Psychosomatic Research*, Vol. 2 (1967).

HOLT, H., and FERBER, R. C. "The Psychological Transition from Management Scientist to Manager," *Management Science*, Vol. 10, No. 3 (April, 1964), pp. 409–20.

HOMANS, G. C. *The Human Group*. New York: Harcourt, Brace & World, 1950.

———. *Social Behavior: Its Elementary Forms*. New York: Harcourt, Brace & World, 1961.

Hood, S. "The BBC: Not So Much a Corporation More an Attitude of Mind," *The Sunday (London) Times Magazine*, July 21, 1968.

Horney, K. *Our Inner Conflicts*. New York: W. W. Norton & Co., 1945.

House, Robert J. "T-Group Education and Leadership Effectiveness: A Review of the Empirical Literature and a Critical Evaluation," *Personnel Psychology*, Vol. 20, No. 1 (1967), pp. 1–32.

————. "A Path-Goal Theory of Leader Effectiveness," *Administrative Science Quarterly*, Vol. 16, No. 3 (September, 1971), pp. 321–38.

————; Filley, A. C.; and Kerr, S. "Relation of Leader Consideration and Initiating Structure to R. and D. Subordinate Satisfaction," *Administrative Science Quarterly*, Vol. 16 (1971), pp. 19–30.

————, and Wahba, M. A. "Expectancy Theory as a Predictor of Job Performance, Satisfaction and Motivation: An Integrative Model and a Review of the Literature," paper presented the American Psychological Association meeting in Hawaii, August, 1972; Working Paper 72–21, Faculty of Management Studies, University of Toronto, 1972.

————, with Wigdor, L. A. "Herzberg's Dual-Factor Theory of Job Satisfaction and Motivation: A Review of the Evidence and a Criticism," *Personnel Psychology*, Vol. 20 (Winter, 1967), pp. 369–89.

Houser, J. D. *What the Employee Thinks*. Cambridge, Mass.: Harvard University Press, 1927.

Hovland, C. I., *et al.* *The Order of Presentation in Persuasion*. New Haven Conn.: Yale University Press, 1957.

Hudson, Liam. *Cult of the Fact*. London: Cape, 1972.

Hulin, Charles L., and Blood, M. R. "Job Enlargement, Individual Differences, and Worker Responses," *Psychological Bulletin*, Vol. 69 (January, 1968), pp. 41–55.

Hunt, E. "Computer Simulation: Artificial Intelligence Studies and Their Relevance to Psychology," *Annual Review of Psychology*, Vol. 19 (1968).

Hunt, J. G. "Fiedler's Leadership Contingency Model: An Empirical Test in Three Organizations," *Organizational Behavior and Human Performance*, Vol. 2 (1967), pp. 290–308.

————, and Hill, J. W. "The New Look in Motivational Theory for Organizational Research," *Human Organization*, Vol. 28 (Summer, 1969), pp. 100–109.

Hunt, R. G. "Role and Role Conflict," in E. P. Hollander and R. G. Hunt (eds.), *Current Perspectives in Social Psychology*. 2d ed. New York: Oxford University Press, 1967.

Hurwitz, J. I.; Zander, A. F..; and Hymovitch, B. "Some Effects of Power on the Relations among Group Members," in D. Cartwright and A. Zander (eds.), *Group Dynamics*. New York: Harper & Row, 1960.

Huxley, Aldous L. *Brave New World*. Garden City, N.Y.: Doubleday & Co., 1932.

James, W. *Principles of Psychology*. New York: Henry Holt & Co., 1890.

Janis, I. L. "Group Identification under Conditions of External Danger," *British Journal of Medical Psychology*, Vol. 36 (1963), pp. 227–38.

JANOWITZ, M. *Sociology and the Military Establishment.* New York: Russell Sage Foundation, 1959.

JAQUES, ELLIOTT. *The Changing Culture of a Factory.* London: Tavistock Publications Ltd., 1951.

———. *Measurement of Responsibility.* London: Tavistock Publications Ltd.; Cambridge, Mass.: Harvard University Press, 1956.

———. *Equitable Payment.* London: William Heinemann, Ltd., 1961.

JASINSKI, F. J. "Use and Misuse of Efficiency Controls," *Harvard Business Review,* Vol. 34 (1956), pp. 105–12.

JENKINS, J. G. "The Nominating Technique, Its Uses and Limitations," paper delivered at Eastern Psychological Association Annual Meeting, Atlantic City, April, 1947, as quoted in D. KRECH and R. S. CRUTCHFIELD, *Theory and Problems of Social Psychology.* New York: McGraw-Hill Book Co., 1948.

JENKINS, P. "Limits of Exhortation," *New Society,* September 22, 1966.

JENNINGS, H. H. "Leadership and Sociometric Choice," in S. E. SWANSON, T. M. NEWCOMB, and E. L. HARTLEY (eds.), *Readings in Social Psychology.* New York: Henry Holt & Co., 1952.

JENNINGS, EUGENE. "Mobicentric Man," *Psychology Today,* July, 1970.

JOHNSON, RICHARD A.; KAST, FREMONT E.; and ROSENZWEIG, JAMES E. "Systems Theory and Management," *Management Science,* Vol. 10 (January, 1964), pp. 367–84.

KAHN, HERMAN; PFAFF, W.; and WIENER, ANTHONY J. (eds). *Appendix to the Next Thirty-four Years: A Context for Speculation.* Croton-on-Hudson, N.Y.: Hudson Institute, Inc., 1966.

———, and WIENER, ANTHONY J. *The Next Thirty-three Years: A Framework for Speculation.* Prepared as Volume II of the *Working Papers* of the Commission on the Year 2000 of the American Academy of Arts and Sciences. Croton-on-Hudson, N.Y.: Hudson Institute, Inc. 1967.

KAHN, R. L., and FRENCH, J. R. P., JR. "Status and Conflict: Two Themes in the Study of Stress," in J. E. McGRATH (ed.), *Social and Psychological Factors in Stress.* New York: Holt, Rinehart & Winston, 1970.

———, and KATZ, D. "Leadership Practices in Relation to Productivity and Morale," in D. CARTWRIGHT and A. ZANDER (eds.), *Group Dynamics.* New York: Harper & Row, 1960.

———; WOLFE, D. M.; QUINN, R. P.; SNOEK, J. K.; and ROSENTHAL, R. H. *Organizational Stress: Studies in Role Conflict and Ambiguity.* New York: John Wiley & Sons, 1964.

KAPLAN, A. D. H. *Big Enterprises in a Competitive System.* Washington, D.C.: Brookings Institution, 1964.

KAST, F. E., and ROSENZWEIG, JAMES E. *Organization and Management.* New New York: McGraw-Hill Book Co., 1970, Chapter 2.

KATZ, DANIEL. "The Functional Approach to the Study of Attitudes," *Public Opinion Quarterly,* Vol. 24 (1960), pp. 163–77.

———. "The Motivational Basis of Organizational Behaviour," *Behavioural Science,* Vol. 9 (1964), pp. 131–46.

————, and KAHN, R. L. *The Social Psychology of Organizations.* New York: John Wiley & Sons, 1966.

KAY, B. R. "Prescription and Perception of the Supervisory Role," *Occupational Psychology*, Vol. 37, No. 3 (1963).

KELLER, R. T.; SLOCUM, J. W.; and SUSMAN, G. I. "Management System, Uncertainty, and Continuous Process Technology," paper presented at 33d meeting of National Academy of Management in Boston, 1973.

KELLY, JOE. "A Study of Leadership in Two Contrasting Groups," *Sociological Review*, November, 1963.

————. "Changing Views of Management Efficiency," *Journal of Industrial Economics*, April, 1964.

————. "The Study of Executive Behaviour by Activity Sampling," *Human Relations*, Vol. 17, No. 3 (1964).

————. *Is Scientific Management Possible?* London: Faber & Faber, Ltd., 1968.

————. "Executive Defence Mechanisms and Games," *Personnel Administration*, July–August, 1968.

————. "The Manager and the Therapist," *Personnel Administration*, July–August, 1968.

————. "Make Conflict Work for You," *Harvard Business Review*, July–August, 1970.

————. "Organizational Concept of Leadership," *Management International*, December, 1970.

————. "Organizational Development via Structured Sensitivity Training," *Management International*, forthcoming.

————, and BILEK, D. "White Collar Unions; Does Middle Management Want Them?" *Canadian Business*, June, 1973.

KELMAN, H. C. "Compliance, Identification, and Internalization: Three Processes of Attitude Change," *Journal of Conflict Resolution*, Vol. 2 (1958).

KERLINGER, F. N. *Foundations of Behavioural Research.* New York: Holt, Rinehart, & Winston, 1964.

KIBBEE, J. M.; CRAFT, C. J.; and NANUS, B. *Management Games.* New York: Reinhold Book Corp., 1961.

KORMAN, A. K. "Consideration, Initiating Structure, and Organizational Criteria—A Review," *Personnel Psychology*, Vol. 19 (1966), pp. 349–62.

KORNHAUSER, ARTHUR. *Mental Health of the Industrial Worker.* New York: John Wiley & Sons, 1965.

KRECH, D., and CRUTCHFIELD, R. S. *Theory and Problems of Social Psychology.* New York: McGraw-Hill Book Co., 1948.

————; ————; and BALLACHEY, E. L. *Individual in Society.* New York: McGraw-Hill Book Co., 1962.

KRETSCHMER, E. *Physique and Character.* New York: Harcourt, Brace & World, Inc., 1925; London: Routledge and Kegan Paul, 1925.

LAING, R. D. *The Divided Self.* London: Tavistock Publications Ltd., 1965.

LANDSBERGER, H. A. *Hawthorne Revisited*. Ithaca, N.Y.: New York State School of Industrial and Labor Relations, Cornell University, 1958.

————. "The Horizontal Dimension in Bureaucracy," *Administrative Science Quarterly*, Vol. 6, No. 1 (1961–62), pp. 299–322.

LATANE, H. A., *et al. The Social Science of Organizations: Four Perspectives*. Englewood Cliffs, N.J.: Prentice-Hall, 1963.

LAWLER, E. E. "Managers' Job Performance and Their Attitudes toward Their Pay," unpublished doctoral dissertation, University of California at Berkeley, 1964.

————. "Ability as a Moderator of the Relationship between Job Attitudes and Job Performance," *Personnel Psychology*, Vol. 10 (1966), pp. 153–64.

————. "Attitude Surveys and Job Performance," *Personnel Administration*, September–October, 1967, pp. 485–87.

————. "Job Design and Employee Motivation," *Personnel Psychology*, Vol. 22 (1969).

————. "Job Attitudes and Employee Motivation: Theory, Research, and Practice," *Personnel Psychology*, Vol. 23 (1970), pp. 223–37.

————. *Pay and Organizational Effectiveness: A Psychological View*. New York: McGraw-Hill Book Co., 1971.

————, and PORTER, L. W. "Antecedent Attitudes of Effective Managerial Performance," *Organizational Behavior and Human Performance*, Vol. 2 (1967), pp. 122–42.

LAWRENCE, PAUL R., and LORSCH, J. W. "Differentiation and Integration in Complex Organizations," *Administrative Science Quarterly*, Vol. 12 (June, 1967), pp. 1–47.

————, and ————. *Organization and Environment: Managing Differentiation and Integration*. Boston: Division of Research, Graduate School of Business Administration, Harvard University, 1967.

LEAVITT, HAROLD J. "Unhuman Organization," *Harvard Business Review*, Vol. 40, No. 4 (1962), pp. 90–98.

————. *Managerial Psychology*. 2d ed. Chicago: University of Chicago Press, 1964.

————. "Applied Organizational Change in Industry: Structural, Technological, and Humanistic Approaches," pp. 1144–70 in JAMES G. MARCH (ed.), *Handbook of Organizations*. Chicago: Rand McNally & Co., 1965.

————, and PONDY, L. R. *Readings in Managerial Psychology*. Chicago: University of Chicago Press, 1964.

————, and WHISLER, THOMAS L. "Management in the 1980's," *Harvard Business Review*, November–December, 1958.

LEVINSON, HARRY. "On Being a Middle-Aged Manager," *Harvard Business Review*, July–August, 1969.

LEWIN, KURT. "Defining the Field at a Given Time," *Psychological Review*, Vol. 50 (1945).

————. *Field Theory in Social Science*. New York: Harper & Bros., 1951.

————; LIPPITT, R.; and WHITE, R. K. "Patterns of Aggressive Behavior in

Experimentally Created Social Climates," *Journal of Social Psychology*, Vol. 10 (1939), pp. 271–99.

LICHTMAN, C. M., and HUNT, R. G. "Personality and Organization Theory: A Review of Some Conceptual Literature," *Psychological Bulletin*, Vol. 76 (1971), pp. 271–94.

LICKLIDER, J. C. R., and TAYLOR, R. W. "The Computer as a Communication Device," *Science and Technology*, Vol. 76 (1968), pp. 21–31.

LIEBOW, ELLIOTT. *Tally's Corner*. Boston: Little, Brown & Co., 1967.

LIKERT, RENSIS. "Motivational Dimensions of Administration," in R. WALKER (ed.), *America's Manpower Crisis*. Chicago: Public Administration Service, 1952.

———. *New Patterns of Management*. New York: McGraw-Hill Book Co., 1961.

———. *The Human Organization*. New York: McGraw-Hill Book Co., 1967.

LINTON, R. *The Study of Man*. New York: Appleton-Century-Crofts, 1936.

———. *The Cultural Background of Personality*. New York: Appleton-Century-Crofts, 1945.

LIPPITT, GORDON L., and SCHMIDT, WARREN H. "Crises in a Developing Organization," *Harvard Business Review*, November–December, 1967.

LIPPITT, R., and WHITE, R. K. "An Experimental Study of Leadership and Group Life," in E. E. MACCOBY, T. M. NEWCOMB, and E. L. HARTLEY (eds.), *Readings in Social Psychology*. 3d ed. New York: Holt, Rinehart & Winston, 1958.

LITTERER, J. A. *The Analysis of Organizations*. 2d ed. New York: John Wiley & Sons, 1973.

LITWIN, G., and STRINGER, R. "The Influence of Organizational Climate on Human Motivation," paper presented at Conference on Organizational Climate, Foundation for Research on Human Behavior, Ann Arbor, Michigan, 1966.

———, and ———. *Motivational and Organizational Climate*. Cambridge, Mass.: Harvard University Press, 1968.

LORENZ, KONRAD. *On Aggression*. London: Methuen & Co., Ltd., 1966.

LORSCH, J. W., and LAWRENCE, PAUL R. *Studies in Organizational Design*. Homewood, Ill.: Richard D. Irwin, 1970, pp. 16–35.

———, and ———. *Organizational Planning*. Homewood, Ill.: Dorsey Press, 1972, pp. 38–48.

LOWE, M. B. "Machiavellianism, Psychological Distance, Social Acceptance and Effectiveness," unpublished M.B.A. thesis, McGill University, 1968.

LUCE, R. D., and RAIFFA, H. *Games and Decisions*. New York: John Wiley & Sons, 1957.

LUCIETTO, LENA L. "Speech Patterns of Administrators," *Administrator's Notebook*, Vol. 18, No. 5 (1970).

LUNDBERG, C. C. "On Plotting Individual Change in Human Relations Training," *Training Development Journal*, Vol. 22, No. 6 (1968), pp. 50–57.

Lupton, T. *On the Shop Floor*. New York: Pergamon Press, 1963.

———. "Industrial Behaviour and Personnel Management," Institute of Personnel Management, London, *Occasional Paper*, 1964.

Luthans, F., and White, D. D., Jr. "Behavior Modification: Application to Manpower Management," *Personnel Admiinstration*, July–August, 1971.

McClelland, D. C. *The Achieving Society*. Princeton, N.J.: D. Van Nostrand Co., 1961.

———. "That Urge to Achieve," *Think*, Vol. 32, No. 6 (November–December, 1966), pp. 19–23.

———. "Business Drive and National Achievement," in G. D. Bell (ed.), *Organization and Human Behavior*. Englewood Cliffs, N.J.: Prentice-Hall, 1957.

———, and Winter, D. C. *Motivating Economic Achievement*. New York: Free Press, 1969.

McDougall, W. *The Principles of Social Psychology*. Washington, D.C.: Robert B. Luce, 1918.

McGregor, D. M. *The Human Side of Enterprise*. New York: McGraw-Hill Book Co., 1960.

McGrath, J. E. (ed.). *Social and Psychological Factors in Stress*. New York: Holt, Rinehart & Winston, 1970.

McLuhan, M. *The Gutenberg Galaxy—The Making of Typographic Man*. Toronto: University of Toronto Press, 1962.

———, and Fiore, Q. *The Medium Is the Massage*. New York: Bantam Books, 1967.

McMurry, R. N. "Clear Communications for Chief Executives," *Harvard Business Review*, March–April, 1965.

McQuade, Walter. "What Stress Can Do to You," *Fortune*, January, 1972.

Maddi, S. R. *Personality Theories*. Homewood, Ill.: Dorsey Press, 1968.

Maier, N. R. F. *Frustration: The Study of Behavior without a Goal*. New York: McGraw-Hill Book Co., 1949.

Malinowski, B. *Introduction* to Hogbin, H. I., *Law and Order in Polynesia*. New York: Harcourt, Brace & World, 1934.

———. *A Scientific Theory of Culture and Other Essays*. Chapel Hill: University of North Carolina Press, 1944.

Manchester, William R. *The Death of a President*. New York: Harper & Row, 1967.

Mann, F. C. "Studying and Creating Change: A Means to Understanding Social Organization," pp. 146–67 in *Research in Industrial Human Relations*. New York: Harper & Bros., 1957.

March, James G. *Handbook of Organizations*. Chicago: Rand, McNally & Co., 1965.

———, and Simon, Herbert A. *Organizations*. New York: John Wiley & Sons, 1958.

Marrow, Alfred J. *The Failure of Success*. New York: American Management Association, AMACOM, 1972.

————; BOWERS, DAVID G.; and SEASHORE, STANLEY E. *Management by Participation: Creating a Climate for Personal and Organizational Development.* New York: Harper & Row, 1967.

MARX, KARL. *Economic and Philosophical Manuscripts of 1844* (trans. by MARTIN MILLIGAN). London: Lawrence & Wishert, 1959.

MARSH, A. *Managers and Shop Stewards.* Institute of Personnel Management, London, *Occasional Paper*, 1963.

MASLOW, A. H. *Motivation and Personality.* New York: Harper & Bros., 1954.

MAY, ROLLO. *The Meaning of Anxiety.* New York: Ronald Press Co., 1950.

————. *Psychology and the Human Dilemma.* Princeton, N.J.: D. Van Nostrand Co., 1967.

MAYFIELD, E. C. "The Selection Interview—A Re-evaluation of Published Research," *Personnel Psychology*, Vol. 17, 1964, pp. 239–60.

MAYO, ELTON. *The Human Problems of an Industrial Civilization.* New York: Macmillan Co., 1933.

————. *The Social Problems of an Industrial Civilization.* Cambridge, Mass.: Harvard University Press, 1947.

MEAD, MARGARET. *Sex and Temperament in Three Primitive Societies.* New York: William Morrow & Co., 1935.

————, and METRAUX, RHODA. "The Anthropology of Human Conflict," in E. B. McNEIL (ed.), *The Nature of Human Conflict.* Englewood Cliffs, N.J.: Prentice-Hall, 1965.

MEADOWS, DENNIS H.; MEADOWS, D. L.; RONDERS, J.; and BEHRENS, W. III. *The Limits to Growth.* New York: Universe Books, 1972.

MECHANIC, D. "Sources of Power of Lower Participants in Complex Organizations," *Administrative Science Quarterly*, Vol. 7 (1962), pp. 349–64.

MELVILLE, D. "The Industrial Rate-Buster—A Characterization," *Journal of Applied Anthropology*, Winter, 1948.

MERTON, R. K. "Bureaucratic Structure and Personality," *Social Forces*, Vol. 18 (1940), pp. 560–68.

————. *Social Theory and Social Structure* (see especially "Social Structure and Anomie"). Glencoe, Ill.: Free Press, 1957.

MEYERSOHN, ROLF. "The Price of Copylation," *New Society*, Vol. 4 (January, 1968).

MICHELS, ROBERT. *Political Parties.* Glencoe, Ill.: Free Press, 1958.

MILES, R. E. "Human Relations of Human Resources," *Harvard Business Review*, Vol. 43, No. 4 (July–August, 1963), pp. 148–57.

MILGRAM, S. "Some Conditions of Obedience and Disobedience to Authority," *Human Relations*, Vol. 18 (1965), pp. 57–75.

MILLER, D. W., and STARR, M. K. *The Structure of Human Decisions.* Englewood Cliffs, N.J.: Prentice-Hall, 1967.

MILLER, E. J., and RICE, A. K. *Systems of Organization: The Control of Task and Sentient Boundaries.* London: Tavistock Publications Ltd., 1967.

MINER, J. B. *Studies in Management Education.* New York: Springer Publishing Co., 1965.

MINTZBERG, H. "The Manager at Work—Determining His Activities, Roles, and Programs by Structured Observation," unpublished Ph.D. dissertation, Sloan School of Management, Massachusetts Institute of Technology, Cambridge, Mass., 1968.

———. *The Nature of Managerial Work.* New York: Harper & Row, 1973.

MISUMI, J., and SHIRAKASHI, S. "An Experimental Study of the Effects of Supervisory Behavior on Productivity and Morale in a Hierarchical Organization," *Human Relations,* Vol. 19 (1966), pp. 297–307.

MITCHELL, G. DUNCAN. *A Hundred Years of Sociology.* London: Duckworth, 1968.

MITCHELL, T. R. "Leader Complexity, Leadership Style, and Group Performance," unpublished doctoral thesis, University of Illinois, 1969.

———. "Leader Complexity and Leadership Style," *Journal of Personality and Social Psychology,* Vol. 16 (1970), pp. 166–74.

———. "The Construct Validity of Three Dimensions of Leadership Research," *Journal of Social Psychology,* Vol. 80 (1970), pp. 89–94.

———; BIGLAN, A.; ONCKEN, G.; and FIEDLER, F. E. "The Contingency Model: Criticism and Suggestions," *Academy of Management Journal,* Vol. 13 (1970), pp. 253–67.

MITFORD, JESSICA. *Kind and Usual Punishment.* New York: Random House, 1973.

MOONEY, J. D., and REILEY, A. M. *Onward Industry.* New York: Harper & Bros., 1931.

———, and ———. *The Principles of Organization.* New York: Harper & Bros., 1947.

MOORE, L. F. "Business Games versus Cases as Tools of Learning," *Training Development Journal,* Vol. 21 (1967), pp. 13–23.

MORENO, J. L. *Who Shall Survive?* Washington, D.C.: Nervous and Mental Diseases Publishing Co., 1934.

MORSE, J., and LORSCH, J. W. "Beyond Theory Y," *Harvard Business Review,* May–June, 1970, pp. 61–68.

MORSE, NANCY, and REIMER, E. "The Experimental Change of a Major Organizational Variable," *Journal of Abnormal Social Psychology,* Vol. 52 (1956), pp. 120–29.

MOSER, G. V. "Consultative Management," *Management Record,* November, 1955.

MULDER, M. "Communication Structure, Decision Structure, and Group Performance," *Sociometry,* Vol. 23 (1960), pp. 1–14.

MUNN, N. L. *Psychology, The Fundamental of Human Adjustment.* London: George G. Harrap Co., Ltd., 1961.

MURCHISON, C. *Handbook of Social Psychology.* Worcester, Mass.: Clark University Press, 1935.

MURPHY, G.; MURPHY, L. B.; and NEWCOMB, T. M. *Experimental Social Psychology.* New York: Harper & Bros., 1937.

MYERS, C. A. "Behavioral Sciences for Personnel Managers," *Harvard Business Review*, July–August, 1966.

MYERS, M. SCOTT. "Conditions for Managerial Motivations," *Harvard Business Review*, January–February, 1964.

———. "Who Are Your Motivated Workers?" *Harvard Business Review*, January–February, 1966.

———. "Every Employee a Manager," *California Management Review*, Vol. 10 (1968).

NATIONAL ECONOMIC DEVELOPMENT COUNCIL. *Conditions Favourable to Faster Growth*. London: H.M. Stationery Office, April, 1963.

———. *Management Recruitment and Development*. London: H.M. Stationery Office, 1965.

NATIONAL INSTITUTE OF INDUSTRIAL PSYCHOLOGY. *Joint Consultation in British Industry*. London: Staples Press, 1952.

NEFF, WALTER S. *Work and Human Behavior*. New York: Atherton Press, 1968.

NEUMAN, J., and VON MORGENSTERN, O. *Theory of Games and Economic Behavior*. Princeton, N.J.: Princeton University Press, 1947.

NEWCOMB, T. M. "Individual Systems of Orientation," in S. KOCH (ed.), *Psychology: A Study of a Science*, Vol. 3. New York: McGraw-Hill Book Co., 1959.

NOVE, A. "Which Way Is Soviet Society Going?" *New Society*, October 7, 1965.

NUNN, SIR T. P. *Education, Its Data and First Principles*. London: Longmans, 1946.

OGILVY, D. *Confessions of an Advertising Man*. New York: Atheneum Publishers; London: Longmans, 1966.

OPSAHL, R. L., and DUNNETTE, M. D. "The Role of Financial Compensation in Industrial Motivation," *Psychological Bulletin*, Vol. 66 (1966), pp. 94–118.

ORWELL, GEORGE. *Animal Farm*. New York: Harcourt, Brace & World, 1946.

OSGOOD, C. E.; SUCI, G. J.; and TANNENBAUM, P. H. *The Measurement of Meaning*. Urbana: University of Illinois Press, 1957.

PAHL, J. M., and PAHL, R. E. "Company Wives," *New Society*, December, 1969.

PARKINSON, C. NORTHCOTE. *Parkinson's Law*. Boston: Houghton Mifflin Co., 1957.

PARSONS, T. "Some Ingredients of a General Theory of Formal Organizations," in A. W. HALPIN, *Administrative Theory in Education*, Chap. 3. Chicago: Midwest Administration Center, University of Chicago, 1958.

———. *Structure and Process in Modern Societies*. New York: Free Press, 1960.

PARTRIDGE, E. D. "Leadership among Adolescent Boys," Teachers College, Columbia University, Contribution to Education, No. 608, 1934.

PASSELL, PETER; ROBERTS, MARC; and ROSS, LEONARD. "The Limits to Growth, World Dynamics, and Urban Dynamics," *New York Times Book Review*, April 2, 1972.

PATERSON, T. T. *Authority*. Department of Administration, University of Strathclyde, 1963.

———. *Glasgow Limited*. Cambridge, England: Cambridge University Press, 1960.

———. *A Methectic Theory of Social Organization*. Department of Social and Economic Research, University of Glasgow, 1957.

———. *Morale in War and Work*. London: Max Parish, 1955.

———. "Towards a Theory of Retribution in Industry," *The Manager*, March, 1963.

PAVLOV, IVAN P. *Conditioned Reflexes* (trans. and ed. by G. V. ANREP). New York: Dover, 1927.

PELZ, D. C. "Creative Tensions in the Research and Development Climate," *Science*, Vol. 157 (July 14, 1967), pp. 160–65.

———. "Influence: A Key to Effective Leadership in the First-Line Supervisor," *Personnel*, Vol. 3 (1952), pp. 3–11.

PERROW, CHARLES. "A Framework for the Comparative Analysis of Organizations," *American Sociological Review*, Vol. 32 (April, 1967), pp. 190–208.

———. *Organizational Analysis, A Sociological View*. Belmont, Calif.: Wadsworth Publishing Co., 1970.

PETER, LAWRENCE J., and HULL, RAYMOND. *The Peter Principle*. New York: William Morrow & Co., 1969.

PFEFFER, JEFFREY. "Merger as a Response to Organizational Interdependence," *Admistrative Science Quarterly*, Vol. 17 (1972).

PFIFFNER, J. M., and SHERWOOD, F. P. *Administrative Organization*. Englewood Cliffs, N.J.: Prentice-Hall, 1960.

PIAGET, J. *The Language and Thought of the Child*. New York: Harcourt, Brace & World, 1926.

PIERSOL, D. T. "Communication Practices of Supervisors in a Mid-Western Corporation," *Advanced Management*, Vol. 23 (1958), pp. 20–21.

PIGORS, P. J. W. *Leadership or Domination*. New York: Houghton Mifflin Co., 1935.

PIOTROWSKI, Z. A., and ROCK, M. R. *The Perceptanalytic Executive Scale: A Tool for the Selection of Top Managers*. New York: Grune & Stratton, 1963.

PLATT, P. L., *et al*. *The MBA in American Corporate Life*. New York: Hobbs, Dorman & Co., 1963.

PLATT, I. R. "Strong Inference," *Science*, Vol. 146 (1964), pp. 346–52.

PONDER, A. D. "The Effective Manufacturing Foreman," *Proceedings of the Tenth Annual Meeting, Industrial Relations Research Association*, Madison, Wis., pp. 41–52.

PORTER, E. H. "The Parable of the Spindle," *Harvard Business Review*, Vol. 40 (1962), pp. 58–66.

PORTER, J. *Vertical Mosaic*. Toronto: University of Toronto Press, 1965.

PORTER, L. W., and LAWLER, E. E. "Properties of Organization Structure in Relation to Job Attitudes and Job Behavior," *Psychological Bulletin*, Vol. 64 (1965), p.. 23–51.

———, and ———. *Managerial Attitudes and Performance.* Homewood, Ill.: Richard D. Irwin, 1968.

PRANDY, K. *Professional Employees.* London: Faber & Faber, Ltd., 1965.

PRITCHARD, R. D. "Equity Theory: A Review and Critique," *Organizational Behavior and Human Performance,* Vol. 4 (1969), pp. 176–211.

PUGH, D. S. "Modern Organizational Theory: A Psychological and Sociological Study," *Psychological Bulletin,* Vol. 66 (1966), pp. 235–51.

———; HICKSON, D. J.; HININGS, C. R.; and TURNER, C. "Dimensions of Organizational Structure," *Administrative Science Quarterly,* Vol. 13 (1968), pp. 65–105.

———; ———; ———; and———. "The Context of Organizational Structures," *Administrative Science Quarterly,* Vol. 14 (1969); pp. 91–114.

PUZO, MARIO. *The Godfather.* New York: G. P. Putnam's Sons, 1969.

READ, W. H. "Upward Communication in Industrial Hierarchies," *Human Relations,* Vol. 15, No. 1 (1962), pp. 3–15.

REDDIN, W. J. *Managerial Effectiveness.* New York: McGraw-Hill Book Co., 1970.

REICH, CHARLES. *The Greening of America.* New York: Random House, 1970.

REISS, ALBERT J., JR. *The Police and the Public.* New Haven, Conn.: Yale University Press, 1971.

REVANS, R. W. "Bigness and Change," *New Society,* January 2, 1964.

RICE, A. K. *Productivity and Social Organization.* London: Tavistock Publications Ltd., 1958.

———. *The Enterprise and Its Environment.* London: Tavistock Publications Ltd., 1963.

RICE, BERKELEY. "Skinner: The Important Influence in Psychology," *New York Times Magazine,* March 17, 1968.

RIDGWAY, W. F. "Dysfunctional Consequences of Performance Measurement," in A. H. RUBENSTEIN and C. J. HABERSTROH (eds.), *Some Theories of Organization.* Rev. ed. Homewood, Ill.: Richard D. Irwin, 1966.

RIESMAN, DAVID. *The Lonely Crowd.* New Haven, Conn.: Yale University Press, 1950.

RIM, YESHAYAHU. "Who Are the Risk-Takers in Decision Making?" *Personnel Administration,* March–April, 1966.

ROBBINS, L. C. R.: see GREAT BRITAIN, COMMITTEE ON HIGHER EDUCATION.

ROBBINS, STEPHEN P. *Managing Organizational Conflict: A Non-Traditional Approach.* Englewood Cliffs, N.J.: Prentice-Hall, 1974.

ROETHLISBERGER, F. J. *Management and Morale.* Cambridge, Mass.: Harvard University Press, 1943.

———. "The Foreman: Master and Victim of Double Talk," *Harvard Business Review,* Vol. 23 (1945), pp. 283–98.

———, and DICKSON, W. J. *Management and the Worker.* Cambridge, Mass.: Harvard University Press, 1959.

ROGERS, C. R., and SKINNER, B. F. "Some Issues Concerning the Control of Human Behavior: A Symposium," *Science,* Vol. 124 (1956) pp. 1057–66.

ROMMETVEIT, R. *Social Norms and Roles.* Minneapolis: University of Minnesota Press, 1954.

ROSZAK, THEODORE. *The Making of a Counter Culture.* Garden City, N.Y.: Doubleday & Co., 1969.

ROWE, P. M. "Individual Differences in Selection Decisions," *Journal of Applied Psychology,* Vol. 47 (1963), pp. 304–7.

ROY, DONALD F. "Quota Restriction and Gold-Bricking in a Machine Shop," *American Journal of Sociology,* Vol. 57 (March, 1952), pp. 430–37.

———. "Banana Time: Job Satisfaction and Informal Interaction," *Human Organization,* Vol. 18 (1960), pp. 158–68.

SALES, S. M. "Organizational Role as a Risk Factor in Coronary Disease," *Administrative Science Quarterly,* Vol. 14 (1969), pp. 325–36.

SALPUKAS, AGIS. "Young Workers Disrupt Key G.M. Plant," *New York Times,* January 23, 1972.

———. "Workers Increasingly Rebel against Boredom on Assembly Line," *New York Times,* April 2, 1972.

SANFORD, N. "Will Psychologists Study Human Problems?" *American Psychologist,* Vol. 20 (1965), pp. 192–202.

SAYLES, L. R. "Wildcat Strikes," *Harvard Business Review,* November–December, 1954, pp. 42–52.

———. *Behavior of Industrial Work Groups.* New York: John Wiley & Sons, 1958.

———. *Managerial Behavior.* New York: McGraw-Hill Book Co., 1964.

SCHEIN, E. H. "Interpersonal Communication, Group Solidarity, and Social Influence," *Sociometry,* Vol. 23 (1960), pp. 148–61.

———. "Management Development as a Process of Influence," *Industrial Management Review,* Vol. 2 (1961), pp. 59–77.

———. *Organizational Psychology.* Englewood Cliffs, N.J.: Prentice-Hall, 1965.

———. "The Problem of Moral Education for the Business Manager," *Industrial Managemenut Review,* Vol. 8 (1966), pp. 3–11.

———. "Attitude Changes during Management Education: A Study of Organizational Influences of Student Attitudes," *Administrative Science Quarterly,* Vol. 11 (1966–67), pp. 601–28.

———. *Process Consultation.* Reading, Mass.: Addison-Wesley, 1969.

———, and BENNIS, W. G. *Personal and Organizational Change through Group Methods: The Laboratory Approach.* New York: John Wiley & Sons, 1965.

SCHELLING, THOMAS C. *Strategy of Conflict.* Cambridge, Mass.: Harvard University Press, 1966.

SCOTT, W. C. *The Management of Conflict.* Homewood, Ill.: Richard D. Irwin, 1965.

SEASHORE, STANLEY E. "Administrative Leadership and Organizational Effectiveness," in R. LICKERT and S. P. HAYES, JR. (eds.), *Some Applications of Behavioural Research.* Paris: UNESCO, 1957.

————, and YUCHTMAN, E. "Factorial Analysis of Organizational Performance," *Administrative Science Quarterly*, Vol. 12 (December, 1967), pp. 377–95.

SEEMAN, M. "On the Personal Consequences of Alienation in Work," *American Sociological Review*, Vol. 32 (1967).——

————. "The Urban Alienations: Some Dubious Theses from Marx to Marcuse," *Journal of Personality and Social Psychology*, Vol. 19 (1971), pp. 135–43.

SELYE, HANS. *The Stress of Life*. New York: Mc-Graw-Hill Book Co., 1956.

SELZNICK, P. *T.V.A. and Grass Roots*. Berkeley: University of California Press, 1949.

————. *Leadership in Administration*. London: Row Peterson, 1957.

SERVAN-SCHREIBER, JEAN-JACQUES. *The American Challenge*. New York: Atheneum, 1968.

SHANNON, C. E. "A Mathematical Theory of Communication," *Bell System Technical Journal*, Vol. 27 (1948), pp. 379–423.

SHELDON, W. H. *The Varieties of Human Physique*. New York: Harper & Bros., 1940.

————. *The Varieties of Temperament*. New York: Harper & Bros., 1942.

————. *The Varieties of Delinquent Youth: An Introduction to Constitutional Psychiatry*. New York: Harper & Bros. 1949.

SHEPARD, H. A. "Explorations in Observant Participation," in L. P. BRADFORD, J. R. GIBB, and K. D. BENNE (eds.), *T-Group Theory and Laboratory Method*. New York: John Wiley & Sons, 1964.

SHEPPARD, HAROLD L., and HERRICK, NEAL. *Where Have All the Robots Gone?* New York: Free Press, 1972.

SHERIF, MUZAFER. "Experiments on Group Conflict and Cooperation," *Scientific American*, Vol. 195 (November, 1956), pp. 54–58.

SHLACHTER, R. "The Perception of Executive Roles by Use of the Semantic Differential Technique," unpublished M.B.A. thesis, McGill University, 1968.

SHONFIELD, ANDREW. *Modern Capitalism*. London: Oxford University Press, 1965.

SHOOK, E. "Spitballing with Flair," *Time*, July 12, 1968.

SHUBIK, M. "Games Decisions and Industrial Organization," *Management Science*, Vol. 6, No. 4 (July, 1960), pp. 455–74.

SIDNEY, E., and BROWN, M. *The Skills of Interviewing*. London: Tavistock Publications Ltd., 1961.

SIEGMAN, J.; BAKER, N. R.; and RUBENSTEIN, A. H. "The Effects of Perceived Needs and Means on the Generation of Ideas for Industrial R&D Projects," *IEEE Transactions on Engineering Management*, December, 1967.

SIMON, HERBERT A. "Recent Advances in Organization Theory," pp. 28–29 in STEPHEN K. BAILEY *et al.*, *Research Frontiers in Politics and Government: Brookings Lectures, 1955*. Washington, D.C.: Brookings Institution, 1955.

————. *Models of Man*. New York: John Wiley & Sons, 1957.

———. "Theories of Decision-Making in Economics and Behavioral Sciences," *The American Economic Review*, Vol. 49, No. 3 (July, 1959).

———. "Comments on the Theory of Organizations," in A. H. RUBENSTEIN and C. J. HABERSTROH (eds.), *Some Theories of Organization*. Homewood, Ill.: Richard D. Irwin, 1966.

SIMPSON, R. L. "Vertical and Horizontal Communication in Formal Organizations," *Administrative Science Quarterly*, Vol. 4 (September, 1959), pp. 188–96.

SINGER, J. D. "The Political Science of Human Conflict," in E. B. McNEIL (ed.), *The Nature of Conflict*. Englewood Cliffs, N.J.: Prentice-Hall, 1965.

SKINNER, B. F. *Science and Human Behavior*. New York: Macmillan Co., 1953.

———. *Walden Two*. New York: Macmillan Co., 1948.

SLOAN, A. P. *My Years with General Motors*. Garden City, N.Y.: Doubleday & Co., 1964.

SMITH, A. G. (ed.) *Communication and Culture, Readings in the Codes of Human Interaction*. New York: Holt, Rinehart & Winston, 1966.

SMITH, E. E., and KNIGHT, S. S. "Effects of Feedback on Insight and Problem-Solving Efficiency in Training Groups," *Journal of Applied Psychology*, Vol. 43 (1959), pp. 209–11.

SMITH, H. C. *Sensitivity to People*. New York: McGraw-Hill Book Co., 1966.

SMITH, P. B., and MOSCOW, D. "After the T-Group Is Over," *New Society*, December, 1966.

SNOW, C. P. "Scientists and Decision Making," in M. GREENBERGER (ed.), *Management and the Computer*. Cambridge, Mass., and New York: published jointly by M.I.T. Press and John Wiley & Sons, 1962.

SOMMER, R. "Small Group Ecology," *Psychological Bulletin*, Vol. 67 (1967), pp. 145–52.

———. *Personal Space*. Englewood Cliffs, N.J.: Prentice-Hall, 1968.

SPEARMAN, C. *The Abilities of Man*. London: Macmillan & Co., Ltd., 1927.

STARKWEATHER, J. A. "Content-Free Speech as a Source of Information about the Speaker," in A. G. SMITH (ed.), *Communication and Culture*. New York: Holt, Rinehart & Winston, 1966.

STEBBING, L. S. *A Modern Introduction to Logic*. London: Methuen & Co., Ltd., 1930.

STEWART, R. "The Use of Diaries to Study Managers' Jobs," *Journal of Management Studies*, Vol. 2, No. 2 (May, 1965), pp. 228–35.

STOGDILL, R. "Personal Factors Associated with Leadership: A Survey of the Literature," *Journal of Psychology*, Vol. 25 (1948).

———, and SHARTLE, C. L. *Methods in the Study of Administrative Leadership*. Columbus: Bureau of Business Research, Ohio State University, 1955.

STOLLER, F. "Use of Video Tape (Focused Feedback) in Group Counselling and Group Therapy," *Journal of Research & Development in Education*, Vol. 1 (1968), pp. 20–43.

STONER, J. A. F. "Risky and Cautious Shifts in Group Decisions: The Influence of Widely Held Values," *Journal of Experimental Social Psychology*, Vol. 4 (1968), pp. 442–59.

STORR, A. "The Concept of Cure," *The (London) Sunday Times*, October 9, 1966.

STRAUSS, GEORGE. "Some Notes on Power Equalization," in HAROLD J. LEAVITT (ed.), *The Social Science of Organizations*. Englewood Cliffs, N.J.: Prentice-Hall, 1963.

————. "Workflow Frictions, Interfunctional Rivalry, and Professionalism: A Case Study of Purchasing Agents," *Human Organization*, Vol. 23 (Summer, 1964).

STROTHER, G. B. *Social Science Approaches to Business Behavior*. Homewood, Ill.: Richard D. Irwin, 1962.

————. "Problems in the Development of a Social Science of Organization," in HAROLD J. LEAVITT (ed.), *The Social Science of Organizations*. Englewood Cliffs, N.J.: Prentice-Hall, 1963.

SWINGLE, P. G. "Illusory Power in a Dangerous Game," *Canadian Journal of Psychology*, Vol. 22, No. 3 (June, 1968), pp. 176–85.

SYKES, A. J. M. "A Study in Changing the Attitudes and Stereotypes of Industrial Workers," *Human Relations*, Vol. 17, No. 2 (1964).

————, and BATES, J. "Study of Conflict between Formal Company Policy and the Interests of Informal Groups," *Sociological Review*, November, 1962.

SYKES, G. M. "The Corruption of Authority and Rehabilitation," in A. ETZIONI (ed.), *Complex Organizations*. New York: Holt, Rinehart & Winston, 1965.

SYMONDS, CHARLES P. "Uses and Abuse of the Term Flying Stress," in AIR MINISTRY, *Psychological Disorders in Flying Personnel of the RAF Investigated during the War, 1939–45*. London: H.M. Stationery Office, 1947.

TAYLOR, DONALD; BERRY, PAUL C.; and BLOCK, CLIFFORD H. "Does Group Participation When Using Brainstorming Facilitate or Inhibit Creative Thinking?" in C. W. BACKMAN and P. F. SECORD (eds.), *Problems in Social Psychology*. New York: McGraw-Hill Book Co., 1966.

TAYLOR, FREDERICK W. *Scientific Management*. New York: Harper & Bros., 1947.

TERREBERRY, SHIRLEY. "The Organization of Environments," unpublished doctoral thesis, University of Michigan, 1968.

————. "The Evolution of Organizational Environments," *Administrative Science Quarterly*, Vol. 12 (March, 1968), pp. 590–613.

THOMAS, E. J., and FINK, C. F. "Effects of Group Size," *Psychological Bulletin*, Vol. 60 (1963), pp. 371–84.

THOMPSON, JAMES D. *Organizations in Action*. New York: McGraw-Hill Book Co., 1967.

THOMPSON, WILLIAM IRWIN. *At the Edge of History*. New York: Harper & Row, 1971.

THOULESS, R. H. *General and Social Psychology*. London: London University Tutorial Press, 1951.

THURSTONE, L. L. "Primary Mental Abilities," *Psychometric Monograph*, No. 1, 1938.

TILLES, SEYMOUR. "The Manager's Job: A Systems Approach," *Harvard Business Review*, Vol. 41 (January–February, 1963), pp. 73–81.

TOFFLER, ALVIN. *Future Shock*. New York: Bantam Books, 1970.

TORRANCE, E. P. "Function of Expressed Disagreement in Small Group Processes," in A. H. RUBENSTEIN and C. J. HABERSTROH (eds.), *Some Theories of Organization*. Homewood, Ill.: Richard D. Irwin, 1966.

TRIST, E. L., and BAMFORTH, K. W. "Some Social and Psychological Consequences of the Long-Wall Method of Coal-Getting," *Human Relations*, Vol. 4 (1951).

———, and SOFER, C. *Exploration in Group Relations*. Leicester: Leicester University Press, 1959.

TURNER, G. *The Car Makers*. London: Eyre & Spottiswoode, Ltd., 1963.

TURNER, A. N., and LAWRENCE, P. R. *Industrial Jobs and the Worker: An Investigation of Response to Task Attributes*. Boston: Harvard University Press, 1965.

UDELL, J. G. "An Empirical Test of Hypotheses Relating to Span of Control," *Administrative Science Quarterly*, Vol. 12, No. 3 (December, 1967).

Understanding How Groups Work. Chicago: Adult Education Association of the U.S.A.

U.S. DEPARTMENT OF HEALTH, EDUCATION, AND WELFARE. *Work in America*. Washington, D.C.: H.E.W., 1973.

URWICK, LYNDALL. *The Elements of Administration*. New York: Harper & Row, 1943.

VENESS, T., and BRIERLEY, D. W. "Forming Impressions of Personality: Two Experiments," *British Journal of Social and Clinical Psychology*, Vol. 2 (1963), pp. 11–19.

VERNON, P. E. *Structure of Human Abilities*. London: Methuen & Co., Ltd., 1950.

———. *Personality Tests and Assessments*. London: Methuen & Co., Ltd., 1953.

———. *Intelligence and Attainment Tests*. London: University of London Press, 1960.

——— (ed.). *Creativity*. London: Penguin, 1970.

———, and PARRY, J. B. *Personnel Selection in the British Forces*. London: University of London Press, 1949.

VERNON, RAYMOND. *Sovereignty at Bay*. New York: Basic Books, 1971.

VON BERTALANFFY, LUDWIG. "The Theory of Open Systems in Physics and Biology," *Science*, Vol. 3 (January, 1950); pp. 23–29.

———. *General Systems Theory*. New York: George Braziller, 1968.

VROOM, VICTOR. "Some Personality Determinants of the Effects of Participation," *Journal of Abnormal and Social Psychology*, Vol. 59 (November, 1959), pp. 322–27.

———. *Work and Motivation.* New York: John Wiley & Sons, 1964.

———. "Motivation in Management," *An American Foundation for Management Research Study*, 1965.

———. "Industrial Social Psychology," in G. Lindzey and E. Aronson (eds.), *Handbook of Social Psychology*, Vol. 5. 2d ed. Reading, Mass.: Addison-Wesley, 1968.

Wald, R. M., and Doty, R. A. "The Top Executive—A Firsthand Profile," "Skills That Build Executive Success," *Harvard Business Review*, September, 1965, pp. 31–40.

Walker, C. R., and Guest, R. H. *The Man on the Assembly Line.* Cambridge, Mass.: Harvard University Press, 1952.

Walker, N. *A Short History of Psychotherapy.* London: Routledge and Kegan Paul, 1957.

Wallach, M. A., and Kogan, N. "The Roles of Information and Consensus in Group Risk Taking," *Journal of Experimental Social Psychology*, Vol. 1 (1965), pp. 1–19.

Walton, Richard E., and Dutton, John M. "The Management of Interdepartmental Conflict," *Administrative Science Quarterly*, Vol. 14 No. 1 (March, 1969).

———, and McKerzie, R. B. *A Behavioral Theory of Labor Negotiations: An Analysis of a Social Interaction System.* New York: McGraw-Hill Book Co., 1965.

Wardwell, W. I. "The Reduction of Strain in a Marginal Social Role," *American Journal of Sociology*, Vol. 61, No. 1 (1955).

Warner, W. L., and Lunt, P. S. *The Social Life of a Modern Community.* New Haven, Conn.: Yale University Press, 1941.

Webber, Ross A. *Culture and Management.* Homewood, Ill.: Richard D. Irwin, 1969.

Weber, Max. *The Protestant Ethic and the Spirit of Capitalism.* New York: Charles Scribner's Sons, 1958 (first ed., London: Allen and Unwin, 1930).

———. *From Max Weber* (ed. H. H. Gerth and C. W. Mills). London: Oxford University Press, 1946.

Webster, M. *Decision Making in the Employment Interview.* Montreal: Industrial Relations Centre, McGill University, 1964.

Weiss, R. S. *Process of Organization.* Ann Arbor: Survey Research Center, University of Michigan, 1956.

———. "A Structure-Function Approach to Organization," *Journal of Social Issues*, Vol. 12, No. 2 (1959).

White, M. "Dunlop Gets a Grip on Rising Costs," *The (London) Times Business News*, January 22, 1968.

Whitehead, R. "The Cybernetic Approach in Business," *Scientific Business*, Vol. 3, No. 9 (May, 1965).

Whitehead, T. N. *Leadership in a Free Society.* London: Oxford University Press, 1936.

WHITMAN, R. M. "Psychodynamic Principles Underlying T-Group Processes," in L. P. BRADFORD, J. R. GIBB, and K. D. BENNE (eds.), *T-Group Theory and Laboratory Method.* New York: John Wiley & Sons, 1964.

WHITSETT, D. A., and WINSLOW, E. K. "An Analysis of Studies Critical of the Motivator-Hygiene Theory," *Personnel Psychology*, Vol. 20, No. 4 (Winter, 1967).

WHYTE, W. F. *Street Corner Society, The Social Structure of an Italian Slum.* Chicago: University of Chicago Press, 1943.

————. "The Social Structure of the Restaurant," *The American Journal of Sociology*, Vol. 54 (1949), pp. 302–10.

————. "Applying Behavioral Science Research to Management Problems," in G. B. STROTHER (ed.) *Social Science Approaches to Business Behavior.* Homewood, Ill.: Richard D. Irwin, 1962.

————. *Organizational Behavior: Theory and Application.* Homewood, Ill.: Richard D. Irwin, 1969.

————, et al. *Money and Motivation.* New York: Harper & Row, 1955.

WHYTE, W. H., JR. "How Hard Do Executives Work?" *Fortune*, January, 1954.

————. *The Organization Man.* New York: Simon & Schuster, 1956.

WIENER, NORBERT. *Cybernetics.* Cambridge, Mass.: M.I.T. Press; and New York: John Wiley & Sons, 1961.

WILENSKY, H. L. *Organizational Intelligence, Knowledge and Policy in Government and Industry.* New York: Basic Books, 1967.

WILLMOTT, P. *The Evolution of a Community.* London: Routledge and Kegan Paul, 1963.

WILSON, A. T. M. "Some Contrasting Socio-Technical Production Systems," *The Manager*, December, 1955.

WILSON, V. F. "Some Personality Characteristics of Industrial Executives," *Occupational Psychology*, Vol. 30, No. 4.

WOLFF, HAROLD. *Stress and Disease.* 2d ed. Springfield, Ill.: C. C. Thomas Press, 1968.

WOODWARD, J. "Management and Technology," *Problems and Progress in Industry.* London: H.M. Stationery Office, 1958.

————. "Industrial Behaviour—Is There a Science?" *New Society*, October, 1964.

———— (ed.). *Industrial Organization: Theory and Practice.* New York: Oxford University Press, 1965.

———— (ed.). *Industrial Organization: Behaviour and Control.* New York: Oxford University Press, 1970.

WOODWORTH, R. S., and SCHLOSBERG, H. *Experimental Psychology.* Rev. ed. New York: Henry Holt & Co., 1955.

WORTHY, J. C. "Organizational Structure and Employee Morale," *American Sociological Review*, Vol. 15 (1950), pp. 169–79.

WORTMAN, MAX S., JR., and LUTHANS, FRED (eds.), *Emerging Concepts in Management.* New York: MacMillan Co., 1969.

WRAY, D. E. "Marginal Men of Industry: The Foremen," *American Journal of Sociology*, Vol. 54 (1949), pp. 298–301.

WRENCH, D. F. "The Perception of Two-sided Messages," *Human Relations*, Vol. 17, No. 3 (1964).

YANKELOVICH, DANIEL. *The Changing Values on Campus: Political and Personal Attitudes on Campus.* New York: Washington Square Press, 1972.

YOUNG, K. *Handbook of Social Psychology.* London: Routledge and Kegan Paul, 1946.

YOUNG, STANLEY. "Organization as a Total System," *California Management Review*, Vol. 10 (Spring, 1968), pp. 21–32.

ZALAZNICK, S. "The M.B.A., the Man, the Myth, and the Method," *Fortune*, May, 1968.

ZALKIND, SHELDON C., and COSTELLO, T. W. "Perception: Some Recent Research and Implications for Administration," *Administrative Science Quarterly*, September, 1962, pp. 218–235.

ZINCK, C. "The Foreman and Productivity," *Advanced Management*, Vol. 23 (1958), pp. 12–16.

ZUCKERMANN, S. *The Social Life of Monkeys and Apes.* London: Routledge and Kegan Paul, 1932.

Acknowledgments

In addition to the source references given in the Bibliography and in the credit lines of the boxes, the publishers of the following selections have requested that acknowledgment be given as follows:

Selection on pp. 12–13 from Scientific Management by F. W. Taylor (pp. 43–46 in "The Principles of Scientific Management"). Copyright, 1911 by Frederick W. Taylor; renewed 1939 by Louise M. S. Taylor. Reprinted by permission of Harper & Row, Publishers.

Selection on p. 76 from *Organizations in Action* by James D. Thompson, Copyright 1967, McGraw-Hill Book Company. Used with permission of McGraw-Hill Book Company.

Selection on p. 99 from *Management and the Worker* by F. J. Roethlisberger and W. J. Dickson, reprinted by permission of the publishers. Copyright, 1939, 1967, by the President and Fellows of Harvard College.

Selection on p. 108 from *Karl Marx: Selected Writings* by T. B. Bottomore and M. Rubel. Reprinted by permission of Pitman Publishing Ltd., London, England and C. A. Watts & Co., Ltd., London, England.

Selection on p. 108 from *The Sane Society*, by Eric Fromm. Reprinted by permission of Holt, Rinehart and Winston, Inc., Publishers.

Selection on pp. 112–13 by Agis Salpukas, from the *New York Times*, January and June 1972. © 1972 by The New York Times Company. Reprinted by permission.

Selection on pp. 114–15 from *Industrial Jobs and the Worker* by A. N. Turner and P. R. Lawrence. Copyright 1965, Harvard University Press. Reprinted by permission of Harvard University Press.

Selection on p. 204 from *Walden Two* by B. F. Skinner, copyright 1948 by the Macmillan Publishing Co., Inc.

Selection on pp. 205–6 from "Skinner: The Most Important Influence in Psychology," by Berkeley Rice. © 1968 by The New York Times Company. Reprinted by permission.

Selections on pp. 210 and 228 are from the *New York Times*. © June 1972 and © April 1972 by The New York Times Company. Reprinted by permission.

Selections on pp. 209 and 280 from *Systems Psychology* by K. B. DeGreene. Copyright © 1970 by McGraw-Hill, Inc. Used with permission of McGraw-Hill Book Company.

Selection on p. 264 from "Description and Measurement of Personality" (1946) and "Personality and Motivation Structure and Measurement" (1957) both by R. B. Cattell. Note: A technical and adequate description of the measurement of these secondary and primary traits is given in Cattell, R. B., Eber, H. W., and Tatsuoka, M., *Handbook for the 16 P.F. Test*, 1970 (Institute for Personality and Ability Testing, Coronado Drive, Champaign, Illinois).

Selection on pp. 275–76 from *Work and the Nature of Man* by Frederick Herzberg. Copyright © 1966 by Frederick Herzberg. With permission of Thomas Y. Crowell Company, Inc.

Selections of pp. 288–91 from "The New Look in Motivational Theory for Organizational Research," by J. G. Hunt and J. W. Hill. Reproduced by permission of the Society for Applied Anthropology from *Human Organization*, Vol. 28, No. 2, 1969.

Selection on p. 292 from *Managerial Behavior, Performance and Effectiveness* by J. P. Campbell, et al. Used with permission of McGraw-Hill Book Company. Copyright 1970 by McGraw-Hill Book Company.

Selection on p. 387 from "Validation and Extension of the Contingency Model of Leadership Effectiveness," by F. E. Fiedler. Copyright 1971 by the American Psychological Association. Reprinted by permission.

Selection on p. 327 from the *New York Times*. © 1972 by The New York Times Company. Reprinted by permission.

Selection on p. 449 from "Managerial Behavior, Performance, and Effectiveness," by J. P. Campbell, et al. Used with permission of McGraw-Hill Book Company. Copyright 1970 by McGraw-Hill Book Company.

Selection on p. 464 from *Managerial Process and Organizational Behavior* by Alan C. Filley and Robert J. House. Copyright © by Scott, Foresman and Company, Reprinted by permission of the publisher.

Selection on p. 468 from "Risky and Cautious Shifts in Group Decisions," by J. A. F. Stoner. Copyright 1969 by the American Psychological Association. Reprinted by permission.

Selection on p. 529 from "A Rare Hamburger Headquarters." Reprinted by permission from *Time*, The Weekly Newsmagazine; Copyright, Time, Inc.

Selection on p. 545 from Wolff, Harold, *Stress and Disease*, 2d. ed., 1968. Courtesy of Charles C Thomas, Publisher, Springfield, Illinois.

Selection on p. 622 from Lena L. Lucietto, "Speech Patterns of Administrators," *Administrator's Notebook*, Volume 18, Number 5. The *Administrator's Notebook* is published by the Midwest Administration Center of the University of Chicago.

Selection on pp. 679, 680–81 from Edgar H. Schein, *Process Consultation: Its Role in Organization Development*, 1969, Addison-Wesley, Reading, Massachusetts.

Selection on p. 684 from Chris Argyris, *Intervention Theory and Method*, 1970, Addison-Wesley, Reading, Massachusetts.

Selection on pp. 696–97 from "The Limits of Growth," by Peter Passell, Marc Roberts, and Leonard Ross. © 1972 by The New York Times Company. Reprinted by permission.

Indexes

Name index

Subject index